Second
Canadian
Edition

Dynamic Physical Education

for Elementary School Children

ROBERT P. PANGRAZI

Arizona State University

SANDRA L. GIBBONS

University of Victoria

PEARSON

Toronto

Library and Archives Canada Cataloguing in Publication

Pangrazi, Robert P.
    Dynamic physical education for elementary school children / Robert
P. Pangrazi, Sandra L. Gibbons. — 2nd Canadian ed.

Includes index.
ISBN 978-0-205-55369-3

    1. Physical education for children—Study and teaching
(Elementary).   I. Gibbons, Sandra Louise, 1956–   II. Title.

GV443.P35 2009   372.86   C2008-900170-2

ISBN-13: 978-0-205-55369-3
ISBN-10: 0-205-55369-9

Vice President, Editorial Director: Gary Bennett
Executive Acquisitions Editor: Christine Cozens
Sponsoring Editor: Lori Will
Marketing Manager: Toivo Pajo
Associate Editor: Brian Simons
Production Editor: Kevin Leung
Copy Editor: Ron Jacques
Proofreader: Martin Tooke
Production Coordinator: Avinash Chandra
Composition: Integra
Art Director, Cover and Interior Design: Julia Hall
Cover Image: Getty Images/Elie Bernager

Photo credits appear on page 614 at the end of this text, which is considered an extension of
this copyright page.

1 2 3 4 5   12 11 10 09 08

Printed and bound in the United States of America.

CONTENTS

PREFACE

Dynamic Physical Education for Elementary School Children, Second Canadian Edition, is designed to build on the strengths of the fifteenth U.S. edition of this popular textbook while incorporating content applicable to the Canadian audience. *Dynamic Physical Education* is written for both physical education teachers and classroom teachers.

Part I, "Instruction and Implementation," contains the theory and knowledge a teacher needs to develop a quality program. The chapters in Part I are separated into three sections that address the need for quality physical education in schools, effective teaching of physical education, and keys to program implementation.

Part I Instruction and Program Implementation

Section 1 Understanding the Need for Physical Education

Chapter 1 Elementary School Physical Education

Chapter 2 Physical Activity for the Growing Child

Chapter 1 provides a brief historical summary of the development of physical education in Canadian schools to help the reader put the current state of elementary school physical education in context. Since the 1970s, Canadian teachers and researchers have shown considerable leadership in the call for quality daily physical education (QDPE) in Canadian schools. Chapter 2 includes current statistics on the physical fitness of children and youth in Canada. Focus on several national surveys on physical fitness in the 1990s and 2000s provides the framework for discussion.

Section 2 The Instructional Process

Chapter 3 Planning for Quality Instruction

Chapter 4 Improving Instructional Effectiveness

Chapter 3 explains a variety of teaching styles as they apply to meeting the diverse learning needs of students. Chapter 4 continues with the discussion of effective teaching, with a particular emphasis on communication skills. This chapter also includes a variety of strategies that help teachers teach for diversity in physical education. Strategies are discussed for addressing equity issues associated with multiculturalism, Aboriginal peoples, and gender.

Chapter 5 Encouraging Positive Behaviour

Chapter 5 provides a comprehensive plan for developing positive student behaviour. The chapter provides proactive and reactive strategies. Two Canadian initiatives (*Fair Play for Kids* and *Peace in the Classroom*) are discussed, both of which focus on positive social skills. Discussion of provincial policies for *Safe and Caring Schools* is also included.

Chapter 6 Assessment and Evaluation of Student Learning

This chapter focuses on student-centred assessment and evaluation strategies. Many provincial ministries of education identify as a goal the active involvement of the student in the assessment/evaluation process. The chapter provides suggestions for authentic assessment in physical education. Examples of assessment rubrics are presented.

Chapter 7 Children with Special Needs

Inclusion of children with special needs in physical education continues to present a variety of challenges for teachers. Chapter 7 provides a basic discussion of the legal framework for inclusion of children with special needs in Canadian schools, along with explanation of the process for development of individual education plans (IEP). Guidelines for successful inclusion are highlighted.

Section 3 Program Implementation

Chapter 8 Curriculum Development

Chapter 8 discusses the curriculum development process from the overall program philosophy and goals, through learning outcomes, to specific lesson plans. Excerpts are included from several provincial physical education curriculum guides.

Chapter 9 Legal Liability and Risk Management

It is crucial to establish a safe environment for students in physical education. Safety is discussed as it relates to a physical education teacher's responsibility for standards of care and legal liability. The chapter provides a basic risk management plan. Excerpts from several provincial physical education safety guidelines are also included.

Chapter 10 Facilities, Equipment, and Supplies

The focus of this chapter is a brief discussion of safe and efficient facilities and equipment. Canadian Standards

Association guidelines provide the basic standard of safety for playground facilities and equipment.

Chapter 11 Making Curriculum Connections

Chapter 11 discusses connecting learning outcomes of physical education with other subjects. Examples of several Canadian resources—including *Heart Smart for Kids*, *Fair Play for Kids*, *Shared Learnings*, *Manitoba Curriculum Framework for Outcomes for Active Healthy Lifestyles*, and *Inuit Games*—show a variety of different ideas for making curriculum connections.

Part II Teaching the Learning Outcomes of Physical Education

Part II is separated into four different sections that are filled with activities and strategies designed to help teachers accomplish the outcomes of a quality physical education program.

Section 4 Personal Health Skills

Section 4 contains many activities and techniques for teaching personal health skills, including methods for teach-ing students how to develop and maintain an active and healthy lifestyle.

Chapter 12 Physical Activity and Fitness

Chapter 12 provides information about the skill- and health-related components of physical fitness. Also included are guidelines for developing and maintaining physical fitness in elementary school children. The chapter includes highlights from *Canada's Physical Activity Guide for Children and Youth*, as well as Daily Physical Activity initiatives in Alberta and Ontario schools. Use of pedometers as a tool to monitor physical activity is highlighted.

Chapter 13 Wellness: Developing a Healthy Lifestyle

Chapter 13 discusses healthy active living, and includes strategies for how to develop this concept in elementary school physical education. Information on the new *Canada's Food Guide* is included. Provincial and territorial *Healthy Schools* initiatives are included.

Section 5 Fundamental Motor Skills

Section 5 brings together methods and activities for teaching fundamental motor skills. The section includes guidance on helping students develop an awareness of movement concepts, fundamental motor skills, and body management skills.

Chapter 14 Movement Concepts

Chapter 15 Fundamental Motor Skills

Chapter 16 Introductory Activities: Applying Fundamental Motor Skills

Chapter 17 Manipulative Skills

Section 6 Specialized Motor Skills

Section 6 is designed to improve specialized motor skills among students of diverse backgrounds. Chapters on body management skills, dance and rhythmic movement skills, gymnastic skills, alternative environment activities, and game skills cover the development of a personalized set of specialized skills in depth.

Chapter 18 Body Management Skills

Chapter 19 Dance and Rhythmic Movement Skills

Chapter 20 Gymnastic Skills

Chapter 20 uses the Dominant Movement Patterns (DMP) approach. The DMP approach forms the basis for gymnastics education in Canada (Russell, 1986). This approach to gymnastics is based on the premise that every skill performed in gymnastics belongs to one of the following six patterns of body movement: (1) landings, (2) statics, (3) locomotions, (4) swings, (5) rotations, and (6) springs.

Chapter 21 Alternative Environment Activities

This chapter presents three sample alternative environment activities—orienteering, cross-country skiing, and curling. Orienteering and cross-country skiing are examples of activities that may be offered in the outdoors during various seasons. Curling is one of the most popular winter recreational activities in many communities in Canada. Suggestions are provided for including these activities in an elementary physical education program.

Chapter 22 Developmental Game Skills

Developmental games included in Chapter 22 provide the opportunity for children to develop the motor skills and tactical understanding to allow for a smooth transition to a variety of sports.

Section 7 Sport Skills

Finally, Section 7 is designed to develop a broad set of sport skills. The chapters contain many teaching tips, lead-up activities, and skill development drills.

Chapter 23 Basketball

Chapter 24 Lacrosse

Lacrosse at the elementary level is a lead-up to the four disciplines of lacrosse practised today in Canada: box lacrosse, men's and women's field lacrosse, and the non-contact inter-lacrosse. Lacrosse at the elementary level is based on non-contact inter-lacrosse.

Acknowledgments

The authors want to thank the following individuals for their specific contributions, without which the second Canadian edition of *Dynamic Physical Education for Elementary School Children* would not have been realized:

■   Dr. Viviene Temple from the University of Victoria provided her expertise and leadership in the adaptation of the content of Chapter 7 "Children with Special Needs" and Chapter 24 "Lacrosse."

■   Edmond Leahy and Kathleen Leahy posed for photographs of lacrosse skills in Chapter 24.

■   Kathleen Leahy posed for Figure 29.3, Figure 29.4a, and Figure 29.4b in Chapter 29.

Very special thanks go to the following reviewers, who provided valuable feedback that helped guide the author's efforts throughout this project:

■   David Chorney, University of Lethbridge

■   Sharon Hamilton, Red Deer College

■   Brenda Kalyn, University of Saskatchewan

■   Jeanne Kentel, Brock University

■   Jack Miller, Thompson Rivers University

■   Joan Thompson, Lakehead University

■   Ralph Wheeler, Memorial University

I would also like to thank the following people at Pearson Education Canada for their assistance and editorial support: Lori Will, Sponsoring Editor; Brian Simons, Associate Editor; and Kevin Leung, Production Editor.

Instruction and Program Implementation

Understanding the Need
for Physical Education

Chapter 1

Elementary School Physical
Education

Chapter 2

Physical Activity for Children

CHAPTER 1

Elementary School Physical Education

Essential Components

I	**Organized around content standards**
II	**Student-centred and developmentally appropriate**
III	**Physical activity and motor skill development form the core of the program**
IV	Teaches management skills and self-discipline
V	Promotes inclusion of all students
VI	Focuses on process over product
VII	Promotes lifetime personal health and wellness
VIII	Teaches cooperation and responsibility and promotes sensitivity to diversity

Physical Education Standards

1	Students are able to move competently using a variety of fundamental and specialized motor skills.
2	Students can monitor and maintain a health-enhancing level of physical fitness.
3	Students are able to apply movement concepts and basic mechanics of skill performance when learning and refining motor skills.
4	Students comprehend the basic principles of wellness and are able to apply concepts that enable them to make meaningful decisions that positively impact their health and wellness.
5	Students participate in a wide variety of physical activities and learn how to maintain a personalized active lifestyle.
6	Students demonstrate empathy, understanding, and respect for the numerous differences exhibited by people in an activity setting.
7	Students exhibit responsible and self-directed behaviours that lead to positive social interactions in physical activity.

OVERVIEW

Physical education is that phase of the general educational program in Canadian schools that contributes to the total growth and development of each child, primarily through movement experiences. Program goals and outcomes provide the framework and direction for the physical education curriculum. Systematic and properly taught physical education can help achieve the major content standards, including developing movement competence, maintaining physical fitness, learning personal health and wellness skills, applying movement concepts and skill mechanics, developing lifetime activity skills, and demonstrating positive personal and social skills. Modern programs of physical education in Canada have been influenced by a variety of social and educational factors.

OUTCOMES

- List program goals and outcomes, and recognize the distinctive contributions of physical education.

- Describe the educational reasons for including physical education as part of the elementary school experience.

- Define physical education and its role in the elementary school experience.

- Articulate various pedagogical influences on elementary school physical education programs.

- Identify essential components of a quality physical education program.

- Explain how several societal influences have had an impact on elementary school physical education.

Physical education is part of the total educational program that contributes, primarily through movement experiences, to the total growth and development of all children. It is an instructional program that gives significant attention to all learning domains: psychomotor, cognitive, and affective. No other area of the curriculum is designed to help children learn motor and lifetime activity skills. This makes physical education a necessary component of the total school curriculum.

Aims and goals of physical education programs from across Canada are consistent in their emphasis on the holistic nature of physical education. The following are aim and goal statements from provincial curriculum guides:

(1) *Alberta*—"The aim of the Kindergarten to Grade 12 physical education program is to enable individuals to develop knowledge, skills and attitudes necessary to lead an active, healthy lifestyle" *(Alberta Learning, 2000).*

(2) *British Columbia*—"Through participation in physical education, students will develop the knowledge, skills and attitudes necessary to incorporate physical activity into regular routines and leisure pursuits to live an active, healthy lifestyle" *(B.C. Ministry of Education, 1995).*

(3) *Manitoba*—". . . to provide students with planned and balanced programs to develop the knowledge, skills, and attitudes for physically active and healthy lifestyles" *(Manitoba Education and Training, 2000).*

(4) *New Brunswick*—". . . to attain healthy levels of physical activity and fitness for all students, to encourage the acquisition of motor skills, to develop knowledge and attitudes supportive of continuing active living habits throughout life and to develop specific objectives designed to meet the physical growth and development needs of children and youth are the goals of the Physical Education program" *(New Brunswick Department of Education, 2002).*

(5) *Newfoundland and Labrador*—"Physical Education fosters personal and community wellness by empowering students to attain healthy, lifelong attitudes and behaviours through physical activity as part of the total education experience" *(Newfoundland and Labrador Department of Education, 2004).*

(6) *Nova Scotia*—"The unique learning opportunities in physical education enable students to acquire the knowledge, skills, and attitudes required to enhance their quality of life through active, healthy living" *(Nova Scotia Education, 2000).*

(7) *Ontario*—"Through the health and physical education curriculum, students will develop an understanding of the importance of physical fitness, health, and well-being and the factors that contribute to them; a personal commitment to daily vigorous physical activity and positive health behaviours; and the basic movement skills they require to participate in physical activities throughout their lives" *(Ontario Ministry of Education and Training, 1998).*

(8) *Prince Edward Island*—"The physical education program should assist the individual in development of (a) efficient and effective motor skills and apply these skills in a wide variety of physical activities; (b) physical fitness; (c) knowledge and understanding of factors involved in attaining competence in and appreciation of physical activity; and (d) positive personal attributes and interpersonal relationships including a positive attitude towards continued participation in physical activity" *(Prince Edward Island Department of Education, 2005).*

(9) *Quebec*—"The Physical Education and Health Program addresses the following three competences: (a) performance of movement skills in different physical activity settings; (b) interaction with others in physical activity settings; and (c) adopt a healthy, active lifestyle" *(Éducation Québec, 2003).*

(10) *Saskatchewan*—"Through participation in physical education, students will develop the knowledge, skills and attitudes necessary to become a physically educated person" *(Saskatchewan Education, 1999).*

Similarly, the Canadian Association for Health, Physical Education, Recreation and Dance (CAHPERD), a national organization that advocates for quality physical education in Canadian schools, highlights the following statement:

Physically educated persons ACQUIRE skills which can help them become physically fit and enable them to perform a variety of physical activities; they PARTICIPATE regularly in physical activity because it is enjoyable and exhilarating; they UNDERSTAND and VALUE physical activity. *(Physical Education 2000)*

Elementary physical education programs provide the initial movement experience for students who are working toward eventually becoming "physically educated."

The Evolution of Elementary School Physical Education

A number of historical events, pedagogical influences, and societal concerns have had a significant impact on elementary school physical education programs.

Education of Canadian Children: A Provincial Responsibility

Perhaps the most notable historical event to influence education in Canada occurred with the creation of Canada as a sovereign nation. Article 93 of the British North America Act in 1867 granted the responsibility and jurisdiction for public education to individual provinces. Each provincial department or ministry of education is responsible for ensuring the education of children and youth in the province. Coupled with Canada's vast geography, this has resulted in diverse educational programs, curricula, and structures across Canada. Like all other subjects, the structure and content of physical education has evolved slightly differently in each province and territory. For example, in terms of structure, what are considered "elementary grades" are not the same across each province and territory. Physical education requirements also differ (see Table 1.1).

Therefore, although this text provides a general Canadian perspective, the reader is alerted to these differences and encouraged to explore his or her respective provincial physical education curriculum guide. Fortunately, CAHPERD has managed to provide a national voice for physical education in Canadian schools by bringing together representatives from each province as part of its board of directors. This has resulted in a much more unified view of physical education among Canadian physical educators.

Enduring Pedagogical Influences

Physical education programs have evolved as Canada has grown as a nation. European immigration and struggles to establish a national identity both influenced physical education programs. The following provide three examples of enduring influences:

Physical Education for Military Training

The health and strength of a country's citizenry has long been considered a significant source of national pride and survival. Even today there is a belief that strong citizens can stand up against all threats. Early physical education programs in Canada provided youth with the physical preparation to defend their country. The Strathcona Trust was an example of such a program. Established in 1909 by Lord Strathcona, the trust provided funding for provinces to include physical training and cadet corps in their school programs. The syllabus of the program was based on the Ling system, a program of gymnastics and calisthenics developed in Sweden. Although the trust eventually ran its course, the notion of physical education as an arena for physical training particularly among youth endured through much of the 20th century.

Movement Education

Specific changes in physical education can be implemented from within the profession by teachers who see a need for different instructional methods and programs. Movement education, which originated in England, is one major approach that has influenced the course of elementary school physical education.

TABLE 1.1

Required physical education in provinces and territories.

	Required PE		Required PE
British Columbia	K–10	Nova Scotia	K–9 & Physically Active Lifestyles 11**
Alberta	K–10	Prince Edward Island	K–9
Saskatchewan	K–9 & one of PE 10, PE 20, or PE 30	Newfoundland & Labrador	K–9 & one full-year of PE over grades 10–12
Manitoba	K–12	Northwest Territories	See Alberta requirements
Ontario	K–8 & one PE credit in grades 9–12 toward graduation. In addition, grades 10–12 students must take 1 credit from one of the following— HPE/Arts/Business Studies toward graduation	Nunavut	See Alberta requirements
		Yukon	See BC requirements
Quebec	1–8		
New Brunswick	K–10 (Francophone schools) K–9/10* (Anglophone schools)		

*Time allocation for PE 9 or 10 may be completed in one year or spread over grades 9 and 10.

**A half-credit course required for graduation.

English physical education teachers who immigrated to Canada during the late 1960s incorporated movement education into Canadian programs. Movement education was based on the work of Rudolf Laban, an Austrian dance teacher who designed a framework for analyzing movement. Educators in England further developed this conceptual framework as a guide for teaching as well as for analyzing movement. Primary physical educators in particular used Laban's concepts of space awareness, body awareness, qualities of movement, and relationships to design movement experiences for children. Movement education programs shifted some of the responsibility for learning to children. The teaching methodology featured problem solving and an exploratory approach. In addition, movement education offered an opportunity for diversity of movement through creative teaching methods and allowed students of all ability levels to find success. To some degree, perhaps, it was a revolt against structured fitness programs, which included calisthenics presented in a formal, command style. This practice created a backlash among some physical educators, who felt that creativity, exploration, and cognition should also be focal points of the movement experience for children.

The pedagogical impact of movement education has been profound and enduring in Canadian physical education programs in terms of providing a conceptual structure and vocabulary for movement. Terminology associated with Laban's framework and movement is evident in almost all contemporary physical education curriculum guides. For further discussion of these movement concepts, see Chapter 14.

Developmental Physical Education

Physical education curriculum guides across Canada use a developmental approach toward learning. The major assumption of the developmental approach is that all children proceed through somewhat orderly stages of development (such as physical, cognitive, affective). To be effective and help children progress, curricular content and teaching strategies in physical education should be consistent with their developmental needs. The content standards mentioned later in this chapter reflect a developmental model.

Contemporary Social Influences

A National Focus: Documenting the Physical Activity and Health of Canadians

Interest in the physical activity of Canadians has endured over the past three decades. The Canada Fitness Survey in 1981 of more than 23000 Canadians provided the first national statistics on physical activity habits, fitness, and health status. Results showed that most adults chose activities such as walking, jogging, swimming, and cycling as their activity of choice. This has contributed to the development of school physical education programs with a focus on lifetime physical activities. In 1988, the Campbell Survey on Well-Being in Canada provided a comprehensive follow-up to the initial 1981 survey. Approximately 4000 of the original respondents completed the 1988 survey, providing some longitudinal information. Perhaps most notable for school physical education programs was the revelation that only one-third of Canadians aged 10 and older were classified as "active" in their leisure time (Stephens & Craig, 1990).

Throughout the 1990s, several extensive national surveys maintained a national profile for physical activity. This profile provided both direct and indirect support for physical education in schools. Health Canada's 1996 publication *Physical Inactivity: A Framework for Action* focused on the major objective to reduce physical inactivity in Canada by 10% by the year 2003, and followed on the heels of the *Surgeon General's Report on Physical Activity and Health* (1996) in the United States. Both documents clearly outlined the health benefits of physical activity for all ages.

In their assessment of physical activity trends from 1998–2003, Craig & Cameron (2004) stated that the "federal, provincial and territorial goal for reducing physical inactivity by 10% (6 percentage points) by the year 2003 has been achieved" (p. 6). However, they emphasized that physical inactivity remained pervasive and a significant risk factor for ill health. For example, results showed that the decrease was primarily in the proportion of the population that was already moderately active. Of major concern was the increase in the proportion of overweight and obese Canadians. Recent statistics show that "23% of adult Canadians, 5.5 million people aged 18 or older, are obese. An additional 36% (8.6 million) are overweight, bringing the total number of adult Canadians who are overweight or obese to over 59%" (Shields, 2005). In addition to the major health concerns this level of obesity presents, the cost of health care continues to rise. Katzmarzyk & Janssen (2004) estimated that the economic burden of physical inactivity was $5.3 billion while the cost associated with obesity was $4.3 billion.

In response to the continued concern (both human and financial), the *Integrated Pan-Canadian Healthy Living Strategy* was published in 2005. This *Healthy Living Strategy* is described as a "conceptual framework for sustained action based on a population health approach" (p. 3). A population health approach focuses on improving the health status of the population, with action directed as the health of the entire population rather than individuals. It is an integrated intersectoral approach involving federal and provincial levels of government. The proposed pan-Canadian Healthy

Living targets seek to obtain by 2015 a 20% increase in the proportion of Canadians who are physically active, eat healthily, and are at healthy body weights.

Focus on Physical Activity of Canadian Children: A Case for Quality Daily Physical Education

The 1995 Physical Activity Monitor, a third nationwide survey of physical activity, provided some specific information on children and physical activity. Highlights included the finding that Canadian children are less active with age, and parents show strong support for the positive outcomes of physical activity (such as increased self-esteem) for their children. Subsequent Physical Activity Monitors in 1997 and 1998 provided further information to support the importance of quality physical education programs for children and youth. In particular, a major finding in the 1998 publication was that three out of five (57%) Canadian children and youth aged 5 to 17 are not active enough for optimal growth and development (Canadian Fitness and Lifestyle Research Institute [CFLRI], 1998). More recently, Craig, Cameron, Russell, & Beaulieu (2001) reported no significant change in children's physical activity levels since 1998. These low physical activity levels are coupled with other disturbing health trends. Childhood obesity is being called an epidemic in Canadian society. Twenty-six percent of Canadian children and adolescents aged 2 to 17 are overweight or obese; 8% are obese (Shields, 2005).

As we enter the new millennium, it is notable that interest in the benefits of physical activity is not a new phenomenon in Canada. In particular, the fitness and health of Canadian children and youth was brought to the forefront in the early 1970s with the publication of several research studies. A benchmark study released in 1973 provided significant impetus for quality physical education programs for children. The Saskatchewan Growth Study (Bailey, 1973) began in 1963–64 and followed a group of children for a 10-year period. A crucial finding in Bailey's study was that children began to decline in physical fitness from the time they began elementary school.

Two major conferences in the early 1970s also highlighted physical activity among children. The National Conference on Fitness and Health in 1972, followed in 1973 by the conference on The Child in Sport and Physical Activity, held at Queen's University, provided similar recommendations for quality daily physical education programs in Canadian schools. An important result of the 1973 conference was the specific recommendation of 30 minutes of physical education on a daily basis for elementary school students. A position paper by CAHPERD in 1974 on daily physical education, and a 1976 report entitled *New Perspectives for Elementary School Physical Education Programs in Canada* continued to expand advocacy for quality daily physical education.

Throughout the 1970s a variety of projects across Canada explored and documented the positive outcomes of quality daily physical education. The most well-known of these projects is the six-year semi-longitudinal study of daily physical education in Trois Rivières, Quebec. The Trois Rivières study is considered one of the pioneer studies of daily physical education both in Canada and internationally. Trudeau, Laurencelle, Tremblay, Rajic, & Shephard (1998, 1999) revisited a group of the original Trois Rivières participants and compared their exercise habits to those of a group of non-participants. Results strongly suggest that the daily physical education experienced by the Trois Rivières participants has had significant positive long-term effects on a variety of exercise habits. As the major aim of many provincial and territorial physical education programs is to enable students to be physically active for a lifetime, the results of the Trois Rivières follow-up provide powerful support for the efficacy of physical education in achieving this aim. As well, the Trois Rivières study demonstrated that even though students received more time for physical education (and less time for academics), their academic performance did not suffer (Shephard, 1997). These results counter the objection that more physical education results in poorer academic performance due to less time spent in the classroom.

Since the mid-1970s CAHPERD has continued to advocate for quality daily physical education (QDPE) in Canadian schools. This advocacy has included the establishment of the Recognition Award Program (RAP) for schools that offer QDPE programs. In 2006, QDPE continues to be CAHPERD's flagship program. According to CAHPERD statistics, approximately 10% of Canadian schools have quality daily physical education programs. Support for quality physical education programs in Canada comes from a range of sources including public health, medical, and education. The CFLRI (1998) reported that 87% of adults polled believe that government should play a significant role in ensuring mandatory daily physical education in elementary and high schools. One of the strongest advocates has been the medical profession. In 1998, the Canadian Medical Association passed a resolution requesting that provincial Ministers of Education implement a minimum requirement of 30 minutes of quality daily physical education for all students in Kindergarten through Grade 12. In 2002, the Canadian Pediatric Society made a similar recommendation. Numerous provincial medical associations also support mandatory physical education in all grades. For example, the Ontario Medical Association (2005) recommended that "communities, including the local school boards, recognize the importance of physical education/ activity as an important part of the curriculum and regulate one hour per day of structured aerobic physical activity and exercise for elementary and secondary school students" (p. 14).

Comprehensive School Health

In the early 1990s, the Comprehensive School Health Model (CSH) was identified as an integrated approach to promoting a healthy school environment. The CSH model comprises four elements: instruction, support services, social support, and a healthy environment. The content and structure of physical education and health curricula provide a major emphasis in the instructional component of the CSH model. Support services in the CSH model can include a wide range of services, including, for example, public health, social services, and recreation services. Examples of the social support component are adult mentoring programs, and public policy that incorporates the needs of youth. The fourth component, a healthy school environment, addresses a variety of issues, including school safety, tobacco regulation, and healthy nutritional options in schools. Promoted throughout Canada, the CSH model continues to grow and develop, and physical education continues to play a prominent role. Several provinces have incorporated the CSH model as a way to increase physical activity and healthy eating in students. Several of these programs will be highlighted in Chapter 13.

Content Standards for Physical Education

A key to providing proper education includes following agreed-upon guidelines, or standards, that have been shown to ensure that children obtain an appropriate education. Content standards are the framework of a program; they determine the focus and direction of instruction. Standards specify what students should know and be able to perform. Standards express what knowledge students should possess and how they should demonstrate that knowledge when they exit a developmental level. The establishment of standards can contribute significantly to the overall goal of school and the greater society. Provincial curriculum guides use a variety of different terms that are similar to the term "content standard" (as described). For example, Alberta refers to "general outcomes," BC uses "prescribed learning outcomes," while New Brunswick uses the term "key elements."

Physical education content standards are taught nowhere else in the school curriculum. Should these standards not be accomplished in physical education classes, children will leave school without a well-developed set of physical skills. Over the 15 years, professionals in the U.S. have worked to identify a set of standards that give direction to physical education. The National Association for Sport and Physical Education (NASPE) (2004) recently identified six major content standards for physical education that provide a basis for describing a physically educated person. Generally, experts agree on the major content of the standards that constitute categories of emphasis for physical education instruction. The NASPE guidelines have been used in this textbook as the organizer for general standards for a quality physical education program. However, the reader is encouraged to consult applicable physical education curriculum documents for individual provinces and territories.

In the following section, we delineate content standards for the *Dynamic Physical Education* program. The standards offer two levels of expected learning: a set of standards for children at developmental level I (grades K–2), and at developmental levels II (grades 3–4) and III (grades 5–7). Following each standard is a detailed explanation and references to chapters the reader can review for further information.

> **STANDARD 1: Demonstrates competency in motor skills and movement patterns needed to perform a variety of physical activities.**

Developmental Level I (grades K–2) students will be able to accomplish the following:

a. Apply movement concepts such as body and space awareness, relationships, and qualities of movement to a variety of locomotor and body management skills;

b. Move efficiently using a variety of locomotor skills such as walking, running, skipping, and hopping;

c. Combine locomotor and nonlocomotor skills into movement themes—for example, supporting body weight, bridges, and receiving and transferring weight;

d. Perform body management skills on the floor and on apparatus including benches, balance beams, individual mats, and jumping boxes;

e. Use a variety of manipulative skills such as tossing, throwing, catching, and kicking;

f. Move rhythmically in a variety of settings including fundamental rhythms, creative rhythms, and simple folk dances;

g. Perform simple gymnastic skills such as animal walks, body rolling, simple balances, and inverted balances; and

h. Use a variety of locomotor skills in low-organized game settings such as running, dodging, evading, and stopping.

Developmental Level II and III (grades 3–7) students will be able to accomplish the following:

a. Perform specialized sport skills with mature form such as throwing, catching, dribbling with foot and hand, kicking and striking, batting, punting, and passing;

b. Use sport skills in a variety of activities such as volleyball pass, basketball dribble, and softball batting;

c. Perform a wide variety of gymnastic skills including tumbling, inverted balances, individual stunts, and partner stunts;

d. Perform body management skills on a variety of apparatus including benches, balance beams, and climbing ropes;

e. Move rhythmically in a variety of settings including folk, square, and line dances, rope jumping, and rhythmic gymnastics;

f. Apply a wide variety of locomotor and manipulative game skills in low-organized game settings; and

g. Incorporate specialized sport skills in a variety of sport lead-up games.

All people want to be skilled and competent performers. The elementary school years are an excellent time to teach motor skills because children have the time and predisposition to learn. Because youngsters vary in genetic endowment and interest, they should have the opportunity to learn about their personal abilities in many types of skills and settings. Major areas of movement competence and motor skill development are described next.

Movement Concepts Skills

Youngsters need to learn about the classification of movement concepts (see also Chapter 14), which includes body and space awareness, qualities of movement, and relationships. This standard is designed to give children an increased awareness and understanding of the body as a vehicle for movement, the acquisition of a personal vocabulary of movement skills, and the ability to perform physical skills in a variety of settings.

Fundamental Motor Skills

Fundamental skills enhance the quality of life. This group of skills is sometimes labelled basic or functional skills. The designation fundamental skills is used because the skills are requisite for children to function fully in the environment. Fundamental skills are divided into three categories: locomotor, nonlocomotor, and manipulative skills.

Locomotor Skills Locomotor skills (see Chapter 15) are used to move the body from one place to another or to project the body upward, as in jumping and hopping. These skills also include walking, running, skipping, leaping, sliding, and galloping.

Nonlocomotor Skills Nonlocomotor skills (see Chapter 15) are performed in place, without appreciable spatial movement. These skills are not as well defined as locomotor skills. They include bending and stretching, pushing and pulling, balancing, rolling, curling, twisting, turning, and bouncing.

Manipulative Skills Manipulative skills (see Chapter 16) are developed through handling some type of object. Manipulation of objects leads to better hand–eye and foot–eye coordination, which is particularly important for tracking items in space. Manipulative skills form the basis of many game skills. Propulsion (throwing, striking, striking with an implement, kicking) and receipt (catching) of objects are important skills. Rebounding or redirecting an object in flight (such as a volleyball) is another useful manipulative skill. Continuous control of an object, such as a wand or a hoop, is also a manipulative activity (see Figure 1.1).

Specialized Motor Skills

Specialized skills are used in various areas of physical education, including gymnastics, dance, and specific games. Specialized skills receive increased emphasis beginning with developmental Level II activities. In developing specialized skills, students achieve progress through planned learning experiences. Many of these skills have

Figure 1.1

Developing manipulative skills.

Figure 1.2

Learning body management skills.

critical points of technique. Learning experiences focus on both repetition of critical points of technique as well as practice of skills in a variety of contexts.

Body Management Skills   Efficient movement of the body (see Chapter 18) demands integration of a number of physical traits, including agility, balance, flexibility, and coordination. In addition, youngsters need to develop an understanding of how to control their bodies while on large apparatuses, such as beams, benches, and jumping boxes (see Figure 1.2).

Rhythmic Movement Skills   Rhythmic movement (see Chapter 19) involves motion with a regular and predictable pattern. The aptitude to move rhythmically is basic to skill performance in all areas. A rhythmic program that includes dance, rope jumping, and gymnastics offers a variety of activities to help attain this objective. Early experiences centre on functional and creative movement forms. Instruction begins with and capitalizes on locomotor skills that children already possess: walking, running, hopping, and jumping. Rhythmic activities provide a vehicle for expressive movement.

Gymnastic Skills   Gymnastic activities (see Chapter 20) make a significant contribution to the overall physical education experience for children in elementary schools. Gymnastic activities develop body management skills. Flexibility, agility, balance, strength, and body control are outcomes that are enhanced through participation in gymnastics. Basic gymnastic skills such as body rolling, balance skills, and inverted balances are learned in a safe and progressive manner.

Game Skills   Many games develop large-muscle groups and enhance the ability to run, dodge, start, and stop under control while sharing space with others (see Chapter 22). Social objectives touched on through games are the development of interpersonal skills, acceptance of rule parameters, and a better understanding of oneself in a competitive and cooperative situation.

Sport Skills   Sport skills (see chapters 23 to 29) are learned in a context of a particular sport. Students learn the basic skills and tactics by doing a variety of practice drills and lead-up games. Lead-up games reduce the number of skills and tactics youngsters have to use to be successful, therefore increasing their chance for successful participation. Where possible, general movement skills and concepts are applied across sports. For example, the concept of "moving into open space" can be generally applied across all invasion sports (e.g., basketball, soccer, floor hockey).

> **STANDARD 2: Demonstrates understanding of movement concepts, principles, and tactics as they apply to the learning and performance of physical activities.**

Developmental Level I (grades K–2) students will be able to accomplish the following:

a. Understand a vocabulary of basic movement concepts such as personal space, qualities of movement, body awareness, and the relationship of movements;

b. Understand words that describe a variety of relationships with objects, such as *around, behind, over, through,* and *parallel;*

c. Implement space awareness concepts and control of movements when performing locomotor movements in a group setting;

d. Understand basic mechanics of skill performance when performing specialized skills such as throwing, kicking, striking, and catching; and

e. Appreciate the value of practice in learning motor skills.

Developmental Level II and III (grades 3–7) students will be able to accomplish the following:

a. Find information regarding skill performance improvement including asking friends and coaches, self-evaluation, and learning to monitor personal accomplishments;

b. Know the importance of repetition and refinement for learning specialized motor skills;

c. Understand how warm-up and cool-down prevent injuries;

d. Incorporate the mechanics of skill performance in a variety of settings; and

e. Use simple strategies when participating in a variety of lead-up games (modified rules, equipment, and number of participants).

The school years are the years of opportunity—the opportunity to experience and learn many different types of physical activities and skills. Related to this standard is the opportunity to learn basic concepts of movement (see Chapter 14). Movement concepts help students understand what, where, and how the body can move. Again, emphasis is placed on experiencing the diversity of human movement. Allied to this experience is learning the correct mechanics of skill performance (see Chapter 3). Students learn about stability, force, leverage, and other factors related to efficient movement.

Instruction focuses on teaching youngsters to be self-directed learners who can evaluate their performance and self-correct their skill technique. Accepting the premise that motor skills are learned through repetition and refinement is necessary if youngsters are to become competent performers. Students need to learn how to warm up for activity and cool down when finished. Understanding simple principles of motor learning (see Chapter 3) such as practice, arousal, and refinement of skills is knowledge that will serve them in future experiences.

STANDARD 3: Participates regularly in physical activity

Developmental Level I (grades K–2) students will be able to accomplish the following:

a. Show willingness to try different physical activities;

b. Understand how activities must be enjoyable for each individual if they are to be used throughout the lifespan;

c. Monitor the amount of time spent in short bouts of activity; for example, "I played tag for five minutes"; and

d. Set aside time for play each day.

Developmental Level II and III (grades 3–7) students will be able to accomplish the following:

a. Show a willingness to try many different activities and to identify those activities best suited to them;

b. Demonstrate the ability to set physical activity goals in terms of time and type of activity;

c. Know where opportunities are available for physical activity such as after-school sports, intramurals, and private clubs and organizations;

d. Identify physical activities that can be performed outside the school environment; and

e. Participate in activities in a variety of settings, including with a friend, with parents, in the community, alone, or with a small group of friends.

The basic premise of this content standard is that active children mature into active adults (Trudeau et al. 1998, 1999). Specifically, important outcomes are learning how to monitor personal activity levels, how to plan meaningful activity programs, and how to make informed decisions about physical activity (see Chapter 12).

There are several basic considerations for lifetime activity. Sallis (1994) classifies into four categories the factors that influence people to be active: psychological, social, physical environmental, and biological. A major role of physical education is to foster those factors that are often referred to as *determinants of active living*. Psychological determinants are among the most powerful. For example, students must derive enjoyment through physical activity if they are expected to participate as adults. Enjoyment increases when there is an adequate level of proficiency in a favoured activity. Learning new motor skills demands time and an opportunity to practise. Childhood is one of the few times in life when there is adequate free time to develop such skill proficiency. Since most adults do not participate in activities unless they have an adequate level of perceived competence, learning skills becomes a priority of childhood.

Social and environmental influences also affect lifetime activity patterns. These factors include having family and peer role models, receiving encouragement from significant others, and having opportunities to participate in activities with others in one's social group. Physical environmental factors include adequate programs and facilities, adequate equipment and supplies, safe outdoor environments, and available opportunities near home and at school. Included are adequate school opportunities such as physical education, intramural programs, recreation programs, and sports. Finally, biological factors include such factors as age, gender, and ethnic and/or socioeconomic status. For more details concerning determinants of physical activity, refer to Sallis's (1994) work.

STANDARD 4: Achieves and maintains a health-enhancing level of physical fitness.

Developmental Level I (grades K–2) students will be able to accomplish the following:

a. Participate daily in at least 60 minutes of physical activity in and out of the school environment;

b. Monitor the basic physiological changes that occur when being active (increased rate of breathing, increased heart rate, and perspiration);

c. Participate in activities that develop muscular strength and endurance (for example, climbing ropes, performing hanging activities, and supporting the body weight with arms and hands);

d. Perform a variety of flexibility activities; and

e. Identify how personal body composition and different body types impact physical performance.

Developmental Level II and III (grades 3–7) students will be able to accomplish the following:

a. Participate daily in at least 60 minutes of moderate to vigorous physical activity in and out of the school environment;

b. Engage in a variety of activities that develop muscular strength ranging from exercises to climbing;

c. Perform activities that increase and maintain flexibility;

d. Know basic elements of safe participation in activity (including performing safe exercises, avoiding overtraining and muscle soreness, and understanding the inherent risk of activities);

e. Monitor the intensity of exercise by counting heart and breathing rates;

f. Understand that all health-related fitness components (body composition, muscular strength and endurance, flexibility, and cardiorespiratory endurance) need to be given attention for total physical fitness;

g. Evaluate personal health-related physical fitness and interpret the meaning of the results; and

h. Understand the basic principles of training, such as frequency, intensity, and time.

Physical fitness instruction (see Chapter 12) concentrates on the process of participating in daily physical activity rather than being concerned about the product of fitness (how many repetitions, how fast, or how far). When students accept responsibility for participating in regular activity, fitness is an authentic learning experience, the results of which may last a lifetime. Meeting this standard means helping students develop positive attitudes that carry over into adulthood.

A portion of each class period should be allotted to learning and experiencing fitness. It is not enough to learn the facts of fitness; there must be a participatory experience in the elementary school years (see Figure 1.3). This is not to say that knowledge is unimportant, but it is not enough. Many people know the facts of fitness but do not stay active because they have not learned the activity *habit*. Students

Figure 1.3

Fitness is a participatory experience.

must participate in physical fitness activity; the best way to learn the amount of effort necessary to maintain personal fitness is to experience it.

Meeting this standard implies students will leave elementary school understanding the basic facts of fitness. Because each individual has unique needs and because programs must be developed according to these needs, an understanding of genetic diversity among people (such as differences in muscle type, cardiorespiratory endurance, and motor coordination) is requisite for helping students understand their physical capabilities. Understanding concepts such as proper exercise form, how much activity is enough, and how to safely participate in activity helps create a positive mindset in youngsters. Finally, students learn to personally evaluate their fitness levels and set personal goals.

> **STANDARD 5: Exhibits responsible personal and social behaviour that respects self and others in physical activity.**

Developmental Level I (grades K–2) students will be able to accomplish the following:

a. Participate in a variety of multicultural activities;

b. Understand how different individuals make a variety of contributions to the group;

c. Explain simple differences and similarities among activities played in different cultural and ethnic backgrounds;

d. Show empathy for the concerns and limitations of peers;

e. Resolve conflicts in an acceptable nonviolent manner;

f. Follow rules and procedures in physical activity settings;

g. Participate safely by observing safety procedures for equipment and apparatus;

h. Understand and follow the rules of low-organized games;

i. Cooperate in a group setting and be willing to take turns and help others;

j. Show the ability to behave responsibly when differences of opinion occur; and

k. Play willingly with all students regardless of race, gender, or disability.

Figure 1.4

Learning to cooperate with others.

Developmental Level II and III (grades 3–7) students will be able to accomplish the following:

a. Understand how sports, games, and dance play a central role in modern-day cultures;

b. React in a positive manner toward individuals who have cultural or ethnic differences, or who have limitations;

c. Demonstrate a willingness to participate with peers regardless of diversity or disability;

d. Enjoy and interact with peers in a variety of physical activity settings;

e. Resolve conflicts in an acceptable nonviolent manner;

f. Reveal the ability to create and modify rules to better meet the needs of the group;

g. Understand that cooperative skills must be developed before competitive games can be played;

h. Understand how sports and games have an impact on issues of gender and diversity;

i. Recognize the benefits (social and physical) derived from participation in group games and activities;

j. Show a willingness to follow rules, procedures, and safety guidelines in all physical activity settings; and

k. Behave in a caring and helping manner toward all peers.

Physical education classes offer a unique environment for learning effective social skills. Children have the opportunity to internalize and practise the merits of participation, cooperation, competition, and tolerance. Some terms, such as *citizenship* and *fair play,* help define the desired social atmosphere. Through listening, empathy, and guidance, children learn to differentiate between acceptable and unacceptable ways of expressing feelings. Youngsters must develop an awareness of how they interact with others, and how the quality of their behaviour influences others' responses to them.

Responsible behaviour (see Chapter 5) implies behaving in a manner that doesn't negatively impact on others. Hellison (2003) and others have developed methodologies for teaching responsible behaviour. Responsible behaviour occurs in a hierarchy of behaviour from irresponsible to caring and behaving in a responsible manner. Youngsters also have the opportunity to learn to win and lose in an acceptable manner and to assume responsibility for their performances. Accepting the consequences of one's behaviour is a lesson that arises regularly in the physical education environment.

Conflicts must be solved in a nonviolent manner (see Chapter 5) that allows all parties to maintain self-esteem and dignity. Physical education offers an excellent opportunity to apply conflict resolution skills because behaviour is easily observed. Students learn to solve conflicts and disagreements in a peaceful and nonthreatening manner. Many diversity and gender issues (see Chapter 4) arise in activity settings, and insightful and caring instruction can minimize negative stereotypes. Learning about the similarities and differences among cultures and how all people share common values and beliefs is an important outcome.

Cooperation precedes the development of competition, which makes it an important behaviour to learn in elementary physical education settings (see Figure 1.4). Without cooperation, competitive games cannot be played. The nature of competitive games demands cooperation and fair play, and when these are not present, the joy of participation is lost. Cooperative games help children learn that all teammates are needed to reach group goals.

STANDARD 6: Values physical activity for health, enjoyment, challenge, self-expression, and/or social interaction.

Developmental Level I (grades K–2) students will be able to accomplish the following:

a. Explain why physical activity is important for good health;

b. Know basic muscle groups and bones related to movement;

c. Know that everybody should be active at least 30 minutes a day; and

d. Understand the importance of eating a balanced diet.

Developmental Level II and III (grades 3–7) students will be able to accomplish the following:

a. Make meaningful decisions about personal wellness by gathering information, considering the alternatives, and understanding the consequences that accompany such choices;

b. Know what types of physical activity are important for feeling good;

c. Understand factors that are detrimental to good health, such as substance abuse and stress;

d. Understand how physical activity is important for weight control;

e. Understand the importance of safety, particularly in activity settings such as bicycling, swimming, sports, and as a pedestrian; and

f. Understand how proper nutrition is important for physical performance.

This standard focuses on the knowledge necessary to make thoughtful decisions that influence an individual's health and wellness (see Chapter 13). Wellness implies developing a lifestyle that is balanced in all phases, with *moderation* being the keyword. Wellness is predicated on developing a clear understanding of choices and alternatives that lead to making wise choices. In elementary school, basic wellness instruction covers how the skeletal, muscular, and cardiorespiratory systems function. In addition, simple principles about nutrition, stress, substance abuse, and safety can be woven into daily instruction so children have an opportunity to learn about healthy lifestyles.

Essential Components of a Quality Program

Physical education teachers need to know the essential components of a quality physical education program. In other words, what are critical elements that should be included to ensure youngsters receive a quality physical education experience? The following components interlock to form a comprehensive physical education program that will be valued by parents, teachers, and students. Each of the components is described briefly in this section. In-depth coverage is offered in the referenced chapters under each point; Figure 1.5 identifies the relevant components.

I. A quality physical education program is organized around content standards that offer direction and continuity to instruction and evaluation. A quality program is driven by a set of content standards. These standards are defined by a number of competencies youngsters are expected to accomplish. Standards are measurable so that both teachers and students know when progress has been made. Previously in this chapter you read about a comprehensive set of physical education content standards.

II. A quality program is student-centred and based on the developmental urges, characteristics, and interests of students. Youngsters learn best when the skills and activities they must learn match their physical and emotional development. See Chapter 8 to learn about the urges, characteristics, and interests of children and how they have an impact on the creation of a quality physical education program. Chapter 4 offers many ideas for understanding and teaching to the personal needs of students. A quality program focuses on the successes of students so that they have the motivation to continue. Developing a positive set of behaviours toward physical activity is a key goal of physical education. Chapter 4 also discusses essential elements of teaching and how to positively reinforce youngsters during learning situations.

III. Quality physical education makes physical activity and motor-skill development the core of the program. Physical education is the only place in the total school curriculum where instruction focuses on teaching motor skills. Physical education is a unique discipline that focuses on physical activity to assure the physical development of students. It is critical that the program centre on skill development and quality physical activity. Chapters 2 and 12 explain the importance of physical activity for the optimal growth and development of youngsters.

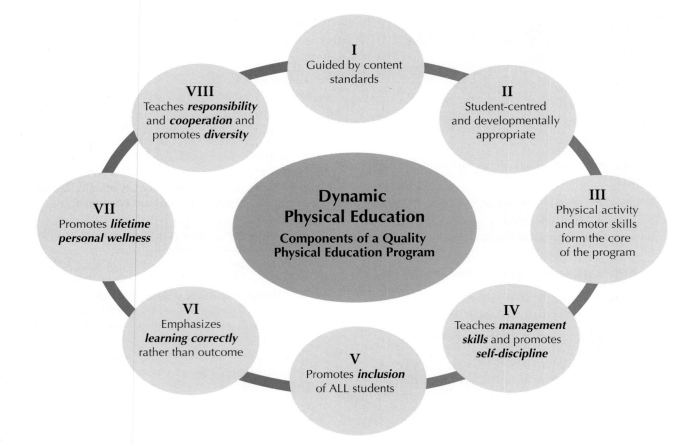

Figure 1.5

Essential components of a quality physical education program.

IV. Physical education programs help students learn personal management skills and prosocial behaviour. Learning outcomes are likely to be achieved when a class is well organized and students are actively involved in productive practice. Chapter 5 offers different methods for teaching personal management skills and promoting prosocial behaviour.

V. Quality programs emphasize inclusion of all students. Physical education should provide opportunity for all youngsters (regardless of ability) to learn skills in a caring and positive environment. All students must feel successful if they are expected to enjoy and value physical activity. See Chapter 7 for inclusion strategies for youngsters who have special needs and for modifying activities so all children can be successful.

VI. In a quality physical education setting, instruction focuses on the process of learning skills. When youngsters are learning new motor skills, performing the skill correctly is more important than the outcome of the skill. Translated, this means it is more important to teach a youngster to catch a

beanbag properly than to worry about how many he catches or misses. Chapter 3 offers strategies for optimizing skill learning. Chapter 6 helps explain when to focus on the process or product evaluation of motor skills.

VII. A quality physical education program teaches lifetime activities that students can use to promote their health and personal wellness. Quality physical education programs prepare youngsters to participate in activities that they can perform when they become adults. If a program is restricted to team sports, the program will be of little value to the majority of adults. Participation in sports activities declines rapidly with age. By far, walking is the most often reported activity for adult Canadians (Craig, Cameron, Russell, & Beaulieu, 2001). Other activities such as bicycling, jogging, swimming, and aerobics are also popular with adults. Quality physical education looks to the future and offers activities youngsters can enjoy and use as adults. Chapter 12 offers information about the importance of teaching lifetime physical activity skills in a physical education setting. Chapter 13 offers instructional strategies for teaching wellness and developing a healthy lifestyle.

VIII. Quality physical education teaches cooperation and responsibility and helps students develop sensitivity to diversity and gender issues. Cooperative skills have to precede competitive skills. Physical education is an effective laboratory for learning to behave responsibly. Chapter 5 presents ways to teach youngsters responsible behaviour and conflict-resolution techniques. Students need to learn about similarities and differences between cultures. Chapter 11 offers ideas for integrating cultural learning and content into physical education. Coeducational activities help students understand how activities cut across gender and stereotypes. When gender differences occur in physical activities, it is an excellent time to point out that individuals differ, regardless of race or gender. Chapter 4 offers a number of strategies for dealing with gender and diversity issues.

Critical Thinking

1. The federal government established the Children's Fitness Tax Credit, effective on January 1, 2007. Examine this program and discuss how it may or may not address concerns associated with physical inactivity of Canadian children.

2. In addition to the societal influences mentioned in this chapter, discuss other factors that may impact elementary school physical education.

References and Suggested Readings

Alberta Learning. (2000). *Physical education kindergarten to grade 12 program of studies.* Edmonton, AB: Author.

Anderson, D., Broom, E., Pooley, J.C., Rhodes, E., Robertson, D.G., & Schrodt, B. (1989). *Foundations of Canadian physical education, recreation and sport studies.* Dubuque, IA: W.C. Brown.

Bailey, D. (1973). Exercise, fitness and physical education for the growing child—A concern. *Canadian Journal of Public Health, 64,* 421–430.

Ball, G. & McCargar, J. (2003). Childhood obesity in Canada: A review of prevalence estimates and risk factors for cardiovascular diseases and Type 2 diabetes. *Canadian Journal of Applied Physiology, 28*(1), 117–140.

British Columbia Ministry of Education. (1995). *Physical education K–7 integrated resource package.* Victoria, BC: Author.

Cameron, C., Craig, C., & Paolin, S. (2005). *Local opportunities for physical activity and sport: Trends from 1999–2004.* Ottawa, ON: Canadian Fitness and Lifestyle Research Institute.

Cameron, C., Craig, C.L., Stephens, T., & Ready, T. A. (2002). *Increasing physical activity: Supporting an active workforce.*

Ottawa, ON: Canadian Fitness and Lifestyle Research Institute.

Canadian Association for Health, Physical Education, Recreation and Dance. (1996). *Physical education 2000—foundations, guidelines and learning outcomes for the future.* Gloucester, ON: Author.

Canadian Fitness and Lifestyle Research Institute. (1983). *Canada fitness survey 1981.* Ottawa, ON: Author.

Canadian Fitness and Lifestyle Research Institute. (1995). *1995 physical activity monitor.* Ottawa, ON: Author.

Canadian Fitness and Lifestyle Research Institute. (1997). *1997 physical activity monitor.* Ottawa, ON: Author.

Canadian Fitness and Lifestyle Research Institute. (1998). *1998 physical activity monitor.* Ottawa, ON: Author.

Canadian Fitness and Lifestyle Research Institute. (1999). *1999 physical activity monitor.* Ottawa, ON: Author.

Chad, K.E. Humbert, M.L., & Jackson, P.L. (1999). The effectiveness of the Canadian quality daily physical education program on school physical education. *Research Quarterly for Exercise and Sport, 70*(1), 55–61.

Cragg, S., Cameron, C., Craig, C.L., & Russell, S. (1999). *Canada's children and youth: A physical activity profile.* Ottawa, ON: Canadian Fitness and Lifestyle Research Institute.

Craig, C.L., & Cameron, C. (2004). *Increasing physical activity: Assessing trends from 1998–2003.* Ottawa, ON: Canadian Fitness and Lifestyle Research Institute.

Craig, C.L., Cameron, C., Russell, S., & Beaulieu, A. (2001). *Increasing physical activity: Supporting children's participation.* Ottawa, ON: Canadian Fitness and Lifestyle Research Institute.

Craig, C., Russell, S., Cameron, C., & Beaulieu, A. (1999). *Foundation for joint action: Reducing physical inactivity.* Ottawa, ON: Canadian Fitness and Lifestyle Research Institute.

Éducation Québec. (2003). *Quebec education program—chapter 9 personal development. Introduction to the physical education and health program.* Quebec City, PQ: Author.

Edwards, P. (1999). Building a healthy future. *Canadian Journal of Public Health.*

Health Canada. (1996). *Physical inactivity: A framework for action.* Ottawa, ON: Author.

Health Canada. (1999). *Toward a healthy future: Second report on the health of Canadians.* Ottawa, ON: Author.

Hellison, D. (2003). *Teaching responsibility through physical activity* (2nd ed.). Champaign, IL: Human Kinetics.

Katzmarzyk, P. & Janssen, I. (2004). The economic costs associated with physical inactivity and obesity in Canada: An Update. *Canadian Journal of Applied Physiology, 29*(1), 90–115.

Krishnamoorthy, J., Hart, C., & Jelalian, E. (2006). The epidemic of childhood obesity: Review of research and implications for public policy. *Social Policy Report, 19*(2), 3–19.

Lalonde, M. (1974). *New perspective on the health of Canadians: A working document.* Ottawa, ON: National Ministry of Health and Welfare.

Manitoba Education and Training. (2000). *Manitoba curriculum framework of outcomes for active healthy lifestyles— kindergarten–senior 4 physical education/health education.* Winnipeg, Manitoba: Author.

Martens, F. (1986). *Basic concepts of physical education: The foundation in Canada.* Champaign, IL: Stipes Publishing.

National Association for Sport and Physical Education. (2004). *Moving into the future: National standards for physical education.* 2nd. Ed. Reston, VA: Author.

New Brunswick Department of Education. (2002). *Middle level physical education.* Fredericton, NB: Author.

Newfoundland and Labrador Department of Education. (2004). *Physical education—primary and elementary curriculum guide.* St. John's, NF: Author.

Nova Scotia Education. (2000). *Physical education curriculum: Grades primary–6.* Halifax, NS: Author.

Ontario Ministry of Education and Training. (1998). *The Ontario curriculum, grades 1–8: Health and Physical Education.* Toronto, ON: Author.

Pate, R., Davis, M., Robinson, T.N., Stone, E., McKenzie, T., & Young, J. (2006). Promoting physical activity in children and youth—A leadership role for schools. *Journal of the American Heart Association, 114,* 1214–1224.

Prince Edward Island Department of Education. (2005). *Elementary program of studies and authorized material 2005–2006.* Charlottetown, PEI: Author.

Rees, R., Kavanagh, J., Harden, A., Shephard, J., Brunton, G., Oliver, S., Oakley, A. (2006). Young people and physical activity: A systematic review matching their views to effective interventions. *Health Education Research, 21*(6), 806–825.

Sallis, J.F. (1994). Influences on physical activity of children, adolescents, and adults or determinants of active living. *Physical and Fitness Research Digest, 1*(7), 1–8.

Saskatchewan Learning. (1999). *Elementary physical education curriculum.* Regina, SK: Author.

Shephard, R.J. (1997). Curricular physical activity and academic performance. *Pediatric Exercise Science, 9,* 113–126.

Shephard, R.J. & Trudeau, F. (2000). The legacy of physical education: Influences on adult lifestyle. *Pediatric Exercise Science, 12,* 34–50.

Shields, M. (2005). Measured obesity: Overweight Canadian children and adults. *Nutrition: Findings from the Canadian community health survey, 1,* 82–620 – MWE 2005001.

Stephens, T. & Craig, C.L. (1990). *The well-being of Canadians: Highlights of the 1988 Campbell's survey.*

Ottawa, ON: Canadian Fitness and Lifestyle Research Institute.

Taras, H. (2005). Physical activity and student performance at school. *Journal of School Health, 75*(6), 214–218.

Telama, R., Yang, X., Hirvensalo, M., & Raitakari, O. (2006). Participation in organized youth sport as a predictor of adult physical activity: A 21-year longitudinal study. *Pediatric Exercise Science, 17,* 76–88.

Thompson, A., Humbert, M.L., & Mirwald, R. (2003). A longitudinal study of the impact of childhood and adolescent physical activity experiences on adult physical activity perceptions and behaviours. *Qualitative Health Research, 13*(3), 358–377.

Thompson, A. Mirwald, R., Faulkner, R., & Bailey, D. (2001). Tracking of physical activity from childhood and adolescence to adulthood. *Canadian Society of Exercise Physiology: From Mechanisms to Action, 67.*

Trudeau, F., Laurencelle, J., Tremblay, J., Rajic, J. & Shephard, R.J. (1998). A long-term follow-up of participants in the Trois-Rivières semi-longitudinal study of growth and development. *Pediatric Exercise Science, 10,* 366–377.

Trudeau, F, Laurencelle, J., Tremblay, J., Rajic, J. & Shephard, R.J. (1999). Daily primary school physical education: Effects on physical activity during adult life. *Medicine and Science in Sports and Exercise,* 111–117.

Trudeau, F. & Shephard, R. (2005). Contribution of school programmes to physical activity levels and attitudes in children and adults. *Sports Medicine, 35*(2), 89–105.

 # Weblinks

Canadian Association for Health, Physical Education, Recreation and Dance: www.capherd.ca/e

This site provides information about the organization, its activities, workshops, conferences, and publications, as well as links to other relevant physical education sites.

Canadian Fitness and Lifestyle Research Institute: www.cflri.ca

CFLRI is a national research agency concerned with educating Canadians about the importance of leading healthy, active lifestyles. This organization is well known for publication of the Physical Activity Benchmarks Program. A wide range of research results are available on their website.

Coalition for Active Living: www.activeliving.ca

The Coalition for Active Living is a national action group of over 80 organizations advocating to ensure that the environments where Canadians live, work, learn and play support regular physical activity. The Coalition is responsible for the development of the *Framework for a Pan-Canadian Physical Activity Strategy.*

CHAPTER 2

Physical Activity for the Growing Child

Essential Components

I	Organized around content standards
II	**Student-centred and developmentally appropriate**
III	**Physical activity and motor skill development form the core of the program**
IV	Teaches management skills and self-discipline
V	Promotes inclusion of all students
VI	Focuses on process over product
VII	Promotes lifetime personal health and wellness
VIII	Teaches cooperation and responsibility and promotes sensitivity to diversity

Physical Education Standards

1	Students are able to move competently using a variety of fundamental and specialized motor skills.
2	Students can monitor and maintain a health-enhancing level of physical fitness.
3	Students are able to apply movement concepts and basic mechanics of skill performance when learning and refining motor skills.
4	Students comprehend the basic principles of wellness and are able to apply concepts that enable them to make meaningful decisions that positively impact their health and wellness.
5	Students participate in a wide variety of physical activities and learn how to maintain a personalized active lifestyle.
6	Students demonstrate empathy, understanding, and respect for the numerous differences exhibited by people in an activity setting.
7	Students exhibit responsible and self-directed behaviours that lead to positive social interactions in physical activity.

OVERVIEW

Physical activity positively affects the growth and development of children. Research supports the value of an active lifestyle for optimum growth and development. There is a positive correlation between the incidence of certain health disorders and a sedentary lifestyle. Lifetime involvement in physical activity often depends on early positive participation. Developing motor skills at an early age provides the tools needed to be physically active throughout life. Guidelines are discussed for safe participation in physical activity including strength training, running, and hot and cold weather.

OUTCOMES

- Describe the need for physical activity.
- Cite stages of the growing child.
- Understand the relationship between physical activity and the development of muscular strength and endurance and skeletal growth.
- Define aerobic capacity and discuss its relationship to health and physical activity.
- Understand the terms *overweight* and *obesity*, and their impact on motor performance and relationship to the health of an individual.
- Discuss the role organized youth sports should play in the proper growth and development of children.
- Identify guidelines to follow when children exercise in hot or cold weather conditions.
- Describe the recommended approach to distance running and strength training for preadolescent children.

*P*hysical activity has a significant impact on the growing child, and this chapter offers an overview. Many of the studies cited offer excellent justification for the inclusion of physical education in the total school curriculum. For example, the high levels of obesity in youth, the need for skill competency so children have tools to be active for a lifetime, and the long-term effects of physical activity are strong arguments for a well-taught, well-organized physical education program.

The Need for Physical Activity

The health risks associated with physical inactivity are well documented in all populations. Clearly, promoting physical activity has been adopted as a new imperative for public health (Sparling, Owen, Lambert, & Haskell, 2000), including calls for public health surveillance of physical activity (Macera & Pratt, 2000). Indeed, the Canadian government in 1995 stated that "physical inactivity represented a major health risk and that physically inactive Canadians were a priority for government action" (*Report on the Health of Canadians*, 1996). The government set a national goal of reducing the number of inactive Canadians by 10% by 2003. Craig and Cameron (2004) reported that this goal of reducing the percentage of adults who are inactive was met. While this represents a positive change in Canadians' activity levels, Craig and Cameron highlighted several concerns including an increase in the proportion of Canadians who are overweight and obese, and the groups who were least active in the initial research (low-income earners and older adults) have fallen further behind. The recent proposed pan–Canadian Healthy Living target, which would increase by 20% by 2015 the proportion of Canadians who participate regularly in physical activity, eat healthily, and maintain a healthy body weight, continues to emphasize the continued health crisis.

Perhaps not surprisingly, data on the physical activity and health status of Canadian children causes alarm. In Canada, it has been estimated that only one-third of children and youth are active enough to reap the benefits for healthy development, and their levels of physical activity decrease with age (Craig, Cameron, Russell, & Beaulieu, 2001). In addition, obesity among Canadian children is becoming an increasing problem. Tremblay and Willms (2000) report that the prevalence of overweight and obese children more than doubled between 1981 and 1996. In addition, the occurrence of overweight and obesity in children tends to be higher among younger children (Willms, Tremblay, & Katzmarzyk, 2003). Active Healthy Kids Canada (2006), a national advocacy group for high-quality, accessible, and enjoyable physical activity experiences for children and youth, recently released their *Report Card on Physical Activity for Children and Youth*, with Canada scoring an overall "D" grade. In addition to the previously mentioned low physical activity levels and high obesity levels, the report card also mentions a high level of television and/or computer "screen time," with only 20% of children meeting the Canadian Paediatric Society guideline of two hours or less of screen time daily. The need for activity as an integral part of children's lifestyles is strong. Because the vast majority of Canadian children are in school, the greatest potential for making a meaningful difference lies in the school context strengthened by community services and policies. Physical education programs that teach lifestyle changes in physical activity can lead to improved health for youngsters (Ernst & Pangrazi, 1999). Programs that focus on activity give all youngsters the opportunity for success and long-term health. The need is clear: Design physical education programs to teach youngsters how to live an active and healthy lifestyle. However, despite this potential less than half of Canadian children aged 6–17 years take physical education classes 3 or more times a week at school and 17% have daily physical education (Craig & Cameron, 2004).

The Growing Child

Growth patterns are generally controlled by genetic makeup at birth. Although an unhealthy environment can have a negative impact on proper growth and development, this section examines maturation patterns that are common to the majority of youngsters. All youngsters follow a general growth pattern; however, each child's timing is unique. Some children are advanced physically for their chronological age, whereas others are slow maturers. There is only cause for concern when aberration from the norm is excessive.

Growth Patterns

Teachers and parents should know if youngsters are maturing normally. When heights and weights are plotted on a graph from year to year, a distance curve can be developed. These curves (see Figure 2.1) give an indication of how tall and heavy children are expected to be during a specific year of life. Another way to examine growth patterns is to look at a velocity curve. The velocity curve reveals how much a child grows on a year-to-year basis (see Figure 2.2). Children go through a rapid period of growth from birth to age five. From age six to the onset of adolescence, growth increases at a slower rate. However, it is not uncommon for some children to experience a *midgrowth*

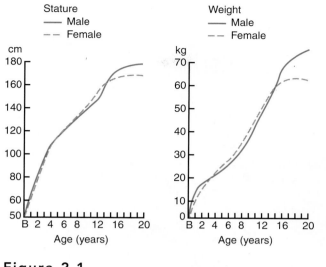

Figure 2.1

Distance curves for height and weight.

Source: Malina, R., 1975. *Growth and development: The first twenty years in man.* Minneapolis: Burgess, 19.

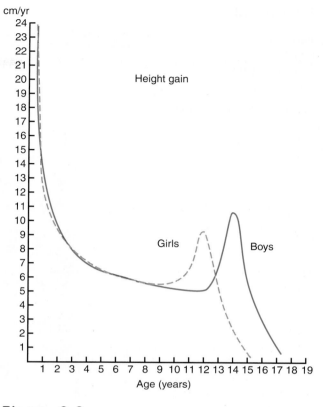

Figure 2.2

Growth velocity curve for height.

Source: Tanner, J.M., Whitehouse, R.H., & Takaishi, M. 1966. *Archives of diseases in childhood,* 41, 466.

spurt in height between 6.5 and 8.5 years of age (Malina, Bouchard, & Bar-Or, 2004). A guideline with regard to motor learning is that when growth is rapid, the ability to learn new skills decreases. Because the rate of growth slows during the elementary school years, this is an excellent window for learning motor skills.

During the elementary school years, on average boys are slightly taller and heavier than girls. Growth accelerates once again before and during puberty. Girls reach the adolescent growth spurt first, and grow taller and heavier during the grade six and grade seven years; boys quickly catch up and grow larger and stronger through to adulthood. Generally, the peak growth rate in boys occurs at about 14 years of age, with girls starting their growth spurt about 2 years earlier (Roche & Sun, 2003). However, it is important to note that age of onset of puberty and completion can vary considerably between individuals. Growth charts based on a large sample of children have been developed by the U.S. National Center for Health Statistics (see Figures 2.3 and 2.4). These tables can be consulted to identify both height and weight percentiles for children ages 2 through 20. The tables offer an opportunity to visualize marked differences among children in a so-called normal population.

Young children have relatively short legs for their overall height. The trunk is longer in relation to the legs during early childhood. The ratio of leg length (standing height) to trunk length (sitting height) is similar for boys and girls through age 11. The head makes up one-fourth of the child's total length at birth and about one-sixth at age six. Figure 2.5 illustrates how body proportions change with growth. Because K–2 students have short legs

in relation to their upper body, they are "top heavy" and fall more easily than adults do. This high centre of gravity will gradually lower and give children increased stability and balance. For discussion of motor skill developmental patterns and expectations see Chapter 3 and Chapter 15.

Developmental Patterns

The learning and development of motor skills varies among children of similar chronological age. However, the *sequence* of skill development in youngsters is similar and progresses in an orderly fashion. Three development patterns typify the growth of primary-grade children:

1. Development, in general, proceeds from head to foot (cephalocaudal): that is, coordination and management of body parts occur in the upper body before they are observed in the lower. For example, children develop throwing skills before kicking competency.

2. Development occurs from inside to outside (proximodistal). Children control their arms before they control their hands. They can reach for objects before they can grasp them.

Figure 2.3

Two to twenty years: Boys' stature-for-age and weight-for-age percentiles.

Source: Developed by the National Center for Health Statistics in collaboration with the National Center for Chronic Disease Prevention and Health Promotion (2000).

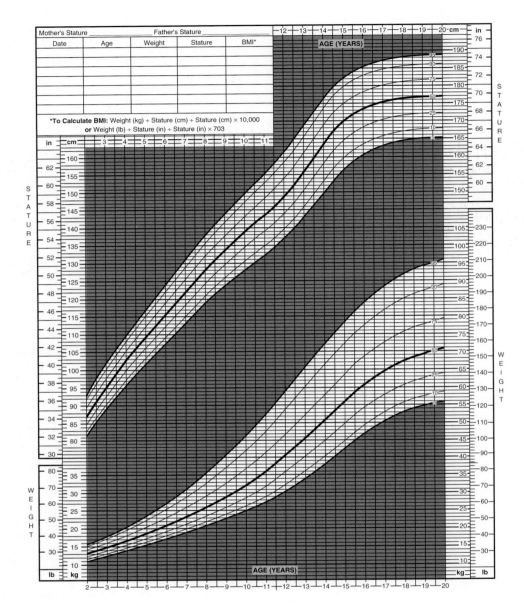

3. Development proceeds from general to specific. Gross motor movements are learned before fine motor coordination and refined movement patterns. As children learn motor skills, nonproductive movement is gradually eliminated. When learners begin to eliminate wasteful and tense movements and are able to concentrate on reproduction of a smooth and consistent performance, motor learning is occurring.

Body Physique

Each of us is born with a body type based on body composition and skeletal frame. Somatotyping is a way to describe these general body types or physiques. Sheldon, Dupertuis, and McDermott (1954) developed the original scheme for somatotyping, identifying three major physiques: *endomorphy, mesomorphy,* and *ectomorphy.* Rating is assessed from standardized photographs on a 7-point scale, with 1

Figure 2.4

Two to twenty years: Girls stature-for-age and weight-for-age percentiles.

Source: Developed by the National Center for Health Statistics in collaboration with the National Center for Chronic Disease Prevention and Health Promotion (2000).

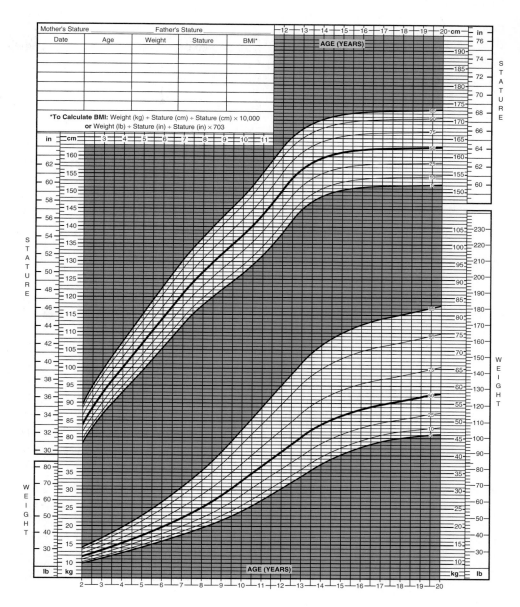

being the least expressive and 7 the most expressive of the specific component. The ratings of each component give a total score that results in identification of an individual's somatotype. A similar system of classification for children is available for teachers who are interested in understanding the body physiques of children (Petersen, 1967).

The *endomorph* is described as pear-shaped (wide hips and narrow shoulders), a protruding abdomen, and soft and round in contour. The *mesomorph* is characterized as having a predominance of muscle and bone, wedge-shaped (broad shoulders and narrow hips), and is often described as "muscled." The *ectomorph* is identified as being extremely thin, with a minimum of muscle development, and is described as "long and lean."

A child's physique (somatotype) affects the quality of his or her motor performance. In general, children who possess a mesomorphic body type perform best in activities requiring strength, speed, and agility. These children

Figure 2.5

Changing body proportions from conception to adulthood.

Source: Whipple, D. (1966). *Dynamics of development: Euthenic pediatrics,* 122. New York: McGraw-Hill.

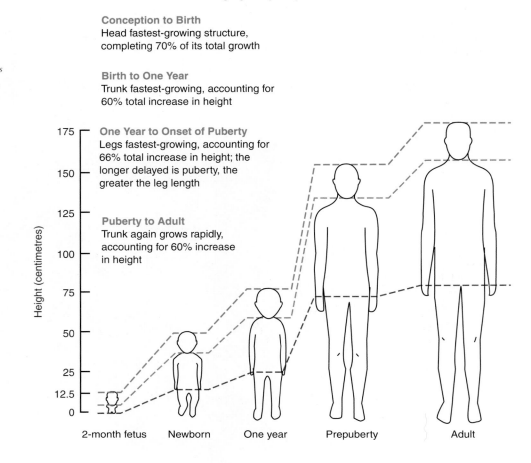

Changing Body Proportions

Conception to Birth
Head fastest-growing structure, completing 70% of its total growth

Birth to One Year
Trunk fastest-growing, accounting for 60% total increase in height

One Year to Onset of Puberty
Legs fastest-growing, accounting for 66% total increase in height; the longer delayed is puberty, the greater the leg length

Puberty to Adult
Trunk again grows rapidly, accounting for 60% increase in height

2-month fetus   Newborn   One year   Prepuberty   Adult

usually perform well in most team sports, because these activities require strength, speed, and agility. Children with an ectomorph body type may perform well in aerobic endurance activities such as jogging, cross-country running, and track and field, and may be less able in activities requiring strength and power. While children with an endomorph body type need more physical activity to maintain a healthy body weight and could be more prone to injury, they can be fit and excel in areas such as aquatics and creative dance. However, it should be emphasized that body type is meant to provide some general guidelines to help teachers plan and provide varied and inclusive programs for all students and body types. Somatotype classification illustrates how dramatically children differ in body physique, and necessitates that instruction accommodate individual differences.

Skeletal Maturity

Teachers often speak about the *maturity* of students. Physical maturity—usually measured by comparing chronological age with skeletal age—has a strong impact on the performance of children in physical education. Ossification (hardening) of the bones occurs in the centre of the bone shaft and at the ends of the long bones (growth plates). The rate of ossification gives an accurate indication of a child's rate of maturation. Maturation rate can be identified by X-raying the wrist bones and comparing the development of the subject's bones with a set of standardized X-rays (Roche, Chumlea, & Thissen, 1988). Children whose chronological age is beyond skeletal age are said to be late (or slow) maturers. If skeletal age is ahead of chronological age, children are labelled early (fast) maturers.

Studies examining skeletal age (Gruelich & Pyle, 1959; Krahenbuhl & Pangrazi, 1983) consistently show that a five- to six-year variation in skeletal maturity exists in a typical classroom of youngsters. For example, a class of grade 3 students who are all 8 years old chronologically would range in skeletal age from 5 to 11 years. This means that some youngsters are actually 5-year-olds skeletally and are trying to compete with others who are as mature as 11-year-olds. Effective programs have to offer activities that are *developmentally appropriate* and suited to children's level of maturity.

Early maturing children of both sexes are generally heavier and taller for their age than are average- or late-maturing students. The motor performance of boys is related to skeletal maturity in that a more mature boy usually performs better on motor tasks (Clarke, 1971). For girls, however, motor performance appears not to be related to physiological maturity; both Malina (1978), and Beunen and Malina (1988) found that late maturation is commonly associated with exceptional motor performance. Students do not mature at the same rate and are not at similar levels of readiness to learn (see Figure 2.6). Offering a wide spectrum of developmentally appropriate activities helps ensure that youngsters will be successful regardless of the maturity factor.

Skeletal Health

It is increasingly well accepted that adult skeletal health is established in childhood. In fact, risk factors for adult osteoporosis such as high levels of physical inactivity already present in childhood and track into adulthood. Weight-bearing exercise is encouraged as part of an overall healthy bone program for children (Greer & Krebs, 2006). According to MacKelvie, McKay, Petit, Moran, & Khan (2002) the ages of ten to twelve years provide a window of opportunity when growing bone appears to respond more positively to physical activity than any other time throughout a lifetime. More specifically, weight-bearing exercise appears to have the greatest effects on bone mineral density. Consider the following when using physical activity to maximize bone health in your physical education classes (Bailey & Martin, 1994):

1. Include weight-bearing activities such as rope jumping, running, and walking on a regular basis.

Figure 2.6

Children the same age vary in size and maturity.

2. Activities should work all large muscle groups.

3. Short, intense daily activity is better than prolonged activity done infrequently.

Muscular Development and Strength

Strength is an important factor in performing motor skills. In the elementary school years, muscular strength increases linearly with chronological age, with changes in strength consistent with changes in body weight (McArdle, Katch, & Katch, 2000). A similar yearly increase occurs until adolescence, at which time a rapid increase in strength occurs, most notably in males. In general, throughout the elementary years boys are about 10% stronger than girls (McArdle, 2000). Despite this difference, boys and girls can participate on somewhat even terms in most activities, particularly if their size and mass are similar. Gender differences in strength become much more apparent and widen after puberty, with males on average stronger than females in most muscle groups. Strength is an important part of a balanced fitness program and offers youngsters a better opportunity to find success in a variety of motor development activities.

Muscle Fibre Type and Performance

The number of muscle fibres an individual possesses is genetically determined. An increase in muscle size is accomplished by an increase in the size of each muscle fibre. The size of the muscles is determined primarily by the number of fibres and secondarily by the size of the fibres. An individual is therefore somewhat muscularly limited by genetic restrictions.

Skeletal muscle tissue contains a ratio of fast-contracting fibres (fast twitch [FT]) to slow-contracting fibres (slow twitch [ST]) (Saltin, 1973). The percentage of fast- versus slow-contracting fibres varies from muscle to muscle and among individuals. At birth and through childhood, slow-twitch fibres constitute about 50% to 60% of all muscle fibres. During this same period, about 25% fast-twitch fibres are found, along with 15% to 20% of undifferentiated fibres (Gabbard, 2004). By adulthood there are very few undifferentiated fibres.

What is the significance of variation in the ratio of muscle fibre type? ST fibres have a rich supply of blood and related energy mechanisms. This results in a slowly contracting, fatigue-resistant muscle fibre that is well suited to endurance-type (aerobic) activities. In contrast, FT fibres are capable of bursts of intense activity but are subject to rapid fatigue. These fibres are well suited to activities demanding short-term speed and power (for example, pull-ups, standing long jump, and shuttle run). ST fibres facilitate performance in the mile run or other endurance-oriented activity.

Surprisingly, elementary-aged children who do best in activities requiring FT fibres also do best in distance running (Krahenbuhl & Pangrazi, 1983). Muscle fibre metabolic specialization does not occur until adolescence; this fact is a strong argument for keeping all youngsters involved in varied physical activity throughout the elementary years. A youngster who does poorly in elementary school may do quite well during and after adolescence, when a high percentage of ST fibres will aid in the performance of aerobic activity. On the other hand, the same child may do poorly in a physical education program dominated by team sports that demand quickness and strength. Designing a program that incorporates activities using a range of physical attributes (that is, endurance, balance, and flexibility) is essential.

Aerobic Capacity

Maximal aerobic power is an individual's maximum ability to use oxygen in the body for metabolic purposes. The oxygen uptake of an individual, all other factors being equal, determines the quality of endurance-oriented performance. Generally, maximal oxygen uptake increases with growth through childhood; both sexes have similar values until approximately 12 years of age. Following puberty, maximum oxygen uptake in males continues to increase until about age 18, while increases in females are minimal beyond 14 years of age (Gabbard, 2004).

Adults interested in increasing endurance-based athletic performance train extensively to increase aerobic power. A frequently asked question is whether training will increase the aerobic performance of children. Research results have been split. Some researchers have found an increase in aerobic power through training, whereas others report that training has no impact on the aerobic system. Payne and Morrow (1993) analyzed 28 studies dealing with the impact of exercise on aerobic performance in children. The results showed that training caused little, if any, increase in aerobic power in prepubescent children. If there is improvement in running performance in young children, Bar-Or (1983) postulates that it may occur because they become more efficient mechanically or improve in anaerobic metabolism. Another theory is that young children are active enough to make intergroup differences negligible (Corbin & Pangrazi, 1992).

Even though children demonstrate a relatively high oxygen uptake, they do not perform up to this level because they are not economical in running or walking activities. An 8-year-old child running at 180 metres per minute is operating at 90% of maximal aerobic power, whereas a 16-year-old running at the same rate is operating at only 75% of maximum. This explains why young children are less capable than adolescents and adults at competing over long distances, even though they can maintain a slow speed for long distances (Bar-Or, 1983).

Children exercising at a certain workload perceive the activity to be easier than do adults working at a similar level. In one study (Bar-Or & Ward, 1989), youngsters were asked to rate their perceived exertion at different percentages of maximal heart rate and usually rated the exertion to be less stressful than did adults. Youngsters also demonstrate a rapid recovery rate after strenuous exercise. This implies that teachers should not judge workloads for children based on how they perceive the difficulty of an activity. Teachers also should use a child's rapid recovery rate to full advantage. Exercise bouts can be interspersed with restful episodes of stretching and nonlocomotor movements. This type of interval training is a particularly effective training method to use with children because it allows them to exercise aerobically and recover.

Obesity and Physical Performance

Obesity restricts children's motor performance due in part to a reduction in *relative strength* (strength in relation to body weight). Obese children may be stronger than normal-weight children in absolute terms, but are less strong when strength is adjusted for body weight. This lack of strength in relationship to body size causes obese children to find a strength-related task (such as a push-up or pull-up) much more difficult than the task would seem to normal-weight children. Isaacs and Pohlman (2000) found that for every kilogram increase in body fat there is a corresponding 65 cm decrease in vertical jump performance in children 7–11 years of age. The need for varied and personalized workloads is important to give all youngsters the opportunity for success in strength-related activities.

As mentioned, obese children seldom perform physical activities on a par with leaner children (Bar-Or, 1983). In part, this is due to the greater metabolic cost of the obese child's exercise. Obese children require a higher oxygen uptake capacity to perform a given task. Obesity takes a great toll on a child's aerobic power because obese children must perform at a higher percentage of their maximal oxygen uptake (see Figure 2.7). Usually, their maximal uptake values are lower than those of lean children. This gives obese children less reserve capacity and causes them to perceive higher exertion (Bar-Or & Ward, 1989) when performing a task. These reactions contribute to the common perception among teachers that "obese children don't like to run." Understand that asking obese children to run as far and as fast as normal-weight children is unrealistic.

Figure 2.7

Body composition has an impact on physical performance.

The task is more demanding for the obese child. Obese children have to work harder than normal-weight children to accomplish the same task and thus need adjusted workloads. There is no acceptable premise, physiological or psychological, for asking all children to run the same distance regardless of ability or body type.

Workloads should be based on time rather than distance. Lean and efficient runners should be expected to move farther than obese youngsters during a stipulated time period. All children *should not* have to do the same workload. Just as one would not expect kindergarten children to perform the same workload as that of grade five students, it is unreasonable to expect obese children to be capable of workloads similar to those of lean, ectomorphic youngsters. Exercise programs for obese subjects should be designed to increase caloric expenditure rather than to improve cardiovascular fitness (Rowland, 1991). The intensity of the activity should be secondary to the amount of time the student is involved in some type of moderate activity.

In addition to decrements in motor performance, the study of childhood obesity has produced some other disturbing findings including increase in risk factors for cardiovascular disease and Type 2 diabetes. Depending on the criteria used to evaluate the ratio of fat, 26% of Canadian youngsters have been identified as overweight or obese, with 8% identified as obese (Shields, 2005). Increase in physical activity has been identified as a crucial factor to deal with obesity levels. Researchers have found a strong relationship between a sedentary lifestyle and obesity in children (Anderson, Crespo, Bartlett, Cheskin, & Pratt, 1998). Obese children who are inactive also report high levels of television watching and video-game playing. Robinson (1999) showed some promising results with a program designed to decrease video-game and television use by grade four students. After a six-month intervention the students in the intervention group showed significant decreases in a variety of adiposity indicators. It is increasingly well accepted that physical activity habits developed in childhood track into adulthood. Similarly, childhood obesity persists into adulthood (Guo & Chumlea, 1999). It is dangerous to assume that excessive weight comes off when the child reaches adolescence. In fact, the opposite is usually true. Fifty percent of overweight children and teens remain overweight as adults (Dietz, 1998). Children clearly do not grow out of obesity—they grow *into* it. Recently, Moore et al. (2003), reported that higher levels of physical activity during childhood lead to the acquisition of less body fat by early adolescence. This emphasizes that childhood obesity must be challenged at an early age, and this challenge must come from increased movement and activity.

Children in Sport Activities

In addition to participation in school physical education, many children in Canada will participate in some type of community sport activity. Given the importance of a youngster's early and continued involvement, physical educators can offer expert advice to parents and community coaches. The following sections discuss some basic guidelines to ensure sport participation is a positive experience for youngsters.

Ensure Success for All Children

The willingness to try new experiences and participate in activities is driven by how people feel about their ability level—their *perceived competence*. Research has consistently shown that perception of competence impacts both sustained participation in sport and achievement behaviour (Weiss, 1993; Weiss & Williams, 2004). Sources of information children use to estimate their physical competence change as they mature. Young students depend primarily on information from adults (parents and teachers) and actual outcomes (performing the skill). While these sources of information remain important as they become older (grades three and four), children start to depend more heavily on comparison with their peers (Horn & Weiss, 1991, Weiss, Ebbeck, & Horn, 1997).

Unfortunately, it is quite possible that the process of feeling incompetent may begin in the elementary school years. Harter's (1978) concept of the *optimal challenge* is a useful framework to help coaches plan for a positive learning experience. An optimal challenge provides a balance between challenge and skill. A challenge that is too easy leads to boredom; one that is too difficult leads to anxiety and simply giving up! A task that is optimally challenging allows the child to experience just enough success that he or she will want to keep trying. With this effort will come increased motivation and skill.

Allow youngsters to play all positions and learn all skills. Because all children deserve equal opportunity to learn sport skills, it should be a mandate to coaches that all children have the opportunity to play all positions and receive similar amounts of practice time. In addition, reinforcement schedules need to be similar for children regardless of their skill level. Children participate in activities that offer them reinforcement; it is easy for them to become discouraged if little encouragement and praise are received when they are trying to learn new skills and positions.

Maturity plays an important role in dictating how youngsters learn motor skills. One of the reasons for helping children learn all skills and play all positions is that it will give them the opportunity to be successful when they reach maturity. Will a youngster be a pitcher or a right fielder, play goaltender or striker? Often, adults answer these questions for young children too early—a decision that may not allow youngsters an opportunity to realize their potential. Many children drop out of sport activities, but would probably have continued to participate if given the opportunity (Petlichkoff, 1992). Unfortunately, some programs start eliminating and "cutting" less gifted players. It is very difficult to justify this approach at the elementary school level. All children should be given the opportunity to participate if they choose to do so. Withdrawal from sport programs should be child-controlled rather than externally controlled (Gould, 1987). In other words, participants should not be forced out of the program due to cost, limitation of participants, or injury. On the other hand, if youngsters choose to withdraw, they should be allowed that opportunity without pressure.

Understand that Starting Young Doesn't Ensure Excellence

There is no evidence to support the idea that starting a child in competitive sport at a young age ensures the child will become an outstanding athlete (see Figure 2.8). It may be more likely that if a child is expected to develop certain skills before he or she is developmentally ready, frustration rather than achievement will result (American Academy of

Figure 2.8

An early start does not guarantee athletic success.

Pediatrics [AAP], 2001a). One reason that many parents and coaches push to have children start competing in a sport at an early age is that this competition offers the perception that a better athlete has been developed by the age of eight or nine. The participating child may seem extremely gifted compared with the non-participant, because he or she has been practising skills for four or five years. Naturally, the "early starter" looks advanced compared with a child who has not been in an organized program. In most cases, a child who is genetically gifted quickly catches up to and surpasses the "early superstar" in one to three years. As Shephard (1984) states, "Any advantage that is gained from very prolonged training probably lies in the area of skill perfection rather than in a fuller realization of physical potential." In addition, children who play a variety of sports through childhood rather than specialize early are more likely to stay involved for a longer period of time (Bompa, 1995). Experts discourage special-ization in a single sport before adolescence (AAP, 2000a).

Children who have been in documented programs for many years may burn out at an early age. A *documented program* is one in which extrinsic rewards are offered. Examples of such rewards are trophies, published league standings, ribbons, and excessive parental involvement. Evidence shows that extrinsic motivation may ultimately decrease intrinsic motivation, particularly in children ages 7 years and older. Whitehead & Corbin (1991) found that younger children (age 5) perceived a reward as a bonus, thus adding to the joy of performing a throwing motor task. This effect decreased with age, and by age 9 the reward was seen as a bribe; intrinsic motivation was undermined. There is no substitute for allowing young children to participate in physical activity for the sheer enjoyment and excitement involved in moving and interacting with peers.

If starting youngsters early can create early burnout, why do some parents feel pressured to enroll their child in a competitive sport program? One explanation is that they compare their children to other children. Parents see other children participating and practising sport skills in an organized setting. They may worry that their children will be unable to "catch up" if they do not get them involved in a similar program immediately. Even though this is not true, parents need reassurance, and they need facts. Physical educators can help parents find programs that minimize pressure and focus on skill development. A key is to find programs that allow the child to participate regard-less of ability, and to have fun while playing. The Coaching Association of Canada (CAC) recommends that children begin to participate in suitably designed competitive sport after the age of about 11 (LeBlanc & Dickson, 1997). The CAC has taken a strong leadership role in helping teachers and coaches provide suitable quality sport programs for children. According to the CAC, suitable developmental sport programs should emphasize fundamental sport skills, fair play, and fun. Similarly, the American Academy of Pediatrics (2001a) recommends that "organized sports programs for preadolescents should complement, not replace, the regular physical activity that is a part of free play, child-organized games, recreational sport, and physi-cal education programs in schools" (p.1461).

Guidelines for Exercising Children Safely

Moderation

As is the case in other areas of wellness, moderation is a way to ensure that children grow up enjoying physical activity. Moderate exercise, coupled with opportunities to participate in recreational activity, helps children develop a lasting desire to move. Some adults are concerned that too much activity might physiologically harm a child. To date, there is no evidence that a healthy child is harmed through vigorous physical activity. Children can withstand a grad-ual increase in workload and are capable of workloads comparable to those of adults when the load is adjusted for height and size. Fatigue causes healthy children to stop exercising long before any danger to health occurs (Shephard, 1984). In addition, the child's circulatory system is similar in proportion to that of an adult and thus is not at a disadvantage during exercise.

Caution should be used when exercising youngsters in hot weather. The arrival of summer does not mean that exercise must stop, but certain measures should be taken to avoid heat-related illness. Children are not "little adults" and do not adapt to extremes of temperature as effectively as adults do, for the following physiological reasons (American Academy of Pediatrics, 2000b; Bar-Or, 1983; Sports Medicine Australia, 2005):

1. Children have higher surface area/mass ratios than those of adults. This allows a greater amount of heat to transfer between the environment and the body.

2. When walking or running, children produce more metabolic heat per unit mass than adults produce. Youngsters are not as efficient in executing movement patterns, so they generate more metabolic heat than do adults performing a similar task.

3. Sweating capacity is not as great in children as in adults, resulting in a lowered ability to cool the body.

4. The ability of the blood to convey heat from the body core to the skin is reduced in children due to a lower cardiac output at a given oxygen uptake.

These physiological differences place children at a dis-tinct disadvantage compared with adults when exercising in an ambient air temperature that is higher than the skin temperature. Individuals do acclimatize to warmer climates. However, children appear to adjust to heat more slowly (up to twice as long) than do adults (Bar-Or, 1989). Also, children do not instinctively drink enough liquids to replenish fluids lost during exercise. The American Academy of Pediatrics Committee on Sports Medicine (2000b) offers the following guidelines for exercising children during hot days:

1. The intensity of activities that last 15 minutes or more should be reduced whenever relative humidity and air temperature are above critical levels. Table 2.1 shows the relationship between humidity and air temperature and when activity should be moderated.

2. At the beginning of a strenuous exercise program or after traveling to a warmer climate, the intensity and duration of exercise should be restrained initially and

TABLE 2.1
Exercising in the Heat

Weather guide: When the humidity and air temperature exceed the corresponding levels, intense activity should be curtailed.

Humidity Level (%)	Air Temperature (°C)
40	32
50	29
60	27
70	24
80	21
90	18
100	16

then increased gradually over a period of 10 to 14 days so that the students can acclimatize to the effects of the heat. When such a period is not available, the length of time for participation should be curtailed.

3. Children should be hydrated 20 to 30 minutes before strenuous activity (see Figure 2.9). During the activity, periodic drinking (for example, 150 ml of cold tap water every 20 minutes for a child weighing 40 kg) should be enforced.

4. Clothing should be lightweight and limited to one layer of absorbent material to facilitate evaporation of sweat and to expose as much skin as possible. Dry garments should replace sweat-saturated ones. Rubberized sweat suits should never be used to produce weight loss.

The committee identifies children with the following conditions as being at a potentially high risk for heat stress: obesity, febrile (feverish) state, cystic fibrosis, gastrointestinal infection, diabetes insipidus, diabetes mellitus, chronic heart failure, caloric malnutrition, anorexia nervosa, sweating insufficiency syndrome, and mental retardation.

Sun Exposure

It is increasingly well accepted that high exposure to sunlight sufficient to cause sunburn in childhood increases the risk of skin cancer in adulthood (AAP, 1999). It is also important to know that approximately 80% of lifetime sun exposure occurs during the childhood and adolescent years (Stern, Weinstein, & Baker, 1986). Therefore, it is important to take appropriate safety precautions when children are participating in outdoor physical activities during

sunny weather. Consider the following (AAP, 1999) when children are participating in outdoor activities:

1. Students should wear hats (with three-inch brims), light cotton clothing with tight weave, and sunglasses that block out ultraviolet rays.

2. Students should stay in the shade whenever possible, and limit extended sun exposure during peak intensity hours (10:00 am to 4:00 pm). (Note: Most local radio stations provide a daily ultraviolet [UV] ray exposure time rating during spring and summer months [e.g., Skin will burn within 30 minutes].)

3. Students should apply sunscreen with an SPF (sun protection factor) of at least 15 approximately 30 minutes prior to outdoor activity.

Exercising in Cold Weather

Exercising in cold weather presents several risks. Frostbite is freezing of the skin or underlying tissue as a result of prolonged exposure to cold. Frostbitten skin looks pale and whitish, is stiff to the touch and feels cold and numb. Sound preparation and preventive strategies can substantively minimize the risks of frostbite. Consider the following:

1. Be aware of local temperature and wind chill conditions. Local weather stations can provide this information. Wind coupled with cold increases potential for frostbite. Follow your school district temperature and wind chill policy for going outdoors during winter months.

2. Ensure participants are dressed appropriately for the activity, including layers, wind protection, hat that covers ears, mitts, and so on.

3. Teach students the signs of frostbite. Use a buddy system to check for "exposed" skin (nose, cheeks, ears, fingers). Build regular buddy checks into your lesson.

Figure 2.9

Water is mandatory for participation in activity in the heat.

4. At first sign of frostbite, protect from further exposure by covering exposed area and moving to shelter.

5. Very early signs of frostbite can be warmed with body heat (for example, put fingers in armpits or warm with breath). If blisters appear (second-degree frostbite), do not break blisters.

6. For deep frostbite, cover the affected area and call for medical assistance. Do not attempt to "thaw" the affected area.

Hypothermia occurs when the body temperature drops below normal. It develops when the body uses heat faster than it can be produced by metabolism and muscle contraction. Early signs that indicate mild to moderate hypothermia include (a) uncontrolled shivering, (b) cold, pale skin, (c) listlessness, and (d) impaired judgment. If the condition worsens, pulse and breathing will slow, the victim will appear drowsy, weak, and incoherent. This is an emergency! Sound preparation and preventive strategies can substantively minimize the risks of hypothermia. Take the following steps:

1. Dress in layers, with protective clothing for wind and rain. Type of clothing should allow the participant to remain warm even when wet.

2. Wear a warm hat. Major loss of body heat is through the head.

3. Early recognition is crucial. Teach students the signs of hypothermia. Use a buddy system to check for signs of hypothermia. If someone starts shivering, stumbling, and appears incoherent, suspect hypothermia.

4. At first sign of hypothermia, protect from further exposure and warm up the victim immediately. Use body heat, warm drink (for example, hot chocolate), and sheltered area (for example, a warm cabin).

Note that the risk of hypothermia is not unique to cold temperatures. Cases of hypothermia are often seen during warmer spring and fall temperatures when participants are unprepared for the conditions.

Strength Training

Whereas development of muscular strength is acknowledged as important to effective motor skill performance, strength training for preadolescent children has also generated concern among educators. Many worry about safety and stress-related injuries, while others question whether such training produces significant strength gains. Accepted thinking for years was that prepubescents are incapable of making significant strength gains because they lack adequate levels of circulating androgens. Evidence is continuing to build that contradicts this point of view. Recent studies have reported significant strength gains following participation in strength training programs (Faigenbaum et al., 2000, 2002). Strength can be increased through strength training in prepubescent youngsters; however, the way prepubescent children gain strength differs from adolescents and adults (Tanner, 1993). In preadolescent children, it appears that strength gains occur from motor learning rather than muscle hypertrophy. Youngsters develop more efficient motor patterns and recruit more muscle fibres, but show no increase in muscle size (Ozmun, Mikesky, & Surburg, 1994).

Note that the terms *resistance training* or *strength training* are used here to denote "the use of resistance methods to increase one's ability to exert or resist force" (American Academy of Pediatrics [AAP], 2001b, p. 1471). This is in contrast to *weightlifting* or *power lifting,* which is a competitive sport for the purpose of determining maximum lifting ability. A third category is bodybuilding, in which muscle size and definition are judged. There is agreement among experts that strength training is acceptable for preadolescents if appropriate training and safeguards are followed, but weightlifting and bodybuilding are undesirable and may be harmful. The following is included in the American Academy of Pediatrics (2001b) policy statement: "Preadolescents and adolescents should avoid competitive weightlifting, power lifting, bodybuilding, and maximal lifts until they reach physical and skeletal maturity" (p. 1471).

Safety and prevention of injury are paramount considerations for those interested in strength training for children. When injuries were reported, most occurred due to inadequate supervision, lack of proper technique, or competitive lifting. A knowledgeable instructor is required to provide an effective and safe program.

There are many safe and effective ways to enhance strength in children (e.g., dynabands). For a number of ways to develop strength see the text by Roberts (1996).

If a decision is made to develop a comprehensive strength-training program for elementary children, it should be done in a thoughtful and studied manner. Proper supervision and technique are key ingredients in a successful program. Consider the following recommendations from AAP (2001b):

1. Aerobic conditioning should be coupled with resistance training if general health benefits are the goal.

2. Strength-training programs should include a warm-up and cool-down component.

3. Strength-training exercise should be learned initially with no load (resistance). Once the exercise skill has been mastered, incremental loads can be added.

4. Resistance should be increased in 1- to 3-pound increments (approximately 0.5 to 1.5 kilograms) only after the prepubescent does 15 repetitions in correct form.

5. All exercises should be carried out through the full range of motion and address all major muscle groups.

In addition, training is recommended for two or three times a week for 20- to 30-minute periods. For additional guidance and advice, the reader is encouraged to read the full policy statement (AAP, 2001b).

Critical Thinking

1. Explain the relationship between obesity and physical inactivity levels in Canadian children.

2. Adults are often cautioned not to view children as "miniature adults." Discuss this statement as it relates to growth and development, and physical activity.

3. There are a variety of gender differences in growth and development. Discuss the challenges and potential these differences present for elementary physical education.

References and Suggested Readings

Active Healthy Kids Canada. (2006). *Canada's report card on physical activity for children and youth—2006*. Toronto, ON: Author.

American Academy of Pediatrics. (1999). Ultraviolet light: A hazard to children. *Pediatrics, 104*(2), 328–333.

American Academy of Pediatrics. (2000a). Intensive training and sports specialization in young athletes. *Pediatrics, 106*(1), 154–157. (Reaffirmed January 2006).

American Academy of Pediatrics. (2000b). Climatic heat stress and the exercising child and adolescent. *Pediatrics, 106*(1), 158–159.

American Academy of Pediatrics. (2001a). Organized sports for children and preadolescents. *Pediatrics, 107*(6), 1459–1462.

American Academy of Pediatrics. (2001b). Strength training by children and adolescents. *Pediatrics, 107*(6), 1470–1472.

Anderson, R.E., Crespo, C.J., Bartlett, S.J., Cheskin, L.J., & Pratt, M. (1998). Relationship of physical activity and television watching with body weight and levels of fatness among children: Results from the Third National Health and Nutrition Examination Survey. *Journal of the American Medical Association, 279*(12), 938–942.

Bailey, D.A., Faulkner, R.A., & McKay, H.A. (1996). Growth, physical activity, and bone mineral acquisition. *Exercise Sport Science Review, 24*, 233–266.

Bailey, D.A. & Martin, A.D. (1994). Physical activity and skeletal health in adolescents. *Pediatric Exercise Science, 6*, 330–347.

Bar-Or, O. (1983). *Pediatric sports medicine for the practitioner*. New York: Springer-Verlag.

Bar-Or, O. (1989). Temperature regulation during exercise in children and adolescents. In C. Gisolfi & D.R. Lamb (Eds.), *Perspectives in exercise sciences and sports medicine II. Youth, exercise and sport* (pp. 335–367). Indianapolis, IN: Benchmark.

Bar-Or, O. & Ward, D. S. (1989). Rating of perceived exertion in children. In O. Bar-Or (Ed.), *Advances in pediatric sport sciences*. Vol. III. Champaign, IL: Human Kinetics.

Beunen, G. & Malina, R.M. (1988). Growth and physical performance relative to the timing of the adolescent growth spurt. In K.B. Pandolf (Ed.), *Exercise and sport sciences reviews*. New York: Macmillan.

Birmingham, C., Muller, J., Palepu, A., Spinelli, J., & Anis, A. (1999). The cost of obesity in Canada. *Canadian Medical Association Journal, 160*, 483–488.

Bompa, T. (1995). *From childhood to champion athlete*. Toronto, ON: Veritas.

Canadian Paediatric Society. (2002). Healthy active living for children and youth. *Paediatric Child Health, 7*(5), 339–345.

Clarke, H.H. (1971). *Physical motor tests in the Medford boys' growth study*. Englewood Cliffs, NJ: Prentice-Hall.

Corbin, C. & Pangrazi, R. (1992). Are American children and youth fit? *Research Quarterly for Exercise and Sport, 63*(2), 96–106.

Craig, C. & Cameron, C. (2004). *Increasing physical activity: Assessing trends from 1998–2003*. Ottawa, ON: Canadian Fitness and Lifestyle Research Institute.

Craig, C.L., Cameron, C., Russell, S., & Beaulieu, A. (2001). *Increasing physical activity: Supporting children's participation*. Ottawa, ON: Canadian Fitness and Lifestyle Research Institute.

Dietz, W.H. (1998). Childhood weight affects morbidity and mortality. *Journal of Nutrition, 128*(2), 411S–414S.

Ernst, M.P. & Pangrazi, R.P. (1999). Effects of a physical activity program on children's activity levels and attraction to physical activity. *Pediatric Exercise Science, 11*, 393–405.

Faigenbaum, A., Milliken, L., Loud, R., Burak, B., Doherty, C., & Westcott, W. (2002). Comparison of 1 and 2 days per week of strength training in children. *Research Quarterly for Exercise and Sport, 73*, 416–424.

Faigenbaum, A., Milliken, L. & Westcott, W. (2003). Maximal strength testing in healthy children. *Journal of Strength and Conditioning Research, 17*, 162–166.

Faigenbaum, A., O'Connell, J., Glover, S., Loud, R., & Westcott, W. (2000). Comparison of different resistance training protocols on upper body strength and endurance development in children. *Medicine and Science in Sports and Exercise, 32*, (5 Supplement), S278.

Fishburne, G., McKay, H., & Berg, S. (2006). *Building strong bones & muscles*. Champaign, IL: Human Kinetics.

Gabbard, C.P. (2004). *Lifelong motor development* (4th ed.). San Francisco, CA: Benjamin Cummings.

Gould, D. (1987). Understanding attrition in children's sport. In *Advances in pediatric sport sciences. Vol. 2. Behavioral issues.* Champaign, IL: Human Kinetics.

Greer, F. & Krebs, N. (2006). Optimizing bone health and calcium intakes of infants, children, and adolescents. *Pediatrics, 117*(2), 578–585.

Gruelich, W., & Pyle, S. (1959). *Radiographic atlas of skeletal development of the hand and wrist.* (2nd ed.). Stanford, CA: Stanford University Press.

Guo, S. & Chumlea, W. (1999). Tracking of body mass index in children in relation to overweight in adulthood. *American Journal of Clinical Nutrition, 70*(1), 145S–148S.

Harter, S. (1978). Effectance motivation revisited. *Child Development, 21*, 34–64.

Haywood, K. & Getchell, N. (2001). *Life Span Motor Development.* (3rd ed.). Champaign, IL: Human Kinetics.

Hellsten, L. (2006). Student obesity in Canada: An epidemic. *Principal Online, 1*(3), 24–28.

Horn, T. & Weiss, M.R. (1991). A developmental analysis of children's self-ability judgments in the physical domain. *Pediatric Exercise Science, 3*, 310–326.

Isaacs, L.D. & Pohlman, R.L. (2000). Effectiveness of the stretch-shortening cycle in children's vertical jump performance. *Medicine and Science in Sports and Exercise, 32* (5 Supplement), S278.

Krahenbuhl, G.S. & Pangrazi, R.P. (1983). Characteristics associated with running performance in young boys. *Medicine and Science in Sports, 15*(6), 486–490.

LeBlanc, J. & Dickson, L. (1997). *Straight talk about children and sport: Advice for parents, coaches and teachers.* Gloucester, ON: Coaching Association of Canada.

Macera, C.A. & Pratt, M. (2000). Public health surveillance of physical activity. *Research Quarterly for Exercise and Sport, 71*(2), 97–103.

MacKelvie, K., McKay, H., Petit, M., Moran, O., & Khan, K. (2002). Bone mineral response to a 7-month randomized controlled, school-based jumping intervention in 121 prepubertal boys: Associations with ethnicity and body mass index. *Journal of Bone Mineral Research, 17*, 834–844.

Malina, R.M. (1978). Physical growth and maturity characteristics of young athletes. In R.A. Magill, M.H. Ash, & F.L. Smoll (Eds.), *Children and youth in sport: A contemporary anthology.* Champaign, IL: Human Kinetics.

Malina, R.M., Bouchard, C., & Bar-Or, O. (2004). *Growth, maturation, and physical activity.* (2nd ed.). Champaign, IL: Human Kinetics.

McArdle, W.D., Katch, F.I., & Katch, V.L. (2000). *Essentials of exercise physiology* (2nd ed.). Philadelphia, PA: Lippincott Williams & Wilkins.

McKenzie, T., Nader, P., Strikmiller, M., Yang, M, Stone, E., Perry, C., Taylor, W., Epping, J., Feldman, H., Luepker, M.,

& Kelder, S. (1996). School physical education: Effect of the child and adolescent trial for cardiovascular health. *Preventive Medicine, 25*, 423–431.

Moore, L., Gao, D., Bradlee, M., Cupples, L., Sundarajan-Ramamurti, A., Proctor, M., Hood, M., Singer, M.R., Ellison, R. (2003). Does early physical activity predict body fat change throughout childhood? *Preventive Medicine, 37*, 10–17.

Mummery, K., Spence, J.C., & Hudec, J.C. (2000). Understanding physical activity intention in Canadian school children and youth: An application of the theory of planned behavior. *Research Quarterly for Exercise and Sport, 71*(2), 116–124.

Ontario Medical Association. (2005). *An ounce of prevention or a ton of trouble—Is there an epidemic of obesity in children? A position paper.* Toronto, ON: Author.

Ozmun, J.C., Mikesky, A.E., & Surburg, P.R. (1994). Neuromuscular adaptations during prepubescent strength training (abstract). *Medicine and Science in Sports and Exercise, 26*, 510–514.

Payne, V.G. & Isaacs, L.D. (2005). *Human motor development: A lifespan approach.* (6th ed.). New York, NY: McGraw-Hill.

Payne, V.G. & Morrow, Jr., J.R. (1993). Exercise and VO2max in children: A meta-analysis. *Research Quarterly for Exercise and Sport, 64*(3), 305–313.

Petersen, G. (1967). *Atlas for somatotyping children.* The Netherlands: Royal Vangorcum.

Petlichkoff, L.M. (1992). Youth sport participation and withdrawal: Is it simply a matter of fun? *Pediatric Exercise Science, 4*(2), 105–110.

Report on the Health of Canadians. (1996). Prepared by the Federal, Provincial and Territorial Advisory Committee on Population Health for the Meetings of Ministers of Health, Toronto, ON: September 10–11, 1996.

Roberts, S., Ciapponi, S., & Lytle, R. (2007). *Strength training for children and adolescents* (2nd ed.). Reston, VA: American Alliance for Health, Physical Education, Recreation, and Dance.

Robinson, T. (1999). Reducing children's television viewing to prevent obesity: A randomized controlled trial. *Journal of the American Medical Association, 282*, 1561–1567.

Roche, A. & Sun, S. (2003). *Human growth: Assessment and interpretation.* Cambridge, England: Cambridge University Press.

Roche, A.F., Chumlea, W.C., & Thissen, D. (1988). *Assessing the skeletal maturity of the hand-wrist: Fels method.* Springfield, IL: Thomas.

Rowland, T.W. (1991). Effects of obesity on aerobic fitness in adolescent females. *American Journal of Disease in Children, 145*, 764–768.

Saltin, B. (1973). Metabolic fundamentals of exercise. *Medicine and Science of Sports, 5*, 137–146.

Sheldon, W.H., Dupertuis, C.W., & McDermott, E. (1954). *Atlas of men: A guide for somatotyping the adult male at all ages.* New York: Harper & Row.

Shephard, R. (1984). Physical activity and child health. *Sports Medicine, 1,* 205–233.

Shields, M. (2005). Measured obesity: Overweight Canadian children and adults. *Nutrition: Findings from the Canadian Community Health Survey, 1,* 82–620 – MWE 2005001.

Sparling, P.B., Owen, N., Lambert, E.V., & Haskell, W.L. (2000). Promoting physical activity: The new imperative for public health. *Health Education Research, 15*(3), 367–376.

Sports Medicine Australia. (2005). *Policy-Preventing Heat Illness in Sport.* Retrieved April 30, 2007, from www.sma.org.au.

Stern, R., Weinstein, M., & Baker, S. (1986). Risk reduction for nonmelanoma skin cancer with childhood sunscreen use. *Archives of Dermatology, 122,* 537–545.

Tanner, S.M. (1993). Weighing the risks: Strength training for children and adolescents. *The Physician and Sportsmedicine, 21*(6), 105–116.

Tremblay, M., Katzmarzyk, P. & Willms, J.D. (2002). Temporal trends in overweight and obesity in Canada, 1981–1996. *International Journal of Obesity, 26,* 583–593.

Tremblay, M. & Willms, J. D. (2000). Secular trends in the body mass index of Canadian children. *Canadian Medical Association Journal, 163*(11), 1469–33.

Warburton, D., Whitney Nichol, C., & Bredin, S. (2006). Health benefits of physical activity: The evidence. *Canadian Medical Association Journal, 174*(1), 801–809.

Weiss, M.R. (1993). Psychological effects of intensive sport participation on children and youth: Self-esteem and motivation. In B.R. Cahill & A.J. Pearl (Eds.), *Intensive Participation in Children's Sport* (pp. 39–69). Champaign, IL: Human Kinetics.

Weiss, M.R., Ebbeck, V., & Horn, T.S. (1997). Children's self-perceptions and sources of competence information: A cluster analysis. *Journal of Sport and Exercise Psychology, 19,* 52–70.

Weiss, M.R. & Williams, L. (2004). The why of youth sport involvement: A developmental perspective on motivational processes. In M.R. Weiss (Ed.), *Developmental sport and exercise psychology: A lifespan perspective* (pp. 223–268). Morgantown, WV: Fitness Information Technology.

Whitehead, J.R. & Corbin, C.B. (1991). Effects of fitness test type, teacher, and gender on exercise intrinsic motivation and physical self-worth. *Journal of School Health, 61,* 11–16.

Willms, J.D., Tremblay, M., & Katzmarzyk, P. (2003). Geographic and demographic variations in the prevalence of overweight Canadian children. *Obesity Research, 11,* 668–673.

 Weblinks

Active Healthy Kids Canada: www.activehealthykids.ca

National organization that advocates for high-quality, accessible, and enjoyable physical activity experiences for children and youth.

American Academy of Pediatrics: http://aappolicy.aappublications.org

This website includes a policy statements and recommendations associated with participation of children and adolescents in a range of physical activities.

Coaching Association of Canada: www.coach.ca

The CAC promotes the education of coaches through a national coaching certification program ranging from community to national team coaching.

CHAPTER 3

Planning for Quality Instruction

Essential Components

I	Organized around content standards
II	**Student-centred and developmentally appropriate**
III	Physical activity and motor skill development form the core of the program
IV	**Teaches management skills and self-discipline**
V	Promotes inclusion of all students
VI	**Focuses on process over product**
VII	Promotes lifetime personal health and wellness
VIII	Teaches cooperation and responsibility and promotes sensitivity to diversity

Physical Education Standards

1	Students are able to move competently using a variety of fundamental and specialized motor skills.
2	Students can monitor and maintain a health-enhancing level of physical fitness.
3	**Students are able to apply movement concepts and basic mechanics of skill performance when learning and refining motor skills.**
4	Students comprehend the basic principles of wellness and are able to apply concepts that enable them to make meaningful decisions that positively impact their health and wellness.
5	Students participate in a wide variety of physical activities and learn how to maintain a personalized active lifestyle.
6	**Students demonstrate empathy, understanding, and respect for the numerous differences exhibited by people in an activity setting.**
7	Students exhibit responsible and self-directed behaviours that lead to positive social interactions in physical activity.

OVERVIEW

Effective teachers are able to use more than one style of teaching and may, in fact, use several styles during a particular lesson. In this chapter, planning strategies associated with quality instruction are described in detail. A number of pre-instructional decisions must be made that influence the quality of the lesson. Quality teachers know how to regulate instructional space and how to use formations to maximize learning. Instructors need to understand the influence that developmental patterns, arousal, feedback, and practice have on learning skills. A productive class environment demands consistent monitoring of student performance, an emphasis on safety, and a method for keeping students on-task. A comprehensive lesson plan format is offered to encourage effective planning.

OUTCOMES

- Describe various teaching styles and the best time to use each style to increase student learning.

- Describe the role of planning in preparing for quality instruction.

- Understand the relationships between instruction and the developmental and experiential level of the students.

- List pre-instructional decisions that must be made before the actual delivery of the lesson.

- Know the basic mechanical principles required for efficient performance of motor skills.

- Cite effective ways to use equipment, time, space, and formations in the instructional process.

- Understand how to optimize skill learning. Include discussions of schema theory, phases of learning a motor skill, arousal, feedback, practice sessions, and skill progression.

- Understand the rationale for the four components of a lesson and describe characteristics of each.

- Know how to improve the quality of instructional presentations through reflection.

*P*lanning is a critical part of teaching that ensures the implementation of a quality lesson and overall program. Pre-instructional decisions, which determine how the lesson will be presented, are discussed here and in Chapter 4, Improving Instructional Effectiveness. They include choosing teaching styles, using equipment effectively, using class time, arranging for teaching space, and properly employing instructional formations. They also involve designing and implementing lesson plans that are both flexible and meaningful. On an average day, teachers must make many unexpected decisions, so the job can be made much easier if as many decisions as possible are made prior to the actual lesson presentation. Pre-instructional decisions are as important as the content of the lesson. If the teacher does not properly address the pre-instructional phase of the lesson, content presentation can be diminished.

Choose from a Variety of Teaching Styles

One of the first steps in planning for instruction is to decide on the teaching styles that will be most effective for each skill. A teaching style provides direction for presenting information, organizing practice, providing feedback, keeping students engaged in appropriate behaviour, and monitoring progress toward goals or learning outcomes. Teaching styles are usually defined in terms of planning and setup of the environment, the instructional approach used, the students' responsibilities during the lesson, and expected student outcomes. Successful teachers are able to incorporate a variety of teaching styles (Harrison, Blakemore, & Buck, 2001; Mosston & Ashworth, 2002; Rink, 2005; Siedentop & Tannehill, 2000).

There is no single "best" or universal teaching style. Even though some educators endorse their favourite approaches, evidence does not suggest that one style is more effective than another. The mark of a master teacher is a repertoire of styles that can be used with different learning outcomes, students, activities, facilities, and equipment. Many variables have to be considered when selecting an appropriate teaching style, including the following:

1. The learning outcomes of the lesson, such as skill development, activity promotion, knowledge, and social behaviours.

2. The activities to be taught, such as body management skills, manipulative skills, or rhythmic movement skills.

3. The students, including individual characteristics, interests, developmental level, socioeconomic status, motivation, and background.

4. The size of the class.

5. The equipment and facilities available for instruction.

6. The unique abilities, skills, and comfort of the teacher.

The use of a different teaching style in an appropriate setting often improves the environment for students and teachers and increases the effectiveness of the program. A new or modified teaching style is not a panacea for all the ills of every school environment or setting and a teaching style cannot be selected without considering a number of variables. Teachers can use combinations of styles in a lesson or unit plan; they do not have to adopt just one style at a time. Figure 3.1 shows a continuum of teaching styles based on the degree of control and decision-making exercised by the teacher and students. At one end of the continuum (command) the teacher makes instructional decisions exclusively. At the other end, children make the majority of decisions about their learning. Along the continuum there is a gradual shift in decision-making and responsibility for learning. Mosston and Ashworth (2002) provide one of the most extensive explanations of how

Figure 3.1

Continuum of teaching styles.

teaching styles apply to physical education. The following discussion adapts and extends their basic continuum of teaching styles.

Direct Teaching Styles

Direct teaching styles (also called teacher-centred, replication, reproduction) are characterized by the teacher providing a model (explanation/demonstration) of the skill to be practised. Direct styles differ primarily in the formats for practising skills and ways students receive feedback on their performance. Directing teaching styles include command, practice, reciprocal, self-check, and inclusion.

Command Style

The *command* style is the most teacher-centred approach. The teacher provides instruction to either the entire class or to small groups, and guides the pace and direction of the class. A common example of this style occurs when a teacher leads an aerobics class or a series of warm-up exercises. The students perform the skills at the same time as the teacher performs the skills. The teacher is the centre of attention. When the teacher stops performing, so do the students. Within this teaching style, the opportunity to provide feedback to individuals is limited.

Practice Style

The *practice* style is the most widely used teaching style in physical education. This style begins with an explanation and demonstration of skills to be practised. Students are organized into partners, small groups, or squads. Independent practice follows and is supervised by an actively involved teacher. While students practise, the teacher actively moves around the area, providing performance feedback, encouraging, and asking questions. Throughout the class, students can be brought together for evaluative comments and instruction, or to focus on another skill. Students spend most of their class time engaged in predetermined subject matter aimed at reaching established goals. This teaching style makes the teacher the major demonstrator, motivator, organizer, disciplinarian, and feedback provider.

The practice style, like any other type of instruction, can be effective or ineffective depending on how it is used and administered. The practice style is an effective strategy for teaching physical skills, especially when there is the possibility of an accident with inexperienced students. It offers an accurate model for replication, an organized practice format and close teacher supervision.

The practice teaching style places emphasis on creating a safe and productive class environment that allows maximum practice opportunity. Effective use of the practice style minimizes time spent passively watching, listening to an explanation-demonstration, or waiting in line. A challenge when using this style is offering activities that meet the needs of all students. Higher-skilled and lower-skilled students may be hindered when learning activities are too easy and unchallenging, or too difficult. This can be avoided, however, by offering learning tasks of varying difficulty. The following two adaptations of this style show ways to accommodate a range of tasks and skill levels.

Practice Style Adaptations: Station or Task Cards

Station or task cards adaptations of the practice style involve arranging and presenting learning tasks at several learning areas or stations. In a station format, students rotate between learning stations and practise a variety of assigned tasks. Each station contains a number of tasks that students practise with a minimum of teacher direction. For example, students might spend five minutes at each of four or five stations, practising one defined task at each. A cue or signal to rotate to a new station is given after time has elapsed. Task cards are similar to stations in that students are presented with a set of tasks. They differ in that students simply move to a non-designated area in the gym to work through the set of tasks on the card.

Using stations or task cards allows teachers to move away from being the central figure in the instructional process. Instruction focuses on visiting learning stations and interacting with students. Less time is spent directing and managing the group as a whole. This approach requires more preparation time for planning and designing tasks. Adequate facilities, equipment, and station/task cards are necessary to keep students productive and working on appropriate tasks. The following guidelines are useful when selecting, writing, and presenting tasks:

1. Select tasks that cover the basic skills of an activity.

2. Select tasks that provide students with success and challenge. Create tasks that are developmentally appropriate. The most skilled student should be challenged, and the least skilled student should be successful.

3. Avoid tasks that carry a high safety risk.

4. Tape station cards on the wall or strap them to boundary cones. Another alternative is to provide a task sheet for each student that can be carried station to station and taken home for practice after school.

5. Write tasks so they are easy to comprehend (use diagrams). Use teaching cues or phrases that students have learned previously. Effective task descriptions explain what the skill is and how to do it (see the example in Figure 3.2). Periodically check to see if students understand and practise the tasks.

6. Incorporate a combination of instructional equipment that offers feedback and motivation, such as targets, music, cones, hoops, ropes, and stopwatches.

Name _____ Class _____ Grade _____

Your expected outcome is to master five of the following individual rope-jumping steps. You must be able to complete a minimum of 10 consecutive jumps when doing one of the steps. Please ask a friend to approve your performance before asking for instructor approval.

Approved by a friend	Approved by teacher	Skill to be completed
		Side Swing. Swing the rope, held with both hands to one side of the body. Switch and swing the rope on the other side of the body.
		Double Side Swing and Jump. Swing the rope once on each side of the body. Follow the second swing with a jump over the rope. The sequence should be swing, swing, jump.
		Running in Place. When the rope passes under the feet, shift the weight alternately from one foot to the other, raising the non-support foot in a running position.
		Spread Legs Forward and Backward. Start in a stride position with weight equally distributed on both feet. As the rope passes under the feet, jump into the air and reverse the position of the feet.
		Side Straddle Jump. Alternate a regular jump with a straddle jump. Perform the straddle jump with the feet spread to shoulder width.
		Cross Legs Sideward. When the rope passes under the feet, spread the legs in a straddle position (sideward) to take the rebound. As the rope passes under the feet on the next turn, jump into the air and cross the feet with the other foot forward. Then repeat with the other foot forward and continue this alternation.
		Toe-Touch Forward. Swing the right foot forward as the rope passes under the feet and touch the right toes on the next count. Then alternate, landing on the right foot and touching the left toes forward.
		Toe-Touch Backward. Same as the Toe-Touch Forward, except that the toes of the free foot touch to the back at the end of the swing.
		Shuffle Step. Push off with the right foot and sidestep to the left as the rope passes under the feet. Land with the weight on the left foot and touch the right toes beside the left heel. Repeat the step in the opposite direction.

Figure 3.2

Task card: Advanced individual rope-jumping steps.

Stations and task cards can use a variety of grouping patterns. Students work alone, with a partner, or in a small group. The partner or reciprocal grouping pattern is useful with large classes, limited amounts of equipment, and in teaching skills where partners can time, count, record, or analyze each other. For example, one partner dribbles through a set of cones, while the other is timing and recording. In a group of three students, one student bounces and catches a ball off the wall, another analyzes the form with a checklist, and the third counts and records the number of catches. (The social aspect of being able to work on tasks with a partner is a form of cooperative learning discussed later.) Arrange learning tasks so students first experience success frequently and later tackle tasks that are more challenging. Learning outcomes can be modified daily or repeated, depending on the progress of the class.

Some teachers are uncomfortable when first using stations because it implies less order and control than when all students are performing the same task. With proper planning, organization, and supervision, however, it offers an opportunity for students to practise a variety of tasks. Students often find stations motivating because of the variety of learning tasks and the self-paced learning.

Reciprocal Style

The *reciprocal* style of teaching (also called peer teaching) builds on the practice style by providing regular personal feedback to each student. This is accomplished by having students work in pairs or small groups in which one student observes and provides feedback to a partner who is practising the skill. As in the practice style, the teacher provides the initial skill demonstration. In addition, the teacher helps students learn to observe the skill and provide effective feedback to a classmate. During practice time, the teacher indirectly impacts the performer by helping the observer share accurate and positive information with his or her classmate. Essential to the efficacy of this style is the teacher's role in providing clear demonstrations with observable cues, and specific guidance to help the observer do an effective job of observing and communicating.

Self-Check Style

The self-check teaching style uses a similar format to the reciprocal style by assisting each student to analyze her or his own performance. Again, the teacher provides the initial demonstration along with guidance for skill analysis. Utility of this style is somewhat limited with younger learners, in that they must rely on kinesthetic sense rather than observation to judge their own performance. Self-check style has considerable potential for self-analysis of learning outcomes associated with individual behaviour. Elementary school learners are able to reflect upon aspects for their own behaviour (e.g., taking turns, using positive words with classmates). See Chapter 6 for assessment ideas that use a self-check teaching style.

Inclusion Style

The inclusion style extends the preceding styles by providing a series of tasks that gradually increase in difficulty and challenge. The intent of this style is to accommodate a range of skills by encouraging each student to choose his or her level of challenge. Ideally this allows the student the opportunity to find a personal "optimal challenge." The teacher's goal is to provide a reasonable range of task progressions to keep all learners challenged and engaged. The following is an example of an inclusive range of tasks for practising the volleyball forearm pass:

1. Receive a beach ball from a toss.
2. Receive a light volleyball from a toss.
3. Receive a regular volleyball from a toss.
4. Receive a regular volleyball tossed a metre to either side.
5. Continuous passing with a partner (in consecutive sets of 10, 20, 30)
6. Play Pepper with a partner.

Inclusion Style Adaptation: Mastery (Outcome-based) Learning

Mastery learning is an adaptation of the inclusion style that takes a general program outcome and breaks it into smaller parts, providing a progression of skills. These sub-skills are the focus of learning and are written as tasks that must be mastered before students are allowed to attempt more complex skills. The number of sub-skills depends on the complexity of the outcome. If mastery is not achieved, corrective activities are offered to help students learn in different ways, such as alternative instructional materials, peer tutoring, or any other learning activity that meets personal preferences. (For an in-depth discussion of mastery learning, see Guskey, 1985.) The following steps are used to implement the mastery style:

1. The outcome or movement competency is divided into sequenced, progressive units.
2. Necessary (prerequisite) competencies are evaluated.
3. Skill outcomes for each of the successive learning units are established.
4. Students informally evaluate themselves to determine whether they are ready for formal evaluation by the teacher or a peer.
5. When a student is ready for formal evaluation, the teacher (or a peer) determines if the performance of the outcome is satisfactory to move on to the next level.
6. If the evaluation is not satisfactory, practice continues, incorporating alternatives or corrective measures.

The following outline demonstrates how a soccer lesson might be broken down to teach the target outcomes for dribbling, trapping, and kicking, using the mastery learning style.

DRIBBLING OUTCOMES

1. Dribble the ball a distance of 9 metres, three consecutive times, making each kick travel no more than 4 metres.
2. Dribble the ball through an obstacle course of six cones over a distance of 9 metres in 20 seconds or less.
3. With a partner, pass the ball back and forth five times while running for a distance of 20 metres, two consecutive times.

TRAPPING OUTCOMES

4. When the ball is rolled to you by a partner 4 metres away, trap it four out of five times, using the instep method with the right and then the left foot.
5. Same as outcome #4, using the sole of the foot.
6. With a partner tossing the ball, trap four out of five shots using the chest method.

KICKING OUTCOMES

7. Kick the ball to a partner, who is standing 4 metres away, five consecutive times with the right and left inside-of-the-foot push pass.

8. Same as outcome #7 using the instep kick. Loft the ball to your partner.

9. Kick four of five shots that enter the goal in the air from a distance of 9 metres.

Mastery learning is useful because students can move at individualized pace and master skills needed to reach the outcomes. It offers a continuum of outcomes youngsters can practise in their spare time. For this reason, the style is well suited for the diverse range of students in physical education class. It accommodates students who may need more time to master skills, and allows for tasks to be broken down into small increments. It also accommodates athletically gifted students who may require tasks beyond the ability of many other students. However, because the style requires self-direction on the part of the students, some may take longer than others to acquire the social skills necessary to use this instructional format. Consider the amount of freedom, flexibility, and choice students can handle and yet still be productive. Mastery learning is most effective when used in short episodes and blended with other styles.

A variety of grouping patterns (individually, with a partner, or with a small group) can be used within the inclusion style depending on available facilities, equipment, learning outcomes, and student choice. During the lesson, the teacher or peers can monitor successful completion of learning outcomes. If class size is small, and the number of learning outcomes also is small, it may be possible for a teacher to do all the monitoring. Otherwise, a combination of procedures is recommended. Student involvement in the monitoring process enhances their understanding of the outcomes and encourages them to share learning responsibility. Monitors can use a performance chart to check learning at each learning station or carry a master list from station to station. Another approach is to develop a performance sheet for each student that combines teacher and peer monitoring (see Figure 3.3). Peers monitor simple learning outcomes while the teacher monitors more difficult ones. Students can also privately monitor themselves on the performance outcomes. Try experimenting with several monitoring approaches depending on the activity, the number learning, the students' abilities, the size of the class, and the available equipment and facilities.

Inquiry Teaching Styles

Whereas the preceding styles replicate a "model," the inquiry style of teaching (similar terms include discovery,

Name: _____		
Instructor approved	**Peer reviewed**	**Skill**
_____	_____	1. Toss and catch with both hands.
_____	_____	2. Toss and catch with right hand.
_____	_____	3. Toss and catch with left hand.
_____	_____	4. Toss and catch with the back of both hands (create soft home).
_____	_____	5. Toss, do a half turn, and catch with both hands.
_____	_____	6. Toss, do a heel click, and catch with both hands.
_____	_____	7. Place beanbag on foot, kick in the air, and catch.
_____	_____	8. Place beanbag on foot, kick in the air, and catch behind back.
_____	_____	9. Put beanbag between feet, jump up with beanbag, and catch.
_____	_____	10. Toss overhead, move to another spot, and catch.
_____	_____	11. Toss overhead, take 3 skipping steps, and catch.
_____	_____	12. Toss overhead, lie down, and catch with hands.

Figure 3.3

Performance objectives: manipulative skills using beanbags.

production, problem-solving, indirect, or student-centred) is process-oriented, thereby placing great importance on the learning process. During this type of approach, students are cognitively active as they experience learning situations that require them to inquire, speculate, reflect, analyze, and discover.

The teacher plays the role of presenting a problem, then guiding students rather than showing or telling. Students are challenged to discover their own answers and solutions. The teacher assumes responsibility for stimulating student curiosity about the subject matter. A combination of questions, problems, examples, and learning activities lead students toward one or more solutions.

In recent years inquiry teaching styles have taken a more prominent place in educational methodology in all subject areas, including physical education. Proponents of these styles believe they enhance students' ability to think, improve creativity, create a better understanding of the subject matter, enhance individual self-concept, and develop lifelong learning patterns. Many provincial physical education curriculum guides emphasize the importance of these teaching styles. For example, in British Columbia "students are challenged to identify and investigate problems, find active ways to solve them, and represent solutions in a variety of ways" (B.C. Ministry of Education, 1995, p. 2). In Nova Scotia "students are enabled to use all of the multiple intelligences in an environment that fosters experiential learning" (Nova Scotia Education, 2000, p. 1). In Manitoba, "the needs of all learners should be addressed through instruction that is relevant, current, meaningful, and balanced, and offers a variety of choices in learning experience" (Manitoba Education & Training, 2000, p. 6). Physical Education in Newfoundland and Labrador "facilitates learning processes which encourage critical thinking, thereby affecting the learners' personal wellness and well-being of society" (Nfld. & Labrador, 2004, p. 3). Similarly, in Quebec "it is essential that a variety of pedagogical approaches be used, such as collaborative learning, problem-solving, and problem-based learning etc." (Éducation Québec, 2003, p. 439).

The efficacy of inquiry teaching styles depends on a great deal of active involvement of students in the learning process. Guided discovery, convergent, and divergent teaching styles are three types of inquiry that give the learner more control over the direction and content of the learning process.

Guided Discovery

Guided discovery is used when there is a predetermined choice or result that the teacher wants students to discover. This process follows a consistent and logical sequence so students can move from one step to the next after a certain amount of thinking. The teacher designs a series of questions and learning activities to "guide" the students toward "discovering" the best solution. The logic underlying this style is that if a student "discovers" a solution, he will be more likely to embrace it than if he were simply being told or shown the solution.

Consider teaching the concept of opposition (e.g., a right-handed thrower should place the feet in a stride position with the left foot forward). Using guided discovery, students are given different foot patterns for experimentation, with the goal of selecting the best pattern. They practise right-handed throwing with the following limitations: feet together, feet in a straddle position, feet in a stride position with the left foot forward, and feet in a stride position with the right foot forward. After practising the four different foot positions, students choose the position that seems best in terms of throwing potential.

Guided discovery is effective when the teacher is interested in having children discover the most suitable movement response when developing a new skill. This allows youngsters to try different ways of accomplishing the task and helps them learn why some solutions work better than others. The teacher's responsibility in planning is to ensure that the students experiment with safe alternatives. The following are examples of skill techniques that students can explore in order to discover the best solution:

1. Placement of the hands when catching.

2. Angles of release for distance throwing with different implements such as the disc, lacrosse ball, and softball.

3. Batting stance and foot pattern alterations for hitting the softball to various fields.

4. The best place to enter in long rope-jumping skills.

5. The role of a person's centre of gravity and momentum in performing activities in gymnastics such as the forward roll.

Convergent Style

The convergent style differs from guided discovery in that the processes used are less structured and sequential, and the teacher provides less direct guidance toward discovery of a solution. Essentially the teacher designs a problem and the students work through the problem using rules of logic and trial-and-error to reach or "converge upon a solution" (Mosston & Ashworth, 2002). A teacher must ensure that problem design takes into account limits of safe experimentation in the trial-and-error process. The following are steps to problem solving in the convergent style:

- *Present the problem.* Present students with a problem in the form of a question or statement that provokes thought and reflection. No demonstration or explanation of appropriate responses is given, because students generate solutions.

- *Determine procedures.* Ask students to think about the procedures necessary for arriving at a solution. With younger children, problems are simple and this phase is minimal. It is important, however, because assessment of how to proceed toward a solution has cognitive value.

- *Experiment and explore.* In experimentation, students try different solutions, evaluate them, and make a choice. In exploration, the goal is to seek breadth of activity. Self-direction is important, and the teacher acts in an advisory role—answering questions, helping, commenting, and encouraging, but not providing solutions.

- *Observe, evaluate, and discuss.* All children have the opportunity to offer a solution and to observe what others have discovered. Various kinds of achievement demonstrations are used—by individuals, by small groups, by squads, or by part of the class. Discussion centres on justifying a particular solution.

- *Refine and expand.* After observing solutions that others have selected, and evaluating the reasoning behind the chosen solutions, all children are given the opportunity to rework their solutions, incorporating ideas from others.

A convergent problem for intermediate children might be this: "What is the most effective way to position and move your feet while guarding an opponent in basketball?" Children learn that problems can be solved and they are able to find solutions. To do so, they must be equipped with techniques so they can proceed under self-direction toward a sound solution.

Divergent Style

Like the convergent style, the divergent style involves input, reflection, choice, and response. The same steps to problem solving are used. However, the problem is structured so there is no one prescribed answer and there are numerous acceptable alternatives. When there is just one answer, problem solving becomes guided discovery or convergent. Whereas guided discovery and convergent problems are helping students eliminate less-desirable solutions and narrow in on a solution, the divergent style uses the problem to open up as many acceptable solutions as possible. A simple divergent problem for primary-level children might be expressed in this manner: "What are all the different ways you can bounce a ball and stay in your personal space?"

One of the most effective uses of a divergent style is to help children work on their creative skills and abilities. For example, in gymnastics a teacher may set a problem such as "put together a roll, balance, and turn in two different ways." This problem allows for students to experiment with a variety of alternatives, all of which are acceptable within the parameters of the problem. This style may also be used to extend learning from the direct styles, essentially going from the "known to the unknown." For example, when teaching pass plays in soccer, you may demonstrate and have students practise one alternative (for example, give and go), then set a problem to encourage them to create another pass play on their own.

Free-exploration Style

Free exploration is the most child-centred style of learning. Guidance by the teacher in the free-exploration style is limited to the selection of the instructional materials to be used and designation of the area to be explored. Two directives might be the following: "Today, for the first part of the period, you may select any piece of equipment and see what you can do with it," or "Get a jump rope and try

creating a new activity." No limits are imposed on children except those dictated by safety. If necessary, forewarn or remind students how to use equipment safely. This style is used effectively to introduce new equipment, concepts, and ideas to children so they generate ideas and responses. It often works best with young children who are experiencing activities and situations for the first time.

With free exploration, the teacher should avoid demonstrations and praising certain results too early because these can lead to imitative and non-creative behaviour. This does not mean, however, that the teacher remains uninvolved. The teacher moves among students—encouraging, clarifying, and answering questions individually. Concentrate on motivating effort, since the student is responsible for being a self-directed learner. It is wise to offer students the opportunity for self-direction in small doses, increasing the time as they become more disciplined. Try to offer exploratory opportunities frequently, as this phase of learning takes advantage of the child's love of movement experimentation and allows the free exercise of natural curiosity.

Cooperative Learning

Cooperative learning focuses on the importance of people working together to accomplish common goals. In cooperative learning, students are assigned to groups where each member works to reach the group's common goals. In cooperative activities, individuals seek outcomes that are beneficial to themselves and to the group. A resource for cooperative learning in physical education is the text by Grineski (1996), *Cooperative Learning in Physical Education.*

There is a strong research base that suggests cooperative learning helps foster constructive relationships among students (Slavin, 1995). Teachers should emphasize joint rather than individual outcomes, and give student peers the opportunity to work with each other regularly. Because students are expected to foster the success of their peers, cooperative learning has the potential to enhance the social and psychological growth of students. Cooperative learning strategies can be included as part of direct and inquiry teaching styles.

In cooperative learning, accomplishments of a group are successful if the outcomes are meaningful and if participation by all group members has occurred. Selected activities should require the knowledge and efforts of all members of the group. If students feel cooperation is not necessary to complete the task, the technique will not be effective. It must be clear that all members of the team are needed, even if amounts of involvement vary. A number of roles can be assigned to group members, including the following:

- A performer who does the skills or tasks
- A recorder who keeps track of statistics, trials, or key points made by the group

- A coach who provides skill feedback to the performer or times practice trials
- A presenter who communicates key points to the rest of the class
- A motivator who encourages and provides general and positive feedback to all group members

Cooperative learning is most successful when students switch roles often and stated group tasks proceed from simple to complex. Teachers need to monitor the groups to ensure all members contribute, but the responsibility for success truly lies with the students' ability to cooperate.

The following are examples of class activities that could be used with cooperative learning:

- Design a fitness routine that requires each member of the group to design one or two exercises for inclusion. The overall routine must show balance (exercise all body parts) and be appropriate for the entire group.
- Modify a sport or game to make it more inclusive. The goal is to redesign the game so all students can play successfully.
- Design a drill (each group member designs one) that enhances skill learning and assures that all members of the group improve. The drills must be cohesive and focus on a single skill to be learned (throwing, rope jumping, and so on).
- Break down a dance into various parts so it is easier to learn. Each member of the group is responsible for teaching one of the parts. The group must determine how the parts will be put together (taught) to the rest of the class.

Optimize Skill Learning

To help students effectively learn motor skills, teachers must understand some basic theory and concepts associated with motor learning. Knowledge of these concepts helps guide the development of content and structure of physical education lessons as well as teaching behaviours.

Motor Programs and Schema Theory

The concept of a *motor program* helps to explain how individuals can perform a vast range of movements without having to re-learn the action each time. Schmidt (1988) describes a motor program as a memory construct that stores information that is necessary to perform an action. In other words, when an individual is required to perform a particular movement, he or she calls upon this motor program rather than going through the entire process of re-learning the movement. Individuals develop and refine their motor programs by repeating and refining movement over time. Schmidt expanded this idea with the concept of a *generalized motor program.* The generalized program stores information on classes of actions rather than unique programs for each individual movement. For example, our generalized motor program for walking provides us with a variety of patterns in the walking action, rather than limiting us to one option. Schmidt's (1988) *schema theory* further explains how humans are able to adapt to new movement situations without having to re-learn or store a distinct program for each unique situation. A *schema*, according to Schmidt, is a generalized set of rules that provide the basis for making movement decisions. In other words, it is a set of rules that the generalized motor program uses to make adjustments to a new situation. One of the most important practical applications of schema theory is the guidance it provides for designing practice sessions. The following sections provide further suggestions for practical application of schema theory.

Offer Variable Practice Experiences

Schema theory suggests providing a wide variety of movement experiences in order to build a broad schema. Motor tasks are usually grouped into classes of tasks. For example, throwing is a collection of a class of movements. Throwing a ball in a sport can be performed in many different ways: the ball can travel at different speeds, different trajectories, and varying distances. Even though throwing tasks are all different, the variations have fundamental similarities. Movements in a class usually involve the same body parts and have similar rhythm but can be performed with many variations. These differences create the need for variable practice in a variable setting. Practice sessions should include a variety of skills in a movement class with a variety of situations and parameters. If a skill to be learned involves one fixed way of performing it (a "closed" skill), such as place-kicking a football or striking a ball off a batting tee, variability is much less important. However, most skills are "open," and responses are somewhat unpredictable, which makes variability in practice the usual mode of operation (for example, catching or batting a ball moving at different speeds and from different angles). Motor skills should be practised under a variety of conditions so students can learn to respond to novel situations.

Use Random Practice Techniques

There are two ways to organize the presentation of activities to be taught. The first is *blocked practice,* where all the trials of one task are completed before moving on to the next task. Blocked practice is effective during the early stages of skill acquisition. Initially, learners find rapid improvement because they are practising the same skill over and over. As a result, learners are often motivated to continue practising. However, a drawback to blocked practice is that it makes learners believe they are more skilled than they actually are. When the skill is applied in a natural setting, performance level lowers.

The other method is *random practice,* where the order of multiple task presentations is mixed and no task is practised twice in succession. Wrisberg and Liu (1991) showed that random practice was the most effective approach to use when learning skills. Students who learned a skill using random practice demonstrated a much higher level of retention and ability to perform the skill in an authentic setting.

Stages of Motor Skill Acquisition

In addition to the information that schema theory provides, it is accepted that the acquisition of motor skills occurs in somewhat predictable and identifiable stages or phases. Fitts and Posner (1967) proposed the following three-part model to explain how individuals learn a motor skill from the first tentative actions through to a refined form. Their model continues to guide the design of practice activities for motor skills. During the initial or *cognitive phase*, the learner is highly cognitively engaged in problem solving as she begins to create a mental plan of the skill. The skill attempts are likely uncoordinated and tentative as the learner works through multiple attempts. Often called the "thinking phase," here the teacher is reminded of the importance of providing simple and specific cues as well as an accurate demonstration to guide the learner's initial skills attempts. More in-depth information on teaching/learning cues is included in Chapter 4. The learner becomes less dependent on external cues and better able to utilize internal cues during the intermediate or *associative phase*, as she begins to refine the skill. The learner becomes both more successful and consistent in her practice attempts. Practice activities for the learner focus on an increased complexity to more closely resemble how the skill is used in an authentic situation. For example, a practice activity for a student at the associative phase of her dribbling skills may include the introduction of a defender to increase the challenge and force the dribbler to make adjustments. During the *autonomous phase*, the skill appears to be performed somewhat effortlessly, and looks automatic, with minimal conscious attention necessary. During this phase, the learner is able to make adjustments in the performance of the skill with ease in response to changes in demands. The following three sections emphasize different applications of this model to the design of effective practice.

Decide on Whole versus Part Practice

Skills can be taught by the whole or part method. The whole method refers to the process of learning the entire skill or activity in one dose. The part method breaks down a skill into a series of parts, and then combines the parts into the whole skill. For example, in a rhythmic activity, each section of a dance is taught and then put together. A simple gymnastics routine might be broken into component parts and put back together for the performance.

Whether to use the whole or part method depends on the complexity and organization of the skills to be learned. Complexity refers to the number of serial skills or components there are in a task. Organization defines how the parts are related to each other. High organization means the parts of the skill are closely related, making separation difficult. An example of a highly organized and complex skill is throwing, which would be difficult to practise without going through the complete motion. A low-organized skill is a simple folk dance, in which footwork and arm movements can be rehearsed separately. Generally, if the skills are high in complexity but low in organization, they can be taught in parts. If complexity is low but organization high, the skills must be taught as a whole. A final consideration is the duration of the skill. If the skill is of short duration, such as throwing, batting, or kicking, trying to teach the skill in parts is probably counterproductive. Imagine trying to slow down kicking while teaching it part by part. The performer would not develop proper pattern and timing.

When skill components are learned separately, students have to learn how to put the parts together. Practice time should be allowed for sequencing. For example, in a gymnastics routine, students might perform the activities separately, but find difficulty sequencing them because they have not learned how to modify each activity based on the previous one.

Length and Distribution of Practice Sessions

Short practice sessions usually produce more efficient learning than do longer sessions. This is due to longer sessions producing both physical and mental fatigue (boredom). The challenge is to try to offer as many repetitions as possible within short practice sessions. Use varied approaches, challenges, and activities to develop the same skill, in order to maintain motivational levels. For example, using many different types of beanbag activities helps maintain motivation but still focuses on tossing and catching skills.

Another way to determine the length of practice sessions is to examine the tasks being practised. If a skill causes physical fatigue, demands intense concentration, or has the potential to become tedious, practice sessions should be short and frequent, with an adequate rest pause between intervals.

Practice sessions that are spread out over many days are usually more effective than sessions crowded into a short time span. The combination of practice and review is effective for youngsters because activities can be taught in a short unit and then practised in review sessions throughout the year. In the initial stages of skill learning, it is particularly important that practice sessions be distributed in this way. Later, when success in skill performance increases motivational levels, teachers can lengthen individual practice sessions.

Know the Effect of Arousal

Arousal is the level of excitement that stress produces (Schmidt & Wrisberg, 2004). The level of arousal can have a positive or negative impact on motor performance. The key to proper arousal is to find the "just right" amount. With too little arousal, a youngster will be uninterested in learning. Too much arousal will fill a youngster with stress and anxiety, resulting in decreased motor performance. The more complex a skill, the more likely it is that arousal may disrupt learning. On the other hand, if a skill is simple, such as running, a greater amount of arousal can be tolerated without causing a reduction in skill performance. Optimally, youngsters should be aroused to a level at which they are excited and confident about participation.

Competition affects the arousal level of children. When competition is introduced in the early stages of skill learning, stress and anxiety reduce a child's ability to learn. On the other hand, if competition is introduced after a skill has been overlearned, it can improve the level of performance. Since most elementary school youngsters have not overlearned skills, teachers should limit use of competitive situations when teaching skills. For example, assume the objective is to practise basketball dribbling. The teacher places youngsters in squads and runs a relay requiring that they dribble to the opposite end of the gym and return. The first squad finished is the winner. The result: Instead of concentrating on dribbling form, students are more concerned about winning the relay. They are overaroused and determined to run as quickly as possible. Dribbling is done poorly (if at all), the balls fly out of control, and the teacher is dismayed by the result. Unfortunately, competitiveness overaroused the youngsters, who had not yet overlearned to dribble.

Offer Meaningful Skill Feedback

Feedback is important in the teaching process because it has an impact on what is to be learned, what should be avoided, and how the performance can be modified. Skill feedback is any kind of information about a movement sss two categories of skill feedback: intrinsic and extrinsic. *Intrinsic feedback* is internal, inherent to the performance of the skill, and travels through the senses, such as vision, hearing, touch, and smell. *Extrinsic feedback* is external and comes from an outside source, such as a teacher, videotape, a stopwatch, and so on.

Extrinsic feedback is further subdivided into *knowledge of results* (KR) and *knowledge of performance* (KP). KR is the information about the outcome of a performance (e.g., time of a run, result of a shot on goal), whereas KP is information about the process leading to the result (e.g., mechanics, technique). As KR is most often visible to the learner (e.g., where a shot lands, score in a game), the teacher is primarily responsible for providing KP (ways to improve the quality of movement). KP can increase a youngster's level of motivation because it provides feedback about improvement. Many youngsters become frustrated because they find it difficult to discern improvement. Knowledge of performance is a strong reinforcement, particularly when a teacher mentions something performed correctly. When using this type of feedback, refer to specific components of the learner's performance—for example, "I like the way you kept your chin on your chest," or "That's the way to step toward the target with your left foot." This feedback motivates youngsters to repeat the same pattern, ultimately resulting in improved performance. The most important aspect of this feedback is that it provides information for future patterns of action. Effective KP helps students associate their actions with an outcome (e.g., the ball popped up because my bat swing came up under the ball). (See Chapter 4 for discussion on the content of feedback and the process for communicating feedback to the learner.)

Use Mental Practice Techniques

Mental practice involves practising a motor skill in a quiet, relaxed environment. The experience involves thinking about the activity and its related sounds, colour, and other sensations. Students visualize themselves doing the activity successfully and at regular speed (Schmidt & Wrisberg, 2004). Mental practice stimulates children to think about and review the activity they are to perform. Some experience or familiarity with the motor task is requisite before the performer can derive value from mental practice. Mental practice is used in combination with regular practice, not in place of it. Before performing the task, prompt students to mentally review the critical factors and sequencing of the act.

Teach Skills in Proper Progression

Skill progression involves moving the learning process through ordered steps from the least challenging to the most challenging facets of an activity. Most motor skills can be ordered in an approximate hierarchy from simple to complex. Instructional progression includes reviewing previously learned steps before proceeding to new material and learning prerequisite skills before trying more difficult activities.

Developmental Levels and Progression

Placing activities into developmental levels makes it easier for the teacher to present activities that are appropriate to the maturity and developmental level of students. Present activities that best suit the individual regardless of the recommended level. Since schools group children by chronological age and grade rather than by developmental level, Table 3.1 shows how developmental levels roughly equate with grades and ages. To help you present skills in proper sequence, activities in Chapters 16 to 29 have been sequenced in approximate order of difficulty.

Developmental level I activities (used most often with Kindergarten through grade 2 children) are the least difficult and form the foundation for more complex skills. Most of these skills are performed individually or with a partner so as to increase the success of primary-grade children. Examples are tossing and catching, striking a stationary object, and playing games that simply incorporate fundamental locomotor movements. With these skills, the number of complex decisions to make while performing is minimized, so youngsters can concentrate on the skill at hand. As youngsters mature and progress into *developmental level II* (usually grades 3 to 4), the tasks become more difficult and many are performed individually or within small groups. Environmental factors such as different speeds of objects, different sizes of objects, and games requiring locomotor movements and specialized skills (throwing, catching, and so on) are introduced at this level. In *developmental level III* (grades 5 to 7), students use skills in a number of sport and game situations. Simple skills previously learned are sequenced into more complex motor patterns. At this level, cognitive

decisions about when to use a skill and how to incorporate strategy into the game are integrated into the learning experiences.

Children learn skills in a natural progression, but not at the same rate. Allow youngsters to progress at a rate that is best suited for them. This usually means that all children will be learning a similar class of skills (throwing or striking, for example) but will progress at different rates and practise different skills within the category. This premise forms the basis for presenting a "developmentally appropriate physical education program" (Barrett, Williams, & Whitall, 1992).

Integrate Mechanical Principles into Instruction

When planning for skill instruction, mechanical principles need to be considered an integral part of skill performance. Young children who are provided with evidence-based (or proper) instruction in performing motor skills experience more successes that lead to the development of mature motor patterns. Many teachers have experienced the difficulty of changing a performer's motor patterns after a skill has been learned incorrectly. Stability, force, leverage, and motion are concepts that are best learned when they accompany a skill being taught. A discussion of each is covered in the following sections.

Stability

Stability reflects balance and equilibrium, which affect the performance of many sport skills. A stable base is necessary when the student applies force to a projectile, or absorbs force. Instability is useful in some activities, such as when a rapid start is desired. Introduce the following concepts:

1. The size of the base of support needs to be increased for greater stability. The base must be widened in the direction of the force being applied or absorbed.

2. The body's centre of gravity must be moved lower, or closer to the base of support, when stopping quickly or applying/absorbing force (as in pushing/pulling). Lowering the centre of gravity is accomplished by bending the knees and hips (see Figure 3.4).

3. The centre of gravity should be kept over the base of support (within the boundaries of the base) for stability and balance. When the centre of gravity passes beyond the boundaries of the base of support, balance is lost. In most activities, keep the head up and eliminate excessive body lean. The ready position (see Figure 3.5) is an example of a stable position used in many sport activities.

TABLE 3.1		
Equating developmental levels to grades and ages		
Developmental Level	**Grades**	**Ages**
I	K–2	5–7
II	3–4	8–9
III	5–7	10–12

Figure 3.4

Pulling.

4. Use the "free" or non-weight-bearing limbs as counterbalances to aid stability. The ready position and fast starts are used in many physical activity settings and illustrate how stability and instability (used in fast starts) can enhance performance.

Figure 3.5

Ready position.

Force

Force is a measure of the push or pull that one object or body applies to another. Force is necessary to move objects of various types and sizes. The larger the object to be moved, the greater the amount of force required to cause the movement. Generating large forces usually requires the involvement of large muscle groups and a greater number of muscles than does the generation of a smaller force.

Torque is the twisting or turning effect that force produces when it acts eccentrically with respect to a body's axis of rotation. Concepts to remember when teaching children include the following:

1. When resisting or applying force, the bones on either side of the major joints should form a right angle to each other. A muscle is most effective at causing rotation when it pulls at a 90-degree angle.

2. To generate greater force, body parts are activated in a smooth, coordinated manner. For example, in throwing, the hips and trunk are rotated first and followed in sequence by the upper arm, lower arm, hand, and fingers.

3. More force is generated when more muscles are used. Muscles are capable of generating high levels of force when the contraction speed is low. For example, it is impossible to lift a very heavy object rapidly.

4. Force should be absorbed over a large surface area and over as long a period of time as possible. An example of absorbing force over a large surface area is a softball player rolling after a dive through the air to catch a ball. The roll absorbs the force with the hands and the large surface area of the body.

5. The follow-through in striking and throwing activities is necessary to ensure maximum application of force and gradual reduction of momentum. An example is the continued swing of the baseball bat after striking the ball.

Leverage and Motion

Body levers amplify force into motion. Levers offer a mechanical advantage so that less effort is needed to accomplish tasks; motion occurs after force has been applied or when force is absorbed. A simple lever is a bar or other rigid structure that can rotate about a fixed point to overcome a resistance when force is applied. Levers serve one of two functions: (a) they allow resistance greater than the applied force to be overcome, or (b) they serve to increase the distance or the speed at which resistance can be moved. The following are characteristics of levers and the effects they have on movement:

1. The three types of levers in the body are first-, second- and third-class levers (see Figure 3.6). Most of the body's levers are third-class levers; they have the point of force (produced by the muscles) between the fulcrum (the joint) and the point of resistance

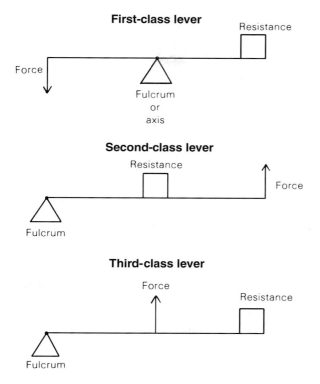

First-class lever

Force

Fulcrum
or
axis

Resistance

Second-class lever

Resistance

Force

Fulcrum

Third-class lever

Force

Resistance

Fulcrum

Figure 3.6

Types of levers.

(produced by the weight of the object to be moved). Also see Chapter 13, Figures 13.3 A, B, C for further information on "body levers."

2. Most of the levers in the body are used to gain a mechanical advantage for speed, not to accomplish heavy tasks.

3. A longer force arm (distance from joint to point of force application) allows greater resistance to be overcome (see Figure 3.7). This concept is useful when manipulating an external lever. For example, to pry open a paint can, force is applied to the screwdriver away from the rim rather than near the paint can: this allows the screwdriver to act as a longer lever.

4. A longer resistance arm (distance from joint to point of resistance) allows greater speed to be generated (see Figure 3.8). Racquets and bats are extensions of the

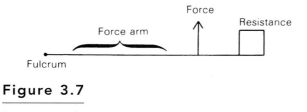

Force

Force arm

Resistance

Fulcrum

Figure 3.7

Longer arm force.

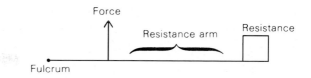

Force

Resistance arm

Resistance

Fulcrum

Figure 3.8

Longer resistance arm.

arm: that is, they offer longer resistance arms for applying greater speed. The longer the racquet or bat, therefore, the greater the speed generated. Longer levers are more difficult to rotate, which is why young baseball players are encouraged to choke up to make the bat easier to swing and control. Even though the lever is shortened, bat velocity (at point of contact with the ball) is probably not much reduced. The important result is that performance improves through increased quality contacts.

Motion and Direction

The majority of skills in physical activities are associated with propelling an object. The following concepts of motion and direction are basic to throwing, striking, and kicking skills learned in physical education:

1. The angle of release determines how far an object will travel. Theoretically, the optimum angle of release is 45 degrees. The human body has various limitations, however, that cause the optimum angle of projection to be well below 45 degrees. For example, the angle of projection for the shot put is 40 to 41 degrees; for the running long jump, it is 20 to 22 degrees.

2. A ball rebounds from the floor or from the racquet at the same angle at which it is hit. However, various factors, such as rotation applied to the ball, the type of ball, and the surface contacted by the ball, can modify the rebound angle.

3. In most throwing situations, the propelled object should be released at a point tangent to the target. During throwing, for example, the arm travels in an arc, and the ball must be released when the hand is in line with the target.

Practical Considerations for the Learning Environment

The environment where youngsters experience physical education can have an impact on the effectiveness of instruction and learning. Practical factors such as space, equipment, and safety are important in the process of planning a quality experience. In general, these environmental factors can be controlled entirely by the teacher.

Predetermine Your Space Needs

A common error is to take a class to a large practice area, give students a task to accomplish, and fail to define or limit the space in which it should be performed. The class spreads out in an area so large that it is impossible for the teacher to communicate and manage the class. The skills being practised and the ability of the teacher to control the class dictate the size of the space. Delineating a small area for participation makes it easier to manage a class because students can see and hear better. As students become more responsive, the size of the area can be enlarged. Regardless of the size of the space, delineate the practice area. An easy way is to set up cones around the perimeter. Natural boundaries can also serve as restraining lines. A factor affecting the size of the practice area is the amount of instruction needed. When students are learning a closed skill and need constant feedback and redirection, it is important for them to stay near the teacher. Establish a smaller area where students can move in closer for instruction, and then return to the larger area for practice.

Available space is often divided into smaller areas to maximize student participation. An example is a volleyball game where only 10 students can play on one available court. In most cases, it is more effective to divide the area into two courts to accommodate a greater number of students. Safety is a related consideration when partitioning space. If the playing areas are too close together, players from one area might run into players from the other area. Include "buffer zones" between play areas. In addition, be sure to teach your students an appropriate safety procedure for retrieving a ball from a neighbouring play space.

Use Equipment Efficiently

Equipment can be a limiting factor. Before beginning the lesson, determine how much equipment is available, since this will determine the structure of the lesson. For example, if there are only 16 paddles and balls for a class of 30, some type of sharing or station work will have to be organized. If possible, know exactly what equipment is available prior to planning a lesson. If equipment is a limitation it will affect your choice of lesson activities.

How much equipment is enough? If it is individual-use equipment, such as racquets, bats, and balls, there should be one piece of equipment for each student (see Figure 3.9). Where sending and receiving is the major focus, it is reasonable to have one ball for a pair of students. If it is group-oriented equipment, such as gymnastics apparatus, there should be enough to assure waiting lines of no more than four students.

What are alternatives when equipment is lacking? One solution is to teach using the station/task style. This

Figure 3.9

All students must have a piece of equipment.

involves dividing students into small groups so each group has enough equipment. For example, in a softball unit, have some students practise fielding, others batting, others pitching, and so on. Another method is the reciprocal teaching approach. While one student practises an activity, a peer is involved in offering feedback and evaluation. The peers share equipment and take turns being involved in practice and evaluation. A third method is the most common—design practice activities that involve taking turns. Keep in mind, however, that waiting in line too long for one's turn does not contribute to skill learning.

Effectively distributing equipment is a key component of a quality lesson. One effective method for distributing individual equipment is to place it around the perimeter of the area. It requires some set-up time prior to the lesson, but makes it easy for students to acquire a piece of equipment without confusion. Efficient equipment distribution reduces the time spent on a task that is not related to learning. Large apparatus should be arranged in the safest possible formation so all pieces are visible from all angles. The initial set-up of equipment also depends on the focus of the lesson. For example, the height of the basket may be reduced to emphasize correct shooting form. Volleyball nets may be placed at different heights to allow different types of practice. Equipment and apparatus should always be modified to best suit the needs of the learner.

Ensure a Safe Environment

One of the most important outcomes of a physical education program is to offer students an opportunity to take risks. Indeed, all activities in physical education have a certain degree of risk because students are moving. However, do not underestimate the importance of a safe environment. When students feel adequate safety precautions are in place, they are less hesitant to learn new activities that involve risk. Injuries are inevitable in physical education classes, but if they are due to poor planning and preparation, you may be found liable and responsible for such injuries (see Chapter 9). You are expected to foresee unsafe situations that might result in student injury. Safe and sensible behaviour needs to be taught and practised. For example, if students are in a tumbling unit, they need instruction and practice in absorbing momentum and force. Practise safety procedures such as taking turns and following directions.

Another component of a safe environment is an approved written curriculum (e.g., provincial curriculum document) that guides planning and implementation of learning activities in proper progression. This curriculum guide offers evidence that proper progression and sequencing of activities were used in the lesson presentation. In addition, proper progression of activities gives students confidence because they develop the skills needed to perform safely before moving on to the next level of difficulty.

Choose an Instructional Formation

Appropriate formations or arrangements facilitate learning experiences. Different formations are needed for activities done in place (nonlocomotor), activities where children move (locomotor), and activities in which balls, beanbags, or other objects are thrown, kicked, caught, or otherwise received (manipulative activities). Select a formation based on providing maximum activity for all students. When small groups are used, try to place no more than four students in a group. This minimizes the amount of time spent standing and waiting for a turn.

Mass or Scattered Formation

Scatter youngsters throughout the area so that each student has a personal space. This formation is useful for in-place activities and when individuals need to move in every direction. Emphasize not bumping into, colliding with, or interfering with classmates. Scattered formation is basic to such activities as wands, hoops, individual rope jumping, and individual ball skills.

Squad Formations

In squad formation, members stand about 1 metre apart in a column. In extended squad formation, the squad column is maintained with more distance (3 to 5 metres) between members. Figure 3.10 shows a regular and an extended squad formation.

Regular Ⓛ **X X X X X X**

Extended Ⓛ **X X X X X X**

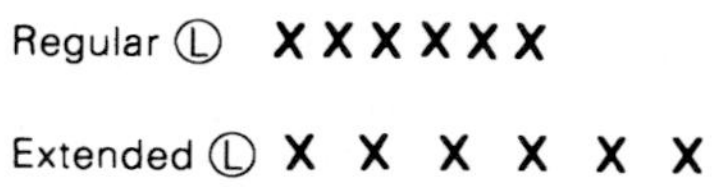

Figure 3.10

Regular and extended squad formations.

Partner Formation

Partner formation is useful for reciprocal teaching, where partners help each other learn new skills. Catching and receiving activities can be practised if each pair has a projectile. It is necessary to keep pairs aligned if space is limited or objects are being caught and thrown (see Figure 3.11).

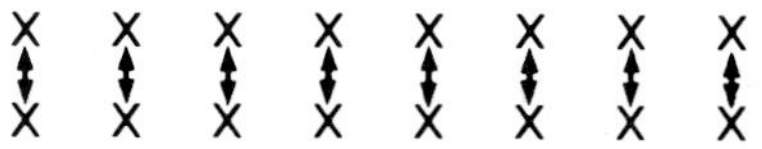

Figure 3.11

Partner formation.

Lane or File

The lane, or file, formation is commonly used with locomotor activity (see Figure 3.12). Students at the front of the lane move as prescribed and take their place at the rear of the lane.

X X X X
X X X X
X X X X
X X X X
X X X X
X X X X

Figure 3.12

Lane, or file, formation.

Line and Leader

Line-and-leader formation (see Figure 3.13) is often used for throwing and catching skills. The leader passes

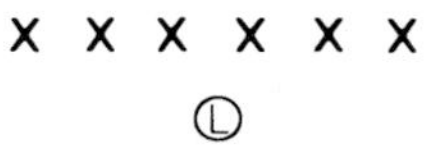

X X X X X X
Ⓛ

Figure 3.13

Line-and-leader formation.

back and forth to each line player in turn. Placing students in a semicircle-and-leader formation (see Figure 3.14) can equalize the distance from the leader for all players.

Figure 3.14

Semicircle-and-leader formation.

Double Line

The double-line formation can be used for passing and kicking. Figure 3.15 shows a zigzag formation in which the ball is passed from one line to the next.

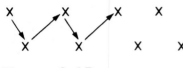

Figure 3.15

Double-line formation.

Regular Shuttle Formation

The regular shuttle formation (see Figure 3.16) is used for practising passing and dribbling skills on the move. It is often used for hockey, soccer, basketball, and football ball-carrying skills. The player at the head of one line dribbles toward, or passes to, the player at the head of the other line. Each player keeps moving forward and takes a place at the end of the other half of the shuttle.

Figure 3.16

Regular shuttle formation.

Shuttle Turn-back Formation

Shuttle turn-back formation (see Figure 3.17) is used for passing, kicking, and volleying for distance. The player at the

Figure 3.17

Shuttle turn-back formation.

head of one shuttle line passes to the player at the head of the other. After passing, players go to the back of their line.

Simultaneous Class Movement

There are times when certain activities require that the entire class move simultaneously. Without some structure and organization, this has the potential to become chaotic. For such activities, the following formations can be useful.

Children can start on opposite sides of the gym and exchange positions (see Figure 3.18). On signal, they cross to the opposite side of the area, passing through the opposite line without contact.

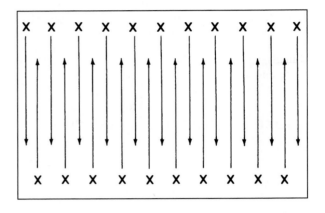

Figure 3.18

Exchanging positions on opposite sides.

You could also have children start on opposite sides of the gym, move toward the centre and then back. A dividing line can be formed with ropes, wands, or cones to mark the centre (see Figure 3.19).

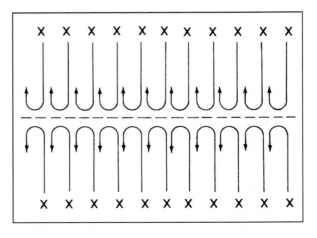

Figure 3.19

Moving to centre and back on opposite sides.

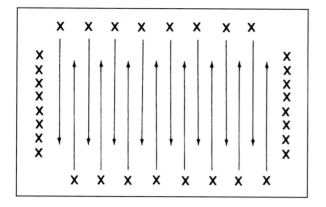

Figure 3.20

Exchanging on four sides.

Finally, children can start on each of four sides of the play area and alternately exchange sides (see Figure 3.20). The children on one pair of opposite sides exchange first and then the others exchange. This formation is useful for class demonstrations—one-half of the class demonstrates while the other half observes and evaluates.

Design a Lesson Plan Format

Written lesson plans vary in form and length, depending on the activity and the background of the teacher. A written plan ensures that the teacher has given thought to the lesson before children enter the activity area. It helps avoid spur-of-the-moment decisions that disrupt the unity and progression of instruction. Lesson plans can and should be modified when needed, but a written plan gives focus and direction to instruction. Progression is more apt to occur in a lesson when instruction is based on activities presented in previous lesson plans. Notes and changes can be written on the lesson plans to give direction for future modifications of the curriculum.

A standardized lesson plan format allows teachers and substitute teachers to interchange plans within a school district. Include the following basic information in your lesson plan:

1. *Learning outcomes.* Learning outcomes are designed and listed for the purpose of accomplishing content standards. Writing effective learning outcomes is discussed in the next chapter.

2. *Equipment required.* Identify amounts of materials and supplies required and how the equipment will be distributed.

3. *Lesson activities.* List actual movements and skill experiences to be taught. Place the activities in proper developmental sequence. Do not describe activities in detail but give enough description so they can be recalled easily.

4. *Teaching points.* Include organizational tips and important learning cues, how equipment is arranged, how students are grouped, and so on.

A common format is the four-part lesson plan, an example of which can be seen in Figure 3.21. Each lesson includes an introductory or warm-up activity, fitness activities, lesson focus, and closing activity. The four parts prepare youngsters for the activity, ensure moderate to vigorous activity, teach skills and concepts, and implement these in a culminating activity.

Lesson planning takes time. Comprehensive lesson plans are best written when you have time to plan and reflect. They give direction to the day's lesson and may include many more activities than can be taught in a typical period. Many teachers use a 10-cm by 15-cm card to write down the actual activities they are teaching. The size of the card and brevity of information make the plan easier to refer to while teaching. The four major parts in a lesson plan consist of the following items.

Introductory (Warm-up) Activity

The introductory (warm-up) activity lasts two to three minutes and sets the tone for the rest of the lesson. The first part of the lesson provides an opportunity to review class management skills, such as stopping on signal, running under control, and so on. An effective guideline is to run and freeze your class three times. If all students are with you after three freezes, proceed to teach an introductory activity (see Chapter 16).

Introductory activities serve several purposes in the lesson format, including the following:

- Students receive immediate activity when they enter the activity area. Youngsters want to move immediately rather than having to sit down, be quiet, and listen to instructions. Offer vigorous activity first; then give instructions or discuss learning outcomes while they recover from vigorous activity.

- They serve as a physiological warm-up, preparing students for physical activity.

- This part of the lesson can be used to review previously learned skills or for an anticipatory set, which pre-focuses on the learning outcomes of the lesson.

Fitness Activity

The second part of the lesson is designed to enhance health-related fitness and promote lifetime physical activity. This

Lesson: Movement Skills and
Concepts Level I

Topic: Twisting, turning, stretching, relaxing
movements

Equipment: None

**Learning outcome(s): "The student will be able to . . . "
(TSWBAT...)**

- Perform several different twisting, turning, stretching, and relaxing tasks in isolation and combination
- Perform a partner challenge game that integrates above skills

Introductory Activities/Warm-up	Organization	Teaching points
• Puppy walk, freeze and stretch, step-hop, freeze and stretch, crab walk, freeze and stretch, robot walk, freeze and stretch, bear walk, freeze and stretch. Find a partner.	Scatter formation	

Fitness Development	Organization	Teaching points
• Follow your partner – using fast walking only with one partner leading and the other following, try to keep up to your partner; on whistle switch leader and follower.	Scatter formation	Look side to side.
Lesson Focus		
• Glue your feet to the floor. Try to twist your body to the right, to the left, twist slowly.		
• Try to bend and twist at the same time.		
• Try to twist one part of body in one direction, another in a different direction.		
• What is the difference between a twist and a turn? Show me a turn, a twist.		Twist (in place). Turn (move in space).
• Turn your body left, right, quarter, half.		
• Show me a turn followed by a twist, a new turn and new twist. Again.		
Culminating Activity		
With a partner: Leader invents a creative combo of turn, twist, turn; follower must copy. Switch leader and follower. New leader invents a "turn, turn, twist." Continue.		Show to class.

Closure

- Let's sit quietly—take a deep breath, hold it tight. Breathe out and relax. Again.
- Reach as high as you can, stretch, and bring your arms down slowly, slowly, slowly. Again.
- Hug yourself as tightly as you can, relax and drop your arms. Again.

Figure 3.21

Example of a lesson plan.

Figure 3.22

Relaxing during the closing activity.

portion of the lesson teaches youngsters the type and amount of activity necessary to maintain a healthy lifestyle. A variety of activities are used so students experience the wide range of options available to increase their heart rate. Physical fitness and activity are discussed in detail in Chapter 12.

Lesson Focus

This portion of the lesson (15 to 20 minutes) affords students the opportunity to *practise skills* and apply movement concepts. It contains learning experiences designed to help students meet the learning outcomes of the lesson. The lesson focus is generally characterized by repetition and refinement of physical skills in a sequential and success-oriented setting. The later part of this section (also called the *culminating activity*) may be a game or equivalent activity (e.g., dance) that applies skills and concepts developed in the lesson focus.

Closing Activity (Closure)

The closing activity brings closure to the lesson through evaluation of the day's accomplishments—stressing and reinforcing skills learned, revisiting performance techniques, and checking cognitive concepts. If a lesson is demanding or spirited, focus closing activities on relaxation and winding down, so students return to the classroom in a calmer state of mind (see Figure 3.22).

Reflect on the Lesson

Quality teachers find time to reflect on their lesson plans. Most teachers admit that their first lesson of the week is not as polished and effective as one taught near the end of

1. *Did I prepare ahead of time?* Mental preparation prior to a lesson assures that flow and continuity occur in a lesson.
2. *Did I understand the "whys" of my lesson?* Knowing why you are teaching something will give you greater strength and conviction in your presentation.
3. *Was my equipment arranged prior to class?* Proper equipment placement reduces management time and allows more time for instruction and practice.
4. *Did I constantly move and reposition myself during the lesson?* Moving allows you to be close to more students so you can reinforce and help them. It usually reduces behaviour problems.
5. *Was I alert for children who were having trouble performing the activities?* Youngsters want to receive relevant but subtle help.
6. *Did I state my instructional goals for the lesson?* Students are more focused if they know what they are supposed to learn.
7. *Did I teach with enthusiasm and energy?* My energy and zest rubs off on my students.
8. *Did I praise youngsters who made an effort or improved?* Saying something positive to children increases their desire to perform at a higher level.
9. *Did I give sufficient attention to the personalization and creativity of each student?* Everybody feels unique and different and wants to deal with learning tasks in a personal manner.
10. *Did I teach students to be responsible for their learning and personal behaviour?* Students need to learn responsibility and self-direction skills. Take time for such learning.
11. *Did I teach for quality of movement or just offer a large quantity of activities in an attempt to keep students on task?* Repetition is a necessary part of learning new skills.
12. *Did I bring closure to my lesson?* This gives you feedback about the effectiveness of your instruction. It also allows students a chance to reflect on what they have learned. Use methods that allow you to check for understanding for all students.
13. *Did I evaluate the usefulness of activities I presented?* Try to find ways to modify activities so they can immediately be implemented and used by students.
14. *Did I evaluate how I handled discipline and management problems?* Did I preserve the self-esteem of my students during behaviour correction episodes? What are some ways I could have handled situations better?

Figure 3.23

Questions that aid the reflection process.

the week; a lesson taught during the first period of the week does not include all the finer points learned through trial and error. Instruction improves when teachers reflect on why some things worked and others didn't. Leave time at the end of the day to consider and note ways the lesson can be improved. Try keeping a portfolio related to inspiration and insight you uncover. Write down personal growth indicators and situations that offer evidence you are developing professionally. Continue to reflect; it is a dynamic and ongoing process. Examine Figure 3.23 for a list of questions that aid the reflection process. Add other questions that are specific and related to your professional growth.

Critical Thinking

1. Discuss the relationship between "theory-driven" choices and "practice-driven" choices a teacher makes during the lesson planning process.

2. How are teaching styles and motor learning theory related?

3. How does the four-part lesson format incorporate aspects of teaching styles, motor learning theory, and personal fitness development?

References and Suggested Readings

Barrett, K.R., Williams, K., & Whitall, J. (1992). What does it mean to have a "developmentally appropriate physical education program?" *The Physical Educator, 49*(3), 113–117.

Byra, M., & Jenkins, J. (2000). Matching instructional tasks with learning ability: The inclusion style of teaching. Teaching style E. *Journal of Physical Education, Recreation, & Dance, 71*(3), 26–30.

British Columbia Ministry of Education. (1995). *Physical education K–7 integrated resource package.* Victoria, BC: Author.

Burk, M. (2002). *Station games.* Champaign, IL: Human Kinetics.

Ebbeck, V. & Gibbons, S.L. (1998). The effect of a team building program on the self-conceptions of grade 6 and 7 physical education students. *Journal of Sport and Exercise Psychology, 20,* 300–310.

Éducation Québec. (2003). *Quebec education program— Chapter 9 personal development. Introduction to the physical education and health program.* Quebec City, PQ: Author.

Fitts, P.M. & Posner, M.I. (1967). *Human performance.* Belmont, CA: Brooks/Cole.

Gabbard, C. (2004). *Physical education for children: Building the foundation* (4th ed.). San Francisco, CA: Benjamin Cummings.

Gallahue, D. & Donnelly, F.C. (2003). *Developmental physical education for all children.* (4th ed.). Champaign, IL: Human Kinetics.

Gibbons, S.L. & Black, K.M. (1997). Effect of participation in team building activities on the self-concepts of middle school physical education students. *AVANTE, 5*(1), 46–60.

Glover, D.R. & Anderson, L. (2003). *Character education: 43 fitness activities for community building.* Champaign, IL: Human Kinetics.

Graham, G., Holt/Hale, S.A., & Parker, M. (2007). *Children moving—a reflective approach to teaching physical education* (7th ed.). New York: McGraw-Hill.

Graham, G., Holt/Hale, S.A., & Parker, M. (2001). *Children moving* (5th ed.). Mountain View, CA: Mayfield.

Grineski, S. (1996). *Cooperative learning in physical education.* Champaign, IL: Human Kinetics.

Guskey, T.R. (1985). *Implementing mastery learning.* Belmont, CA: Wadsworth.

Harrison, J.M., Blakemore, C.L., & Buck, M.M. (2001). *Instructional strategies for secondary school physical education* (5th ed.). New York: McGraw-Hill.

Johnson, D.W. & Johnson, F. (2003). *Joining together: Group theory and group skills* (8th ed.). Boston, MA: Allyn & Bacon.

Manitoba Department of Education and Training. (2000). *Kindergarten to senior 4 physical education/health education— Manitoba curriculum framework of outcomes for active healthy lifestyles.* Winnipeg, MB: Author.

Metzler, M.W. (2000). *Instructional models for physical education.* Boston: Allyn and Bacon.

Midura, D.W. & Glover, D.R. (1995). *More team building challenges.* Champaign, IL: Human Kinetics.

Mosston, M. & Ashworth, S. (2002). *Teaching physical education* (5th ed.). San Francisco, CA: Benjamin Cummings.

Newfoundland and Labrador Department of Education. (2004). *Physical education—Primary and elementary curriculum guide.* St. John's, NF; Author.

Nova Scotia Education. (2000). *Physical education curriculum: Grades primary–6.* Halifax, NS: Author.

Orlick, T. (2006). *Cooperative games and sports* (2nd ed.). Champaign, IL: Human Kinetics.

Rink, J.E. (2005). *Teaching physical education for learning* (5th ed.). Boston: McGraw-Hill.

Robinson, D. (2006). A call for PE consultants and specialists: Let's get serious about implementing quality PE. *Physical and Health Education Journal, 72*(3), 6–11.

Schmidt, R.A. (1988). Motor and action perspectives on motor behavior. In O.G. Meijer & K. Roth (Eds.), *Complex motor behaviour: "The" motor-action controversy* (pp. 3–44). Amsterdam: Elsevier.

Schmidt, R.A. & Wrisberg, C. (2004). *Motor learning and performance* (3rd ed.). Champaign, IL: Human Kinetics.

Siedentop, D. & Tannehill, D. (2000). *Developing teaching skills in physical education* (4th ed.). Mountain View, CA: Mayfield.

Slavin, R. (1995). *Cooperative learning: Theory, research & practice* (2nd ed.). Boston, MA: Allyn & Bacon.

Wrisberg, C. & Lui, Z. (1991). The effect of contextual variety on the practice, retention, and transfer of an applied motor skill. *Research Quarterly for Exercise and Sport, 62,* 406–412.

 Weblinks

The following websites provide a variety of lesson planning resources for physical education teachers:

http://ednet.edc.gov.ab.ca/physicaleducationonline/ lessonplans

www.ocup.org/units/units55.php?grade=ALL&subject= Health%20and%20Physical%20Education

www.pecentral.com

www.pe4life.org

CHAPTER 4

Improving Instructional Effectiveness

Essential Components

I	Organized around content standards
II	Student-centred and developmentally appropriate
III	Physical activity and motor skill development form the core of the program
IV	Teaches management skills and self-discipline
V	**Promotes inclusion of all students**
VI	**Focuses on process over product**
VII	Promotes lifetime personal health and wellness
VIII	**Teaches cooperation and responsibility and promotes sensitivity to diversity**

Physical Education Standards

1	Students are able to move competently using a variety of fundamental and specialized motor skills.
2	Students can monitor and maintain a health-enhancing level of physical fitness.
3	Students are able to apply movement concepts and basic mechanics of skill performance when learning and refining motor skills.
4	Students comprehend the basic principles of wellness and are able to apply concepts that enable them to make meaningful decisions that positively impact their health and wellness.
5	Students participate in a wide variety of physical activities and learn how to maintain a personalized active lifestyle.
6	**Students demonstrate empathy, understanding, and respect for the numerous differences exhibited by people in an activity setting.**
7	**Students exhibit responsible and self-directed behaviours that lead to positive social interactions in physical activity.**

OVERVIEW

There are instructional elements in quality lessons that cut across all presentations regardless of the students' age or grade, or lesson content. Instructional effectiveness can be improved by using teaching cues, demonstration, modelling, and feedback. Communication with students clearly increases if the teacher offers several points while simultaneously demonstrating the desired behaviour. Listening skills are as important as speaking skills when trying to establish meaningful relationships with students. Instructional cues—words or phrases—can be used as quick and efficient communication regarding proper technique in the performance of a particular skill or movement. Feedback to students can be delivered in various ways, including positive, negative, and corrective. Over time, positive feedback is the most effective for developing positive attitudes toward activity. Three aspects of diversity, including meeting the needs of the multicultural classroom, Aboriginal students, and gender, are discussed as they relate to effective instruction in physical education. Strategies for enhancing diversity are outlined in this chapter.

OUTCOMES

- Know how to teach for the promotion of diversity in physical education classes.
- Identify various ways to communicate effectively with youngsters in a physical education learning environment.

- Understand the procedures needed to develop effective teaching cues.

- Cite various ways to enhance the clarity of communication between the teacher and the learner.

- Identify essential elements of instruction and discuss the manner in which each relates to the learning environment.

- Describe the value of nonverbal behaviour in the physical education setting.

- Describe various demonstration skills that facilitate an environment conducive to learning.

- Understand how instructional cues can be used to increase student performance.

- Articulate techniques that supply youngsters with meaningful feedback regarding performance.

*E*ffective teachers create a positive atmosphere for learning. They may not know more about skills and activities than less capable teachers, but they are able to apply a set of effective instructional skills. Becoming an effective teacher demands an inward look at one's teaching personality and the impact it has on learning. How teachers interact with students, in large part, influences how those students feel about themselves.

Characteristics of a Quality Lesson

Regardless of the teaching style used, an effective learning environment is characterized by a set of instructional behaviours that occur regularly. These behaviours do not describe a specific method or style and allow significant room for individual approaches to teaching. The focus is less on what the teacher does and more on what students are doing. For example, any style of teaching that produces high rates of student-engaged time and positive attitudes toward the subject matter is considered an effective learning environment. Evidence from teacher effectiveness research (Rink, 2003; Siedentop & Tannehill, 2000) indicates that, regardless of the teacher's teaching style, an educational environment is most effective when the following elements are present:

1. Students are engaged in appropriate learning activities for a large percentage of class time. Effective teachers use class time wisely. They plan carefully and insist on appropriate learning activities that deal with the subject matter. Students need time to learn; effective teachers assure that students are engaged in productive practice. Developmental learning activities are matched to students' abilities and contribute to overall learning outcomes.

2. The learning atmosphere is success-oriented, with a positive, caring climate. Evidence shows that teachers who develop a supportive atmosphere foster learning and positive student attitudes toward school.

3. Students are given clear learning outcomes and receive high rates of information feedback from the teacher. Students know that they are going to be held accountable for their progress in the physical education class. Class activities are designed so students spend large amounts of time on the required learning outcomes. The environment is also designed so students receive regular feedback on learning attempts even if the teacher is not available.

4. Student progress is monitored regularly, and students are held accountable for learning in physical education. Students are expected to make progress toward learning outcomes. They are able to assess and record their progress toward these outcomes, and they know what is expected of them and how the expectations are tied to the accountability system.

5. Low rates of management time and smooth transitions from one activity to another characterize the environment. Students move from one learning activity to another smoothly and without wasting time. Equipment is organized to facilitate smooth transitions.

6. Students spend a limited amount of time waiting in line or in other unproductive behaviours. Effective environments are characterized by high rates of time engaged in subject matter. In physical education, this means high rates of time spent practising and playing.

7. Teachers are organized, with high but realistic expectations for student achievement. Learning activities are structured to challenge students. Activities are not too easy or too difficult. Expect students to learn, and hold them accountable for their progress.

8. Teachers are enthusiastic about what they are doing and are actively involved in the instructional process. Students need an enthusiastic model—someone who incorporates physical activity into his or her lifestyle.

Incorporate Essential Elements of Instruction

Education is effective when both a quality curriculum and able instruction are smoothly meshed. The curriculum is a critical component of the educational process; however, when the curriculum is poorly taught, student progress is limited. The following sections discuss aspects of effective instruction that are necessary to ensure a quality curriculum is maximized.

Writing Learning Outcomes

Learning outcomes are statements of what students are expected to know and do as a result of a learning experience (e.g., a lesson, a unit). Learning outcomes give a lesson direction and meaning and guide the choice of learning activities. Outcomes that are stated clearly and expressed in measurable terms let learners know what needs to be accomplished. It is helpful for teachers to adopt a regular stem for writing outcomes: for example, "The student will be able to . . ." (TSWBAT). Learning outcomes are characterized as follows:

- *First, outcomes must define observable behaviour.* Teachers and students must know when an outcome is reached. If an outcome is not visible, neither party knows when it has been reached. This is easier in physical education than in some other areas because most activities are overt and easy to observe.

- *Second, learning outcomes must identify clearly and specifically the content to be learned.* Teachers and students will be comfortable when everyone clearly understands what is expected. Problems arise when students have to guess what the teacher wants them to learn. Students have a right to know what is expected and what they need to accomplish to reach the stated outcome. If outcomes are ambiguous or nonexistent, they provide little guidance for the student or teacher.

Outcomes can be written for the three learning domains—psychomotor, cognitive, and affective. Psychomotor domain outcomes are defined most commonly in physical education and cover areas such as learning physical skills and developing health-related physical fitness. Cognitive outcomes for physical education aim toward knowledge and comprehension of skill performance principles and precepts related to fitness and activity. Affective outcomes focus on attitudes and behaviours, such as learning to cooperate with peers on a team or behave in a responsible manner. Figure 4.1 provides examples of learning outcomes.

The organization of learning outcomes in provincial physical education curriculum guides has changed in recent years. In many previous curricula, outcomes were often organized by domain (for example, all the cognitive outcomes grouped together). In most current curricula, these outcomes are grouped under a variety of major concepts. For example, in the *Manitoba Curriculum Framework of Outcomes for Active Healthy Lifestyles* (2000), learning outcomes are grouped under these General Student Learning Outcomes: Movement, Fitness Management, Safety, Personal and Social Management, and Healthy Lifestyle Practices. Each general outcome includes cognitive, affective, and psychomotor outcomes. In the *British Columbia Integrated Resource Package* (IRP) (1995), learning outcomes are grouped under three curriculum organizers: Active Living, Movement, and

Psychomotor

"The student will demonstrate four ways to perform a forward roll."

"Using a jump rope, the student will be able to perform three consecutive forward crossover moves."

Cognitive

"The student will show an understanding of soccer rules by explaining when a corner kick is awarded."

"The student will demonstrate knowledge and understanding of rhythmic gymnastics routines by diagramming a sample floor routine for balls."

Affective

"After participating in physical activity, the students will be able to express their personal satisfaction in their accomplishments."

"The students will be able to share how they feel about participating in physical activities with friends."

Figure 4.1

Examples of measurable outcomes.

Personal and Social Responsibility. Each organizer includes learning outcomes from all three domains. Alberta's (2000) general learning outcomes for physical education are organized under four general outcomes: activity, benefits of health, cooperation, and do it daily for life. Both Nova Scotia (2000) and New Brunswick (2002) organize their physical education learning outcomes under the three broad terms of "doing," "knowing," and "valuing." Most recently, the Newfoundland and Labrador (2004) physical education curriculum guide organized learning outcomes under the concepts of "in movement," "about movement," and "through movement." These different ways of grouping learning outcomes emphasize the interrelatedness and interdependence of outcomes in the three traditional learning domains.

Determine the Instructional Entry Level

A challenge common to most teachers is this issue: "At what skill level do I begin teaching my class?" It is challenging to select the level of difficulty for skill instruction because students show a wide variation in ability and maturation. An important step in determining a proper instructional entry level is to formulate a desired outcome (one that is just beyond the grasp of the most skillful student in the class). Ask yourself, "When this lesson is over, where do I want the students to be?" Then develop a progression of essential learning activities that lead to the outcome.

A way to determine entry level is to move through a progression of activities until a majority of students have difficulty performing successfully. This accomplishes two things: It offers a review of skills that makes students feel successful, and gives the teacher an estimate of the students' ability levels. Another approach is to let students self-determine a level of performance they feel is best suited for them. For example, when teaching with balance beams, use task charts that list skills students are to perform on the beam. Students pick activities they feel competent in performing and progress at their own rate through the tasks. Teaching and learning is effective when students find an entry level that is appropriate for them.

Use Anticipatory Set

Anticipatory set refers to a technique designed to focus students on the learning outcomes of the lesson. The opening sequence in a lesson is one of the more difficult, yet most important. It sets the stage for the lesson activities that follow. Just as it is important to have a physical warm-up (see Chapter 3), it is important to have a mental warm-up. Use an anticipatory set to "mentally warm up" a class. Anticipatory sets are most effective when they tie in to students' past personal or learning experiences. For example, in a basketball unit, asking students to identify why they are missing so many shots encourages them to think about technique. Instructional focus might involve discussing hand placement, eyes on the basket, or keeping the shooting elbow in. Anticipatory set is also used to remind students of what they practised in previous lessons. For example, asking students "What are three things we have to remember when tossing and catching beanbags?" reveals whether they remember the basic tenets of catching skills. Figure 4.2 shows some examples of anticipatory sets.

Deliver Meaningful Skill Instruction

Instruction is a cornerstone of learning because it is the way information is shared with students. For direct teaching styles, such information can include the definition of the skill; the elements or parts of the skill; and when, why, and how the skill should be used. In inquiry teaching styles where the information may be different, the need for clarity and brevity is equally important. The following are suggestions for effective instruction:

1. *Focus instruction on a maximum of three key points.* It is difficult to remember a series of instructions. Telling students a long list of points related to skill performance leaves them baffled and frustrated. Strong emphasis

- "On Monday we practised the skills of passing, dribbling, and shooting lay-ins. Yesterday we used those skills in a game of three-on-three. Take a few moments to think about the problems you had with dribbling or passing skills. [Allow time for thought and discussion.] Today we are going to use some drills that will help you improve in these areas."

- "Think of activities that require body strength and be ready to name some when called upon. [Allow time for thinking and discussion.] This week we are going to learn some activities that help us become stronger."

- "What is it called when we change direction quickly? Think of as many activities as you can that require agility, and be ready to share with the class. [Allow time for thinking and discussion.] This week we are going to learn how to do Tinikling. This rhythmic activity will improve your agility level."

Figure 4.2

Examples of anticipatory sets.

on no more than three key points makes it easier for students to focus their concentration.

2. *Refrain from lengthy skill descriptions.* When instructions last longer than 30 to 60 seconds, students become listless because they can't comprehend and remember all the input. Develop a pattern of short, concise presentations, alternated with practice sessions. Short practice sessions offer an opportunity to refocus many times on key points of a skill.

3. *Present information in its most basic, easy-to-understand form.* Check for understanding (discussed further in the next section) to see if students comprehend the material.

4. *Separate management and instructional episodes.* Consider the following instructions during the presentation of a new game: "In this game, we will break into groups of five. Each group will get a ball and form a small circle. On the command 'Go,' the game will start. Here is how you play the game. . . . " A lengthy discussion of game rules and conduct follows. Because the instructions are long, students forget what they were asked to do earlier. Or, they think about whom they want in their group rather than the game rules. Instead, move the class into game formation (management) and then discuss the activity to be learned (instruction). This serves two purposes: It reduces the length of the episode, and makes it easier for students to conceptualize how the game is played.

Monitor Student Performance

Monitoring class performance ensures that students stay on task and practise activities correctly. Effective monitoring involves the teacher being in a position where she or he makes eye contact with all students. Try to be unpredictable when positioning yourself throughout the teaching area. If students know where you like to stand to teach and observe, some of them will move away from you. You will find students who enjoy being nearby and students who like to move as far away as possible. Random positioning ensures contact and proximity, at various points during the lesson, with all students in the class.

Teacher movement coupled with effective observation keeps students on task. Moving into position to observe skill performance enhances your ability to improve student learning. For example, if you are observing kicking, stand to the side rather than behind the student. A judgment that needs to be made when observing performances is how long to stay with a single group of students. Spending too much time with one student may cause the rest of the class to move off task. Give one student one or two points upon which to focus and then move to another student. Follow up later in the lesson to check student progress.

Because teacher movement affects observational effectiveness, it is a part of instruction that is best planned. To facilitate coverage, divide the instructional area into four (or more) equal areas and make an attempt to move into the far corner of each area a certain number of times. Try to give instructions and reinforcement from all four quadrants of the area.

Use Teaching Cues

Teaching cues are keywords that quickly and efficiently communicate proper technique and performance of skills and movement tasks. Children learning new skills need a clear understanding of critical skill points because motor learning and cognitive understanding of the skill are developed simultaneously (see Chapter 3). Planning skill and movement activities without teaching cues can result in ineffective learning if students do not clearly understand proper technique and key points of performance. When using teaching cues, consider the following points.

Develop Precise Cues

Cues are short, descriptive phrases that call to the learner's attention key points of skill technique. Cues must be precise and accurate. They should guide learners and be part of instruction that enhances the quality of learning. Cues make it easier for learners to remember a sequence of new motor patterns. Study an activity and design cues that focus student learning on correct skill technique.

All teachers occasionally have to teach activities that they know little about. To develop cues in areas of less expertise, study. Many textbooks and media aids delineate key points of skills. For example, Fronske and Wilson (2002) offer teaching cues for a wide variety of physical activities. Other avenues of information are teachers who have strengths in different activities.

Use Short, Action-oriented Cues

Effective cues are short and to the point. They should encourage the learner to focus on one phase of a skill during practice. For example, if learning to throw is the skill being learned, offer a cue such as, "Begin with your throwing arm farthest from the target." This cue reminds the student not to face the target, which precludes trunk rotation in later phases of the throw. Other examples of throwing cues are as follows:

"Step toward the target."

"Follow through toward the target."

"Shift your weight from the rear to the front foot."

To examine the effectiveness of cues, see if they communicate the skill as a whole. Have all the critical points of throwing been covered, or is the skill incorrect in certain phases? With most skills, the performance can be broken into three parts: preparation, action, and recovery. Focus on one phase of a skill at a time, as most beginners can best concentrate on only one thing at a time. Action-oriented words are effective with children, particularly if they have an exciting sound. For example, "*Pop up* at the end of the forward roll," "*Twist* the body during the throw," or "*Explode* off the starting line." In other situations, let the voice influence the effectiveness of the cue. For example, if a skill is to be done smoothly and softly, speak in a soft tone and ask students to "let the movement *flooooooow*" or to "move *smooooooothly* across the balance beam." The most effective cues use voice inflections, body language, and action words to signal the desired behaviour.

Integrate Cues

Integration of cues involves putting the parts of a skill together so learners can focus on the skill as a whole. Integrated cues depend on prior cues used during the presentation of a skill, and assume the understanding of concepts from earlier phases of instruction. Examples of integrated cues are as follows:

"Step, rotate, throw."

"Run, jump, and forward roll."

"Stride, swing, follow through."

The first integrated cue ("step, rotate, throw") reminds students to sequence parts of the skill. The second set of words

- Students are in partners spread out about 20 metres apart, with one partner having a football. "When kicking the football, take a short step with your kicking foot, a long step with the other foot, and kick (demonstrate). Again, short step, long step, kick (teaching cue)."

- "Listen to the first verse of this schottische music. I'll do the part of the schottische step we just learned starting with the second verse (demonstrate). Ready, step, step, step, hop (teaching cue). When I hit the tambourine, begin doing the step."

Figure 4.3

Combining demonstration and teaching cues.

("run, jump, and forward roll") helps young children remember a sequence of movement activities. Integrated cues help learners to remember proper sequencing of skills and to form mental images of the performance. Figure 4.3 offers examples for combining teaching cues and demonstration.

Enhance Instruction by Demonstrating Skills

A quick and effective way to present a physical activity is to demonstrate (see Figure 4.4). Effective demonstration accentuates critical points of performance. While demonstrating, simultaneously verbalize key focal points so students know what to observe.

Teachers cannot be expected to demonstrate all physical activities. All teachers need to devise substitutions for an instructor demonstration. Through reading, study, and analysis of movement it is possible to develop an understanding of how to present activities. If performing an activity is impossible, know what key points of the activity should be emphasized. Use visual aids and media to enhance instruction.

When possible, slow down the demonstration and present it step by step. Many skills can be videotaped and played back in slow motion. The replay can be stopped at critical instances so students can emulate a position or technique. For example, in a throwing unit, freeze at a point that illustrates the position of the arm. Have students imitate moving the arm into proper position based on the stop-action pose.

Use Students to Demonstrate Skills

Students are helpful demonstrators. Usually, it is possible to find a capable student by asking the class to perform the desired skill. Identify a student who is correctly

Figure 4.4

Effective teachers demonstrate skill techniques.

performing the skill during the practice session and ask if he or she would be willing to demonstrate. As the student demonstrates the skill, identify key points of the action.

Student demonstration interjects original ideas into the lesson sequence (see Figure 4.5). It also helps to build self-esteem if youngsters can successfully demonstrate. If you are unsure about a student's ability to demonstrate, ask him or her to try the activity while all students are engaged. At opportune times, stop the class and let children volunteer to show what they have done. Ensure all students are selected at one time or another.

Check for Understanding

Checking to see if students comprehend lesson content is necessary to monitor student progress. Students are effective at displaying an exterior that says they understand even when they do not. Additionally, a common (but bad) habit of teachers is to ask periodically, "Does everybody understand?" It appears they are checking for understanding; however, this seldom is the case. Rather than asking students if

Figure 4.5

Using a student to demonstrate a skill.

they understand, ask if they have questions. The following are suggestions for monitoring student understanding:

1. *Use hand signals.* Examples might be "Thumbs up if you understand," or "If you think this demonstration is correct, balance on one foot," or "Raise the number of fingers to signal which student you think did a correct forward roll." If the signals are given quickly and without comment, students will signal immediately and without embarrassment.

2. *Ask questions that can be answered in choral response.* Some students may mouth an answer even though they do not know the correct response. An indicator of the number of students who understand can be estimated by the intensity of the group response. A strong response by the class indicates the majority of youngsters understand.

3. *Direct a forthcoming check to the entire class rather than to a specified student*—for example, "Be ready to demonstrate the grapevine step." This encourages all members of the class to focus on the activity, knowing they may be called on to demonstrate. Even though it does not ensure that everyone understands, it increases the possibility that students will think about the skill check.

4. *Use peer-checking methods.* Have students pair up and evaluate each other's performance using a criteria checklist. Different students can perform more than one evaluation to help ensure the reliability of the scoring.

Offer Guided Practice

Guided practice helps ensure that students are performing a skill correctly. Correct practice develops correct skill patterns, whereas practising skills with incorrect technique ingrains mistakes. Guided practice helps a class move through each step of a skill. During the early phases of guided practice, small amounts of information are presented. New skills build on previously learned skills so students can see the importance of prerequisite learning. Offer practice sessions as quickly as possible after a skill demonstration.

Bring Closure

Closure is a time to review learning that has taken place during the lesson. Closure helps increase retention because students review what they have learned. Closure is not simply a recall of activities that were completed, but a discussion of the application of skills and knowledge learned through practice. The following prompts are ways to initiate closure discussions:

"Describe two or three key parts of the forward roll to your partner."

"Demonstrate the proper skill when I (or a peer) say the cue."

"Describe and demonstrate a key point for a new skill learned in the lesson."

Effective Feedback: Positive, Specific, and Immediate

Delivering meaningful feedback to students is an important part of instruction. Used properly, feedback enhances a student's self-concept, improves the focus of performance, increases the rate of on-task behaviour, and improves student understanding. Consider the following points to enhance the quality of your feedback.

Forms of Feedback

Mosston and Ashworth (2002) identify four forms of feedback: (a) *value* offers a judgment; (b) *neutral* is factual and descriptive; (c) *corrective* identifies and corrects errors; and (d) *ambiguous*, which is imprecise and vague. Much of the feedback delivered by teachers is corrective, with a focus on improving student performance. Students expect some corrective feedback; however, when it is the only feedback offered, students focus on errors rather than on strengths. Adding specific information (neutral feedback) and value to feedback improves desired student performance (see Figure 4.6). The value content of a feedback statement tells students why it is important to perform a skill in a certain manner. Students clearly understand why their performance was positive and can build on this information. Examples of positive feedback with neutral information and value content include the following:

"Good throw. When you look at your target, you are much more accurate."

"Excellent catch. You bent your elbows while catching, which created a soft home for the ball."

"That's the way to stop. When you bend your knees, you always stop under control."

Figure 4.6

Delivering meaningful feedback.

Here are some examples of feedback with specific content:

"That's the way to tuck your head on the forward roll."

"Wow! Everybody was dribbling the ball with their heads up."

"I'm impressed with the way you kept your arms straight."

Try to focus feedback on positive student performance. A positive atmosphere makes it easier for students to accept a challenge and to risk error. Positive feedback helps students focus on their strengths. Siedentop and Tannehill (2000) suggest a 4:1 ratio of positive to corrective feedback as desirable.

It is easy to develop patterns of interaction that are positive, yet ambiguous. For example, statements such as "Nice job," "Way to hustle," "Right on," and "Great move," are used over and over. When used habitually, students may "tune out" and fail to feel the positive nature of the comments. These general comments also contain little specific information or value content, thus allowing for misinterpretation. For example, after a student performs a forward roll, "Nice job" reinforcement is delivered. You were pleased with the performance because the student's head was tucked. However, the student thought you were pleased because her legs were bent.

Offer feedback to students as soon as possible after a correct performance. When feedback is delayed, allow opportunity for immediate practice so students can apply the feedback information.

Distribute Feedback Evenly

Feedback should be evenly distributed to all students by moving systematically from student to student. Observe carefully, offer feedback, move to another student, and recheck progress at a later time. This approach fosters contact with students a number of times during the lesson. In addition, it keeps students on task because they know the teacher is moving and "eyeballing" the class regularly. If skills are complex and refinement is a goal, it is better to take more time with individual students. This involves watching a student long enough to offer specific and information-loaded feedback. The result is high-quality feedback to fewer students.

Nonverbal Feedback

Nonverbal behaviour is another way to deliver feedback. Nonverbal feedback is effective because it is easily interpreted by students and often perceived as more meaningful than words. Many types of nonverbal feedback can be used to reinforce a class: a finger in the air to signify "you're number 1," a thumbs-up, a high five, a handshake, and so

Figure 4.7

Using nonverbal communication.

on (see Figure 4.7). In contrast to the positive nonverbal behaviours, negative signals can be delivered, including hands on the hips, finger to the lips, frowning, and staring. Effective use of nonverbal feedback increases the validity and strength of verbal communication.

When using nonverbal feedback, find out how the customs and mores of different cultures influence the response of youngsters to different types of gestures. For example, Hmong and Laotian children may be touched on the head only by parents and close relatives. A teacher who pats the child on the head for approval is interfering with the child's spiritual nature. The "okay" sign—touching thumb and forefinger—is an indication of approval in Canada. However, in several Asian cultures it is a "zero," indicating the child is not performing properly. In many South American countries, the okay sign carries a derogatory sexual connotation. Ask for advice when using nonverbal gestures with youngsters from other cultures.

Consider the Personal Needs of Students

If teaching only involved presenting physical activities to students, it would be a rather simple endeavour. The uniqueness of each student in a large class is a factor that makes teaching complex and challenging. Teachers who are able to make each student feel important have an impact on the lives of their students. This section focuses on ways to make instruction meaningful and personal.

Allow Students to Make Educational Decisions

Decision-making is a large part of behaving in a responsible manner, but responsibility is a learned skill that takes practice. Students' cognitive development can be enhanced if we allow them to be an integral part of the lesson—choosing content, implementing the lesson, and assessing their own and each other's learning. Allowing students to make decisions provides an opportunity for them to learn. If youngsters are not given the opportunity to make choices, they may not know, as they age, how to make serious decisions that affect their future. The following are some ways to incorporate aspects of student choice to accommodate the range of skill among youngsters:

1. *Limit the number of choices.* With this strategy, the teacher retains ultimate control, but gives students a chance to decide, in part, how the outcome is reached. Use this technique when learners have had little opportunity to make decisions in the past. If you have a new class and know little about the students, limit their choices. For example, permit students the choice of practising either a drive or a pass shot in a hockey unit. The desired outcome is that students practise striking skills, but they can decide which striking skill to practise.

2. *Modify the conditions.* Modify tasks and activities to help all children experience success. For example, move partners closer together if they are learning to catch, use a slower-moving object such as a beach ball or balloon, increase the size of the target, change the size of boundaries or goal areas, allow students to toss and catch individually, or increase the size of the striking implement. Recall the *optimal challenge* mentioned in Chapters 2 and 3.

3. *Use self-competition.* Surprising as it sounds, if the success rate is too high, students may become bored. When teaching individual activities, encourage students to set personal goals for themselves. For example, ask youngsters to see if they can beat their personal best performance. Offer challenges by asking students to accomplish higher levels of performance, use a faster-moving object, increase the distance to the goal, or decrease its size. Students respond best to challenges that are personal and slightly above their current skill level.

4. *Offer different task challenges.* All students do not have to be working on the same tasks simultaneously. Offer a number of tasks of varying complexity so students can find personal challenges. Task cards and station teaching allow students to learn at an optimum rate. When difficult skills are listed on task cards, ensure that there is a balance of less demanding tasks as well. For example,

students who have limited upper-body strength might find inverted balances to be difficult, if not impossible. Include some activities using the legs so all students can work on balance skill challenges. Be sure to revisit the discussion of teaching styles in Chapter 3.

5. *Offer open-ended tasks.* This approach offers wide latitude for making decisions about the content of the lesson. Students get to decide how the task should be accomplished. You decide the learning outcome and students determine the means to reach it—for example:

   a. "Develop a game that requires four passes before a shot at the goal."

   b. "Plan a floor exercise routine that contains a forward roll, a backward roll, and a cartwheel."

   c. "Design a long-rope jumping routine that involves four people and two pieces of manipulative equipment."

These tasks have no predetermined answer. Students apply principles they have learned previously and transfer learned skills to new situations. Ultimately, the problem is solved through a movement response that has been guided by cognitive involvement. Recall the divergent teaching style described in Chapter 3.

Employ Effective Communication Skills

Communicating with a learner—indeed, with all learners—is critical, and communication skills can always be improved. Effective teachers seem able to create a positive atmosphere for learning. They may not know more about skills and activities than less able teachers, but they often know how to communicate effectively. For children to learn essential information, communication must occur in a manner that encourages students to listen.

Students want to communicate openly and honestly with adults. Behaviour used when talking to students can help keep relationships strong. When talking with students, assume a physical pose that expresses interest and attention. Kneel at times so youngsters do not always have to look up. Check to see if facial and verbal cues reinforce your interest and concern. Some of the following suggestions can help you to establish a positive bond with students and create a learning environment enjoyed by everyone:

1. *Speak about the behaviour of students, not about their personal character.* The following is an example of speaking about a student's *behaviour:* "Talking when I am talking is unacceptable behaviour." Such feedback identifies behaviour that can be improved upon and avoids questioning the self-worth of the student. In contrast, saying something like "Why do you always have to act like a fool?" reflects on the child's character and undermines his or her self-esteem.

2. *Understand the child's point of view.* Imagine if someone embarrassed you in front of a class. These and other emotions make listening difficult for youngsters. Unrestrained feedback can stress a youngster and increase behaviour problems. When suggesting ways to improve behaviour, do so in a private manner (so other youngsters can't hear you).

3. *Accentuate the positive.* When teaching key points of a skill, accent the positive. For example, stress the fact that children "land lightly," rather than saying, "Don't land so hard." An easy way to emphasize key points positively is to say, "Do this because . . ." If there are several different and acceptable ways to perform movement patterns, be explicit with your points.

4. *Speak precisely.* Limit the use of open-ended directives and substitute those with precise goals. Instead of saying, "How many times can you . . . ?" or "See how many times you can . . . ," give children a definite target goal. Use directives such as "See if you can . . . five times without missing," or "Show me five different ways to . . ." Encourage youngsters to set personal target goals.

5. *Optimize speech patterns.* Certain teacher mannerisms require attention and change. Avoid sermonizing at the least provocation. Excessive reliance on certain words and phrases—"Okay," "All right," and the irritating "and, uh"—are unappealing to children. Acquire a broad vocabulary of effective phrases that indicate approval and good effort. A common list used by teachers shows 100 ways to say "Good job." Also, a period of silence can be effective; it allows students time to internalize and digest the information.

Be a Good Listener

Listening skills are as important to effective teaching as speaking techniques. Poor communication often occurs because of a breakdown in listening rather than speaking. Listening to what students say can provide valuable insight for teachers. There is truth in the adage "You were given two ears and one mouth so you could listen twice as much as you speak." Each of the following promotes effective listening skills:

1. *Be an active listener.* Active listeners convince the speaker they are interested in what the speaker is saying. Much of this is done through nonverbal behaviour, such as eye contact, head nodding, facial expressions, and movement toward the speaker.

2. *Listen to the hidden message of the speaker.* Young children sometimes find it difficult to express their feelings clearly. The words expressed may not signal what the child is actually feeling. For example, a child may say, "I hate P.E." Most children do not hate all phases of physical education, and most likely something more immediate (such as, "I don't like jumping rope") is the problem. Try acknowledging their feelings with a response such as, "You sound angry. Are you having a problem you want to discuss?" This helps students realize their feelings are important and gives them an opportunity to clarify concerns.

3. *Paraphrase what the student said.* Paraphrasing is restating in your words what was said to you, including your interpretation of their feelings. For example, you might respond, "Do I hear you saying you are frustrated and bored with this activity?" If the paraphrasing is correct, it makes the student feel validated and understood. If the interpretation is incorrect, the student has an opportunity to restate his or her concern. It offers the teacher an indication of how students perceive various situations.

4. *Let students know you value listening.* Teachers who listen to students can learn about their students' feelings. Let students know you will listen, and then do something about it. If you are a good listener you will hear things that are not always positive. For example, students may state honestly which activities they enjoy and which they do not. They may express how they felt when they were criticized. This communication can provide you with constructive information that will ultimately help you create a more productive learning environment.

Teach for Diversity

Increasing diversity in the Canadian population presents both opportunities and challenges for educators. According to Levin and Riffel (1994), "while diversity is a potential source of vitality, creativity, and growth . . . at the same time, diversity can be a source of conflict which educators and others have difficulty channeling in constructive directions" (p. 1). The following discussion addresses three kinds of diversity—multiculturalism, Aboriginal peoples, and gender—as each relates to the learning environment in physical education.

Multicultural Classroom

In 1971, the Canadian federal government enacted a policy of multiculturalism. During the subsequent 35 years, Canadian society has evolved and changed to reflect this policy. According to the 2001 Census data, about 4 million Canadians identify themselves as being members of a visible minority group (13% of Canada's total population of almost 32 million). As well, in 2002, approximately one-quarter

million new immigrants came to Canada, with almost 75% settling in Canada's three largest cities (Montreal, Toronto, Vancouver). The evolution of Canadian society has not been without struggle and challenge, often amplified in the education system. Consider the findings from a report entitled *Immigrant Youth in Canada*, from the Canadian Council on Social Development (2000a):

- Between 1996 and 1998, an estimated 230,000 immigrant children and youth arrived in Canada. Nearly half came from Asia and the Pacific region. Many had little knowledge of English and French when they arrived. Like their adult counterparts, immigrant children and youth generally stayed in large urban centres, especially Toronto, Vancouver, and Montreal.

- Recent immigrant youth viewed North American culture as a double-edged sword. Most said they enjoyed the freedom that the youth culture in Canada afforded them, but many felt somewhat overwhelmed and alienated by what they perceived to be its rampant consumerism and superficiality. Some said this caused them to feel socially isolated, particularly in high school.

- School is at the centre of these young peoples' lives. The trials and tribulations of the often-difficult high school years—which most youth tend to encounter—were magnified for immigrant youth. Most reported experiencing some ostracism, bullying, and difficulties with schoolwork. Many felt that teachers and other staff constituted part of the problem, rather than being providers of solutions.

Despite these experiences, Canadian schools today are making strides to better address the challenges and potential associated with multiculturalism. From a general perspective, many provinces have developed powerful policy and/or philosophy statements (and supporting documents) that guide their educational actions. For example, Manitoba Education, Citizenship and Youth (2006) describes diversity as "encompassing all the ways in which human beings are both similar and different. It means understanding and accepting the uniqueness of all individuals as well as respecting their differences. It is ultimately about acceptance and respect for difference" (p. 12). Similarly, in *Diversity in BC Schools: A Framework* (2004), diversity refers to the

> *ways in which we differ from each other. Some of these differences may be visible (e.g., race, ethnicity, gender, age, ability), while others are less visible (e.g., culture, ancestry, language, religious beliefs, sexual orientation, socioeconomic background). Honouring diversity is based on the principle that if these differences are acknowledged and utilized in a positive way, it is of benefit to the quality of our learning and working environment. (B.C. Ministry of Education, 2004, p. 7)*

Saskatchewan Learning (2002) emphasizes that "diversity is not perceived as an obstacle, but rather as an opportunity to enrich school culture... providing students and adults with experiences to increase their knowledge, understanding and appreciation of differences while strengthening their commitment to one another, their community and shared future" (p. 4).

Saskatchewan Education (1994) provides a comprehensive guide for teachers, including the following statement:

Multicultural education fosters understanding, acceptance, empathy and constructive and harmonious relations among people of diverse cultures. It encourages learners of all ages to view cultures different from their own as sources of learning and enrichment .... While the first and most lasting influence on a child is that of the home environment, educators and educational institutions have a responsibility for preparing children to function in our culturally diverse society. (p. 2)

Multicultural Education and Heritage Language Education Policies identifies goals that provide a foundation for multicultural education in the classroom. These goals include self-concept development, understanding and relating to others, spiritual development, and membership in society. There are a number of ways that teachers can demonstrate and promote cultural respect and understanding:

(1) Affirm each student's language use as unique and important.

(2) Accept and respect the language that each student brings to the classroom.

(3) Become educated about the cultural backgrounds of the student.

(4) Determine if unexpected behaviours and actions reflect a student's culture.

(5) Respect each student's knowledge about his or her own culture.

(6) Build a classroom environment that discourages racial put-downs of others' language usage and abilities, and their cultural and ethnic backgrounds.

(7) Deal with racial incidents in a positive manner, if they occur.

(8) View students of all cultures as having equal potential.

(9) Become informed about a variety of cultures and inform students about these cultures.

(10) Give students opportunities to select and respond to the resources that they listen to, read, and view.

(11) Encourage students to read, view, and listen to a variety of resources and media that are representative of cultural groups with which they do and do not identify.

(12) Use interpreters for second-language speakers (for example, parents, community members).

(13) Use a variety of instructional and assessment strategies to accommodate students' cultural learning preferences and backgrounds.

(14) Develop students' collaborative and cooperative skills and attitudes through group work, problem-solving discussions, and consensus activities.

(15) Encourage students to talk and write about their experiences and places that they have travelled.

(16) Choose resources and media selections that represent a diversity of cultures and cultural perspectives.

(17) Discuss stereotypic beliefs and cultural biases in resources and media.

(*Source:* Saskatchewan Education. (1994). *Multicultural education and heritage language education policies*. Regina, SK: Author. Reprinted with permission.)

The inclusion of multicultural content, perspectives, and resources in physical education helps students to develop multicultural perspectives that prepare them to live more enriched and compassionate lives while contributing harmoniously to a pluralistic society.

Saskatchewan educators provide a productive framework for cultural awareness and action in physical education (see Figure 4.8). They have fashioned their work after the Levels of

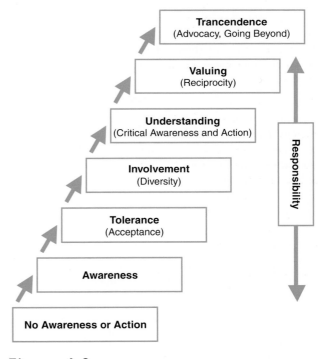

Figure 4.8

Cultural awareness and levels of action continuum in physical education settings.

Source: Saskatchewan Education (1999). *Elementary Physical Education Curriculum*. Regina, SK: Author. Reprinted with permission.

Responsibility Model by Hellison (1985) and describe it as a framework in which to consider their developmental work with children (Saskatchewan Education, 1999).

Level 0: No Awareness or Action *Students at Level 0 are unaware of the values and cultural ways of groups other than their own. Discrimination and racism may characterize relations with other groups and individuals. Teachers at this level do not consider exposure to other cultures to be a priority in their teaching. Diversity of experience in cultural matters is not valued.*

Level I: Awareness *Students and teachers at Level I have some knowledge of other cultures, universal rights, and the ways that other people live, work, and play. They have some knowledge of the games and physical culture of other people. There is little, if any, variation in the physical education curriculum from traditional western forms of physical activity.*

Level II: Tolerance (Acceptance) *Students and teachers at Level II show an acceptance of other cultures. Teachers operating at this level begin to include games and dance activities from other countries, which are not mainstream. Assimilation is a governing principle in the curriculum. Human and material resources of the community are integrated into the existing curriculum.*

Level III: Involvement (Diversity) *Students and teachers at Level III openly welcome the opportunity to teach and learn about other cultures. Knowledge of other cultures is generated through a much broader and diverse curriculum; the experiences and values of students, teachers, and the broader community are all introduced and explored. Activities are much more diverse.*

Level IV: Understanding (Critical Awareness and Action) *At Level IV students and teachers recognize the need to place cultural understanding as a high priority in their curriculum. There is considerable freedom to explore and develop topics in depth; integration with other school subjects is emphasized.*

Level V: Valuing (Reciprocity) *At this level both students and teachers come to value other cultures as just as important as their own. Curriculum boundaries are broadened so that many activities and events from the community are included in the curriculum. Activities occur frequently in community settings as well as in the school; participation in community events and festivals is common.*

Level VI: Transcendence (Advocacy, Going Beyond) *At Level VI, major links between the school curriculum and the broader community education and recreation programs are forged. Service becomes a priority. Students assume much more responsibility in the governance of their affairs. Teachers become strong advocates for youth and youth culture. Intergenerational activities are more frequent. Authentic dialogue among students and between students and adults is*

the norm. Emphasis is on growth and transformation. The ethic of social justice permeates the curriculum. Programs are consistent with Article 31 of the United Nations Convention on the Rights of the Child.

(Source: Elementary Physical Education Curriculum. Regina, SK: Author. Reprinted with permission.)

Multiculturalism education stresses the promotion of understanding, respect, and acceptance of cultural diversity within our society (B.C. Ministry of Education, 1995). It assumes that children come from different backgrounds and helps them make sense of their everyday life. Our responsibility as educators is to teach children to live comfortably and to prosper in this diverse and changing world.

Aboriginal Peoples

Aboriginal peoples[1] occupy a unique place in Canadian society. According to the 2001 Census, Aboriginal peoples number about 800,000, approximately 3.3% of the Canadian population. They have a rich cultural history and represent tremendous diversity. For example, there are more than 30 major Aboriginal language groups within British Columbia alone (B.C. Ministry of Education, 2006). In addition, consider the following statistics as they affect the education system:

- About one-third of Canada's Aboriginal population are children under the age of 14—significantly higher than the corresponding 18% proportion among the non-Aboriginal population. While Aboriginals represent 3.3% of Canada's total population, they comprise 5.6% of all children in Canada. (Canadian Council on Social Development, 2006)

- The Aboriginal population in Canada is growing. Between 1996 and 2001, the Aboriginal population increased by 22%. (Canadian Council on Social Development, 2006)

- More than three-quarters of Aboriginal youth smoke, half report problems of drug abuse, and the rate of suicide of Aboriginal youth between ages 10 and 19 is four times greater than that of their non-Aboriginal counterparts. (Grantham, 2000b)

The third statistic is particularly disturbing and has implications for the future. High rates of school absenteeism and dropping out among Aboriginal students is related to their feeling unwelcome in the school system (Grantham, 2000b). Teachers can play a vital role in making the classroom a more welcoming environment. Here are a few suggestions:

1. Become the initiator of staff inservice about Aboriginal education. Contact resource personnel available for inservice.

2. Become informed about the community's various cultures and cultural differences.

3. Talk to the children and parents in the school's community. Learn about the various traditions regarding good manners and approaches to discipline. Talk to someone with whom the school has a trusting relationship. Find out about the community's protocol for contacting elders and visiting homes.

4. Know the homes from which the students come. This will give you some idea of the daily environments in which students live. Invite parents into the classroom; organize several parent nights. Show parents what goes on in class and how the various activities relate to daily community life.

5. If parents are unable to attend, search out individuals who can act as liaisons for the families.

6. Become visible and involved in cultural activities.

7. Use appropriate terms when discussing Aboriginal history and cultures.

8. Practise listening skills. Teachers sometimes neglect to consider that a question from a student is, in fact, a compliment! The student is expressing trust and a need for input. Nodding, maintaining eye contact (even if this is absent on the speaker's part), leaning forward, and paraphrasing are examples of very simple yet effective techniques used to communicate the fact that you are hearing and understanding what the student is saying.

9. When developing listening skills among students, allow them to see each other's faces during group discussions.

10. Use a talking stick when discussions are being held in small groups. This technique allows students to become involved in the discussions, to pass when the stick is offered to them, and to appropriately control those who dominate the conversation by monopolizing the stick.

11. Be a bridge builder. Seek commonalties rather than differences. We are products of our past. People do things the way their families did them. Rather than emphasize differences, concentrate on the human experiences we all share: birth, kinship, friendship, learning, celebrating, gift giving, and a sense of humour.

(*Source:* Adapted from Saskatchewan Education, 1999, *Elementary Physical Education Curriculum Guide.* Used with permission.)

In addition to these general considerations, specific focus on learning styles and/or preferences of Aboriginal students will further contribute to creation of a learning environment that better meets their needs. Toward this goal, Hill (1999) proposed an educational model based on the concept of holistic learning. According to Hill, herself an Aboriginal educator, "in Aboriginal thought a whole person consists of spirit, heart, mind and body—the capacity to see, feel, know and do.

Therefore, in the learning process, a whole person engages his or her physical, mental, emotional and spiritual capacities in receiving data or information for the brain to process" (p. 100). She has developed a graphic representation of the learning cycle process in the form of a circle to show these four elements: namely to see (spirit), to do (body), to feel (heart), and to know (mind) (see Figure 4.9). According to Hill, each type of learner can be accommodated in the model. Given the encompassing holistic nature of the model, physical education teachers are particularly well positioned to use the model as a guide for designing learning experiences. Physical education has long been viewed and organized around the concepts of knowing, doing, and valuing.

Gender Equity

As mentioned in previous chapters, there is evidence that high rates of physical inactivity start in the childhood years. Girls and young women appear to be particularly vulnerable. The *2000 Physical Activity Monitor* reported that between ages 5 and 12, only 44% of females were considered active enough for optimal growth and development. This statistic worsens through adolescence. Results of the fourth cycle of the Health Behaviour in School-Aged Children (HBSC) survey in Canada showed that an average of only 27% of female

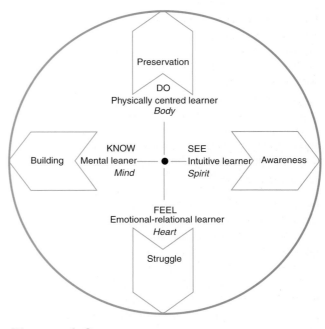

Figure 4.9

Holistic Learning Process Circle.

Source: Used with permission from Diane Hill, Ph.D. (abd), *Holistic Learning: A Model of Education based on Aboriginal Cultural Philosophy* (unpublished master's thesis, St. Francis Xavier University, Antigonish, Nova Scotia, 1999). Several initiatives for integrating Aboriginal perspectives into the physical education curriculum will be discussed in Chapter 11.

youth (Gr. 6–10) reported they were physically active at least 60 minutes each day for five days out of a typical week (Boyce, 2004). These statistics present a very troubling possibility of long-term health consequences. There is evidence that if females do not have a history of involvement in physical activity during childhood and adolescence they are significantly less likely to be physically active as adults (Thompson, Humbert, & Mirwald, 2003).

The goal of physical education programs across Canada is to both promote and facilitate lifelong involvement in physical activity. However, research suggests that this goal is being less frequently realized for female students and that inequity begins as early as elementary school (Fenton, Frisby & Luke, 1999; Gibbons, Wharf Higgins, Gaul, & Van Gyn, 1999). Girls as young as 10 or 11 years of age are able to articulate their needs, likes, and dislikes about their PE experiences (Fenton et al., 1999; Gibbons & Humbert (in press). They are beginning to develop some very strong opinions that have the potential to guide participation in PE as they approach their adolescent years.

There is some promising research that supports the notion that if the needs and interests of young women are incorporated into PE programs, they will willingly participate. Female students place considerable importance on the opportunity for personal accomplishment, choice of physical activity, and a feeling of safety in the learning environment (Gibbons & Gaul, 2004). In an examination of the PE experiences of girls in grades 7 and 8, Gibbons and Humbert (in press) highlighted the importance these girls placed on fun, fairness, and safety. When they perceived these aspects were present in PE, the girls expressed a sense of enjoyment of PE class; when absent, a strong expression of dislike. As well, another theme focused on the perception of a power imbalance between these female students and their male classmates. The girls expressed frustration with the aggressive behaviour of the boys, dominance during game play, and apparent favouritism by the teacher toward the physical activity preferences of the boys.

Clearly, if female students do not find value in their PE programs, it is unlikely that they will choose to continue when given the choice. From a more positive perspective, it follows that the earlier we can meet the needs of female students in their PE classes, the more likely it will be for them to want to continue the experience. Establishing an environment in physical education where both girls and boys feel safe, find value, and feel valued is key (Gibbons, Susut, & Fenton, 1999). The following suggestions are provided to help elementary school teachers increase the likelihood that girls will develop a positive view of physical education.

1. Create a fair and equitable physical environment.

Creating a respectful and safe environment is based on the assumption that everyone has a right to participate fully in physical education class. Most educators and coaches believe they treat people fairly and equally. However the principle of equal treatment tends to ignore that fact that girls and boys differ in their interests, resources, and previous experiences. To treat children equally ignores their individuality and limits the extent to which we value their differences. Our goal should be to treat children fairly. Girls and boys thrive in environments where they receive fair treatment. Teachers are encouraged to:

- Establish respectful routines for processes such as picking partners or organizing teams.
- Offer a variety of activities that allow both boys and girls to participate in the class. These activities should reflect a balance of various movement categories suggested in most physical education curricula.
- Avoid using elimination games that frequently reward highly skilled children.
- Shorten activity units: students may participate more in an activity they do not like if they know it won't last too long.
- Avoid using "girl rules" (e.g., must pass to a girl before you can shoot). Such rules reinforce the stereotypic belief that girls are less skilled.
- Modify the equipment and the rules so that students of all abilities can experience joy and success.
- Balance competition with a variety of ways to participate.
- Utilize assessment and evaluation methods that focus on a variety of learning outcomes in physical education (e.g., fair play, leadership, knowledge).

2. Be aware that boys' behaviour may negatively impact girls' experiences in physical education.

The attitudes, beliefs, and behaviours of boys are often a key barrier to girls enjoying their physical education and physical activity experiences. Incidents of verbal and physical harassment and exclusion are reasons that girls frequently give for their lack of participation in their physical education classes. Equitable physical education means that each student, regardless of gender, age, motor ability, race, religion, or socio-economic level has the opportunity for successful and full participation and instruction in a variety of physical activities. Teachers are encouraged to:

- Take every opportunity to model fair and equitable behaviour.
- Establish rules of conduct, behaviour, and equitable language.
- Establish a "no tolerance" policy for any behaviour that frightens, embarrasses, demoralizes, or negatively affects students' self-esteem.

- Establish routines/policies that limit opportunities for harassment (e.g., allow the girls to wear clothing they feel comfortable in as long as it is safe and appropriate).

- Discuss what it means with your students to be a "good sport" or a "bad sport."

3. Be aware that girls may be reluctant to participate in physical education classes but that does not mean they do not want to be physically active.

   Girls are less likely than boys to be encouraged by parents, family, and friends (and society) to be physically active. Boys are more likely to be given adequate coaching in sport, to be exposed to a variety of physical activity opportunities and have visible role models. In general, physical activity is highly valued for boys and not for females. Girls often want to be active but they feel they do not possess the skills needed, and their opportunities tend to be in traditional male sports.

   Teachers are encouraged to:

- Offer a program with a wide variety of activity opportunities.

- Be aware that you may have to spend extra time developing the fundamental motor patterns of girls; they may need to be "caught up."

- Show girls and young women that you believe in their abilities and support their efforts in physical activity.

- Ensure that the images in your gymnasium reflect the accomplishments of both genders.

- Provide leadership opportunities for both boys and girls.

4. Model gender-inclusive language.

   Language is particularly powerful in children. The words we use with children should be respectful, accurate and inclusive. Using masculine words to describe a group of girls and boys can reinforce the powerful stereotype that the male term includes everyone. This is not the case.
   Teachers are encouraged to:

- Use gender-inclusive language and expect its use among students.

- Compile a list of alternative words or phrases to replace words commonly used in elementary physical education classes (e.g., *sportsmanship* to *fair play*; *tom boy* to *active child*; *guys* to *children, class,* or *everyone*; *man-to-man defence* to *player-to-player defence*).

- Avoid the use of terms that demean girls such as "Girl's push-ups"; "throws like a girl"; "runs like a girl".

Notes

1. *Aboriginal peoples* is a term defined in the *Constitution Act of 1982*, and refers to all indigenous peoples in Canada, including Indians, Métis people, and Inuit people (B.C. Ministry of Education, 2006).

Critical Thinking

1. A student in your grade 4 physical education class tells you that you favour certain students. Considering the instructional elements discussed in this chapter, how do you address her or his concern?

2. Further explore the Holistic Learning Process Circle (Figure 4.9). How can this model be used as a guide for teaching effectiveness in elementary physical education?

References and Suggested Readings

Alberta Education. (2005). *Our words, our ways: Teaching First Nations, Métis and Inuit learners.* Edmonton, AB: Author.

Alberta Learning. (2000). *Physical education kindergarten to grade 12 program of studies.* Edmonton, AB: Author.

Boyce, W. (2004). *Young people in Canada: Their health and well-being.* Ottawa, ON: Health Canada.

British Columbia Ministry of Education. (1995). *Physical education K–7 integrated resource package.* Victoria, BC: Author.

British Columbia Ministry of Education. (2006). *Shared learnings—Integrating BC aboriginal content K–10.* Victoria, BC: Author.

British Columbia Ministry of Education. (2004). *Diversity in BC schools: A framework.* Victoria, BC: Author.

Canadian Council on Social Development. (2000a). *Immigrant youth in Canada: Highlights.* Ottawa: ON: Author.

Canadian Council on Social Development. (2000b). *The progress of Canada's children toward the millennium—Progress report at a glance.* [Online], 1, Available: www.ccsd.ca/pccy/2006/pdf/pccy_2006.pdf

Canadian Council on Social Development. (2006). *Demographic profile of Canada.* Retrieved January 7, 2007, from www.ccsd.ca/factsheets/demographics/demographics.pdf

Canadian Fitness and Lifestyle Research Institute. (2001). *2000 physical activity monitor.* Ottawa, ON: Author.

Condon, R. & Collier, C. (2002). Student choice makes a difference in physical education. *Journal of Physical Education, Recreation, & Dance, 73*(2), 97–115.

Critchley, K.A., Walton, F., Timmons, V., Bryanton, J., McCarthy, M., & Taylor, J. (2006). Personal health practices around physical activity as perceived by the aboriginal children of Prince Edward Island. *Journal of Aboriginal Health,* 26–33.

Dyck, M., Wong, I.E., & Breadner, S. (2000). Teacher feedback in physical education: Listening for equity. *CAHPERD Journal, 66*(1), 18–22.

Fenton, J., Frisby, W., & Luke, M. (1999). Multiple perspectives on organizational culture: A case study of physical education for girls in a low income multiracial school. *AVANTE, 5*(2), 1–22.

Fronske, H. & Wilson, R. (2002). *Teaching cues for basic sport skills for elementary and middle school students.* San Francisco, CA: Benjamin Cummings.

Gibbons, E. (2004). Feedback in the dance studio. *Journal of Physical Education, Recreation, & Dance, 75*(7), 38–43.

Gibbons, S.L. (2001). Gender equity in physical education: Resources for teachers. *Physical and Health Education Journal, 67*(1), 36–40.

Gibbons, S.L. & Gaul, C.A. (2004). Making physical education meaningful for young women: Case study in educational change. *AVANTE, 10*(2), 1–16.

Gibbons, S.L. & Humbert, M.L. (in press). What are girls looking for in middle school physical education? *Canadian Journal of Education.*

Gibbons, S.L., Susut, J., & Fenton, J. (1999). *Girls and boys in elementary physical education: Issues and action.* Gloucester, ON: Canadian Association for Health, Physical Education, Recreation and Dance.

Gibbons, S.L., Van Gyn, G.H., Wharf Higgins, J., & Gaul, C.A. (2000). Reversing the trend: Girls' participation in physical education. *CAHPERD Journal, 66*(1), 26–32.

Governments of Alberta, British Columbia, Manitoba, Yukon Territory, Northwest Territories, & Saskatchewan. (2000). The common curriculum framework for aboriginal language and culture programs: Kindergarten to grade 12 [Electronic version]. *Western Canadian protocol for collaboration in basic education.*

Grantham, A. (2000a). Promoting positive race relations, cross cultural understanding and human rights. *CAHPERD Journal, 66*(1), 10–11.

Grantham, A. (2000b). Ensuring diversity within aboriginal and non-aboriginal classrooms. *CAHPERD Journal. 66*(1), 39–41.

Hellison, D. (2003). *Teaching responsibility through physical activity* (2nd ed.). Champaign, IL: Human Kinetics.

Hill, D. (1999). *Holistic learning: A model of education based on Aboriginal cultural philosophy.* Unpublished thesis. St. Francis Xavier University, Antigonish, Nova Scotia, Canada.

Levin, B. & Riffel, J.A. (1994). Dealing with diversity: Some propositions from Canadian education. *Education Policy Analysis Archives, 2*(2), 1–7.

Lyn-Harrison, J. (2002). Thoughtful language—Activities for gender-inclusive language in school, recreation, and sport. *CAHPERD Journal, 68*(4), 12–13.

Manitoba Education and Training. (2000). *Manitoba curriculum framework of outcomes for active healthy lifestyles—Kindergarten–senior 4 physical education/health education.* Winnipeg, Manitoba: Author.

Manitoba Education, Citizenship, & Youth. (2006). *Belonging, learning, and growing—kindergarten to grade 12 action plan for ethnocultural equity.* Winnipeg, MB: Author.

Manitoba Education and Youth. (2003). *Integrating aboriginal perspectives into curricula.* Winnipeg, MB: Author.

Mosston, M. & Ashworth, S. (2002). *Teaching physical education* (5th ed.). San Francisco, CA: Benjamin Cummings.

New Brunswick Department of Education. (2006). *Boys and girls and learning—K–12 handbook.* Fredericton, NB: Author.

New Brunswick Department of Education. (2002). *Middle level physical education.* Fredericton, NB: Author.

Newfoundland & Labrador Department of Education. (2004). *Physical education—Primary and elementary curriculum guide.* St. John's, NF; Author.

Nova Scotia Education. (2000). *Physical education curriculum: Grades primary–6.* Halifax, NS: Author.

Parson, M. (1998). Focus student attention with verbal cues. *Strategies, 11*(3), 30–33.

Rink, J.E. (2003). Effective instruction in physical education. In S. Silverman & C. Ennis (Eds.), *Student learning in physical education—Applying research to enhance instruction* (2nd ed., pp. 165–186). Champaign, IL: Human Kinetics.

Rink, J.E. (2005). *Teaching physical education for learning* (5th ed.). Boston: McGraw-Hill.

Saskatchewan Education. (1994). *Multicultural education and heritage language education policies.* Regina, SK: Author.

Saskatchewan Education. (1999). *Elementary physical education curriculum guide.* Regina, SK: Author.

Saskatchewan Learning. (2002). *Children's services policy framework.* Regina, SK: Author.

Service, D. (2000). Equity issues and physical education. *CAHPERD Journal, 66*(1), 4–9.

Siedentop, D., & Tannehill, D. (2000). *Developing teaching skills in physical education* (4th ed.). Mountain View, CA: Mayfield.

Thompson, A.M., Humbert, M.L., & Mirwald, R.L. (2003). A longitudinal study of the impact of childhood and adolescent physical activity perceptions and behaviors. *Qualitative Health Research, 13*(3), 358–377.

Van Holst, A. (1997). The use of demonstration in teaching physical education. *CAHPERD Journal, 63*(2), 20–22.

Willows, N. (2005). Overweight in first nations children: Prevalence, implications, and solutions. *Journal of Aboriginal Health,* 76–86.

Weblinks

Canadian Council on Social Development: www.ccsd.ca

Non-profit research and social policy organization with a focus on issues such as social inclusion, poverty, disability, child well-being, and cultural diversity.

The Canadian Association for the Advancement of Women and Sport and Physical Activity: www.caaws.ca/girlsatplay

The Canadian Association for the Advancement of Women and Sport and Physical Activity hosts a great website aimed at getting girls involved in sports and physical activity. The site targets a young audience and highlights the On the Move (OTM) initiative. OTM is designed to increase opportunities for inactive girls and young women to participate in physical activity and sport.

Aboriginal Sport Circle: www.aboriginalsportcircle.ca

National website for Aboriginal sport. Includes links to provincial and territorial Aboriginal sport organizations. Explains the Aboriginal Athlete & Youth Role Model Program.

Aboriginal Canada Portal: www.aboriginalcanada.gc.ca

This is a comprehensive portal to Canadian online resources, contacts, government programs, and services. Includes a range of educational and health resources.

C H A P T E R   5

Encouraging Positive Behaviour

Essential Components

I	Organized around content standards
II	Student-centred and developmentally appropriate
III	Physical activity and motor skill development form the core of the program
IV	**Teaches management skills and self-discipline**
V	Promotes inclusion of all students
VI	Focuses on process over product
VII	Promotes lifetime personal health and wellness
VIII	**Teaches cooperation and responsibility and promotes sensitivity to diversity**

Physical Education Standards

1	Students are able to move competently using a variety of fundamental and specialized motor skills.
2	Students can monitor and maintain a health-enhancing level of physical fitness.
3	Students are able to apply movement concepts and basic mechanics of skill performance when learning and refining motor skills.
4	Students comprehend the basic principles of wellness and are able to apply concepts that enable them to make meaningful decisions that positively impact their health and wellness.
5	Students participate in a wide variety of physical activities and learn how to maintain a personalized active lifestyle.
6	**Students demonstrate empathy, understanding, and respect for the numerous differences exhibited by people in an activity setting.**
7	**Students exhibit responsible and self-directed behaviours that lead to positive social interactions in physical activity.**

of this chapter discusses guidelines for productive response to misbehaviour. Finally, a variety of provincial and territorial initiatives and policies focusing on safe and caring schools are discussed.

OUTCOMES

■ Describe the role of the teacher as it pertains to encouraging positive behaviour in a physical education setting.

■ Implement management and behavioural skills that result in a positive and constructive learning environment.

■ Identify management techniques used to start and stop the class, organize the class into groups and formations, use teams, and prepare youngsters for activity.

■ Cite positive responses to misbehaviour in physical education.

■ Describe teaching strategies that focus on personal and social learning outcomes in physical education.

OVERVIEW

An effective learning environment requires implementing a proactive approach to encouraging positive student behaviour. First, the chapter presents effective class management skills that improve the efficiency and productivity of instruction, and reduce the opportunity for misbehaviour. Second, a variety of teaching strategies in physical education are presented that focus on learning outcomes associated with personal and social responsibility. The third part

Create a Positive Learning Environment

A class of children is really a group of individuals, each of whom must be uniquely treated and understood. A productive learning environment allows children a reasonable degree of flexibility to learn effectively without encroaching on the rights of others. Most children choose to cooperate and participate in the educational setting. In fact, the learner is largely responsible for allowing the teacher to teach. No one can be taught who chooses not to cooperate. It is a teacher's responsibility to fashion a learning environment in which all children feel comfortable, safe, and have the opportunity to learn. Creating and maintaining such a learning environment involves a blend of management skills that allow PE classes to run smoothly, and learning experiences specifically focused on the development of positive personal and social skills.

Proactive Management Strategies

Class management skills are prerequisites to effective teaching and learning. In a well-managed class, teacher and students both assume responsibility for learning that works toward target goals. Well-managed classes function with little wasted time and disruption. They run smoothly and are characterized by routines students expect and follow. The climate in a productive class setting is learning-oriented, yet relaxed and pleasant. Effective class management and organizational skills create an environment that gives students freedom of choice in harmony with class order. Because a teacher has the ability to prevent problems before they occur, less time is spent dealing with inappropriate behaviour. Many incidents of misbehaviour can be prevented through proactive management strategies. Figure 5.1 lists some typical situations that may lead to misbehaviour in physical education class.

The following section presents management strategies that if followed will allow attention to be focused on learning rather than behaviour.

Determine Rules and Procedures for the School Year

Rules are an expected part of the school environment. Most teachers want students to be respectful to them and to other students. It is not unreasonable to expect students to behave. Managing students is a necessary and important part of teaching; in fact, it is requisite to a productive learning

- Confused student expectations about pre-instruction routines.
- Unclear instructions to students regarding day's activities.
- Excess time spent on equipment set-up and take-down.
- Long waits for activity or equipment. (This "wait time" provides opportunity for misbehaviour.)
- Activities that are too easy or too difficult.
- Insufficient equipment for number of students.
- Inadequate spacing between practice groupings.

Figure 5. 1

Situations that may lead to misbehaviour.

environment. When creating your rules, select general categories rather than specific behaviour. For example, "Respect your classmate" means many things, from taking turns to helping a partner. The following are examples of general rules:

- *Stop, look, and listen.* This implies freezing on signal, looking at the teacher, and listening for instructions.
- *Take care of equipment.* This includes caring for equipment, and distributing, gathering, and using it properly.
- *Respect the rights of others.* This includes behaviour such as taking turns, sharing, and using positive language.

The number of rules should be minimized. Try not to exceed three to five rules; more than this number makes it difficult for students to remember all the details. Numerous rules also make students rule-specific. A youngster may choose to chew gum in the multipurpose room because the rule is "No gum chewing in the halls." Rules are guidelines for desired behaviour rather than negative statements telling students what they can't do. In addition to establishing a few general rules, consider the following points:

- Involve students in the development of rules.
- Identify observable behaviour. This makes it easy to determine whether a person is following a rule and does not involve subjective judgment.
- Make rules reasonable for the age level of students. Meaningful rules cut across all ages and can be used throughout the elementary school years.
- State rules in positive terms. For example, say, "Be kind to others," rather than "Don't be mean to others."

Communicate High Standards

Students respond to your expectations. If you expect students to perform at high levels, the majority of them will strive to do so. A common but accurate expression is "You get what you ask for." If you expect students to perform to the best of their abilities, they probably will do so. On the other hand, if you act as if you don't care whether they try, some students will do as little as possible.

Discuss Rules and Consequences

Discuss rules and consequences with your class. Explain why such rules are necessary and how consequences will be used. Ask for and listen to student input; this is an opportunity for the class to discuss the ramifications of the rules and how they will be enforced. It is possible that students will add new interpretations to the rules and help peers understand how the consequences will come about.

Have the Class Practise Rules Systematically

Rules stipulate expected class behaviour. If a rule is in place for proper care of equipment, students need the opportunity to practise handling equipment the way the teacher wants it handled. If a rule requires students to stop and listen, they have to practise such behaviour and be reinforced for proper response. Continue to allow time throughout the school year for students to practise desired behaviour.

Enforce Rules Consistently

One of the best ways to earn students' respect is to treat them all in a fair and caring manner. Most students are willing to accept the consequences of their misbehaviour if they think they will be treated in a manner consistent with and equal to the way other students were treated. Animosity occurs when students sense that you play favourites. One reason for defining consequences prior to misbehaviour is that it allows you to administer the consequences equitably.

Give Positive Group Feedback

Positive feedback delivered to a class develops group morale. Classes will learn to view themselves as units that work together and are rewarded when they meet group goals. Students have to work within groups as adults, so learning about group cooperation and pride in accomplishment will help to ensure a smoothly running class, and benefit students in the long run.

Establish Pre- and Post-teaching Routines

Children enjoy the sense of security that comes from knowing what to do from the time they enter the instructional area until they leave. There are a number of procedures that need to be routinely handled. The following are situations that occur before and after teaching and need to be planned for prior to the lesson.

Dealing with Nonparticipation

An efficient system should be devised for identifying children who are not to participate in the lesson. Each school will have a procedure for dealing with nonparticipation or modified participation. A common procedure is to require a note from a parent or guardian describing the nature of the situation and the degree of participation that is possible. For long-term nonparticipation due to illness or injury, it's advised to have specific discussion with parents to establish a plan to keep the student as actively involved as possible. For those students who arrived unprepared to participate (e.g., inappropriate physical activity clothing), try to have a selection of clean shorts and T-shirts the student may borrow for the period. This practice presents a positive alternative to "sitting out" of class, a consequence that is desirable for neither the student nor teacher.

Entering the Physical Activity Area

Meet your class at the door before they enter the area. Remind the students of the procedure for entering the gymnasium. Another successful approach is to have the class enter the area and begin jogging around. After telling them to "freeze," describe the day's activities. Regardless of the method used, students should enter the area under control and know where they are supposed to meet.

Discussing the Lesson Content

Students enter the activity area expecting to move. Take advantage of this desire to move by having them participate in some activity before discussing the content of the lesson. Students are more willing to listen after they have participated in vigorous activity. Allow students to try an activity before offering instruction on points of technique. This allows you an opportunity to assess the performance level of the students.

Closing a Lesson

A regular routine for closing the lesson is beneficial. It allows time for closure of the instructional content, and a procedure for leaving the physical activity area. This may involve lining up at the door, returning to teams, or kneeling in a semicircle. Using a routine at the end of the lesson tends to calm and quiet children, in preparation for returning to the classroom. Another way to calm students is to take a few minutes for relaxation activities.

Deliver Instruction Efficiently

If students are not listening when instructions are given, little learning will occur. Deliver instructions in small doses, focusing on one or two points at a time. Instructions should be specific and seldom last longer than 30 to 45 seconds. An effective approach is to alternate short instructional episodes with periods of activity.

When giving instructions, tell students "when before what." Tell the class when to perform an activity before stating what the activity is. An effective way to implement "when before what" is to use a keyword, such as *Begin!* or *Start!* to start an activity. For example, "When I say *start,* I'd like you to . . . . " or, "When I say *Go!* I want you to jog to a beanbag, move to your own space, and practise tossing and catching." Since the keyword is not given until all directions have been issued, students have to listen to all instructions before starting.

Stop and Start a Class Consistently

The most basic and important management skill is to be able to start and stop a class. Pick a consistent signal you want to use to stop a class. It does not matter what the signal is, as long as it always means the same thing. Using both an audio signal (such as a hand clap, whistle, or music) and a visual signal (such as raising the hand overhead) is useful because some youngsters may not hear the audio signal when engrossed in activity. Whereas a loud audio signal is used to stop a class, a voice command should be used to start the class. Regardless of the signal used to indicate a stop, it is best to select a different signal from the one used to start the class. If children do not respond to the signal to stop, take time to practise the procedure. Reinforce students when they perform management behaviour properly (see Figure 5.2).

Move Students into Groups and Formations Quickly

It is necessary on a regular basis to move students into small groups and instructional formations. Simple techniques can be used to accomplish this in an enjoyable and rapid fashion. For example, use the activity Toe to Toe (see Chapter 11) to teach children to find partners quickly. The

Figure 5.2

Class in freeze position.

goal of the game is to get toe-to-toe with a partner as fast as possible. Other challenges are to get elbow-to-elbow or shoulder-to-shoulder with a partner. Students without a partner go to the centre of the teaching area (marked by a cone or spot) and find someone else without a partner. This gives students a designated spot to locate themselves, as opposed to feeling unwanted while running around the area looking for a partner.

To divide a class into two equal groups, have students get toe-to-toe with a partner. One partner sits down while the other remains standing. Those standing are asked to go to one area, after which those sitting are then moved to the desired space. Getting into groups is a skill that needs to be learned and practiced regularly.

Another activity for arranging students in groups of a selected size is Whistle Mixer. When the whistle is blown a certain number of times, students form groups corresponding to the number of whistles and sit down to signify that they have the correct number in their group. Students left out go to the centre of the area, find the needed number of members, and move to an open area. When this skill is mastered, students are able to move quickly into appropriate groups. The use of hand signals to show the size of the desired group will make it easier for all students to recognize the instruction.

Other suggestions for finding partners are to ask students to find a partner wearing the same colour, with a birthday during the same month, and so on. To arrange students in equal-size groups, place an equal number of different-coloured beanbags or hoops on the floor. Students are asked to move throughout the area. On signal, they sit on a beanbag. All students with a red beanbag are in the same group, green beanbags make up another group, and so on.

An effective technique for moving a class into a single-file line or circle is to have students run randomly throughout the area until a signal is given. On the signal to "fall in," students continue jogging, move toward the perimeter of the area, and fall in line behind someone until a circle is formed. This exercise can be done while students are running, jogging, skipping, or walking. As long as students continue to move behind another person, a circle will form automatically. Either you or a student leader can lead the line into a desired formation or position.

Another method of moving a class into formation is to ask students to get into various formations without talking. Youngsters can use visual signals but cannot ask someone verbally to move. Groups hustle to see how quickly they can form the desired formation. Another method is to hold up a shape drawn on a large card to signal the desired formation. Young students learn to visualize various shapes through this technique.

Use Teams to Expedite Class Organization

Some teachers find that placing students into teams helps them manage a class effectively. Teams offer a place for students to meet, work positively with classmates, and make it easier to learn students' names. The following are guidelines for using team formation to maximize positive behaviour:

1. A designated location should be used for assembling students into team formation. On signal, children move to the designated area, with team leaders in front and the rest of the team behind.

2. Teams provide opportunities for leadership and following among peers. Use team leaders so youngsters have an opportunity to learn leadership skills. Examples of leadership activities are moving teams to a specified location, leading teams through exercises or introductory activities, and appointing team members to certain positions in game activities.

3. The composition of teams can be predetermined. It may be important to have equal representation of the sexes on each team. Teams can also be used to group students in a way that may allow for maximum diversity in the group, thus allowing students to learn to work with a variety of classmates. So that students get to work with all students in the class, change team members on a regular basis.

4. Make the use of teams an exciting activity, not an approach that restricts movement and creativity. For example, place numbered cones in various locations around the activity area. When students enter the gym, instruct them to find their team number and assemble. The numbers can be written in a different language or hidden in a mathematical equation or story problem.

Know Students' Names

Effective class management requires the teacher to learn the names of students. Praise, feedback, and correction go unheeded when students are addressed as "Hey, you!" Develop a system to expedite the task of learning names. Grouping children into teams of five to six is very helpful. This allows you to focus the students in each team rather than one large group of 30 students. Another approach is to memorize five or six names per class period. Write the names on a notecard, and identify those students at the start and throughout the period. At the end of the period, identify the students again. Once the first set of names has been memorized, a new set can be learned. The next time the class meets, those names learned previously can be reviewed and new students identified. Identification is also easier with students in teams, because they will be in the same location. Another effective way to learn names is to take a photograph of each class in teams and identify students by keying names to the picture.

Tell students you are trying to learn their names. Asking students to say their name before performing a skill or answering a question can help you to learn names. Once a name is learned, you may precede the question or skill performance with the student's name. For example, say, "Simi, it's your turn to jump." Greet students by name when they enter the gymnasium.

Using Equipment Effectively

Make students responsible for securing equipment they use. Teach students how you want them to get the equipment and how to return it at the end of the lesson. Distribute equipment to students as rapidly as possible. A common practice is to assign several student leaders to get the equipment for their team. When students have to wait in line for a piece of equipment, time is wasted and behaviour problems occur. Regardless of the method used to acquire equipment, clearly state what students are supposed to do with the equipment once they have it. This allows them to start practising immediately. When using small equipment, such as balls, hoops, and jump ropes, be sure (if possible) that every youngster has a piece for personal use. Teach students where the equipment is to be placed during instruction. Equipment should be placed in the same (home) position when the class is called to attention. For example, beanbags are placed on the floor, basketballs between the feet, and jump ropes folded and placed behind the neck. Placing the equipment in home position avoids the problem of children striking one another with the equipment, dropping it, or practising activities when they should be listening. To avoid their playing with the equipment when it is placed on the floor, ask students to take a giant step away from it. When large equipment or apparatus is used, establish as many stations or groups as possible. For a class of 30, a minimum of six benches, mats, or jumping boxes should be available so students have only a short wait in line.

Developing Responsible Student Behaviour

Physical education offers opportunities for developing responsible behaviour. There are almost daily occasions to learn to share, express feelings, set personal goals, and function independently. Teamwork—learning to be subordinate to a leader, as well as being a leader—is learned. Effective instruction in PE includes teaching the whole person, rather than focusing just on physical skills. Much is lost when youngsters leave physical education with well-developed physical skills but negative attitudes toward physical activity, and a lack of respect for other participants. Ponder the following situation:

You ask one of your students to perform his gymnastics sequence in front of the class. As he is performing, several classmates giggle and laugh. One student shouts, "Nice try, Ravi!"

Few people have positive feelings about an activity if they are embarrassed. Students have to sense that you care about their feelings and want to avoid placing them in embarrassing situations. It is never justified to knowingly place students in an embarrassing situation. The attitudes and values that students form are based in part on how they were treated by teachers and peers. Learning and performing in physical education is a very public process at all phases of skill development. All students need to feel safe both physically and emotionally when they are performing. Therefore it is important to ensure you have established clear expectations for your students when they are observing performances of classmates. Typical audience expectations may be to "observe quietly and attentively . . . then clap and cheer with enthusiasm at the end of the performance!"

To enhance the affective domain, how you teach is as important as what you teach. Have you established a positive environment where students feel safe trying new skills and performing for their peers? Students must be acknowledged as human beings with needs and concerns and should be treated in a courteous manner. How youngsters feel about themselves and their classmates affects their motivation to learn. Therefore, when planning, analyze whether the lesson will result in experiences that enhance this motivation. Effective teaching communicates to students that they are capable, important, and self-sufficient. Stressing a positive self-concept and offering experiences to promote success are invaluable aids to learning. The following describes some general strategies that focus on developing responsible behaviour.

Model Desirable Behaviour

How you interact with your students encourages responsible behaviour. Treat youngsters with dignity and respect, and follow through with responsible action and words. In return, expect students to treat you and others with the same dignity and respect. In addition, you perform the behaviour desired, with the expectation that students respond in similar fashion. For example, placing your piece of equipment on the floor when stopping the class will remind the class to do likewise.

Acknowledge and Reinforce Desired Behaviour

Effective teachers use praise and facial expressions to acknowledge desired behaviour in their students. The following are examples of words of praise that can be used with students in a physical education setting:

Words of Praise

Great job at helping your partner!

Perfect arm placement.	That's the best one yet.
Nice hustle.	Thank you for running in quickly.

Physical Expressions

Smiling	Winking
Nodding	Clenched fist overhead
Thumbs up	Clapping
Handshake	High five

Just as specific corrective feedback helps students improve their skill performance, praise is effective when it refers to specific behaviour exhibited by the youngster. This contrasts with general statements such as, "Good job" or "You are an excellent performer." General and non-specific statements do not tell the youngster what was done well. It leaves it to the student to try to identify what you had in mind. To improve the specificity and effectiveness of feedback, describe the behaviour to be acknowledged. For example, consider the following:

"Janelle, I saw you helping your partner. Thank you!"

In this example, the child is identified and the specific performed behaviour is acknowledged. To increase desired behaviour, describe what makes the performance effective or noteworthy. In addition, try using positive reinforcement to increase desired behaviour with the hope that it will replace negative behaviour. For example, if a skilled student is always criticizing less able young-sters, ask that student to help others and serve as a student assistant. The intent is to teach the youngster to deliver positive and constructive feedback rather than criticism.

Offer Time for Reflection

Allow time for students to think about the attitudes and behaviours and how they affect others. Ask the students to fill out a self-responsibility checklist at various times of the year. See Figure 5.3 for an example of a checklist.

My Self-responsibility Checklist

Name: _____

Date: _____

Self-control:

_____ I did not call others names.

_____ I had self-control when I became mad.

_____ I listened when others were talking.

_____ Other (describe)

Involvement:

_____ I listened to all directions before starting.

_____ I was willing to try all activities.

_____ I tried activities even when I didn't like them.

_____ Other (describe) _____

Self-responsibility:

_____ I followed directions without being told more than once.

_____ I did not blame others.

_____ I worked on activities by myself.

_____ Other (describe) _____

Caring:

_____ I helped someone today.

_____ I said something nice to someone.

_____ I asked someone to do something with me.

_____ Other (describe) _____

Figure 5. 3

Example of a responsibility checklist.

Allow Student Sharing

Offer students a chance to give their opinions about responsible behaviour. Accept all students' feelings as important. Focus on ways to encourage higher levels of responsible behaviour. Brainstorming to identify consequences of high and low behaviour is an effective approach. Another practice is to ask various students to give examples of responsible behaviour at different levels.

Encourage Goal-Setting

Help students set goals for responsible behaviour that they want to exhibit. This can be done at the start of the lesson by asking each student to tell a partner the behaviour they want to use today. At the end of the lesson, partners evaluate each other to see if the behaviour was exhibited. Examples of behaviours are listening, hustling, being courteous, and complimenting others.

Offer Opportunities for Responsibility

There are a number of times when students can be given responsibility in a class setting. Group leader, team captain, referee, scorekeeper, or dispute resolver—all are roles that encourage students to exhibit high-level behaviour.

Allow Student Choice

Responsible behaviour is best learned when students make choices. The natural consequences of self-selected choices are often the best teachers. Students can make choices about games they choose to play, fitness activities they select, and friends they make.

Personal and Social Learning Outcomes in Physical Education

Concern about student behaviour has increased the emphasis on learning outcomes in physical education that focus on personal and social responsibility. In addition to contributing to a positive class environment, these learning outcomes play an important part in provincial and territorial physical education curriculum guides. For example, one of the major curriculum organizers in the British Columbia PE curriculum is entitled *Personal and Social Responsibility*. This curriculum organizer includes specific learning outcomes (PLOs) for each grade level. In kindergarten/grade 1 (BC Ministry of Education, 1995, p. 28) within *Personal and Social Responsibility,* for example, it is expected that students will:

- show a willingness to listen to directions and simple explanations
- use safe behaviours when responding to simple movement tasks
- demonstrate self-confidence while participating in activities from different movement categories
- stay on task when participating in physical activity
- display a willingness to work with others
- identify different roles in a variety of physical activities

Similarly, in Alberta, the PE curriculum guide includes the following as one of four general outcomes: "Students will interact cooperatively with others." This general outcome is divided into four concepts—Communication, Fair Play, Leadership, and Teamwork. Specific learning outcomes at each grade level are identified for each of these concepts. For example, the following learning is expected of students in grade 1 (Alberta Learning, 2000, p. 23):

- *Communication*: Develop and demonstrate respectful communication skills applied to the appropriate context.
- *Fair Play*: Identify and demonstrate etiquette and fair play.
- *Leadership*: Identify different roles in a variety of physical activities.
- *Teamwork*: Display willingness to play cooperatively with others in large and small groups.

In a third example, the Manitoba PE/Health curriculum provides one of the most inclusive frameworks of personal and social learning outcomes. The PE/Health curriculum identifies *Personal and Social Management* as one of five general learning outcomes. Within the *Personal and Social Management* learning outcome, "the student will the ability to develop self-understanding, to make health-enhancing decisions, to work cooperatively and fairly with others, and to build positive relationships with others" (Manitoba Education and Training, 2000, p. 6). This general learning outcome is further delineated into a very comprehensive and cohesive framework of strands, sub-strands, and grade-specific learning outcomes (see Figure 5.4).

General Learning Outcome: The student will demonstrate the ability to develop self-understanding, to make health-enhancing decisions, to work cooperatively and fairly with others, and to build positive relationships with others.

Knowledge Strand	Sub-Strands	Example: Grade 1 Learning outcomes for sub-strands
A. Personal Development	1. Self-awareness/self-esteem 2. Goal-setting 3. Decision-making/problem-solving process	1. Recognize positive attributes of self, family, and classmates. 2. (a) Recognize that it takes time, effort, and cooperation to achieve simple individual tasks/goals. (b) Discuss behaviours that demonstrate personal responsibility and irresponsibility in a classroom. 3. Identify initial steps for making simple personal and/or guided decisions regarding home and classroom situations.
B. Social Development	1. Social responsibility 2. Relationships 3. Conflict resolution process 4. Avoidance and refusal strategies	1. Discuss how feelings and experiences associated with participation in physical activities . . . can be the same or different from person to person. 2. (a) Identify different ways of expressing feelings and emotions that contribute to getting along with others.

Figure 5.4

Sample organization of personal and social management learning outcomes in elementary physical education (adapted from Manitoba Education & Training, 2000).

		(b) Identify ways to get along with others for developing healthy relationships. 3. (a) Identify what can happen when someone becomes angry . . . and healthy ways to deal with anger. (b) Identify several causes of conflicts that may occur in class or play situations. (c) Identify ways to avoid or reduce potential conflict situations. 4. Identify ways to exercise caution, avoidance, and/or refusal in potentially dangerous situations.
C. Mental-Emotional Development	1. Feelings and emotions 2. Elements of stress 3. Effects of stress 4. Stress management strategies	(Outcomes in this sub-strand continued from Kindergarten.) 1. (a) Identify a range of feelings and emotions in a range of contexts. (b) Recognize ways emotions are expressed by others. 2. (a) Identify situations that cause feelings of anxiety and stress. (b) Identify the personality traits that are conducive to handling stress and showing resiliency. 4. Identify the people who can support stressful situations.
Skills Strand		
A. Acquisition of Personal and Social Management Skills related to Physical Activity and Healthy Lifestyle Practices	1. Goal-setting/ planning 2. Decision-making/problem solving 3. Interpersonal skills 4. Conflict resolution skills 5. Stress-management skills	1. Set simple short-term goals and participate in strategies for goal attainment. 2. Demonstrate ways to expand knowledge and explore different options for making informed and health-enhancing decisions. 3. Demonstrate behaviours that show social responsibility in daily routines. 4. Demonstrate ways to resolve conflict in a peaceful manner with limited teacher input. 5. Experience activities for relaxation.

Figure 5.4

Continued

Clearly, PE curricula in Canadian schools have accepted responsibility for helping children learn positive personal and social skills. Whether described as fair play, participation, leadership, effort, or cooperation, all these outcomes involve the notion of developing a sense of personal responsibility and accountability for one's behaviour. Teachers are charged with the design of learning experiences to help students achieve these outcomes. The following section describes two examples of approaches to teaching strategies for personal and social learning outcomes in physical education.

Fair Play for Kids

Teachers and students at Rimbey Elementary School in Rimbey, Alberta, have embraced the notion that the concept of fair play can guide responsible behaviour both within and beyond the gymnasium. Not surprisingly, initial efforts to focus on fair play at Rimbey Elementary started with the physical education teacher, Joanne Susut. She was concerned that through their behaviour, some students were interfering with their own right to learn, with the rights of other students to learn, and with her right to teach. To address this concern, the teacher made a concerted effort to help students learn respect for others by focusing on fair play in her physical education classes. Fortunately, fair play has the potential to reach beyond the physical education classroom. Soon other teachers began to use the fair play theme in a variety of subjects. Eventually teachers and students integrated the ideals of fair play into the school philosophy. The ideals of fair play included (a) respect for the rules, (b) respect for officials and their decisions, (c) respect for the opponent, (d) providing all individuals with an equal opportunity to participate, and (e) maintaining self-control at all times (Fair Play Canada, 1995). In the school, fair play now forms a common language that spans the grades. It is the language used in the gymnasium, in the classroom, and on the playground. The school has become a safer and more secure place where each individual is respected and valued.

Teachers at Rimbey Elementary selected and adapted activities from the *Fair Play for Kids* (1995) resource manual. This manual was designed to provide elementary school teachers with a variety of teaching strategies that focused on the ideals of fair play, and could be readily incorporated into a variety of subjects. Teaching strategies in the manual focused primarily on a blend of social learning and problem-solving tasks associated with the identification and resolution of moral dilemmas in sport and everyday life. The effectiveness of teaching strategies included in *Fair Play for Kids* has been supported in several recent field experiments (Gibbons & Ebbeck, 1997; Gibbons, Ebbeck, & Weiss, 1995). To establish and maintain a consistent emphasis on the principles of fair play at different grade levels, the teachers used a variety of school-wide and subject-specific strategies. The following are some of these actions.

Fair Play Assemblies

The principles of fair play grew beyond the physical education classes to become part of the school philosophy. This was accomplished by using the five principles of fair play as themes for the school assemblies. Each assembly highlights one of the fair play principles and at these assemblies several students from each of the intermediate classes are recognized as fair play award winners in the school. These students are given a fair play certificate, adapted from the *Fair Play for Kids* manual, and their pictures are placed on the Fair Play Super Star bulletin board. The fair play award winners are recognized in the school's monthly newsletter.

Fair Play Rap

The primary classes have chosen not to recognize individual award winners as they feel the task of identifying these children and selecting only two to receive the award is difficult. Every child is encouraged to strive for the fair play ideals and all of the children in the primary grades take part in fair play assemblies by performing songs, cheers, and word raps related to the fair play philosophy. The following is a word rap adapted from a library word rap (adapted by Mrs. Wilson & Mrs. Coambs) and performed by the grade 1 students at an assembly:

Fair Play Rap

We have a little rap for you today,

We want to tell you about fair play.

We think you should know that rules are cool,

So follow them at home and follow them at school.

Whether you're inside or out in the sun,

Playing by the rules is much more fun.

So always remember the number one rule—

Fair Play is cool at R.E.S. School!!!

Physical Education

The following teaching strategies are used on an ongoing basis in physical education: (a) role-modelling of the expected fair play behaviour; and (b) verbal praise to reinforce appropriate fair play behaviour. Examples of specific strategies include the implementation of a fair play awards program, and a self-monitoring and peer-monitoring program based on an established code of fair play. The following are samples of several of the fair play teaching strategies.

Compliment Cards

Students document examples of fair play displayed by their classmates. These are collected and some examples are highlighted at the beginning of each week.

Fair Play Code

Students discuss ways they will put the ideals of fair play into action in their physical education class (for example, "We will cheer good plays by our opponents as well as our own team"). This list is posted in the gym.

My Fair Play Agreement

Each student lists several fair play behaviours he or she will endeavour to exhibit during a particular activity. The student signs this list as a contract between himself or herself and other members of the class. Similar strategies are also used to teach children to behave in a respectful manner when they are officials and spectators. The following are examples:

Discuss ways to encourage others, how to be positive, how to cheer in positive ways that are not distracting.

Create spectator opportunities through which students can observe fair play.

In classroom sessions pose questions: "What does it mean to be respectful?" "If the environment in the gymnasium was a respectful one, what would it look like, sound like?"

Levels of Responsible Behaviour

Don Hellison (2003) developed strategies and programs for teaching responsibility to older students. Elementary school teachers also have adapted many of Hellison's concepts to elementary school programs. Jim Roberts, a physical education specialist in the Mesa, Arizona, public schools, has implemented much of the material that follows in this section.

A basic premise for learning responsible behaviour is that it must be planned for, taught, and reinforced. Responsible behaviour takes time and practice to learn, much like any other skill. Hellison (2003) suggests there is a hierarchy of responsible behaviour. The suggestions described in this section subscribe to the idea that there are different levels of responsible behaviour that can be learned. Teaching responsible behaviour as described here involves five levels of behaviour. Each is defined next, followed by applicable examples of typical student behaviour for that level.

Level 0: Irresponsibility Level 0 students are unmotivated and undisciplined. Their behaviour includes discrediting other students' involvement and interrupting, intimidating, manipulating, and verbally or physically abusing other students and perhaps the teacher.

Behaviour examples:

- At home: Blaming brothers or sisters for problems; lying to parents
- On the playground: Calling other students names; laughing at others
- In physical education: Talking to friends when the teacher is giving instructions; pushing and shoving when selecting equipment

Level 1: Self-Control Students at this level do not participate in the day's activity or show much mastery or improvement. These students control their behaviour enough so they do not interfere with other students' right to learn or the teacher's right to teach.

Behaviour examples:

- At home: Refraining from hitting a brother or sister even though angry
- On the playground: Standing and watching others play; not getting angry at others because they did something to upset them
- In physical education: Waiting until an appropriate time to talk with friends; having control and not letting others' behaviour bother them

Level 2: Involvement These students show self-control and are involved in the subject matter or activity.

Behaviour examples:

- At home: Helping clean up the dishes after dinner; taking out the trash
- On the playground: Playing with others; participating in a game
- In physical education: Listening and performing activity; trying even when they don't like the activity; doing an activity without complaining or saying, "I can't."

Level 3: Self-Responsibility Level 3 students take responsibility for their choices and for linking these choices to their own identities. They are able to work without direct supervision, eventually taking responsibility for their intentions and actions.

Behaviour examples:

- At home: Cleaning up without being asked
- On the playground: Returning equipment after recess

- In physical education: Following directions; practising a skill without being told; trying new activities without encouragement

Level 4: Caring   Students behaving at this level are motivated to extend their sense of responsible behaviour by cooperating, giving support, showing concern, and helping.

Behaviour examples:

- At home: Helping take care of a younger brother or sister or a pet

- On the playground: Asking others (not just friends) to join them in play

- In physical education: Helping someone who is having trouble; helping a new student feel welcome; working with all students; showing that all people are worthwhile

Responsible behaviour is taught using a number of strategies. Post the levels of responsibility in the teaching area. Explain the different levels of behaviour and identify acceptable behaviours at each level. After students have received an introduction to responsible behaviour, implement the program by reinforcing desired behaviour and redirecting inappropriate behaviour. The program is based on this two-pronged approach: (1) Catch students using responsible behaviour and reinforce them; and (2) Redirect students behaving at level 0 by asking, "At what level are you performing and what level would be more acceptable?" An example is the following discussion between teacher and student. You see a student behaving at level 0 and open dialogue with the student in a nonconfrontational manner:

"Reza, it appeared you were making fun of someone . . . "

"I wasn't making fun of anyone!"

"Maybe not, but if you were, what level of behaviour would it be?"

"Zero!"

"If you were at level 0, how do you think you can make some changes? What kinds of things can you do to move to level1? Remember at level 1 you are practising self-control. What does self-control look like?

Positive Strategies for Responding to Misbehaviour

Even within a positive and productive learning environment, there will be situations where students misbehave. Try to respond to this misbehaviour with a positive approach where you decrease the likelihood that the misbehaviour will reoccur and increase the likelihood that appropriate behaviour will take its place. Consider the following when responding to misbehaviour.

Monitor Your Own Behaviour

1. *Maintain composure.* Students don't know your trigger points unless you reveal them. If you "lose it," students lose respect for you and believe you are an ineffective teacher.

2. *Acknowledge your feelings when student misbehaviour occurs.* Do you feel angry, threatened, challenged, or fearful?

3. *Design a plan for yourself when such feelings occur.* For example, count to 10 before responding, or take five deep breaths. Avoid dealing with the student misbehaviour until you are aware of how you feel.

4. *Know the options you have for dealing with the inappropriate behaviour.* Talking with students is best done after class if it is going to take more than a few seconds. Limited time options include the following: Quietly warn the student; quietly remove the student from class; or quietly send another student for help if the situation is severe.

5. *Examine your own actions that lead up to the inappropriate behaviour.* Did you inadvertently contribute to the student's actions? For example, having students wait in line for long periods of time will often provide the opportunity for misbehaviour. This opportunity is significantly reduced when students are actively engaged in activity.

Verbal Interactions with Students

Your everyday verbal interactions with your students should focus on positive behaviour. Given this focus, it is also important to be aware of several negative interaction habits teachers may develop. The following types of negative interactions may work immediately but cause greater problems later:

- *Threatening.* Threats are ultimatums given in an attempt to terminate undesirable behaviour. The supposed power of this type of threat lies in the real belief by the students that you will fulfill the ultimatum. However, often the teacher makes a threat that he or she has no wish to actually enact! Thus, it becomes an "idle threat." When students hear enough idle threats, they start to tune out.

- *Ordering and commanding.* If you are bossy, students begin to think they are nothing more than pawns to be moved around the area. Use patterns of communication that ask students to carry out tasks. Courtesy and politeness are requisites for effective teacher–student relationships.

- *Interrogating.* When there is a problem (such as an argument between students), an initial reaction is to figure out who started the argument rather than deal with the feelings of the combatants. Little is gained by trying to solve "who started it." Try calmly saying, "You know arguing is not accepted in my class. You must have been very angry to place yourself in this situation." This encourages youngsters to talk about feelings rather than place blame. It also communicates your caring and concerned attitude toward youngsters even when they misbehave.

- *Labelling.* Labelling is characterized by telling children "Stop acting like babies" or "You're behaving like a bunch of grade ones." On an individual level, it might sound like "You're always the troublemaker." This is degrading and dehumanizes youngsters. Often, labelling is done with the intent of improving performance. In actuality, it is usually destructive and leaves youngsters with negative feelings.

Start with Minimal Response

Start with the least intrusive response to the misbehaviour. If possible stop the undesirable behaviour with a look or signal, moving toward the student (proximity control), or a quick verbal reminder. If these responses stop the behaviour, then there is no need to use a more intrusive intervention, and no need for any further consequence.

Make Consequences Clear, Immediate, and Productive

Students must know what will occur if they misbehave. Therefore, when discussing rules and expectations include the consequences for misbehaviour. As well, apply a consequence as soon after misbehaviour as possible, just as positive feedback is delivered immediately following desired behaviour. Consequences, even though negative, should be productive and educational rather than menial and demeaning. Just as you need to know what reinforces students, you also need to know effective consequences for students who misbehave. Use consequences to help youngsters learn how to behave properly, rather than to punish them. Consequences that have been shown to be productive in decreasing undesirable behaviour include verbal reprimands, removal of positive consequences, and time-out.

Verbal Reprimands

A verbal reprimand is telling an individual that his behaviour is unacceptable and why it is unacceptable, followed by provision of an acceptable alternative behaviour (Lavay, French, & Henderson, 2006). Verbal reprimands are a common approach used to decrease undesirable behaviour. If done in a caring and constructive manner, reprimands can serve as very effective reminders to behave. Consider the following when delivering a verbal reprimand.

- Identify the unacceptable behaviour, state briefly why it is unacceptable, and communicate to students what behaviour is desired. For example, "You were talking while I was speaking. It bothers other students, so please listen to me."

- Address the student privately. A public reprimand is seldom productive. Not only does it embarrass the student, but also it can diminish his or her self-esteem. When students feel belittled, they may lash out and react in a manner more severe than the original behaviour. Buy some time for talking with the student privately by giving the class a task to perform. This affords you the opportunity to discuss the situation with the misbehaving student. Deal with one student at a time. Often, a couple of students are misbehaving together. Separate them and deal with their unacceptable behaviour one-on-one.

- Reprimands should speak about behaviour, not the person. Ask the behaviour to stop rather than telling a student "You are always causing problems in this class." Avoid general and negative statements related to the personality of the student.

- After reprimanding and asking for acceptable behaviour, reinforce such behaviour when it occurs. Be vigilant in looking for the desired behaviour, since acknowledging such behaviour may cause it to occur more often in the future.

Removal of Positive Consequences

This common approach is to remove something positive from the student when misbehaviour occurs. Some examples include the following: (a) students lose some of their free time; (b) they lose points related to a grade; (c) they are not allowed to participate in an activity that is exciting to them. For removal of positive consequences to be effective, make sure the removal activity is meaningful to the student. A few key principles should be followed when using this technique:

- Assure that the magnitude of the removal fits the *misbehaviour.* In other words, children who commit a minor infraction shouldn't have to miss recess for a week.

- Be consistent in removal, treating all students and occurrences the same. Students believe teachers are unfair if they are more severe with one student than another.
- Make sure students understand the consequences of their misbehaviour before the penalties are implemented. If students know what the consequences will be, they are making the choice to accept the consequences when they choose to misbehave.

Time-out

The time-out approach moves youngsters who misbehave out of the class activity and places them in a designated area (see Figure 5.5). Being placed in time-out communicates to youngsters that they have disrupted learning and must be removed so that the rest of the class can participate as desired. During the time-out, the student reflects on the misbehaviour in a somewhat secluded area in the gymnasium while the rest of the class continues in the

Figure 5.5

Student assigned to time-out.

activity. The time-out provides the opportunity for the teacher to interact with the individual student. The child stays in the time-out area until ready to re-enter the activity. Be certain that the child knows why she or he was required to take a time-out. When determining if a student is ready to return, ask them to state the appropriate behaviour before returning to the class activity. It is also acceptable for children to voluntarily use the time-out area as a cooling-off spot if they become angry, embarrassed, or frustrated. If youngsters have been placed in the time-out area for fighting or arguing, they should be placed at opposite ends of the area so that the behaviour does not rekindle.

When Misbehaviour Continues

Typically, effective teachers establish a series of steps for responding to recurring misbehaviour. Generally, in response to a first misbehaviour, the student is warned or lightly reprimanded quietly on a personal basis. At times, students are not aware that they are bothering others, and a gentle reminder is sufficient to refocus the youngster. A second misbehaviour may involve going to the time-out area. The student stays there until ready to re-enter the activity and behave properly. If the misbehaviour continues and a student is a frequent visitor to the time-out area, a more involved intervention is necessary (e.g., behaviour contract).

Behaviour Contracts

A behaviour contract is a written statement specifying certain behaviours the students must exhibit in order to earn specified rewards or privileges. The contract is drawn up after a private conference to decide on the appropriate behaviours and rewards. It is agreed upon and signed by the student and teacher. This approach allows students to make decisions that will improve their own behaviour.

The behaviour contract may be a successful strategy for intermediate-grade students with severe behaviour problems. Every attempt should be made to find rewards that occur naturally in physical education class (such as Frisbee play, aerobics, or basketball). If not possible, different types of rewards may have to be used. For example, a student who is interested in music could be allowed to spend some time selecting CDs to be used for class during the next week. The contract is gradually phased out over a period of time as the youngster gains control of the behaviour and can participate in the regular class environment.

Contracts can be written for a small group of students or for an entire class with similar problems, but teachers must be careful about setting up a reward system for too many students. The system can become too complex or time-consuming to be supervised properly. The contract is

---

Individual Behaviour Contract

Date: _____

I, _____, agree to follow the rules as listed below:

1. Listen when the teacher is talking.

2. Do not touch others during class.

If all the rules are followed during physical education class, I will earn 10 minutes of basketball activity for a friend and myself after school on Thursday anytime between 3:00 and 3:45.

Signed: _____, Student

Signed: _____, Teacher

Figure 5.6

Individual behaviour contract.

best used with a limited number of students who have severe problems. Examples of behaviour contracts are shown in Figures 5.6 and 5.7.

Resolving Conflict between Students

Conflict is a part of daily life, and youngsters should understand that it is necessary to deal with conflict in an effective manner. If left unresolved, conflict between students has the potential to result in aggression and violence. Students can learn ways to respect others' opinions and feelings while maintaining their own worth and dignity.

Conflict resolution can help students learn to solve conflicts in a peaceful manner. This approach takes a cooperative approach to solving problems. Such an approach often builds positive feelings between students and leads to better group cohesiveness. The following are steps typically followed to resolve conflicts (Gordon & Browne, 1996).

1. *Stop the conflict immediately.* Students in conflict are separated immediately and given an opportunity to cool down. Time-out areas are often an excellent place to send students to relax and unwind.

2. *Gather data about what happened and define the problem.* Find out what happened, who was involved, and how each youngster is feeling. Ask open-ended questions, such as, "What happened?" "How did you feel about...?" so youngsters can talk freely about the problem.

3. *Brainstorm possible solutions.* Keep in mind that brainstorming is a nonjudgmental process where all solutions are accepted regardless of their perceived value. Encourage youngsters to think of as many options as possible by asking open-ended questions, such as, "How could we solve this problem?" and "What other ways could we deal with this?"

4. *Test the solutions generated through brainstorming.* Ask a question such as, "What solutions might work best?" Help students understand the implications of the solutions and how the solutions can be implemented. Accept solutions that may differ from your way of solving the problem.

Group Behaviour Contract

Our team agrees to follow the rules listed below:

1. Listen when the teacher is talking.

2. Take care of the equipment.

3. Treat others as we would like to be treated.

One point is earned each time the music stops and every member of the team is following the rules.
No points are awarded if one or more members of the team are not following the rules.
Each point is worth 1 minute of free activity time to be awarded every other Friday.

Signed: Team Number _____   _____

_____   _____

_____   _____

_____   _____

Figure 5.7

Group behaviour contract.

5. *Help implement the plan.* Walk students through the solution so they develop a perception of the approach. Guide them through the steps by asking, "Who goes first?" and "Who will take the next step?" As the solution is implemented, there may be a need to change it, which can be agreed on by the involved students.

6. *Evaluate the approach.* Observe to see that the plan is accomplishing the desired outcome. Encourage students to change the plan if necessary.

The conflict resolution process takes practice and time. It demands that the teacher play certain roles and take an objective approach to resolution. The conflict resolution process demands certain behaviours from the teacher. Listening carefully to both parties is necessary. Both sides of the problem must be explored, and students must feel as though the process was equitable. Students must trust that the process will be fair and objective and that they will receive a fair shake if they deal with the issue cooperatively.

An extension of this conflict resolution process is *peer mediation.* Peer mediation is a strategy that has student mediators help resolve minor conflict among their peers. In the peer mediation process, students trained as mediators or conflict managers apply steps very similar to those described in Conflict Resolution (primarily steps 2–5). The intent of peer mediation is to help students begin to monitor their own behaviour, take responsibility, move away from blaming each other, and lead all parties toward to mutually acceptable solutions. As a teaching strategy, the peer mediation process is designed to provide students with alternatives for solving problems and resolving conflict.

Safe and Caring Schools: Policies and Educational Initiatives

It is important to remember that the Physical Education classroom does not exist in a vacuum. Thus, helping students learn positive behaviour is not limited to PE. However, the preceding discussion does provide a framework for the discussion of strategies for encouraging positive behaviour in the greater school community. The classroom management skills that allow PE classes to run smoothly, coupled with learning experiences in PE specifically focused on the development of positive personal and social skills, have their equivalent in the broader education community. The following sections present a range of policies (classroom management equivalent) and educational initiatives (personal and social skills equivalent) focused on establishing and maintaining safe and caring schools.

Sadly, the concept of the safe and caring school has its roots in violence. High-profile incidents of appalling violence in schools (e.g., shootings, bullying, harassment, beating deaths) in Canada and internationally have shocked and horrified educators. These tragic incidents have been somewhat of a catalyst for the critical examination of the environments in which children are expected to learn. Fortunately, there has been considerable positive action as a result of this examination, albeit small comfort to the victims of these violent acts.

Positive Learning Environments in Schools: A Pan-Canadian Consensus Statement provides a solid base from which to discuss the variety of actions different provinces have taken. This consensus statement was a result of a national meeting in June 2000 of representations from over 30 organizations from education, justice, and other community groups, for the purpose of facilitating school-community partnerships that will lead toward safer schools and ultimately safer communities. The following is an excerpt from the statement:

> *Participating and contributing to a safe, respectful and positive learning environment is both the right and responsibility of children and youth, their parents/caregivers, school personnel and all community members. Schools, acting in partnership with their communities, can create and maintain these environments that foster a sense of belonging, enhance the joy of learning, honour diversity and promote respectful, responsible and caring relationships. (Safe, Healthy Schools, 2000, p. 1)*

Provincial/territorial departments/ministries of education have either adopted this statement, or created one for their own context. The following are sample safe and caring schools goal statements:

- *Caring and Respectful School* environment focuses on the concept of community and the need for schools to be caring and respectful learning communities with an unconditional commitment to help every child and young person succeed in school and life (Saskatchewan Learning, 2004, p. 2).

- In *Safe Schools Policy and Practice*, a "school is a place that promotes responsibility, respect, civility and academic excellence in a safe learning and teaching environment. All students, parents, teachers and staff have the right to be safe, and feel safe, in their school community" (Ontario Ministry of Education, 2006, p. 12).

Toward this end, provincial ministries/departments of education have created policy documents that help define both the structure and content of a safe and caring school. For example, the *Safe and Caring Schools Policy* from Newfoundland & Labrador Department of Education (2006) states that the goal is to "provide a framework for the development and implementation of provincial, district and school-level policies and action plans to ensure that learning and teaching can take place in a safe and caring environment" (p. 4). Correspondingly, the purpose of BC's *Safe, Caring and Orderly Schools Strategy* is to "help make schools places where students are free from harm, where clear expectations of acceptable behaviour are held and met and where all members of the school community feel they belong" (BC Ministry of Education, 2004, p. 4). In Saskatchewan, *Caring and Respectful Schools* offers a "conceptual framework for strengthening schools as caring and respectful centres of learning, support and community for children, youth and their families" (Saskatchewan Learning, 2004, p. 2). New Brunswick Department of Education (2002) describes its *Positive Learning Environment Policy* as a "tool designed to help school staff, students and parents build safe and peaceful environments where people feel accepted and respected and where learning is the main focus" (p. 1).

Generally, in terms of structure, these documents are grounded in their respective School/Education Acts, which ultimately define acceptable and unacceptable behaviour of students and teachers. As well, they specify in clear terms the rights and responsibilities of those involved in the education system (e.g., students, parents, teachers, school boards). The following are excerpts from several provincial School/Education Acts:

- "A board shall ensure that each student enrolled in a school operated by the board is provided a safe and caring environment that fosters and maintains respectful and responsible behaviour" (Alberta School Act, Section 45[8], 1999).

- "A student must comply . . . with the code of conduct and other rules and policies of the board or Provincial school" (BC School Act c. 412, Section 6[b] 1996).

- "It is the responsibility of a student to (a) participate fully in learning opportunities; (b) attend school regularly and punctually; (c) contribute to an orderly and safe learning environment; (d) respect the rights of others; and (e) comply with the discipline policies of the school and the School board" (Nova Scotia Education Act, 24, 1, 1995–96).

- "It is mandatory that a pupil be suspended from his or her school and from engaging in all school-related activities if the pupil commits any of the following infractions while he or she is at school or is engaged in a school-related activity: (a) uttering a threat to inflict serious bodily harm on another person; (b) possessing alcohol or illegal drugs; (c) being under the influence of alcohol; (d) swearing at a teacher or at another person in a position of authority; (e) committing an act of vandalism that causes extensive damage to school property . . . ; and (f) engaging in another activity that, under a policy of the boards, is one for which suspension is mandatory" (Ontario Education Act, 13, c. 12, s. 3, 2000)

Standards of acceptable behaviour in schools and consequences for not meeting these standards are delineated further in official Codes of Conduct. For example, the *Ontario Schools Code of Conduct* (2001) denotes standards of behaviour (encompassing civility, respect, physical safety, and responsible citizenship) and the mandatory consequences (e.g., suspension, expulsion) for actions that do not meet the standards. In addition to what is described in the Ontario document, the *School Code of Conduct* for Nova Scotia also includes consequences that are specifically forbidden for any type of misconduct. These include: (a) corporal punishment; (b) use of collective responsibility (group punishments) in disciplinary procedures; (c) use of academic work as a disciplinary procedure—i.e., assigning extra academic work to punish misbehaviour; and (d) use of evaluation as a disciplinary procedure—i.e., arbitrarily assigning a test to an individual or class that is behaving inappropriately (Nova Scotia Department of Education, 2001).

Just as class management skill alone does not guarantee appropriate student behaviour in physical education, policies, statutes, and codes of conduct do not guarantee appropriate behaviour in the wider school context. These structures must be accompanied by applicable learning experiences for students. The following describe examples of the types of school-wide educational initiatives that are helping students learn and practise positive behavioural skills.

Peace in the Classroom

Similar to the PE-focused *Fair Play for Kids,* Hetty Adams's (1994) *Peace in the Classroom* takes a proactive student-centred cross-curricular approach to developing responsible behaviour. A longtime educator in Nova Scotia, Adams emphasizes that we must "provide our children with the tools they will need for living in harmony with one another" (p. 2). These tools include self-esteem, respect for others, communication skills, and conflict resolution skills. The following are examples of teaching strategies focused on some of these tools (adapted with permission from Adams, H. [1994]. *Peace in the classroom.* Winnipeg, MB: Peguis Publishers).

Things We Do Well

This is to foster the development of self-esteem in each child by identifying one thing he or she does well. Assemble the children and ask each to think of one thing that he or she does well. Start the discussion by telling the children something you do well. Allow each child to share if he or she wishes to do so. Then have the children draw pictures of themselves doing what they do well and use these drawings as a bulletin board display.

Helping Hands

This is to encourage children to think of ways in which they can help others. Discuss with the children ways they can help others—in class, at home, and on the playground. Stress that helping someone involves the giving of oneself, not of material possessions. Ask for suggestions and record their ideas on the chalkboard or on chart paper. Encourage students to add to the list throughout the year.

Friendly Words

This is to help develop a vocabulary that is conducive to creating a peaceful environment. Discuss with the children the importance of using friendly words; brainstorm an ABC of friendly words (a friendly word for each letter of the alphabet).

Peace Is...

This is to enable children to examine their notions of peace and come to a mutual understanding. In the centre of a piece of chart paper, print the word *peace*. Ask the children to offer words or phrases that they can associate with peace. From these contributions, come up with a simple definition of *peace*.

For further information on successful peaceful school models see Van Gurp (2002), *The Peaceful School Models that Work.*

Bullying Prevention Programs

Bullying is defined as a "form of repeated aggressive behaviour directed at an individual or group from a position of power" (Saskatchewan Learning, 2006). This type of behaviour is doubly troubling because in addition to being damaging on its own, if left unchecked it is very likely to lead to even worse behaviour and further poison the school environment. Therefore, addressing potential bullying behaviour as early as possible is crucial. Fortunately, there is a considerable knowledge base to demonstrate that well-designed bullying prevention programs can prevent, reduce, and eliminate many bullying problems, and notably improve the general school environment (Canadian Public Health Association, 2005).

Effective bullying prevention programs at the elementary level most often include a parent education portion, some community organization involvement (e.g., police), along with a range of cross-curricular learning activities that progress through the grade levels. For example, *Focus on Bullying*, a prevention program in BC elementary schools, includes lesson plans for three educational modules (Defining Bullying, The School Plan, Dealing with Bullying), which appear across the K–7 elementary grades.

The intent is to have the lessons in the modules build each year as the needs of children change. A promising curricular initiative for the primary-age child is the WITS program. WITS is a social skills program that helps K–3 children learn and practise social skills for handling conflicts with peers (Rock Solid Foundation, 2004). The WITS acronym represents "Walk away," "Ignore," "Talk it out" (use words not fists), and "Seek help." The acronym is a valuable tool to remind even the youngest child to use acceptable ways to resolve conflict. It also provides a variety of options for the child. This simple acronym is a helpful reminder for children to "use their WITS" when confronted with conflict. The WITS program has a strong literacy focus where students read a range of stories; teachers are supplied with a variety of strategies to embed aspects of the WITS message in follow-up discussions.

Critical Thinking

1. Peer mediation was briefly discussed as an alternative strategy for resolving minor conflict between students. Discuss potential strengths and caveats for using this strategy in physical education. Investigate programs for training elementary school–aged peer mediators.

2. Effective class management does not guarantee appropriate behaviour. Discuss this statement as it relates to creating and maintaining a positive learning environment in physical education.

3. Investigate the approach that the Ministry/Department of Education in your province/territory takes toward realizing the concept of safe and caring schools (e.g., policies, codes of conduct, bullying prevention initiatives).

References and Suggested Readings

Adams, H. (1994). *Peace in the classroom.* Winnipeg, MB: Peguis Publishers.

Alberta Education. (2005). *The heart of the matter: Character and citizenship in Alberta schools.* Edmonton, AB: Author.

Alberta Learning. (2000). *Physical education kindergarten to grade 12 program of studies.* Edmonton, AB: Author.

Alberta Learning. (2002). *Supporting the social dimension: Resource guide for teachers, grades 7–12.* Edmonton, AB: Author.

Alberta Learning. (2003). *Working together for safe and caring schools: Resource manual for students, staff and parents, grades 7–12.* Edmonton, AB: Author.

Alberta School Act, Section 45(8) (1999).

British Columbia Confederation of Parent Advisory Councils. (2003). *Call it safe: A parent guide for dealing with bullying in elementary schools.* Victoria, BC: Author.

British Columbia Ministry of Education. (1995). *Physical education k–7 integrated resource package.* Victoria, BC: Author.

British Columbia Ministry of Education. (1998). *Focus on bullying: A prevention program for elementary school communities*. Victoria, BC: Author.

British Columbia Ministry of Education. (2001). *Social responsibility: A framework*. Victoria, BC: Author.

British Columbia Ministry of Education. (2003). *Facing our fears—Accepting responsibility: Report of the safe schools task force. Bullying, harassment and intimidation in BC schools*. Victoria, BC: Author.

British Columbia Ministry of Education. (2004). *Safe, caring and orderly schools: A guide*. Victoria, BC: Author.

British Columbia School Act c.412, Section 6(b) (1996).

Canadian Association for Health, Physical Education, Recreation and Dance. (1998). *Positive environment: How to eliminate harassment and abuse from happening in your school*. Gloucester, ON: Author.

Canadian Public Health Association. (2005). *Bullying prevention in schools. National crime prevention strategy*. Ottawa, ON: Author.

Coloroso, B. (2002). *The bully, the bullied, and the bystander*. Toronto, ON: Harper Collins.

Doolittle, S. & Demas, K. (2001). Fostering respect through physical activity. *Journal of Physical Education, Recreation, & Dance, 72*(9), 28–33.

Fair Play Canada. (1995). Fair play for kids—A handbook of activities for teaching fair play (2nd ed.). Ottawa, ON: Author.

Gibbons, S.L. & Ebbeck, V. (1997). The effect of different teaching strategies on the moral development of physical education students. *Journal of Teaching in Physical Education, 17*, 85–98.

Gibbons, S.L., Ebbeck, V., & Weiss, M.R. (1995). Fair play for kids: Effects on moral development of children in physical education. *Research Quarterly for Exercise and Sport. 66*(3), 1–9.

Goyette, R., Doré, R., & Dion, É. (2000). Pupils' misbehaviors and the reactions and causal attributions of physical education teachers: A sequential analysis. *Journal of Teaching in Physical Education, 20*, 3–14.

Hawkins, D.L. Pepler, D., & Craig, W. (2001). Naturalistic observations of peer interventions in bullying among elementary school children. *Social Development, 10*, 512–527.

Hellison, D. (2003). *Teaching responsibility through physical activity* (2nd ed.). Champaign, IL: Human Kinetics.

Lavay, B.W., French, R., & Henderson, H.L. (2006). *Positive behavior management strategies for physical educators* (2nd ed.). Champaign, IL: Human Kinetics.

Manitoba Education and Training. (2000). *Manitoba curriculum framework of outcomes for active healthy lifestyles—Kindergarten–senior 4 physical education/health education*. Winnipeg, MB: Author.

New Brunswick Education. (2002). *The positive learning environment policy* (Policy 703). Fredericton, NB: Author.

Newfoundland & Labrador Department of Education. (2005). *Meeting behavioural challenges— creating safe and caring learning environments: A teacher resource*. St. John's, NL: Author.

Newfoundland & Labrador Department of Education. (2006). *Safe & caring schools policy*. St. John's, NL: Author.

Nova Scotia Department of Education. (2001). *School code of conduct*. Halifax, NS: Author.

Nova Scotia Education Act, 24 1, 1995–96.

Ontario Education Act, 13, c.12, s.3, 2000.

Ontario Ministry of Education. (2001). *Ontario schools code of conduct*. www.edu.gov.on.ca/eng/document/brochure/conduct.html.

Ontario Ministry of Education. (2005). *Shaping safer schools: A bullying prevention action plan*. Toronto, ON: Author.

Ontario Ministry of Education. (2006). *Safe schools policy and practice: An agenda for action*. Toronto, ON: Author.

Pellegrini, A.D. (2002). Bullying, victimization, and sexual harassment during the transition to middle school. *Educational Psychologist, 37*(3), 151–163.

Platt, K. & Fairholm, J. (2004). *Beyond the hurt: Preventing bullying* (2nd ed.). Vancouver, BC: Canadian Red Cross.

Rock Solid Foundation. (2004). *WITS: The rock solid primary program resource manual*. Victoria, BC: Author.

Safe, Healthy Schools. (2000). *Positive learning environments in schools: A Pan-Canadian consensus statement*. Retrieved January 19, 2007, from www.safehealthyschools.org/positivelearning/htm.

Saskatchewan Learning. (2004). *Caring and respectful schools: Toward school PLUS*. Regina, SK: Author.

Saskatchewan Learning. (2006). *Caring and respectful schools: Bullying prevention: A model policy*. Regina, SK: Author.

Siedentop, D. & Tannehill, D. (2000). *Developing teaching skills in physical education* (4th ed.). Mt. View, CA: Mayfield.

Van Gurp, H. (2002). *The peaceful school models that work*. Winnipeg, MB: Portage & Main Press.

 Weblinks

Safe, Healthy Schools: www.safehealthyschools.org/positivelearning.htm

This website includes the Pan-Canadian Consensus Statement for Positive Learning Environments in Schools.

Provincial Organizations for Safe, Caring Schools:
Alberta: www.learning.gov.ab.ca/safeschools

British Columbia: www.bced.gov.bc.ca/sco/resources.htm

Saskatchewan: www.leagueofpeacefulschools.sk.ca

Manitoba: www.safeschoolsmanitoba.ca

Ontario: www.edu.gov.on.ca/eng/teachers/safeschools.html

Newfoundland & Labrador:
www.gov.nf.ca/edu/dept/safesch.htm

Each website contains a variety of resources and programs designed to establish and maintain safe school learning environments. Topics include bullying prevention, anti-racism strategies, and violence prevention.

ProTeacher: www.proteacher.com/030000.shtml

This website includes a variety of strategies and resources to assist teachers in promoting positive behaviour. Information on classroom routines, conflict resolution, and codes of conduct is included.

Dr. Mac's Amazing Behaviour Management Advice Site: www.behavioradvisor.com

This website includes a wide range of resources and guidelines for promoting responsible behaviour. A bulletin board is available where you can post advice on behavioural challenges.

You Can Handle Them All: www.disciplinehelp.com

This website presents strategies for redirecting a wide range of inappropriate behaviours in more positive directions.

CHAPTER 6

Assessment and Evaluation of Student Learning

Essential Components

I	Organized around content standards
II	Student-centred and developmentally appropriate
III	Physical activity and motor skill development form the core of the program
IV	Teaches management skills and self-discipline
V	**Promotes inclusion of all students**
VI	**Focuses on process over product**
VII	Promotes lifetime personal health and wellness
VIII	Teaches cooperation and responsibility and promotes sensitivity to diversity

Physical Education Standards

1	Students are able to move competently using a variety of fundamental and specialized motor skills.
2	Students can monitor and maintain a health-enhancing level of physical fitness.
3	Students are able to apply movement concepts and basic mechanics of skill performance when learning and refining motor skills.
4	Students comprehend the basic principles of wellness and are able to apply concepts that enable them to make meaningful decisions that positively impact their health and wellness.
5	Students participate in a wide variety of physical activities and learn how to maintain a personalized active lifestyle.
6	Students demonstrate empathy, understanding, and respect for the numerous differences exhibited by people in an activity setting.
7	Students exhibit responsible and self-directed behaviours that lead to positive social interactions in physical activity.

OVERVIEW

Assessment and evaluation is done to increase learning and improve instruction. Ways to evaluate student learning include the use of checklists, logs, tests, authentic assignments, and rubrics. The use of portfolios and other student-centred assessment strategies enables students to be actively involved in the assessment process. Student progress reports and student-led conferences are useful approaches for helping parents understand their child's progress in physical education.

OUTCOMES

- Explain the relationship between assessment, evaluation, grading, and reporting.
- Explain the major purposes of evaluating student achievement.
- Cite a number of methods that can be used to assess psychomotor, cognitive, and affective learning outcomes in physical education.
- Explain effective methods for reporting student achievement.
- Define and explain the features of authentic assessment.
- Describe the nature and purpose of student portfolios.
- Differentiate between assessment *for* learning, assessment *as* learning, and assessment *of* learning.

The purpose of assessment and evaluation is to determine whether progress is being made toward learning
outcomes. To achieve this purpose effectively, the process of
assessment and evaluation should gather, interpret, and
communicate specific information to students, parents,
and teachers. An effective process not only documents
students' ongoing progress, but also provides guidance on
how each student might improve.

Major Concepts

To establish a framework for discussion, the following
definitions are provided. *Assessment* is the "systematic gathering of information about student learning, what they know,
are able to do, and are trying to do" (Ministry of Education,
1995, p. 125). In turn, *evaluation* involves the interpretation
of the information collected during assessment in order to
make a judgment as to the degree of progress made toward
an outcome. These two terms are intricately related and
are often used interchangeably. However, it is important to
distinguish between them. In short, assessment is the process
of *gathering* information, and evaluation involves *interpretation* and *judgment*. Fortunately, most effective assessment
tools (ways to gather information) are designed to provide
for easy and accurate evaluation, thus allowing evaluation to
occur at the same time as the information is gathered. For
example, an effective observation checklist for a skill will be
organized to differentiate between levels of achievement,
allowing teachers to judge (evaluate) each student's progress
(see Figure 6.6 on p. 102).

Following assessment and evaluation, the teacher
communicates the results in a meaningful way to students
and parents. This involves the completion of two complementary tasks. *Grading* involves the determination and
assignment of a meaningful value or symbol to the level of
student achievement. Common grading symbols in
Canadian schools include letter grades and numerical values
(such as percentages). In many instances, these symbols
(grades) are complemented by anecdotal comments. Finally,
reporting involves communicating the information gained
through assessment, evaluation, and grading to students
and parents. Reporting is most often done in writing and
scheduled conferences. The following sections will expand
on these definitions.

Assessment and Evaluation: Frequently Used Terminology

The reader should be familiar with *criterion-referenced*
evaluation and *norm-referenced* evaluation, as these terms
are frequently used to discuss the types of information

collected during the assessment and evaluation process.
Criterion-referenced evaluation methods (the most
common type of evaluation in physical education) compare
student performance to established criteria rather than
to the performance of other students. For example, when a
teacher uses a skill checklist with specific technique
cues to judge a student's skill, he or she is using a form
of criterion-referenced evaluation. Norm-referenced evaluation uses the comparison of a student's performance
to a similar reference group to judge achievement.
Standardized fitness tests provide an example of norm-
referenced evaluation in physical education. A student's
score on this type of fitness test will allow comparison
to a specific reference group (for example, norms on the
sit-and-reach test for Canadian 10-year-old girls). Norm-
referenced evaluations systems are most appropriate for
large-scale system analysis (a Canada-wide fitness test)
rather than classroom assessment. If these types of norms
are used in the classroom, they should be limited to
providing some general baselines and comparisons.

Summarizing the purposes of classroom assessment, the
*Western and Northern Canadian Protocol for Collaboration in
Education* (Manitoba Education, Citizenship and Youth,
2006) offers the following three concepts: (a) assessment *for*
learning, (b) assessment *of* learning, and (c) assessment *as*
learning. Assessment *for* learning (also called *formative*
assessment) refers to gathering data about student progress
throughout a unit of instruction in order to provide
meaningful feedback to students. In other words, formative
assessment provides students with information along the way
toward an outcome. In this process, the teacher helps
students decide what to work on, and where their strengths
are. Assessment *of* learning or *summative* assessment
provides the information as to the degree that learning
outcomes are achieved. Achievement denotes a student's
demonstration of knowledge/skills/attitudes relative to
expected learning outcomes. It answers the question "How
did the student do in the unit or course?" The final grade in
a unit or course is an example of assessment *of* learning.

Assessment *as* learning refers to the active involvement
of students in their own assessment (or self-assessment
and/or aspects of peer assessment). The intent of assessment *as* learning is to assist students toward becoming
self-sufficient learners. In other words, students reflect
upon and take responsibility for their own learning in
order to make adjustments and continue to improve.

Effective Assessment and Evaluation

As stated earlier, the gathering and interpretation of
information (assessment and evaluation) are crucial to
guiding students toward the achievement of learning

outcomes. To be effective, assessment and evaluation tools and procedures must be *valid* (measure what they are supposed to measure), *reliable* (be consistent), *feasible* (be realistic in terms of time, effort, and cost), and *fair* (give each student an equal opportunity to demonstrate his or her achievement). Teachers are constantly challenged to find a balance and compromise among these factors.

Authentic Assessment

In addition to the preceding factors, effective assessment and evaluation should be as meaningful as possible to the student and a realistic indication of their achievement and progress. This concept of providing meaning and realism for the student has contributed to the notion of "authentic assessment." Hensley (1997) suggests "assessment is said to be more authentic when the assessment task is designed to take place in a real-life setting, one that is less contrived and artificial" (pp. 19–20). This authenticity means that the task will be more meaningful to students and will provide a more realistic and accurate indication of their progress. In addition to the above-mentioned factors—validity, reliability, feasibility, and fairness—consider the following guidelines to make assessment as authentic as possible. Authentic assessment should

1. *Be regular and ongoing.* This will provide a truer indication of a student's progress over time and minimize the notion of a "one shot" test, where a student may do poorly on that particular day.

2. *Involve meaningful tasks and contexts.* For example, when assessing a student's physical skills, try to observe these skills in the context in which the skills are used (that is, during game play).

3. *Require a close connection between daily instructional tasks and assessment tasks.* In other words, the types of tasks students do when learning and practising in physical education should be very similar (if not identical) to tasks used for assessment purposes.

4. *Emphasize the active involvement of students in the assessment process.* Self-assessment as part of the concept of authenticity is emphasized as an ongoing process in which students get to know themselves as learners and take responsibility for their learning by reflecting on their own performance.

5. *Be comprehensive and use a variety of assessment methods.* Gathering information from a variety of sources and in a variety of ways provides for a realistic picture of student performance.

6. Involve an open line of communication between teacher, student, and parents.

Portfolios

Teachers can accomplish authentic assessment in many different ways. The use of portfolios has become a popular and effective method for elementary school teachers to achieve the positive outcomes in student learning associated with authentic assessment. Although used somewhat less frequently in physical education than in some other subjects, portfolios hold considerable promise as a method for helping teachers and students assess and evaluate the progress toward a variety of learning outcomes (see Figure 6.1).

Portfolio Possibilities for Physical Education

A portfolio is a purposeful and systematic gathering of student work that shows the student's effort, progress, or achievement over time (Ministry of Education, 1995). An effective portfolio can implement many of the concepts of authentic assessment. It should include a wide range of student work that is meaningful to both student and teacher. Collected over a period of time, the contents of a portfolio will allow for ongoing focus on individual improvement, effort, and achievement. In addition, the portfolio allows for the active involvement of students in the assessment process, in that they become aware of and accountable for their own learning in a very concrete way. In terms of communication, the contents of a portfolio provide a valuable starting point for the collaborative discussion between student and teacher. In many cases the portfolio can become the guide for reporting conferences. The Portfolio Entry Conference shown in Figure 6.2 is an example of such a conference guide.

Movement Skill Outcomes (Psychomotor Domain)

The two major tools for assessment and evaluation of movement skill learning outcomes (psychomotor domain) in elementary physical education are rubrics and skill checklists. Both tools are designed to allow teachers to observe movement skills and compare students' performance to predetermined criteria.

Rubrics

A rubric is a "set of clear expectations or criteria used to help teachers and students focus on what is valued in a subject, topic, or activity" (Airasian, 2000, p. 166). Rubrics define varied levels (from lower to higher) of accomplishment by identifying several characteristics associated with each level. The criteria are performance levels students are

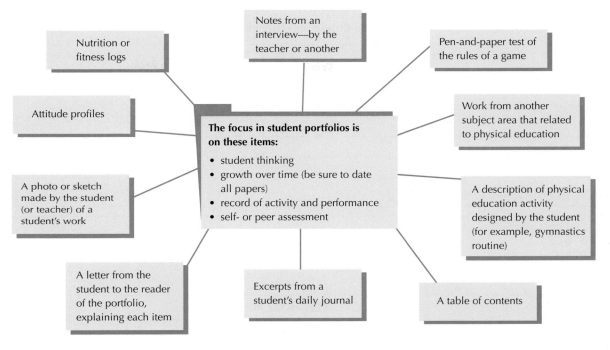

The focus in student portfolios is on these items:
- student thinking
- growth over time (be sure to date all papers)
- record of activity and performance
- self- or peer assessment

Nutrition or fitness logs

Notes from an interview—by the teacher or another

Pen-and-paper test of the rules of a game

Attitude profiles

Work from another subject area that related to physical education

A photo or sketch made by the student (or teacher) of a student's work

A description of physical education activity designed by the student (for example, gymnastics routine)

A letter from the student to the reader of the portfolio, explaining each item

Excerpts from a student's daily journal

A table of contents

Figure 6.1

Portfolios in physical education.

expected to achieve. In addition, the rubric includes a simple rating scale used to designate each level (see Figure 6.3).

A question common to most motor skill assessment is this: "Can the child perform the stated motor pattern using correct technique?" Teachers who employ this type of assessment require accurate knowledge of various learning stages so the child's pattern of development can be observed and categorized. Videotaping is useful for viewing the skill performance a number of times and in slow motion. For example, a 9-year-old youngster at the expected developmental level should be able to demonstrate stage 4 catching form. If a child of this age tests at stage 2, a developmental

---

Portfolio Entry Conference

Student Name: _____   Dates: _____

Project: _____

Student Comments:

Two reasons I chose this item are:

I want you to notice:

Next time I might:

Other comments:

Signature: _____ Date: _____

Teacher Comments:

Two positive things I noticed are:

One specific area to work on is:

Other comments:

Signature: _____ Date: _____

Figure 6.2

Portfolio entry conference.

Scoring Rubric for Catching Skills				
	Stage 1—Arms held out and ball trapped against body	Stage 2—Anticipatory movement made to catch ball	Stage 3—Contact made with the hands first	Stage 4—Catch with the hands absorbs the force of the ball
Students				
Mikal				
Kesha				
Lise				
Alex				

Figure 6.3

Form showing rubric for scoring ball-catching skills.

Game-Play Rubric for Softball	
What softball team should you be on?	*What best describes your playing ability?*
4 (Exceeds Expectations)	✓ I was always involved in the game and showed a tremendous amount of respect for others. ✓ I showed and applied my extensive knowledge of the rules during game play. ✓ I consistently demonstrated a high level of skill and completed no errors. ✓ I consistently demonstrated a high level of offensive strategy (batting and base running). ✓ I consistently demonstrated a high level of defensive strategy (catching, throwing, and field position).
3 (Fully Meets Expectations)	✓ I was usually involved in the game and showed a good level of respect for others. ✓ I showed and applied a good knowledge of the rules during game play. ✓ I consistently demonstrated a good level of skill and completed very few errors. ✓ I consistently demonstrated a good level of offensive strategy (batting and base running). ✓ I consistently demonstrated a good level of defensive strategy (catching, throwing, and field position).
2 (Minimally Meets Expectations)	✓ I was sometimes involved in the game and showed an adequate amount of respect for others. ✓ I showed and applied basic knowledge of the rules during game play. ✓ I consistently demonstrated a basic level of skill and completed some errors. ✓ I consistently demonstrated a basic level of offensive strategy (batting and base running). ✓ I consistently demonstrated a basic level of defensive strategy (catching, throwing, and field position).
1 (Not Yet Within Expectations)	✓ I was rarely involved in the game and showed a very little amount of respect for others. ✓ I showed and applied very little knowledge of the rules during game play. ✓ I consistently demonstrated a low level of skill and completed many errors. ✓ I consistently demonstrated a low level of offensive strategy (batting and base running). ✓ I consistently demonstrated a low level of defensive strategy (catching, throwing, and field position).

Figure 6.4

Softball game-play rubric.

deficiency is indicated. Figure 6.3 is an example of a scoring rubric for catching skills. This rubric lists the four stages of catching. Evaluation involves judging the student's ability to catch, and matching the degree of skill with these stages. A more in-depth explanation of design and use of rubrics is included in Personal and Social Responsibility Outcomes.

Rubrics may also be used for assessment and evaluation of "game play" skills that involve a complex interaction between a student's ability to perform the physical skills, and understanding and application of the strategic concepts that allow him or her to "play the game." The softball game play rubric in Figure 6.4 has been adapted from a generic game play scoring rubric. Note that the terminology on this rubric is worded directly to the student, which helps make this assessment tool not only valuable for the assessment *of* and *for* learning, but also includes assessment *as* learning. This more actively engages students in the learning outcomes included in the rubric. The rubric shown in Figure 6.5 provides further support for involving students in development of their game play skills and assessment of their own learning. Using the rubric to guide observation over several class periods, a teacher should be able to make a reasonable judgment of a student's game-play ability. This, coupled with scores on checklists of individual skills, will provide a clear picture of the progress of each student.

Skill Checklists

Another means of assessing and evaluating movement skill is use of a skill checklist. The teacher lists criteria governing proper technique for the movement pattern, and then checks the child's performance against these points. Limiting coverage to two or three of the critical points of technique is usually best. Ratings for each point can be on a 3-point scale: above developmental level, at developmental level, and below developmental level. These can be numbered 3, 2, and 1, respectively, providing a point scale for ease of recording. The record sheet can also be organized so achievement levels are listed, and the evaluator circles the appropriate number. Figure 6.6 is an example of a skill checklist for some of the fundamental locomotor skills. A slightly different checklist includes the specific and observable criteria. For example, use the same technique cues in the original skill demonstration on the checklist (see Figure 6.7). Where possible, also design the checklist for efficient recording (for example, all student names on a single sheet), and include space for anecdotal comments. This space allows teachers to record specific information about individual students.

Checklists have long been used as a system for summarizing and reporting progress to students and parents.

	Floor Hockey Game Play Self-Assessment 4 R's of Game Play—Check 4 Circles That Define Your Play
4 **Team Leader** (Exceeds Expectations)	○ **Read**—I create plays by interpreting the play ○ **React**—I am able to anticipate what is going to happen ○ **Respond**—My actions helped my team succeed ○ **Recover**—I ready for the next play and reading what is going on
3 **Part of the Team** (Fully Meets Expectations)	○ **Read**—I always see what is going to happen ○ **React**—I always move into the right space ○ **Respond**—I always interact with the play appropriately ○ **Recover**—I always fall back to cover my position and opponent
2 **Becoming a Team Player** (Minimally Meets Expectations)	○ **Read**—I usually see what is going to happen ○ **React**—I usually move into the right space ○ **Respond**—I usually interact with the play in the right way ○ **Recover**—I usually move back to cover my position and opponent
1 **Getting Started** (Not Yet Within Expectations)	○ **Read**—I miss what is happening in the game ○ **React**—I move to the wrong space ○ **Respond**—I rarely do the right play ○ **Recover**—I rarely move back into position or cover my opponentt

Figure 6.5

Involving Students in Game-Play Assessment.

(Adapted by John-Michael Gareau & Jon Lawrence)

Class _____   Grade _____   Date _____

Scoring:
  3 = above developmental level
  2 = at developmental level
  1 = below developmental level

Student's Name	Running			Jumping			Hopping			Skipping		
	Arm Action	Leg Action	Composite	Arm Action	Leg Action	Composite	Arm Action	Leg Action	Composite	Arm Action	Leg Action	Composite

Figure 6.6

Observation checklist for locomotor skills.

*Place 'X' in box for each cue performed.	Heading the ball 1. Contact ball on forehead 2. Lean into ball (flex at waist) 3. Head facing target				Dribbling (inside of foot) 1. Head up 2. Ball close to body 3. Head & body above ball				Shooting 1. Strike with instep (laces) 2. Non shooting foot beside ball 3. Keep head down & follow through			
Name of student	1	2	3	Comments	1	2	3	Comments	1	2	3	Comments

Figure 6.7

Soccer skills checklist.

Rope-jumping Checklist

Student		Jump in place	Jump, turn both ends	Jump, pendulum swing	Slow time	Fast time	Alternate-foot step	Swing step forward	Rocker step	Spread legs, forward	Toe-and-heel touch	Shuffle step	Cross arms	Cross arms, backward	Double jump	

Figure 6.8

Sample skill checklist.

A class roster with skills listed across the top of the sheet is a common method used for recording class progress. Checklists are usually most effective when skills are listed in the sequence in which they should be learned. In this way, you can gear the teaching process to diagnosed needs. To avoid disrupting the learning process, it is best to record student progress informally while students are practising. Figure 6.8 is a sample checklist for rope jumping.

Personal and Social Responsibility Outcomes (Affective Domain)

Teachers are responsible for the design of learning experiences to help students achieve a variety of personal and social responsibility outcomes (affective domain) in physical education. In turn, teachers assess and evaluate student learning associated with these outcomes. The design of valid, reliable, and practical assessment tools for personal and social responsibility outcomes provides a challenge to physical education teachers. The degree of subjectivity and variability often associated with many of these outcomes has made their assessment difficult. With the move toward authentic means of assessment in physical education,

rubrics have shown considerable promise and development as a productive assessment tool for identifying and clarifying criteria associated with personal and social outcomes (Lund, 2000; O'Sullivan & Henninger, 2000). A well-designed rubric has the potential to provide a valid, reliable, and practical learning and assessment option for these outcomes.

Rubrics

A rubric is particularly helpful in the assessment of personal and social outcomes in that it allows teachers to identify and organize often diverse and complex behaviours into an orderly framework. This helps to reduce subjectivity and potential misunderstanding. The following steps assist in the design of an effective rubric.

1. Identify and organize criteria associated with outcome

This step includes the formulation of a list of criteria that are to be judged, then placing them into various levels of performance. This is undoubtedly the most difficult task associated with the design of rubrics! One way to approach this process is to describe what you see in students performing at a particular level. For example, in Figure 6.9 "Team Captain"(Level 4) describes what we would expect to see from a PE student at the highest level for personal

	Personal and Social Responsibility Outcomes **Today I was . . .**
4 **Team Captain!** (Exceeds Expectations)	• on time and dressed appropriately • on task and tried my best • demonstrated positive behaviours that show respect for my classmates and teacher • played safe, fair, and hard all of the time
3 **Team Player!** (Fully Meets Expectations)	• on time and dressed appropriately • usually on task and tried my best usually • demonstrated positive behaviours that show respect for my classmates and teacher most of the time • played safe, fair, and hard most of the time
2 **In the Game!** (Minimally Meets Expectations)	• on time and dressed appropriately • sometimes on task and tried my best some of the time • demonstrated positive behaviours that show respect for classmates and teacher some of the time • played safe, fair, and hard some of the time
1 **Getting Started** (Not Yet Within Expectations)	• late and/or inappropriately dressed • on task minimally and did not try my best • rarely demonstrated positive behaviours that show respect for my classmates and teacher • rarely played safe, fair, and hard

Figure 6.9

General personal and social responsibility rubric: four levels.

and social responsibility learning outcomes. Conversely, "Getting Started"(Level 1) describes a participant at a level that is below an acceptable standard. To make a rubric a practical tool, consider using three to five performance levels, with a limited number of criteria (four to five) for each level.

To avoid having to create a new rubric for every outcome in each activity, try to create a generic rubric that identifies the general behaviours associated with acceptable participation and effort in physical education (often a general curriculum outcome). This sort of rubric may then be adapted to all activities (see Figures 6.9 and 6.10).

In addition to these general expectations, some activity-specific outcomes may be added. This allows the teacher to highlight different personal and social outcomes in particular activities, as well as continue with the general expectations.

2. Involve students in design process

One of the most productive aspects of a well-designed rubric is that it can assist students to monitor their own progress and that of their peers. With the concept of

personal accountability so predominant throughout personal and social outcomes, a rubric can be a learning tool as well as an assessment tool. It is helpful to involve students in the design of the rubric. Not only will they become more familiar with the criteria—both its meaning and importance—but also students have the opportunity to take more ownership and responsibility for their own behaviour if they have been involved in the process. Input from students will also allow the criteria to be defined in student-friendly terms, making it easier for them to understand and discuss. The examples of rubrics in Figures 6.9 and 6.10 are designed for students in intermediate grades. Terminology for younger students should be consistent with their level of understanding and reading ability.

3. Hold students accountable for learning

Equally important is the strong link between instruction and assessment in order to establish a valid means of assessment. Using the defined criteria and levels in the rubric not only clarifies expectations for students, but also gives teachers an important guide for designing appropriate

I am a star student	• I showed up early for class, in my PE clothes, and helped set up the equipment. • I showed respect for my classmates and my teacher. • I put in maximal effort when playing and was always on task. • I always played fair, followed the rules, and shared gym space and equipment. • I had the best possible attitude and was always encouraging others.
I am a high performer	• I was on time for class and in PE clothes. • I consistently showed respect for my classmates and my teacher. • I put in a very good effort when playing and was most often on task. • I was most often playing fair, following the rules, and sharing gym space and equipment. • I had a very positive attitude and encouraged others often.
I am doing a good job today	• I was on time for class and in PE clothes. • I showed respect for my classmates and my teacher. • I put in good effort when playing and was usually on task. • I usually played fair, followed the rules, and shared gym space and equipment. • I had a positive attitude and encouraged others.
I need to tighten up my shoelaces	• I was late for class and/or did not have PE clothes. • I sometimes showed respect for my classmates and teacher. • I put in some effort when asked by the teacher and was not always on task. • I sometimes played fair, followed the rules, and shared gym space and equipment. • I sometimes had a positive attitude and rarely encouraged others.
We need to talk	• I was late for class and/or did not have PE clothes. • I never showed respect for my classmates or my teacher. • I put in no effort when playing and was rarely on task. • I did not follow the rules, and did not share gym space or equipment. • My attitude was not acceptable and I never encouraged others.

Figure 6.10

General personal and social responsibility rubric: five levels.

learning experiences. Rubrics are shared with the students from day one to describe the expectations in the major outcome areas. In PE, teachers refer to the rubrics on a regular basis in informal conversations with students, asking them to reflect on and indicate their current performance relative to one or more items on the rubric. If their performance is less than desirable, they are asked to indicate what they need to do to move up to the next standard (or higher). Rubrics also provide a guide to help students become more articulate and reflective in discussing their own achievement based on the criteria. Students ultimately take more responsibility for their actions and learning, as they are aware of the expectations. The rubrics may be posted on the physical education bulletin board and are always present during parent–teacher–student interviews. Rubrics provide an important tool to increase consistency in assessment of student performance. Rubrics help to objectify what is required and expected. There is no "mystery marking"; students, teachers, and parents know the expectations and how students are progressing on an ongoing basis.

Try to make the rubric "memorable" for both students and teacher. For example, do the different levels have titles that are easy to remember and comfortable to discuss? (See Figures 6.9 and 6.10). These friendly titles make the rubric a part of the daily class environment and provide an alternative to the focus on the numbers associated with each level. These titles can also provide a quality of gentle humour, which may be particularly helpful when encouraging students who are struggling in the lower levels. Consider using these title phrases to open discussion with a student.

Rubrics are designed to be regular and consistent over time, and in this way can guide both instruction and assessment. The rubric becomes integrated with the day-to-day class activities. However, it often takes some time for both teacher and students to become comfortable with their use. Especially where an aspect of self-assessment (a valuable learning strategy for many personal and social outcomes) is included, considerable time and guidance may be required to help each student develop the skills and confidence to assess his or her behaviour accurately.

Anecdotal Record Sheet

Class _____ *Ms. Massoney* _____   Date _____ *2/14* _____

Bob: Is making progress on the backward jump. Sent a jump rope home with him for practice.

Gene: Seems to be discouraged about rope jumping. Called parents to see if there is a problem outside of school.

Linda: Discussed the need for helping others. She is going to be a cross-aged tutor for next two weeks, as her performance in batting is excellent.

Figure 6.11

Sample anecdotal record sheet.

Anecdotal Record Sheets

A record sheet that contains student names and has room for comments about student behaviour can be used to assess student progress toward a variety of personal and social learning outcomes. Anecdotal records of student progress can be reinforcing to both student and teacher, as it is often difficult to remember how much progress has been made over a period of time. A rubric listing specific criteria is a helpful guide for recording anecdotal comments.

Comments can be recorded during observation. This process can help you learn the names and behaviour patterns of students and can lead to an increased understanding of student performance. Observations should be recorded throughout the unit as instruction proceeds. A sample anecdotal record sheet is illustrated in Figure 6.11.

Student Self-assessment

Students in the intermediate grades are capable of self-assessment. The ability to assess oneself is an important outcome of any effective program. With the use of learning outcomes as guides, students can begin to set some personal goals and develop action plans for their own progress. The process of setting realistic goals, developing plans to reach these goals, and assessing the outcome is an important learning outcome in and of itself! Figure 6.12 shows a general type of goal-setting form that can become a regular part of the student portfolio.

Peer Assessment

Peer assessment tasks provide exciting possibilities for enhancing student learning in a number of different ways. There are potential benefits for both the student who is being assessed and the student who is doing the assessing. Benefits

---

Goal-setting Action Planner

Student Name: _____   Date: _____

My goal:

Steps to attain my goal:

Timeline for achieving my goal:

People and resources that I might need to achieve my goal:

How I will know when my goal is achieved:

How I will celebrate achieving my goal:

Figure 6.12

Student goal-setting planner.

Source: Copyright © 1995 Province of British Columbia. All rights reserved. Reprinted with permission of the Province of British Columbia.

for the former include receiving from a fellow learner helpful feedback that will improve subsequent performances. The student providing the feedback will benefit by improving

~ Gymnastics ~

Peer Assessment of Individual Routines

Judge's Name: _____   Gymnast's Name: _____

Date: _____

* Did your partner perform the following skills within his or her routine? Put a ✔ in the box as they complete **at least one** of the skills in **each of the required categories.**

* **beginning pose** (v-sit, knee-scale, star, tuck)	
* **forward roll** (straddle roll, straight-leg roll, shoulder roll)	
* **backward roll** (straddle roll, straight-leg roll, shoulder roll)	
* **1 turn & jump** (half turn, full turn, star jump, tuck jump)	
* **balance** (handstand, headstand, teddy bear stand, stork stand)	
* **end pose** (v-sit, knee-scale, star, tuck)	
Add up the total number of ✔ and write the total here:	/6

Two Stars...

Describe two things you liked about the routine

* **Two stars and a Wish!** After your partner has finished, evaluate their performance. Write two "stars" and one wish that will give your partner some constructive feedback.

A Wish...

Something they could do that would make the routine even better!

Figure 6.13

Gymnastics peer assessment.

observation skills (knowledge). In both cases, the students also benefit by simply learning to work together and share in a positive way (personal and social responsibility). In Figure 6.13, several young teachers (Andrea Hughes, Kris Van Wieren, and Shawna Horpestad) adapted the Two Stars and a Wish strategy in a peer assessment tool for intermediate gymnastics routines. This peer assessment form provides specific guidance for the assessor by guiding the observation of specific skills (see instructions to the judge in Figure 6.13), and then asks the assessor to provide some positive and constructive feedback to the performer in the form of "two stars and a wish." This tool also shows how students can be actively involved in productive formative assessment. A peer assessor is not pressured to "grade" the performance, but simply provides productive feedback to help the performer improve (assessment *for* learning [formative]).

Figure 6.14 further expands the notion of assessment *for* learning and *as* learning by providing guidance for both the student performing the skills (participant) and the student observing the skill (assessor). For both students,

---

Partner Activity: Orienteering

Name of Participant: _____

Name of Assessor: _____

In the box provided, place a checkmark (☑) if your partner performs the skill consistently (C), Sometimes (S), or Never (N).

Attack! (the use of attack points): Orienteering

Cues:	C	S	N
1. Chooses an attack point.	☐	☐	☐
2. Chosen attack point is easy to find.	☐	☐	☐
3. The control can be seen from the attack point.	☐	☐	☐

Give your partner two stars and a wish!

☆ _____

☆ _____

❞ _____

Which Way? (the use of a compass): Orienteering

Cues:	C	S	N
1. Holds the map horizontally.	☐	☐	☐
2. Places the compass flat on the map.	☐	☐	☐
3. Keeps the compass oriented to the north lines on the map.	☐	☐	☐

Give your partner two stars and a wish!

☆ _____

☆ _____

❞ _____

Figure 6.14

Peer assessment—example of assessment *as* learning.

(Adapted by Jelena Burgess)

learning is happening (assessment for learning *for* the participant and assessment *as* learning for the assessor).

Student Logs

Intermediate-grade youngsters are capable of maintaining a log that indicates progress toward a goal over time. Assume students want to increase the amount of physical activity they accomplish each day. The teacher and students could discuss some goals that would help them become more active. Another approach is to ask students to develop behaviours they need to accomplish to reach their goals. The log should include goal behaviours they have accomplished over time—including decisions and choices made, time spent on goal behaviours, and a reflection area to record their perceptions of the experience (see Figure 6.15). Students can share the details of activities they have tried, as well as their experiences and feelings about them.

Knowledge Outcomes (Cognitive Domain)

The two major tools for assessment and evaluation of knowledge learning outcomes (cognitive domain) in elementary physical education are written quizzes and assignments. Knowledge outcomes most often complement movement skill outcomes (i.e., rules, strategic concepts, and fitness concepts).

Written Quizzes

Teachers may administer written quizzes to check the cognitive learning that has accompanied physical skill learning. The tests can be true–false or multiple choice for ease of correction. On the other hand, short answer or essay questions encourage students to apply knowledge to a variety of

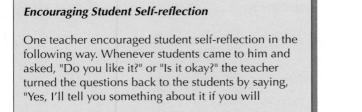

Encouraging Student Self-reflection

One teacher encouraged student self-reflection in the following way. Whenever students came to him and asked, "Do you like it?" or "Is it okay?" the teacher turned the questions back to the students by saying, "Yes, I'll tell you something about it if you will

* tell me two things that you like about it."
* tell me your two stars and a wish about your work."
* tell me what is important to you."
* tell me one piece of advice that you would give someone else working on a similar project."

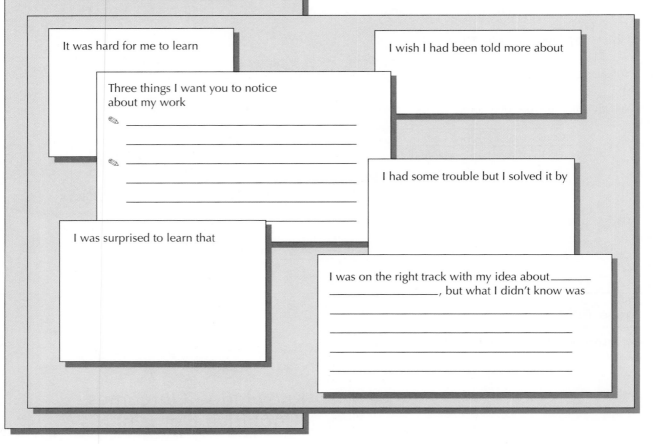

It was hard for me to learn

I wish I had been told more about

Three things I want you to notice about my work

I had some trouble but I solved it by

I was surprised to learn that

I was on the right track with my idea about _____ _____, but what I didn't know was

Figure 6.15

Encouraging student reflection.

Source: *Together is Better: Collaborative Assessment, Evaluation and Reporting*, by Anne Davies, Caren Cameron, Colleen Politano, and Kathleen Gregory. © Winnipeg: Peguis Publishers, 1992. Reprinted with permission.

situations. Where possible, consider authentic questions that allow students to demonstrate their knowledge in a meaningful context. For example, in "Make the Call in Volleyball" (see Figure 6.16), the student must show knowledge of volleyball rules and game procedures by keeping score in a hypothetical game. In this way the student must be able to both know and interpret rules in a "real life" context. When writing tests, consider the reading level of students. A student may be unable to demonstrate his or her knowledge if limited by reading ability. Oral presentation of questions is often best for younger students.

Assignments

A wide range of assignments may be used in physical education. For example, assignments may be structured as

Make the Call in Volleyball

Cadboro Bay Elementary and Royal Oak Elementary are involved in a thrilling final match for the city championships. It is two minutes before game time and the referee still has not shown up. Having just finished taking a volleyball unit, you joke that you will step in. Surprisingly, they accept. Now you have to "make the call."

CADBORO BAY 0 ROYAL OAK 0

Scenario 1
The score is 5–4 Royal Oak. Cadboro Bay serves the ball to Royal Oak, who returns the ball with a winning hit. The ball lands on the Cadboro Bay court. The new score is:

CADBORO BAY _____   ROYAL OAK _____

Scenario 2
The score is 8–5 Cadboro Bay. Royal Oak serves the ball to Cadboro Bay. Cadboro Bay makes two good passes and sets up for a hit. Royal Oak goes up for the block and in doing so crosses the plane of the net but does not touch the net and successfully blocks the ball. The block did not interfere with the hit. As referee you call a point. The new score is:

CADBORO BAY _____   ROYAL OAK _____

Scenario 3
The score is tied 10–10. Royal Oak having just served has assumed a defensive formation. Cadboro Bay on their third hit plays the ball over the net and it bounces off the knee of a Royal Oak player and back into the Cadboro Bay court, landing in bounds. As a ref you call a point. The new score is:

CADBORO BAY _____   ROYAL OAK _____

Scenario 4
Both teams are tired as the score is 20–19 with Cadboro Bay in the lead. The Royal Oak server plays a beautiful serve over the net where Cadboro Bay passes it into the net. A front row player for Cadboro Bay kicks the ball over the net before it hits the ground and it lands on the back line of the Royal Oak court. The crowd looks confused and the Royal Oak team looks confused. Make the call! The new score is:

CADBORO BAY _____   ROYAL OAK _____

Scenario 5
The score is 24–23 Cadboro Bay. Royal Oak is receiving the serve from Cadboro Bay. It is a high floater and as a Cadboro Bay player is turning to watch the ball, she brushes up against the net. Seeing that a Cadboro Bay player has touched the net, the Royal Oak receiver doesn't bother to make a play on the ball and it lands dead in the centre of the court. Royal Oak celebrates, thinking they are still in the game. Cadboro Bay celebrates, thinking they just won. Make the call! The new score is:

CADBORO BAY _____   ROYAL OAK _____

Figure 6.16

Include authentic questions to test knowledge.

informal questions: "Why do you think your heart beats faster when you exercise? See what you can find out for next class," to more formal research projects for students in the intermediate grades. As with written quizzes, also consider authentic tasks or questions that allow students to demonstrate their knowledge in a meaningful context. For example, if you are teaching intermediate students about rules and scorekeeping in basketball, as an assessment option students might assist in scorekeeping duties during a home game, with the guidance of a trained scorekeeper. To receive credit, students would have the official scorekeeper sign their scorekeeping sheet.

Grading

The purpose of a grade is to provide a meaningful symbol that represents a student's progress toward an outcome. In turn, an effective grading system must be easily understood and interpreted by parents and students.

There is wide variation in physical education grading policies in elementary schools, ranging from no assignment of grades to using letter grades similar to high school classes. Generally, grading policies across all subject areas are established at the ministry level in each province/territory. For example, in British Columbia, criterion-referenced letter grades are required in grades 4 to 12 to indicate students' levels of performance as they relate to the expected learning outcomes set out in provincial guides for each subject or course and grade. No letter grades are required for kindergarten to grade 3. Letter grades will appear on report cards in grades 4 to 7 unless the district chooses an alternative way of communicating to parents (Policy for Reporting Student Progress in British Columbia, 2005). Letter grades alone tell parents very little about the performance of their youngsters in physical education. Learning outcomes and anecdotal comments to accompany the letter grade provide parents with more information and help to communicate the goals of the program. The reader is encouraged to examine specific grading policies and procedures for her or his respective province/territory.

Reporting Student Progress: What, When, How?

In general, a teacher has three general responsibilities with regard to reporting on student progress. First, teachers must follow provincial/territorial legislation and policy for reporting on student progress. These policies will differ slightly within each provincial/territorial ministry of education and in some cases, where the policies allow for choice, from district to district. Second, teachers must provide parents with complete, easily understood, and accurate evaluations of their children's performance based on the provincial/territorial curriculum learning outcomes. And third, teachers must indicate in relation to these expected learning outcomes what each student is able to do, the areas in which the student requires further attention or development, and ways of supporting the student in his learning (Policy for Reporting Student Progress in British Columbia, 2005).

Learning Outcomes (What)

Learning outcomes (LO) provide the basis for the content of student progress reports. These outcomes describe what a student is expected to know and do as a result of active participation in the learning experiences designed by the teacher.

Learning outcomes in physical education are identified in provincial/territorial curriculum guides using a variety of different organizational frameworks. For example, in British Columbia, physical education prescribed learning outcomes (PLO) are grouped under three curriculum organizers: active living, movement, and personal and social responsibility. Similarly, the Manitoba physical education/health education curriculum groups outcomes in the following five categories: movement, fitness management, safety, social and personal management, and healthy lifestyle practices. The Alberta physical education curriculum is grouped in four general outcomes—the ABCDs of physical education for life: A—Activity, B—Benefits to Health, C—Cooperation, and D—Do it Daily. In each case, within these categories, learning outcomes are further delineated by grade level (for example, "A student in grade 4 will be able to . . . ").

Frequency and Format of Reporting (When and How)

Provincial and territorial regulations for reporting student progress provide minimum requirements for both frequency and format. For example, in British Columbia reporting regulations require that parents be provided with a minimum of the following:

- Three formal written report cards (on a form approved by the Ministry of Education)
- Two informal reports each school year—teachers determine how they will communicate informally with parents (telephone calls, interim reports [written or oral], conferences [parent–teacher, three-way, student-led])

The reader is encouraged to examine specific reporting policies and procedures for his or her respective province/territory. In addition to specifying frequency of reporting, provincial/territorial policies also provide guidelines for the type of information that must be shared with students and parents. For example, in British Columbia comments in a structured written progress report describe, in relation to curriculum, the following:

- What the student is able to do
- Areas of learning that require further attention or development
- Ways the teacher is supporting the student's learning needs
- Comments (written or oral) about student progress with reference to the expected development for students in a similar age range
- Written comments to describe student behaviour, including information on attitudes, work habits, and effort

Conferences

In recent years, traditional parent–teacher conferences where the teacher reports a student's progress to parents have evolved to allow for more collaboration among teacher, student, and parent(s). In some cases conferences may involve a three-way meeting of teacher, parent(s), and student to discuss the student's learning. Figure 6.17 shows an example of a typical guide for a three-way conference.

Portfolios may also play an important role in guiding conferences. This may be a two-way conference between teacher and student as in the example of the Portfolio Entry Conference in Figure 6.2 on p. 99, or may be a student-led conference, in which the student uses the types of questions and comments shown in Figure 6.18, Conference Guide for Students.

CONFERENCE GUIDE FOR TEACHERS

Student's Name: _____   Date: _____

Areas of strength	Areas needing improvement
Notes for the conference	Additional notes

Action Plan
Goal:

Student will…	Teacher will…	Parent will…

Other notes:

Figure 6.17

Conference guide for teachers.

Source: *Together is Better: Collaborative Assessment, Evaluation and Reporting,* by Anne Davies, Caren Cameron, Colleen Politano, and Kathleen Gregory. © Winnipeg: Peguis Publishers, 1992. Reprinted with permission.

CONFERENCE GUIDE FOR STUDENTS	
Student's Name: _____	Date: _____

Things I am really good at…

Two things I need to improve…

Things to show…

My next term goal is…

Figure 6.18

Conference guide for students.

Source: Together is Better: Collaborative Assessment, Evaluation and Reporting, by Anne Davies, Caren Cameron, Colleen Politano, and Kathleen Gregory. © Winnipeg: Peguis Publishers, 1992. Reprinted with permission.

Critical Thinking

1. Brainstorm as many purposes for assessment in physical education as possible. Try to group your responses into assessment *for* learning, assessment *of* learning, and assessment *as* learning. Which grouping is the largest? Smallest? Why?

References and Suggested Readings

Airasian, P. (2000). *Assessment in the classroom—A concise approach* (2nd ed.). Boston: McGraw-Hill.

Alberta Assessment Consortium. (1997). *A framework for student assessment.* Edmonton, AB: Author.

Alberta Assessment Consortium. (1999). *A framework for communicating student learning.* Edmonton, AB: Author.

Alberta Assessment Consortium. (2001a). *How to . . . develop and use performance assessments in the classroom.* Edmonton, AB: Author.

Alberta Assessment Consortium. (2001b). *Smerging data: Grading . . . more than just number crunching.* Edmonton, AB: Author.

Alberta Education. (2005). *Guide to education.* Edmonton, AB: Author.

Alberta Learning. (2003). *Classroom assessment toolkit: 1–6.* www.education.gov.ab.ca/k_12/curriculum/bysubject/ict/div1_2.pdf

British Columbia Ministry of Education. (1994a). *Performance assessment.* Victoria, BC: Author.

British Columbia Ministry of Education. (1994b). *Portfolio assessment.* Victoria, BC: Author.

British Columbia Ministry of Education. (1994c). *Student-centered conferences.* Victoria, BC: Author.

British Columbia Ministry of Education. (1994d). *Student self-assessment.* Victoria, BC: Author.

British Columbia Ministry of Education. (1995). *K–7 Physical education integrated resource package.* Victoria, BC: Author.

British Columbia Ministry of Education. (2005). *Policy for reporting student progress in British Columbia.* Victoria, BC: Author.

Cone, T. & Cone, S. (2005). *Assessing dance in elementary physical education.* Reston, VA: National Association for Sport and Physical Education.

Davies, A., Cameron, C, Politano, C., & Gregory, K. (1992). Together is better: *Collaborative assessment, evaluation and reporting.* Winnipeg, MB: Peguis Publishers.

Earl, L. (2003). *Assessment as learning: Using classroom assessment to maximize student learning.* Thousand Oaks, CA: Corwin.

Easley, S. & Mitchell, K. (2003). *Portfolios matter: what, where, when, why and how to use them.* Markham, ON: Pembroke.

Gallo, A.M. (2004). 5 simple steps to designing a rubric. *Strategies, 15*(5), 21–24.

Gibbons, S.L., Anderson, E., Balzer, J., Baylis, J., Bohemier, D., Duke, D., Duyndam, J., & Soon, G. (2004). Making every question count: Designing authentic quizzes for physical education. *Physical and Health Education Journal, 70*(2), 4–12.

Gibbons, S.L., & Robinson, B.A. (2005). Student-friendly rubrics for personal and social learning in physical education. *Physical and Health Education Journal, 70*(4), 4–9.

Giles-Brown, L. (2006). *Physical education assessment toolkit.* Champaign, IL: Human Kinetics.

Hensley, L. (1997). Alternative assessment for physical education. *JOPERD, 68*(7), 19–24.

Hopple, C. (2005). *Elementary physical education teaching & assessment.* Champaign, IL: Human Kinetics.

Johnson, R. (2004). Peer assessments in physical education. *Journal of Physical Education, Recreation & Dance, 75*(8), 33–40.

Lambert, L.T. (1999). *Standards-based assessment of student learning: A comprehensive approach.* Reston, VA: National Association for Sport and Physical Education.

Lund, J. (1997). Authentic assessment: Its development & application. *JOPERD, 68*(7), 25–28, 40.

Lund, J. (2000). *Creating rubrics for physical education.* Reston, VA: National Association for Sport and Physical Education.

Manitoba Education, Citizenship and Youth. (2006). *Rethinking classroom assessment with purpose in mind: assessment for learning, assessment as learning, assessment of learning. Western and Northern Canadian Protocol for Collaboration in Education.* www.wncp.ca.

Markos, N. (2007). *Self-and peer-assessment for elementary school physical education programs.* Reston, VA: National Association for Sport and Physical Education.

Melograno, V.J. (2006). *Professional and student portfolios for physical education* (2nd ed.). Champaign, IL: Human Kinetics.

Newfoundland & Labrador Department of Education. (2000). *The evaluation of students in the classroom: A handbook and policy guide* (2nd ed.). St. John's, NL: Division of Evaluation, Testing & Certification.

Northwest Territories Education, Culture and Employment. (2001). *Educating all our children: Departmental directive on student assessment, evaluation and reporting.* Yellowknife, NWT: Author.

Ontario Ministry of Education and Training. (1998). *Guide to the provincial report card, grades 1–8.* Toronto, ON: Author.

O'Sullivan, M. & Henninger, M. (2000). *Assessing student responsibility and teamwork.* Reston, VA: National Association for Sport and Physical Education.

Principles for fair student assessment practices for education in Canada. (1993). Edmonton, AB: Joint Advisory Committee, Centre for Research in Applied Measurement and Evaluation, University of Alberta, Edmonton, Alberta.

Quebec English Schools Network. (2003). *Portfolio process.* www.learnquebec.ca/en/

Robinson, B.A. & Turkington, H.D. (1994). Do you involve students in the assessment of student performance in physical education? *Canadian Association for Health, Physical Education, Recreation and Dance Journal, 60*(2), 18–22.

Saskatchewan Education. (1991). *Student evaluation: A teacher handbook.* Regina, SK: Author.

Saskatchewan Learning. (2003). *Portfolios: More than just a file folder.* Regina, SK: Saskatchewan Professional Development Unit.

Schiemer, S. (1999). *Authentic assessment strategies for elementary physical education* (2nd ed.). Champaign, IL: Human Kinetics.

Smith, T.K. (1997). Authentic assessment: Using a portfolio card in physical education. *JOPERD, 86*(4), 46–52.

Steffen, J. & Grosse, S. (2003). *Assessment in outdoor adventure physical education.* Reston, VA: National Association for Sport and Physical Education.

Stiggins, R. (2001). *Student-involved classroom assessment.* Upper Saddle River, NJ: Prentice-Hall.

 Weblinks

Quebec English Schools Network: www.learnquebec.ca/en/

This website provides a wide range of resources to support both students and teachers in the portfolio formulation process. Includes extensive bibliography.

Electronic Portfolio Resources: www.uvm.edu/~jmorris/ecresources.html

This website includes information developing on electronic portfolios for a variety of grade levels.

Alberta Assessment Consortium: www.aac.ab.ca

The Alberta Assessment Consortium is a not-for-profit organization dedicated to enhancing student learning through effective classroom assessment. Provides information on a wide range of assessment resources and workshops for teachers.

CHAPTER 7

Children with Special Needs

Essential Components

I	**Organized around content standards**
II	**Student-centred and developmentally appropriate**
III	Physical activity and motor skill development form the core of the program
IV	Teaches management skills and self-discipline
V	**Promotes inclusion of all students**
VI	**Focuses on process over product**
VII	Promotes lifetime personal health and wellness
VIII	**Teaches cooperation and responsibility and promotes sensitivity to diversity**

Physical Education Standards

1	**Students are able to move competently using a variety of fundamental and specialized motor skills.**
2	Students can monitor and maintain a health-enhancing level of physical fitness.
3	Students are able to apply movement concepts and basic mechanics of skill performance when learning and refining motor skills.
4	Students comprehend the basic principles of wellness and are able to apply concepts that enable them to make meaningful decisions that positively impact their health and wellness.
5	Students participate in a wide variety of physical activities and learn how to maintain a personalized active lifestyle.
6	**Students demonstrate empathy, understanding, and respect for the numerous differences exhibited by people in an activity setting.**
7	Students exhibit responsible and self-directed behaviours that lead to positive social interactions in physical activity.

OVERVIEW

Contemporary classrooms are diverse; and differences are to be expected, respected, and planned for. In this chapter the concept of inclusion is discussed and processes and procedures associated with inclusion are explained. A program planning model to address the needs of students with special needs is introduced. The model suggests that the core curriculum is the starting point for educational planning for students with special needs. The next step is to gather information about the student and the student's needs. Relevant health, medical, educational, and behavioural information will be part of the student's individual education plan; however teachers should also consider physical education–specific information. When necessary, adaptations can be made to equipment, the environment (curriculum and instructions modifications), and how personnel are used. Both general principles and disability-specific ideas to address students' needs are presented in this chapter.

OUTCOMES

- Describe the principle of inclusion and the legislative framework for inclusion in Canada.

- Articulate the process of developing an individual education plan (IEP).

- Explain the concept of individualization and how to develop an individualized approach to physical education.

- List guidelines for successful inclusion of students.

- Describe ways to modify the environment and equipment for inclusion; and the potential roles for peer tutors, teacher's assistants, and volunteers as instructional assistants.

- Describe characteristics of specific disabilities and ways to modify learning experiences in physical education to accommodate students with disabilities.

It is estimated that 155,000 Canadian children between 5 and 14 years old (4% of all children in this age group), have some form of disability (Human Resources and Social Development Canada, 2006). Accordingly, contemporary classrooms are diverse. Student diversity includes difference in culture, heritage, language, abilities, and needs. Differences are to be expected, respected, and planned for (Saskatchewan Learning, 2002).

Inclusive education values diversity and is based on the principle that all students are entitled to equitable access to learning, achievement, and the pursuit of excellence in all aspects of their education. Equal access does not mean treating everyone the same. In practice, equal access often means treating students differently depending on their needs and overcoming barriers to learning so that students can truly access education. The Manitoba Education, Citizenship and Youth (2006, p. 1) definition of inclusion is indicative of how inclusion is viewed in Canadian education:

[Inclusion is] a way of thinking and acting that allows every individual to feel accepted, valued and safe. An inclusive community consciously evolves to meet the changing needs of its members. Through recognition and support, an inclusive community provides meaningful involvement and equal access to the benefits of citizenship.

This principle of inclusion goes beyond simple physical location (integration) and extends to basic values that promote participation, friendship, and interaction. This does not mean, however, that students with special needs will necessarily spend all of their time in an integrated setting. Resource rooms, community-based training facilities, or other specialized classrooms or settings might also be appropriate. However, in all educational jurisdictions in Canada, these alternatives are pursued only after all reasonable efforts to integrate have been exhausted, and always with a view to returning students to an integrated setting as soon as is feasible.

The main beliefs underpinning the principle of inclusion have been summarized by Tripp, Piletic, and Babcock (2004, pp. 8–9) as:

Social Justice: All people have equal value and each person has a right to an equal share of the services and materials available.

Equal Opportunity: All people have the right to be treated equally, to have choices and to take risks. No person should be discriminated against; neither should rules or conditions exist that make it more difficult for some people to participate than others.

Non-categorization: People are individuals with many things in common and some things different. There is no such thing as a "category" of people that are all the same.

Non-segregation: People need contact with a variety of people; this helps us all understand about various ways of life and allows us to make choices with greater awareness.

Legislative Framework for Inclusion

Each province and territory constructs its own set of policies, procedures, and guidelines that provide a framework for educating children with special needs. These documents have been written to be in accordance with the Canadian Charter of Rights and Freedoms (1982) (see Table 7.1) and jurisdictional codes of human rights. For example, the Saskatchewan Human Rights Code (1979) stipulates the right to an education in any school, institution, or place of learning, without discrimination. Specific rights and responsibilities related to education and education of students with special needs are defined in legislation and ministerial directives. In the Northwest Territories, Section 7(1) of the Education Act (1996) is titled Inclusive Schooling and states that "every student is entitled to have access to the education program in a regular instructional setting" and the British Columbia School Act "requires that school boards make available educational programs to all school-age residents of that district." In addition, Ministerial Order 150/89, Amended by M32/04 [BC] requires school boards to provide "a student with special needs with an educational program in a classroom where that student is integrated with other students who do not have special needs." (BC Ministry of Education, 2004) Similar positions on inclusion have been adopted in most jurisdictions in Canada, and the philosophy of inclusion has been expressed in a variety of ways (see Table 7.2).

TABLE 7.1

Excerpt from Canada's Charter of Rights and Freedoms [Section 15(1)]

"Every individual is equal before and under the law and has the right to the equal protection and equal benefit of the law without discrimination and, in particular, without discrimination based on race, national or ethnic origin, colour, religion, sex, age or mental or physical disability."

TABLE 7.2	
Inclusion across jurisdictions in Canada	
Province/Territory	**Expression of Philosophy of Inclusion**
Alberta	. . . *regular education in neighbourhood schools . . . first placement option . . .*
British Columbia	. . . *equitable access to learning by all students . . .*
Manitoba	. . . *student with special learning needs in regular classroom settings . . .*
Ontario	. . . *integration as the first consideration . . .*
New Brunswick	. . . *with same age peers in most enabling environments . . .*
Newfoundland and Labrador	. . . *that programming is delivered with age peers . . .*
Northwest Territories	. . . *access to the education program in a regular instructional setting . . .*
Nova Scotia	. . . *within regular instruction settings with peers in age . . .*
Prince Edward Island	. . . *most enabling environment that allows opportunities to interact with peers . . .*
Quebec	. . . *a view to facilitate their learning and social integration . . .*
Saskatchewan	. . . *students with exceptional needs . . . should experience education . . . in inclusive settings . . .*
Yukon Territory	*As much as possible, students will have their special needs met in class, alongside their peers.*

Source: Adapted from Saskatchewan Special Education Review Committee (2000, p. 18).

As might be expected, documents outlining rights and responsibilities as well as documents designed to provide support and guidance are similar in nature but not exactly the same. It is important that teachers familiarize themselves with the process and procedures of inclusion in their own province or territory. A key document in the process of inclusion in every jurisdiction is the individual education plan or IEP. This document is developed by a coordinated team (learning team) that includes teachers, the parents, the student (as appropriate), other professionals (e.g., psychologist, occupational therapist), and often members of the community. The purpose of the document is to ensure appropriate planning and programming for students with special needs.

Process of Developing an Individual Education Plan (IEP)

There is a clear trend across Canada to move from a categorical approach to providing funding and support based on labelling, toward focusing on the needs of students within inclusive settings. The delivery of supports to students occurs via implementation of an IEP developed with the student as the focus and in collaboration with the

learning team. The IEP is a written commitment of intent to ensure appropriate planning for students with special needs. These written commitments are known variously across Canada as Individual Education Plans in British Columbia, Manitoba, Northwest Territories, and Ontario; Individualized Education Plans in Quebec, and Yukon Territory; Personal Program Plans in Saskatchewan; Individual Program Plans in Nova Scotia; Individualized Program Plans in Alberta; and Individual Support Services Plans in Newfoundland and Labrador. For this chapter, Individual Education Plan will be used as it is most common. Each of these documents is . . . "a concise plan of action designed to address students' special education needs, and is based on diagnostic information which provides a basis for intervention strategies. . . . " (Alberta Education 2004, p. 4)

The IEP is developed to address the specific needs of learners through collaborative effort involving the student, parents, teachers, and other staff who work closely with the student. The document is a planning tool that helps monitor and evaluate education planning and progress and is also a tool to communicate student growth and progress. The IEP provides a summary of the individualized learning goals and objectives, a summary of adaptations (modification, adjustment, or accommodation) that will help the student achieve these goals and objectives, and provides an ongoing record to ensure continuity of programming.

Generally an IEP is developed when a student has need of special education programming. How special education programming is defined varies across jurisdictions. In Québec, for example, an IEP is established when one or more of the following occurs:

1. *The student's complex situation is such that a sustained and coordinated effort is needed (e.g., agencies/staff from outside the school)*

2. *The student's situation calls for the introduction of specialized resources or adjustments (e.g., the teacher needs to adjust his/her actions to the student's needs)*

3. *The student's situation requires decisions that impact on the student's educational path (e.g., departures from typical curriculum)*

Source: Ministère de l'Éducation (2004).

Often, an IEP is developed when the student has been formally identified or designated as having a special need. In Ontario, regulation 181/98 of the Education Act requires that an IEP be developed for each student identified as exceptional by an Identification, Placement and Review Committee. This does not preclude an IEP being written for a student who has not been formally identified. An IEP can be written if the school principal determines that a student requires a modified program or adaptations for instructional or assessment purposes.

The development of the IEP is a collaborative process; however, the responsibility to ensure the IEP is developed resides with the principal. The IEP is part of a dynamic, ongoing process in which the success of the student should be the constant motivation. Typically, the process of developing an IEP involves the following phases:

1. Gather information.
2. Set the direction.
3. Develop the IEP (student program and services).
4. Implement the plan.
5. Review and update the plan.

Figure 7.1 is an overview of the phases of developing, implementing, and reviewing an IEP in Ontario (Ontario Ministry of Education, 2004). Most IEPs are written for a school year or semester. Minimally, the IEP is reviewed annually. However, the IEP may be revised more frequently, particularly if the needs of the student change. Figure 7.2 is an example of an IEP form from Ontario. The IPRC referred to in the document is the Identification, Placement and Review Committee that operates at the district school's board level. This committee is similar to committees in other provinces and territories. The role of the IPRC includes reviewing relevant information about the student, deciding whether or not the student should be identified as exceptional, and deciding on an appropriate placement

for the student. The commitment to inclusion and the regulation governing the identification and placement of exceptional students in Ontario charges the IPRC to consider the inclusion of exceptional students into regular classes, before considering the option of placing a student in a special education class.

An important concept in the provision of services and programs for students with special needs is the concept of the least restrictive environment (LRE). The LRE is the environment most like that of other students in which the student can succeed. The LRE is individually determined by the circumstance in which the student can learn cognitively, physically, and socially. This refers not only to the student's physical location, but also to how the student is taught. The preference is that the student be included in regular education activities as much as possible. It is important to understand that any educational environment may be the least restrictive one for a particular student, depending on that student's learning and behavioural needs and characteristics. For example, a student who needs an adult teaching assistant to help with literacy in the classroom may not require an adult assistant in physical education. Having the adult assistant in the classroom may be least restrictive in that context, whereas providing and using an adult assistant as a partner in physical education may be more restrictive because it might restrict the student's social interaction.

Creating the Least Restrictive Environment

It is inappropriate to place a student in an environment in which success is impossible. On the other hand, it is debilitating to put a student in a setting that is more restrictive than necessary. The least restrictive environment varies depending on the instructional content, the learning context, and learning tasks. For example, for a student who uses a wheelchair during a unit on soccer, the physical education class could be very restrictive, whereas when the same class is swimming this may not be restrictive. For a student with a cognitive disability, direct styles of teaching might be the least restrictive environment, while an exploration style of instruction may be more restrictive. When curriculum content and teaching styles vary, the type of environment for the student may need to be modified. It is also necessary to continue to monitor the student's progress in order to make adjustments if necessary. Prudent use of a least restrictive educational environment means ensuring the setting is as normal as possible (normalization), while attempting to ensure that the student can achieve success in that context.

Creating the least restrictive environment is accomplished by considering what supports and services

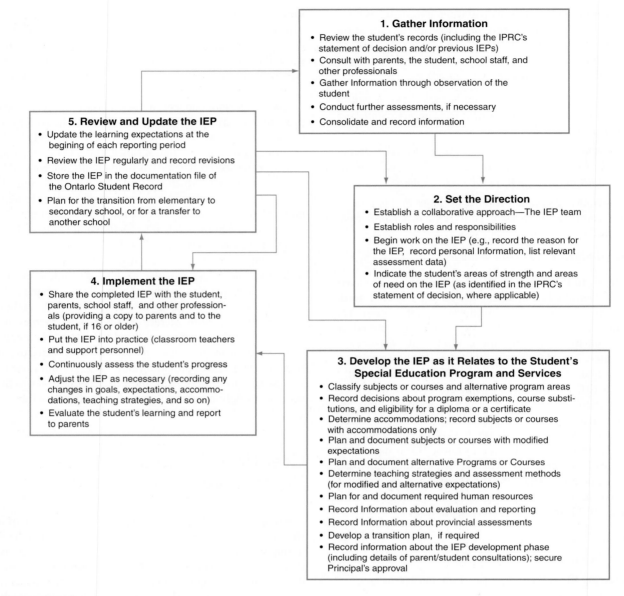

Figure 7.1

Overview of the process of developing, implementing, and reviewing an IEP.

are needed for the student to learn successfully and in what context that support/service will be delivered. A continuum of support to ensure success in a regular physical education context is shown in Table 7.3 and using paraprofessionals and peers tutors as teacher's assistants are discussed on pages 127 and 128 of this chapter.

Placing students in a separate context is appropriate when it is in the best interest of the child. The thrust of programs in these contexts is to establish a level of skill, health, and social proficiency that eventually enables students to engage successfully in an inclusive environment.

The cornerstone of the educational process is emphasis on placement in the least restrictive environment in which the child can profit most. Students with special needs, working on their own, often are denied opportunities to interact with peers and become a part of the social and academic classroom network.

The education of students with special needs is the responsibility of the teacher. It is important that physical educators do not devolve physical education programming to paraprofessionals or other support personnel. But physical education teachers should maintain contact with support personnel such as the special education teacher,

Figure 7.2

Individual education plan.

**Individual
Education Plan**

IEP

REASON FOR DEVELOPING THE IEP

☐ Student identified as exceptional by IPRC   ☐ Student not formally identified but requires education program/services, Including modified/alternative learning expectations and/or accommodations

STUDENT PROFILE

Name:_____ Gender: _____ Date of Birth: _____

School: _____

Student OEN/MIN: _____ Principal: _____

Current Grade/Special Class: _____ School Year: _____

Most Recent IPRC Date: _____ Date Annual Review Waived by Parent/Guardian: _____

Exceptionality: _____

IPRC Placement Decision (*check one*)
☐ Regular class with indirect support
☐ Regular class with resource assistance
☐ Regular class with withdrawal assistance

☐ Special education class with partial integration
☐ Special education class full-time

ASSESSMENT DATA

List relevant educational, medical/health (hearing, vision, physical, neurological), psychological, speech/language, occupational, physiotherapy, and behavioural assessments.

Information Source	Date	Summary of Results

STUDENT'S STRENGTHS AND NEEDS

Areas of Strength	Areas of Need

Health Support Services/Personal Support Required   ☐ Yes (list below)   ☐ No

1

(*continued*)

---

school psychologists, and speech therapists. Although the students are the responsibility of the physical education teacher, support personnel should serve as a source of information and support.

Guidelines for Successful Inclusion

The concern is not whether to plan for inclusion, but how to include *effectively*. An IEP is a guide. It provides a summary of individualized goals and objectives that the student will work toward, and a summary of adaptations that will help the student learn more effectively. It does not usually provide specific day-to-day strategies.

Figure 7.3

Children using wheelchairs for mobility participate in parachute activities with their peers.

Figure 7.2

Continued

SUBJECTS, COURSES, OR ALTERNATIVE PROGRAMS TO WHICH THE IEP APPLIES

Identify each of Modified (MOD), Accommodated only (AC), or Alternative (ALT)

1. _____ ☐ MOD ☐ AC ☐ ALT   6. _____ ☐ MOD ☐ AC ☐ ALT
2. _____ ☐ MOD ☐ AC ☐ ALT   7. _____ ☐ MOD ☐ AC ☐ ALT
3. _____ ☐ MOD ☐ AC ☐ ALT   8. _____ ☐ MOD ☐ AC ☐ ALT
4. _____ ☐ MOD ☐ AC ☐ ALT   9. _____ ☐ MOD ☐ AC ☐ ALT
5. _____ ☐ MOD ☐ AC ☐ ALT   10. _____ ☐ MOD ☐ AC ☐ ALT

Elementary Program Exemptions or Secondary School Compulsory Course Substitutions
☐ Yes (*provide educational ratinale*) ☐ No
_____
_____

Complete for secondary students only:
Student is currently working towards attainment of the

☐ Ontario Secondary School Diploma ☐ Ontario Secondary School Certificate ☐ Certificate of Accomplishment

ACCOMMODATIONS

(Accommodations are assumed to be the same for all subjects, unless otherwise indicated)

Instructional Accommodations	Environmental Accommodations	Assessment Accommodations

Individualized Equipment   ☐ Yes (*list below*)   ☐ No
_____   _____
_____   _____

PROVINCIAL ASSESSMENTS (accommodations and exemptions)

Provincial assessments applicable to the student in the current school year: _____

Accommodations: ☐ Yes(list below)   ☐ No
_____   _____
_____   _____

Exemptions: ☐ Yes (*provide explanatory statement from relevant EQAO document*)   ☐ No
_____
_____

2

Inclusion should allow children to make commendable educational progress, to achieve in those areas outlined in the IEP, and to develop their personality, talents, and mental and physical abilities to their fullest potential. Following are some general guidelines for successful inclusion of children with special needs into physical education:

1. Beyond the regular program of activities, meet target goals as specified in the IEP. This may involve resources beyond the physical education class, including special work and homework.

2. Build ego strength; stress abilities. Eliminate established practices that unwittingly contribute to embarrassment and failure.

3. Foster peer acceptance, which begins when the teacher accepts the child as a functioning, participating member of the class.

4. Concentrate on the child's physical education needs and not on the disability. Give strong attention to fundamental skills and physical fitness qualities.

5. Provide continual monitoring and assess the child's target goals periodically. Anecdotal and periodic record-keeping are implicit in this guideline.

6. Be constantly aware of the student's feelings and anxiety concerning progress and inclusion. Provide positive feedback as a basic practice.

TABLE 7.3

Continuum of support for physical education

Level	Support	Example
Level 1	No support needed.	1.1 After the whistle is blown to stop the activity, a student who is deaf moves himself to a position where he can watch the teacher's face.
	1.1 The student can make necessary modification on his or her own.	
	1.2 The regular teacher of physical education feels comfortable working with the student and making necessary adjustments to the environment or equipment.	1.2 In a tee-ball game the teacher has the fielding team throw the ball to each base rather just one base to give a student with mobility difficulties more time to get to the base.
Level 2	Regular PE plus supplementary instructional support/services.	2.1 The physical educator may consult a visiting physiotherapist about how muscular dystrophy affects the student's balance and any contraindications for physical education.
	2.1 Physical educator consults the IEP learning team or other professional for assistance then teaches without additional support. The teacher makes the adjustments to the environment or equipment.	2.2 When assigned to groups and a student with a cognitive disability is unsure where to go; her peer tutor ensures she moves to the correct group.
	2.2 Peer tutor watches out for student.	
	2.3 Peer tutor assists student.	2.3 The peer tutor reinforces the cues provided by the teacher—e.g., "Bat back, watch the ball . . . "
	2.4 Paraprofessional assists the student.	2.4 To assist with transitions, teacher's assistant pre-warns a student with autism that an activity will change in 30 seconds time.
Level 3	Part-time regular PE, part-time supplementary or alternative PE.	A student who uses a wheelchair for mobility may find soccer a restrictive activity. For this unit of instruction the student could work on strength, wheelchair mobility, or other less restrictive activity such as swimming or tennis.
Level 4	Separate classes, school, home, or hospital.	At times children are in separate placements when in the best interests of the child.

Source: Adapted from Block & Krebs (1992) and Sherrill (1998).

7. Modify the regular program to meet the unique capacities, physical needs, and social needs of students with special needs.

8. Provide individual assistance and keep students active. Peer or paraprofessional help may be needed.

9. Consult regularly with the learning team (therapists, inclusion coordinator, etc.).

10. Give consideration to more individualization within the program so students with special needs are smoothly integrated. Individual attention is based on the target goals of the IEP.

An Individualized Approach to Physical Education

The success of inclusion " . . . depends in large part upon the quality of the regular physical education program and the extent to which it meets individual differences" (Sherrill, 1993, p. 3). An individualized approach does not mean one-on-one instruction but, rather, adaptations to the instructional process based on the needs of students. Figure 7.4

Figure 7.4

Program planning model for individualizing instruction.

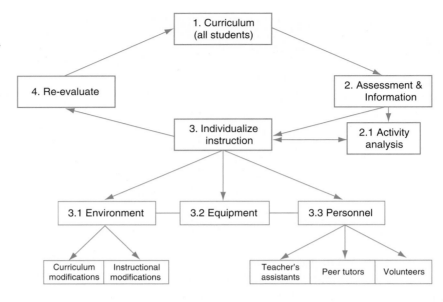

illustrates a program planning model for adapting instruction to the needs of students. The following sections of this chapter describe the processes involved in program planning.

1. Start with the core curriculum

The provincial/territory core curriculum and the teacher's planned curriculum for the entire class should be the starting point for educational programming for students with special needs. Some students with special needs will engage in the regular curriculum with adaptations to facilitate and foster success and learning; and other students will need a modified program (or parts of a program). These decisions will be based on the IEP and assessments conducted specifically for physical education. The IEP will describe the special education program and/or services for the student. It will also describe the learning expectations that are modified from or alternative to the expectations from the core curriculum documents. However, the IEP is not a daily or weekly lesson plan itemizing every detail of how to instruct the student.

2. Make decisions about how to adapt based on assessment and activity analysis

Student and program evaluation is an integral part of teaching and learning, and integral to the success of inclusion. Assessment refers to a wide variety of methods and strategies to gather information about the student. These methods can include informal approaches such as observation in a variety

of settings, and reports from other teachers, parents, or the student; or more formal approaches such as criterion-related checklists, screening tests, evaluations from therapists, and relevant medical information. The IEP will provide information about relevant educational, medical/health (e.g., physical conditions, hearing, vision), psychological, speech/language, occupational, physiotherapy, and behavioural assessments. It is particularly important that teachers of physical education make themselves aware of medical/health conditions to ensure student safety and well-being.

There are also physical education–specific assessments that need to occur to enhance the teacher's ability to meet student needs. For example, the IEP may contain a physiotherapist's evaluation of motor functioning that places the child in the 10th percentile for age. There may also be an accompanying recommendation for the student to develop both fine and gross motor skills. However, how this information translates to a unit of instruction on dance requires assessment by the teacher of physical education.

Let's think about a hypothetical dance unit of instruction. During this unit children will be asked to hop, jump, skip, slide, chassé, move to a beat, pretend, take turns, and invent. Based on past experience, the teacher does not plan to teach the skills of sliding, hopping, and jumping with this grade because the children usually have these skills; but she does intend to work on consolidating skipping and to introduce the chassé. Assessment of whether the student with special needs has these skills is important. If the student can jump but she cannot yet hop, skip, slide, or chassé, it is unrealistic to expect that student to master all of these skills in the same time frame that the rest of the class is consolidating skipping and the chassé. Choosing one new locomotor skill to work on and master during the unit may be more appropriate. This new skill and her existing jumping skill may form the basis of her movement patterns during dance.

The important concept of *Activity Analysis* arises here. Activity Analysis is a technique for determining the basic characteristics of an activity and relating them to desired student outcomes. In making this analysis the teacher considers the cognitive, physical (movement skills and physiological demands), affective, and social domains. When examining the physical domain the teacher would list the fitness requirements of the activity (e.g., sufficient strength to hold their body weight), the motor skills needed, and the sensory systems used (e.g., listen to the beat of the drum). Cognitive analysis would include the complexity of instructions/rules to be followed, literacy skills needed (e.g., reading, counting, charting), and the need to memorize and to think abstractly. Social analysis involves the type of social interaction needed (e.g., sharing, cooperating), and affective factors include the need to persist and frustration tolerance. Table 7.4 is an activity analysis for the Mexican Hat Dance. This type of detail helps identify areas of need for students with special needs and opportunities to teach to adapt the task, equipment, or personnel. For example, some students with autism have unusual responses to sensory stimuli, including adverse reactions to tactile stimulation. A student with this adverse reaction may prefer not to touch or be touched by a partner. A logical adaptation of this dance would be to perform the action of clapping without actual physical contact.

3. Individualizing instruction

Armed with information about the strengths and needs of the particular student and knowledge of the demands of the activity (Activity Analysis), the teacher can now individualize instruction by selecting appropriate adaptations. Three broad areas of the instructional process can be targets of adaptation in physical education: the environment, equipment, and personnel. Ideally, only needed adaptations are made so that the activities and instruction are as typical as possible.

3.1 Environment

Within the instructional environment it may be necessary to adapt the specific student learning outcome associated with the curriculum. The example in Table 7.5 from the Physical Education/Health Education Curriculum from Manitoba Education and Training (2000) illustrates this point.

It is evident from the wheelchair use example in Table 7.5 above that although the specific student outcome has changed, the general learning outcome of movement is still central to these activities and also relevant to lifelong skills for the student.

Instructional modifications include using additional instructional strategies, and making changes to skills and rules of games. Typically, students gain information through sight and hearing. However, sometimes using kinesthetic information from one's own body position and using tactile information can supplement or replace verbal and/or visual information. Tactile information obtained by

---

TABLE 7.4

Activity analysis for the Mexican Hat Dance

Activity analysis of the Mexican Hat Dance

Cognitive	**Psychomotor**
Listens to the music	Performs motor skills
Understands when to begin	• Hop step
Remembers the cues	• Clap
Remembers the steps (type, number)	• One-hand clap with partner
Attends and responds to the teacher's instructions	• Slaps knees
Understands the reciprocal	• Skip
Affective	Cardiovascular fitness to perform dance
Understands role as a partner	
Cooperates with partner	
Holds hands, links elbow, and claps hands with a partner	

TABLE 7.5

Adaptation of a student learning outcome

Type of disability:	The student has a mobility impairment and uses a wheelchair for mobility
General student learning outcome:	Movement
Specific student outcome (grade 3)	Demonstrate proficiency in basic transport skills (i.e., running, hopping, galloping, jumping, and skipping [S.1.3.A.1])
Accommodation* (*for student with special needs*)	Demonstrate proficiency in wheeling techniques (e.g., stopping with control, turning to the right, turning to the left, turning quickly, backing up, weaving around obstacles)
Teacher's comments on student's progress and achievement	The student has demonstrated mastery of the given skills in a specific circuit and in cooperative activities

* An accommodation is a change or alteration in the regular way a student is expected to learn, complete assignments, or participate in classroom activities (Alberta Education, 2006).

Brailling is described in the visual impairment section of this chapter. A kinesthetic instructional strategy that can be very useful involves a continuum of assistance (see Table 7.6). Ideally, the physical guidance is faded out as the student masters the skill with that particular level of assistance. It is important to use the same cues throughout the process so that the cues can eventually replace physical guidance. The continuum of assistance described in Table 7.6 can be very useful for students with cognitive difficulties and motor planning challenges.

Modifying the rules of games, the spaces used, and the requirement of a skill are also useful instructional modifications. The teacher can adjust player positions, teaming of players, numbers on a team and the like. For instance, after a student with mobility difficulties hits the ball off the tee, another student may push her wheelchair to first base. Rules of games can be adjusted in so many ways to enhance inclusion. For example, to get a student out who may take longer to run to a base in softball, the fielding team throws the ball to each base. The area defined to play pickle ball

may be smaller for a student who moves slowly than for her opponent, or the ball may bounce twice and still be in play. A child with delayed skill development may be allowed to bounce and catch the basketball while dribbling, or the teacher may use a six-second time limit with the ball rather than allow opponents to steal the ball away. The list of adaptations to rules, spaces, and skills is limited only by the creativity of the teacher; there is nothing sacred about the rules of major games in physical education lessons.

3.2 Equipment

Adapting equipment can make a great deal of difference to success in physical education for many students with special needs. The size, texture, weight, colour, and function of equipment can be modified. Many specific examples of adaptations are provided in the sections that follow on Modifications for Students with Limited Strength and Endurance, Modification for Students with Coordination

---

TABLE 7.6

Continuum of assistance

Physical assistance	The student is physically manipulated or guided through the activity in conjunction with verbal cues—e.g., "look at the pins," "step long and low."
Partial assistance	The student is given physical prompts; body parts to be moved are specified prior to the movement. Same cues (above) are used as the student moves.
Demonstration	Important aspects of the activity are highlighted or modelled for the student; again, same cues are used.
Verbal cue	The student is provided with the verbal cues only.
No cue	The student is able to self-initiate the activity; he/she may say the cues him/herself.

Difficulties, Modifications for Students with Balance and Agility Challenges, and in the disability-specific sections. However, here we will give some examples of how modifications to equipment can facilitate learning.

Function of equipment: Placing a fan or auditory signal behind bowling pins will orientate a student with a visual impairment to the target.

Size and **weight** of equipment: For a student who is having difficulty catching, using a larger foam ball will increase the likelihood of success and be less frightening. Use a short-handled putter in golf for students using a wheelchair.

Colour of equipment: Using cone colours that contrast highly with the floor or grass will help students who have difficulty separating an object from the environment identify the boundaries.

Texture of equipment: Carpet squares can be used to define a space in the gymnasium for students who are visually impaired or for students who would benefit from a tangible reminder of their space.

Equipment adaptations that are helpful for students with special needs may also be beneficial for other students. By providing a range of options for all students e.g., four types of balls to choose from, or three different bench heights to practise soft knee landings in gymnastics, the teacher is creating an inclusive style of teaching (Mosston & Ashworth, 1994) (see Chapter 3). Not only will the teacher meet the needs of diverse learners, but he/she will create a classroom environment where children see that doing things a little differently is the norm.

3.3 Personnel

The teacher's assistant

Teacher's assistants are variously described across educational jurisdictions as paraprofessionals, educational assistants, paraeducators, and teacher associates. The role of the teacher's assistant includes helping the student with learning activities, assisting to provide appropriate adaptations as described in the IEP, monitoring and recording student achievement and progress, maintaining ongoing communication with the student's teachers, and assisting with student care. It is important to note that the education of the student with special needs and implementation of the IEP is the responsibility of the physical education teacher. The teacher's assistant works to support the student in physical education under the direct supervision of the teacher.

When available, teachers' assistants provide a wealth of knowledge about the student, and can improve time-on-task for the student and enhance program quality. To make effective use of teachers' assistants it is important to clarify roles and responsibilities. Usually, the teacher's assistant does not have formal training in physical education; therefore it is not appropriate to assume that the individual

will be knowledgeable about the content of the lesson, about how to adapt and sequence physical activities, or how to ensure the safety of the activity. These responsibilities lie with the teacher of physical education. The physical educator and the teacher's assistant should engage in an ongoing dialogue about the goals of objectives of instruction, how activities will be modified if necessary, and any safety or medical aspects that may be pertinent.

While having a teacher's assistant work directly with a child with special needs can be efficient and effective, the teacher of physical education should also consider that the teacher's assistant can take a less direct role— perhaps by supporting a peer tutor or a small group that includes the child with special needs. A human rights principle that should underpin inclusion and curriculum decisions is the principle of normalization (Wolfensberger, 1972). This principle states that the living, learning, and working conditions of people with a disability should be as close as possible to the norms of able-bodied society. When applied in the context of physical education, this means that children with special needs should be working with their peers, rather than adults, whenever possible.

Peer tutor

Peer tutoring involves same-age or cross-age (older) students helping with instruction. Peer tutoring is a strategy that can help provide quality physical education to students with special needs in regular classrooms. It is an approach where selected students receive formal tutor training including how to cue, provide feedback, and task analyze. The process can be very beneficial for both tutors and those being tutored, as they both develop skills such as decision making, communication, and learning to disagree constructively. Peer tutoring is an effective support for success in regular physical education for children with special needs. DePaepe (1985) compared the effectiveness of three physical education instructional environments for students with intellectual disability: (a) peer tutoring, (b) self-contained (segregated), and (c) integrated. The peer-tutor environment, in which each student with intellectual disability worked with a peer chosen by the physical education teacher, produced significantly higher time-on-task for the included students than either of the other two environments. These findings are supported by other research, which demonstrated that peer tutors improved time-on-task for students with disabilities (Webster, 1987) and can lead to improvements in fundamental motor skills (Strickland, Temple, & Walkley, 2005). Advantages of peer tutoring include the following:

- Enables the student with a disability to receive individualized instruction and immediate feedback

- Maximizes on-task time

- Can improve the skills, self-concept, and attitude of the student with a disability relative to physical education
- Can develop or reinforce leadership skills, self-concept, task-specific skills, and attitude of the tutor
- Encourages socialization

A peer tutor is not just a partner. The tutor is part of the instructional process. To enhance the likelihood of success the following guidelines are useful: (1) the tutor should be trained in what to do, how to give feedback; (2) task cards or worksheets should be provided for the tutor to refer to; (3) the tutor should have demonstrated good behaviour in physical education classes and the ability to follow directions; (4) the tutor should have a strong desire to be a tutor; (5) tutors should have opportunities to participate themselves and tutors should be rotated (e.g., after a unit of instruction); and (6) the teacher must provide feedback to the tutor about his or her role as a tutor.

The task card shown in Figure 7.5 is an example of a tutor task card that was used to help grade 4–5 students with intellectual disability develop the striking fundamental movement skill. The teacher highlighted one or two key cues for the peer tutor to focus on each lesson; over a six-week period the children's intellectual disability decreased and the peer tutors improved their skill (Temple, 2006).

Figure 7.5

Example peer-tutor task sheet.

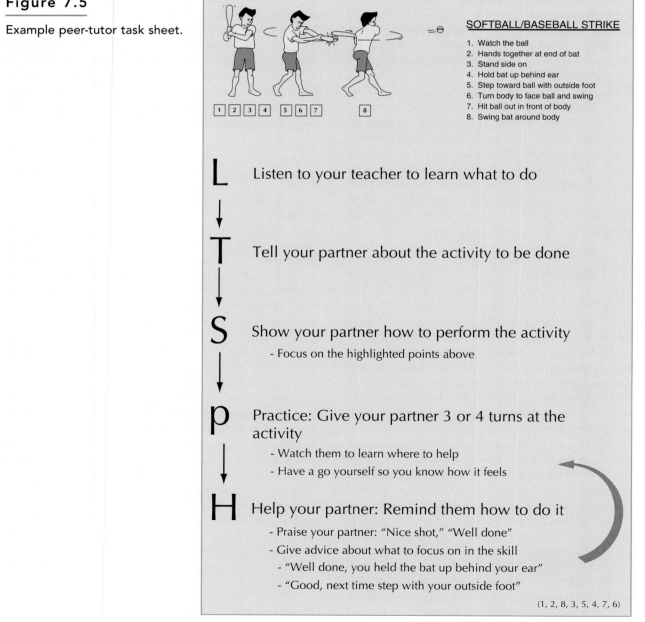

SOFTBALL/BASEBALL STRIKE

1. Watch the ball
2. Hands together at end of bat
3. Stand side on
4. Hold bat up behind ear
5. Step toward ball with outside foot
6. Turn body to face ball and swing
7. Hit ball out in front of body
8. Swing bat around body

L Listen to your teacher to learn what to do

T Tell your partner about the activity to be done

S Show your partner how to perform the activity
- Focus on the highlighted points above

P Practice: Give your partner 3 or 4 turns at the activity
- Watch them to learn where to help
- Have a go yourself so you know how it feels

H Help your partner: Remind them how to do it
- Praise your partner: "Nice shot," "Well done"
- Give advice about what to focus on in the skill
- "Well done, you held the bat up behind your ear"
- "Good, next time step with your outside foot"

(1, 2, 8, 3, 5, 4, 7, 6)

Recruiting and Training Volunteer Aides

Recruiting and using volunteers can be an effective way to increase the amount of instruction and practice for students. Most communities in Canada are serviced by a volunteer bureau. Alternatively, volunteers might be recruited from groups such as service clubs, schools, and recreation organizations. High school students can serve as volunteers (cross-age tutors) and have been shown to work effectively with elementary school students. An initial meeting with volunteer aides should explain the needs of students they will be working with and what responsibilities are entailed. Training should teach aides how they can be most effective in assisting the instructor. Include learning how to work effectively with individuals, recording data, and developing special materials and instructional supplies. In addition, give potential aides an introductory experience in working with students, to see if they are capable and enjoy such work. Working with aides takes time and prior planning. The task of organizing and supervising aides can be burdensome if you have not learned to supervise and organize experiences.

Aides can assume many roles to increase the effectiveness of the instructional situation. They can gather and locate equipment and supplies prior to the lesson. They may referee games and ensure that the games run smoothly. Experienced aides enjoy and are capable of offering one-on-one or small-group instruction to students. Aides are not to be used to reduce the need for teacher involvement; rather they are there to implement instruction strategies that have been organized and developed by the professional educator.

In summary, the core curriculum is the starting point for educational planning for students with special needs. The next step is to gather information about the student and the student's needs. The IEP will also provide relevant health, medical, educational, and behavioural information, and assessments from other therapists. The physical educator should also collect physical education–specific information and conduct activity analyses of core curriculum. If necessary, adaptations can be made to equipment, the environment (curriculum and instructions modifications), and how personnel are used to individualize instruction.

The next section of this chapter provides general suggestions for meeting the needs of students with limited strength and endurance, for students with coordination difficulties, and for students with balance and agility challenges.

Modifications for Students with Limited Strength and Endurance

1. *Lower or enlarge the size of the goal.* In basketball, the goal can be lowered; in soccer, the goal might be enlarged.

2. *Modify the tempo of the game.* For example, games might be performed using a brisk walk rather than

Figure 7.6

Modifying an activity for successful participation.

running. Another way to modify tempo is to stop the game regularly for substitution. Auto-substitution is an excellent method for allowing students to determine when they are fatigued. They ask a predetermined substitute to take their place.

3. *Reduce the weight and/or modify the size of the projectile.* A lighter object moves more slowly and inflicts less damage on impact. A larger object is easier to track visually and to catch.

4. *Reduce the distance that a ball must be thrown or served.* Options are to reduce the dimensions of the playing area or add more players to the game. In serving, others can help make the serve playable. For example, in volleyball, other teammates can bat the serve over the net as long as it does not touch the floor.

5. *In games that are played to a certain number of points, reduce the number required for a win.* For example, play volleyball games to 7 or 11, depending on the skill and intensity of the players.

6. *Modify striking implements by shortening and reducing their weight.* Rackets are much easier to control when they are shortened. Softball bats are easier to control when the player "chokes up" or selects a lighter bat.

7. *In some games it is possible to slow down the ball by letting out some of the air.* This reduces the speed of rebound and makes the ball easier to control in a restricted area. It also keeps the ball from rolling away from players when it is not under control.

8. *Play the games in a different position.* Some games may be played in a sitting or lying position, which is easier and less demanding than standing or running.

9. *Provide matching or substitution.* Match another child on borrowed crutches with a child on braces. Two players can be combined to play one position. A student in a desk chair with wheels can be matched against a child in a wheelchair.

10. *Students can substitute for each other for certain skills.* For example, a child may be able to strike an object but may lack the mobility to run. Permit substitute courtesy runners.

Modifications for Students with Coordination Difficulties

1. *Increase the size of the goal or target.* Increasing the size of a basketball goal increases the opportunity for success. Another alternative is to offer points for hitting the backboard or getting near a goal. Since scoring is self-motivating, modification should occur until success is ensured.

2. *Offer protectors.* The lack of coordination will make the student more susceptible to injury from a projectile. Use various types of protectors (glasses, chest protectors, face masks, and so on).

3. *When teaching throwing, allow opportunity to throw at maximum velocity without concern for accuracy.* Use small balls that can be grasped easily. Fleece balls and beanbags are easy to hold and release.

4. *When learning to strike an object, begin with one that is held stationary.* The use of a batting tee or tennis ball fastened to a string offers students the opportunity for success. In addition, a larger racquet or bat can be used and the student can choke up on the grip.

5. If a great deal of time is spent on recovering the projectile, children receive only a few practice trials and feel frustrated. Place them near a backstop or use a goal that rebounds the projectile to the shooter.

6. *When learning to catch, use soft, lightweight, and slow-moving objects.* Beach balls and balloons are excellent for beginning catching skills because they allow the student to track their movement visually. In addition, foam rubber balls eliminate the student's fear of being hurt by a thrown or batted projectile.

Modifications for Students with Balance and Agility Challenges

1. *Increase the width of rails, lines, and beams when practising balance.* Carrying a long pole helps minimize rapid shifts of balance and is a useful lead-up activity.

2. *Increase the width of the base of support.* Teach students to keep their feet spread at least to shoulder width.

3. *When beginning balance practice, emphasize controlled movement using as many body parts as possible.* The more body parts that are in contact with the floor, the easier it is to balance the body.

4. *Increase the surface area of the body parts in contact with the floor or beam.* For example, walking flatfooted is easier than walking on tiptoes.

5. *Lower the centre of gravity.* This offers more stability and greater balance to the child. Place emphasis on bending the knees and leaning slightly forward.

6. *Ensure that surfaces offer good friction.* Floors and shoes should not be slick or children will fall. Carpets or tumbling mats increase a child's traction.

7. *Some children will require balance assistance.* A barre, cane, or chair can be used to keep the child from falling.

8. *Children with balance problems will inevitably fall.* Offer practice in learning how to fall so they gradually learn to absorb the force of the fall.

Understanding Specific Disabilities

A crucial piece of the Program Planning Model shown in Figure 7.4 is Assessment/Information: finding out as much as possible about the student, the student's disability, and the associated needs of the child. Understanding the disability and what it means to the child is essential if teachers are going to plan for successful inclusion. Basic information is provided here, and additional materials may be obtained from national disability-specific associations, from books, from journals such as *Adapted Physical Activity Quarterly*, the Active Living Alliance for Canadians with a Disability (see Figure 7.7), and through professional development workshops.

Intellectual Disability

Intellectual disability originates before age 18 and is characterized by significant limitations both in intellectual functioning and in adaptive behaviour as expressed in conceptual, social, and practical adaptive skills.

The Active Living Alliance for Canadians with a Disability offers a resource package entitled *Moving to Inclusion* designed specifically for teachers of physical education classes and leaders of community-based active living programs. Their vision was and remains that children and youth with disabilities will always be included in physical education leading to a healthy active lifestyle. First published in 1994, these resources assist in assessing strengths and weaknesses of students with disabilities as well as providing ideas and plans for making appropriate activity and equipment modifications. *Moving to Inclusion* was developed with the assistance of provincial education departments and the Canadian Associations for the following:

- Amputee Sports;
- Disabled Skiing;
- Health, Physical Education, Recreation and Dance;
- Cerebral Palsy Sports;
- Council of the Blind;
- Blind Sports;
- Deaf Sports;
- Hard of Hearing Special Olympics; and
- Wheelchair Sports.

Moving to Inclusion offers an abridged version, which can be used as a quick reference tool and consists of one introductory and nine disability specific resources, and a series of comprehensive versions containing more complete information pertaining to students with specific disabilities. Each volume gives great hints and helpful suggestions about the inclusion of children with a disability in physical activities such as aquatics, games, dance, gymnastics, and outdoor pursuits, and includes sections on safety concerns, equipment and rules, instructional strategies, learning objectives, and assessment techniques. The Comprehensive Versions are as follows:

- The Student with an Amputation;
- The Student with Cerebral Palsy;
- The Student who is Deaf or Hard of Hearing;
- The Student with and Intellectual Disability;
- The Student with Multiple Disabilities;
- The Student with a Visual Impairment;
- The Student who uses a Wheelchair;
- The Student who is Physically Awkward; and
- Skiing for the Student with a Disability.

This K–12 resource is available in both English and French (Abridged Version: $25.00 each, Comprehensive versions: $25.00 each or $200.00 for the full set of nine comprehensive resources) from:

Active Living Alliance for Canadians with a Disability
720 Belfast Rd. #104
Ottawa, ON K1G 0Z5
Ph: 1-800-771-0663   Fax: (613) 244-4857
Email: info@ala.ca   Web: www.ala.ca

Figure 7.7

Moving to Inclusion: An adapted physical activity model.

Many terms have been used to describe intellectual disability. In the past *mental retardation* was used, and often the term *developmental disability* is used as a synonym. However, developmental disability is not a synonym as it is a broader term that refers to the following:

- Is attributable to mental or physical impairment or a combination of mental and physical impairments;
- Is manifested before the person is 22 years of age;
- Is likely to continue indefinitely;
- Results in substantial functional limitations in three or more of the following areas of major life activity: self-care, receptive and expressive language, learning, mobility, self-direction, capacity for independent living, and economic self-sufficiency;

- Reflects the person's need for a combination and sequence of special, interdisciplinary, or generic care, treatment, or other services that are of lifelong or extended duration and are individually planned and coordinated.

If you compare the definition of *intellectual disability* with the term *developmental disability,* you will notice that developmental disability is a more all-encompassing term and that intellectual disability is indeed one developmental disability.

A number of characteristics are typically associated with having an intellectual disability. It is important to determine the extent to which each of the following is experienced by the individual and how this may impact learning in physical education.

Medical Considerations: Students with an intellectual disability are more likely to experience epilepsy; therefore it is important to determine whether and how the student experiences epilepsy, whether it is controlled by medication, whether there are factors that may induce a seizure, and what to do if the student has a seizure. Among students with Down syndrome it is also important to find out whether the student has a congenital heart condition and/or atlanto-axial instability. Atlanto-axial instability is an orthopedic problem present in 10–20% of persons with Down syndrome. It refers to instability of the first two cervical vertebrae associated with laxity of ligaments and muscles surrounding the joint.

Cognitive Characteristics: Students with an intellectual disability may have some or all of the following cognitive challenges: learn at a slower rate, short attention span, more frequently distracted, difficulty understanding abstract concepts, difficulty transferring skills from one context to another, lower levels of receptive and expressive language, and deficits in short- and long-term memory. However, often students with intellectual disability show a strong ability to copy and follow a lead.

Affective Characteristics: Students with an intellectual disability may have a poor self concept; difficulty in adapting to new people, places, and changes in routine; lower motivation for physical activity; and a low tolerance of frustration.

Psychomotor/Physical Fitness: It is not uncommon for the motor development (both locomotor and manipulative) of children with intellectual disability to lag behind their peers by approximately one to two standard deviations of the average motor performance of children of the same age (Rarick, 1980). In addition, students often experience difficulties with motor planning, task speed and reaction time, static and dynamic balance (may be task-specific), and cardiovascular fitness and strength.

The extent to which some of the characteristics described above are related to lack of opportunity and inadequate instruction rather than limited learning capabilities is sometimes unclear. For example, students with intellectual disability often have lower fitness and strength; however it has been demonstrated that children and youth with intellectual disability can improve these components of fitness. Students with an intellectual disability may have difficulty with a jog around a field because they may not understand the purpose, or are unsure of, or scared of, the feeling of breathlessness. Additional assistance to understand the value of physical fitness to health, and understanding that increased heart rate and breathing rates are normal and "OK" can be helpful.

Severity of intellectual disability and motor performance are related; and the motor proficiency of children with mild intellectual disability tends to lag behind their peers. However, we also know that motor skills develop in a similar pattern to students who are typically developing, and that children with intellectual disability can master movement skills. Generally, the greatest difficulty for students with intellectual disability is in attention and comprehension, rather than execution once the task is understood (Rarick, 1980).

Instructional Considerations

Although it is not uncommon for the motor development of children with intellectual disability to lag behind their peers, children with mild intellectual disability should be able to master these skills—albeit at a slower rate. The greatest difficulty in teaching movement skills to children with intellectual disability lies in attention and comprehension rather than execution (Sherrill, 1998). This, and the ability of children with intellectual disability to copy and follow a lead, suggests visual demonstrations, peer tutors, and teaching assistants are very helpful in the learning process. Peer tutoring (discussed earlier) has been associated with increases in the level of active engagement of students with intellectual disability in physical education lessons.

Setting challenging yet attainable goals is also very important. The pace of learning depends on the degree of the delay. If students are learning at a slower rate it will be necessary to reduce the number of goals to ensure mastery. Mastery of skills is much more important than exposure to a wider variety of skills. Often, past experiences have placed children with intellectual disability in a cycle of failure, where the time available is insufficient to learn what is asked. The satisfaction of accomplishment must supplant poor self-image that can arise from cycles of failure.

Teach activities that are presented through demonstration rather than verbalization. Many of the skills may have to be accompanied by manual assistance to help children get the "feel" of the skill. To avoid boredom and frustration, practice periods should be short. Allow ample opportunity for students to show off skills they can perform so that they can enjoy the feeling of accomplishment. Shape behaviour by accepting approximation of the skill; this will encourage the student to keep trying. Progress arrives in small increments, and teachers must be sensitive to improvement and accomplishment, no matter how small. Reward trying. Many students are reluctant to try a new activity. Instructions should be repeated a number of times. Pay close attention to safety as students may not understand the risk of injury in physical education.

Ensure a student with Down syndrome has a medical clearance for atlanto-axial instability or avoid forceful forward or backward bending of the neck. If the medical clearance is not noted in the IEP, teachers of physical education should restrict the student from participating in gymnastics; diving, butterfly stroke, and diving starts in swimming; high jump; pentathlon; soccer heading, and any activities that place pressure on the head and neck. Once an X-ray clears the student of atlanto-axial instability these activities can be added to his or her physical education activities.

Epilepsy

Epilepsy is a dysfunction of the electrical impulses emitted by the brain. It is not an organic disease. It can happen at any period of life but generally shows up during early childhood. With proper care and medication, many children overcome this condition and live normal lives. One challenge is that epilepsy is a hidden problem. A child with epilepsy looks, acts, and is like other children, except for unpredictable seizures. Unfortunately, epilepsy carries an unwarranted social stigma. A child with epilepsy meets with a lack of acceptance, even when adequate explanations are made to those sharing the child's environment. A major seizure can be frightening to others.

Gaining control of seizures is often a long procedure, involving experimentation with appropriate anticonvulsive medication in proper doses. Fortunately, with proper medication most epilepsy eventually can be controlled or minimized. Very important in controlling epilepsy is ensuring that the child is taking the medication as prescribed. Sometimes a child can recognize signs of seizure onset and should know he or she can move to the sideline without permission. A seizure may, however, occur without warning. Know the signs of a seizure and respond accordingly.

Three kinds of seizures are identified. A *petit mal seizure* involves a brief period (a few seconds) of blackout. Often no one is aware of the problem, including the child. Sometimes it is labelled inattention and thus is difficult to identify. A *psychomotor epileptic seizure* is longer lasting (perhaps a few minutes) and is characterized by involuntary movements and twitching. The child acts like a sleepwalker and cannot be stopped or helped. The student does not respond when addressed and is unaware of the seizure. A *grand mal seizure* is a total seizure with complete neurological involvement. The child may become unconscious and lose control of the bladder or bowels, resulting in loss of urine, stool, or both. Rigidity and tremors can appear. The seizure must run its course.

Two points are important. First, throughout any seizure or incident, preserve a matter-of-fact attitude. Second, educate other children to understand and empathize with the problem. Stress what the condition is and, later, what it is not. Explain that the behaviour during a seizure is a response to an unusual output of electrical discharges from the brain. Everyone needs these discharges to function in normal living, but the person with epilepsy is subject to an unusual amount of the discharges, which results in unusual activity. The condition involves a natural phenomenon that gets out of control.

Information about epilepsy should be a part of the standard health curriculum in the school, rather than a reaction to an epileptic seizure or to the presence of a student who may have seizures. Epilepsy can be discussed as a topic relevant to understanding the central nervous system. Certain risks are involved if the lessons have as their focus the problems of a particular child, because this may heighten the child's feelings of exclusion and place disproportionate attention on what might have been a relatively inconsequential aspect of the student's life. (This caution does not rule out helpful information being given to peers when a seizure has taken place.)

In the event of a grand mal seizure, some routine procedures should be followed. Have available a blanket, a pillow, and towels for clean-up. Make the child comfortable if there is time. Do not try to restrain the child. Put nothing in the mouth. Support the child's head on the pillow, turning it to one side to allow the saliva to drain. Remove from the area any hard or sharp objects that might cause harm. Secure medical assistance if the seizure continues more than three or four minutes or if seizures occur three or more times during a school day. Always notify the school administration and the parents that a seizure has occurred. Assure the class that the seizure will pass and that the involved child will not be harmed or affected.

Instructional Considerations

Recommendations regarding special modes of conduct and guidelines governing participation in school activities must come from the child's physician, since most children with epilepsy are under medical supervision. The instructor should stay within these guidelines while avoiding being overprotective. Most children whose seizures are well controlled rarely have seizures during physical activity. However for students whose seizures have not been under control for two years or longer, extra safety precautions (e.g., not participating alone) should be taken during participation in activities that would result in injury if consciousness was lost (such as swimming and bicycling).

Today's approach is to bring epilepsy into the open. A concerted effort should be made to educate today's children so as to alter incorrect information about the condition.

The child with epilepsy is a fully functional person except at the time of a seizure. Epilepsy is not a form of mental illness, and most people with epilepsy do not have an intellectual disability.

Visual Impairment

Vision impairment refers to any condition that interferes with vision, including total blindness. Blindness is a low-incidence condition in childhood; therefore there are usually very few students with severe vision problems in a school. However there are likely to be more students with vision impairment that may include tunnel vision, blurred vision, loss of central vision, motion perception only, or light perception. It is important to find out what the student can see and how to maximize use of existing sight.

A number of characteristics are typically associated with having vision impairment, including fear of injury within activities, delay in motor development milestones (such as when the child walks), poor fundamental movement skills, poor posture due to deficits in balance or from fear of falling, difficulty interpreting body language, and low cardiovascular fitness and strength. Students with vision impairment may develop excellent abilities to memorize information and enhanced ability to learn from touch, feel, and sound.

Instructional Considerations

Children with visual impairments will be successfully included in physical education if the teacher encourages them to be independent and instructs to their strengths. Students with visual impairments have to develop confidence in their ability to move freely and surely within the limits of their abilities. Since limited mobility often leads to reduced activity, this inclination can be countered with a personalized program in which the lack of sight does not prove insurmountable. Children can take part in group fitness activities with assistance as needed. Exercises should pose few problems. Rope jumping, for example, is an excellent activity. Individual movement activities, stunts and tumbling, rhythms and dances (particularly partner dances), and selected apparatus activities can be appropriate. Even low balance beams, bench activities, climbing apparatus, and climbing ropes may be within the child's capacity. If the child has some vision, brightly coloured balls against a contrasting background in good light can permit controlled throwing, tracking, and catching. However, games that rely heavily on catching and throwing are often difficult for students with a visual impairment. These student's sense of balance should be regularly challenged to contribute to their sureness of movement.

The student with a visual impairment cannot ordinarily take visual cues from other children or the teacher, so explanations must be precise and clear. When possible, verbal explanations should be combined with brailling, physical guidance, or demonstrations. Brailling in physical education is a technique akin to reading braille with one's fingers. But in this case the student with the visual impairment will feel objects or the body position of the physical educator, teaching assistant, or peer tutor. Importantly, it is the student with the visual impairment who examines the demonstrator's body, and the movement required; the student isn't manipulated through the movement. For example, the demonstrator may assume a series of positions in gymnastics (e.g., v-sit, long-sit, tuck sit) which the student can braille and then copy. The demonstration should be accompanied by the verbal cue for the skill so that the student can add these to his or her gymnastics repertoire.

Physical guidance is another technique that can be used with students with visual impairment. It is the technique of performing the movement with the student. The student will eventually get the feel of the motion.

Hearing (Auditory) Impairment

Children with hearing impairments are those who are deaf or hard of hearing. In physical education classes, children who experience these conditions are capable of performing most, if not all, activities that students without a disability can perform. Because most instruction is verbal, a student who has a hearing impairment may be isolated and can be frustrated in a regular physical education context, unless other means of communication are established.

Teaching the deaf is a challenging and specialized process, requiring different communication techniques. Many children with hearing impairments have poor or unintelligible speech and inevitably develop a language gap with the hearing world. Sign language, speech reading, and speech training are all important facets of communicative ability for the deaf (see Figure 7.8).

Instructional Considerations

To enhance learning in physical education for students who are deaf or have a hearing impairment, physical educators can augment communication and employ specialized teaching strategies.

To *enhance communication* when giving instructions, reduce ambient noises by turning off any music and not allowing others to talk. Also, ensure that the student who is

Figure 7.8

Signing to student with an auditory impairment.

speech reading is allowed to move to where he/she can best see the person speaking and ensure the face of the person speaking is well lit. Arrange for a buddy or peer tutor to repeat the instructions if necessary. For controlling movement patterns, use hand signals for starting, stopping, moving to an area, assembling near the teacher, sitting down, and so on. If the student signs, learn as much sign language as possible.

Some students who are deaf have vestibular damage. If the semicircular canals of the inner ear are damaged, balance problems may arise. These balance problems may give rise to delays in motor development. Students with balance difficulties should be provided with many opportunities to engage in safe static, dynamic, and inverted balance activities. Students with vestibular damage should also have extra supervision when swimming underwater.

Provide additional information to students who are deaf or hard of hearing. Task cards and cues on a chalkboard can be useful, as can a "do as I do" approach utilizing a partner, peer tutor, or teacher's assistant. During activities involving rhythm or music the vibration from speakers placed on the floor can be sensed if students dance in bare feet. A light that flashes in rhythm with the music can provide a visual cue.

Physical Disabilities

People with physical disabilities climb mountains, compete in marathons, sail yachts, play tennis, and engage in all sorts of sports and recreational activities. Because of the vast array of conditions that fall into this category it is not possible to fully address all possible disabilities that could arise in a school setting. Many children with physical disabilities function on an academic level with

other children and are regular members of a classroom. They should also participate in regular physical education classes.

Instructional Considerations

Focus on what the child can do and on the physical needs that are to be met. Mobility is a problem for most, and modification is needed if the class activity demands running or agility. When collecting information about the student relevant to physical education it is important to ask what muscles and limbs can be moved independently or with minimal assistance; and what functional skills the student can demonstrate; whether the condition is stable or degenerative (such as muscular dystrophy); and whether any activities are contraindicated. It is also helpful to know what the student does with his or her family for physical activity.

Like other students with special needs, individualization is important because achievement goals can be set within the child's capacity to perform (see Figure 7.7 on

Figure 7.9

A student using a wheelchair for mobility participates with his peers.

p. 131). Skills and activities that have the greatest carry-over for lifetime participation should be given time and attention. Although wheelchair volleyball and basketball are popular team sports, there will be few leisure opportunities for individuals to participate in these activities due to the difficulty of getting enough participants together for team play. Strong emphasis should be placed on individual and dual sports such as tennis, track and field, road racing, table tennis, badminton, and swimming. This allows the individual with a physical disability to play a dual sport with an opponent or to participate individually in activities such as road racing and swimming.

Linked to the concept of the least restrictive environment, it is important to know the student's preferred mode of locomotion and the range of assistive devices used. Using a walking frame may be the least restrictive option for a student with cerebral palsy for some activities; however when playing indoor curling the same student may find using her wheelchair less restrictive as she is more stable and has her hands free to curl the rock.

For children who are wheelchair users, physical conditioning is important. Activities should be designed and chosen to develop general musculature, to improve conditions for coping with the disability, and to prevent muscle atrophy. In particular, children who use wheelchairs need strong arm and shoulder musculature to transfer in and out of the wheelchair without assistance. Emphasize flexibility training to prevent and relieve permanent muscle shortening (contracture). Cardiorespiratory training is needed to maintain or improve aerobic capacity, as immobility in the chair decreases activity. From these experiences, the child who uses a wheelchair should derive a personal, functioning program of activity that can carry over into daily living.

Time devoted to specific health care and hygiene after physical education class must be considered for children who use braces or wheelchairs. Children with braces should inspect skin contact areas to look for irritation. If they have perspired, a washcloth and towel will help them freshen up and remove irritants. Children who use wheelchairs can transfer to a sturdy chair that is rigid and stabilized, while allowing their activity wheelchair time to dry out. Better yet, a specialized sport wheelchair might be provided for use in the gym, or on the court or the playing field.

Provide adequate cushioning for any surface to which a person with an orthopedic disability transfers—such as chairs, weight machines, and pool decks—to prevent pressure sores and skin abrasions. Schedules should be adjusted so that time for this care is available. Scheduling the class just before lunch or recess or at the end of the day allows this time.

Fetal Alcohol Spectrum Disorder

Fetal Alcohol Spectrum Disorder (FASD) is used to collectively refer to a range of disabilities caused by alcohol consumed during pregnancy. Alcohol is a neurobehavioural teratogen (a negative factor influencing prenatal life) because it can cause damage to the brain and can subsequently change behaviour. There are four diagnostic categories within this umbrella term: Fetal Alcohol Syndrome (FAS), Partial Fetal Alcohol Syndrome (pFAS), Alcohol-Related Birth Defects (ARBD), and Alcohol-Related Neurodevelopmental Disorder (ARND). Although every individual is unique, there are some common characteristics associated with FASD. Common primary disabilities include:

- Delay in reaching developmental milestones
- Physical and health conditions such as hearing and visual impairments, cardiac and/or respiratory problems and weakened immune systems
- Difficulty controlling impulses
- Memory problems
- Inconsistent performance
- Difficulty generalizing from one situation to another
- Difficulties processing abstract information
- Over- and under-sensitivity to stimuli
- An inability to understand a consequence

All of the primary disabilities listed above affect the student's potential for learning (Saskatchewan Learning, 2004). The effect alcohol has on the central nervous system can also lead to poor motor coordination, increased reaction time, low muscle tone, and fine motor impairment.

Instructional Considerations

Physical difficulties: Students with FASD may have vision problems due to optic nerve damage, and they may be sensitive to bright or fluorescent lights. Providing extra time to read and watching for light sensitivity are useful practices. Students may also be hard of hearing, in which case the instructional considerations described in the Hearing (Auditory) Impairment section are relevant. Because hearing and vision difficulties often present along with distractibility, it can be difficult for students with FASD to develop good listening and observing skills. You can assist students to focus and encourage them to listen to instruction by drawing their attention to key parts of a demonstration before it occurs (e.g., "watch where I place my hands on the ball"). Partners, peer tutors, or teacher's assistants can also assist the student with FASD to focus on important verbal and visual cues.

Students may also be hyper- or hypo-sensitive to light, sound, touch, taste, and smell; and hyposensitive to cold. Students can also display irritability, frustration, loss of temper, hyperactivity, and inattentiveness when senses are overloaded. It is therefore important to monitor the environment and the student's reactions to the environment; and adapt the environment where you can. Structuring the environment and the activities to decrease that amount of stimulation will be beneficial to children with FASD. For example, keep equipment out of the way until it is time to use it. Equipment that is left lying around may be difficult for students with FASD to resist. Noise levels can be a problem for students with FASD. While many students with FASD have hearing problems, they may still be sensitive to loud noises such as loud music or other students' cheering or shouting. It can be helpful to keep the music volume at a level that does not agitate students with FASD (Loftus & Block, 1996). Providing a quieter space for a student with FASD to calm down can be useful. It may also be necessary to monitor what the student wears outside when it is cold. Hyposensitivity to cold may mean that the student doesn't dress appropriately for the conditions. Focusing on fewer movement skills and giving students with FASD plenty of time to work on achievable goals reduces their frustration and enhances their learning.

Social difficulties: Students with FASD often have delayed social skills. Social skills can be taught, and physical education is an excellent context for the development and practice of social skills. In particular, physical education affords opportunities to share with others, take turns, invite others to participate, assist others, give and receive compliments, develop an awareness of personal space, negotiate, and display control. Saskatchewan Learning (2004) suggests the steps to teaching social skills can be organized as follows: Identify the skill on which to focus; teach, review, reteach; model and role-play; provide feedback and reminders; and transfer and generalize to other locations. Imagine a grade 2 class, where students have been asked to design—with a partner—a game that uses a bowling action and has a way to keep count or score. The students can use pins, balls, cones, and/or a hoop. An activity analysis suggests that in the psychomotor domain there is predominantly the skill of bowling; but in the affective domain there are numerous demands. Students will need to agree upon which equipment to use, design their game together through discussion and negotiation, perhaps take turns to bowl, and accept the consequences of their scoring system. A game this like presents both students an opportunity to develop social skills; but it could also be very difficult for a child with FASD if the child was not prepared for this learning activity. Using the program planning model in Figure 7.4 on p. 124, adaptations of personnel (peer tutor, teacher's assistant) or the environment would be useful. The instructional task could be modified for the student with FASD—for example, removing the need to keep count or score would mean that students would not be put in a position of losing a game.

Behavioural challenges: "For students who are affected by prenatal alcohol exposure it is important to remember that these students have permanent neurological damage that will make changing behaviour difficult" (Saskatchewan Learning, 2004, p. 8). Students often do not seem to learn from their experiences, do not connect cause and effect, and have difficulty generalizing to other contexts. Notably, students with FASD are often hyperactive and have difficulty paying attention. There are effective practices that include building a caring and respectful environment, developing and teaching classroom procedures, using positive discipline practices, communicating with home, and having corrective classroom strategies.

Direct, very structured styles of teaching work best for students with FASD. For example "Show me how you can log roll along this mat" is very direct and provides clear instruction about what to do. It is also important that the teacher is as consistent as possible. Stop or freeze signals should be kept constant, and consequences for not following signals should be clearly explained and carried out consistently. Some students with FASD may have difficulty stopping immediately upon hearing a cue. Two strategies that can help are to forewarn the student that you are going to stop (e.g., "I'm going to blow my whistle to stop in five seconds") or to give the group 10 seconds to stop once they hear the cue.

Most importantly, plan on teaching and reviewing rules and appropriate behaviour often; do not assume that the student with FASD understands the rules of the physical education class or proper social behaviour. Henderson and French (1993) suggest that it can be useful to set up situations in which the student with FASD can practise abiding by various rules, social structures, and routines used in physical education. When the student does keep to the rules or routines ensure he or she is praised for the behaviour. Students with FASD probably need more praise than typical students in order to stay in control, stay on task, and to comply with directions (Loftus & Block, 1996). If a student with FASD (or any other student for that matter) does not follow a rule, consistently provide a predetermined consequence (see Chapter 5).

Autism Spectrum Disorders

Autistic disorder, more commonly called autism, is a condition in which the individual exhibits communication difficulties, impaired sociability, inappropriate behaviour, and language problems. It may or may not be accompanied by intellectual disability. There are multiple other "autistic-like" conditions that, together with autism, are referred to as Autism Spectrum Disorders (ASD). Other conditions include Asperger's Syndrome and Pervasive Developmental Disorder Not Otherwise Specified (PDD-NOS). The severity of symptoms can range from almost imperceptible to profoundly disabling. ASD comprises the third most common developmental disability, nearing the prevalence rate of Down syndrome, and males are three to four times more likely to be affected than females.

Individuals with ASD display a wide range of behaviours, such that two children with ASD can differ enormously. Different levels of functioning may also be confounded by intelligence since the full range of intelligence scores is found among individuals with ASD (National Academy of Sciences, 2001). Furthermore, as children develop, behaviours continue to change and evolve. Considerable breadth of abilities among individuals with ASD must be expected. Students with ASD exhibit impairments in communication, reciprocal social interaction, and often have restricted repetitive patterns of interests and behaviours.

Motor delays and movement skill differences are recognized as deficit areas for many individuals with ASD. Delays in motor development can be recognized in some infants with ASD as early as six months and progressive delays are demonstrated in additional infants with increasing age. Movement differences become more obvious during the performance of increasingly challenging tasks that involve sequencing movements or coordinating movements with objects.

Instructional Considerations

The following is a synopsis of selected strategies suggested by Staples, Todd, and Reid (2006) for physical activity instruction with students with ASD.

1. **Familiarization:** Students with ASD can be anxious in new situations, especially with new people; therefore, it is important to give students time to adjust without interference and give them time to explore. The teacher, teacher's assistant, or peer can gradually get closer and increase the level of interaction. The student may or may not directly engage in joint attention with you, but demonstrating that you (and their peers) are interested in interacting with them is important.

2. **Communication:** Use the preferred methods of communication (i.e., signs, pictorial symbols, verbal). Instructions should be concise and straightforward. For younger students with ASD, instructions and questions should be phrased as statements or choices. Avoid questions that can be answered with "no." For example, use "1, 2, 3, run" or "Do you want to run or skip?" instead of "Do you want to run?"

3. **Structure:** Students with ASD benefit from structure. As previously described with FASD, routines provide a predictable environment. A schedule of planned activities can be presented as pictures, words, or real objects. The schedules will ease transitions between activities, but it is also helpful to incorporate verbal reminders. For example, "In 30 seconds we will be moving to the next station to your left" or "We are going to shoot five more baskets each and then put the balls away."

4. **Continuum of assistance:** The continuum of assistance described in Table 7.6 on p. 126 can be helpful for students with ASD. Research does support a prompting (cues, demonstration, physical manipulation) with verbal and visual cues for motor tasks. Students with ASD may demonstrate overselectivity by focusing on only one cue, so it is helpful to focus students on the most important cues. Part of the continuum of assistance is physical manipulation. Allow students who are sensitive to touch to hold onto you; in this manner they regulate how much pressure is applied during contact. Instructors can also give an advanced warning: "I am going to lift your hand." Physical manipulation can also be provided using a piece of equipment. In order to complete an obstacle course and stay on task, two children can work together holding onto a Hula Hoop or piece of rope and never have to touch one another, but still accomplish the task goal. Of course, not all children with ASD are touch-sensitive.

5. **Sensory issues:** Many students with ASD have a preferred sensory modality, which means they may prefer and pay greater attention to instructional cues received through one type of stimuli. Instructors try to gain attention from the children by stating "Look at me, look at me"; however in movement environments "Watch Megan run" followed by actually running is often effective. Students who are visually orientated are attracted to movement; therefore attention will frequently be directed toward the demonstration. Similarly, those who prefer auditory stimulation will become focused on the sounds generated by the movement pattern—such as galloping or a bouncing ball—and will pay attention. Some students with ASD may demonstrate strong aversive

reactions to specific sensory stimuli such as touch or sound. As noted previously, advanced warning is usually enough to avoid extreme reactions.

Learning Disabilities

Learning disabilities encompass a range of problems that lack a clear definition. Examples of terms used to describe various learning disabilities are *perceptual handicaps, brain injury, minimal brain dysfunction, dyslexia,* and *developmental aphasia.* This definition is so broad that over 40% of school-aged students can qualify as being learning disabled. More boys than girls (a 2:1 ratio) are identified as having learning disabilities in today's schools. In addition, many more elementary than secondary school children are identified. Students with learning disabilities may experience the following: hyperactivity, short attention span, perceptual-motor problems, poor self-concept, clumsiness, poor short- or long-term memory, and an unwillingness to persevere when learning motor tasks. The largest single disabling condition in this category is Attention Deficit Hyperactivity Disorder (ADHD), a chronic behaviour disorder characterized by persistent and intrusive inattention, impulsiveness, and hyperactivity.

The causes of learning disabilities are poorly understood. Two major theories are currently popular for explaining these problems (Horvath, 1990). The first theory supposes that learning disabilities are organically based, with one of the major causal factors being an injury to the brain. The individual with a brain injury is unable to receive and integrate sensory impulses efficiently. The second hypothesis is that learning disabilities are biochemically based. This theory supposes that several biochemical factors, such as allergies, mineral and vitamin deficiencies, and glandular disorders cause learning disabilities. Modify the physical education program on an individualized basis for these children, since each will present unique needs.

Instructional Procedures

Structure the program and conduct it in a similar fashion on a day-to-day basis. Students should not be surprised with unexpected changes in the routine. Arrange the activity area so that distractions are kept to a minimum. An unchanging structure allows the child to explore the environment with confidence. The teaching area should be restricted to the smallest possible size so that student–teacher distance is kept to a minimum. An environment without limits may cause some students to feel threatened or out of control. Students with learning disabilities often find it difficult to learn independently or

wait for a turn. Insist on active participation and require students to be on task for a large share of the lesson time. Introduce cross-aged tutoring or invite volunteers in to work individually with students. Attention based on firmness and concern will help these students learn motor skills and deal with extraneous distractions in their environment.

Asthma

Children with asthma have restricted breathing capacity. In the past, doctors were quick to excuse children with asthma from participating in physical education classes. However, recent research shows that physical activity is not contraindicated for children with asthma. A study by Varray, Mercier, Terral, and Prefaut (1991) showed that children with asthma could participate in high-intensity exercise without complications. Children who were 11 years old participated in a swimming program and reached an intensity level within 5% of their maximal heart rate. These children showed a significant increase in cardiovascular fitness. Parents of the participants reported their children showed a decrease in the intensity of wheezing attacks, and the ability to control asthmatic attacks through relaxation and breathing exercises. The researchers concluded that when workloads are individualized for asthmatic children, their cardiovascular fitness can be enhanced through aerobic training.

Instructional Procedures

Check with the school nurse or another health professional to gather background information on students with asthma. Know how to recognize symptoms and deal with severe asthmatic bouts. Working with children with asthma requires the teacher to develop an awareness of the symptoms that require prompt action. If a student is coughing or wheezing, has difficulty breathing, or complains of chest tightness or pressure, take immediate action. Recommended steps are to stop the student's current activity, follow the student's asthma management plan, help the student with medication, and then closely observe the effect. If the student fails to improve or is straining to breathe or speak without pausing for a breath, call for help immediately.

Talk to children with asthma about their asthma and discuss their concerns about being active. Offer reassurance that you are aware of their condition and understand the need to modify activity. The students are often the best judges of their own abilities, as long as they don't feel pressured to push themselves excessively. Try to develop a shared understanding of what is an acceptable modification of the activity you are teaching. Include adequate warm-up activity for students with asthma. Ask children to suggest modifications. If an activity is too demanding and cannot be modified, allow students to help with equipment, keep score, or referee.

Cardiac Problems and Diabetes

Children with cardiac problems are generally under the guidance of a physician. Limitations and restrictions should be followed to the letter. The child should, however, be encouraged to work to the upper limits of the prescription.

Diabetes is an inability to metabolize carbohydrates that results from the body's failure to supply insulin. Serious cases are controlled with insulin, orally or by injection. If the child is overweight, programs of weight reduction and moderate exercise are partial solutions. Children with diabetes are usually under medical supervision. It is important to know when a child with diabetes is in your physical education class, because the child must be monitored to detect the possibility of hypoglycemia (abnormally low blood sugar level). Trembling, weakness, hunger, incoherence, and even coma or convulsions can accompany the condition. The solution is to raise the blood sugar level immediately through oral consumption of simple sugar (for example, skim milk, orange juice) or some other easily converted carbohydrate. The student usually carries carbohydrates, but a supply should be available to the instructor. Immediate action is needed because low blood sugar level can be dangerous, even leading to loss of life. The student probably has enough control to participate in almost any activity. This is illustrated by the number of professional athletes living with diabetes who successfully meet the demands of high activity.

Critical Thinking

1. Design a gymnastics lesson consistent with your province/territory curriculum. Conduct an activity analysis to identify the psychomotor (and physical fitness), affective, and cognitive demands of the lesson. Now consider that you have a student with an autism spectrum disorder, or with an amputation, or with an intellectual disability in the class. Describe how you might individualize instruction for this lesson.

2. Explain how the principles of the least restrictive environment and normalization might influence how a physical educator utilizes a teacher's assistant in a physical education class.

References and Suggested Readings

Alberta Education. (2006). *Identifying student needs. Selecting accommodations and strategies*. Edmonton, AB: Crown in Right of Alberta.

Alberta Education. (2004). *Standards for Special Education*. Edmonton, AB: Crown in Right of Alberta.

BC Ministry of Education. (2004). *Special needs students order*. School Act, sections 75 and 168 (2) (t). Ministerial Order 150/89 (M150/89), Amended M32/04 Effective February 18, 2004.

Block, M.E. (1994). *A teacher's guide to including students with disabilities in regular physical education*. Baltimore: Brookes.

Block, M.E., Klavina, A., & Flint, W. (2007). Including students with severe, multiple disabilities in general physical education. *Journal of Physical Education, Recreation and Dance, 78*(3), 29–32.

Cheatum, B.A. & Hammond, A. (2000). *Physical activities for improving children's learning and behavior*. Champaign, IL: Human Kinetics.

DePaepe, J. (1985). The influence of three least restrictive environments on the content motor-ALT and performance of moderately mentally retarded students. *Journal of Teaching Physical Education, 5*, 34–41.

Davis, R. W. (2002). *Inclusion through sports—A guide to enhancing sport experiences*. Champaign, IL: Human Kinetics.

Dickinson, J., Perkins, D., & Bikek, I. (1988). Integrated versus special schools. *Canadian Association for Health, Physical Education, Recreation and Dance*, Jan./Feb., *35–39*.

Dobbins, D.A., Garron, R., & Rarick, G.L. (1981). The motor performance of educable mentally retarded and intellectually normal boys after covariate control for differences in body size. *Research Quarterly, 52*, 6–7.

Dunn, J.M. (1997). *Special physical education: Adapted, individualized, developmental*. Madison: Brown & Benchmark.

Eichstaedt, C.B. & Kalakian, L.H. (1993). *Developmental/adapted physical education: Making Ability Count*. New York: Macmillan.

Emes, C. & Veide, B. (2005). *Practicum in adapted physical activity*. Champaign, IL: Human Kinetics.

Government of Canada. (1982). *Canadian Charter of Rights and Freedoms, Schedule B to the Canada Act 1982 (U.K.)*.

Henderson, H.L., & French, R.W. (1993). *Creative approaches to managing student behavior in physical education* (Vol. 2nd). Park City, UT: Family Development Resources, Inc.

Horvath, M. (1990). *Physical education and sport for exceptional students*. Dubuque, IA: Wm. C. Brown.

Human Resources and Social Development Canada. (2006). *Advancing the inclusion of people with disabilities 2006*. Ottawa, ON: Government of Canada.

Jansma, P. & French, R. (1994). *Special physical education: Physical activity, sports, and recreation*. Englewood Cliffs: Prentice Hall.

Kasser, & Lytle, R. (2005). *Inclusive physical activity—A lifetime of opportunities.* Champaign, IL: Human Kinetics.

Laurence, M. (1988). Making adventure accessible: Innovations in adapted physical education/recreation curricula. *Canadian Association for Health, Physical Education, Recreation and Dance,* May/June, 10–13.

Levinson, L.J. & Reid, G. (1991). Patterns of physical activity among youngsters with developmental disabilities. *Canadian Association for Health, Physical Education, Recreation and Dance,* Summer, 24–28.

Lieberman, L.J. & Houston-Wilson, C. (2002). *Strategies for inclusion: A handbook for physical educators.* Champaign, IL: Human Kinetics.

Lieberman, L.J., James, A.R., & Ludwa, N. (2004). The impact of inclusion in general physical education for all students. *Journal of Physical Education, Recreation, & Dance, 75,* 37–41, 55.

Loftus, J., & Block, M. E. (1996). Physical education for students with fetal alcohol syndrome. *Physical Educator 53,* 147–151.

Manitoba Education Citizenship and Youth. (2006). *Appropriate educational programming in Manitoba: Standards for student services.* Winnipeg, MB: Crown in Right of Manitoba.

Ministère de l'Éducation. (2004). *Learning difficulties: Reference framework for intervention.* Government du Québec.

Mosston, M., & Ashworth, S. (1994). *Teaching physical education* (4th ed.). Ontario: Maxwell Macmillan.

Ministry of Education. (1995). *Special education services: A manual of policies, procedures and guidelines.* Victoria, British Columbia: Special Education Branch.

Murphy, R. & Sidney, K. (1992). Diabetes and physical activity: what the physical educator and coach should know. *Canadian Association for Health, Physical Education, Recreation and Dance,* Summer, 7–11.

National Academy of Sciences. (2001). *Report of the committee on educational interventions in children with autism: Educating children with autism.* Washington, DC: National Academy of Sciences Press.

Nichols, D.R. (1997). Alternative physical education activities: An example of inclusion. *Canadian Association for Health, Physical Education, Recreation and Dance, 63,* 22–24.

Ontario Ministry of Education. (2004). *The individual education plan (IEP): A resource guide.* www.edu.gov.on.ca.

Rarick, G. L. (1980). Cognitive-motor relationships in the growing years. *Research Quarterly for Exercise and Sport, 51,* 174–192.

Reid, G. (1981). Perceptual-motor training: Has the term lost its utility? *JOPERD, 52*(6), 38–39.

Rouse, P. (2004). *Adapted games & activities—From tag to teambuilding.* Champaign, IL: Human Kinetics.

Saskatchewan Human Rights Code, S.S. 1979, c. S-24.1

Saskatchewan Learning. (2002). *Children's Services Policy Framework.* Planning, Evaluation and Children's Services, Saskatchewan Learning.

Sherrill, C. (1993). *Adapted physical activity, recreation and sport: Cross disciplinary and life span.* (4th ed.). Madison, WI: Brown & Benchmark.

Sherrill, C. (1998). *Adapted physical activity, recreation and sport: Cross disciplinary and life span.* (5th ed.). Boston: WCB/McGraw-Hill.

Strickland, J., Temple, V.A., & Walkley, J.W. (2005). Peer tutoring as an instructional design methodology to improve fundamental movement skills. *ACHPER Healthy Lifestyles Journal, 52,* 22–27.

Taylor, M. J. (1984). The plight of physically awkward children in our schools or "Why they hate physical education." *Canadian Association for Health, Physical Education, Recreation and Dance,* May/June, 26 & 36.

Temple, V.A. (2006). Getting a head-start on movement for life. *Snapshots Primary Edition: The Specialist Schools Trust Journal of Innovation in Education, 3,* 8–10.

Tripp, A., Piletic, C., & Babcock, G. (2004). *A position statement on including students with disabilities in physical education.* Reston, VA: Adapted Physical Activity Council of the American Association for Active Lifestyles and Fitness.

Ulrich, D.A. (1983). A comparison of the qualitative motor performance of normal, educable, and trainable mentally retarded students. In R.L. Eason, T.L. Smith, & F. Caron (Eds.), *Adapted physical activity.* Champaign, IL: Human Kinetics.

U.S. Department of Health and Human Services. (1995). *Asthma & physical activity in the school.* (NIH Publication No. 95-3651). Washington DC: National Institutes of Health.

Varray, A.L., Mercier, J.G., Terral, C.M., & Prefaut, C.G. (1991). Individualized aerobic and high intensity training for asthmatic children in an exercise readaption program. *Chest, 99,* 579–586.

Vogler, E.W. (2003). Students with disabilities in physical education. In S. Silverman & C. Ennis (Eds.), *Student learning in physical education: Applying research to enhance instruction* (2nd ed.) (pp. 83–105). Champaign, IL: Human Kinetics.

Webster, G.E. (1987). Influence of peer tutors upon academic learning time-physical education of mentally handicapped students. *Journal of Teaching Physical Education, 6,* 393–403.

Winnick, J.P. (2005). *Adapted physical education and sport* (4th ed.). Champaign, IL: Human Kinetics.

Wolfensberger, W. (1972). *The principle of normalization in human services.* Toronto: National Institute of Mental Retardation.

Zhang, J. & Griffin, A. (2007). Including children with autism in general physical education. *Journal of Physical Education, Recreation and Dance, 78*(3), 33–37, 50.

Weblinks

The SNOW Project: www.snow.utoronto.ca

The SNOW Project (Special Needs Ontario Windows) is a provider of online resources and professional development opportunities for educators and parents of students with special needs. The website offers tools and information, online workshops, curriculum materials, discussion fora, and other resources.

The British Columbia Wheelchair Sports Association: www.bcwheelchairsports.com

This association's website has information for both children and adult wheelchair athletes, with event listings, programs, coaching and sports science information, and links to other resources.

Petro-Canada Paralympic Schools Program: www.paralympic.ca

An online educational resource that helps students learn about the Paralympic Games. Includes cross-curricular lesson plans.

Active Living Alliance for Canadians with a Disability: www.ala.ca

Includes information about *Moving to Inclusion*, a series of nine disability-specific resource binders. Each binder includes a wide range of strategies to enable inclusion of students with different disabilities in physical activity programs.

National Center on Physical Activity and Disability (NCPAD): www.ncpad.org

This website is an information centre concerned with physical activity and disability. The broad goal of the site and NCPAD is health promotion through physical activity for persons with a disability.

Program Implementation

CHAPTER 8

Curriculum Development

Essential Components

I	**Organized around content standards**
II	**Student-centred and developmentally appropriate**
III	**Physical activity and motor skill development form the core of the program**
IV	Teaches management skills and self-discipline
V	**Promotes inclusion of all students**
VI	**Focuses on process over product**
VII	**Promotes lifetime personal health and wellness**
VIII	Teaches cooperation and responsibility and promotes sensitivity to diversity

Physical Education Standards

1	**Students are able to move competently using a variety of fundamental and specialized motor skills.**
2	Students can monitor and maintain a health-enhancing level of physical fitness.
3	Students are able to apply movement concepts and basic mechanics of skill performance when learning and refining motor skills.
4	Students comprehend the basic principles of wellness and are able to apply concepts that enable them to make meaningful decisions that positively impact their health and wellness.
5	Students participate in a wide variety of physical activities and learn how to maintain a personalized active lifestyle.
6	Students demonstrate empathy, understanding, and respect for the numerous differences exhibited by people in an activity setting.
7	Students exhibit responsible and self-directed behaviours that lead to positive social interactions in physical activity.

ensure that the curriculum will meet the needs of all students.

OUTCOMES

- Define *scope, sequence,* and *balance* as each relates to curriculum development.

- List elements common to quality curriculum.

- Delineate your philosophy of physical education for children.

- List environmental factors that have an impact on curriculum development.

- Specify the seven-step approach in developing a quality curriculum.

- Specify the needs, characteristics, and interests of children and explain how these age and maturity factors influence program development.

- Cite the three learning domains and discuss characteristics of each.

OVERVIEW

This chapter offers a systematic approach for developing a curriculum and suggests formats for organization and evaluation. A sequence of steps is provided for planning, designing, and implementing a comprehensive curriculum. The concepts of scope, sequence, and balance help

Designing a Quality Curriculum

The steps that follow offer a sequential approach for constructing a meaningful, well-planned physical education program. The first four steps are designed to establish the framework that guides selection of activities for the curriculum.

Step One: Be Familiar with Physical Education Curriculum Guide

An approved curriculum guide is the foundation document for physical education programs in Canadian schools. Familiarity with this document is essential.

Conceptual Framework for the Curriculum

The development of a curriculum includes a set of beliefs, goals, and learning outcomes that form a conceptual framework. A conceptual framework is a series of statements that characterize the desired curriculum. These concepts establish the criteria that will be used to select activities and experiences included in the curriculum. The framework not only directs the activities but also reflects beliefs about education and the learner. Following are general conceptual statements that define a developmentally appropriate physical education curriculum.

- *Curriculum goals and learning outcomes are appropriate for all youngsters.* This implies a balanced curriculum that covers fundamental skills, sport skills, games, rhythms and dance, gymnastics, and individual and dual activities. Emphasis is placed on developing a broad foundation of motor skills for all students.

- *Activities in the curriculum are selected based on their potential to help students reach curriculum goals.* The elementary years are a time of experimentation, practice, and decision-making involving all movement possibilities. The criterion for inclusion of activities is not based on whether teachers or students *prefer* certain activities. Activities are included in the curriculum because they contribute to student progress toward goals and learning outcomes.

- *The curriculum helps youngsters develop lifelong physical activity habits and understand basic fitness concepts.* Regardless of the philosophy of the curriculum, it should be designed so youngsters leave school with active lifestyle habits. Fitness is an important component of the curriculum and should be varied, positive, and

educational. The fitness program is experiential: that is, students participate in fitness activities rather than just being told the facts of fitness. A meaningful curriculum helps students understand that physical activity and fitness are personal in nature, need to be maintained throughout life, and contribute to better health.

- *The curriculum includes activities that enhance cognitive and affective learning.* Children are whole beings and need to learn more than the physical performance of skills. They must understand skill performance principles and develop cognitive learning related to physical activity and wellness. Affective development, the learning of cooperative and social skills, is fostered through group activities that are inclusive of all children regardless of their widely varying skills and abilities.

- *The curriculum provides experiences that allow all children to succeed and feel satisfaction.* Quality programs focus on minimizing failure and emphasizing success. Activities that emphasize self-improvement, participation, and cooperation encourage the development of positive self-concepts.

- *Activities in the curriculum are presented in an educationally sound sequence.* Progression is the soul of learning, and the curriculum should reflect progression vertically (between developmental levels) and horizontally (within each level and within each activity).

- *The curriculum includes an appropriate means of assessing student progress.* Student assessment includes health-related fitness, skill development, cognitive learning, and attitude development toward physical activity. Any assessment program should enhance the effectiveness of the program and should help teachers individualize instruction, communicate with parents, and identify youngsters with special needs.

Provincial and Territorial Physical Education Curriculum Guides

Each province and territory has a prescribed curriculum guide for physical education. This curriculum guide provides the conceptual framework for the learning experiences of students in physical education. Although there are strong commonalities in both content and structure, there are also differences in physical education curricula across Canada. The following conceptual frameworks from Manitoba and British Columbia demonstrate some of these similarities and differences. Figure 8.1 shows a graphic of the conceptual framework for Manitoba Physical Education/Health Education (2000). This graphic is helpful in showing the relationships of major concepts that form the basis for the physical education curriculum.

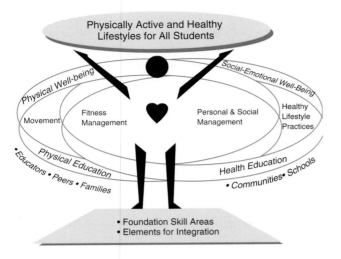

Figure 8.1

Conceptual Framework for Physical Education/Health Education (Manitoba).

Source: Manitoba Education and Training. (2000). *Kindergarten to senior 4 physical education/health education—Manitoba curriculum framework of outcomes for active healthy lifestyles*. Winnipeg, MB: Author. Reproduced by permission of Manitoba Education, Citizenship and Youth. All rights reserved.

The content and structure of this framework is delineated in Figure 8.2, Manitoba Curriculum Framework of Outcomes for Active Healthy Lifestyles (2000). Here the learning outcomes are organized into five sections (Movement, Fitness Management, Safety, Personal and Social Management, Healthy Lifestyle Practices). The specific learning outcomes in these categories are further delineated into knowledge and skill strands.

Figure 8.3 shows the general conceptual framework for the physical education curriculum in British Columbia. Three concepts (Active Living, Movement, Personal and Social Responsibility) are used as organizers for the learning outcomes in physical education. Each curriculum organizer includes learning outcomes from the three general learning domains (psychomotor, cognitive, affective). Figure 8.4 shows the conceptual framework for the physical education program in Alberta schools. Four general outcomes (Activity, Benefits Health, Cooperation, and Do it Daily . . . for Life) are used to organize specific learning outcomes in much the same manner as shown in Figure 8.3.

The method of organizing outcomes under specific physical education concepts in the Manitoba, British Columbia, and Alberta examples shows a departure from earlier curriculum documents in which outcomes were typically organized under the three general learning domains.

The reader is encouraged to examine the particular physical education curriculum guide for her or his respective province or territory.

Step Two: Develop a Personal Philosophy

A philosophical statement defines how physical education fits into the total school curriculum and what it will accomplish for each student. A personal philosophy of physical education reflects the educator's value orientation, and in turn guides the choices she will make when interpreting and implementing the provincial or territorial curriculum.

Value orientation is a set of personal and professional beliefs that provides a basis for determining curricular decisions. In other words, a teacher's value orientation determines what he considers to be the most important outcomes in physical education. Often, physical educators have several value orientations, and physical education programs reflect a blend of different values. For example, a chosen model might include participating over the lifetime in physical activities, developing sport skills, acquiring fitness knowledge, improving social skills, acquiring disciplinary knowledge, or a combination of orientations.

When implementing or revising an existing curriculum, the value orientation of the physical education staff toward the existing curriculum and toward proposed changes is a necessary consideration (Jewett, Bain, & Ennis, 1995).

Determining the value orientation of the curriculum involves consideration of three major components: the subject matter to be learned, the students for whom the curriculum is being developed, and the society that has established the schools. Priorities in curriculum vary depending on the value orientations of the physical educators involved in the planning. For example, physical educators who place highest priority on subject matter mastery include an emphasis on sport, dance, outdoor adventure activities, physical fitness activities, and aquatic activities. This in turn places strong emphasis on learning skills and gaining knowledge, so students have the opportunity to learn the subject matter and continue active participation for a lifetime. In contrast, instructors who favour a student-centred approach prize activities that develop the individual student. They emphasize helping students find activities that are personally meaningful. Other physical educators see student autonomy and self-direction as the most important goals. They focus instruction and curricula on lifetime sport skills and nontraditional activities, such as cooperative games and group activities, in an attempt to foster problem-solving and interpersonal skills. The examples above illustrate a few of the different value orientations of physical educators. Finding common ground among value orientations makes it easier for a staff to present lessons that teach common goals and learning outcomes.

General Student Learning Outcomes	1. Movement	2. Fitness Management	3. Safety	4. Personal and Social Management	5. Healthy Lifestyle Practices
Description	The student will demonstrate competency in selected movement skills, and knowledge of movement development and physical activities with respect to different types of learning experiences, environments, and cultures.	The student will demonstrate the ability to develop and follow a personal fitness plan for lifelong physical activity and well-being.	The student will demonstrate safe and responsible behaviours to manage risks and prevent injuries in physical activity participation and in daily living.	The student will demonstrate the ability to develop self-understanding, to make health-enhancing decisions, to work co-operatively and fairly with others, and to build positive relationships with others.	The student will demonstrate an ability to make informed decisions for healthy living related to personal health practices, active living, healthy nutritional practices, substance use and abuse, and human sexuality.
Knowledge Strands (Acquiring knowledge/ understanding)	A. Basic Movement (Science, Math, The Arts) B. Movement Development C. Activity-specific Movement	A. Fitness Components (SC, MA) B. Fitness Benefits C. Fitness Development	A. Physical Activity Risk Management (SC) B. Safety of Self and Others (SC, SS)	A. Personal Development (All Subject Areas) B. Social Development (All) C. Mental–emotional Development (All)	A. Personal Health Practices (SC) B. Active Living (SC, MA) C. Nutrition (SC, MA) D. Substance Use and Abuse Prevention (SC) E. Human Sexuality (SC, MA)
Skills Strands (Acquiring and applying skills)	A. Acquisition of Movement Skills (The Arts, SS) B. Application of Movement Skills to Sport/Games C. Application of Movement Skills to Alternative Pursuits D. Application of Movement Skills to Rhythmic/Gymnastic Activities	A. Acquisition/ Application of Fitness Management Skills to Physical Activity and Healthy Lifestyle Practices (SC, MA)	A. Acquisition/ Application of Safe Practices to Physical Activity and Healthy Lifestyle Practices	A. Acquisition of Personal and Social Management Skills to Physical Activity and Healthy Lifestyle Practices	A. Application of Decision-making/ Problem-solving Skills to Physical Activity and Healthy Lifestyle Practices

Figure 8.2

Manitoba Curriculum Framework of Outcomes for Active Healthy Lifestyles.

Source: Manitoba Education and Training. (2000): *Kindergarten to senior 4 physical education/health education—Manitoba curriculum framework of outcomes for active healthy lifestyles.* Winnipeg, MB: Author. Reproduced by permission of Manitoba Education, Citizenship and Youth. All rights reserved.

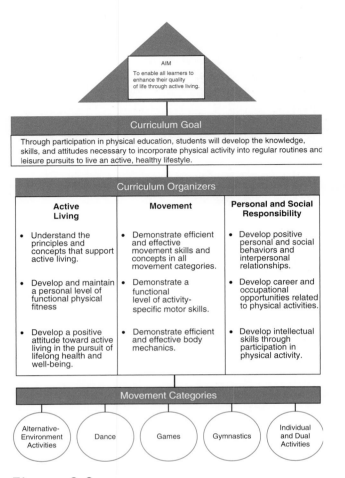

Figure 8.3

Conceptual Framework for Physical Education (British Columbia).

Source: British Columbia Ministry of Education. (1995). *Physical education K–7 integrated resource package*. Victoria, BC: Author. Reprinted with permission.

The following is an example of a typical philosophical platform for physical education. Physical education is that portion of the child's overall education that is accomplished through movement. It is education about and involving movement. Physical education must be largely an instructional program if it is to acquire a full partnership in the child's overall education. Only high-quality programs based on developmental goals with demonstrable outcomes achieve this respect. Although physical education stresses psychomotor goals, it also contributes to cognitive and affective learning domains. Three major and unique contributions of physical education to the total school curriculum are as follows:

1. *To develop personal activity and fitness habits.* The program teaches children the conceptual framework under which personal fitness and lifetime activity habits are developed. This implies teaching the concept

of human wellness (that is, teaching students how to maintain a vibrant and functional lifestyle throughout adulthood). Emphasis is placed on lifetime activity and personal habits that can be used in adulthood.

2. *To develop and enhance movement competency and motor skills.* Movement competency is rooted in developing a broad base of body management skills. The focus is on developing motor skills in a positive and nurturing environment. Personal competency in a wide variety of skills is an overriding theme of instruction.

3. *To gain a conceptual understanding of movement principles.* To move efficiently requires learning basic concepts of movement and understanding anatomical and mechanical principles. Physical education instruction integrates knowledge and skill performance to develop students who know how to move.

Step Three: Consider Environmental Factors

Environmental factors are all those conditions within the community and school district that limit or extend the scope of the curriculum. Examples of environmental factors are the amount and type of equipment, budget size, and cultural make-up of the community. Other factors—such as the support of school administrators—can affect the type of scheduling or amount of required physical education in the school. Different communities may value certain types of activities or experiences for their children. Although environmental factors need to be examined carefully, they should not circumvent and limit curriculum scope and sequence. Rather, these factors should give direction to the curriculum development process. Consider various environmental factors and try to use them to enhance the creativity and scope of the curriculum.

Following are examples of environmental factors that can limit the development of a quality curriculum. However, these factors can be handled creatively to ensure an effective curriculum. Think big; develop a comprehensive and ideal curriculum that is as varied, broad, and creative as possible.

School Administrators

The support of school administrators has a significant impact on the curriculum. It is important to communicate program goals to administrators. Like the public, administrators may have misconceptions about physical education and its contribution to the overall education of students. In most cases, administrators will support physical education if they perceive that the program is built on sound educational principles that are documented and evaluated.

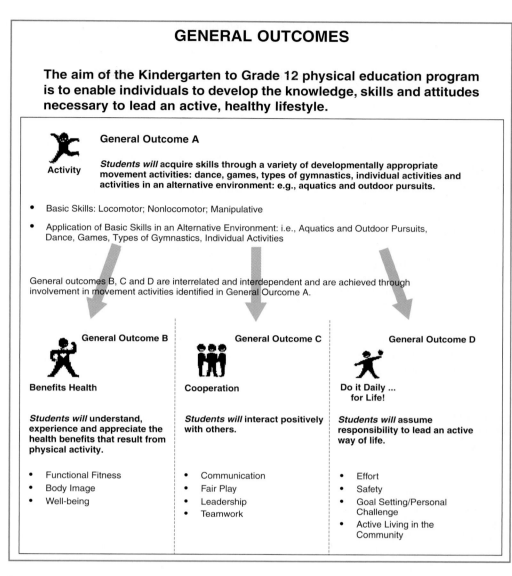

Figure 8.4

Conceptual Framework for Alberta Physical Education Curriculum.

The Community: People and Climate

Occupations, religions, educational levels, cultural values, and physical activity habits within the community are factors that might affect curriculum development. Parents have a strong influence on the activity interests and habits of their children. The geographical location and the climate of the area are also important factors for consideration. The terrain (mountains, plains, and so on), combined with the weather conditions particular to each area, has an effect on people's activity interests. Extremely hot or cold climates influence markedly what activities are included in the curriculum and at what time of year they should be scheduled.

Facilities and Equipment

Available teaching facilities influence which activities can be offered. Facilities include on-campus as well as off-campus areas in the neighbouring community. Off-campus facilities might be a community swimming pool or park. Equipment must be available in quality and quantity. If students are to learn at an optimum rate, one piece of equipment per child is ideal. Equipment can be purchased with school funds or through school fund-raising events. The amount of funding allocated for purchasing new equipment and replacing old supplies has an impact on the quality of the curriculum. In some cases, sets of expensive large apparatus (for example, gymnastics apparatus) may be purchased by the district and moved from school to school throughout the year.

Scheduling

The schedule or organizational pattern of the school has an impact on curriculum development. Factors to consider are how many times per week classes meet and the length of class periods. In some provinces and territories, the curriculum guide provides guidelines for frequency and duration of physical education. For example, in Saskatchewan "core curriculum guidelines recommend that 150 minutes per week be allotted to the instructional physical education program. Daily physical education is preferred" (Saskatchewan Education, 1992, p. 12). Similarly, the Nova Scotia physical education guideline for primary through grade 6 is 150 minutes per week. New Brunswick (Francophone program) recommends the following for PE: gr. 1–2, 80 min/week; gr. 3–6, 100 min/week; and gr. 7–8, 115 min/week. In addition, some provincial curriculum documents provide a guideline for the percentage PE should utilize in overall instruction time. For example, in Manitoba the following minimum time allotments are recommended: "11 percent of instructional time (75 percent of the time spent on physical education-related student learning outcomes/25 percent of the time spent on health education-related student learning outcomes" (Manitoba Education, 2000, p. 8). Similarly, the British Columbia physical education curriculum guide states "schools are expected to allocate 10 percent of instructional time to the subject [physical education]" (B.C. Ministry of Education, 1995, p. 1). As mentioned in Chapter 1, since the mid-1970s the Canadian Association for Health, Physical Education, Recreation and Dance (CAHPERD) has continued to advocate for quality daily physical education (QDPE) in Canadian schools. Their general guideline for frequency and duration of physical education is a minimum of 150 minutes per week. Where your provincial or territorial curriculum guide does not specify, the reader is encouraged to use the CAHPERD guidelines.

Regardless of the various parameters, most elementary schools put together a scheduling committee. This committee is responsible for scheduling time and facilities in order to meet whatever guidelines are provided. Consider several factors when developing schedules. Most often, 30 to 45 minutes is the amount of time scheduled for physical education classes. Some teachers prefer 45 minutes for youngsters in the intermediate grades; however, such periods may be long for primary grade children.

Step Four: Determine Learning Outcomes

Curriculum goals and learning outcomes provide the direction of the program as mandated and desired by the province or territory, district, or individual school. They determine what students should know and be able to do when they complete their schooling. These goals and learning outcomes guide what criteria will be used to select instructional activities for the curriculum.

Learning Outcomes

Learning outcomes describe what a student is expected to know and do as a result of active participation in the learning experiences designed by the teacher. They may be stated in general terms such as the ones listed in Figures 8.2, 8.3, and 8.4 when used to describe overall curriculum outcomes, or in more specific terms when referring to actual lesson outcomes. Learning outcomes (similar terms—behavioural objectives, student learning outcomes, prescribed learning outcomes) are usually written in behavioural terms. Generally, learning outcomes comprise three key characteristics: (a) a desired behaviour that is observable; (b) a behaviour that is measurable; and (c) a criterion for success that can be measured. Learning outcomes are written for all three of the learning domains—psychomotor, cognitive, and affective. The reader is reminded that the organization of the learning outcomes from these general learning domains is unique to each provincial and territorial physical education curriculum (see examples in Figures 8.2, 8.3, and 8.4). A description of each domain follows.

1. *Psychomotor domain.* This domain is the primary focus of instruction for physical educators. The seven levels in psychomotor domain taxonomy are movement vocabulary, movement of body parts, locomotor movements, movement of implements and objects, patterns of movement, movement with others, and movement problem solving. This graduated list progresses in line with the developmental level of learners. Children learn the vocabulary of movement before proceeding to simple body-part movements. Youngsters learn more complex movements to enable them to participate in activities with others and to solve personal movement dilemmas.

2. *Cognitive domain.* The cognitive domain was defined by Bloom (1956) and includes six major areas: knowledge, comprehension, application, analysis, synthesis, and evaluation. The focus of the cognitive domain for physical education is knowing rules, health information, safety procedures, and so on, and being able to understand and apply such knowledge. As students mature, they learn to analyze different activities, develop personalized exercise routines (synthesis), and evaluate their fitness levels.

3. *Affective domain.* The affective domain (Krathwohl et al., 1964) deals with feelings, attitudes, and values. The major categories of learning in this area are receiving, responding, valuing, organization, and characterization. Typically, changes in the affective domain happen more slowly than do changes in the psychomotor and cognitive domains.

The following are examples of learning outcomes related to content standards listed in Chapter 1.

Psychomotor Domain

The student will be able to (TSWBAT) accomplish the following:

1. Move efficiently using a variety of locomotor skills such as walking, running, skipping, and hopping.

2. Perform body management skills on a variety of apparatus including climbing ropes, benches, and balance beams.

Cognitive Domain

The student will be able to (TSWBAT) accomplish the following:

1. Demonstrate an understanding of words that describe a variety of relationships with objects such as *around, behind, over, through,* and *parallel.*

2. Demonstrate an understanding of how warm-up and cool-down prevent injuries.

Affective Domain

The student will be able to (TSWBAT) accomplish the following:

1. Show empathy for the concerns and limitations of peers.

2. Demonstrate a willingness to participate with peers regardless of diversity or disability.

Step Five: Select Developmentally Appropriate Activities

When selecting activities for a developmentally appropriate physical education curriculum, a clear understanding of children is requisite. The task of designing a program that flows with children and doesn't run contrary to their characteristics and interests requires a clear view of their nature.

Know the Basic Urges of Children

The urges of children represent broad traits that are typical regardless of their age, developmental maturity, sex, or race. A basic urge is a desire to do or accomplish something. All children have similar urges, which are influenced by heredity or environment. Basic urges are linked closely to societal influences and are affected by teachers, parents, and peers. Usually, basic urges are similar among youngsters of all ages and not affected by developmental maturity. These urges provide direction for creating child-centred experiences.

The Urge for Movement Children have an insatiable appetite for moving, performing, and being active. They run for the sheer joy of running. For them, activity is the essence of living. Design a physical education program that takes advantage of this craving for movement.

The Urge for Success and Approval Children like to achieve and have their achievements recognized. They wilt under criticism and disapproval, whereas encouragement and friendly support can promote growth and development. Failure can lead to frustration, lack of interest, and inefficient learning. Successes should far outweigh failures, and students should achieve a measure of success during each class meeting. Organize and present activities in the curriculum in a manner that assures students will achieve an adequate amount of success.

The Urge for Peer Acceptance and Social Competence Peer acceptance is a basic human need. Children want others to accept, respect, and like them. Teach and encourage peer acceptance in physical education and the overall school environment. Learning to cooperate with others, being a contributing team member, and sharing accomplishments with friends are important outcomes of the program.

The Urge to Cooperate and Compete Children want to work and play with other children. They find satisfaction in being a needed part of a group and experience sadness when others reject them. Cooperation needs to be taught prior to competitive experiences since competition is impossible when people choose not to cooperate or follow the rules. Often, the joy of being part of a group far outweighs the gains from peer competition.

The Urge for Adventure The drive to participate in something different, adventurous, or unusual impels children to participate in interesting new activities. Youngsters are motivated by unexpected activities and teaching methodologies, and this is what they are seeking when they want to know "What are we going to do today?"

The Urge for Creative Satisfaction Children like to try different ways of doing things, to experiment with different implements, and to find creative ways of accomplishing goals. Finding different ways to express themselves physically satisfies the urge for creative action.

The Urge for Rhythmic Expression Physical education offers a variety of rhythmic activities that students can learn well enough to achieve satisfaction. Emphasize the natural rhythm involved in all physical activity, be it walking, running, or skipping. Many effective and beautiful sport movements can be done rhythmically, including shooting a lay-up, jumping a rope, and running hurdles.

The Urge to Know Young people are naturally curious. They are interested not only in what they are doing but also in why they are doing it. Knowing why is a great motivator. It takes little time or effort to share with a class why an activity is performed and the contributions it makes to physical development.

Understand the Characteristics and Interests of Children

While the urges of children represent broad traits regardless of age, sex, or race, *characteristics* and *interests* are age- and maturity-specific attributes that influence learning outcomes. The characteristics and interests chart (see Table 8.1) provides information that influences appropriate selection and sequencing of curriculum activities. The information in the chart is broken out by the three learning domains—psychomotor, cognitive, and affective—and is grouped by developmental levels.

Activities are most often grouped by grade level or developmental level. This textbook uses developmental levels to group activities and units of instruction because the method allows for greater variation of skill development among students. Figure 8.5 illustrates the continuum of skill development through which most youngsters progress. Even though this developmental skill continuum is common to all youngsters, there are large variations among children. Placing activities in developmental levels offers activities that are appropriate for the maturity and developmental levels of all youngsters. On occasion, it may be necessary to move to a higher or lower developmental

level to accommodate youngsters. Table 8.2 on p.156 shows how developmental levels roughly equate with grades and ages. The following section describes characteristics of learners at each level and identifies skills and competencies typical of children in each of the levels.

Developmental Level I For the majority of children, activities placed in developmental level I are appropriate for kindergarten through grade 2. Most activities for younger children are individual in nature and centre on learning movement concepts through theme development. Children learn about movement principles, and educational movement themes are used to teach body identification and body management skills. By stressing the joy and personal benefits of physical activity, positive behaviours can be developed that last a lifetime.

Developmental Level II Developmental level II activities are usually appropriate for the majority of children in grades 3 and 4. In developmental level II activities, refinement of fundamental skills occurs and the ability to perform specialized skills begins to surface. Practising manipulative skills enhances visual–tactile coordination. This is a time when children explore, experiment, and create activities without fear. Children learn the how and why of activity patterns. Cooperation with peers receives more emphasis through group and team play. Initial instruction in sport skills begins in developmental level II, and a number of lead-up activities allow youngsters to apply newly learned skills in a small-group setting.

Developmental Level III Developmental level III activities place more emphasis on specialized skills and sport activities. The majority of activities at this level are used with students in grades 5 to 7. Basketball, softball, track and field, and volleyball are typically added to sport offerings. Students learn and improve sport skills while participating in cooperative sport lead-up games. Adequate time is also included for physical activities in the other movement categories, including dance, individual and dual activities, gymnastics, and alternative environment activities.

Step Six: Organize Selected Activities into Instructional Units

The major criterion when selecting activities for the curriculum is this: Do the activities contribute to the goals and learning outcomes of physical education? This approach contrasts with selecting activities because they are fun or because you enjoy them. Some teachers fail to include activities in the curriculum if they lack confidence or feel

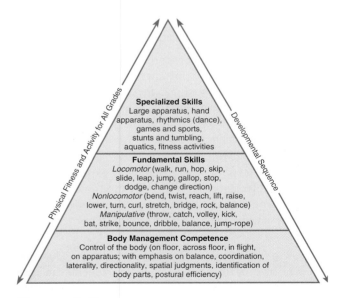

Figure 8.5

Continuum of skill development.

TABLE 8.1
Characteristics and interests of children

Characteristics and Interests	Program guidelines
Developmental Level I	
Psychomotor Domain	
Noisy, constantly active, egocentric, exhibitionistic. Imitative and imaginative. Want attention.	Include vigorous games and stunts, games with individual roles (hunting, dramatic activities, story plays), and a few team games or relays.
Large muscles more developed; game skills not developed.	Challenge with varied movement. Develop specialized skills of throwing, catching, and bouncing balls.
Naturally rhythmic.	Use music and rhythm with skills. Provide creative rhythms, folk dances, and singing movement songs.
May become suddenly tired but soon recover.	Use activities of brief duration. Provide short rest periods or intersperse physically demanding activities with less vigorous ones.
Hand–eye coordination developing.	Give opportunity to handle different objects, such as balls, beanbags, and hoops.
Perceptual abilities maturing.	Give practice in balance—unilateral, bilateral, and cross-lateral movements.
Pelvic tilt can be pronounced.	Give attention to posture problems. Provide abdominal strengthening activities.
Cognitive Domain	
Short attention span.	Change activity often. Give short explanations.
Interested in what the body can do. Curious.	Provide movement experiences. Pay attention to educational movement.
Want to know. Often ask *why* about movement.	Explain reasons for various activities and the basis of movement.
Express individual views and ideas.	Allow children time to be creative. Expect problems when children are lined up and asked to perform the same task.
Begin to understand the idea of teamwork.	Plan situations that require group cooperation. Discuss the importance of such.
Sense of humour expands.	Insert some humour in the teaching process.
Highly creative.	Allow students to try new ways of performing activities; sharing ideas with friends encourages creativity.
Affective Domain	
No gender differences in interests.	Set up same activities for boys and girls.
Sensitive and individualistic; self-concept very important.	Teach taking turns, sharing, and learning to win, lose, or be caught gracefully.
Accept defeat poorly. Like small-group activity.	Use entire class group sparingly. Break into smaller groups.
Sensitive to feelings of adults. Like to please teacher.	Give frequent praise and encouragement.
Can be reckless.	Stress and tumbling.
Enjoy rough-and-tumble activity.	Include rolling, dropping to the floor, and so on, in both introductory and program activities. Stress simple stunts and tumbling.
Seek personal attention.	Recognize individuals through both verbal and nonverbal means. See that all have a chance to be the centre of attention.
Love to climb and explore play environments.	Provide play materials, games, and apparatus for strengthening large muscles (e.g., climbing towers, climbing ropes, jump ropes, miniature Challenge Courses, and turning bars).

(continued)

TABLE 8.1

Characteristics and interests of children (continued)

Characteristics and Interests	Program guidelines
Developmental Level II	
Psychomotor Domain	
Capable of rhythmic movement.	Continue creative rhythms, singing movement songs, and folk dancing.
Improved hand-eye and perceptual-motor coordination.	Give opportunity for manipulating hand apparatus. Provide movement experience and practice in perceptual-motor skills (right and left, unilateral, bilateral, and cross-lateral movements).
More interest in sports.	Begin introductory sport and related skills and simple lead-up activities.
Sport-related skill patterns mature in some cases.	Emphasize practice in these skill areas through simple ball games, stunts, and rhythmic patterns.
Developing interest in fitness.	Introduce some of the specialized fitness activities to grade 3.
Reaction time slow.	Avoid highly organized ball games that require and place a premium on quickness and accuracy.
Cognitive Domain	
Still active but attention span longer. More interest in group play.	Include active big-muscle program and more group activity. Begin team concept in activity and relays.
Curious to see what they can do. Love to be challenged and will try anything.	Offer challenges involving movement problems and more critical demands in stunts, tumbling, and apparatus work. Emphasize safety and good judgment.
Interest in group activities; ability to plan with others developing.	Offer group activities and simple dances that involve cooperation with a partner or a team.
Affective Domain	
Like physical contact and belligerent games.	Include dodging games and other active games, as well as rolling stunts.
Developing more interest in skills. Want to excel.	Organize practice in a variety of throwing, catching, and moving skills, as well as others.
Becoming more conscious socially.	Teach need to abide by rules and play fairly. Teach social customs and courtesy in rhythmic areas.
Like to perform well and to be admired for accomplishments.	Begin to stress quality. Provide opportunity to achieve.
Essentially honest and truthful.	Accept children's word. Give opportunity for trust in game and relay situations.
Do not lose willingly.	Provide opportunity for children to learn to accept defeat gracefully and to win with humility.
Gender difference still of little importance.	Avoid separation of genders in any activity.

(continued)

TABLE 8.1

Characteristics and interests of children (continued)

Characteristics and Interests	Program guidelines
Developmental Level III	
Psychomotor Domain	
Steady growth. Girls often grow more rapidly than boys.	Continue vigorous program to enhance physical development.
Muscular coordination and skills improving. Interested in learning detailed techniques.	Continue emphasis on teaching skills through drills, lead-up games, and free practice periods. Emphasize correct form.
Differences in physical capacity and skill development.	Offer flexible standards so all find success. In team activities, match teams evenly so individual skill levels are less apparent.
Posture problems may appear.	Include posture correction and special posture instruction; emphasize effect of body carriage on self-concept.
Sixth-grade girls may show signs of maturity; may not wish to participate in all activities.	Have consideration for their problems. Encourage participation on a limited basis, if necessary.
Sixth-grade boys are rougher and stronger.	Keep genders together for skill development but separate for competition in certain rougher activities.
Cognitive Domain	
Want to know rules of games.	Include instruction on rules, regulations, and traditions.
Knowledgeable about and interested in sport and game strategy.	Emphasize strategy, as opposed to merely performing a skill without concern for context.
Question the relevance and importance of various activities.	Explain regularly the reasons for performing activities and learning various skills.
Desire information about the importance of physical fitness and health-related topics.	Include in lesson plans brief explanations of how various activities enhance growth and development.
Affective Domain	
Enjoy team and group activity. Competitive urge strong.	Include many team games, relays, and combatives.
Much interest in sports and sport-related activities.	Offer a variety of sports in season, with emphasis on lead-up games.
Little interest in the opposite gender. Some antagonism may arise.	Offer coeducational activities with emphasis on individual differences of all participants, regardless of gender.
Acceptance of self-responsibility. Strong increase in drive toward independence.	Provide leadership and followership opportunities on a regular basis. Involve students in evaluation procedures.
Intense desire to excel both in skill and in physical capacity.	Stress physical fitness. Include fitness and skill surveys both to motivate and to check progress.
Sportsmanship a concern for both teachers and students.	Establish and enforce fair rules. With enforcement include an explanation of the need for rules and cooperation if games are to exist.
Peer group important. Want to be part of the gang.	Stress group cooperation in play and among teams. Rotate team positions as well as squad makeup.

TABLE 8.2
Equating developmental levels to grades and ages

Developmental Level	Grades	Ages
I	K–2	5–7
II	3–4	8–9
III	5–7	10–12

incompetent to teach those particular activities. This results in a curriculum that is designed for the teacher's benefit rather than students'. If an activity contributes to curricular goals, it is necessary to develop requisite teaching competency. Imagine a math teacher choosing not to teach fractions or multiplication tables to students because of feelings of incompetence. It is your responsibility to learn to teach new activities so students experience and achieve learning outcomes. After selecting appropriate activities that contribute to goals and learning outcomes, design a delivery system that ensures you teach all activities.

There are several options for organizing and scheduling units of instruction in elementary physical education. (Note: for the purpose of this discussion a "daily physical education" scenario is used.) Using *solid block* units is a common approach in the intermediate grades. When using this approach, instruction focuses on an activity for a series of sequential lessons (for example, a 10-lesson block). There are a number of strengths to the solid block. First, it allows for continuity. Instructional sequences for each day are built on the preceding lesson. Second, less orientation instruction is needed after the first day. Safety factors, teaching hints, and key points need only a brief review each day and equipment needs are similar from day to day. Third, progression and learning sequences are evident to both teacher and children.

A disadvantage raised by some teachers is that a solid block unit does not have enough variety, causing some children to tire of the same activities presented over a longer period. A *modified solid block* allows for major time allotment for one activity and a minor time allotment for one or more other activities. For example, a 4+1 modified block features four days focused on the major activity with one day allowed each week for another activity. Use a different activity to provide a change of pace when the motivational level of the class appears to be waning. Table 8.3 shows an example of this, where the grade 6–7 teacher has developed a 4+1 modified solid block with one day per week allocated for a fitness focus ("Fitness Fridays"). A modified solid block provides a reasonable compromise between continuity and variety and allows for a degree of flexibility.

The *multiple block* unit allows for teaching two or more activities concurrently, usually alternating days. This type of scheduling is frequently used in the primary grades when motor skill development is at a general stage. This approach takes a set of skills or movements and offers a wide variety of activities for instruction related to the same skill. An assortment of equipment is needed since the same skills are taught using different activities and equipment. Table 8.4 shows a sample multiple block format for two activities.

Table 8.5 illustrates the parallel listing of the four parts of the lesson in the yearly plan using a multiple-block format. This plan ensures that youngsters learn many ways of warming up for activity and approximately 15 different types of fitness activity. In addition, they are exposed to 20 to 25 lesson activities that focus on skill development and 60 to 80 low-organized game activities.

Check the Scope, Sequence, and Balance of the Curriculum

An important step in creating a quality program is to review and monitor the scope, sequence, and balance of the curriculum. These are important concepts that assure the curriculum is comprehensive and varied.

Scope is the yearly content of the curriculum. Scope is also referred to as the horizontal articulation of the curriculum. Monitoring the scope of the curriculum ensures that the entire content of the program will be covered in a systematic and accountable fashion. In elementary school physical education, the scope of the curriculum is broad; teachers present many activities rather than covering just a few activities in depth. Elementary school physical education is designed to help students learn about all the available types of physical activity.

Sequence, or vertical articulation, of the curriculum defines the skills and activities to be covered on a year-to-year basis. Sequence ensures that youngsters receive different instruction and activities at each developmental level. Of particular importance is the articulation of program material throughout elementary, junior, and senior high school programs.

Provincial and territorial physical education curriculum guides provide learning outcomes for each grade level (or splits, such as grades 3/4). To a certain extent this provides a general guide for both scope and sequence. It is helpful in your elementary school to involve all teachers in planning the physical education program. This will allow articulation between teachers and grade levels, and avoid needless repetition.

Balance ensures that all learning outcomes in the program receive adequate coverage. When reviewing the scope and sequence of the curriculum, checking for balance avoids a skewing toward one particular area. To assure balance, major areas of emphasis are determined based on program goals and outcomes. These areas can be allotted a percentage of program time based on the characteristics and

TABLE 8.3

Sample modified solid block

YEAR PLAN SAMPLE Month/Week	PHYSICAL EDUCATION Modified solid block Gr. 6/7 (4+1) (1=fitness each Fri)		YEAR PLAN SAMPLE Month/Week	PHYSICAL EDUCATION Modified solid block Gr. 6/7 (4+1) (1= fitness each Fri)	
SEPTEMBER			**FEBRUARY**		
Week #1	Group problem solving	F	Week #1	Gymnastics (large app.)	F
Week #2	Soccer/minor games	F	Week #2	Gymnastics (large app.)	F
Week #3	Soccer	F	Week #3	Gymnastics (large app.)	F
Week #4	Soccer	F	Week #4	Dance (hip-hop)	F
OCTOBER			**MARCH**		
Week #1	Gymnastics (all categories) Floor work/routines	F	Week #1	Orienteering	F
Week #2	Gymnastics (all categories) Floor work/routines	F	Week #2	Orienteering	F
			Week #3	**SPRING BREAK**	
Week #3	Volleyball	F	Week #4	Minor games	F
Week #4	Volleyball	F	**APRIL**		
NOVEMBER			Week #1	Aerobics/rhythmics	F
Week #1	Volleyball	F	Week #2	Racquet games	F
Week #2	Skipping, fitness circuits	F	Week #3	Racquet games	F
Week #3	Skipping (double dutch)	F	Week #4	Bike safety week	F
Week #4	Basketball lead-ups	F	**MAY**		
DECEMBER			Week #1	Frisbee games	F
Week #1	Minor games/line dance	F	Week #2	Soccer	F
Week #2	Line dance	F	Week #3	Outdoor Ed. Week	F
Week #3	**CHRISTMAS VACATION**		Week #4	Track and field	F
Week #4	**CHRISTMAS VACATION**		**JUNE**		
JANUARY			Week #1	Track and field	F
Week #1	Basketball	F	Week #2	Track and field	F
Week #2	Basketball	F	Week #3	Softball	F
Week #3	Basketball	F	Week #4	Softball	F
Week #4	Hacky sack/skipping	F			

(4 + 1)–1 alternates between the following:
- fitness focus
- classroom active health
- off-campus days—e.g., skating, swimming, bowling

interests of students. This determination reveals to administrators, teachers, and parents the direction and emphasis of the program. All areas have a proportionate share of instructional time, and the percentage of time allotted to each area reflects the needs and characteristics of the students.

Several provincial and territorial curriculum guides provide specific guidelines for maintaining balance in course offerings. For example, the British Columbia curriculum recommends that no less than 15% of instructional time is spent in any one of the five movement categories.

Saskatchewan guidelines provide even more specific time allotment recommendations across the categories: Alternative Environment Activities—10%, Rhythmics and Dance—15%, Educational Games—25%, Educational Gymnastics—25%, and Individual and Dual Activities—10%. The optional 15% may be used to increase offerings in any of the five categories.

Another phase of balance is to alternate units based on the type of student interaction required: that is, individual, dual (partner), small group, or large group activities. Team

TABLE 8.4
Multiple block unit

WEEK 1	ACTIVITY	LESSON #
Monday	Rhythmics	Lesson 1
Tuesday	Games	Lesson 1
Wednesday	Rhythmics	Lesson 2
Thursday	Games	Lesson 2
Friday	Rhythmics	Lesson 3
WEEK 2	**ACTIVITY**	**LESSON #**
Monday	Rhythmics	Lesson 4
Tuesday	Games	Lesson 3
Wednesday	Rhythmics	Lesson 5
Thursday	Games	Lesson 4
Friday	Rhythmics	Lesson 6

sports require organization in a large group, whereas a movement concept lesson is individual in nature. Learning to catch is a partner activity, whereas a lead-up game requires small groups. A small or large group activity will often follow individual and partner activities. Balance ensures children do not have to stay with one type of activity too long. It gives them a chance to experience the type of organization they enjoy on a regular basis.

Step Seven: Evaluate and Modify the Curriculum

Evaluation schedules and suggested techniques for modifying the curriculum are an integral part of the curricular structure. A number of sources can supply evaluative data: pupils, teachers, consultants, parents, and administrators. The type of data desired can vary. The evaluation schedule can select a limited area for assessment, or assessment can be broadened to cover the entire program. Collecting information is only the first step; the information must be translated into action. Modification of possible program deficiencies is based on sound educational philosophy. If the program has weak spots, identifying the weaknesses and determining the causes are important steps to take.

A pilot or trial project can be instituted if the new curriculum represents a radical change. One school in the district might be chosen to develop a pilot program. Site selection should offer the program a strong opportunity to succeed, for success depends in large part on the educational climate of the school. In some cases, just one class in the school might implement the experimental program.

TABLE 8.5
An example of a yearly plan: Developmental level II

Week	Introductory Activity	Fitness Development Activity	Lesson Focus Activity	Game Activity
1	Move and freeze on signal	Teacher leader movement challenges	Orientation	Back to Back Get-up Whistle Mixer
2	Fundamental movements and stopping	Teacher leader exercises	Manipulative skills with hoops and beanbags	Beanbag Touch & Go Cageball Kickover
3	Move and assume pose	Teacher leader exercises	Throwing skills (1)	Whistle Mixer Couple Tag
4	Creative routines	Agility run	Lacrosse-related activities	Continuous Shuttle Pick-up Hideaway
5	Four-corners movement	Agility run	Manipulative skills using playground balls	Bounce Ball One Step
6	Run, stop, and pivot	Circuit training		Nonda's Car Lot
7	European running	Circuit training	Stunts and tumbling Skills (1)	Whistle Mixer Alaska Baseball
8	Magic number challenges	Astronaut drills	Soccer-related activities (1)	Circle Kickball Soccer Touch Ball Diagonal Soccer

(continued)

TABLE 8.5

An example of a yearly plan: Developmental level II (continued)

Week	Introductory Activity	Fitness Development Activity	Lesson Focus Activity	Game Activity
9	New leader	Astronaut drills	Soccer-related activities (2)	Soccer Touch Ball Diagonal Soccer Dribblerama Bull's-eye
10	Group over and around	Aerobic fitness	Fundamental skills using parachutes	Trees Box Ball
11	Bend, stretch, and shake	Aerobic fitness	Orienteering	Map Symbol Relay Sardines
12	Crossing the River	Walk, trot, and jog	Orienteering activities	Memory Orienteering Follow the Leader
13	Jumping and hopping patterns	Challenge course fitness	Rhythms (1)	Whistle March Home Base
14	Squad tag	Walk, trot, and jog	Long rope-jumping skills	Jump the Shot Home Base Fox Hunt
15	Moving to music	Challenge course	Stunts and tumbling skills (2)	Loose Caboose Crows and Cranes
16	Ball activities	Challenge course	Rhythms (2)	Fox Hunt Steal the Treasure Addition Tag
17	Partner leaping	Aerobic fitness and partner resistance	Basketball-related activities (1)	Birdie in the Cage Dribblerama Team 5 Passes
18	Bridges by three	Aerobic fitness and partner resistance	Basketball-related activities (2)	Captain Ball Five Passes—Ten Passes Around the Key
19	Locomotor and manipulative activity	Exercise to music	Throwing skills (2)	Bounce Ball Club Guard
20	Balance tag	Exercise to music	Fundamental skills using benches	Cageball Kickover Squad Tag
21	Low organizational games	Continuity drills	Hockey-related activities (1)	Circle Keep-away Lane Hockey Circle Straddleball
22	Following activity	Continuity drills	Hockey-related activities (2)	Modified Hockey Lane Hockey
23	Moving to music	Aerobic fitness	Manipulative skills using paddle and balls	Steal the Treasure Trees
24	Stretching activities	Stretching activities	Track-and-field skills (1): Sprints/Starts	Beanbag Shuttles Nature Run
25	Stretching activities	Stretching activities	Track-and-field skills (2): Relays Passing, etc.	Circle Relays Shuttle Relays One-on-one contents

(continued)

TABLE 8.5
An example of a yearly plan: Developmental level II (continued)

Week	Introductory Activity	Fitness Development Activity	Lesson Focus Activity	Game Activity
26	Move and perform task	Walk, trot, and jog	Manipulative skills using beanbags (curling in the gym activities)	Draw Contest
27	Long rope routine	Parachute fitness	Rhythms (3)	Jump the Shot Beach Ball Batball Club Guard
28	Squad leader movement	Parachute fitness	Stunts and tumbling skills (3)	Beach Ball Batball
29	European running with equipment	Exercise to music	Individual rope-jumping	Loose Caboose Wolfe's Beanbag Exchange Tag
30	Marking	Circuit training	Volleyball-related skills (1)	Beach Ball Volleyball Informal Volleyball
31	Tag games	Agility Run	Volleyball-related skills (2)	Beach Ball Volleyball Shower Service Ball
32	Combination movement patterns	Continuity drills	Rhythms (4)	Alaska Baseball Addition Tag
33	European running with variations	Aerobic fitness	Manipulative skills using Frisbees	Frisbee Golf
34	Tortoise and hare	Aerobic fitness	Fundamental skills using balance beams	Nonda's Car Lot
35	Move and perform task	Parachute exercises	Softball-related activities (1)	Throw It and Run Two-pitch Softball Hit and Run
36	Walk, trot, and sprint	Teacher leader exercises	Softball-related activities (2)	Beat Ball Kick Softball In a Pickle

Enthusiastic, skilled direction is necessary for such projects. Much information can be derived from this pilot process before an entire program is implemented throughout the school system.

Critical Thinking

1. Explore two different Ministry/Department of Education websites. Compare how Physical Education is organized and presented in each province/territory. Discuss some possible reasons for differences and similarities.

2. Formulate a statement that reflects your value orientation toward physical education. How does it relate to your provincial/territorial physical education curriculum guide?

References and Suggested Readings

Alberta Learning. (2000). *Physical education kindergarten to grade 12 program of studies.* Edmonton, AB: Author.

Barrett, K.R., Williams, K., & Whitall, J. (1992). What does it mean to have a "developmentally appropriate physical education program"? *The Physical Educator, 49*(3), 113–117.

Bloom, B.S. (Ed.). (1956). *Taxonomy of educational objectives, the classification of educational goals, handbook I: The cognitive domain.* New York: David McKay.

British Columbia Ministry of Education. (1995). *Physical education K–7 integrated resource package.* Victoria, BC: Author.

Chepko, S. & Arnold, R.K. (Eds.). (2000). *Guidelines for physical education programs, K–12: Standards, objectives and assessments.* Boston: Allyn and Bacon.

Ennis, C. (2003). Using curriculum to enhance student learning. In S. Silverman & C. Ennis (Eds.), *Student Learning in Physical Education: Applying Research to Enhance Instruction* (2nd ed., pp. 109-127), Champaign, IL: Human Kinetics.

Gabbard, C. (2004). *Physical education for children: Building the foundation* (4th ed.). San Francisco, CA: Benjamin Cummings.

Gallahue, D. & Donnelly, F.C. (2003). *Developmental physical education for all children.* (4th ed.). Champaign, IL: Human Kinetics.

Graham, G. (2005). *Teaching children physical education: Becoming a master teacher* (2nd ed.). Champaign, IL: Human Kinetics.

Graham, G., Holt/Hale, S.A., & Parker, M. (2007). *Children moving—a reflective approach to teaching physical education* (7th ed.). New York: McGraw-Hill.

Jewett, A., Bain, L., & Ennis, K. (1995). *The curriculum process in physical education.* Dubuque, Iowa: Wm. C. Brown and Benchmark.

Kelly, L. & Melograno, V.J. (2004). *Developing the physical education curriculum an achievement-based approach.* Champaign, IL: Human Kinetics.

Krathwohl, D.R., Bloom, B.S., & Masia, B.B. (1964). *Taxonomy of educational objectives, handbook II: Affective domain.* New York: David McKay.

Manitoba Education, Citizenship and Youth. (2007). *Scheduling kindergarten to grade 8 physical education/health education: a resource for school administrators.* Winnipeg, MB: Author.

Manitoba Education and Training. (2000). *Kindergarten to senior 4 physical education/health education—Manitoba curriculum framework of outcomes for active healthy lifestyles.* Winnipeg, MB: Author.

Mosston, M. & Ashworth, S. (2002). *Teaching physical education* (5th ed.). New York: Benjamin Cummings.

National Association for Sport and Physical Education. (2004). *Moving into the future: National standards for physical education.* St. Louis, MO: Mosby-Year Book.

Rink, J.E. (2005). *Teaching physical education for learning* (5th ed.). Boston: McGraw-Hill.

Saskatchewan Education. (1992). *Policy for instructional physical education: kindergarten to grade 12.* Regina, SK: Author.

Siedentop, D. & Tannehill, D. (2000). *Developing teaching skills in physical education* (4th ed.). Mountain View, CA: Mayfield.

 Weblinks

Provincial and Territorial Ministries/Departments of Education

Current information for K-12 Physical Education programs in each province and territory can be found below:

Alberta Learning: www.education.gov.ab.ca

British Columbia Ministry of Education: www.gov.bc.ca/bced

Manitoba Education, Citizenship and Youth: www.edu.gov.mb.ca

New Brunswick Department of Education: www.gnb.ca/0000

Newfoundland & Labrador Department of Education: www.gov.nf.ca/edu

Northwest Territories Ministry of Education, Culture and Employment: www.ece.gov.nt.ca

Nova Scotia Department of Education: www.ednet.ns.ca

Nunavut Department of Education: www.gov.nu.ca/ education.htm

Ontario Ministry of Education: www.edu.gov.on.ca

Prince Edward Island Department of Education: www.edu.pe.ca

Éducation Québec: www.mels.gouv.qc.ca/GR-PUB/ m_englis.htm

Saskatchewan Learning: www.sasked.gov.sk.ca

Yukon Department of Education: www.education.gov.yk.ca

CHAPTER 9

Legal Liability and Risk Management

Essential Components

I	Organized around content standards
II	Student-centred and developmentally appropriate
III	Physical activity and motor skill development form the core of the program
IV	Teaches management skills and self-discipline
V	Promotes inclusion of all students
VI	Focuses on process over product
VII	Promotes lifetime personal health and wellness
VIII	Teaches cooperation and responsibility and promotes sensitivity to diversity

Physical Education Standards

1	Students are able to move competently using a variety of fundamental and specialized motor skills.
2	Students can monitor and maintain a health-enhancing level of physical fitness.
3	Students are able to apply movement concepts and basic mechanics of skill performance when learning and refining motor skills.
4	Students comprehend the basic principles of wellness and are able to apply concepts that enable them to make meaningful decisions that positively impact their health and wellness.
5	Students participate in a wide variety of physical activities and learn how to maintain a personalized active lifestyle.
6	Students demonstrate empathy, understanding, and respect for the numerous differences exhibited by people in an activity setting.
7	**Students exhibit responsible and self-directed behaviours that lead to positive social interactions in physical activity.**

OVERVIEW

This chapter explains the various legal terms and situations associated with physical education and describes instructional and administrative procedures common to the responsible conduct of the physical education program. It is a teacher's legal responsibility to create a safe environment in which risk and the opportunity for injury are minimized and to provide a standard of care that any reasonable and prudent professional with similar training would apply under the given circumstances. Safety instruction is designed to prevent accidents and should be included in lesson plans to ensure coverage. A comprehensive safety checklist is provided.

OUTCOMES

- Define *tort, negligence, liability, malfeasance, misfeasance, nonfeasance,* and other terms common to legal suits brought against educators.

- List major points that must be established to determine negligence on the part of the teacher.

- Explain how to examine all activities, equipment, and facilities for possible hazards and sources of accidents.

- Identify common defences against negligence.

- Describe supervisory responsibilities expected of all teachers.

- List guidelines for the proper supervision of instruction, equipment, and facilities.

- Understand how to ensure safety, focusing on prevention.

- Outline an emergency action plan.

S*chool district personnel, including teaching and non-teaching members, are obligated to exercise ordinary care for the safety of students. This duty is manifested as the ability to anticipate reasonably foreseeable dangers and the responsibility to take necessary precautions to prevent problems from occurring.*

Compared with other subject matter areas, physical education is particularly vulnerable to accidents and resultant injuries. In Ontario, for example, recent statistics show that half of all school injuries are a result of physical activity (Dougherty, Goldberger, & Carpenter, 2002). Thus, physical education teachers are more exposed to litigation than other staff members because physical education involves actions that may be inherently risky due to the physical movement demands within the wide range of activities in which students engage. In Canada, legal suits are conducted under both provincial and federal statutes. Principles underlying legal action are similar, but certain regulations and procedures vary among provinces and territories. You should acquire a copy of the legal liability policy for your school district.

*All students have the right to freedom from injury caused by others or due to participation in a program. Courts have ruled that teachers owe their students a **duty of care** to protect them from harm. Teachers must offer a **standard of care** that any reasonable and prudent professional with similar training would apply under the given circumstances. A teacher is required to exercise the teaching skill, discretion, and knowledge that members of the profession in good standing normally possess in similar situations. Lawsuits usually occur when citizens believe that this standard of care was not exercised.*

*   **Liability** is the responsibility to perform a duty to a particular group. It is an obligation to perform in a particular way that is required by law and enforced by court action. Teachers are bound by contract to carry out their duties in a reasonable and prudent manner. Liability is always a legal matter. Before one can be held liable, it must be proved in a court of law that **negligence** occurred.*

Torts

In education, a *tort* is concerned with the teacher–student relationship and is a legal wrong that results in direct or indirect injury to another individual or to property. *Black's Law Dictionary* (1996) defines a tort as a private or civil wrong or injury, other than breach of contract, for which the court will provide a remedy in the form of an action for damages. There are three elements of every tort action: existence of legal duty from defendant to plaintiff, breach of duty, and damage as proximate result.

As the result of a tort, the court can give a monetary reward for damages that occurred. The court can also give a monetary reward for punitive damages if a breach of duty can be established. Usually, the court rewards the offended individual for damages that occurred due to the negligence of the teacher or other responsible individual.

Liability and Negligence

Liability is usually concerned with a breach of duty through negligence. In general terms, negligence is the failure to act as a reasonably careful and prudent person would act in a specific situation. Lawyers examine the situation that gave rise to the injury, to establish if liability can be determined. Four major elements must be established to find a teacher negligent:

1. *Duty.* The first element considered is that of duty owed to the participants. Did the school or teacher owe students a *duty of care* that implies conforming to certain standards of conduct? When examining duty or breach of duty, the court takes some initial guidance from the standards described in provincial school acts. For example, as defined in the British Columbia School Act (1995), teachers have the responsibility to maintain reasonable standards in the interest of student safety. According to the School Act, inherent in these duties is the responsibility to protect students from risk of injury:

   > *Reg. 76/91 4. (a) provide teaching and other educational services . . . as required or assigned by the board or the minister; (b) providing such assistance as the board or principal considers necessary for the supervision of students on school premises and at school functions, whenever and wherever held; and (c) ensuring that students understand and comply with the codes of conduct governing their behaviour and with the rules and policies governing the operation of the school. (BC School Act, 1995, D-75)*

   In the province of Saskatchewan, the Education Act (1993) goes further by defining the classroom duties of a teacher. In Saskatchewan, the teacher shall do the following:

   > *Plan and organize the learning activities of the class with due regard for individual differences and the needs of the pupil; maintain good order and general discipline in the classroom and on school premises; and exclude any pupil from the class for overt opposition to the teacher's authority or other gross misconduct and, by the conclusion of that day, report in writing to the principal the circumstances of that exclusion. (pp. 111–112)*

In addition to defining the duties of teachers, most provincial/territorial School/Education Acts provide statements regarding the duties of students. For example, in the Nova Scotia Education Act (1995–96) it is the duty of a student to: (a) participate fully in learning opportunities; (b) attend school regularly and punctually; (c) contribute to an orderly and safe learning environment; (d) respect the rights of others; and (e) comply with the discipline policies of the school and the school board.

2. *Breach of duty.* A teacher commits a breach of duty by failing to conform to the required duty. After it is established that a duty was required, it must be proved that such duty was not performed. A determining factor in deciding whether there has been a breach of the duty is the level, expertise, or competence of the defendant and the standard of care that is expected and applied. Historically, the *careful parent of a large family* standard is the one that the Canadian judicial system has applied to teachers. However, more recently, the professional standard of care has been applied in cases involving physical education teachers. In a landmark case *Thornton v. Board of School Trustees of School District No. 57* (1978), the *ordinary competent instructor* test extended a teacher's responsibility beyond that of a careful parent. This test recognized that "in certain circumstances teachers, because of their expertise, should be able to foresee danger of which a careful parent might not be aware" (Nicholls, 1988, p. 62). For example, a physical education teacher may be presumed to know more about the dangers inherent in artistic gymnastics than the average careful parent (Manitoba Education, 2000). Accordingly, the teacher may be held to the ordinary competent instructor standard of care.

Another significant outcome of the Thornton case was the establishment of criteria for standard of care applied to school physical education. The following four criteria were identified and applied:

(a) Is the activity suitable to the age, and condition (mental and physical) of the participating student?

(b) Have the students been progressively taught and coached to perform the activity(ies) properly to avoid the dangers inherent in the activity(ies)?

(c) Is the equipment adequate and suitably arranged?

(d) Is the activity being supervised properly in light of the inherent dangers involved?

3. *Injury.* An injury must have occurred if liability is to be established. If no injury or harm occurs, there is no liability. Further, it must be proved that the injured party is entitled to compensatory damages for financial loss or physical discomfort.

4. *Proximate cause.* The failure to conform to the required standard must be the proximate cause of the resulting injury. It must be proved that the injury was caused by the teacher's breach of duty. It is not enough to prove simply that a breach of duty occurred. It must simultaneously be shown that the injury was a direct result of the teacher's failure to provide a reasonable standard of care.

Foreseeability

A key to the issue of negligence is foreseeability. Courts expect that a trained professional is able to foresee potentially harmful situations. Was it possible for the teacher to predict and anticipate the danger of the harmful act or situation and to take appropriate measures to prevent it from occurring? If the injured party can prove that the teacher should have foreseen the danger involved in an activity or situation (even in part), the teacher will be found negligent for failing to act in a reasonable and prudent manner. This points out the necessity of examining all activities, equipment, and facilities for possible hazards and sources of accident.

Types of Negligence

The courts define *negligence* as conduct that falls below a standard of care established to protect others from unreasonable risk or harm. Several types of negligence can be categorized.

Malfeasance

Malfeasance occurs when a teacher does something improper by committing an act that is unlawful and wrongful, with no legal basis (often referred to as an *act of commission*). Malfeasance can be illustrated by the following incident. A male student misbehaved on numerous occasions. In desperation, the teacher gave the student a choice of punishment—a severe spanking in front of the class or running many laps around the field. The student chose the former and suffered physical and emotional damage. Even though the student was given a choice whereby he could have avoided the paddling, the teacher is still liable for any physical or emotional harm caused.

Misfeasance

Misfeasance occurs when a teacher follows proper procedures but does not perform according to the required standard of conduct. Misfeasance is based on performance of the proper action, but not up to the required standard. It is usually the sub-par performance of an act that might have been otherwise lawfully done. An example would be the teacher's offering to spot a student during a tumbling routine and then not doing the spotting properly. If the student is injured due to a faulty spot, the teacher can be held liable.

Nonfeasance

Nonfeasance is based on lack of action in carrying out a duty. This is usually an *act of omission*. The teacher knew the proper procedures but failed to follow them. Teachers can be found negligent if they act or fail to act. It is essential that teachers understand and carry out proper procedures and duties in a manner befitting members of the profession. In contrast to the misfeasance example, nonfeasance occurs when a teacher knows that it is necessary to spot certain gymnastic routines but fails to do so. For example, a physical education teacher is expected to know the importance of hydration when exercising in hot weather and make water readily available to students. If he or she doesn't make water available and remind students to drink, the teacher is at risk of nonfeasance. Teachers are expected to behave with greater competency because they have been educated to give students a higher standard of professional care than do parents.

Contributory Negligence

The situation is different when the injured student is partially or wholly at fault. Students are expected to exercise sensible care and to follow directions or regulations designed to protect them from injury. Improper behaviour by the injured party that causes the accident is usually ruled to be *contributory negligence*, because the injured party contributed to the resulting harm. This responsibility is directly related to the maturity, ability, and experience of the child. For example, most provinces have laws specifying that a child under 6 years of age is incapable of contributory negligence (Dougherty et al., 2002). To illustrate contributory negligence, assume that a teacher has thoroughly explained safety rules to be followed while hitting softballs. As students begin to practise, one of them runs through a restricted area that is well marked and is hit by a bat. Depending on the age and maturity of the child, the possibility is strong that the student will be held liable for such action.

Comparative or Shared Negligence

Under the doctrine of comparative negligence, the injured party can recover only if found to be less negligent than the defendant (the teacher). Where statutes apply, the amount of recovery is generally reduced in proportion to the injured party's participation in the circumstances leading to the injury.

Common Defences against Negligence

Negligence must be proved in a court of law. Many times, teachers are negligent in carrying out their duties, yet the injured party does not take the case to court. If a teacher is sued, some of the following defences are used in an attempt to show that the teacher's action was not the primary cause of the accident.

Act of God

The act of God defence places the cause of injury on forces beyond the control of the teacher or the school. The defence is made that it was impossible to predict an unsafe condition, but through an act of God, the injury occurred. Typical acts would be a gust of wind that blew over a volleyball standard or a cloudburst of rain that made a surface slick. The defence lawyer can use the act of God defence only in cases in which the injury still would have occurred even if reasonable and prudent action had been taken.

Proximate Cause

This defence attempts to prove that the accident was not caused by the negligence of the teacher. There must be a close relationship between the breach of duty by the teacher and the injury. This is a common defence in cases dealing with proper supervision. Imagine a student is participating in an activity supervised by the teacher. When the teacher leaves the playing area to answer a phone call, the student is injured. The defence lawyer will try to show that the accident would have occurred regardless of whether the teacher was there.

Assumption of Risk

Clearly, physical education is a high-risk activity when compared with most other curriculum areas. The participant assumes the risk accompanying the activity when choosing to be part of that activity. Physical education teachers, because of the unique relationship between school and student, seldom use the assumption of risk defence. The student is compelled by law to attend, and the school is bound to care for and educate the child; therefore the situation differs from voluntary participation in a recreational physical activity (Bezeau, 2006).

Contributory Negligence

Contributory negligence is often used by the defence in an attempt to convince the court that the injured party acted in a manner that was abnormal. In other words, the injured individual did not act in a manner that was typical of students of similar age and maturity. The defence attempts to demonstrate that the activity or equipment in question was used for years with no record of accident. A case is made based on the manner of presentation—how students were taught to act in a safe manner—and that the injured student acted outside the parameters of safe conduct. A key point in this defence is whether the activity was suitable for the age and maturity level of the participants.

Areas of Responsibility

A two-tiered approach for analyzing safety is useful for determining responsibility for injury. The first tier includes duties the administration must assume in support of the program. The second tier defines duties of the teacher or staff member charged with teaching or supervising students. Each party has a role to fill, but some overlap occurs. The following example illustrates the differences.

A student is hurt while performing a tumbling stunt. A lawsuit ensues, charging the teacher with negligence for not following safe procedures. By law, a school board is responsible for the protection of its students by maintaining a reasonable level of supervision of its students and maintaining the safety of its premises (Bezeau, 2006). Therefore, the administration is often included in the suit. Two levels of responsibility should be considered when delegating responsibility, for the following reasons:

1. They identify different functions and responsibilities of the teaching staff and administration.

2. They provide a framework for reducing injuries and improving safety procedures.

3. They provide perspective for following legal precedents.

4. In the following described responsibilities, both administrative and instructional duties are presented.

Supervision

All activities in a school setting must be supervised, including recess, lunchtimes, and field trips. The responsibilities of the school are critical if students are to be supervised properly.

Administration

Two levels are identified in supervision: general and specific. General supervision (for example, playground duty) refers to broad coverage, when students are not under direct control of a teacher or a designated individual. A plan of supervision should be made, designating the areas to be covered and including where and how the supervisor should rotate. This plan, kept in the principal's office, should cover rules of conduct governing student behaviour. Rules should be posted prominently on bulletin boards, especially in classrooms. In addition to the plan, administrators must select qualified personnel, provide necessary training, and monitor the plan properly.

The general supervisor is concerned primarily with student behaviour, focusing on the student's right to a relaxing recreational experience. Supervisors should observe the area, looking for breaches of acceptable behaviour. The supervisor needs to look for physical hazards such as broken glass and debris on the play area. If it becomes necessary to leave the area, the supervisor must find a qualified substitute to prevent the area from going unsupervised.

Staff

General supervision is necessary during recess, before and after school, during lunch-hour break, and during certain other sessions when instruction is not offered. The supervisor should know the school's plan for supervision as well as the emergency care procedures to follow in case of an accident. Supervision is a positive act that requires the supervisor to be actively involved and moving throughout the area. The type of activity, the size of the area, and the number and age of the students should determine the number of supervisors. The reader is encouraged to become familiar with school district supervision policies.

Specific supervision requires that the teacher be with a certain group of students (a class). An example is direct monitoring of students during a tackling drill in soccer. Merriman (1993) offers five general recommendations to ensure that adequate supervision occurs:

1. The supervisor must be in the immediate vicinity (within sight and hearing).

2. If required to leave, the supervisor must have an adequate replacement in place before departing. Adequate replacements do not include paraprofessionals, student teachers, or custodial help.

3. Supervision procedures must be preplanned and incorporated into daily lessons.

4. Supervision procedures should include what to observe and listen for, where to stand for the most effective view, and what to do if a problem arises.

5. Supervision requires that age, maturity, and skill ability of participants always be considered, as must be the inherent risk of the activity.

Three categories of specific supervision are identified in provincial safety guidelines for physical education (e.g., Alberta Centre for Injury Control and Research, 2003; Ontario Physical and Health Education Association, 1999). These include (a) *constant supervision* where a teacher is physically present and watching a particular activity (e.g., present at the rope climbing station); (b) *on-site supervision* where the teacher is in the vicinity but not specifically viewing a single activity (e.g., while at the rope climbing stations, teacher is also monitoring the students doing forward rolls); and (c) *in-the-area supervision* where the teacher is in the vicinity but may not always have visual contact with all students (e.g., students doing a fitness run around the school may be out of sight for a period of time). Consider Merriman's five recommendations (with particular emphasis on number five) when determining the appropriate category of supervision.

Instruction

Instructional responsibility rests primarily with the teacher, but administrative personnel have certain defined functions.

Administration

The administration should review and approve the curricular plan. The curriculum should be reviewed regularly to ensure that it is current and updated. Be sure that activities included in the program are based on the goals and learning outcomes of the physical education curriculum guide. It makes little sense in a court of law to say that an activity was included "for the fun of it" or "because students liked it." Instead, make sure activities are included because they meet curriculum learning outcomes. Of particular note to both administrators and teachers should be familiarity with position statements and recommendations published by pertinent professional organizations. For example, in a position statement *Appropriate Practices for Elementary School Physical Education,* the Council on Physical Education for Children (2000) identifies dodgeball as an inappropriate activity for K–12 school physical education programs. Other organizations such as the American Academy of Pediatrics also publish a range of position statements and recommendations (e.g., medical conditions affecting sports participation). These types of documents are used consistently in litigation.

The principal and higher administrators should visit the program periodically. Familiarity with program content and operation obviates the possibility that practices were occurring without adequate administrative supervision.

Instructional Staff

With regard to instruction, teachers have a duty to protect students from unreasonable physical or mental harm. This includes avoiding any acts or omissions that might cause such harm. Teachers are educated, experienced, and skilled in physical education and must be able to foresee situations that could be harmful.

The major area of concern involving instruction is whether the student received adequate instruction before or during activity participation. Adequate instruction means (a) teaching children how to perform activities correctly and use equipment and apparatus properly, and (b) teaching youngsters necessary safety precautions. If instructions are given, they must be correct, understandable, and include proper technique, or the instructor can be held liable. The teacher must communicate to the learner the risk involved in an activity.

The age and maturity level of students plays an important role in the selection of activities. Younger students require more care, instructions that are easy to comprehend, and clear restrictions in the name of safety. Some students have a lack of appropriate fear, and the teacher must be aware of this when discussing safety factors. A very young child may have little concern about performing a high-risk activity if an instructor is nearby. This places much responsibility on the teacher to give adequate instruction and supervision.

Careful planning is a necessity. Written curriculum guides and lesson plans can offer a well-prepared approach that withstands scrutiny and examination by other teachers and administrators. Written lesson plans should include proper sequence and progression of skill. Teachers are on defensible grounds if they can show that the progression of activities was based on presentations designed by experts and were followed carefully during teaching. Closely check district and provincial or territorial guidelines enforcing instructional sequences and restricted activities.

Proper instruction demands that students not be forced to perform a skill beyond their capabilities. The line between helpful encouragement and forcing students to try new activities is not always clear. If you force a youngster to perform an activity unwillingly, you may be open to a lawsuit. For example, in *Boise v. Board of Education of St. Paul's Roman Catholic Separate School Division* (1979), an obese and inexperienced 13-year-old boy was injured when he was required to make a 2-metre vertical jump, even after expressing hesitancy and concern about the task. The teacher was found negligent in this case, as it was held that the boy's injury was foreseeable when considering his physical condition and lack of experience. To ensure that the proper sequence of skills and lead-up activities have been presented properly, it may be useful to post them.

The following points help ensure safe instruction:

1. Sequence all activities in units of instruction and develop written lesson plans. Problems occur when snap judgments are made under the daily pressure and strain of teaching.

2. Scrutinize high-risk activities to ensure that all safety procedures have been implemented. If in doubt, discuss the activities with experienced teachers and administrators.

3. Activities used in the curriculum must be within the developmental limits of the students. Since the range of maturity and development of youngsters in a class is usually wide, activities may be beyond the ability level of some students.

4. The lesson plan should detail how equipment should be arranged, where mats should be placed, and where the instructor will carry out supervision.

5. Establish a policy and procedure for dealing with nonparticipation or modified participation. Be sure to communicate this information to parents. A common procedure is to require a note from a parent or guardian describing the nature of the situation and the degree of participation that is possible. For long-term nonparticipation due to illness or injury, specific discussion with parents is advisable in order to establish a plan to keep the student as actively involved as possible within their limitations.

6. Make sure activities included in the instructional process are in line with the available equipment and facilities. An example is the amount of space available. If a soccer lead-up activity is brought indoors because of inclement weather, it may no longer be a safe and appropriate activity.

7. Where student aides are used (for example, senior students assisting in primary classes), they must be assigned tasks within their level of knowledge. The reader is encouraged to check school district policies regarding use of student aides.

8. If students are working independently at stations, carefully constructed and written task cards can help eliminate unsafe practices.

9. Post a written emergency care plan in the gymnasium. This plan should be approved by health care professionals and should be followed to the letter when an injury occurs.

Medical Information

All districts have specific policies and procedures regarding the handling of student medical information. In general, records must be kept on file and should be identified prominently (consistent with confidentiality rules) when physical restrictions or limitations exist. It is the parents' responsibility to inform the school of any emergency requirements so staff can be prepared to administer appropriate treatment where necessary. For example, if a student is allergic to bee stings and carries a "bee kit," then various school staff members should be trained to administer the medication. It is important to provide parents with basic information about the curricular and safety requirements in physical education. This information will minimize potential misunderstandings. Figure 9.1 shows a sample letter to parents. Again, since policies will differ from district to district, be sure you are familiar with those in your school district.

Equipment and Facilities

The school is responsible for equipment and facilities required for both non-instructional and class use. The following provides some general guidelines regarding care and use of equipment. In addition, check specific school district equipment policies and procedures.

Administration

The principal, custodial staff, and district maintenance staff should oversee the fields and playground equipment that are used for recess and outside activities. Students should be instructed to report broken and unsafe equipment, as well as hazards (such as glass, cans, rocks), to the principal's office. If equipment is faulty, remove it from the area. Regular inspection of equipment and facilities should be consistent with specific school district policies and procedures.

In general, administrators are required to have a written checklist of equipment and apparatus for the purpose of recording scheduled safety inspections. Note the date of inspection to show that inspection occurs at regular intervals. If a potentially dangerous situation exists, post rules or warnings so students and teachers are made aware of the risk.

Proper installation of equipment is critical. The appropriate qualified personnel should handle installation of all equipment, in accordance with district policy. Maintenance of facilities is also important. Grass should be kept short, and the grounds inspected for debris. Holes in the ground should be filled, and loose gravel removed. Hazards found on playing fields need to be repaired and eliminated. A proper finish that prevents excessive slipping should be used on indoor floors. Shower rooms should have a roughened floor finish applied, to prevent falls when the floors are wet.

Safe participation in activity can be enhanced by the selection of equipment and facilities. Choice of apparatus and equipment should be based on the growth and developmental levels of students. For example, allowing elementary school children to use a horizontal ladder that was designed for high school students may result in a fall that causes injury. Understand the legal concept of an *attractive nuisance*. This implies that some piece of equipment or apparatus, usually left unsupervised, is attractive to children that they cannot be expected to avoid it. When an injury occurs, even though students may have been using the apparatus incorrectly, teachers and school administration are often held liable because the attractive nuisance should have been removed from the area when unsupervised.

Instructional Staff

Indoor facilities are of primary concern to physical education teachers. Even though the administration is charged with overall responsibility for facilities and equipment, including periodic inspection, the teacher should make a regular safety inspection of the instructional area. If corrective action is needed, the principal or another designated administrator should be notified in writing. Verbal notification is not enough, since it offers little legal protection to the teacher.

Arrange facilities in a safe manner. The side and end lines of playing fields and gymnasium for sports such as basketball, soccer, and field hockey must provide a sufficient buffer between wall and fences. These boundaries allow adequate room for deceleration. School district safety guidelines will include the specific dimensions and requirements.

Proper use of equipment and apparatus is important. Regardless of the state of equipment repair, if the equipment is misused, it may result in an injury. Give students instruction in the proper use of equipment and apparatus before the equipment is issued to the students and used. Include safety instruction in the written lesson plan to ensure that all points are covered. If certain pieces of apparatus require special care and proper use, post rules and regulations near the apparatus (for children in intermediate grades).

Dear Parent/Guardian:

Vigorous physical activity is essential for normal, healthy growth and development. Growing bones and muscles require not only good nutrition, but also the stimulation of vigorous physical activity to increase the strength and skills necessary for a physically active lifestyle. Active participation in games, dance and gymnastics provides opportunities for students to discover and trust themselves and gain the confidence necessary to play and work cooperatively and competitively with their peers. Physical education programs at both the curricular and co-curricular level provide opportunities for students to experience the fitness feeling and to help them understand and make decisions regarding personal fitness and the value of physical activity in their daily lives.

Individual schools should highlight various curricular Physical Education topics and identify unique programs which take students into the immediate community e.g. in-class cross country running and skating are important components of the physical education program (this does not include downhill skiing etc. which are bus trips requiring parent/guardian consent forms). Please be advised that these activities will take your child off the school grounds. Supervision will be provided.

Schools should identify examples of intramural activities, which may be offered to students during the school year.

ELEMENTS OF RISK NOTICE

The risk of injury exists in every athletic activity. However, due to the very nature of some activities, the risk of injury may increase. Injuries may range from minor sprains and strains to more serious injuries. The safety and well being of students is a prime concern and attempts are made to manage as effectively as possible, the foreseeable risks inherent in physical activity.

Figure 9.1

Sample letter to parents/guardians (continued)

Source: Ontario Physical and Health Education Association. (1997). *Ontario physical education safety guidelines* (pp. 66–67). North York, ON: Author. Reprinted with permission.

It is important that your child participate safely and comfortably in the physical education program. In your child's best interests we recommend the following:

a) An annual medical examination.

b) Appropriate attire for safe participation (T-shirt, shorts or track pants and running shoes). Hanging jewellery must not be worn. Jewellery which cannot be removed and which presents a safety concern must be taped.

c) The wearing of an eyeglass band and/or shatterproof lens if your child wears glasses, which cannot be removed during physical education classes.

d) The wearing of sun protection for all outdoor activities.

e) Safety inspection at home of any equipment brought to school for personal use in class, e.g. skis, skates, and helmets.

Please complete the medical information form attached and have your child return it to his/her teacher. If you require further information, please contact the school.

MEDICAL INFORMATION FORM

Name of Student _____ Grade _____ Teacher _____

I would like to inform the school about these facts pertaining to my child's physical/medical condition related to his/her participation in Physical Education Curricular and Intramural Programs.

1. Please indicate if your son/daughter/ward has been subject to any of the following and provide pertinent details:

   epilepsy, diabetes, orthopedic problems, heart disorders, asthma, allergies.

   _____

   head or back conditions or injuries (in the past two years):

   _____

   arthritis or rheumatism; chronic nosebleeds; dizziness; fainting; headaches; dislocated shoulder; hernia; swollen, hyper mobile or painful joints; trick or lock knee: _____

2. What medication(s) should the participant have on hand during the sport activity?

   _____

   Who normally administers the medication?

   _____

3. Does your son/daughter/ward wear a medic alert bracelet _____, neck chain _____, or carry a medic alert card? _____

   If yes, please specify what is written on it:

   _____

4. Any other relevant medical condition that will require modification of the program:

   _____

   In signing this form, I acknowledge the element of risk information noted above.

Parent/Guardian Signature: _____ **Date:** _____

PLEASE NOTE: FREEDOM OF INFORMATION The information provided on this form is collected pursuant to the Board's education responsibilities as set out in the Education Act and its regulations. This information is protected under the Freedom of Information and Protection of Privacy Act and will be utilized only for the purposes related to the Board's Policy on Risk Management. Any questions with respect to this information should be directed to your school principal.

Figure 9.1

Continued

Equipment should be purchased on the basis of quality and safety as well as potential use. Many lawsuits occur because of unsafe equipment and apparatus. The liability for such equipment may rest with the manufacturer, but this has to be proved, which means that the teacher must state, in writing, the exact specifications of the desired equipment. The Canadian Standards Association (CSA) has developed the only recognized national standards on children's play spaces and equipment. As equipment and play spaces are continually being improved, the reader is encouraged to check with the CSA regarding current equipment safety standards.

Field Trips

A variety of activities in physical education may require travel to off-campus facilities (for example, swimming pools, skating rinks, and parks). This requires the teacher to deal with consent forms and transportation concerns.

Consent Forms

When students travel off-campus, teachers must provide the following information to parents prior to the trip: educational outcomes, field trip agenda, itinerary, level of supervision, safety concerns, cost, and mode of transportation.

This sort of information is often sent home with the student in the form of a letter, and the student returns a signed consent form (see Figure 9.2).

Transportation of Students

Whenever students are transported, teachers are responsible for their safety both en route and during the activity. If the school must provide transportation, licensed drivers and school-approved vehicles should always be used. Travel plans should include official approval from the appropriate school administrator. Figure 9.3 shows the typical information that must be completed if a private vehicle is used to transport students to official school activities.

School District # 56

FIELD TRIP CONSENT FORM

Name of Student: _____

❏ Yes   I have read the attached information about the planned field trip (including possible information such as education outcomes, field trip agenda, itinerary, level of supervision, safety concerns, cost, etc.) I feel that I have received sufficient information from the school and give my consent.

Signature of Parent or Guardian: _____

❏ No   I do not give my consent for the following reasons:

_____

_____

_____

_____

Signature of Parent or Guardian: _____

Please return this form as soon as possible.

School: _____

Sponsoring Teacher: _____

Name of Field Trip: _____

Date(s) of Field Trip: _____

Figure 9.2

Sample field trip consent form.

School District #56

SCHOOL USE OF PRIVATE VEHICLE

(Original to be filed in the school office)

To be completed by drivers of all vehicles that transport students to official school activities.

_____   _____
Driver's Name (please print clearly)   Registered Owner's Name (please print clearly)

_____
Address of Registered Owner

_____   _____
Vehicle Licence Number   Model/Year of Vehicle

Board Policy requires that a minimum of $1,000,000 liability insurance be carried on any vehicle used to transport students to or from a school function.

The above vehicle has _____ seat belts in good working order.

Check one:

- The above vehicle has a minimum of $1,000,000 liability insurance.   ❑ Yes ❑ No
- The driver has a valid driver's licence, will act in accordance with *BC Motor Vehicle Act,*   ❑ Yes ❑ No
  and ensure that there is one seat belt for each passenger.
- The vehicle is in good mechanical shape and road worthiness.   ❑ Yes ❑ No

_____   _____
Driver's Signature   Date

Figure 9.3

Sample form for school use of private vehicle.

Physical Education Safety Guidelines: Emphasis on Risk Management

The major concept that ties together the common areas of negligence (supervision, instruction, and equipment/facilities) is risk management (Goodman & McGregor, 1993; Hart & Ritson, 2002; Robertson & Robertson, 1988; Watson, 1996). There are inherent risks in every physical education activity. However, learning to "manage" risk is an important factor in creating a safe environment for students. Watson (1996) defines *risk management* as "developing a complete and thorough understanding of an activity to be able to develop policies and procedures that will eliminate, or significantly reduce, foreseeable risks" (p. 13). In other words, teachers must possess a clear understanding of the hazards and potential dangers of an activity before they can establish controls. Provincial safety guidelines for physical education

provide helpful documentation and guidance for teachers. Ontario Physical and Health Education (1999) states the purpose of provincial safety guidelines is to "focus teachers' attention on safe instructional practices for each class activity in order to minimize the inherent element of risk" (p. 3). They further state that a guideline alone "does not eliminate risk regardless of how well it is written or how effectively it is implemented. Safety awareness, practised by the teacher, based on up-to-date information, common sense observation, action and foresight, is the key to safe programming" (p. 3). For examples of comprehensive physical education safety guidelines, see Alberta Centre for Injury Control and Research (2003), Manitoba Education and Training (1997), New Brunswick Department of Education (2002), Nova Scotia Department of Education (2001), Ontario Physical and Health Education Association (1999), and Saskatchewan Education (1998). The reader is encouraged to consult physical education safety guidelines for their province or territory, and individual school district.

General Guidelines for Managing Risk

The following are some guidelines for risk management in physical education:

1. Experienced and knowledgeable teachers should administer in-service sessions in safety. Giving credit to participating teachers offers strong evidence that the district is concerned about using proper safety techniques.

2. Teachers must meet the minimum first aid certification requirements. These requirements differ greatly from province to province or territory. Administrators and teachers are encouraged to go beyond minimum requirements and make training sessions available.

3. Medical records should be reviewed at the start of the school year and on a regular basis throughout the year. Records must be kept on file and should be identified prominently (consistent with confidentiality rules) when physical restrictions or limitations exist. See the discussion on medical information in Figure 9.1.

4. Throughout the school year, safety orientations should be conducted with students. Discussions should include potentially dangerous situations, class conduct, and rules for proper use of equipment and apparatus. Teachers should urge students to report any conditions that might cause an accident.

5. Safety rules for specific units of instruction should be discussed at the onset of each unit. Rules should be posted and brought to the attention of students regularly. Posters and bulletin boards can promote safety in an enjoyable and stimulating manner.

6. If students are to serve as teaching aides, they should be trained and assigned duties within their level of knowledge. Be familiar with school policy on the use of student aides.

7. Instructional practices need to be monitored for possible hazards. Prior to activity, there should be proper instruction necessary for safe participation. The instructional area should be properly prepared for safe participation; if the area is lacking necessary apparatus and safety devices, instruction should be modified to meet safety standards.

8. An inventory of equipment and apparatus should include a safety checklist. Whenever necessary, send equipment in need of repair to proper agents.

9. When an injury occurs, it should be recorded and reported in a manner consistent with school district policies and procedures.

10. Safety should be publicized regularly throughout the school, and a mechanism should exist that allows students, parents, and teachers to voice concerns about unsafe conditions.

11. Safety policies and procedures should be reviewed and updated on a regular basis.

Emergency Action Plan

Before any emergency arises, teachers should prepare themselves by learning about special health and physical conditions of their students (Gray, 1993). Most schools have a method for identifying students with special health problems. If a student has a problem that may require treatment, a consent-to-treat form should be on file in case the parent or guardian is unavailable. Make sure necessary first aid materials and supplies are available in a kit and are readily accessible.

Establishing procedures for emergency care and notification of parents in case of injury is of utmost importance in providing a high standard of care for students. *First aid* is the immediate and temporary care given at an emergency before a physician is available. Its purposes are to save lives, prevent aggravation of injuries, and alleviate severe suffering. If there is evidence of life-threatening bleeding or if the victim is unconscious or has stopped breathing, the teacher or another properly qualified person must administer first aid. When already injured persons may be further injured if they are not moved, then moving them is permissible. As a general rule, however, an injured person should not be moved unless absolutely necessary. If there is indication of back or neck injury, the head must be immobilized and should not be moved without the use of a spine board. Remember, the purpose of first aid is to save lives. Figure 9.4 shows an example of a comprehensive emergency action plan.

Reporting an Accident

School districts have established specific procedures for reporting accidents. These procedures are designed to document the particulars of the accident for insurance purposes, for protection of the injured party, and for protection of the applicable school personnel. Figure 9.5 shows a sample accident/injury report form. For the protection of all concerned, it is imperative that teachers involved complete these forms accurately and in a timely fashion.

Safety Checklists

The following checklists can be used to monitor the physical education environment. Immediately rectify any situations that deviate from safe and legally sound practices.

There is the potential for injury in all physical activities. Therefore, it is important to have an emergency action plan. The key to any emergency action plan is getting professional care to the student as quickly as possible.

Know the following information:

1) Location and means of access to a first aid kit.
2) Location of a telephone.
3) Telephone number of ambulance and hospital.
4) Directions and best access routes to hospital.
5) Location of vehicles on the school site which could be used to transport students to hospital.

When an injury occurs:

1) Take control and assess the situation.
2) Remember the basic first aid rule:
   Do not move the injured student. If student cannot start a movement by himself/herself, do not move the body part for him/her.
3) Tell bystanders to leave the injured student alone.
4) Leave the student's equipment in place.
5) Evaluate the injury. Once you have assessed the severity of the injury, decide whether further assistance is required.
6) If an ambulance is not needed, decide how to remove the injured student from the playing surface.
7) If an ambulance is required:
   a) Request assistance from another person (teacher/administrator/parent);
   b) Have the second person call an ambulance and give the following information:
   - state that it is a medical emergency;
   - state what the emergency is; and
   - give the exact location and the name of the closest cross streets.
   c) Give the telephone number from which you are calling.
   d) After the other person has called the ambulance, he/she should report back to the person in charge, confirm the call, and give the estimated time that the ambulance will arrive.
   e) Have someone go to the entrance and wait for the ambulance.
8) Once the ambulance has been called, observe the injured person carefully for any change in condition, and try to reassure the injured student until professional help arrives.
9) Do not move the injured person unnecessarily.
10) Do not give the injured person food or drink.
11) Stay calm. Keep an even tone in your voice.
12) When ambulance attendants arrive, tell them what happened, how it happened, and what you have done. If possible, inform the ambulance attendants about any medical problems or past injuries that the injured person may have experienced.
13) Accompany the injured person to the hospital to help reassure him or her and to give the relevant medical history and injury circumstances to the physician.
14) If the injured person is a student, contact the parents/guardians as soon as possible after injury.
15) Complete an accident report and file it with appropriate school board officials and school administrator.

For after-school and outdoor activities, have access to a cellular phone.

Figure 9.4

Sample Emergency Action Plan.

Source: Saskatchewan Education (1998). *Saskatchewan physical education: Safety guidelines for policy development*, p. 115. Regina, SK: Author. Reprinted with permission.

Supervision and Instruction

1. Are teachers adequately trained in all of the activities that they are teaching?
2. Do all teachers have evidence of a necessary level of first-aid training?
3. When supervising, do personnel have access to a written plan of areas to be observed and responsibilities to be carried out?
4. Have students been warned of potential dangers and risks, and advised of rules and the reasons for the rules?
5. Are safety rules posted near areas of increased risk?
6. Are lesson plans written? Do they include provisions for proper instruction, sequence of activities, and safety?
7. When a new activity is introduced, are safety precautions and instructions for correct skill performance always communicated to the class?

MARSH & McLENNAN (SASK.) LTD.
SUITE 205–2222–13TH AVENUE
REGINA, SK S4P 3M7

Phone No. (306) 525-5120
FAX No. (306) 352-9633

SASKATCHEWAN SCHOOL TRUSTEES ASSOCIATION
400–2222–13th AVENUE   Phone No. (306) 569-0750
REGINA, SK S4P 3M7   FAX No. (306) 352-9633

SCHOOL/COLLEGE/INSTITUTE INCIDENT REPORT FORM FOR INSURANCE PURPOSES

1. GENERAL

Name/Number of School or Name and Location of College/Institute Facility:

_____

Name of School Division:

_____

Date of Incident (M/D/Y) _____ Time _____ : _____ a.m./p.m.   Telephone # _____

Description of how incident occurred:

_____

_____

_____

_____

Location of Incident:

C01 ( )	Basement	L12 ( )	Playing Fields
L02 ( )	Cafeteria/Lunchroom	L13 ( )	Playground Equipment
L03 ( )	Classroom	L14 ( )	Pool
L04 ( )	Shops/Lab/Kitchen	L15 ( )	Rink
L05 ( )	Doors/Entrance Areas	L16 ( )	Sidewalks/Roads off Facility Property
L06 ( )	Dormitories	L17 ( )	Stairs within Building
L07 ( )	Gymnasium/Auditorium	L18 ( )	Stairs/Sidewalks within Grounds
L08 ( )	Hallways/Lockers	L19 ( )	Washrooms/Changing Rooms/Showers
L09 ( )	Library/Office/Lounge/ Study Room	L20 ( )	Other • (Please Explain)
L10 ( )	Park/Grounds		
L11 ( )	Parking Lot		

WITNESSES:

(1) Name: _____

Teacher/Instructor/Other: _____

Witness Activity at time: _____

(2) Name: _____

Teacher/Instructor/Other: _____

Witness Activity at time: _____

Figure 9.5

Sample accident/injury report form (continued)

Source: Saskatchewan Education (1998). *Saskatchewan physical education: Safety guidelines for policy development*, pp. 116–120. Regina, SK: Author. Reprinted with permission.

2. COMPLETE THE APPROPRIATE SECTION
For Bodily Injury/Other Party, Damage complete Section "A"   For Loss or Damage to Facility and/or Contents complete Section "B"

SECTION A

Name of Person Involved _____   Age: _____   M/F: _____

Address: _____   Postal Code: _____   Grade/Year/Night School: _____
(Schools Only)

Student/Visitor/Other: (Explain) _____

Division/Program: _____

Parent/Guardian/Emergency Contact: _____   Notified? (Y/N) _____

How? _____

Telephone # _____

Parent/Guardian/Emergency Contact Instructions: _____

Emergency Treatment: (Y/N) _____   What? _____   By Whom? _____

Advised to seek medical treatment: (Y/N) _____   Hospitalized? (Y/N) _____   Where? _____

How transported? _____

Nature of Injury/Damage:

N01 ( )	Bruise/Abrasion/Swelling	N10 ( )	No Information	
N02 ( )	Burn	N11 ( )	Nosebleed	
N03 ( )	Concussion (Suspected)	N12 ( )	Open Wound/Laceration	
N04 ( )	Crushed	N13 ( )	Sprain/Strain (Suspected)	
N05 ( )	Dental Damage	N14 ( )	Winded	
N06 ( )	Dislocation	N15 ( )	Property Damage/Other Party	
N07 ( )	Fatality/Death	N16 ( )	Bites/Stings	
N08 ( )	Fracture	N17 ( )	Other ● (Please Explain)	
N09 ( )	Imbedded Object			

Cause of Injury or Damage:

C01 ( )	Assault ● No Weapon	C10 ( )	Horseplay	
C02 ( )	Assault with Weapon	C11 ( )	Maintenance Activity	
C03 ( )	Choking/Suffocation	C12 ( )	Motor Vehicle Accident	
C04 ( )	Drowning	C13 ( )	Poison/Allergic Reaction	
C05 ( )	Exposure to Flame/ Electricity or Hot Caustic Substance	C14 ( )	School Bus Accident	
		C15 ( )	Sports Injury	
C06 ( )	Fall at Same Height	C16 ( )	Struck Against Person	
C07 ( )	Fall from Different Height	C17 ( )	Struck/Crushed By/Against Object	
C08 ( )	Fatigue/Over Exertion	C18 ( )	Other ● (Please Explain)	
C09 ( )	Foreign Body			

Body Area:

B01 ( )	Arms/Shoulder/Elbow	B08 ( )	Legs/Knees/Ankles	
B02 ( )	Chest/Abdomen/Pelvis	B09 ( )	Multiple Areas	
B03 ( )	Eyes	B10 ( )	Neck	
B04 ( )	Face	B11 ( )	No Information	
B05 ( )	Feet/Toes	B12 ( )	Spine/Back	
B06 ( )	Fingers/Hands/Wrists	B13 ( )	Teeth/Mouth	
B07 ( )	Head/Forehead	B14 ( )	Other ● (Please Explain)	

Activity at Time of Incident:

A01 ( )	Academic Classroom	A06 ( )	Sports Event	
A02 ( )	Between Classes	A07 ( )	Sports-Related Class	
A03 ( )	Extra-Curricular (i.e. Club)	A08 ( )	Travel to or from Facility	
A04 ( )	Out-of-Class Field Trip	A09 ( )	Unorganized Sports	
A05 ( )	Recess/Pre- or Post- Class/Noon Hour	A10 ( )	Work Placement	
		A11 ( )	Maintenance Activity	
		A12 ( )	Other ● (Please Explain)	

Figure 9.5

Continued

SECTION B

Property Involved (Describe property involved and extent of loss and/or damage): _____

_____

_____

Fire Department Attended: (Y/N) _____   Report Number: _____

Were Police Notified? (Y/N) _____

Branch/Detachment: _____   Case Number: _____

Date (M/D/Y) _____   Time _____ : _____ a.m./p.m.

Were there visible signs of forced entry?   (Y/N) _____

What? (Explain) _____

_____

Cause of Loss/Damage:

C01	( ) Burglary/Forcible Entry	C10	( ) Robbery
C02	( ) Collapse	C11	( ) Smoke
C03	( ) Dishonesty/Infidelity	C12	( ) Theft
C04	( ) Explosion	C13	( ) Transportation
C05	( ) Falling Object	C14	( ) Vandalism/Malicious Acts
C06	( ) Fire/Lightning	C15	( ) Water Escape/Rupture/ Freezing
C07	( ) Glass Breakage	C16	( ) Windstorm/Hail
C08	( ) Impact by Vehicle/Aircraft	C17	( ) Other • (Please Explain)
C09	( ) Riot		

3. SIGNATURES AND DATE

Name of Person Completing Report: _____

_____   _____   (Signature)
(Please Print or Type)

Name of Administrator: _____

_____   _____   (Signature)
(Please Print or Type)

Date: _____   Incident Report Form used with permission of Marsh & McLellan (Sask.) Ltd.

Figure 9.5

Continued

8. Are the activities taught in the program consistent with prescribed learning outcomes?

9. Do the methods of instruction recognize individual differences among students, and have the necessary steps been taken to meet the needs of all students, regardless of gender, ability, or disability?

10. Are substitute teachers given clear and comprehensive lesson plans so that they can maintain the scope and sequence of instruction?

11. Is appropriate dress required for students? This does not imply uniforms, only dress (including shoes) that ensures the safety of the student.

12. When necessary for safety, are students grouped according to ability level, size, or age?

13. If students are used as teacher aides or to spot others, are they given proper instruction and training?

Equipment and Facilities

1. Is all equipment inspected regularly and are the inspection results recorded on a form and sent to the proper administrators?

2. Is a log maintained recording the regular occurrence of inspections, the equipment in need of repair, and when repairs were made?

3. Are "attractive nuisances" eliminated from the gymnasium and playing field?

4. Are specific safety rules posted on facilities and near equipment?

5. Are the following inspected periodically?
   a. playing field for presence of glass, rocks, and metal objects
   b. fasteners holding equipment, such as climbing ropes, horizontal bars, or baskets
   c. goals for games, such as soccer and field hockey, to be sure that they are fastened securely
   d. padded areas, such as goal supports

6. Are mats placed under apparatus from which a fall is possible?

7. Are playing fields arranged so participants will not run into each other or be hit by a ball from another game?

8. Are landing pits filled and maintained properly?

Emergency Care

1. Is there a written procedure for emergency care?

2. Is a person properly trained in first aid available immediately following an accident?

3. Are emergency telephone numbers readily accessible?

4. Are telephone numbers of parents available?

5. Is an up-to-date first-aid kit available? Is ice immediately available?

6. Are medical files maintained that list restrictions, allergies, and health problems of students?

7. Are medical files reviewed by teachers on a regular basis?

8. Are accident reports filed promptly and analyzed regularly?

Transportation of Students

1. Have parents been informed that their students will be transported off campus?

2. Are detailed travel plans approved by the site administrator and kept on file?

3. Are school vehicles used whenever possible?

4. Are drivers properly licensed and vehicles insured in accordance with district policy?

Managing Personal Safety: Learning Outcomes in Physical Education

The teacher will always be ultimately responsible for the safety of his or her students; however, an integral part of the establishment and maintenance of a safe environment involves students learning to take responsibility for their behaviour. This includes development of learning outcomes associated with safe behaviour as part of the physical education curriculum. Most provincial PE curriculum guides identify safety as a major concept. For example, Manitoba includes *Safety* as one of five major outcomes in its PE/Healthy curriculum framework. The *Safety* curriculum outcome states that the "student will demonstrate safe and responsible behaviours to manage risks and prevent injuries in physical activity participation and in daily living" (Manitoba Education and Training, 2000, p. 20). This outcome is further subdivided into two knowledge strands including *physical activity risk management* (relates to safe participation in physical activity), and *safety of self and others* relating to safety practices associated with everyday living (e.g., fire safety). Similarly, both BC and Ontario include explicit knowledge and skill learning outcomes associated with personal safety and injury prevention as part of their PE curriculum guides.

Critical Thinking

1. *Considering the Elements of Negligence:* A group of grade 7 students are playing a game of Diagonal Soccer. When their numbers are called, three students from each team run to the centre to try and get the ball first and gain scoring advantage. One of the students is a small student who weighs about 32 kilograms. A student on the other team is physically mature and weighs nearly 64 kilograms. As they approach the ball, the larger student basically runs over the smaller student, knocking him down and causing a head injury. Within two weeks, the student has a seizure and the parents are considering legal action. Was the accident foreseeable? Could the game have been modified to avoid this injury? Consider the following elements in your discussion: duty of care, breach of duty, proximate cause, and injury.

2. *Considering a Teacher's Duty of Care:* A group of students in grade 5 are playing softball during physical education class. The teacher has provided the students with thorough softball hitting practice, review of related safety rules, and has marked out restraining lines that are easy for students to see. During class, students are engaged in a number of softball stations. One of the students runs through the restricted area and is hit by a batted ball. Was the student old enough to know better? Should the teacher have foreseen that an accident might happen even if students were prewarned? Consider the four criteria for standard of care applied to physical education in your discussion.

3. Examine your provincial/territorial PE curriculum guide for learning outcomes focused on the development of safe behaviour in physical activity. Discuss the suggested teaching strategies associated with these learning outcomes.

References and Suggested Readings

Alberta Centre for Injury Control & Research. (2003). *Safety guidelines for physical activity in Alberta schools.* Edmonton, AB: Author.

American Academy of Pediatrics. (2001). Medical conditions affecting sports participation. *Pediatrics, 107*(5), 1205–1209.

Appenzeller, H. (2003). *Managing sports and risk management strategies* (2nd ed.). Durham, NC: Carolina Academic Press.

Barnes, J. (1996). *Sports and the law in Canada.* Toronto, ON: Butterworths.

Bezeau, L.M. (2006). *Educational administration for Canadian teachers* (6th ed.). Retrieved from www.unb.ca/education/bezeau/eact/eactcvp.html.

Black, H.C. (1996). *Black's law dictionary.* St. Paul, MN: West.

Boise v. Board of Education of St. Paul's Roman Catholic Separate School Division, District 20. (1979) DLR (3d) 643. (Sask. QB).

British Columbia School Act (7th ed.). (1995). Victoria, BC: Queen's Printer.

Canadian Standards Association. (1991). *A guideline for children's playspaces and equipment.* Toronto, ON: Author.

Council on Physical Education for Children. (2000). *Appropriate practices for elementary physical education: A position statement of the National Association for Sport and Physical Education.* Reston, VA: NASPE/AAHPERD.

Dickinson, G.M. (2006). Teaching within the Law: Liability for physical harm and the need for proper risk management. In E. Singleton & A. Varpalotai (Eds.), *Stones in the sneaker—Active theory for secondary school physical and health educators* (pp. 277–302). London, ON: Althouse Press.

Dougherty, D. (2002). *Principles of safety in physical education & sport.* Reston, VA: American Alliance for Health, Physical Education, Recreation and Dance.

Dougherty, N.J., Goldberger, A.S., & Carpenter, A.S. (2002). *Sport, physical activity, and the law.* Champaign, IL: Sagamore.

Goodman, S.F., & McGregor, I. (1993). *Legal liability and risk management.* Toronto, ON: Risk Management Associates.

Gray, G.R. (1993). Providing adequate medical care to program participants. *Journal of Physical Education, Recreation, and Dance, 64*(2), 56–57.

Hart, J.E & Ritson, R.J. (2002). *Liability and safety in physical education and sport.* Reston, VA: American Alliance for Health, Physical Education, Recreation and Dance.

MacKay, A.W. (1984). *Education law in Canada.* Toronto: Emond-Montgomery Publishing.

Manitoba Education and Training. (1997). *Safety guidelines for physical activity in Manitoba schools.* Winnipeg, MB: Author.

Manitoba Education and Training. (2000). *Kindergarten to senior 4 physical education/health education—Manitoba curriculum framework of outcomes for active healthy lifestyles.* Winnipeg, MB: Author.

Merriman, J. (1993). Supervision in sport and physical activity. *Journal of Physical Education, Recreation, and Dance, 64*(2), 20–23.

New Brunswick Department of Education. (2002). *Physical education elementary & middle school level curricular guidelines.* Fredericton, NB: Author.

Nichols, A.C. (1988). *An introduction to school case law.* Vancouver, BC: EduServ Inc.

Nova Scotia Education Act, 24 1, 1995–96.

Nova Scotia Department of Education. (2002). *Physical education safety guidelines: Grades primary–12.* Halifax, NS: Author.

Ontario Ministry of Education and Training. (1998). *The Ontario curriculum, grades 1–8: Health and physical education.* Toronto, ON: Author.

Ontario Physical and Health Education Association. (1999). *Ontario safety guidelines for physical education—Elementary: Curriculum guidelines.* North York, ON: Author.

Robertson, B.W. & Robertson, B.J. (1988). *Sport and recreation liability and you!* Vancouver, BC: Self-Counsel Press.

Safe Kids Canada. (1997). *Child's Play—A playground safety guide for daycares, schools, and communities.* Toronto, ON: Author.

Saskatchewan Education Act. (1993). Regina, SK: Queen's Printer.

Saskatchewan Education. (1998). *Saskatchewan physical education: Safety guidelines for policy development.* Regina, SK: Author.

Thornton et al. v. Board of Trustees of School District No. 57 (Prince George) et al. (1977). *Dominion Law Reports (3d). 73*: 35–62. 5 W.W.R. 240, [1978] 1 W.W.R. 607, (1976) 73 D.L.R. (3d) 35, [1978] 2 S.C.R. 267.

Watson, R. (1996). Risk management: A plan for safer activities. *Canadian Association for Health, Physical Education, Recreation and Dance Journal, 61*(1), 13–17.

 Weblinks

Stay Alert . . . Stay Safe: www.sass.ca

Includes a program that focuses on helping children and adults become more aware of potential dangers and developing proactive skills to avoid these dangers. Includes a variety of classroom resources.

Think First for Kids: www.thinkfirst.ca

This organization helps increase understanding of brain and spinal cord safety associated with a variety of recreational physical activities. Includes educational resources for grades K–6, 7–8.

Canadian Institute of Child Health: www.cich.ca

Website includes a variety of resources that focus on Healthy and Safe schools.

CHAPTER 10

Facilities, Equipment, and Supplies

Essential Components

I	Organized around content standards
II	Student-centred and developmentally appropriate
III	Physical activity and motor skill development form the core of the program
IV	Teaches management skills and self-discipline
V	Promotes inclusion of all students
VI	Focuses on process over product
VII	Promotes lifetime personal health and wellness
VIII	Teaches cooperation and responsibility and promotes sensitivity to diversity

Physical Education Standards

1	Students are able to move competently using a variety of fundamental and specialized motor skills.
2	Students can monitor and maintain a health-enhancing level of physical fitness.
3	Students are able to apply movement concepts and basic mechanics of skill performance when learning and refining motor skills.
4	Students comprehend the basic principles of wellness and are able to apply concepts that enable them to make meaningful decisions that positively impact their health and wellness.
5	Students participate in a wide variety of physical activities and learn how to maintain a personalized active lifestyle.
6	Students demonstrate empathy, understanding, and respect for the numerous differences exhibited by people in an activity setting.
7	**Students exhibit responsible and self-directed behaviours that lead to positive social interactions in physical activity.**

OVERVIEW

This chapter presents procedures associated with the design, purchase, maintenance, and construction of physical education facilities, equipment, and supplies. The term *equipment* refers to items that are more or less fixed in nature. Equipment has a relatively long life span, needs periodic safety checks, and requires planned purchasing.

Supplies are nondurable items that have a limited period of use.

OUTCOMES

- Identify standards to follow in the construction of outdoor and indoor physical education facilities.

- Understand that safety is an essential consideration in facility design.

- List recommended equipment for outdoor and indoor physical education areas.

- Outline a systematic plan for the storage of physical education equipment and supplies.

- Describe procedures for the care and repair of physical education equipment and supplies.

- Illustrate floor lines and markings that enhance management potential and increase ease of instruction.

- List essential equipment and supplies for physical education in the elementary school.

The facilities for physical education usually fall into one of two categories: outdoor and indoor. Usually, outdoor space provides enough room for several classes to work simultaneously. Ideally, indoor facilities should allow for all classes to receive daily physical education.

Outdoor Facilities

Standards for outdoor play areas are defined by provincial and territorial facilities guidelines, with numerous differences across Canada. Therefore, discussion will be limited to some general requirements. The reader should refer to his or her respective guidelines for specific requirements. Ideally, the outdoor areas should include field space for games, a track, hard-surfaced areas, apparatus areas, play courts, age-group–specific play areas, and covered play space.

Fields should be levelled, drained, and turfed, because grass is the most usable field surface. An automatic sprinkler system is desirable, but sprinkler heads must not protrude to become safety hazards. Automatic installations permit sprinkling during the evening and night, so that the fields are not too soggy for play the next day.

A hardtop area should be marked for a variety of game courts, such as volleyball and basketball. Four-square courts, hopscotch layouts, and circles for games are examples of other markings that can be put on these surfaces. Simple movement pattern courses can also be marked.

As a minimum, space should be provided for a track, and it should be placed in an area where it will not interfere with other activities. For schools where a permanent installation is not practical, a temporary track can be laid out each spring.

Separate play spaces for different age groups should be included in the planning. Such areas should contain apparatus designed for each age group. The play area for primary-level children should be well away from areas where soccer balls and softballs are used.

Small, hard-surfaced play courts can be located strategically near the edges of the outdoor area, thus spreading out the playgroups. These courts, approximately 12 by 18 metres, can be equipped for basketball or volleyball or for both. A covered shed can be divided for use by different age groups. Climatic conditions would dictate the need for such facilities.

A jogging trail can stimulate interest in jogging. Small signs indicating the distances covered and markers outlining the trail are all that are needed. Stations with exercise tasks can be placed at intervals. For example, a station could have directions to accomplish a specified number of push-ups or sit-ups. Such a circuit is popularly called a *parcourse*.

An area set aside as a developmental playground is an important part of the total play space. The area should contain equipment and apparatus and should be landscaped to have small hills, valleys, and tunnels for children. A recommended approach is to divide the playground into various developmental areas so that children must exercise different body parts in different areas of the play space. For example, one area might contain a great deal of climbing equipment to reinforce arm–shoulder girdle development, and another area might challenge the leg and trunk regions. Equipment and apparatus should be abstract in nature; creation and imagination are left to the children. Apparatus can be manipulated and changed to suit the needs and desires of the youngsters.

Safety on the Playground

The following section provides some general guidelines for playground equipment and play spaces. The Canadian Standards Association (CSA) has developed the only recognized national standards on children's play spaces and equipment. The reader is encouraged to consult CSA standards for specific information. A recent research study demonstrated that when school playgrounds were upgraded to the CSA standard, injuries declined by 49% (Howard, et al., 2005).

Safe Kids Canada (2004) reports that more than 28,500 Canadian children receive hospital treatment for playground-related injuries. Close to 75% of non-fatal injuries (including head injuries) are caused when children fall from an apparatus and strike the underlying surface (Lesage & Laforest, 1997). In addition, most falls involve climbers, slides, or swings (Canadian Hospitals Injury Reporting and Prevention Program, 1996). Roughhousing, improper usage, and slipping are the most prominent causes of accidents. Rules should be established so that only one person is on the platform, with the next user waiting at the base of the ladder.

The type of surface under the equipment is a major factor affecting the severity of injuries associated with falls from apparatus. Concrete, asphalt, and other paved surfaces placed under an apparatus require little or no maintenance. However, hard surfaces do not provide injury protection from accidental fall impacts and therefore are unsuitable for use.

No playground surface is safe under all circumstances. The CSA recommends a variety of natural (sand, pea gravel, or wood chips) and synthetic (poured in-place rubber or rubber mats) options. To examine the pros and cons of each surface consult the Canadian Standards Association's (2003) *A Guideline on Children's Playspaces and Equipment*. The choice of material needs to be based on local conditions and the availability of funds. Continuous and correct maintenance is as important as the selection of the proper material. Allied to proper maintenance is the need for a checklist of proper procedures to be followed. This form should be filled out and dated on a regular basis.

For natural options, the depth and spread is the critical safety feature. The deeper the surface, the better it cushions a fall. The CSA recommends a minimum depth of 15 cm throughout a playground, and 30 cm inside fall zones—the area under and around equipment where children usually land when they fall. Frequent levelling, grading, and replacement of the material are necessary, as children will push the material away from the impact areas. The synthetic surfaces are more expensive to install; however, they require less maintenance. In addition, the synthetic surfaces allow for better wheelchair accessibility.

Outdoor Apparatus and Equipment

The continued emphasis on physical fitness should dictate the selection of outdoor equipment. Equipment that offers "sit and ride" experiences (swings, merry-go-rounds, and teeter-totters) does not meet this criterion. A second criterion is that of safety. Each piece of equipment should minimize the potential for injury. As a general rule, moving parts on equipment increase its potential for injury. Suggestions for equipment are offered below based on their potential to develop various components of fitness. The categories can be useful if you want to establish a challenge course that develops all parts of the body. Outdoor equipment should stimulate children's creative drives and their desire to move.

Equipment for Upper Body Development

Most children do not receive enough activity that develops upper body strength. In order to develop arm–shoulder girdle strength on the playground, youngsters need the opportunity to climb and swing, and to elevate their bodies. Climbing is important for physical development and to help children learn to overcome the fear of new situations. The reader is reminded to consult specific CSA standards for general suggestions. The following are examples of equipment that could be used to develop arm–shoulder girdle strength:

- Large telephone cable spools that are fastened securely so they will not move or tip over. Youngsters can climb on and jump off the spools.
- Climbing poles placed next to platforms that children can reach by climbing the poles.
- Logs and clean railroad ties, positioned vertically, with handholds or handles placed in strategic locations for climbing.
- Tires attached to telephone poles or logs for climbing through and around.

- Jungle gyms that are attached securely.
- Horizontal ladders in a variety of combinations and forms. Arched ladders are quite popular and allow children to reach the rungs easily. Uniladders, consisting of a single beam with pegs on each side, offer a different ladder challenge to children.
- Logs anchored vertically with handholds provided for climbing.

Equipment for Lower Body Development

Equipment and apparatus for enhancing lower body development should encourage youngsters to use locomotor movements throughout the available space. Allow enough distance and area to ensure movement. Here are some suggestions for lower body development:

- Large spaces, which encourage free movement and running games.
- Railroad ties anchored vertically at varying heights and distances, which encourage children to walk, run, hop, and jump from one to the other.
- Used automobile tires fastened on the ground in different patterns to stimulate moving in and out, around and over the tires using different movements.
- Stairways and platforms for climbing on and jumping off.
- Stepping stones to encourage movement patterns. Stones can be placed so they encourage oppositional patterning while moving.
- Miniature challenge courses that contain tires to move over and through, sand pits to run or jump into, and poles or cones arranged for moving around and dodging.

Equipment for Balance Skills

Balance is improved through regular practice. A number of pieces of equipment can be used to challenge youngsters' balance skills. Youngsters should be encouraged to move under control while practising balance. The following are suggestions for offering balance challenges:

- Balance beams made of 10-by-10-cm beams can be permanent installations. They can be arranged in various patterns but should not be more than 30.5 to 46 cm above the ground.
- Logs, anchored securely, can be used as balance beams.
- Include balance beams that start with a wide width of 29 cm and progress in difficulty to 15 cm.
- Wooden ladders secured 15 cm above the ground offer opportunities to walk on the rungs and rails.

Equipment for Sport Skills

Outdoor basketball goals may or may not be combined with a court. Youngsters play a lot of one-goal basketball, and a regulation court is not needed for this game. The goals should be in a surfaced area, however. Outdoor baskets for elementary school use should be designed to allow for easy adjustment of the height of the basket. Volleyball standards should have flexible height adjustments. Softball backstops can be either fixed or portable.

Jumping standards, bars, and pits should be available. These must be maintained properly.

Indoor Facilities

The gymnasium must be well planned for maximum use. It should be located in a separate wing connected to the classrooms by a covered corridor and should provide ready access to play areas. Isolating the gym from the rest of the school minimizes the noise problem and allows after-school and community groups to use the facilities without access to other parts of the school. The indoor facility should be planned in such a way that athletic contests can be scheduled there at times, but the primary purpose of the gymnasium is not as an athletic facility. Consideration for spectators should not be a major planning concern. Only after planners have met basic physical education needs should they consider needs of spectators.

In the gymnasium, put markings and boundaries on the floor to outline convenient areas for the more common activities. The markings should be painted on the floor after the first or second sealer coat has been applied. A finish coat should then be applied on top of the line markings. Figure 10.1 is an example of how floor markings can maximize the usefulness of a facility.

Temporary lines needed occasionally during the year can be applied with pressure-sensitive tape. These tapes are, however, difficult to remove completely and are likely

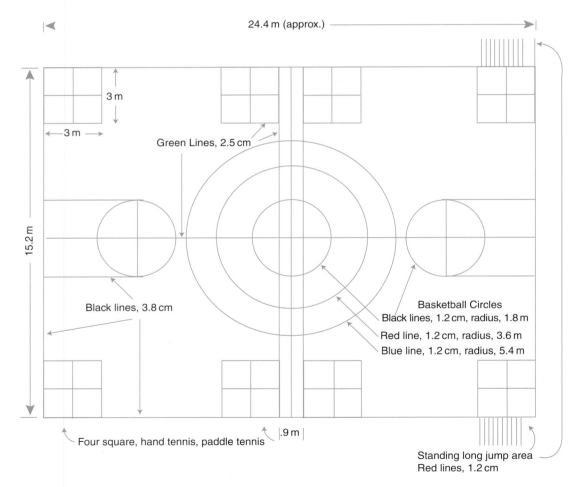

Figure 10.1

Floor markings to maximize gymnasium use.

to take off the finish when removed. A hardwood (preferably maple) floor is recommended for the gymnasium. Other surfaces limit community use and create both safety and maintenance problems.

For safety reasons and for rebound practice, walls should have a smooth surface 2.5 to 3 metres up from the floor. Walls and ceilings should have acoustical treatment. In original construction, a recess for each set of ropes on tracks is an excellent feature. Insulation should conform to modern health standards, and older buildings should be scrutinized for unacceptable insulation materials, such as asbestos fibres and certain formaldehyde-based plastics.

The lighting should be of sufficient intensity, and fixtures should be recessed to prevent damage. Lights should be arranged so that they can be serviced from the floor. Exposed beams should be available for attaching apparatus, and all walls should have electrical out-lets. A permanent overhead public address system is desirable, permitting permanent installation of a record, tape, or CD player for easy and quick access. Windows should be placed high on the long sides of the gymnasium. Protection from glare and direct sun should be provided.

If baskets and backboards need to be raised and lowered often, a motor-driven system eliminates labourious hand cranking. The system switch should be activated with a key.

Give careful thought to adequate storage space. The storage space needed for the equipment and instructional supplies used in present-day physical education is considerable, and the area should be designed so that the materials are readily available.

One problem frequently associated with a combination auditorium–gymnasium facility is the use of the physical education storeroom for storage of bulky auditorium equipment, such as portable chairs on chair trucks, portable stages, lighting fixtures, and other paraphernalia for dramatic productions. Unless the storage facility is quite large—and most are not—the result is an unworkable and cluttered facility. The best solution is two separate storerooms for the dual-purpose facility, or at least one very large storeroom.

A separate storage area of cabinets is essential for outside groups that use the facility. These groups should not have access to the regular physical education supply room. For the physical education teacher, an office-dressing room is desirable. The office should contain a toilet and shower.

Equipment and Supplies

Equipment refers to items of a more or less fixed nature. Supplies are those nondurable items that have a limited period of use. To illustrate the difference, a softball is listed under supplies, but the longer-lasting softball backstop comes under the category of equipment. Equipment needs periodic replacement, and budget planning must consider the life span of each piece of equipment. Supplies generally are purchased on a yearly basis. It is important to have adequate financing for equipment and supplies and to use funds wisely.

If the goals and learning outcomes of the physical education program are to be fulfilled, instructional materials must be available in sufficient quantity. Enough equipment should be present so that the children do not waste practice time waiting for turns.

It is necessary for policies to cover the purchase, storage, issuance, care, maintenance, and inventory of supplies if administrators are to realize maximum return on the allotted budget. Decide program features first, followed by a purchasing plan based on these features. Using a minimal operational list of instructional supplies stabilizes the teaching process.

Purchasing Policies

The purchase of supplies and equipment involves careful study of need, price, quality, and material. The safety of the children who will use the equipment is of vital concern. Quantity buying by pooling the funds of an entire school district generally results in better use of the tax dollar. However, cooperative purchasing may require compromises on equipment type and brand to satisfy different users in the system. If bids are requested, careful specifications are necessary. Bids should be asked for only on specified items, and "just as good" merchandise should not be accepted as a substitute.

One individual within a school should be made responsible for the physical education supplies and for keeping records of equipment, supplies, and purchasing. Needs will vary from school to school, and it is practical for school district authorities to deal with a single individual at each school. Prompt attention to repair and replace supplies is possible under this system. The individual designated should also be responsible for testing various competing products to determine which will give the best service over time. If this is to be accomplished, some kind of labelling or marking of materials is needed.

Take an accurate inventory of equipment at the start and end of each school year. Through a sound inventory system, the teacher can establish the durability of equipment and supplies and make an accounting of supplies lost or misplaced. Order supplies and equipment by the end of the school year or earlier, if possible. A delivery date in August should be specified so that orders can be checked and any necessary adjustments made before the school year begins.

Most equipment of good quality will last from five to seven years, thus keeping replacement costs to a minimum. Budgetary practices should include an allotment for the yearly purchase of instructional supplies as well as major replacement and procurement costs for large items, which are usually staggered over a number of years. Once you have procured sufficient equipment and supplies, the budget considerations are for replacement and repair only.

Indoor Equipment

Several principles should govern the choice of indoor equipment. First, a reasonable variety and amount of equipment should be available to keep children active. Included should be items to facilitate arm–shoulder girdle development (for example, climbing ropes, climbing frames, ladders, and similar apparatus). A criterion for selection is that most, if not all, indoor equipment should be of the type that the children themselves can carry, assemble, and disassemble. A regular trampoline, for example, would not meet this criterion.

Mats for Tumbling and Safety

Mats are basic to any physical education program. Enough mats—at least eight—must be available to provide a safe floor for climbing apparatus. The light,

Figure 10.2

Tumbling mats stored on wall with Velcro® fasteners.

folding mats are preferable because they are easy to handle and store. They stack well and can be moved on carts. Mats should have fasteners so that two or more can be joined (see Figure 10.2). The covers should be plastic for easy cleaning. Folding mats are generally 1.2 by 1.2 m or 1.2 by 1.8 m (in 0.6-m panels) with 2.2-kg density rebonded foam.

Other mats that might be considered are thick, soft mats (somewhat similar to mattresses) and inclined mats. Soft mats are generally 10 cm or more thick and may entice the timid to try activities that they otherwise would avoid. Inclined mats are wedge-shaped and provide downhill momentum for rolls.

Tape/CD Player

A portable combination tape and CD player with remote control is the most affordable and versatile choice.

Balance-Beam Benches

Balance-beam benches have double use. They can serve as regular benches for many types of bench activity, and, when turned over, they can be used for balance-beam activities. Wooden horses or their supports can serve as inclined benches. Six benches are a minimum for class activity.

Climbing Ropes

Climbing ropes are essential to the program. At least eight ropes should be present, but more than eight allow for better group instruction. The most efficient to handle are climbing rope sets on tracks (see Figure 10.3). With little effort or loss of time, the ropes are ready for activity. Ropes on tracks are available in a variety of materials, but good-quality manila hemp seems to be the most practical. Ropes should be either 28.5 or 29 cm in diameter.

Jumping Boxes

Small boxes used for jumping and for allied locomotor movements extend the opportunities to work on basic movement skills. Boxes should be 21.5 and 41 cm high (see Figure 10.4).

Balance Beams

A wide beam (10 cm) is recommended for kindergarten and grade 1 students. Otherwise, a 5-cm beam can be used. Balance beams with alternate surfaces (5 cm and 10 cm) can be constructed from common building materials.

Figure 10.3

Climbing ropes on tracks.

Volleyball Standards

Volleyball standards should adjust to various heights for different grade levels and games.

Figure 10.4

Grade 1 students using 41-cm jumping boxes.

Supply Cart

A cart to hold supplies is desirable. Other carts can be used for the audio equipment and for regular and individual mats.

Horizontal Ladder Sets

Horizontal ladders that fold against the wall make an excellent addition to indoor equipment. The ladder may be combined with other pieces of apparatus in a folding set.

Other Indoor Items

A portable chalkboard is desirable, as is a wall screen for viewing visual aids. A large bulletin board and a wall chalkboard should be located near the main entrance to the gym. The wall chalkboard permits quick announcements or notes. An audiovisual cart or stand for projectors is helpful, and should contain sufficient electrical cord to reach wall outlets.

Equipment and Supplies for Physical Education

Knowing what equipment to obtain for your program and where to find it can be difficult, but it doesn't need to be a major obstacle. Figure 10.5 identifies the equipment and supplies needed to teach a quality physical education program. This is a general list only; specific requirements will differ from district to district, in each province or territory.

Storage Plans

When a class goes to the gymnasium for physical education, the teacher has a right to expect sufficient supplies to be available to conduct the class. The teacher should create a master list stipulating the kinds and quantities of supplies in storage. Expect a reasonable turnover, and make sure supply procedures reflect this. Supplies in the storage facility should be available for physical education classes and for organized after-school activities. A system should be established for the storage of equipment and supplies. "A place for everything and everything in its place" is the key to good housekeeping. Bins, shelves, and other assigned areas where supplies and equipment are to be kept should be labelled. Both teachers and students must accept responsibility for maintaining order in the storage facility. Squad leaders or student aides can assume major responsibility.

Some schools use small supply carts of the type pictured in Figure 10.6 on p. 191. The carts hold those articles used most frequently. They take up some additional space but do save time in accessing needed items. A cart that holds the

SMALL EQUIPMENT

CURRENT NUMBER	NEED TO ORDER	DESCRIPTION OF EQUIPMENT
		48 Beanbags (10/pkg)
		35 Skipping Ropes (speed)
		35 Skipping Ropes (sash)
		24 Utility Balls (19cm/7″)
		24 Utility Balls (15cm/6″)
		24 Sponge Balls (8cm)
		36 Hoops (76cm/30″)
		12 Elephant Skin Balls (3.5″)
		12 Elephant Skin Balls (2.75″)
		12 Beach Balls
		1 Large Bag Balloons

SMALL EQUIPMENT (OPTIONAL)

CURRENT NUMBER	NEED TO ORDER	DESCRIPTION OF EQUIPMENT
		12 Nerf Balls (19cm/7″)
		12 Quoits
		24 Hoops (90cm/36″)

TEAM SPORTS

SOCCER

CURRENT NUMBER	NEED TO ORDER	DESCRIPTION OF EQUIPMENT
		18 Soccer Balls (Rubber)
		4 Soccer Balls (Leather) Size 5
		18 Soccer Balls (Rubber) Size 4
		10 Soccer Balls Foam Sponge
		2 Soccer Balls Indoor

BASKETBALL

CURRENT NUMBER	NEED TO ORDER	DESCRIPTION OF EQUIPMENT
		18 Basketballs (Rubber) Size 6
		4 Basketballs (Leather) Size 6
		18 Mini Basketballs Size 5
		4 Replacement Nets
		1 Possession Indicator

VOLLEYBALL

CURRENT NUMBER	NEED TO ORDER	DESCRIPTION OF EQUIPMENT
		18 Volleyballs (Leather)
		10 Volleyballs (Training Pr/Jr)
		1 Volleyball Nets (9m)
		2 Volleyball Nets (6.4m)
		9 Volleyball Knee Pads (Large)
		9 Volleyball Knee Pads (Medium)

Figure 10.5

Basic equipment and supplies for quality physical education (continued).

FLOOR HOCKEY

CURRENT NUMBER	NEED TO ORDER	DESCRIPTION OF EQUIPMENT
		1 Super Safe Hockey Kit
		6 Pucks
		6 Balls

SOFTBALL

CURRENT NUMBER	NEED TO ORDER	DESCRIPTION OF EQUIPMENT
		12 Softballs (Very Soft 30cm/12")
		12 Softballs (Red Dot)
		2 Sets of Bases
		2 Bats (29")
		2 Bats (32")
		2 Bats (34")
		2 Dom Invinci Bats
		2 Softball Masks
		2 Umpire Indicators
		1 Softball Protector (Small)
		1 Softball Protector (Large)
		2 Helmets (Large)
		2 Helmets (Medium)
		1 Adjustable Batting Tee
		1 Home Plate Extension
		6 Mushballs
		1 Primary Jumbo Bat
		1 Set Extension First Base
		1 Indoor Set Bases

LOW ORGANIZATIONAL GAMES

CURRENT NUMBER	NEED TO ORDER	DESCRIPTION OF EQUIPMENT
		1 Parachute (Large)
		1 Parachute (Small)
		18 Scooter Boards
		5 Elephant Skin Balls

LOW ORGANIZATION GAMES (OPTIONAL)

CURRENT NUMBER	NEED TO ORDER	DESCRIPTION OF EQUIPMENT
		1 Cricket Set
		18 Frisbees (Ultimate)
		18 Frisbees (Nerf)
		18 Scoopball Sets
		1 Table Tennis Table
		12 Table Tennis Racquets
		24 Table Tennis Balls
		15 Gymnastics Ribbons
		1 Bowling Set (Indoor)

Figure 10.5

Continued

INDIVIDUAL & DUAL ACTIVITIES
GYMNASTICS—ESSENTIAL

CURRENT NUMBER	NEED TO ORDER	DESCRIPTION OF EQUIPMENT
		24 Tumbling Mats (with Velcro fasteners)
		1 Beat Board
		6 Benches

GYMNASTICS—OPTIONAL

CURRENT NUMBER	NEED TO ORDER	DESCRIPTION OF EQUIPMENT
		Box Horse
		Mini Tramp
		Climbers

TRACK AND FIELD—ESSENTIAL

CURRENT NUMBER	NEED TO ORDER	DESCRIPTION OF EQUIPMENT
		1 Crash Mat
		1 Fibreglass Crossbar
		6 High Jump Cords
		1 Pair High Jump Risers
		4 Tape Measures
		12 Relay Batons
		1 Shot Put (3kg Outdoor)
		2 Shot Put (4kg)
		4 Digital Stop Watches
		1 Rake

TRACK AND FIELD (OPTIONAL)

CURRENT NUMBER	NEED TO ORDER	DESCRIPTION OF EQUIPMENT
		1 Crash Mat
		1 Starter Pistol
		50 Cartridges (6mm, 100/box)
		2 Starting Blocks
		1 Indoor Shot Put (3kg)
		1 Shot Put Ring & Toe Board
		1 Toe Board Long Jump

RACQUET SPORTS—ESSENTIAL

CURRENT NUMBER	NEED TO ORDER	DESCRIPTION OF EQUIPMENT
		18 Badminton Racquets
		36 Shuttlecock—Indoor
		18 Mini Tennis Racquets
		36 Mini Tennis Balls
		2 Badminton Nets

Figure 10.5

Continued

ALTERNATIVE ENVIRONMENT ACTIVITIES—OPTIONAL

CURRENT NUMBER	NEED TO ORDER	DESCRIPTION OF EQUIPMENT
		24 Orienteering Compasses
		12 Orienteering Control Markers

MISCELLANEOUS

CURRENT NUMBER	NEED TO ORDER	DESCRIPTION OF EQUIPMENT
		1 Megaphone
		1 Tape/CD Player
		1 Portable Scoreboard
		2 Goalie Nets
		1 First Aid Kit
		12 Pinnies (Red, numbered 1–12)
		24 Pylons
		Whistles
		1 Electric Ball Inflator
		1 Manual Pump
		6 Nylon Bags
		2 Ball Carts
		Storage Bins
		12 Large Plastic Pails
		24 Team Uniforms (Girls)
		24 Team Uniforms (Boys)
		12 Water Bottles
		Ball Inflator Needles
		Floor Tape (Red)
		Ice Packs (20 per case)

Figure 10.5

Continued

audio equipment, and carts that store and move mats and balls, are helpful.

Care, Repair, and Marking

Develop a system for repairing supplies and equipment. A quick decision must be made about whether to repair an item locally or to send it out of the area for repair. If the repair process is lengthy and not cost-efficient, using the article until it can no longer be salvaged may be preferable to being deprived of its use. An area should be established for equipment needing repair, so that all articles to be repaired are evident at a glance.

Balls must be inflated to proper pressures. This means using an accurate gauge and checking the pressures periodically. Moisten the inflation needle before inserting it into the valve. Children should kick only those balls made specifically for kicking (soccer balls, footballs, and playground balls). Cuts, abrasions, and breaks in rubber balls

Figure 10.6

Portable ball cart.

should be repaired immediately. In some cases, make repairs with a vulcanized patch, such as those used for repair of tire tubes. In other cases, try a hard-setting rubber preparation. In instances where the repair is beyond the school's capability, send the ball away for repair.

Mats are expensive, and proper care is needed if they are to last. Provide a place where they can be stacked properly, or hang up mats with handles. A mat truck is another storage solution if there is space for storing the truck. The newer plastic or plastic-covered mats should be cleaned periodically with a damp, soapy cloth. For small items, clean, plastic ice-cream buckets make adequate storage receptacles.

All equipment and supplies should be marked. This is particularly important for equipment issued to different classrooms. Marking can be done with indelible pencil, paint, or stencil ink. Few marking systems are permanent, however, and it's necessary to re-mark at regular intervals.

Rubber playground balls come in different colours, and the physical education teacher can assign them to classrooms on the basis of colour. A code scheme with different-coloured paints can be used also. It is possible to devise a colour system to designate the year of issue, which allows the teacher to document equipment usage and care.

Critical Thinking

1. There will always be a certain level of risk of injury when children use playground equipment. Discuss the procedures you will use to ensure the level of risk is acceptable.

References and Suggested Readings

Canadian Hospitals Injury Reporting and Prevention Program (CHIRPP). (n.d.) *Injuries associated with playground equipment. CHIRPP database for 1996.*

Canadian Standards Association. (2003). *A guideline on children's playspaces and equipment* (3rd ed.). Toronto, ON: Author.

Fissel, D., Pattison, G., & Howard, A. (2005). Severity of playground fractures: Play equipment versus standing height falls. *Injury Prevention, 11*, 337–339.

Howard, A.W., MacArthur, C., Willan, A., Rothman, L., Moses-McKeag, A., & MacPherson, A.K. (2005). The effect of safer play equipment on playground injury rates among school children. *Canadian Medical Association Journal, 172*(11), 1443–1446.

Lesage, D. & Laforest, S. (1997). Playground equipment injuries: Circumstances, natures of injuries and opportunities for action. *Chapter 12 in For the Safety of Canadian Children and Youth: From Injury Data to Preventive Measures.* Ottawa, ON: Health Canada.

Pless, B. & Millar, B. (2000). *Unintentional injuries in childhood: Results from Canadian health surveys.* Ottawa, ON: Health Canada.

Public Health Agency of Canada. (n.d.). *Canadian Hospitals Injury Reporting and Prevention Program—Data Sampler: Injuries Associated with Playground Equipment.* Retrieved February 14, 2007, from www.phac-aspc.gc.ca/injury-bles/

Safe Kids Canada. (2000). *Canada playground safety survey.* www.safekidscanada.ca

Safe Kids Canada. (2004). *Playground safety fact sheet.* www.safekidscanada.ca

Safe Kids Canada. (1997). *Child's play—A playground safety guide for daycares, schools and communities.* Toronto, ON: Author.

Thompson, D., Hudson, S., & Olsen, H. (2007). *S.A.F.E. play areas.* Champaign, IL: Human Kinetics.

 ## Weblinks

Safe Kids Canada: www.safekidscanada.ca

Includes classroom resources to help children learn injury prevention. Includes lesson plans, learning activities for safety education curriculum.

The Canada Safety Council: www.safety-council.org/index.html

The Canada Safety Council acts as Canada's voice and resource on topics of safety. The council has a wealth of information on the topic of children's safety and ensuring a safe environment.

CHAPTER 11

Making Curriculum Connections

OVERVIEW

Children use knowledge learned in many settings. Integrating learning from other subjects with physical education content furthers the total development of children in both areas. Classroom teachers can be asked to enhance physical education concepts. Many concepts from other subjects can also be presented through physical education instruction.

OUTCOMES

- Know how to make curriculum connections between physical education and other subject areas in elementary school.

- Describe several activities that connect math, language arts, science, and/or social studies into a quality physical education lesson.

- Develop strategies for including cultural content and learning in physical education.

Curriculum Connections

Learning is holistic; students use what they have learned in one area in many other areas. There is little doubt that learning to apply concepts in different settings is an important practice. Only the ingenuity of the teacher and the interests of youngsters limit the variety of curriculum connections between physical education and other subject areas. The first part of the chapter deals with making curricular connections (also called "subject integration") between physical education

and other subjects in elementary school. Integration of content is a two-way street. Classroom-based subjects can be integrated into physical education, and physical education content can also be integrated into other subjects. The second part of the chapter deals with including cultural content and learning in physical education with a particular focus on Aboriginal peoples.

Figure 11.1 provides a framework for helping teachers identify connections between subject areas. Consider using this framework as a starting point for making connections, and add to it. Not only does it suggest ways to "reinforce

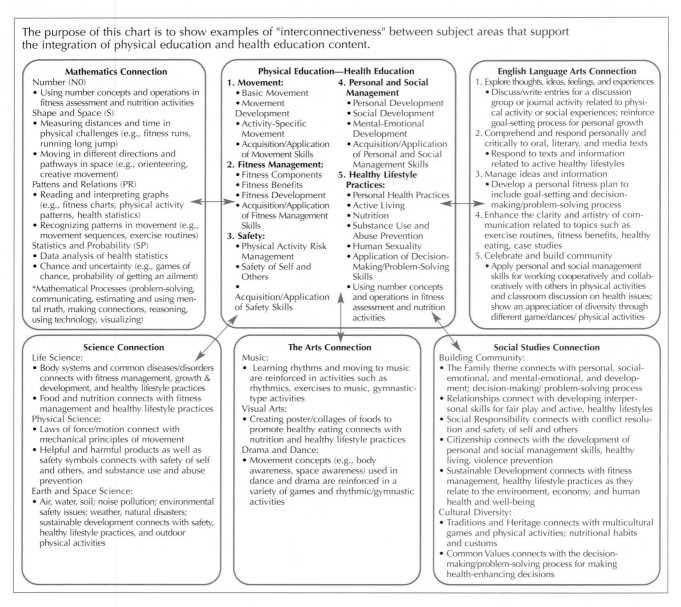

Figure 11.1

Suggested curricular connections with other subject areas.

Source: Manitoba Education and Training. (2000). *Kindergarten to senior 4 physical education/health education—Manitoba curriculum framework of outcomes for active healthy lifestyles.* Appendix B (pp. 201–202). Winnipeg, MB: Author. Reproduced by permission of Manitoba Education, Citizenship and Youth. All rights reserved.

concepts and skills to make student learning more relevant and meaningful," but also it helps to "reduce redundancy and repetition between subject areas" (Manitoba Education, 2000, p. 201).

The purpose of this chart is to show examples of "interconnectiveness" between subject areas that support the integration of physical education and health education content.

Ideas for Making Other Subject Connections with Physical Education

Learning activities in this section are organized into four subjects: math, language arts, science, and social studies. Each area is then subdivided into "Connection Tips" and "Connection Activities." Connection Tips are simple strategies that teachers may use to teach content from another subject in physical education. Connection Tips are not specific to a lesson; they can be used in a variety of lessons. For each Connection Activity that follows, these four components are listed: the connecting subject concept, the PE concepts, the PE lesson part where the concept should be integrated, and the supplies necessary to teach the concept. The connecting subject concept is the general concept being taught or reinforced through the activity. The PE concept provides the general physical education concepts being emphasized during the activity. The PE lesson part shows where the connection activity can be taught during a four-part lesson. If the activity is part of a lesson focus, ideas for the types of lessons are provided.

Math

During the early elementary years, students learn math concepts such as number recognition and meaning, counting, shapes, addition, subtraction, measuring, and patterns. As they progress through the grades, students learn numbers through one million, multiplication, division, fractions, percent, degrees, geometry, and statistics.

Connection Tips

Counting (Skipping Numbers)
Any time counting is used during a lesson (e.g., keeping score, timing a stretch), instruct students to count by a given number. For example, rather than saying that one goal equals one point, say that each goal is worth three points. Thus, as the number of goals accumulates, students must count by threes.

Math Terms
Many mathematical terms such as *diameter* and *perimeter* can easily be integrated into many physical education lessons. For example, rather than instructing students, "Jog around the outside of the gym floor," tell them, "Jog around the perimeter of the gym." When discussing the influence the size of a ball has on throwing, instead of saying, "Is a bigger ball easier to throw or harder to throw?" say, "If a ball has a larger diameter, is it easier to throw? Remind me what *diameter* means before you answer." These examples allow math terms to be integrated without interfering with the physical education lesson.

Degrees and Fractions
In many physical education lessons, students are told, "Turn facing away from the teacher" or "Turn all the way around." Early in physical education experiences, these basic terms are necessary; however, as students become older, more challenging directions can be used to teach math concepts. For example, have students turn "360 degrees" or "180 degrees" before catching a beanbag or when dismounting from a balance bench. Similarly, incorporate fractions by having students make a half turn or a three-quarter turn.

Estimating
Because numbers are often used during physical education, estimating can be naturally integrated into a variety of lessons. The following are just two examples. Messy Back Yard is a game in which students attempt to rid their backyard (side of the court) of yarn balls by throwing them over the net to the other team's side. Meanwhile, the other team tries to rid its side as well. After a set amount of time, the teacher stops the game, and yarn balls on each side are counted. To teach estimation, before counting the number of balls on each side, the teacher can instruct children to estimate how many balls are on each side and keep that number in their heads. When the teacher announces the actual number, the children then self-assess their estimates. Another example is to ask students to estimate how many times they can toss their beanbags a certain height and catch them in 30 seconds. This activity can be repeated two or three times to allow students to make adjustments to their estimates.

Measurement
Measurement is often included during the physical education lesson. Concepts related to measuring distance, height, weight, and time can all be integrated into physical education lessons. During a jumping lesson, students can be

Figure 11.2

Checking the length of the long jump.

asked to jump as far as they can and then quickly measure the distance of their jump using tiles on the floor (see Figure 11.2). Floor tiles are generally 30 cm square. Track and field lessons also offer numerous opportunities for students to measure. Students can time each other in a run, measure the length of a person's long jump, or measure the height of a high jump.

Connection Activities

MYSTERY NUMBERS

Math Concepts: Number recognition and number sequencing

PE Concepts: Locomotor skills, spacing, sequencing skills

PE Lesson Part: Introductory activity

Supplies: Laminated signs with numbers or sequences of numbers

The teacher holds one of the laminated signs in the air so that the students can see it and she cannot. The students are instructed to perform their favourite locomotor skill the same number of times indicated on the sign. When they finish they should stop and then pick a different locomotor skill and perform it the same number of times. For example, if the sign has the number 8 on it, a child may choose to walk eight steps, stop, and then skip eight times. The teacher, by watching the students, tries to determine the mystery number.

For older students, a sequence of numbers is placed on the sign. For example, a sign could read "7, 3, 15." For each number, students choose a locomotor movement and perform it. One student may choose to gallop 7 times, walk 3 steps, and jump 15 times. When these are completed,

Figure 11.3

Number challenge sign.

the students start over with a different sequence of 7, 3, and 15. Again, the teacher tries to determine the number sequence on the card. If desired, specific locomotor movements can be provided for each number, as shown in Figure 11.3.

SHAPES

Math Concept: Shape recognition

PE Concepts: Locomotor skills, low-organized games

PE Lesson Part: Game activity

Supplies: Differently coloured laminated circles, squares, triangles, and rectangles

Each student stands in a circle with a laminated shape on the floor in front of him or her. When the teacher calls out a specific shape, all students with that shape step back out of the circle and begin running around the circle in a designated direction. Their goal is to get back to their shape as quickly as possible. As soon as all runners have returned to their position, the teacher calls out another shape. While the runners are running, the remainder of the class is responsible for running in place and cheering on the runners. To add some challenge for older students, rather than say, "Triangle," the number of sides of the shape ("Three") can be used as the signal. As a variation, rather than shapes, the colour of the shape can be used. When the teacher says, "Red," all students with a red shape are runners. Because this activity involves movement of light intensity, it works well as a game following a vigorous activity such as individual rope jumping.

SYMMETRY ASYMMETRY

Math Concepts: Symmetric and asymmetric balance

PE Concepts: Nonlocomotor skills, balance, body awareness

PE Lesson Part: Lesson focus (gymnastics)

Supplies: Tumbling mats

During a gymnastics lesson students are often asked to perform balances while meeting various challenges (e.g., balancing on two body parts; balancing on three body parts, one being a hand, etc.). For this activity, students are asked to perform a symmetric or asymmetric balance with a specific challenge. Examples include a symmetric balance with only three body parts touching the mat or an asymmetric balance with both feet flat on the mat.

BODY NUMBERING

Math Concept: Number recognition

PE Concepts: Nonlocomotor skills

PE Lesson Part: Lesson focus (movement concepts)

Supplies: None

When teaching nonlocomotor skills such as bending, ask students to make the shape of a number with their bodies. This can be accomplished while lying on the floor or standing. Students can also work together to form a larger number.

HUMAN PENCIL (SHAPES AND NUMBERS)

Math Concept: Number recognition

PE Concepts: Spacing, locomotor skills

PE Lesson Part: Lesson focus (movement concepts)

Supplies: None

Tell students that the gym floor is one big piece of paper and that they are human pencils. Ask students to walk and make a circle, a triangle, and a square. Following this activity, ask questions such as, "How many turns did you make to create a triangle?" Since they already know how to make a circle, as a transition to making numbers, ask

students to skip and make the number 0. Next, have them make numbers or a sequence of numbers using a variety of locomotor skills. For an added challenge, give number problems such as 2 + 2 and have the students "write" the answer as human pencils.

PEDOMETER RECORDING

Math Concept: Place values

PE Concepts: Importance of physical activity, measuring physical activity, logging physical activity

PE Lesson Part: Lesson focus

Supplies: Pedometers, pedometer recording card, pencils

One effective use of pedometers is to have students record their physical education steps. Using the card in Figure 11.4, students record their data and learn the place values of the numbers. Although the number of steps children accumulate will vary depending on the lesson, in a 30-minute physical education lesson, most students will accumulate between 1,500 and 2,000 steps. By recording their data on a place value card, students learn ones, tens, hundreds, and thousands.

COMPUTING AVERAGE NUMBER OF STEPS

Math Concept: Computing an average

PE Concept: Tracking physical activity

PE Lesson Part: Lesson focus

Supplies: Pedometer recording card, pedometers, pencils

For older children, after they have recorded several days of physical education data, ask them to compute the average number of steps they take during physical education. Because this activity is sedentary, it is best either to coordinate with the classroom teacher so he can complete the activity in the classroom or to have this activity as one station in a circuit. When students reach this station, they compute their average of previous physical education classes and then begin working on a task assigned by the teacher or the station sign.

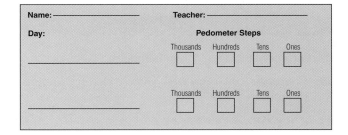

Figure 11.4

Pedometer data card with place values.

NUMBER WIZARD

Math Concept: Positive and negative numbers

PE Concepts: Locomotor skills, low-organized games

PE Lesson Part: Game activity

Supplies: None

The entire class stands on a line in the middle of the teaching area, and the teacher explains that the gym floor is going to be their number line. The line they are standing on is zero. One child, designated the "Number Wizard," stands in the middle of the line. The Number Wizard calls out either a positive or a negative number. For a positive number, all students take that many steps forward. For a negative number, all students take that many steps backward. Throughout the game the entire class remains in a straight line. When the Number Wizard yells, "Zero," the class attempts to get back to zero before being tagged by the Number Wizard. Children who are tagged join the Number Wizard.

ODDS

Math Concept: Odd and even numbers

PE Concepts: Chasing, fleeing, locomotor skills, spacing, low-organized games

PE Lesson Part: Introductory activity or game activity

Supplies: None

Partners stand facing each other on a line. One partner is designated "odd" and the other "even." Similar to Rock, Paper, Scissors, students place one fist in the palm of the other hand. The game is played one-on-one and begins with both players hitting the palms of their hands twice, saying, "Math rocks"; on the third strike, rather than a fist they extend one to five digits. Both partners should have one hand out in front. The partners quickly count the number of fingers on both hands. If the total is odd, the person designated "odd" chases her partner. If she can tag him before he takes three steps, she gets a point. If the total number of fingers is even, the "even" person becomes the chaser.

ODDS AND EVENS

Math Concept: Odd and even numbers

PE Concepts: Low-organized games, chasing, fleeing, locomotor skills

PE Lesson Part: Game activity

Supplies: Large die (optional)

This game is played with the same rules as Crows and Cranes except that teams are "Odds" and "Evens." To start, the teacher calls out a team name to identify who will be chased. For added challenge, the teacher also calls out actual numbers and students must determine if they are odd numbers or even numbers. Finally, the teacher calls out math equations. Students must then solve the equation and decide if the solution is odd or even. If available, a large die can be rolled to determine the number rather than the teacher calling it out.

Language Arts

In the elementary years, students explore language and learn to express ideas by writing, speaking, listening, and communicating nonverbally. Concepts such as giving and following directions, reading, learning vocabulary, thinking critically, taking notes, spelling, and interacting with others are taught.

Connection Tips

Reading

Reading is just one of the areas in language arts that can be integrated into physical education. An effective strategy for integrating reading without sacrificing activity time is to use instruction signs. Figure 11.5 involves simple word recognition. Once students read the word, they perform the skill while moving to one of the other stations throughout the teaching area. The effective use of instructional signs efficiently integrates reading into physical education and allows the teacher to move about the teaching area, helping those who need assistance.

Spelling

Often in physical education, students are asked to count to a given number to determine the length of time to stretch. This can be used to teach skip-counting as discussed earlier; this can also be a great time to teach the spelling of physical education terms or terms being used in the classroom (e.g., vocabulary words from a specific

Figure 11.5

Word recognition.

content area). Instructions to implement spelling could be, "Grade fours, choose your favourite lower body stretch that we have learned in physical education. Instead of counting today, we are going to spell words as we stretch. We are studying Antarctica in Socials Studies, so let's spell it." The teacher then slowly starts the class spelling with a counting tempo.

Parts of Speech

Physical education is full of action words such as *skip, run, throw, roll, tap,* etc., which offers an excellent chance to teach about verbs. An effective strategy is to quiz students following a bout of instructions. After saying, "Everyone jump," briefly stop and ask, "What was the verb in that sentence?" If the students do not immediately respond with "Jump," quickly say, "It was *jump*; remember, verbs show action." The key to this strategy is to allow students to take no more than five seconds to determine the verb. As this process continues, students learn which words are verbs and begin responding quickly. This same process can be used to teach other parts of speech (e.g., nouns, adverbs, adjectives, and prepositions).

Antonyms and Synonyms

Physical education offers many contrasting and similar words, thereby offering an excellent opportunity for teaching antonyms and synonyms. During a locomotor lesson, you can ask students to skip at a slow level. Next, ask them to skip at the level that is the antonym for *slow*. As part of a nonlocomotor activity in which you tell students, "Stretch to make yourself large," ask for examples of synonyms for *large*. If students have not learned the words *antonym* and *synonym,* use the words *opposite* and *same*.

Connection Activities

BODY SPELLING

LA Concept: Spelling

PE Concepts: Spacing, nonlocomotor skills

PE Lesson Part: Lesson focus (movement concepts, gymnastics), game activity

Supplies: None

Working in groups of four to five, students are given the task of using their bodies to make letters to spell out words provided by the teacher. Students can make the words standing or lying on the ground (see Figure 11.6). For younger students, short words are used and each child is usually one letter of the word. For example, to

Figure 11.6

Making letters.

spell *dog,* one child would be the *D,* one the *O,* and one the *G.* With older students, longer words can be used; however, the entire group may have to make each letter. That is, to spell *locomotor,* the entire group would make an *L,* then an *O,* and so on. Classroom vocabulary words or physical education terms work well for this activity.

ALPHABET FREEZE

LA Concept: Letter recognition

PE Concepts: Body awareness, spacing, nonlocomotor skills

PE Lesson Part: Introductory activity, game activity

Supplies: None

Students begin the activity by moving about the teaching area. When the teacher says, "Alphabet freeze," the students select a letter and freeze in the shape of that letter. The activity continues with the stipulation that students must select a different letter with each freeze. The teacher may also choose the letter by saying, "Alphabet freeze—*A,*" and all students freeze while forming an *A* with their bodies. The teacher may also designate whether students should freeze in a standing position or on the ground.

LETTER TAG

LA Concept: Letter recognition

PE Concepts: Body awareness, spacing, nonlocomotor skills

PE Lesson Part: Introductory activity, game activity

Supplies: None

This game is played in the fashion of Frozen Tag. If a youngster is tagged, she freezes in the shape of any letter.

Figure 11.7

Playing Letter Tag.

To unfreeze her, a classmate must either say the letter or make the letter with her (Figure 11.7). The teacher can also designate the letter shape that students must freeze as; in this case, the student must make the letter to unfreeze a classmate.

HUMAN PENCIL (SPELLING)

LA Concept: Spelling

PE Concepts: Locomotor skills, spacing

PE Lesson Part: Lesson focus (movement concepts)

Supplies: None

Students are instructed to spell a specific word using locomotor skills. They are pencils and the entire teaching area floor is their paper. Teachers may wish to lead into the activity with the following instructions: "Show me how you would walk to make an *O*." "Now show me how you would walk to spell *cat*." "Okay, now show me how you can skip and spell *education*. I know that is one of your spelling words this week."

NOUNS AND VERBS

LA Concept: Parts of speech

PE Concepts: Chasing, fleeing, locomotor skills, low-organized games

PE Lesson Part: Game activity

Supplies: None

This game is played in the fashion of Crows and Cranes, except that teams are called "Nouns" and "Verbs." To assist students in learning the game, begin by simply using "Noun" or "Verb" as the chase word. Then call out nouns or verbs as the chase word, but use caution when choosing them. Many words such as *jump* can be either a noun or a verb. Students who skateboard are likely to think of a jump, whereas other students may think of jumping as they learned it in physical education. Early on, when calling out the chase word, it may be helpful to point the direction in which students should be moving to help students who are having difficulty determining if a word is a noun or a verb.

IN A LINE

LA Concept: Alphabetizing

PE Concept: Cooperation

PE Lesson Part: Game activity

Supplies: None

The activity begins with the entire group standing on a line. The challenge is for the students to get in alphabetical order by first name; however, the group must have at least one foot on the line at all times. Once students achieve this, their final challenge is to get into alphabetical order by their last names without speaking. They may use gestures, but they must keep one foot on the line at all times. During this activity, students can become creative by using letters on their shirts, shoes, or jewellery. However, it is important that the teacher let them establish such strategies on their own.

LANGUAGE LION SAYS

LA Concepts: Listening, following directions

PE Concepts: Nonlocomotor skills, locomotor skills, manipulative skills, fitness challenges

PE Lesson Part: Introductory activity, game activity

Supplies: None

This is played just like Simon Says but with "Language Lion" as the leader. Commands that tie in physical education movements should be used throughout. Typically, in Simon Says, the students remain in one position. For Language Lion Says, students should be moving throughout the teaching area. At the end of the game, the teacher can briefly comment, "When most students think of language arts, they think of words that we write or say. However, an important part of language is being able to listen, and playing Language Lion Says helped all students practise their listening skills."

Science

Elementary students are often fascinated by science. Thus, teaching concepts such as the senses, animals, the environment, the solar system, climate, matter, energy, force, and plants are often met with great enthusiasm. Concepts associated with human anatomy and physiology are particularly applicable.

Connection Tips

Body Part Identification

One skill students learn in science is the ability to identify body parts. Since taking care of the body through physical activity is an important component of physical education, body part identification can be integrated easily. Some teachers simply have students copy them by saying, "Touch your eyes, your nose, your femur, your triceps." This not only teaches body parts, but it also works on listening skills. Also, touching a specific body part can be the "Go" signal. For example, the teacher can say "When I touch my humerus bone, hustle to the line on the east side of the gym" and then immediately touch her humerus or touch other bones to check for student understanding.

Influence of Physical Activity on the Body

During a vigorous lesson such as jogging/walking or individual rope-jumping, children often need a quick break. These breaks offer a great opportunity to teach the influence of physical activity on the body. Concepts such as increased heart rate and why it happens, sweating and why it happens, why we get tired, and many others can quickly be discussed during short breaks. Using this strategy throughout the year can be an effective method for teaching these concepts.

Connection Activities

MUSCLE AND BONE TAG

Science Concept: Muscle and bone identification

PE Concepts: Fleeing, chasing, locomotor skills, low-organized games

PE Lesson Part: Introductory activity, fitness development, game activity

Supplies: None

This tag game starts with five people chosen by the teacher as taggers. If they tag someone, they "give up the tag" and the tagged person becomes the tagger. Before the game, the teacher designates a bone or muscle that is the "base." If a child touches the predetermined bone or muscle and repeats its name three times, she is safe from being tagged for five seconds. She may only use her base once per game, and taggers may not stand by her waiting for the five seconds to expire. This is called the "no guarding" rule.

PONIES IN THE STABLE

Science Concept: Animal habitats

PE Concepts: Locomotor skills, low-organized games, spacing

PE Lesson Part: Game activity

Supplies: One Poly spot per student

Students are in scattered formation with a Poly spot at their feet. When given the signal, they begin galloping around the teaching area. When the teacher says, "Ponies in a stable," they quickly find a spot and stand on it. To teach other animal habitats, the game could be called "Whales in the Ocean," "Rabbits in a Burrow," or "Gorillas in the Jungle." For each of these games, the children's locomotor movement should be consistent with the animal.

PALM PUSH

Science Concept: Force, pushing, pulling

PE Concepts: Balance, body awareness

PE Lesson Part: Introductory activity, fitness development, lesson focus (gymnastics), game activity

Supplies: None

Players face each other, standing approximately 30 cm apart. They place the palms of their hands together and must keep them together throughout the game. The object of the game is to get the opponent to move one of her feet. Following a few rounds, the teacher then asks a few brief questions: "How does force affect this game?" "Is it better to have a lot of force or not much?" "How could you use a little bit of force and still move your opponent off balance?"

FINGER FENCING

Science Concept: Force, pushing, pulling

PE Concepts: Balance, body awareness

Figure 11.8

Finger fencing.

PE Lesson Part: Lesson focus (gymnastics), game activity

Supplies: None

Partners start balanced on one foot facing each other with index fingers hooked. The object is to push or pull the opponent off balance. See Figure 11.8 for the starting position. If a person causes her opponent to lose his balance, she receives a point and they start over. After a few minutes of play the teacher stops the class to discuss strategies related to pushing and pulling. "Is pushing better or is pulling the best?" "Can you use both?" Be sure that partners are matched by size for this game.

LEVERS

Science Concept: Levers, force

PE Concepts: Throwing, striking with a racquet, cooperation

PE Lesson Part: Lesson focus (throwing skills, racquet activities, tennis, softball, soccer)

Supplies: Racquets, yarn balls, playground balls

Since many motions and activities used in physical education involve levers (see Figure 11.9 for activities that can be used to teach about levers), the concept of levers can easily be integrated into a variety of lessons. As a break from skills involving throwing, kicking, or racquet skills, have students find a partner and assume the wheelbarrow position. Ask questions such as: "What part of your body is making a lever?" "What part was making a lever when we were

Figure 11.9

Levers in physical education.

throwing? Or kicking? Or using the racquet?" Allow students to perform a variety of skills learned in PE and then ask, "What type of levers are you using?" A large picture similar to Figure 11.10 may help students answer this question.

SCIENCE OF THROWING

Science Concepts: Trajectory and distance, weight and distance

PE Concepts: Cooperation, throwing

PE Lesson Part: Lesson focus (throwing skills, softball)

Supplies: Tennis balls, yarn balls

Introduce three trajectories in which a ball can be thrown such as straight up, straight out, or up and out. In an open space, have students experiment with the distance a tennis ball travels when thrown at these three different trajectories. Then challenge the students to throw the yarn balls using the three trajectories (see Figure 11.11). Follow this activity with a brief discussion regarding the influence trajectory and the weight of the ball had on distance travelled. After the discussion, allow time for more throwing so that students can experiment.

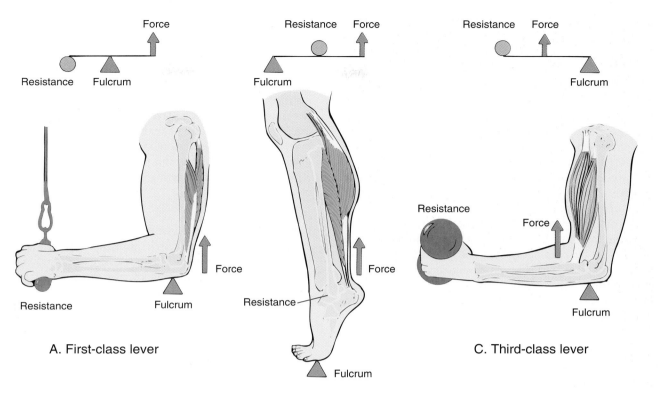

Figure 11.10

Types of levers in human joints.

Figure 11.11

Checking the trajectory of the throw.

Science Concepts: Changes in matter, states of water

PE Concepts: Locomotor skills, spacing

PE Lesson Part: Introductory activity

Supplies: None

Students begin by moving around the teaching area. Challenge the class to keep moving but in half of the space. Further compress the space by asking the class to move in half of that space, or one-quarter of the original space. Remind the class that the goal is to not touch anyone. Next, ask the students to recall what they know about molecules of water when it is in a solid, liquid, or gas state. After the brief discussion, have the class move like gas molecules, solid molecules, and liquid molecules.

BOUNCE REBOUNCE

Science Concepts: Forces, influence of weight on reaction, action and reaction

PE Concepts: Volleying, bouncing, dribbling, catching, passing

PE Lesson Part: Lesson focus (playground ball activities, basketball, volleyball)

Supplies: One playground ball and one balloon per student

Begin the activity by having students bounce or dribble a playground ball in general space. Ask them to experiment by applying different forces to the ball to see how that influences the bouncing. After a brief discussion about how increased force makes the ball bounce higher, have students trade their playground balls for balloons. Next have students volley the balloon using different amounts of force. Challenge students to bounce the balloon as if it were the playground ball. Freeze the class and ask them what would happen if they struck the playground ball with the same force and why. Ask: "Why does the playground ball bounce back up better than the balloon?" Next, have partners stand side by side while bouncing the ball off the wall to each other. After each pass they should take one step away from each other. Ask them: "What happens to your pass? What happens if you pass it like you did when you were close together?" Conclude with the notion that the ball bounces off the wall and the floor at the same angle that it hits them.

ANIMALS MOVE

Science Concept: Animal locomotion

PE Concepts: Animal movements, spacing

PE Lesson Part: Introductory activity

Supplies: None

The game begins with the teacher calling out different animals and a method of movement. For instance, the teacher might call out, "Horses fly. Birds crawl. Salmon swim." When the leader states a correct relationship, the class must move accordingly. In this example, students make a swimming movement. When an incorrect relationship is given, the children should not move. Games should be kept short so that all children have a chance to lead.

Social Studies

Social studies includes geography, history, social responsibility, and other areas. At the elementary level, concepts such as directions, rules and laws, the geography of different regions, Canadian history, cultural diversity, and community are taught.

Connection Tips

Directions
Directions are an important part of geography and can easily be taught throughout a physical education curriculum. The

first step is to place large north, south, east, and west signs on the appropriate walls. Early in the curriculum, teachers can simply refer to lines using a direction. For instance, "When I say, 'Go,' hustle to the line by the south wall." Initially it may be helpful to point to the line as well. As students mature, instruction can refer to the "southwest wall" or "the cone closest to the northeast basket." If teaching outside, students can be taught to use the sun to determine direction. In order to do this, students need to know only the time of day and the direction from which the sun rises. These concepts will be especially useful if orienteering is taught later in the year to older students.

Games from Other Countries
The physical education curriculum is filled with activities from other countries. When teaching these activities, simply take a few minutes to discuss the country, show where it is on a map, and talk about the languages spoken there.

Class Greeting
Prepare a list of greetings that are used in other countries. Each week have a greeting of the week to use when the class arrives. The students should then attempt to determine the country in which the greeting is used. Gestures such as bowing or handshaking can also be used.

Conversation
Often in physical education, students work on skills with partners. During these activities, remind students to concentrate on the skills, but also teach them how to have conversations. Discuss appropriate questions, how to ask questions, or what to say if you say something wrong. These skills are often assumed to be learned by children, and are often neglected. Social time during physical education is important, and physical education is a great time to teach social skills.

Connection Activities

RULES

SS Concept: The need for rules and laws

PE Concepts: Classroom management skills

PE Lesson Part: Introductory activity

Supplies: None

Early in the school year, rules for physical education are established. This is an excellent time to discuss the importance of rules outside of physical education and outside of school. During the activity, the importance of following directions is discussed. To have students practise this, a variety of instructions are given with one set leading to a game. An example of a series of instructions follows:

"When I say, 'Toe-to-toe,' quickly get toe-to-toe with the person closest to you. Toe-to-toe [pause]. Thank you for doing that quickly. Now one partner remains standing while the other sits. If you are standing, please report to the line by the south wall. If you are sitting, please report to the line by the north wall."

After these directions, the teacher has the class play a game. Following the game, the teacher asks, "What would have happened if the class had decided not to follow directions?" It is important to teach students early in the year that following rules leads to more enjoyment for everybody.

MOVING ACROSS CANADA

SS Concepts: Geography, history, famous people

PE Concepts: Jumping rope, locomotor skills, tracking physical activity

PE Lesson Part: Lesson focus (individual rope-jumping, long rope-jumping, walking and jogging skills)

Supplies: Pedometers, jump ropes, maps, tracking sheets

One important use of pedometers in physical education is to teach students to track their physical activity levels across a number of different lessons. Using recording cards, students track their number of strides during each lesson. Then, using their stride length, they calculate the distance they travelled in kilometres. The teacher totals the distance travelled by the entire class. Prior to teaching this activity, the teacher determines a route across a given area and tracks the class's progress across a map. It may be best to start with the school's town and then progress to larger areas such as provinces or well-known trails. As the class moves across the route, historic facts or historic figures related to students' present location could be discussed. The book *Pedometer Power* (Pangrazi, Beighle, & Sidman, 2003) has more examples regarding the implementation of this activity.

HOW DO I GET THERE?

SS Concepts: Travel, evolution of transportation, rural and urban settings

PE Concept: Locomotor skills

PE Lesson Part: Introductory activity, lesson focus (movement concepts)

Supplies: None

For this activity, students are asked to demonstrate how they would travel to a specific place if they lived during a given time in history. For example, the teacher could say, "If I lived in the 1700s and wanted to get to my neighbour's house, show me how I could get there." The teacher then points out students who are walking, jogging, skipping, or galloping like a horse, which would have been methods of travel during this time. Depending on their age, some students will pretend to drive a car. This is a teachable moment for discussing the modes of transportation available in the 1700s and the distances between neighbours during this time.

COURTESY TAG

SS Concept: Social responsibility

PE Concepts: Low-organized games, body management, locomotor skills, chasing, fleeing

PE Lesson Part: Introductory activity, game activity

Supplies: None

This game is similar to Frozen Tag. Several students are designated taggers. When tagged by a tagger, the tagged person must freeze. While frozen, the student stands with his hands raised, calling out, "Please help me!" He must say, "Please." When not frozen, players move around giving high fives to the players who are frozen. After getting a high five, the frozen player must say, "Thank you" and the other player must say, "You are welcome" before the frozen player can re-enter the game. To add variety to the game, the teacher can designate a specific greeting (see the previous activity) that frozen students must perform with unfrozen students before re-entering the game. As with all tag games, the game is stopped often and new taggers are selected.

Thematic Approach

Using curricular connections between subject areas to develop a central theme, topic, or concept is a well-used teaching strategy in many elementary schools. Themes drawn from physical education have shown considerable promise. For example, the theme of "fair play" has received attention in both resource development and implementation. In terms of resource development, the *Fair Play for Kids* (Fair Play Canada, 1995) resource manual was designed to provide teachers (grades 4–7) with a variety of interdisciplinary teaching strategies that focused on the ideals of fair play and could be readily incorporated into a variety of subjects. (See Chapter 5 for sample teaching strategies from the manual.) Examination of a systematic implementation of these teaching strategies has also shown promising results. In a recent study, Gibbons, Ebbeck, and Weiss (1995) conducted a field experiment to investigate the effectiveness of teaching strategies selected from this manual on several indicators of moral development. Results provided initial validation of the strategies in *Fair Play for Kids* for effecting change in the moral development of elementary school students.

Other prominent themes from physical education outcomes often focus on physical activity, health, and wellness.

Activity	Personal Planning	Physical Education	Science	Other Curriculum Connections
Active Living 2 (Heart Acts to follow) Objective: Compare various physical activities with heart health recommendations. Activities: • Review magazine • Measure heart rates for activities • Prepare display of results	• Select and apply behaviours that promote a balanced, healthy lifestyle • Identify and describe global health issues • Access sources of information to enhance their personal well-being • Identify factors that can affect their personal futures • Demonstrate an appreciation of the impact of decisions that they have made	• Describe how activity affects physical fitness • Demonstrate and describe ways to achieve a personal functional level of physical fitness	• Identify relevant variables in an experiment • Classify and order based on a set of keys and criteria • Use appropriate technologies to record, measure, save, and retrieve data	• Math • Art • EXTENSION ACTIVITIES include learning outcomes related to: • Physical Education • Drama

Figure 11.12

Sample Heart Smart Kids curriculum connections with subject learning outcomes (grade 5).

Source: Based on Heart and Stroke Foundation of British Columbia and Yukon. (1995). *Heart Smart Kids—Gr. 4–7*. Vancouver, BC: Author.

For example, the *Heart Smart Kids Educator's Guide* (Heart and Stroke Foundation of BC & Yukon, 1995, 1999) integrates the central theme of heart health across the curriculum. The educational activities in the guide focus on three modifiable risk factors: making informed, heart-healthy food choices; being physically active; and being smoke-free. Each activity is tied to prescribed learning outcomes of different subject areas (see Figure 11.12). "Built around an integrated approach, the activities allow students to relate heart health concepts to their other knowledge and skills, both in school and in the rest of their lives" (Heart & Stroke Foundation of B.C. and Yukon, 1995, p. 5). Chapter 12 will include further discussion on integration of heart health concepts in physical education.

Connecting Cultural Content and Learning

Another type of connection that goes beyond the "between subjects" connection is the integration of cultural content and learning among all subjects, including physical education. In Canada, an important challenge for educators is to look for ways to help students better understand the unique culture(s) of the Aboriginal peoples. Several provinces have made significant strides toward this goal.

In British Columbia, for instance, a curriculum guide entitled *Shared Learnings: Integrating B.C. Aboriginal Content K–10* (2006) was designed to provide teachers with guidance for integrating authentic Aboriginal content in all subject areas. Developed with direct participation of Aboriginal teachers, Elders, and other members of Aboriginal communities in British Columbia, *Shared Learnings* presents the knowledge in a way that is accurate and reflects the Aboriginal concept of teaching and learning (B.C. Ministry of Education, 2006). The information in the curriculum guide is organized by subject area and grade level. Figure 11.13 shows shared learnings for 4–7 physical education. Each page includes three sections: (a) shared learnings—the Aboriginal content that is appropriate for subjects and grade groupings; (b) suggested instructional strategies for integrating the specific content; and (c) recommended resources. Each page also includes a teaching tip and an interesting "Did you know?" fact about Aboriginal peoples. Both Alberta and Manitoba have also

<SHARED Learnings box>

SHARED Learnings

† There are many traditional Aboriginal games and sports.

† Games and sports have specific values in Aboriginal cultures.

† Traditional Aboriginal dance is based on specific movement elements.

TEACHING TIP

Celebrate the contributions of Aboriginal peoples to Canada and the world.

DID YOU KNOW?

Aboriginal peoples invented lacrosse and hockey.

INSTRUCTIONAL STRATEGIES

Active Living, Movement

Invite a knowledgeable member of the local Aboriginal community to lead the class in traditional Aboriginal games and sports. Have your guest share with the students the value and purpose of these games in traditional Aboriginal societies.

Arrange a field trip to a gathering or large pow wow where there is likely to be dance performed. If it is an option, expand a student's involvement by contributing to the event by setting up, packing, or giving gifts. Have students think about the following questions in preparation for the field trip:

- "What will we see, hear, smell, taste, feel?"
- "How will we show respect?"

Debrief through class discussion about the various movements they may have observed in the dance. These may include an erect stance, starting with the music, hand movements, footwork, sequence of left right steps, quick steps, stomping steps; imitating animal movements, or changing facial expressions.

Personal and Social Responsibility

Provide opportunities for students to observe and later participate in Aboriginal dance, obtaining support from the local Aboriginal communities by inviting knowledgeable visitors.

Have children explore traditional foods from the local Aboriginal community and the health and nutritional aspects of these.

If they exist in the local Aboriginal community, look at how canoe races, snowshoeing, cross-country skiing, local basketball or soccer tournaments reflect historical gatherings in that same community. Examine the responsibilities involved.

RESOURCES

See Appendix H for detailed descriptions of provincially recommended resources and for a list of locally developed resources that have been created through partnerships between school districts and Aboriginal communities.

Figure 11.13

Shared learnings curriculum for 4–7 physical education.

Source: *Shared Learnings: Integrating B.C. Aboriginal Content K–10.* (2006) (p. 43). Copyright © Province of British Columbia. All rights reserved. Reprinted with the permission of the Province of British Columbia.

adopted an *infusion approach* to Aboriginal content. In the resource *Our Words, Our Ways—Teaching First Nations, Métis and Inuit Learners*, this approach "includes the infusion of Aboriginal perspectives across the subject areas at all grade levels" (Alberta Education, 2005, p. 53). They further suggest "the infusion of Aboriginal content into the regular curriculum ensures that all students have opportunities to learn about the historical and contemporary contributions and cultures of Aboriginal peoples" (p. 53). Similar to the *Shared Learning* curriculum in British Columbia, Manitoba Education and Youth (2003) identifies learning outcomes associated with Aboriginal perspectives across all subject areas and grade levels. For example, for K–4 Physical Education/Health Education (p. 23), the following outcomes are identified:

Students will

- *demonstrate understanding of the value of traditional Aboriginal games and sports they have played*

- *describe a traditional Aboriginal diet*

- *demonstrate willingness to participate in traditional dance(s)*

Another educational initiative, co-sponsored by the Saskatchewan Department of Education and the Saskatchewan Teachers' Federation, invited teachers to submit units on any K–12 subject in which Aboriginal content or learning was the focus. These units were then compiled and made available for use by Saskatchewan teachers. The reader is encouraged to examine one unit in particular, entitled *Aboriginal Physical Education for Middle Years (Grades Six to Nine)* by Rachel Desnomie (1996). In her introductory comments, the author states that "it is the traditional teachings of the First Nations to have a balance of the four elements of an individual . . . spiritual, emotional, mental, and physical . . . it is the purpose of this unit to develop awareness of the four domains and to meet the physical needs of an individual as defined by the

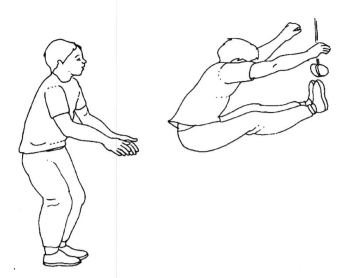

Figure 11.14

Two-Foot High Kick.

Source: Reprinted with permission of Northwest Territories Department of Education. (1989). *Inuit games*. Rankin Inlet, NWT: Regional Resource Centre.

Saskatchewan Physical Education Curriculum" (p. 2). Using activities that originate with First Nations peoples, the author integrates the four elements of the individual into the movement categories in the Saskatchewan physical education curriculum. (A full text of this innovative unit is available online at **www.stf.sk.ca**).

Finally, much of the cultural content and learning included in physical education focuses on exploring some of the traditional games of Aboriginal peoples. To this end,

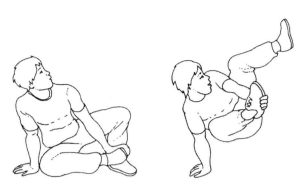

Figure 11.16

Alaskan High Kick (start and action).

Source: Reprinted with permission of Northwest Territories Department of Education. (1989). *Inuit games*. Rankin Inlet, NWT: Regional Resource Centre.

in 1989, the Keewatin Inuit Association compiled an exciting resource manual, the purpose of which was to "record the traditional games played by the Inuit and to preserve a unique form of sports and recreation experienced by the people of Northern Canada" (NWT Department of Education, 1989, p. 3). In addition to providing a variety of traditional games, the manual includes the history of many of the games within the Inuit culture. Figures 11.14 to 11.20 are examples of some of the games from this manual. The reader should note that some of these games might be particularly challenging for some elementary school children. Consider building in progressions toward these games in early years and then introducing some of the easier games with your intermediate students.

Figure 11.15

One-Foot High Kick.

Source: Reprinted with permission of Northwest Territories Department of Education. (1989). *Inuit games*. Rankin Inlet, NWT: Regional Resource Centre.

Figure 11.17

Arm Pull.

Source: Reprinted with permission of Northwest Territories Department of Education. (1989). *Inuit games*. Rankin Inlet, NWT: Regional Resource Centre.

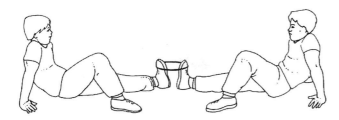

Figure 11.18

Foot Pull.

Source: Reprinted with permission of Northwest Territories Department of Education. (1989). *Inuit games.* Rankin Inlet, NWT: Regional Resource Centre.

TWO-FOOT HIGH KICK

Equipment: High-kick stand

Stance and Start: Start from a standing position

Movement: Walk or run toward the target. Jump from both feet and, keeping feet together, kick target. Land on two feet and maintain balance.

Judging and Scoring: The competitors and judge establish the starting height based on skill levels. Three tries are given each competitor at each height. The target is raised two inches (5 cm) at a time. When it begins to get difficult, the competitor may decide to raise the target only one inch (2.5 cm). The target must be clearly hit with two feet. If there is a tie, the number of failed kicks at all attempted heights is counted. The person with the fewest failed kicks wins.

ONE-FOOT HIGH KICK

Equipment: High-kick stand

Stance and Start: Start from a standing position under the target or up to 3 m (10 feet) from the target.

Movement: Walk or run toward target. Jump from two feet, kick target with one foot only (left or right), and land

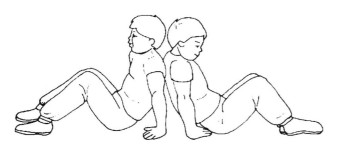

Figure 11.19

Back Push (Third Trial).

Source: Reprinted with permission of Northwest Territories Department of Education. (1989). *Inuit games.* Rankin Inlet, NWT: Regional Resource Centre.

Figure 11.20

Owl Hop.

Source: Reprinted with permission of Northwest Territories Department of Education. (1989). *Inuit games.* Rankin Inlet, NWT: Regional Resource Centre.

on the same foot that you kicked the target with. Maintain balance by bouncing on the one foot that landed before dropping the other foot to the floor.

Judging and Scoring: Same as for Two-Foot High Kick except that the target must be clearly kicked by one foot.

ALASKAN HIGH KICK

Equipment: High-kick stand

Stance and Start: Sit on the floor with one hand placed on the floor behind the rump. Grab the opposite foot with the free hand. This opposite foot is the non-kicking foot.

Movement: Lift the body off the floor and kick the target with the free foot. The kicking foot must return to the floor before the rump does.

Judging and Scoring: Three tries for each height. Target is raised 5 cm at a time and 2.5 cm when it gets higher.

ARM PULL

Equipment: None

Stance and Start: In pairs, competitors face each other, sitting on the floor. One leg is bent and the other is straight. Competitors lock legs and hook right arms at the elbow. The other hand is holding the ankle of the opponent's bent leg. (See diagram. Take watches off.)

Movement: On signal, opponents pull slowly and steadily at the elbow. The object is to try to pull the other opponent over or to force the opponent's hand to touch the chest of the winner.

Judging and Scoring: If hand touches floor, slips off opponent's ankle, or if opponent turns sideways to touch floor, start over. Best out of three attempts.

FOOT PULL

Equipment: Leather thong or belt

Stance and Start: Competitors sit on floor with line between them at an equal distance. One leg is thrust straight out in front and the other leg is bent at the knee. Either leg may be used. A belt or thong is placed around the upturned feet about 30 to 45 cm apart.

Movement: On a signal, opponents pull back with the foot using full body strength and arms. The opponent who pulls the competitor over the line or causes the thong to come off the foot wins.

Judging and Scoring: Best out of three attempts

BACK PUSH

Equipment: None

Stance and Start: Both opponents sit on floor with backs together. Place right hand on floor between the legs and the left hand on the outside of the left leg. Knees are bent with feet flat on floor.

Movement: Opponents may be in a circle, or have two lines at either end. Using leg, arm, and body strength, try to push the opponent out of the circle or over the line.

Judging and Scoring: The loser's foot has to go out of the circle or over the line. Three tries are given with the best out of three. One try with right hand between legs, one with left hand between legs, and the third try, if a tie, will be Eastern style with both hands outside the legs.

OWL HOP

Equipment: None

Stance and Start: Start on set line. Hook one foot behind the knee and bend halfway down. Either leg will do.

Movement: Bounce or hop as far as you can without quitting.

Judging and Scoring: Greatest distance wins. Hops must be continuous.

Quiet Games

Consider the following three games from *Inuit Games* (1989) for cool down and change of pace.

Anutujuak

A group of people gets together and each person faces a partner. No one can smile. The last person to smile is the winner (p. 92).

Acserk (Chanting Game)

Everyone sits in a circle or group and chants a song. On a signal, the chant stops and no one makes a noise. The first person to make a noise breaks the silence and the game starts over (p. 94).

Iglagunerk (Laughing Contest)

A group of people gets together and each person faces a partner. Partners hold hands. On signal, everyone begins to laugh. The couple that laughs the hardest and longest is declared the winner (p. 95).

Critical Thinking

1. The "subject connection" ideas presented in this chapter have focused primarily on using Physical Education to consolidate learning outcomes from other subjects (e.g., how to bring Math learning into PE). Explore ideas for consolidating learning outcomes from Physical Education in other subjects (e.g., how to bring PE learning into Math).

References and Suggested Readings

Alberta Education. (2005). *Our words, our ways: Teaching First Nations, Métis and Inuit learners.* Edmonton, AB: Author.

Barbarash, L. (1997). *Multicultural games.* Champaign, IL: Human Kinetics.

British Columbia Ministry of Education. (2006). *Shared learnings—Integrating BC Aboriginal content K–10.* Victoria, BC: Author.

Clancy, M. E. (2006). *Active bodies, active brains.* Champaign, IL: Human Kinetics.

Fair Play Canada. (1995). *Fair play for kids* (2nd ed.). Gloucester, ON: Author.

Gibbons, S.L., Ebbeck, V., & Weiss, M.R. (1995). Fair play for kids: Effects on the moral development of children in physical education. *Research Quarterly for Exercise and Sport, 66*(3), 1–9.

Governments of Alberta, British Columbia, Manitoba, Yukon Territory, Northwest Territories, & Saskatchewan. (2000). The common curriculum framework for Aboriginal language and culture programs: Kindergarten to grade 12 [Electronic version]. *Western Canadian protocol for collaboration in basic education.*

Heart and Stroke Foundation of BC & Yukon. (1995). *Heart smart kids—Gr. 4–7.* Vancouver, BC: Author.

Heart and Stroke Foundation of BC & Yukon. (1999). *Heart smart kids—Gr. K–3.* Vancouver, BC: Author.

Manitoba Education & Training. (1997). *Curricular connections: Elements of integration in the classroom.* Winnipeg, MB: Author.

Manitoba Education and Training. (2000). *Kindergarten to senior 4 physical education/health education—Manitoba curriculum framework of outcomes for active healthy lifestyles.* Appendix B (pp. 201–202). Winnipeg, MB: Author.

Manitoba Education and Youth. (2003). *Integrating Aboriginal perspectives into curricula: A resource for curriculum developers, teachers, and administrators.* Winnipeg, MB: Author.

Northwest Territories Department of Education. (1989). *Inuit games.* Rankin Inlet, NWT: Regional Resource Centre, Author.

Oliver, M., Schofield, G., McEvoy, E. (2006). An integrated curriculum approach to increasing habitual physical activity in children: A feasibility study. *Journal of School Health, 76*(2), 74–79.

Organizing Your Own Arctic Winter Games. (2000). *Physical and Health Education Journal, 66*(4), 37–40.

Pangrazi, R.P., Beighle, A., & Sidman, C. (2003). *Pedometer power.* Champaign, IL: Human Kinetics.

Placek, J. (2003). Interdisciplinary curriculum in physical education: Possibilities and Problems. In S. Silverman & C. Ennis (Eds.), *Student learning in physical education: Applying research to enhance instruction* (2nd ed., pp. 255–271), Champaign, IL: Human Kinetics.

Right to Play. (2006). *Playbook—a grade 4–6 social studies, literacy, and physical education resource.* Toronto, ON: Company for Education Communications.

Saskatchewan Education (1994). *Indian and Métis resource kit for K–12.* Regina, SK: Saskatchewan Education, Training and Employment.

Wnek, B. (2006). *Celebration games.* Champaign, IL: Human Kinetics.

 Weblinks

Right to Play: www.righttoplay.com

Right to Play is an athlete-driven international humanitarian organization that uses sport and play as a tool to provide children in disadvantaged areas of the world with opportunities for development, health, and peace. Lesson resources are available for teachers.

Canadian Olympic School Challenge: www.olympic.ca/EN/education/school_challenge.shtml

This website includes the cross-curricular Canadian Olympic Resource Kit for schools.

Heart and Stroke Foundation: www.heartandstroke.ca

This website explains Heartsmart Kids, a cross-curricular program (gr. K–3 & 4–8) related to three themes including active living, healthy eating, and living smoke-free. Also includes a Heartsmart Kids program for Aboriginal students.

Teaching the Learning Outcomes of Physical Education

SECTION 4

Personal Health Skills

CHAPTER 12

Physical Activity and Fitness

Essential Components

I	Organized around content standards
II	**Student-centred and developmentally appropriate**
III	Physical activity and motor skill development form the core of the program
IV	Teaches management skills and self-discipline
V	**Promotes inclusion of all students**
VI	Focuses on process over product
VII	**Promotes lifetime personal health and wellness**
VIII	Teaches cooperation and responsibility and promotes sensitivity to diversity

Physical Education Standards

1	Students are able to move competently using a variety of fundamental and specialized motor skills.
2	**Students can monitor and maintain a health-enhancing level of physical fitness.**
3	**Students are able to apply movement concepts and basic mechanics of skill performance when learning and refining motor skills.**
4	**Students comprehend the basic principles of wellness and are able to apply concepts that enable them to make meaningful decisions that positively impact their health and wellness.**
5	**Students participate in a wide variety of physical activities and learn how to maintain a personalized active lifestyle.**
6	Students demonstrate empathy, understanding, and respect for the numerous differences exhibited by people in an activity setting.
7	Students exhibit responsible and self-directed behaviours that lead to positive social interactions in physical activity.

OVERVIEW

This chapter discusses the value of a healthy lifestyle and the importance of teaching lifetime physical activity and fitness. An understanding of the difference between health-related and skill-related fitness helps clarify the need for emphasizing lifetime activity. High-level fitness performance is not the major goal for the majority of children. Instead, the goal is to increase the activity level of all students in order to improve their health status. Activity for children can be moderate in intensity and still offer many health benefits. Suggestions are included for developing a fitness module, motivating children to maintain fitness, and developing positive attitudes toward activities. The chapter describes a variety of exercises and proper performance techniques that can form a health-related program to meet the needs of all students.

OUTCOMES

- Differentiate between skill-related and health-related physical fitness.

- Explain the guidelines in *Canada's Physical Activity Guide for Children and Youth*.

- Explain the role that a broad program of physical fitness and activity plays in the elementary school curriculum.

- Identify the various components of health-related versus skill-related physical fitness.

- Develop a fitness module.

- Cite strategies and techniques to motivate children to maintain physical fitness.

- Categorize various exercises by the muscle group exercised.

- Identify harmful physical activities and exercises.

- Explain how to incorporate pedometers into physical education classes.

- Plan and demonstrate numerous activities and exercises that can improve the physical fitness of children.

A consistent and repeated challenge for physical education programs is to teach youngsters how to maintain an active lifestyle that promotes health and vitality. Schools teach children how to achieve academically in order to live productive lives, and few question the importance of learning to read and write. However, there is no higher priority in life than health. Without it, all other skills lack meaning and utility.

The Integrated Pan-Canadian Healthy Living Strategy (2005) focuses on the major objective of increasing by 20% the proportion of Canadians who participate in 30 minutes of regular moderate to vigorous physical activity, by 2015. The 2000 Physical Activity Monitor nationwide survey of physical activity, and subsequent monitor in 2004, provided some specific information on children and physical activity. Major results of this report included the following:

- *There has been no significant change in children's physical activity levels since the baseline year of 1998, when 61% of children and youth 5–17 were considered insufficiently active.*

- *Children's activity levels decrease with age, going from 49% among children aged 5–12 to 36% among teenagers aged 13–17.*

- *Half of Canada's children aged 6–17 years reportedly take physical education classes three or more days a week at school and 17% have daily physical education classes.*

- *Three-quarters of Canadians think that governments have a major role to play in ensuring that daily physical education is mandatory in schools.*

Never before has a body of research been compiled to show the strong need for activity and fitness in the lives of youth. Activity programs are an absolute requisite for healthy youngsters. Physical education today has a clearer mandate than ever to play an important role in the total school curriculum. The fitness and activity program must produce an enjoyable and positive social experience so children develop a positive attitude toward activity.

What Is Physical Fitness?

A general definition regarding the precise nature of physical fitness has never been universally accepted. However, two types of physical fitness are most often

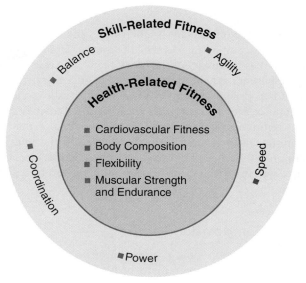

Figure 12.1

Components of physical fitness.

recognized: health-related physical fitness and skill-related physical fitness. The differentiation between *physical fitness related to functional health* and *physical performance related to athletic ability* makes it easier to develop appropriate fitness outcomes and goals for youngsters. The components of health-related physical fitness are a subset of skill-related fitness components (see Figure 12.1).

Health-related fitness is characterized by moderate and regular physical activity, and health-related fitness activities can be integrated into regular everyday activities that are often characterized as lifetime activities. In contrast, skill-related physical fitness includes the health-related components, but includes additional components that are somewhat related to genetic factors. The following discussion describes and contrasts health-related and skill-related fitness.

Health-related Physical Fitness

Health-related physical fitness includes aspects of physiological function that offer protection from diseases resulting from a sedentary lifestyle. Health-related fitness is often called *functional fitness* because it helps ensure that a person will be able to function effectively in everyday tasks. Such fitness can be improved or maintained through regular and moderate physical activity. Specific components include cardiovascular fitness, body composition (ratio of leanness to fatness), abdominal strength and endurance, and flexibility. The following are the major components of health-related fitness.

Cardiovascular Fitness

Aerobic fitness offers many health benefits and is often seen as the most important element of fitness. *Cardiovascular endurance* is the ability of the heart, the blood vessels, and the respiratory system to deliver oxygen efficiently over an extended period of time. To develop cardiovascular endurance, activity must be aerobic in nature. Activities that are continuous and rhythmic in nature require that a continuous supply of oxygen be delivered to the muscle cells. Activities that stimulate development in this area are paced walking, jogging, biking, rope jumping, aerobics, and swimming.

Body Composition

Body composition—the proportion of body fat to lean body mass—is an integral part of health-related fitness. After measuring the thickness of selected skinfolds, one can calculate the percentage of lean body mass by using formulas based on other, more accurate methods of measuring body composition. Teachers can communicate to parents the conversion of skinfold thickness to percentage of lean body mass more easily than they can the more involved measurements.

Flexibility

Flexibility is the range of movement of a joint or sequence of joints. Inactive individuals lose flexibility, whereas active individuals retain the range of movement. Stretching activities increase the length of muscles, tendons, and ligaments. The ligaments and tendons retain their elasticity through constant use. Flexibility is important to fitness; a lack of flexibility can create health problems for individuals. People who are flexible usually have good posture and may have less lower-back pain. Many physical activities demand a range of motion to generate maximum force, such as serving a tennis ball or kicking a soccer ball.

Muscular Strength and Endurance

Strength is the ability of muscles to exert force. Most activities do not build strength in areas where it is needed—the arm–shoulder girdle and the abdominal–trunk region. *Muscular endurance* is the ability to exert force over an extended period. Endurance postpones the onset of fatigue so that a person can perform activity for lengthy periods. Sport activities require muscular endurance, because a person must be able to perform throwing, kicking, and striking skills many times without fatigue.

Skill-related Physical Components

Whereas health-related fitness is primarily sought for functional health, skill-related fitness is necessary for athletic accomplishment. It is strongly influenced by genetic factors. In addition to the health-related components, skill-related fitness components include agility, balance, coordination, power, and speed. Specific components of skill-related fitness are discussed below.

Agility

Agility is the ability of the body to change position rapidly and accurately while moving in space. Wrestling and football are examples of sports that require agility.

Balance

Balance refers to the body's ability to maintain a state of equilibrium while remaining stationary or moving. Maintaining balance is essential to all sports but is especially important in gymnastic activities.

Coordination

Coordination is the ability of the body to perform smoothly and successfully more than one motor task at the same time. Needed for football, baseball, tennis, soccer, and other sports that require hand–eye and foot–eye skills, coordination can be developed by practising the skill to be learned over and over.

Power

Power is the ability to transfer energy explosively into force. To develop power, a person must practise activities that are required to improve strength, but at a faster rate involving sudden bursts of energy. Skills requiring power include high jumping, long jumping, shot putting, throwing, and kicking.

Speed

Speed is the ability of the body to perform movement in a short period of time. Usually associated with running forward, speed is essential for the successful performance of most sports and general locomotor movement skills.

TABLE 12.1				
Five-month plan for increasing physical activity				
	Daily increase in *moderate* physical activity (minutes)	**Daily increase in *vigorous* physical activity (minutes)**	**Total daily increase in physical activity (minutes)**	**Daily decrease in non-active time (minutes)**
Month 1	At least 20 +	10 =	30	30
Month 2	At least 30 +	15 =	45	45
Month 3	At least 40 +	20 =	60	60
Month 4	At least 50 +	25 =	75	75
Month 5	At least 60 +	30 =	90	90

Source: Adapted from *Canada's Physical Activity Guides* for Children.

Skill-related or Health-related Fitness?

It is helpful for students to learn the difference between the types of fitness so they understand the purposes of each. Skill-related fitness helps improve performance in motor tasks related to sport and other forms of physical activity. The ability to perform well is influenced by predetermined genetic skills. When skill-related fitness is taught in elementary school, it should be accompanied with an explanation about why some people perform well with a minimum of effort whereas others, no matter how hard they try, never reach high levels of performance. Many examples illustrate this, such as individual differences in speed, jumping ability, strength, and physical size.

Health-related physical fitness focuses on how much activity is required for good health. Emphasis is placed on the process of activity and participation rather than on the product of high-level performance. This approach teaches students the importance of maintaining a personal level of fitness through regular activity rather than comparing one's fitness level with others.

How Much Physical Activity?

Canada's Physical Activity Guides for Children and Youth (2002) provides a set of national guidelines designed to enhance healthy growth and development of children and youth through regular physical activity. The *Guides* recommend that children (ages 6–9) and youth (ages 10–14) accumulate at least 90 minutes of physical activity per day. The 90 minutes are described as a combination of 60 minutes of moderate physical activity (e.g., brisk walking, bike riding, playing outdoors) with 30 minutes of vigorous physical activity (e.g., running, soccer). In addition, the Guides recommend a decrease by at least 90 minutes per day on the amount of time spent on non-active activities such as watching television or sitting at a computer. The *Guides* also provide a six-month plan for gradually increasing physical activity toward the 90-minute target (see Table 12.1).

Figure 12.2 shows the decrease in total daily activity of children as they age. Where *Canada's Physical Activity*

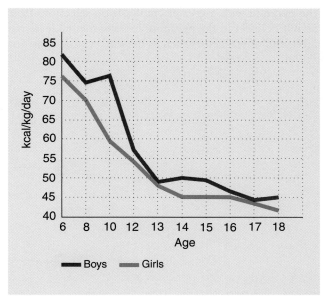

Figure 12.2

Total daily energy expenditure.

Source: Adapted from Rowland, T. W. (1990). *Exercise and children's health*, Champaign, IL: Human Kinetics.

Guides recommend 90 minutes of daily physical activity (60 minutes moderate plus 30 minutes vigorous), it also allows for the accumulation of physical activity throughout the day in periods of at least 5–10 minutes.

Youngsters learn through movement, and physical activity should constitute a relatively large part of the child's day, including some periods that are more active than others. The natural movement pattern of children is an intermittent style of all-out activity alternating with periods of rest and recovery. Continuous moderate to vigorous physical activity periods lasting more than five minutes without rest or recovery are rare among children younger than age 13. Because typical activities of children involve sporadic bursts of energy, what is recommended is a greater time involvement rather than a greater intensity of continuous involvement.

What Type of Activity?

Youngsters need to participate in a wide variety of physical activities. The Physical Activity Pyramid (see Figure 12.3) is a model used to help teachers and students develop a balanced fitness approach. The following discussion explains each level of the pyramid and recommends how such activity should be delivered to children. In general, the Physical Activity Pyramid encourages participation in activities from the lowest three levels of the pyramid with a greater emphasis on selections from activities lower in the pyramid. Developmental level, age level, and other factors such as hereditary predisposition

ultimately determine the optimal amounts of activity required at the different levels of the pyramid.

Lifestyle Activities

Lifestyle activities are at the base of the pyramid because an accumulation of daily minutes of involvement in these activities has been shown to have positive health benefits. These activities are widely accessible and relatively easy to perform for people of all ages throughout their life span. These types of activities are often done as part of daily routine, and involve large muscles. Examples are walking to or from school, climbing the stairs rather than using the elevator, raking the leaves, and doing chores around the house that require greater calorie expenditure. For young children, active play involving large muscles is the most common type of lifestyle activity.

Recommendations for Developmental Level I

The greatest portion of accumulated minutes of physical activity for children of this age usually comes from lifestyle activities. Lifestyle activities for this age include active play and games involving the large muscles of the body. Climbing, tumbling, and other activities that require lifting the body or relocating the body in space are desirable when they can be performed safely. Activities are typically intermittent in nature rather than continuous (those done for long periods of time without stopping). These activities normally involve few rules and little formal organization.

Figure 12.3

The physical activity pyramid.

Source: Adapted from Corbin, C.B., and Lindsey, R. (1997). *Fitness for Life* (4th ed.) Glenview, IL: Scott, Foresman.

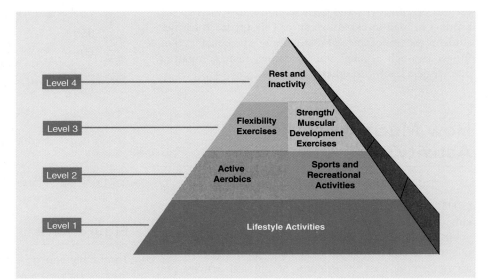

Lifestyle activities such as walking to school, when appropriate, and being involved in chores around the home are also appropriate.

Recommendations for Developmental Level II & III

As with young children, a large portion of accumulated minutes of physical activity for children of this age will typically come from lifestyle activities. Lifestyle activities for this age include active play and games involving the large muscles of the body. Activities are typically intermittent in nature, though children at this age are more likely to be involved in continuous activities (those done for long periods of time without stopping). Lifestyle activities such as walking to school and being involved in chores around the home are appropriate.

Active Aerobics

Activities that are done for relatively long periods of time without stopping are considered to be aerobic in nature. Examples of active aerobics are brisk walking, jogging or running, biking, swimming, hiking, and other similar activities. For optimal health benefits, some of these activities should be done at a moderate to vigorous intensity level.

Recommendations for Developmental Level I

Some aerobic activities are appropriate if children are not expected to participate in them continuously for a long duration. More appropriate are intermittent aerobic activities such as recreational swimming, family walking, or aerobic activities that are included in the lifestyle activity category, such as walking or riding a bicycle to school or in the neighbourhood. Participation in continuous aerobic activities of long duration is not recommended for this age group.

Recommendations for Developmental Level II & III

Participation in aerobic activities of longer duration is appropriate for this age group. Most children do not voluntarily choose to participate in continuous activity, so it is important to clearly discuss reasons for such activities. Intermittent involvement in aerobic activities is appropriate (several short bouts of activity followed by rest intervals) and is preferred by children of this age.

Active Sports and Recreational Activities

Sports such as tennis, soccer, racquetball, and basketball, and recreational activities such as canoeing and water skiing are included in this category. Some activities such as bowling and golf are also included because even activities that require relatively low energy expenditure have health benefits when included as part of a total physical activity program.

Recommendations for Developmental Level I

When young children choose to be involved in sports it is appropriate that sports be modified to meet their developmental level. In general, active sports should not comprise the major proportion of activity for developmental level I and II. Age-appropriate recreational activities such as fishing or boating with the family are suggested for children at this level; however, activities of this type are not typically high in energy expenditure. It is important that children at developmental level I and II have time to learn basic skills that are prerequisite to performing sports and other recreational activities such as catching, throwing, walking, jumping, running, and striking objects.

Recommendations for Developmental Level II & III

At this developmental level youngsters start to become involved in active sports. For this reason a greater amount of time is dedicated to this type of activity. Lead-up games and emphasis on skill development are necessary to make the activities suitable for this age. However, an emphasis on conditioning for sport is unnecessary for this age group. More of the time spent in this type of activity will be dedicated to learning skills and playing games rather than conditioning. Teachers should encourage age-appropriate recreational activities that have a lifetime emphasis or that can be done with family and friends.

Flexibility Exercises

Exercises and physical activities designed and performed specifically to increase the length of muscles and connective tissues and to improve the range of joint motion are included in this category. Some activities at lower levels in the pyramid may contribute to the development of flexibility, but specific exercises are often necessary to develop this part of fitness, even for the most active people.

Recommendations for Developmental Level I

In general, the amount of time spent on flexibility exercises for developmental level I and II is minimal. Children are more flexible than adults. For this reason this type of exercise is relatively easy for most children. Teaching some stretching exercises is helpful in illustrating the importance of flexibility. Active play activities such as tumbling and climbing are encouraged for flexibility development.

Recommendations for Developmental Level II & III

More time is spent teaching and performing flexibility exercises at this level. Children, especially boys, begin to lose flexibility at this age. Some regular stretching is appropriate either in the form of age-appropriate flexibility exercises, or activities such as tumbling and stunts that promote flexibility.

Strength and Muscular Endurance Exercises

Exercises and physical activities designed and performed specifically to increase strength (the amount of weight one can lift) and muscular endurance (the ability to persist in muscular effort) are included in this category. Some activities at lower levels in the pyramid may contribute to the development of these aspects of muscle fitness, but extra exercises are often necessary to build strength and muscular endurance, even for the most active people.

Recommendations for Developmental Level I

Participation in some strength exercises as part of a physical education class or a regular family fitness program is appropriate. However, as long as children are engaged in adequate daily activities from lower levels in the pyramid, it is not necessary for them to spend a large amount of time performing organized calisthenics on a regular basis. Modified fitness activities are an excellent way to help youngsters learn about exercises in a positive manner.

Recommendations for Developmental Level II & III

Youngsters at developmental level III participate in strength development activities that require them to move and lift their body weight. Participation in active play, games, and sports that require muscle overload is desirable for these youngsters. Exercises using body weight are appropriate when alternative exercises are offered to allow all children to be successful. It is important to show children the relevance of these exercises. Formal exercises and conditioning programs should play a minor role in physical education classes. Children who are highly motivated may benefit from greater exposure to these types of programs. Children of this age can develop modest gains in strength and muscular endurance using resistance training (see Chapter 2). However, other activities are generally better suited to the needs of most children, particularly in a class setting.

Rest and Inactivity

Total sedentary living (virtually no activity) as well as activities involving little large muscle activity—such as computer games—are included in this category. Involvement in reading, television watching, and relatively inactive recreational activities is beneficial to participants, and abstinence from these activities is not necessary if they do not limit involvement in other activities in the pyramid. They are recommended, however, primarily as a supplement to greater involvement in the activities in the first three levels of the pyramid.

Recommendations for Developmental Level I

Children at this level need some private time to be involved in play of types other than those using the large muscles. However, discourage long periods of sedentary living (not typically a characteristic of young children).

Recommendations for Developmental Level II & III

Like younger children, children at this level need some private time to be involved in types of play other than those involving large muscles. However, as with developmental level I, discourage long periods of sedentary living (not typically a characteristic of children of this age). Time between activity periods can be less than for younger children.

Fitness Testing

Consider a number of issues before implementing a testing program. The overriding consideration is to be sure the testing experience is positive and educational. Children can learn about their personal fitness and how to develop a lifestyle that maintains good health, without being turned off by the testing experience. For an example of in-depth coverage of fitness assessment see *Guidelines for fitness assessment in Manitoba schools* (Manitoba Education, Citizenship and Youth, 2004).

A Fitness Test for the Right Purpose

Fitness tests are designed to evaluate and educate youngsters about the status of their physical fitness. Obviously, fitness tests have limitations, so the important thing is how the tests are used. The three major purposes of fitness tests are as follows: (1) to offer personalized, informal self-testing; (2) to measure personal best fitness performance; and (3) to evaluate institutional accomplishment of fitness goals. A personalized self-testing approach is usually the best choice for the majority of students because it can be done in the least amount of time and it is administered as an educational process.

The *personalized self-testing approach* is student centred, concerned with the process of fitness testing, and places less emphasis on performance scores (product). When using this technique, students find a friend with whom they would like to work, or they can work alone if desired. Partners evaluate each other as they develop personal fitness profiles. The focus is on learning the process of fitness testing so they know how to evaluate their health status during adulthood. Students are asked to do their best. The teacher supports rather than directs the process. Results are the property of the student and are not posted or shared with other students. The self-testing program allows for more frequent evaluation because it can be done quickly, privately, and informally.

Figure 12.4 is an example of a self-testing form for the Fitnessgram test. It contains a column to check off whether students have met the minimum criterion-referenced health standard for each test item. The purpose of recording the data is to help students learn to self-evaluate.

Figure 12.4

My personal fitness record (Fitnessgram items).

My Personal Fitness Record

Name _____ Age _____ Grade _____ Room _____

	Score	HFZ*
Body Composition		
Calf (leg) Skinfold		
Triceps (arm) Skinfold	+	
Total (leg and arm)	=	
Cardiovascular Endurance PACER		
Abdominal Strength Curl-ups		
Upper Body Strength Push-ups		
Back Strength Trunk Lift		
Lower Back Flexibility Sit and Reach	L R	
Upper Body Flexibility Shoulder Stretch	L R	

* HFZ means you have scored in the Healthy Fitness Zone. You have achieved or passed the minimum fitness standard required for good health and feeling good. Regardless of whether you scored in the HFZ for all the tests, you must maintain an active lifestyle for good health. Try to accumulate at least 60 minutes of activity every day.

You do not have to share the results of your personal fitness record. It is for your information and should help you determine your health status. Ask your teacher if you need ideas for increasing your physical activity level.

Students are learning the process of evaluating their fitness. The scores recorded may not be accurate.

Health-related Physical Fitness Testing

Use a health-related fitness test (Fitnessgram, 2004) to provide students, teachers, and parents with information about health. The Fitnessgram system consists of a test battery and software for reporting health-related fitness results. In addition, a manual accompanies the software and covers test administration and software information. The test battery allows teachers to select test items if they choose to develop a customized test battery. The software also includes an Activitygram component that allows students to input information about their physical activity accomplishments. The Activitygram is a recall instrument that asks students to grade the intensity, level, and type of activity they participated in the previous day.

Fitnessgram Test Items

The test items in the Fitnessgram are briefly described. Where more than one item is offered, teachers have the choice of selecting the test they desire to use.

Aerobic Capacity The PACER (Progressive Aerobic Cardiovascular Endurance Run) or 1-mile (1.6-km) run/walk is used to measure aerobic performance. The PACER is a more acceptable alternative to the mile, as it involves a 20-m shuttle run and can be performed indoors. The test is progressive; it begins at a level that all youngsters can perform and gradually increases in difficulty. The objective of the PACER is to run back and forth a 20-m distance within a specified time that gradually gets shorter. The 20-m distance is not intimidating to youngsters (compared to the mile, or 1.6 km) and avoids the problem of trying to teach young children to pace themselves rather than running all-out and fatiguing rapidly. Additionally, the least fit youngster drops out of the PACER first rather than being the last person left on the track.

Body Composition Body composition is evaluated using percentage of body fat, which is calculated by measuring the triceps and calf skinfolds or Body Mass Index (calculated using height and weight).

Abdominal Strength Curl-up. This item uses a cadence (one curl-up every three seconds). The maximum is 75. Students lie in a supine position with the knees bent at a 140-degree angle. The hands are placed flat on the mat alongside the hips. The objective is to gradually sit up and move the fingers down the mat a specified distance.

Upper Body Strength Push-up. This test is done to a cadence (one every three seconds) and is an excellent substitute for the pull-up. A successful push-up is counted when the arms are bent to a 90-degree angle. This item allows many more students to experience success as compared to the pull-up and flexed arm hang. Alternative test items are the modified pull-up, the pull-up, and the flexed arm hang.

Trunk Extensor Strength and Flexibility Trunk lift. From a facedown position, this test involves lifting the upper body 15 to 30 cm off the floor using the muscles of the back. The position must be held until the measurement can be made.

Flexibility The back-saver sit-and-reach is similar to the traditional sit-and-reach test except that it is performed with one leg flexed to prevent students from hyperextending. Measurement is made on both the right and left legs.

Criterion-referenced Health Standards

The Fitnessgram uses criterion-referenced health standards. These standards represent a level of fitness that offers some degree of protection against diseases that result from sedentary living. The Fitnessgram uses an approach that classifies fitness performance into two areas: Needs Improvement, and Healthy Fitness Zone (HFZ). All students are encouraged to score in the HFZ.

Criterion-referenced health standards for aerobic fitness are based on a study by Blair et al. (1989). This study reported a significant decrease in all-cause mortality when moderate activity lifted participants above the bottom 20% (least active segment) of the population. Risk level continues to decrease as activity level increases, but not as dramatically as simply getting out of the bottom 20% of the population. Aerobic capacity standards for the Fitnessgram HFZ correspond with achieving a fitness level above the lower 20% of the population. The upper end of the HFZ corresponds to a fitness level that excludes all but the top 20% (most active segment) of the population.

Criterion-referenced health standards for percentage of fat are calculated from equations reported by Slaughter et al. (1988). Detailed information on the development of these equations and other issues related to the measurement and interpretation of body composition information is available in Lohman (1992). Williams et al. (1992) reported that children with body fat levels above 25% for boys and 30 to 35% for girls are more likely to exhibit elevated cholesterol levels and hypertension. The lower limit of the Fitnessgram HFZ corresponds to these levels of body fat.

Criterion-referenced health standards have not been established for abdominal strength, upper body strength, and flexibility. Instead, criterion-referenced training standards are used for these areas of fitness. The lower limit represents a performance level that youngsters should be able to accomplish if they are reasonably active. Stated another way, these standards reflect a reasonable expectation for students who are sufficiently active.

Daily Physical Activity Initiatives in Elementary Schools

Two provinces (Alberta and Ontario) have implemented a requirement for Daily Physical Activity (DPA) to complement the physical education curriculum. As of September 2005, all students in grades 1–9 in Alberta schools are required to participate in 30 minutes of planned DPA. The major purposes of Alberta's DPA Initiative are to optimize students' physical activity during each school day, and to help them better acquire knowledge, skills, and attitudes associated with active healthy living. According to Alberta Education's DPA Policy Statement, in order to maximize DPA, the activities should: (a) vary in form and intensity; (b) take into account each student's ability; (c) consider resources available within the school and the larger community; and (d) allow for student choice (Alberta Education, 2005, p. 2). In October 2005, Ontario implemented a requirement for at least 20 minutes of sustained moderate to vigorous DPA each day during instruction time, for students in grades 1–8.

Create Positive Attitudes toward Activity

Teachers can do a number of things to increase the probability of students being "turned on" to activity. Fitness activity is neither good nor bad. Rather, how fitness activities are taught determines how youngsters will feel about making fitness a part of their lifestyle. The following strategies can help make activity a positive learning experience.

Personalize Fitness Activities

Students who find themselves unable to perform exercises are not likely to develop a positive attitude toward physical activity. Fitness experiences should allow children to determine their personal workloads. Use time as the workload variable and ask children to do the best they can within a time limit. Voluntary long-term exercise is more probable when individuals are internally driven to do their best. Fitness experiences that allow children to control the intensity of their workouts offer better opportunities for them to develop positive attitudes toward activity.

Expose Youngsters to a Variety of Fitness Activities

Presenting a variety of fitness opportunities decreases the monotony of doing the same routines week after week and increases the likelihood that students will experience fitness activities that are personally enjoyable. Youngsters are willing to accept activities they dislike if they know that in the future there will be a chance to experience routines they do enjoy. A year-long routine of "calisthenics and running a kilometre" forces children, regardless of ability and interest, to participate in the same routine whether they like it or not. Avoid potential boredom by systematically changing fitness activities in order to help students perceive fitness in a positive light.

Start Easy and Progress Slowly

Fitness development is a journey, not a destination. A useful starting point is to allow students to start at a level that they can *accomplish*. This usually means self-directed workloads within a specified time frame. Don't force students into heavy workloads too soon. It is impossible to start a fitness program at a level that is too easy. Start with success and gradually increase the workload. When students successfully accomplish activities, they develop a system of self-talk that looks at their exercise behaviour in a positive light. This minimizes the practice of self-criticism where students fail to live up to their own or others' standards.

Use Low-intensity Activity

Make activity appropriate for the developmental level of the youngster. The amount of activity needed for good health is dictated by two variables—the intensity of the activity and the duration of the activity. Most children participate in high volume–low intensity activity as they exercise sporadically all day. This naturally occurring activity is consistent with the developmental level of children.

Avoid Harmful Practices and Exercises

The following points contraindicate certain exercise practices and should be considered when offering fitness instruction. For in-depth coverage of contraindicated exercises, see Corbin, Lindsey, and Welk (2000).

1. Keep the following techniques (Macfarlane, 1993) in mind when performing abdominal exercises that lift the head and trunk off the floor:

   - Avoid placing the hands behind the head or high on the neck. This may cause hyperflexion and injury to the discs when the elbows swing forward to help pull the body up.

   - Keep the knees bent. Straight legs cause the hip flexor muscles to be used earlier and more forcefully, making it difficult to maintain proper pelvic tilt.

   - Don't hold the feet on the floor. Having another student secure the feet places more force on the lumbar vertebrae and may lead to lumbar hyperextension.

   - Don't lift the buttocks and lumbar region off the floor. This also causes the hip flexor muscles to contract vigorously.

2. If forward flexion is done from a sitting position in an effort to touch the toes, the bend should be from the hips, not from the waist, and should be done with one leg flexed. To conform to this concern, the new Fitnessgram sit-and-reach test item is now performed with one leg flexed to reduce stress on the lower back.

3. Straight-leg raises from a supine position should be avoided because they may strain the lower back. The problem can be somewhat alleviated by placing the hands under the small of the back, but it is probably best to avoid such exercises.

4. Deep knee bends (full squats) and the duck walk should be avoided. They may cause damage to the knee joints and have little developmental value. Much more beneficial is flexing the knee joint to 90 degrees and returning to a standing position.

5. When doing stretching exercises from a standing position, the knees should not be hyperextended. The knee joint should be relaxed rather than locked. It is often effective to have students do their stretching with bent knees; this will remind them not to hyperextend the joint. In all stretching activities, participants should be allowed to judge their range of motion. It is an unrealistic goal to expect all students to be able to touch their toes. If concerned about touching the toes from this position, do so from a sitting position with one leg flexed.

6. Activities that place stress on the neck should be avoided. Examples of activities in which caution should be used are the Inverted Bicycle, Wrestler's Bridge, and abdominal exercises with the hands behind the head.

7. Avoid the so-called hurdler's stretch. This activity is done in the sitting position with one leg forward and the other leg bent and to the rear. Using this stretch places undue pressure on the knee joint of the bent leg.

Substitute a stretch using a similar position with one leg straight forward and the other leg bent with the foot placed in the crotch area.

8. Avoid stretches that demand excessive back arching. An example: While lying in prone position, the student reaches back and grabs the ankles. By pulling and arching, the exerciser can hyperextend the lower back. This places stress on the discs and stretches the abdominal muscles.

Implement a Year-long Fitness Plan

Developing a year-long plan of fitness instruction helps ensure that you offer a variety of experiences to learners. It also allows for progression and ensures that youngsters receive a well-rounded program of instruction. Plan physical fitness instruction in a manner similar to skill development sequences. Figure 12.5 is a sample one-year plan.

When organizing a one-year plan for fitness instruction, units of fitness instruction should vary in length depending on the age of the youngster. Children at developmental level I need to experience a variety of routines to maintain a high level of motivation and to understand the different facets of fitness.

During these years, exposure to many different types of activities is more important than is a progressive, demanding fitness routine. Make the first experiences of fitness instruction positive and enjoyable. The yearly plan should offer activities that allow all types of youngsters to find success at one time or another during the school year.

The yearly plan reveals that routines become much more structured as youngsters grow older. Most of the activities listed for kindergarten through grade 2 children are unstructured and allow for wide variation of performance. For older-grade children, emphasis on proper technique and performance increases.

Develop Quality Fitness Routines

Fitness routines are exclusively dedicated to the presentation of a variety of fitness activities. The following are suggestions for successful implementation of the fitness routines:

1. Precede fitness instruction with a 2- to 3-minute warm-up period. Introductory activities are useful for this purpose because they allow youngsters an opportunity to loosen up and prepare for strenuous activity.

2. The fitness portion of the daily lesson, including warm-up, should not extend beyond 10 to 13 minutes.

Developmental Level I

Week

1 Fitness Games and Challenges
2 Four-Corners Movement
3 Astronaut Drills
4 Fitness Games and Challenges
5 Fitness Challenges
6 Circuit Training
7 Animal Movements and Fitness Challenges
8 Astronaut Drills
9 Fitness Challenges
10 Parachute Fitness
11 Astronaut Drills
12 Walk, Trot, and Jog
13 Parachute Fitness
14 Circuit Training
15 Mini-Challenge Course
16 Mini-Challenge Course
17 Four-Corners Fitness
18 Fitness Games and Challenges

Week

19 Parachute Fitness
20 Jump-Rope Exercises
21 Walk, Trot, and Jog
22 Fitness Challenges
23 Jump-Rope Exercises
24 Four-Corners Fitness
25 Fitness Games and Challenges
26 Animal Movements and Fitness Challenges
27 Jump-Rope Exercises
28 Parachute Fitness
29 Four-Corners Movement
30 Walk, Trot, and Jog
31 Animal Movements and Fitness Challenges
32 Parachute Fitness
33 Fitness Challenges
34 Astronaut Drills
35 Circuit Training
36 Walk, Trot, and Jog

Developmental Level II

Week

1 Teacher Leader Movement Challenges
2 Teacher Leader Exercises
3 Teacher Leader Exercises
4 Hexagon Hustle
5 Hexagon Hustle
6 Circuit Training
7 Circuit Training
8 Astronaut Drills
9 Astronaut Drills
10 Aerobic Fitness
11 Aerobic Fitness
12 Astronaut Drills
13 Challenge Course Fitness
14 Walk, Trot, Jog
15 Challenge Course
16 Challenge Course
17 Aerobic Fitness and Partner Resistance
18 Aerobic Fitness and Partner Resistance

Week

19 Exercises to Music
20 Exercises to Music
21 Continuity Drills
22 Continuity Drills
23 Aerobic Fitness
24 Stretching and Jogging Activities
25 Stretching and Jogging Activities
26 Walk, Trot, and Jog
27 Parachute Fitness
28 Parachute Fitness
29 Exercises to Music
30 Circuit Training
31 Hexagon Hustle
32 Continuity Drills
33 Aerobic Fitness
34 Aerobic Fitness
35 Parachute Exercises
36 Teacher Leader Exercises

Figure 12.5

Yearly plan of fitness activities (continued)

Developmental Level III	
Week	**Week**
1 Teacher Leader Exercises	19 Exercises to Music
2 Teacher Leader Exercises	20 Exercises to Music
3 Teacher Leader Exercises	21 Continuity Drills
4 Hexagon Hustle	22 Continuity Drills
5 Hexagon Hustle	23 Aerobic Fitness
6 Circuit Training	24 Stretching Activities
7 Circuit Training	25 Stretching Activities
8 Astronaut Drills	26 Stretching Activities
9 Astronaut Drills	27 Parachute Fitness
10 Aerobic Fitness	28 Parachute Fitness
11 Aerobic Fitness	29 Exercises to Music
12 Astronaut Drills	30 Circuit Training
13 Challenge Course	31 Hexagon Hustle
14 Stretching Activities	32 Continuity Drills
15 Challenge Course	33 Squad Leader Exercises with Task Cards
16 Challenge Course	34 Squad Leader Exercises with Task Cards
17 Partner Aerobic Fitness and Resistance Exercises	35 Parachute Exercises
18 Partner Aerobic Fitness and Resistance Exercises	36 Squad Leader Exercises with Task Cards

Figure 12.5

Continued

Some might argue that more time is needed to develop adequate fitness. However, the reality is that many elementary PE classes allow for a 20- to 45-minute period of instruction. Because skill instruction is part of a balanced physical education program, compromise is necessary to ensure teachers cover all phases of the lesson.

3. Use activities that exercise all body parts and cover the major components of fitness. Children are capable performers when workloads are geared to their age, fitness level, and abilities.

4. A variety of fitness routines comprising sequential exercises for total body development is the recommended alternative to a year-long program of regimented calisthenics. Use a diverse array of activities that appeal to the interest and fitness level of children.

5. Exercises, in themselves, are not sufficient to develop cardiovascular endurance. Add aerobic activity, such as jogging, rope jumping, or walking, so youngsters learn the concept of a balanced approach to fitness.

6. Assume an active role in fitness instruction. Children respond positively to role modelling. If you actively exercise with children, and are able to make exercise fun, your actions will instill in children the value of an active lifestyle.

7. When determining workloads for children, the available alternatives are time or repetitions. Base the workload on time rather than on a specified number of repetitions, so youngsters can adjust their workload within personal limits. Beginning dosages for exercises should start at a level at which *all* children will succeed.

8. Use audiotapes to time fitness activity segments so you are free to move throughout the area and offer individualized instruction. Participation and instruction should be enthusiastic and should focus on positive outcomes.

9. Avoid using fitness activities as punishment. Such a practice teaches students that "push-ups and running are things you do when you misbehave." The opportunity to exercise should be an enjoyable one.

Fitness Activities for Developmental Level I

Fitness activities for young children have the potential to teach components of physical fitness and exercise the various body areas. All the fitness routines that follow alternate strength and flexibility activities with cardiovascular activity. For most routines, strength and flexibility activities are listed.

Together, the introductory and fitness activities provide broad coverage by including activities for each of these five areas: arm–shoulder girdle, trunk, abdomen, legs and cardio respiratory system, and flexibility.

Modified Fitness Activities

Many modified activities can be used to develop fitness routines for children at this level. Nonlocomotor activities should be alternated with locomotor activities to avoid excessively fatiguing youngsters. When youngsters are pushed too hard aerobically, they will express their fatigue in many different manners (by complaining, quitting, misbehaving, or sitting out). Know when to ease up. Instruction and activities should be sensitive to the capacities of youngsters.

ARM–SHOULDER GIRDLE DEVELOPMENT ACTIVITIES

The push-up (see Figure 12.6) and crab (tummy toward the ceiling) positions are excellent for developing upper body strength. Allow students to rest with one knee on the floor in the up position rather than lying on the floor. Many of the directives listed for the push-up position can be used for the crab position. One way to develop a sequence of push-up challenges is to have the students begin with one knee on the floor while practising a number of challenges. As youngsters develop strength, they can make a controlled descent to the floor from the up position. The following are examples of movement challenges that can be done with one knee down (beginning) or in the regular push-up (more challenging) position.

1. Hold your body off the floor (push-up position).
2. Wave at a friend. Wave with the other arm. Shake a leg at someone. Do these challenges in the crab position.
3. Lift one foot high. Now the other foot.
4. Bounce both feet up and down. Move the feet out from each other while bouncing.

Figure 12.6

Push-up position.

5. Inch the feet up to the hands and go back again. Inch the feet up to the hands and then inch the hands out to return to the push-up position.
6. Reach up with one hand and touch the other shoulder behind the back.
7. Lift both hands from the floor. Try clapping the hands.
8. Turn over so that your back is to the floor. Now complete the turn to push-up position.
9. Walk on your hands and feet. Try two hands and one foot. Walk in the crab position.
10. With one knee on the ground, touch your nose to the floor between your hands. As you get stronger, move your head forward a little and touch your nose to the floor. (The farther the nose touches the floor in front of the hands, the greater the strength demands.)
11. Lower the body an inch at a time until the chest touches the floor. Return to the up position any way possible.
12. Gradually lower yourself to the floor as if you were a tire going flat.

TRUNK DEVELOPMENT ACTIVITIES

Trunk development movements include bending, stretching, swaying, twisting, reaching, and forming shapes. Examples of different trunk movements follow.

Bending

1. Bend in different ways.
2. Bend as many parts of the body as you can.
3. Make different shapes by bending two, three, and four parts of the body.
4. Bend the arms and knees in different ways and on different levels.
5. Try different ways of bending the fingers and wrist of one hand with the other. Use some resistance. (Explain *resistance*.) Add body bends.

Stretching

1. Keep one foot in place and stretch your arms in different directions; move with the free foot. Stretch at different levels.
2. Lie on the floor and stretch one leg different ways in space. Stretch one leg in one direction and the other in another direction.
3. Stretch as slowly as you can and then snap back to original position.

4. Stretch with different arm–leg combinations in several directions.

5. See how much space on the floor you can cover by stretching.

6. Combine bending and stretching movements.

Swaying and Twisting

1. Sway your body back and forth in different directions. Change the position of your arms.

2. Sway your body, bending over.

3. Sway your head from side to side.

4. Select a part of the body and twist it as far as you can in one direction and then in the opposite direction.

5. Twist your body at different levels.

6. Twist two or more parts of your body at the same time.

7. Twist one part of your body while untwisting another.

8. Twist your head to see as far back as you can.

9. Twist like a spring. Like a screwdriver.

10. Stand on one foot and twist your body. Untwist.

11. From a seated position, make different shapes by twisting.

ABDOMINAL DEVELOPMENT ACTIVITIES

The basic position for exercising the abdominal muscles is supine on the floor or on a mat. Movements should lift the upper and lower portions of the body from the floor, either singly or together. Since developmental level I children are top-heavy (large head, short legs), they find it difficult to perform most abdominal exercises. Early abdominal development should begin with youngsters lying on the floor and lifting the head. Follow by starting in a sitting position and gradually lowering the upper body (with head tucked) to the floor. The following activities stimulate children to develop abdominal and shoulder girdle strength. In addition, selected abdominal exercises can be modified to provide suitable challenges. Use a directive such as "Show me how you can . . ."

1. Lift your head from the floor and look at your toes. Wink your right eye and wiggle your left foot. Reverse.

2. In a supine position, "wave" a leg at a friend. Use the other leg. Use both legs.

3. Lift your knees up slowly, an inch at a time.

4. Pick your heels up about 15 cm off the floor and swing them back and forth. Cross them and twist them.

5. Sit up any way you can and touch both sets of toes with your hands.

6. Sit up any possible way and touch your right toes with your left hand. Do it the other way.

7. In a sitting position, lean the upper body backward without falling. How long can you hold this position?

8. From a sitting position, lower the body slowly to the floor. Vary the positions of the arms (across the tummy, the chest, and above the head).

9. From a supine position curl up by pulling up on your legs.

10. From a supine position, hold your shoulders off the floor.

11. From a supine position, lift your legs and head off the floor.

LEG AND CARDIORESPIRATORY DEVELOPMENT ACTIVITIES

Leg and cardiorespiratory development activities include a range of movement challenges in general space or in place. Youngsters fatigue and recover quickly, so take advantage of this trait by alternating cardiorespiratory activities with arm, trunk, and abdominal exercises.

Running Patterns

Running in different directions

Running in place

Ponies in the Stable

Tortoise and Hare

European Rhythmic Running

Running and stopping

Running and changing direction on signal

Jumping and Hopping Patterns

Jumping in different directions back and forth over a spot

Jumping or hopping in, out, over, and around hoops, individual mats, or jump ropes laid on the floor

Jumping or hopping back and forth over lines, or hopping down the lines

Rope Jumping

Individual rope jumping—allow choice

Combinations

Many combinations of locomotor movements can be used to motivate youngsters. Following are possible challenges that might be used.

1. Run in place. Do some running steps in place without stopping.

2. Skip or gallop for 30 seconds.

3. Slide all the way around the gymnasium.

4. Alternate hopping or jumping for 30 seconds with 30 seconds of rest.

5. Jump in place while twisting the arms and upper body.

6. Do 10 skips, 10 gallops, and finish with 30 running steps.

7. Hold hands with a friend and do 100 jumps.

8. Jump rope as many times as possible without missing.

9. Hop back and forth over this line from one end of the gym to the other.

10. Try to run as fast as you can. How long can you keep going?

Animal Movements

Animal movements are enjoyable for primary-grade children who love to mimic the sounds and movements of animals. Most of the animal movements are done with the body weight on all four limbs, which helps develop the arms and shoulders. Challenge youngsters to move randomly throughout the area, across the gymnasium, or between cones delineating a specific distance. Increase the distance or the amount of time each walk is performed to increase the workload. To avoid excessive fatigue, alternate the animal movements with stretching activities. The following are examples of animal movements that can be used. See Chapter 20 for descriptions of more animal movements.

Puppy Walk: Move on all fours (not the knees). Keep the head up and move lightly.

Lion Walk: Move on all fours while keeping the back arched. Move deliberately and lift the "paws" to simulate moving without sound.

Elephant Walk: Move heavily throughout the area, swinging the head back and forth like an elephant's trunk.

Seal Walk: Move using the arms to propel the body. Allow the legs to drag along the floor much as a seal would move.

Injured Coyote: Move using only three limbs. Hold the injured limb off the floor. Vary the walk by specifying which limb is injured.

Crab Walk: Move on all fours with the tummy facing the ceiling. Try to keep the back as straight as possible.

Rabbit Jump: Start in a squatting position with the hands on the floor. Reach forward with the hands and support the body weight. Jump both feet toward the hands. Repeat the sequence.

Fitness Games

Fitness games are excellent for cardiovascular endurance and create a high degree of motivation. Place emphasis on all students moving. One of the best ways to be sure this occurs is to play games that do not eliminate players. Players who tag someone are no longer the chaser and the person tagged becomes the new chaser. This makes it difficult for players to tell who is the chaser, which is desirable because players cannot stop and stand when the chaser is a significant distance from them. Also consider having multiple chasers, allowing all participants to move more vigorously. If various games stipulate a "safe" position, allow players to maintain this position for a maximum of five seconds. Because fitness games primarily focus on cardiovascular fitness, alternate the games with strength and flexibility activities. The following are examples of games that can be played.

Back-to-back tag: Players are safe when they stand back to back with another. Other positions can be designated such as toe-to-toe, knee-to-knee, and so on.

Train tag: Form groups of three or four and make a train by holding the hips of the other players. Three or four players are designated as chasers and try to hook onto the rear of the train. If it is successful, the player at the front of the train becomes the new chaser.

Colour tag: Players are safe when they stand on a specified colour. The leader may change the "safe" colour at any time.

Elbow swing tag: Players cannot be tagged as long as they are performing an elbow swing with another player.

Balance tag: Players are safe when they are balanced on one body part.

Push-up tag: Players are safe when they are in push-up position. Other exercise positions, such as bent knee curl-up, V-up, and crab position, can be used.

Group tag: The only time a player is safe is when all are in a group (stipulated by the leader) holding hands. For example, the number might be "4," which means that to be safe, students must be holding hands in groups of four.

Run-on-the-spot tag: When a player is "frozen," he or she must run on the spot until freed.

Miniature Challenge Courses

Miniature Challenge Courses (see Figure 12.7) can be set up indoors or outdoors. The distance between the start and finish lines depends on the type of activity. A good starting point is a distance of about 30 m, but this can be adjusted. Mark the course boundaries with cones.

Each child performs the stipulated locomotor movement from the start to the finish line, then turns and jogs back to the start. Movement is continuous. Give directions in advance so that no delay occurs.

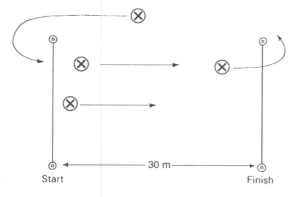

Figure 12.7

Miniature challenge course.

Sample Routine

1. Crawl under a wand set on two cones.

2. Roll down an inclined mat.

3. Log-roll up an inclined mat.

4. Move up and down on jumping boxes. Climb on the last box, jump, and roll.

5. Crawl through hoops or bicycle tires held by individual mats.

6. Walk a balance beam.

7. Pull the body down a bench in prone position.

8. Leap over five carpet squares.

9. Move through a tunnel created by four jumping boxes (or benches) covered with a tumbling mat.

10. Hang on a climbing rope for 10 seconds.

11. Crab walk from one cone to another and back.

12. Run and weave around a series of five cones.

Parachute Fitness Activities

The parachute has been a popular item in elementary physical education for many years. Usually used to promote teamwork, provide maximum participation, stimulate interest, or play games, the parachute can be used as a tool to develop physical fitness. Exciting fitness routines can be developed by having the youngsters combine vigorous shaking movements, locomotor circular movement, and selected exercises while holding onto the chute.

Sample Routine

1. Jog while holding the chute in the left hand. (music)

2. Shake the chute. (no music)

3. Slide while holding the chute with both hands. (music)

4. Sit and perform curl-ups. (no music)

5. Skip. (music)

6. Freeze, face the centre, and stretch the chute tightly. Hold for 8–12 seconds. Repeat five to six times. (no music)

7. Run in place while holding the chute taut at different levels. (music)

8. Sit with legs under the chute. Do a seat walk toward the centre. Return to the perimeter. Repeat four to six times. (no music)

9. Place the chute on the ground. Jog away from the chute and return on signal. Repeat. (music)

10. Move into push-up position holding the chute with one hand. Shake the chute. (no music)

11. Shake the chute and jump in place. (music)

12. Lie on back with feet under the chute. Shake the chute with the feet. (no music)

13. Hop to the centre of the chute and return. Repeat. (music)

14. Sit with feet under the chute. Stretch by touching the toes with the chute. Relax with other stretches while sitting. (no music)

TEACHING TIP

Tape alternating segments (20 seconds in length) of silence and music to signal the duration of the exercise. Music segments indicate aerobic activity with the parachute while intervals of silence announce using the chute to enhance flexibility and strength development.

Space youngsters evenly around the chute.

Use different hand grips (palms up, down, mixed).

Walk, Trot, and Jog

Four cones outline a square or rectangular area 30 to 40 m on a side. (Indoors, use the circumference of the gymnasium.) Children are scattered around the perimeter, all facing in the same direction. Signals are given with a whistle. On the first whistle, children begin to walk. On the next whistle, they change to a trot. On the third whistle, they jog faster, but still under control. Finally, on the fourth whistle, they walk again. The cycle is repeated with faster-moving youngsters passing on the outside of the area.

Another way to signal change is by drumbeat. One drumbeat signals walk, two beats signals trot, and three means run. The three movements can be presented in a random order. Different locomotor movements such as running, skipping, galloping, and sliding can be used for variation. At regular intervals, stop students and perform various stretching activities and strength development exercises. This allows short rest periods between bouts of activity. Examples of activities are one-leg balance, push-ups, curl-ups, touching the toes, and any other challenges.

Sample Routine

Move to the following signals:

1. One drumbeat—walk.
2. Two drumbeats—trot.
3. Three drumbeats—jog.
4. Whistle—freeze and perform exercises.

Perform various strength and flexibility exercises between bouts of walk, trot, and jog. Examples of exercises are as follows:

1. Bend and Twist
2. Sitting Stretch
3. Push-up Challenges
4. Abdominal Challenges
5. Body Twist
6. Standing Hip Bend

TEACHING TIP

Tape alternating segments (30 seconds in length) of silence and music to signal the duration of the exercise. Music segments indicate walk, trot, and jog activity. Intervals of silence signal performance of the strength and flexibility exercises. Any exercises can be substituted. Try to maintain a balance by having youngsters exercise all body parts.

Jump Rope Exercises

Jump ropes are used in a number of exercises and aerobic activities. Playing music with taped intervals of silence is an excellent method for alternating periods of rope jumping and exercises. During the periods of silence, youngsters perform an exercise; during the music, children pick up their ropes and begin jumping.

Sample Routine

1. Jump rope—30 seconds. If not able to jump, practise swinging the rope to the side while jumping.
2. Place the rope on the floor and perform locomotor movements around and over the rope. Make different shapes and letters with the rope.

3. Hold the folded rope overhead. Sway from side to side. Twist right and left.
4. Jump rope—30 seconds.
5. Lie on back with rope held with outstretched arms toward ceiling. Bring up one leg at a time and touch the rope with toes. Lift both legs together. Sit up and try to hook the rope over the feet. Release and repeat.
6. Touch toes with the folded rope.
7. Jump rope—30 seconds.
8. Place rope on the floor and do various Animal Walks along or over the rope.
9. Do Push-up variations with the rope folded and held between the hands.
10. Jump rope—30 seconds.

TEACHING TIP

Tape alternating segments (30 seconds in length) of silence and music to signal the duration of the exercise. Music segments indicate aerobic activity with the jump ropes while intervals of silence announce using the jump ropes to enhance flexibility and strength development.

Four-corners Movement

Delineate a rectangle with four cones. Youngsters move around the perimeter of the rectangle. Each time they pass a corner, they change their movement pattern. On long sides, rapid movement such as running, skipping, or sliding is designated. Moving along short sides, students hop, jump, or do animal walks. Vary clockwise and counterclockwise directions. On signal, stop and perform flexibility and strength development challenges in place.

Using the four-corners idea as a basis, devise other combinations. For example, the pattern in Figure 12.8 requires

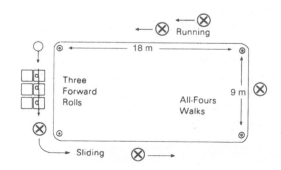

Figure 12.8

Four-corners movement formation.

running along one of the long sides and sliding along the other. One of the short sides has mats and requires three forward rolls, and the other short side requires an animal walk on all fours. Another variation that stimulates children is to place different equipment around the perimeter of the area. On signal, youngsters stop, pick up a piece of equipment, and manipulate it for a specified time. By interspersing four-corners movement (aerobic movement) with equipment handling (resting), teachers implement interval training. Try using beanbags, scooters, balance beams, benches, balls, and hoops.

Fitness Activities for Developmental Levels II and III

In contrast to the program of developmental level I activities, emphasis shifts to more structured exercises and routines. Start off the year with teacher–leader exercises, as these are the basic exercises that can be used in other routines.

Exercises for Fitness Routines

Exercises selected fall into the following categories: (a) flexibility, (b) arm–shoulder girdle, (c) abdominal, (d) leg and agility, and (e) trunk-twisting and bending. Recommended exercises are presented under each of the five categories. Stress points, modifications, variations, and teaching suggestions are presented when appropriate. Include 6 to 10 exercises in a fitness routine, with two exercises from the arm–shoulder girdle group and at least one from each of the other categories.

Flexibility Exercises

BEND AND TWIST

Starting position: Stand with the arms crossed, hands on opposite shoulders, knees slightly flexed, and feet shoulder-width apart.

Movement: Bend forward at the waist (count 1). Twist the trunk and touch the right elbow to the left knee (count 2). Twist in the opposite direction and touch the left elbow to the right knee (count 3). Return to the starting position (count 4). Knees can be flexed.

SITTING STRETCH

Starting position: Sit on the floor with one leg extended forward and the other bent at the knee. The foot is placed in the area of the crotch. The toes of the extended foot are

Figure 12.9

Sitting stretch position.

touched with the fingertips of both hands as the chest gradually moves forward (see Figure 12.9).

Movement: Gradually bend forward, taking three counts to bend fully. Recover to sitting position on the fourth count.

Stress point: Bend from the hips.

PARTNER ROWING

Starting position: Partners sit facing each other, holding hands with palms touching and fingers locked. The legs are spread and extended to touch soles of partner's feet.

Movement: One partner bends forward, with the help of the other pulling backward, to try to bring the chest as close to the floor as possible (see Figure 12.10). Reverse direction.

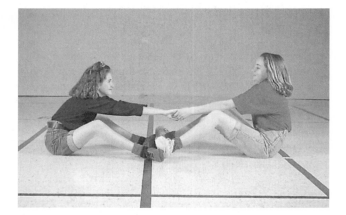

Figure 12.10

Partner rowing.

Variation: Steam Engine. Have both partners in the sitting position, and alternate pulling hands back and forth like a pair of steam engine pistons. Do eight sets, right and left combined twists.

LOWER LEG STRETCH

Starting position: Stand facing a wall with the feet about shoulder-width apart. Place the palms of the hands on the wall at eye level (see Figure 12.11).

Movement: Slowly walk away from the wall, keeping the body straight, until the stretch is felt in the lower portion of the calf. The feet should remain flat on the floor during the stretch.

ACHILLES TENDON STRETCH

Starting position: Stand facing a wall with the forearms on it. Place the forehead on the back of the hands. Back a half-metre away from the wall, bend, and move one leg closer to the wall.

Movement: Flex the bent leg with the foot on the floor until the stretch is felt in the Achilles tendon area. The feet should remain flat on the floor as the leg closer to the wall is flexed. Repeat, flexing the other leg.

BODY TWIST

Starting position: Sit on the floor with the left leg straight. Lift the right leg over the left leg and place it on the floor outside the left knee (see Figure 12.12). Move the left elbow outside the upper right thigh and use it to maintain pressure on the leg. Lean back and support the upper body with the right hand.

Movement: Rotate the upper body toward the right hand and arm. Reverse the position and stretch the other side of the body.

STANDING HIP BEND

Starting position: Stand with the knees slightly flexed, one hand on the hip and the other arm overhead.

Movement: Bend to the side with the hand resting on the hip. The arm overhead should point and move in the direction of the stretch with a slight bend at the elbow. Reverse and stretch the opposite side.

Arm–Shoulder Girdle Exercises

Arm–shoulder girdle exercises for this age group include both arm-support and free-arm types.

PUSH-UPS

Starting position: Assume the push-up position (see Figure 12.6 on p. 229), with the body straight from head to heels.

Figure 12.11

Lower leg stretch.

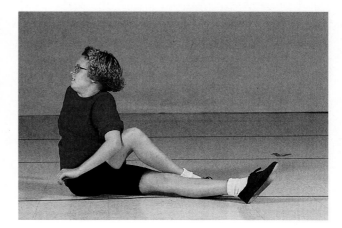

Figure 12.12

Body twist.

Movement: Keeping the body straight, bend the elbows and touch the chest to the ground; then straighten the elbows, raising the body in a straight line.

Stress points: The movement should be in the arms. The head is up, with the eyes looking ahead. The chest should touch the floor lightly, without receiving the weight of the body. The body remains in a straight line throughout, without sagging or humping.

TEACHING TIP

Variation: Some youngsters develop a dislike for push-ups because they are asked to perform the exercise without any modification. Instead of asking an entire class to perform a specified number of push-ups, personalize the workload by allowing each youngster to accomplish as many repetitions as possible of a self-selected push-up challenge in a specified amount of time.

RECLINING PULL-UPS

Starting position: One pupil lies in supine position. Partner is astride, with feet alongside the reclining partner's chest. Partners grasp hands with interlocking fingers, with some other suitable grip, or with an interlocked wrist grip.

Movement: The pupil on the floor pulls up with arms until the chest touches the partner's thighs. The body remains straight, with weight resting on the heels (see Figure 12.13). Return to position.

Figure 12.13

Reclining pull-ups.

Stress points: The supporting student should keep the centre of gravity well over the feet by maintaining a lifted chest and proper head position. The lower student should maintain a straight body during the pull-up and move only the arms.

TEACHING TIP

Variation: Raise as directed (count 1), hold the high position isometrically (counts 2 and 3), return to position (count 4).

TRICEPS PUSH-UP

Starting position: Assume the inverted push-up position with the arms and body held straight.

Movement: Keeping the body straight, bend the elbows and touch the seat to the ground, then straighten the elbows and raise the body.

Stress points: The fingers should point toward the toes or be turned in slightly. The body should be held firm, with movement restricted to the arms.

ARM CIRCLES

Starting position: Stand erect, with feet apart and arms straight out to the side (see Figure 12.14).

Movement: Do forward and backward circles with palms facing forward, moving arms simultaneously. The number of circles executed before changing can be varied.

Stress points: Avoid doing arm circles with palms down (particularly backward circles) as it stresses the shoulder joint. Correct posture should be maintained, with the abdominal wall flat and the head and shoulders held back.

CRAB KICK

Starting position: Crab position, with the body supported on the hands and feet and the back parallel to the floor. The knees are bent at right angles. On all crab positions, keep the seat up and avoid body sag.

Movement: Kick the right leg up and down (counts 1 and 2) (see Figure 12.15). Repeat with the left leg (counts 3 and 4).

CRAB ALTERNATE-LEG EXTENSION

Starting position: Assume crab position.

Movement: On count 1, extend the right leg forward so that it rests on the heel. On count 2, extend the left leg forward and bring the right leg back. Continue alternating.

Figure 12.14

Arm circles.

Figure 12.15

Crab kick.

CRAB FULL-LEG EXTENSION

Starting position: Assume crab position.

Movement: On count 1, extend both legs forward so that the weight rests on the heels. On count 2, bring both feet back to crab position.

CRAB WALK

Starting position: Assume crab position.

Movement: Move forward, backward, sideward, and turn in a small circle right and left.

FLYING ANGEL

Starting position: Stand erect, with feet together and arms at sides.

Movement: In a smooth, slow, continuous motion, raise the arms forward with elbows extended and then upward, at the same time rising up on the toes and lifting the chest, with eyes following the hands (see Figure 12.16). Lower the arms sideward in a flying motion and return to starting position.

Stress points: The abdominal wall must be kept flat throughout to minimize lower back curvature. The head should be back and well up. The exercise should be done slowly and smoothly, under control.

TEACHING TIP

Variation: Move the arms forward as if doing a breaststroke. The arms are then raised slowly, with hands in front of the chest and elbows out, to full overhead extension. Otherwise, the movement is the same as the Flying Angel.

Abdominal Exercises

For most exercises stressing abdominal development, start from the supine position on the floor or on a mat. When lifting the upper body, begin with a roll-up (curling) action, moving the head first so that the chin makes contact or near contact with the chest, thus flattening and stabilizing the lower back curve. The bent knee position better isolates the abdominal muscles and avoids stressing the lower back region. When doing abdominal exercises, avoid moving the trunk up to the

Figure 12.16

Flying Angel.

sitting position (past 45 degrees) since it may cause pain and exacerbate back injury in susceptible individuals (Macfarlane, 1993).

REVERSE CURL

Starting position: Lie on back with the hands on the floor to the sides of the body.

Movement: Curl the knees to the chest. The upper body remains on the floor. As abdominal strength increases, the child should lift the buttocks and lower back off the floor.

Stress points: Roll the knees to the chest and return the feet to the floor after each repetition. The movement should be controlled, with emphasis on the abdominal contraction.

Variations:

1. Hold the head off the floor and bring the knees to the chin.

2. Instead of returning the feet to the floor after each repetition, move them 2.5 to 5 cm off the floor. This activity requires greater abdominal strength as there is no resting period (feet on floor).

PELVIS TILTER

Starting position: Lie on the back with feet flat on the floor, knees bent, arms out in wing position, and palms up.

Movement: Flatten the lower back, bringing it closer to the floor by tensing the lower abdominals and lifting up on the pelvis. Hold for 8–12 counts. Tense slowly and release slowly.

KNEE TOUCH CURL-UP

Starting position: Lie on the back, with feet flat and knees bent, and with hands flat on top of thighs.

Movement: Leading with the chin, slide the hands forward until the fingers touch the kneecaps and gradually curl the head and shoulders until the shoulder blades are lifted off the floor (see Figure 12.17). Hold for eight counts and return to position. To avoid stress on the lower back, do not curl up to the sitting position.

Figure 12.17

Knee Touch Curl-up.

Trunk-twisting and Bending Exercises

TRUNK TWISTER

Starting position: Stand with feet shoulder-width apart and pointed forward. The hands are cupped and placed loosely over the shoulders, with the elbows out and the chin tucked.

Movement: Bend downward, keeping the knees relaxed. Recover slightly. Bend downward again and simultaneously rotate the trunk to the left and then to the right (see Figure 12.22). Return to original position, pulling the head back, with chin in.

BEAR HUG

Starting position: Stand with feet comfortably spread and hands on hips.

Movement: Take a long step diagonally right, keeping the left foot anchored in place. Tackle the right leg around the thigh by encircling the thigh with both arms. Squeeze and stretch (see Figure 12.23). Return to position. Tackle the left leg. Return to position.

Stress point: The bent leg should not exceed a right angle.

Figure 12.22

Trunk Twister.

Figure 12.23

Bear Hug.

SIDE FLEX

Starting position: Lie on one side with lower arm extended overhead. The head rests on the lower arm. The legs are extended fully, one on top of the other.

Movement: Raise the upper arm and leg diagonally (see Figure 12.24). Repeat for several counts and change to the other side.

TEACHING TIP

Variation: Side Flex, supported. Similar to the regular Side Flex but more demanding. A side-leaning rest position is maintained throughout (see Figure 12.25).

Figure 12.24

Side Flex.

Figure 12.25

Side Flex, supported.

BODY CIRCLES

Starting position: Stand with feet shoulder-width apart, hands on hips, and body bent forward.

Movement: Make a complete circle with the upper body. A specified number of circles should be made to the right and the same number to the left.

TEACHING TIP

Variations:

1. Circle in one direction until told to stop, then reverse direction.

2. Change to a position in which the hands are on the shoulders and the elbows are kept wide. Otherwise, the exercise is the same.

WINDMILL

Starting position: Stand with feet shoulder-width apart and arms extended sideward with palms down.

Movement: Bend and twist at the trunk, bringing the right hand down to the left toes. Recover to starting position. Bend and twist again, but bring the left hand to the right toes. Recover to starting position.

Partner Resistance Exercises

Partner resistance exercises are used in conjunction with activities that demand considerable endurance, such as Aerobic Fitness Routines, jogging, or Astronaut Exercises. The exercises are simple and enjoyable; children can do them as homework with parents or friends. Partners should be roughly matched in size and strength so that they can challenge each other. The exercises are performed throughout the full range of motion at each joint and should take 8 to 12 seconds to complete. The partner providing the resistance counts the duration of the exercise; partners then reverse position.

ARM CURL-UP

The exerciser keeps the upper arms against the sides with the forearms and palms forward. The partner's fists are placed in the exerciser's palms (see Figure 12.26). The exerciser attempts to curl the forearms upward to the shoulders. To develop the opposite set of muscles, partners reverse hand positions. Push down in the opposite direction, starting at shoulder level.

FOREARM FLEX

The exerciser extends the arms and places the hands, palms down, on the partner's shoulders. The exerciser attempts to push the partner into the floor. The partner

Figure 12.26

Arm Curl-up.

may slowly stoop lower to allow the exerciser movement through the range of motion. Try with the palms upward.

FIST PULL-APART

The exerciser places the fists together in front of the body at shoulder level. The exerciser attempts to pull the hands apart while the partner forces them together with pressure on the elbows. As a variation, with fists apart, the exerciser tries to push them together. The partner applies pressure by grasping the wrists and holding the exerciser's fists apart.

BUTTERFLY

The exerciser starts with arms straight and at the sides. The partner, from the back, attempts to hold the arms down while the exerciser lifts with straight arms to the sides. Try with arms above the head (partner holding) to move them down to the sides.

CAMEL BACK

The exerciser is on all fours with head up. The partner pushes on the exerciser's back, while the exerciser attempts to hump his or her back like a camel.

BACK BUILDER

The exerciser spreads the legs and bends forward at the waist with head up. The partner faces the exerciser and places the hands on top of the shoulders. The exerciser attempts to stand upright while the partner pushes downward (see Figure 12.27).

SCISSORS

The exerciser lies on one side, while the partner straddles the exerciser and holds the upper leg down. The exerciser attempts to raise the top leg. Reverse sides and lift the other leg.

BEAR TRAP

Starting from a supine position on the floor, spread the legs and then attempt to move them together. The partner, who tries to keep the legs apart, provides resistance.

KNEE BENDER

The exerciser lies in prone position with legs straight and arms pointing out to sides on the floor. The partner places the hands on the back of the exerciser's ankles.

Figure 12.27

Back builder.

The exerciser attempts to flex the knees while the partner applies pressure (see Figure 12.28). Try in the opposite direction, starting with the knee joint at a 90-degree angle.

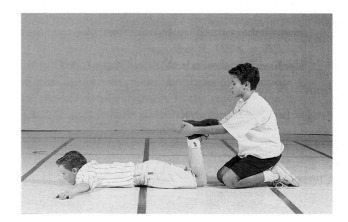

Figure 12.28

Knee bender.

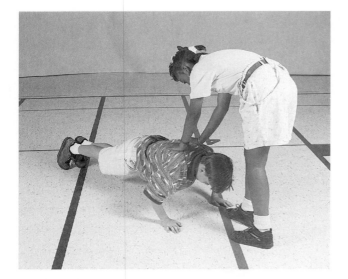

Figure 12.29

Push-up with resistance.

PUSH-UP WITH RESISTANCE

The exerciser is in push-up position with arms bent, so that the body is about halfway up from the floor. The partner straddles or stands alongside the exerciser's head and puts pressure on the top of the shoulders by pushing down (see Figure 12.29). The partner must judge the amount of pressure. Too much causes the exerciser to collapse.

Examples of Fitness Routines

When planning fitness routines, establish variety in activities and include different approaches. This minimizes the inherent weaknesses of any single routine. The routines should exercise all major parts of the body. Additionally, when sequencing fitness activities into a routine, try not to overload the same body part with two sequential exercises. For example, if push-ups are being performed, the next exercise should not be crab walking, as it also stresses the arm–shoulder girdle.

Measure exercise dosage for youngsters in time rather than repetitions. It is unreasonable to expect all youngsters to perform the same number of exercise repetitions.

Student Leader Exercises

Students in the intermediate grades enjoy leading their peers in single exercises or in an entire routine. Students need prior practice, however, if they are to lead their peers effectively in a stimulating exercise session. The following routine is an example of student leader exercises.

STUDENT LEADER EXERCISES

Encourage youngsters to do the best they can within the specified time limit.

Arm Circles	30 seconds
Push-up Challenges	30 seconds
Bend and Twist	30 seconds
Treadmill	30 seconds
Sit-up Challenges	30 seconds
Single-leg Crab Kick	30 seconds
Knee to Chest Curl	30 seconds
Run in Place	30 seconds
Standing Hip Bend	30 seconds

Conclude the routine with 2–4 minutes of jogging, rope jumping, or other aerobic activity.

TEACHING TIP

Do not require each youngster to do the same workload. Children differ and their ability to perform fitness workloads differs. Make fitness a personal challenge.

Tape alternating segments of silence (10 seconds) to signal a change of exercise, and music to signal the duration of exercise (30 seconds).

Squad Leader Exercises

Squad leader exercises give students an opportunity to lead exercises in a small group. This approach is an effective method for teaching students how to lead others and to help them learn to put together a well-balanced fitness routine. A student within each squad is given a task card specifying a sequence of exercises (see following sample routine). After the first student has led the exercise for the desired amount of time, the card is passed to another member of the squad, who becomes the leader. To ensure a balanced routine, place exercises in groups on the task card (arm–shoulder girdle, abdominal strength, leg strength, and so on). Each new leader then selects an exercise from a different group of exercises. The following routine is an example of squad leader exercises.

SQUAD LEADER EXERCISES

Sitting Stretch
Push-up Challenges
Body Circles
Jumping Jack variations
Crab Kick combinations
Abdominal Challenges
Treadmills
Toe Touchers
Leg Extensions

If there is a delay in starting an exercise, advise the squad to walk or jog rather than stand in place.

TEACHING TIP

The class is divided into groups of four to five students. Each group is given a task card that lists eight to ten exercises. One of the group members begins as the leader and leads the group through an exercise. Each time an exercise is completed, the card is passed to a new leader.

Use alternating intervals of music to signal exercising (30 seconds) with silence (5–8 seconds) to indicate passing the card.

Exercises to Music

Exercises to music add another dimension to developmental experiences. Many commercial CD sets with exercise programs are available. Using a homemade tape with alternating intervals of silence and music signals time for exercises and aerobic activity. For example, if doing Random Moving, students could run/walk as long as the music is playing and stretch when the silent interval occurs. Having the music pre-taped frees you from having to keep an eye on a stopwatch. Many exercise modules work well with music, including Circuit Training, Aerobic Fitness Routines, Continuity Exercises, Astronaut Exercises, Squad Leader Exercises, and Rope-jumping Exercises. A routine using music follows.

EXERCISES TO MUSIC	
Forward Lunges	30 seconds
Alternate Crab Kicks	25 seconds
Windmills	30 seconds
Walk and do Arm Circles	25 seconds
Abdominal Crunchers	30 seconds
Side Flex	25 seconds
Triceps Push-ups	30 seconds
Two-step or Gallop	25 seconds
Jumping Jack variations	30 seconds
Aerobic Jumping	25 seconds
Leg Extensions	30 seconds

Push-up Challenges	25 seconds
Walking to cool down	30 seconds

TEACHING TIP

Select music with a strong rhythm and easy-to-hear beat. When the music is on, students perform aerobic activities (for 30 seconds). When the silent interval is playing, students perform the strength development and flexibility exercises (25 seconds).

Use scatter formation.

Circuit Training

Circuit Training incorporates several stations, each with a designated fitness task. The student moves from station to station, generally in a prescribed order, completing the designated fitness task at each station. Exercises for the circuit should contribute to the development of all parts of the body. In addition, activities should contribute to the various components of physical fitness (strength, power, endurance, agility, and flexibility).

Instructional Procedures

1. Each station provides an exercise task to perform without the aid of a partner. Exercises that directly follow each other should make demands on different parts of the body. This ensures that performance at any one station does not cause fatigue that could affect the ability to perform the next task.

2. Place an equal number of youngsters at each station. This keeps demands on equipment low and activity high.

3. Music, whistle signals, and even verbal directions can be prerecorded to signal students to the next station. The tape provides time control and gives a measure of consistency to the circuit. Using tapes also allows you to help youngsters without worrying about timing each interval.

4. The number of stations can vary but probably should be no fewer than six and no more than nine. (Figures 12.30 and 12.31 show a six- and a nine-station

Six-station course

1 Running in place	2 Curl-ups	3 Arm Circles
6 Crab Walk	5 Trunk Twister	4 Agility Run

Figure 12.30

Sample six-station circuit training course.

Supplies and equipment: Mats for Curl-ups (to hook toes)
Time needed: 4 minutes—based on 30-second activity limit, 10 seconds to move between stations

Figure 12.31

Sample nine-station circuit training course.

Nine-station course

1	2	3	4
Rope jumping	Push-ups	Agility Run	Arm Circles
8	7	6	5
Windmill	Treadmill	Crab Walk	Reverse Curl

9 Hula-Hooping (or any relaxing "fun" activity)

Supplies and equipment: Jumping ropes, mats for knee Push-ups (if used), hoops (if used)
Time needed: 6 minutes–based on 30-second activity limit, 10 seconds to move between stations

course, respectively.) Signs at the different stations can include the name of the activity and any necessary cautions or stress points for execution. When children move between lines as limits (as in the Agility Run), traffic cones or beanbags can mark the designated boundaries.

Timing and Dosage

A fixed time limit at each station is the easiest way to administer Circuit Training. Children do their personal best during the time allotted at each station. Establish a 10-second interval to allow children to move from one station to the next. Students start at any station, as designated, but follow the established station order. A second method of timing is to sound only one signal for the change to the next station. With this plan, the class ceases activity at their station, moves to the next, and immediately begins the task at that station without waiting for another signal.

Increase the activity demands of the circuit by changing the exercises to more strenuous ones. For example, a station could specify knee or bench push-ups and later change to regular push-ups, a more demanding exercise. Another method of increasing intensity is to have each child run a lap around the circuit area between station changes. Dividing the class into halves can enhance cardiovascular endurance. One half exercises on the circuit while the other is running lightly around the area. On signal to change, the runners go to the circuit and the others run.

Another method of organizing a circuit is to list several activities at each station. The circuit can be performed more than once so students do a different exercise each time they return to the same station. If the circuit is to be done only once, children can perform their favourite exercise. Exercises at each station should emphasize development of the same body part. An example of a circuit training routine follows.

Ask students to do the best they can at each station within the time limit. This implies that youngsters are not required to do the same workload. Children differ, and their ability to perform fitness workloads differs. Make fitness a personal challenge.

Rope jumping

Triceps Push-ups

Agility Run

Body Circles

Hula Hoops

Reverse Curls

Crab Walk

Tortoise and Hare

Bend and Twist

Conclude circuit training with 2–4 minutes of walking, jogging, rope jumping, or other self-paced aerobic activity.

TEACHING TIP

Tape alternating segments of silence and music to signal the duration of the exercise. Music segments (begin at 30 seconds) indicate activity at each station; intervals of silence (10 seconds) announce it is time to stop and move forward to the next station.

Use signals such as *start*, *stop*, and *move up* to ensure rapid movement to the next station.

Suggested Circuit Training Activities

Always include activities for exercising the arm–shoulder girdle and for strengthening the abdominal wall. A variety of activities are suggested and they are classified in the following section. One activity can be selected from each classification.

GENERAL BODY ACTIVITIES

Rope Jumping: Use single-time speed only.

Jumping Jacks: See page 240.

Running in Place: Lift the knees.

ARM–SHOULDER GIRDLE EXERCISES

Crab Walk: Two parallel lines are drawn 2 to 3 metres apart. Start with hands on one line and feet pointing toward the other. Move back and forth between the lines in crab position, touching one line with the heels and the other with the hands.

Crab Kick: Start in crab position and alternate with the right and the left foot kicking toward the ceiling.

LEG EXERCISES

Step-ups: One bench is needed for every three children at this station. Begin in front of the bench, stepping up on the bench with the left foot and then up with the right foot. Now step down in rhythm, left and then right. The next class period, begin with the right foot to secure comparable development. Be sure that the legs are fully extended and that the body is erect when on top of the bench.

Straddle—Bench Jumps: Straddle a bench and alternate jumping to the top of the bench and back to the floor. Since the degree of effort depends on the height of the bench, benches of various heights should be considered.

Agility Run—Touch with the Toes: Two lines are established 3 metres apart. Move between the two lines as rapidly as possible, touching one line with the right foot and the other with the left.

Agility Run—Touch with the Hand: Same as above, except touch the lines with alternate hands instead of with the feet.

ARM AND SHOULDER EXERCISES

Standing Arm Circles: See page 236.

Lying Arm Circles: Lie prone, with arms out to the sides. Alternate forward and backward arm circling, changing after five circles in each direction. The head and shoulders are lifted from the ground during the exercise.

Reverse Curls: See page 238.

Alternate Toe Touching: Begin on the back with arms extended overhead. Alternate by touching the right toes with the left hand and vice versa. Bring the foot and the arm up at the same time and return to the flat position each time.

FLEXIBILITY AND BACK EXERCISES

Bend and Twist: See page 234.

Windmill: See page 242.

Trunk Twister: See page 241.

CONTINUITY EXERCISES

Continuity Exercises originated in Europe. Children are scattered, each with a jump rope. They alternate between rope jumping and exercises. A specified time period governs the length of the rope-jumping episode. At the signal to stop rope jumping, children drop the ropes and take position for the exercise selected. Many of the exercises can use a 2-count rhythm. When children are positioned for the exercise, the leader says, "Ready!" The class completes one repetition of the exercise and responds, "One, two!" This occurs for each repetition. To increase the enjoyment, a number of brief phrases can be used, such as "Work hard; keep fit." An example of a routine of continuity exercises follows.

Rope jumping—forward	25 seconds
Double Crab Kick	30 seconds
Rope jumping—backward	25 seconds
Knee Touch Curl-up	30 seconds
Jump and turn body	25 seconds
Push-ups	30 seconds
Rocker Step	25 seconds
Bend and Twist	30 seconds
Swing-step forward	25 seconds
Side Flex	30 seconds
Free jumping	25 seconds

Relax and stretch for a short time.

TEACHING TIP

Make a tape with music segments (25 seconds) alternated with silence segments (30 seconds). When the music is playing, students jump rope; when silence occurs, students do a flexibility and strength development exercise.

Exercises can be done in two-count fashion. Exercises are done when the leader says "Ready." The class answers "One–two" and performs a repetition.

Allow students to adjust the workload to their level. This implies resting if the rope jumping is too strenuous.

Hexagon Hustle

A large hexagon is formed using six cones. Students perform the "hustle" by moving around the hexagon, changing their movement patterns every time they reach one of the six points on the hexagon. On signal, the "hustle" stops and selected exercises are performed.

Instructional Procedures

1. To create a safer environment, children should move in the same direction around the hexagon.

2. Laminated posters with colourful illustrations should be placed by the cones to inform children of the new activity to be performed.

3. Faster children pass to the outside of slower children.

4. The direction of the "hustle" should be changed after every exercise segment.

HEXAGON HUSTLE

Tape alternating segments of silence and music to signal duration of exercise. Music segments (25 seconds) indicate moving around the hexagon; intervals of silence (30 seconds) announce flexibility and strength development activities.

Hustle	25 seconds
Push-up from knees	30 seconds
Hustle	25 seconds
Bend and Twist (8 counts)	30 seconds
Hustle	25 seconds
Jumping Jacks (4 counts)	30 seconds
Hustle	25 seconds
Curl-ups (2 counts)	30 seconds
Hustle	25 seconds
Crab Kick (2 counts)	30 seconds
Hustle	25 seconds
Sit and Stretch (8 counts)	30 seconds
Hustle	25 seconds
Power Jumper	30 seconds
Hustle	25 seconds
Squat Thrust (4 counts)	30 seconds

Conclude the Hexagon Hustle with a slow jog or walk.

TEACHING TIP

Outline a large hexagon with six cones. Place signs with locomotor movements on both sides of the cones. Locomotor movements to use are the following: jogging, skipping, galloping, hopping, jumping, sliding, leaping, and animal movements. Sport movements such as defensive sliding,

running backward, and running and shooting jump shots can also be used. The signs identify the hustle activity students are to perform as they approach a cone.

During the hustle, faster moving students should pass on the outside of the hexagon.

Change directions at times to keep students properly spaced.

Astronaut Exercises

Astronaut Exercises are performed in circular or scatter formation. Routines are developed by moving using various locomotor movements, alternated with stopping and performing exercises in place. The following movements and tasks can be incorporated into the routine:

1. Various locomotor movements, such as hopping, jumping, running, sliding, skipping, taking giant steps, and walking high on the toes.

2. Movement on all fours—forward, backward, or sideward—with respect to the direction of walking. Repeat backward and forward using the Crab Walk.

3. Stunt movements, such as the Seal Walk, Gorilla Walk, and Rabbit Jump.

4. Upper torso movements and exercises that can be done while walking, such as Arm Circles, bending right and left, and body twists.

5. Various exercises are performed in place when the music stops. A balance of arm–shoulder girdle and abdominal exercises should be included.

Astronaut Exercises can be adapted successfully to any developmental level. The type of movements selected will determine the intensity of the routine. More active children pass on the outside. Enjoyment comes from being challenged by a variety of movements.

ASTRONAUT EXERCISES

Walk, do Arm Circles	35 seconds
Crab Full-leg Extension	30 seconds
Skip sideways	35 seconds
Body Twist	30 seconds
Slide; change lead leg	35 seconds
Jumping Jack variations	30 seconds
Crab Walk	35 seconds
Curl-ups with Twist	30 seconds
Hop to centre and back	35 seconds
Four-Count Push-ups	30 seconds
Gallop Backward	35 seconds

Bear Hugs	30 seconds
Grapevine Step (Carioca)	35 seconds
Trunk Twisters	30 seconds
Power Jumper	35 seconds

Cool down with stretching and walking or jogging for 1–2 minutes.

TEACHING TIP

Tape alternating segments of music and silence to signal the duration of the exercise. Music segments indicate aerobic activity; intervals of silence announce flexibility and strength development activities.

Use scatter formation; ask students to change directions from time to time in order to keep spacing.

Allow students to adjust the workload pace. They should be allowed to move at a pace that is consistent with their ability level.

Challenge Courses

Challenge Courses are popular as a tool for fitness development in the elementary schools. Students move through the course with proper form rather than run against a time standard. The course is designed to exercise all parts of the body through a variety of activities. Equipment such as mats, parallel bars, horizontal ladders, high-jump standards, benches, and vaulting boxes can make effective Challenge Courses. A variety of courses can be designed, depending on the length of the course and the tasks included. Some schools have established permanent courses. A sample indoor course, including a climbing rope, is illustrated in Figure 12.32. The total equipment list for this course is as follows:

Three balance benches
Four tumbling mats
Four hoops
One pair of high-jump standards with magic rope
One climbing rope
One jumping box
Five chairs or cones

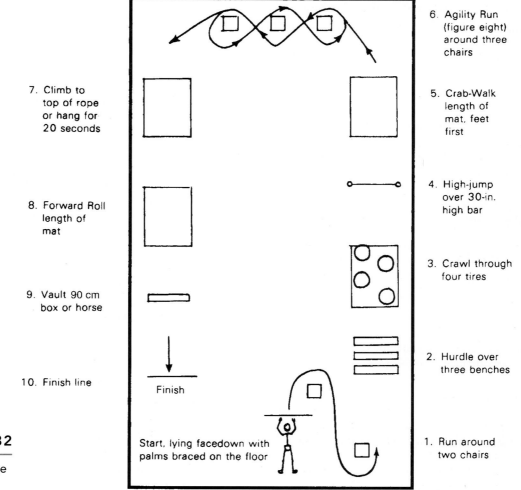

Figure 12.32

Indoor challenge course.

6. Agility Run (figure eight) around three chairs

7. Climb to top of rope or hang for 20 seconds

5. Crab-Walk length of mat, feet first

4. High-jump over 30-in. high bar

8. Forward Roll length of mat

3. Crawl through four tires

9. Vault 90 cm box or horse

2. Hurdle over three benches

10. Finish line

Finish

Start, lying facedown with palms braced on the floor

1. Run around two chairs

Aerobic Fitness Routines

Aerobics is a fitness activity that develops cardiorespiratory endurance plus strength and flexibility. A leader is designated who performs a series of movements that the other students follow. There are few limits to the range of activities a leader can present. The leader may integrate manipulative equipment (including balls, jump ropes, hoops, and wands) with the movement activities.

Instructional Procedures

1. Use movement patterns that are organized by units of 4, 8, or 16 counts.

2. Vary movements so stretching and flowing movements are alternated with the more strenuous aerobic activities.

3. Keep steps relatively simple. Focus on activity rather than becoming competent rhythmic performers. Stress continuous movement (moving with the flow) rather than perfection of routines. Running and bouncing steps are easily followed and motivating.

4. Routines are best when they are not rigid. Youngsters shouldn't have to worry about being out of step.

5. Establish cue words to aid youngsters in following routines. Examples are *Bounce*, *Step*, *Reach*, and *Jump*.

Basic Steps

The following are examples of basic steps and movements that can be used to develop a variety of routines. The majority are performed to 4 counts, although this can be varied.

RUNNING AND WALKING STEPS

1. *Directional runs*—forward, backward, diagonal, sideways, and turning.

2. *Rhythmic runs with a specific movement on the fourth beat.* Examples are knee lift, clap, jump, jump-turn, and hop.

3. *Runs with variations.* Run while lifting the knees, kicking up the heels, or slapping the thighs or heels; or run with legs extended as in the goose step.

4. *Runs with arms in various positions*—on the hips, in the air above the head, and straight down.

MOVEMENTS ON THE FLOOR

1. *Side leg raises.* Do these with a straight leg while lying on the side of the body.

2. *Alternate leg raises.* While on the back, raise one leg to meet the opposite hand. Repeat, using the opposite leg or both legs.

3. *Rhythmic push-ups.* Do these in 2- or 4-count movements. A 4 count would be as follows: halfway down (count 1), nose touched to the floor (count 2), halfway up (count 3), and arms fully extended (count 4).

4. *Crab kicks and treadmills.* Do these to 4 counts.

UPRIGHT RHYTHMIC MOVEMENTS

1. *Lunge variations.* Perform a lunge, stepping forward on the right foot while bending at the knee, and extending the arms forward and diagonally upward (counts 1 and 2). Return to starting position by bringing the right foot back and pulling the arms into a jogging position (counts 3 and 4). The lunge can be varied by changing the direction of the move and the depth and speed of the lunge.

2. *Side bends.* Begin with the feet apart. Reach overhead while bending to the side. This movement is usually done to four beats: bend (count 1), hold (counts 2 and 3), and return (count 4).

3. *Reaches.* Reach upward alternately with each arm. Reaches can be done sideways also and are usually 2-count movements. Fast-alternating 1-count movements can be done, too.

4. *Arm and shoulder circles.* Make Arm Circles with either one or both arms. Vary the size and speed of the circles. Shoulder shrugs can be done in a similar fashion.

JUMPING JACK VARIATIONS

1. *Jump with arm movements.* Alternately extend arms upward and then pull in toward the chest.

2. *Side Jumping Jacks.* Use regular arm action while the feet jump from side to side or forward and backward together.

3. *Feet variations.* Try different variations such as forward stride alternating, forward and side stride alternating, kicks or knee lifts added, feet crossed, or heel–toe movements (turning on every fourth or eighth count).

BOUNCE STEPS

1. *Bounce and clap.* This is similar to a slow-time jump-rope step. Clap on every other bounce.

2. *Bounce, turn, and clap.* Turn a quarter- or half-turn with each jump.

3. *Three bounces and clap.* Bounce three times, and bounce and clap on the fourth beat. Turns can be performed.

4. *Bounce and rock side to side.* Transfer the weight from side to side, or forward and backward. Add clapping or arm swinging.

5. *Bounce with body twist.* Hold the arms at shoulder level and twist the lower body back and forth on each bounce.

6. *Bounce with floor patterns.* Bounce and make different floor patterns such as a box, diagonal, or triangle.

7. *Bounce with kick variations.* Perform different kicks, such as knee lift and kick; double kicks; knee lift and knee slap; and kick and clap under knees. Combine the kicks with 2- or 4-count turns.

ACTIVITIES WITH MANIPULATIVE EQUIPMENT

1. *Jump ropes.* Perform basic steps, such as forward and backward, and slow and fast time. Jump on one foot, cross the arms, and while jogging, swing the rope from side to side with the handles in one hand.

2. *Beanbags.* Toss and catch while performing various locomotor movements. Use different tosses for a challenge.

3. *Hula hoops.* Rhythmically swing the hoop around different body parts. Perform different locomotor movements around and over hoops.

4. *Balls.* Bounce, toss, and dribble, and add locomotor movements while performing tasks.

AEROBIC FITNESS ROUTINE

The following aerobic movements are suggestions only. When youngsters begin to fatigue, stop the aerobic fitness movements and perform flexibility and strength development. This allows students time to recover aerobically.

1. Rhythmic run with clap

2. Bounce turn and clap

3. Rhythmic 4-count Curl-ups (knees, toes, knees, back)

4. Rhythmic Crab Kicks (slow time)

5. Jumping Jack combination

6. Double knee lifts

7. Lunges (right, left, forward) with single-arm circles (on the side lunges) and double-arm circles (on the forward lunge)

8. Rhythmic trunk twists

9. Directional run (forward, backward, side, turning)

10. Rock side-to-side with clap

11. Side leg raises (alternate legs)

12. Rhythmic 4-count push-ups (If these are too difficult for students, substitute single-arm circles in the push-up position.)

TEACHING TIP

Use music to stimulate effort. Any combination of movements can be used.

Keep the steps simple and easy to perform. Some students will become frustrated if the learning curve is steep.

Signs that explain the aerobic activities will help students remember performance cues.

Partner Resistance and Aerobic Fitness Exercises

Partner resistance exercises combined with Aerobic Fitness Routines make an excellent fitness activity. Partner resistance exercises develop strength but offer little aerobic benefit. Combine them with Aerobic Fitness Routines to offer a well-balanced program. The exercises listed below refer to partner resistance exercises mentioned earlier in this chapter. Enough time is allotted so each partner has the opportunity to resist and exercise.

PARTNER RESISTANCE AND AEROBIC FITNESS EXERCISES

Students find a partner and lead each other in aerobic activities. Partners switch leader and follower roles after each partner resistance exercise. See the aerobic fitness section for descriptions of activities.

Bounce and Clap	25 seconds
Arm Curl-up	45 seconds
Jumping Jack variations	25 seconds
Camel Back	45 seconds
Lunge variations	25 seconds
Fist Pull-apart	45 seconds
Directional Runs	25 seconds
Scissors	45 seconds
Rhythmic Running	25 seconds
Butterfly	45 seconds
Bounce with Body Twist	25 seconds
Resistance Push-up	45 seconds

Walk, stretch, and relax for a minute or two.

TEACHING TIP

Tape alternating segments of music and silence to signal the duration of the exercise. Music segments indicate aerobic activity (25 seconds); intervals of silence announce partner resistance exercises (45 seconds).

Teach the exercises first. A sign with aerobic activities on one side and partner resistance exercises on the other helps students remember the activities. The signs can be held upright by cones and shared by 2–4 students.

Take 6–10 seconds to complete a resistance exercise.

Interval Training

All fitness routines in this chapter take advantage of interval training principles. Interval training is effective with elementary school children because they fatigue and recover quickly. Interval training involves alternating work and recovery intervals. Intervals of work (large muscle movement dominated by locomotor movements) and recovery (dominated by nonlocomotor activity or walking) are alternated at regular timed intervals. The following are examples of motivating activities that can be alternated with recovery activities.

HIGH FIVES

Youngsters run around the area and, on signal, run to a partner, jump, and give a "high five." Various locomotor movements can be used, as can different styles of the "high five."

OVER AND UNDER

Students find a partner. One partner makes a bridge on the floor while the other moves over, under, and around the bridge. This continues until a signal is given to "switch," which notifies them to change positions. This assures that one child is moving (working), while the other is resting. Try different types of bridges and movements to offer variety to the activity.

ROPE JUMP AND STRETCH

Each student has a jump rope and is jumping it during the work interval. On signal, the student performs a stretch using the jump rope. For example, fold the rope in half and hold it overhead while stretching from side to side and to the toes.

STICK AND STRETCH

Working with a partner, one partner is the chaser and tries to stick like glue to the partner, who attempts to escape. Students should move under control. Upon signal, the chaser leads the other person in a stretching (resting) activity. On the next signal, the roles are reversed.

Using Pedometers to Monitor Physical Activity

Pedometers are a natural fit in a chapter on monitoring and promoting physical activity because they measure the daily amount of physical activity a person accumulates. Pedometers do not measure the intensity of physical activity, only the quantity of physical activity. These devices electronically detect movement through a spring-loaded, counterbalanced mechanism that records vertical acceleration at the hip.

Pedometers are small, unobtrusive, and easily fastened to a belt or waistband. In their most basic form, pedometers measure the number of steps a person takes. Counting steps is an effective way to measure how active a person is throughout the day even though pedometers can't measure all types of activity. To measure distance covered, the length of the step must be entered into the pedometer. The pedometer then calculates distance covered by multiplying the step length times the number of steps. Using pedometers to measure the physical activity levels of youth is now an accepted instructional and research methodology (Beighle, Pangrazi, & Vincent, 2001).

There are a number of pedometers that have features other than counting steps. Walk4Life pedometers (**www.walk4life.com**) have a function that measures activity time as well. Every time a person moves, the pedometer starts accumulating time. When the person stops moving, the timing function stops. This function shows the total hours and minutes of exercise time accumulated throughout the day.

The Accuracy of Pedometers

Activity recommendations in terms of daily minutes of physical activity for children and youth (Health Canada, 2002) have created an interest in accurately measuring personal movement. With children, some type of objective measuring tool is helpful for documenting activity levels because it avoids depending on recollection and reading of questionnaires. The pedometer is an objective way to measure physical activity, and its validity and reliability have been studied by a number of researchers. A recent study (Crouter et al., 2003) evaluated the validity of 10 different electronic pedometers and found them to be "most accurate." The next section explains how to find an accurate placement point for difficult cases. In spite of these limitations, pedometers are still one of the most accurate and reasonably priced tools for measuring physical activity.

Teaching Students about Pedometer Placement and Accuracy

Pedometers are designed to be worn at the waistline directly in line with the midpoint of the front of the thigh and kneecap. This positioning is accurate for the majority of users. However, it is not always the best placement for 20 to 30% of users. Therefore, the first thing that students need to learn is a placement point where the pedometer measures most accurately. Using the following protocol will help to ensure that the pedometer measures accurately:

1. Place the pedometer on the waistband in line with the midpoint of the thigh and kneecap. The pedometer must be parallel with the body and upright. If it is angled in any direction, it will not measure accurately. Teach students to open their pedometer (without removing it from the waistband) and reset it to zero steps. Have them walk at their normal cadence while counting the number of steps they are taking. Ask them to stop immediately when 30 steps are reached. Open the pedometer and check the step count. If the step count is within plus or minus two steps of 30, this placement is an accurate location for the pedometer. If the step count is less accurate, try Step 2.

2. Move the pedometer on the waistband until an accurate position is found. Adjust the pedometer so it is positioned slightly closer to the belly button or the hip. Open the pedometer, clear it, and have the students take 30 steps as described in Step 1. Again, if the step count is within plus or minus two steps of 30, this new placement is accurate and the user should always position the pedometer in that position. If not, try another placement and repeat the step test.

3. If it is difficult to find an accurate measuring position, consider the following: Pedometers must remain in an upright plane (with the pedometer display perpendicular to the floor and parallel to the body) in order to accurately register step counts. Loose-fitting clothing will impact accuracy because the clothing absorbs the slight vertical force that occurs with each step. Excess body fat may also tilt the pedometer away from the body and negate accuracy. In these cases, placement at waist level behind the hip and on the back may offer an accurate measurement. Another alternative is to use a Velcro belt to ensure that the pedometer is maintained in an upright position. Placing the Velcro belt above the waist may be necessary to find a position where the pedometer remains in the vertical plane. Repeat the 30-step process until an accurate placement has been identified.

Pedometers and Personal Goal Setting

The approach recommended here is the baseline and goal-setting technique (Pangrazi, Beighle, & Sidman, 2003). This method requires that each individual identify his or her average daily activity (baseline) level. For preadolescent youth, four days of monitoring step counts (or activity time) are required to establish an average activity level (Trost et al., 2000). Baseline data can be entered in a chart similar to the one shown in Figure 12.33.

After the baseline level of activity has been established, each individual has a reference point for setting a personal goal. The personal goal is established by taking the baseline activity level and adding 10% more steps (or time in whole minutes) to that level. For example, assume a baseline of 6,000 steps per day. The personal goal would be 6,000 steps plus 600 more steps for a total of 6,600 steps. This will be the personal goal for the next two weeks. If the goal is reached for a majority of the days during this two-week period, another 10% (600 steps) is added to the goal and the process repeated. For most people, a top goal of 4,000 to 6,000 steps above their baseline level is a reasonable expectation.

This baseline and goal-setting approach takes into consideration the fact that all individuals are unique. It gradually increases personal goals so that they seem achievable to even inactive individuals. Most individuals are interested in establishing their baseline levels of activity and this can be a good way to motivate students to increase their current activity levels.

Using Pedometers in a Class Setting

Using pedometers in physical education requires teaching proper protocol to students. Teachers quickly become frustrated with students fussing with their pedometers if they don't set standard procedures that students are to follow. Here is an example of a procedure that seems to minimize pedometer handling time, resulting in maximum instructional time. Number each of the pedometers and store no more than six pedometers in each container (Figure 12.34). Make sure that you have the same number of pedometers in each container so it is easy to see when a pedometer is missing (and which student has it).

The process of teaching students to secure, fasten, and put away the pedometers is critical to successful integration of pedometers into the program. Students should be taught to enter the teaching area, pick up their assigned pedometer, and put it on while moving around the area. When all students have their pedometers on, freeze the class and have students reset their pedometers (Figure 12.35). Class then begins as usual. At the end of class, students remove their pedometers, put them back into the proper container, record their steps or activity time on the sheet next to their container, and prepare to exit class.

The following activities illustrate a number of ways to use pedometers in a school setting. They are explained in greater detail in the resource book *Pedometer Power* (Pangrazi, Beighle, & Sidman, 2003).

MOVING ACROSS CANADA

Students accumulate steps and measure their stride length so they can figure out how far they have travelled across a map. As they reach different checkpoints, class

Step 1: Calculate Your Baseline Step Counts

Name: _____

Date: _____

Day 1 Step Count: _____

Day 2 Step Count: _____

Day 3 Step Count: _____

Day 4 Step Count: _____

Total Step Count: _____ divided by 4 equals _____. This number is your average **baseline step count** and will be used to determine your personal activity goal.

Step 2: Calculate Your Step Count Goal

The next step is to calculate your personal step count goal. A couple of examples are shown below. The first person discovered that she had a baseline step count of 4,000 steps. After ten weeks her step count goal increases to 6,000 steps. For the person who has a baseline of 6,000 steps, her step count goal will increase to 9,000 steps by the final weeks. Thus, both individuals will increase their number of steps by one-third.

Baseline	Personal Goal (10 percent of your baseline plus your baseline)	Weeks	Total Step Counts
4,000 steps	$4,000 \times 0.10 = 400$; $400 + 4,000 = 4,400$ Every two weeks thereafter, the goal will be increased by 400 steps.	1 & 2 3 & 4 5 & 6 7 & 8 9 & 10	4,400 4,800 5,200 5,600 6,000
6,000	$6,000 \times 0.10 = 600$; plus $6,000 = 6,600$ Every two weeks thereafter, the goal will be increased by 600 steps.	1 & 2 3 & 4 5 & 6 7 & 8 9 & 10	6,600 7,200 7,800 8,400 9,000
	_____ $\times 0.10 =$ _____; plus _____ = _____ Every two weeks thereafter, the goal will be increased by _____ steps.	1 & 2 3 & 4 5 & 6 7 & 8 9 & 10	

Figure 12.33

Setting personal activity goals using pedometers.

discussions on various locations across Canada can be included (e.g., walking to each provincial and territorial capital city).

ACTIVE OR INACTIVE

Students can participate in a variety of physical education lessons and try to predict which lessons are high activity and which are low activity. An enjoyable related activity is to have students try to guess how many steps they will take in the activity.

A SAFE WALK TO SCHOOL

Walking to school can add 1,000 to 2,000 steps each day to a student's activity level. This is a good activity for teaching students about walks that are safe, walks that increase in distance (and steps), and walks that avoid traffic.

Figure 12.34

A method of storing pedometers.

This is a school-wide contest with all classes participating. The step counts of all students in each class, and the teacher, are added and then divided by the number of students. Finding the average number of steps for the entire class makes this a group competition and avoids putting down students who are less active.

Walking: The "Real" Lifetime Activity

Walking is an activity that almost all people can do. In fact, it forms the basis for all lifestyle physical activity. Therefore,

Figure 12.35

Students resetting their pedometers.

a strong focus of physical education should be to teach the joy of moving and walking and trying to accumulate physical activity. Walking has the advantages of not requiring any special equipment and of having a low injury rate. Walking, probably more than any other activity, will be done by students when they reach adulthood. One of the things that makes walking such a valuable skill for health maintenance is its simplicity. To receive the best health results, walking should be done at least five times per week for 30 minutes or more per session. Certainly, any amount of time for walking is beneficial. There are only a few things that students need to remember to achieve maximum benefit:

1. They should walk at a brisk pace with a comfortable stride and a good arm swing.

2. Their walking pace should allow them to carry on a conversation without difficulty. If students find they can't walk and talk at the same time, encourage them to slow the pace slightly.

3. The walking program in school is a great place to coordinate pedometer use. Students can begin to see how many steps they typically gather in a specified amount of time.

Walking and Weight Management

Currently, it is estimated that nearly 26% of Canadian children and youth (ages 2–17) are overweight or obese (Shields, 2005). The chance for childhood obesity persisting into adulthood increases from 20% at four years of age to 80% by adolescence (Guo & Chumlea, 1999), making it important to establish regular physical activity patterns in the elementary school years. Weight management always deals with both caloric intake and expenditure, and people who are successful in maintaining proper body weight have usually learned to manage the balance between their food intake and physical activity.

Walking is likely the activity of choice for overweight students. It is easy on the joints, doesn't overly stress the cardiovascular system, and is not painful to perform. When coupled with pedometers, a new interest in being active may be ignited. Recently, walking (or trekking) poles have become popular, and may be an option for developmental level III students. They have been used for years in the Scandinavian countries and research has shown that 25–30% more calories are burned compared to walking without poles (Church et al., 2002). The poles increase heart rate by 10 to 15 beats and put more than 90% of the body's muscle mass to work. Additionally, they help absorb some of the impact on the knees and ankles, which results in an increase in upper body strength and a decrease in hip, knee, and foot injuries. Adding walking poles to a physical education program is another way to help students realize greater results from their walking.

Websites on using and purchasing walking poles can be found at **www.walkingpoles.com** or **www.trekking poles. com**.

Suggested Walking Activities

I SPY

On their walk students take a scorecard with them that has a challenge on it. For example, "Identify as many different makes of cars as possible," or, "List as many different birds and animals as you can." Different cards can be designed to create varying challenges. When the students complete their walks, the items they have identified can be discussed.

INTERVAL WALK

Set up a walking circuit that includes stretching and strength activities at each corner of the football field. For example, instruct students to walk a lap, then do a standing stretch for 30 seconds, then walk half a lap to a sitting stretch, then walk another lap, then do some abdominal activities, then walk to a push-up station.

WALKING GOLF

Set up a walking "golf" tournament around your teaching space with Hula Hoops for holes, cones for the tees, and a tennis ball for each student to throw. Students throw the ball and then walk with their group to the hoop. Students use a scorecard to keep track of the number of throws needed at each hole.

TREASURE HUNT

Set up a walking course with a set of clues to follow to get to 10 sites. At the sites you can tape a set of words that can later be arranged in a particular order to spell a popular saying or jingle. Examples of the clues to follow could include "a place for extra points on the south side"; "a place for H_2O"; "long jumpers take off here"; "stand under this for the score of the game."

POKER WALK

Set out several decks of cards at various locations around the teaching area. Students walk to the areas and pick up one card at each without looking at it. They walk to as many areas as possible within a time limit and then add up the points. Set it up so that anyone can win by just walking to the card areas, picking up the cards, and then adding up the points at the end of the time limit.

WEEKLY WALKING CALENDAR

Each week give students a five-day calendar that stipulates different types of things to do on their walk. For example:

Monday: Walk with a friend. Tuesday: Walk with walking poles. Wednesday: Walk, stop, and stretch periodically. Thursday: Walk 15 minutes in one direction and return to the starting spot by retracing your path. Friday: Walk and use a pedometer to count your steps.

Critical Thinking

1. *Canada's Physical Activity Guides for Children and Youth* (2002) includes a Teacher's Guide. Examine this guide and discuss possibilities and challenges for implementing the recommendations as part of a Physical Education program.

2. Two provinces (Alberta and Ontario) have implemented mandatory Daily Physical Activity (DPA) programs. Examine the support materials provided for teachers to implement DPA. How do these resources help teachers?

   Alberta:
   www.education.gov.ab.ca/ipr/DailyPhysAct.asp

   Ontario: www.edu.gov.on.ca/eng/teachers/ healthyschools.html

References and Suggested Readings

Alberta Education. (2005). *Daily physical activity (DPA) school handbook*. Edmonton, AB: Author.

American Academy of Pediatrics. (2006). Active healthy living: Prevention of childhood obesity through increased physical activity. *Pediatrics, 117*(5), 1834–1842.

Beighle, A., Pangrazi, R., & Vincent, S. (2001). Pedometers, physical activity, and accountability. *Journal of Physical Education, Recreation & Dance, 72*(9), 16–19.

Blair, S.N., Kohl, H.W., Paffenbarger, R.S., Clark, D.G., Coopert, K.H., & Gibbons, L.W. (1989). Physical fitness and all-cause mortality: A prospective study of healthy men and women. *Journal of the American Medical Association, 17*, 2395–2401.

Boyce, W. (2004). Young people in Canada: their health and well-being. Ottawa, ON: Health Canada.

Church, T.S., Earnest, C.P., & Morss, G.M. (2002). Field testing of physiological responses associated with Nordic walking. *Research Quarterly for Exercise and Sport, 73*(3), 296–300.

Cooper Institute. (2004). *Fitnessgram/Activitygram test administration manual.* M. Meredith & G. Welk (Eds.). 3rd ed. Champaign, IL: Human Kinetics.

Corbin, C.B., Lindsey, R., & Welk, G. (2000). *Concepts of physical fitness and wellness: A comprehensive lifestyle approach.* Boston: McGraw-Hill.

Craig, C.L. & Cameron, C. (2004). *Increasing physical activity: Assessing trends from 1998–2003.* Ottawa, ON: Canadian Fitness and Lifestyle Research Institute.

Craig, C.L., Cameron, C., Russell, S.J., & Beaulieu, A. (2001). *Increasing physical activity: Supporting children's participation.* Ottawa, ON: Canadian Fitness and Lifestyle Research Institute.

Crouter, S.C., Schneider, P.L., Karabulut, M., & Bassett, D.R. (2003). Validity of 10 electronic pedometers for measuring steps, distance, and energy cost. *Medicine and Science in Sports and Exercise, 35*(8), 1455–1460.

Decker, J. & Mize, M. (2002). *Walking games and activities.* Champaign, IL: Human Kinetics.

Guo, S.S. & Chumlea, W.C. (1999). Tracking of body mass index in children in relation to overweight in adulthood. *American Journal of Clinical Nutrition, 70,* 145S–148S.

Halas, J. & Gannon, G. (2006). Principles of physical fitness development: Implications for fitness assessment. *Physical and Health Education Journal, 71*(4), 4–9.

Halas, J., Gannon, G., & Ng, C. (2006). The challenges of teaching "fitness" in an era of physical inactivity: Examples of effective practice. *Physical and Health Education Journal, 72*(1), 4–9.

Health Canada. (2002). *Canada's physical activity guides for children.* Ottawa, ON: Author.

Lohman, T.G. (1992). *Advances in body composition.* Champaign, IL: Human Kinetics.

Macfarlane, P.A. (1993). Out with the sit-up, in with the curl-up. *Journal of Physical Education, Recreation, and Dance, 64*(6), 62–66.

Manitoba Education, Citizenship and Youth. (2004). *Guidelines for fitness assessment in Manitoba schools—A resource for physical education/health education.* Winnipeg, MB: Author.

Morgan, C.F., Pangrazi, R., & Beighle, A. (2003). Using pedometers to promote physical activity in physical education. *Journal of Physical Education, Recreation & Dance, 74*(7), 33–38.

Ontario Medical Association. (2005). *An ounce of prevention or a ton of trouble: Is there an epidemic of obesity in children.* Toronto, ON: Author.

Ontario Ministry of Education. (2005a). *Daily physical activity in schools—grades 1 to 3 resource guide.* Toronto, ON: Author.

Ontario Ministry of Education. (2005b). *Daily physical activity in schools—grades 4 to 6 resource guide.* Toronto, ON: Author.

Ontario Ministry of Education. (2005c). *Daily physical activity in schools—grades 7 to 8 resource guide.* Toronto, ON: Author.

Pangrazi, R.P., Beighle, A. & Sidman, C. (2003). *Pedometer power—67 lessons for K–12.* Champaign, IL: Human Kinetics.

Rowland, T.W. (1990). *Exercise and children's health.* Champaign, IL: Human Kinetics.

Shields, M. (2005). Measured obesity: Overweight Canadian children and adults. *Nutrition: Findings from the Canadian Community Health Survey, 1,* 82–620 – MWE 2005001.

Slaughter, M.L., Lohman, T.G., Boileau, R.A., Horswill, C.A., Stillman, R.J., Van Loan, M.D., & Benben, D.A. (1988). Skinfold equations for estimation of body fatness in children and youth. *Human Biology, 60,* 709–723.

Stewart, A., Elliot, S., Boyce, A. & Block, M. (2005). Effective teaching practices during physical fitness testing. *Journal of Physical Education, Recreation & Dance, 76*(1), 21–24.

Taras, H. (2005). Physical activity and student performance at school. *Journal of School Health. 75*(6), 214–218.

Trost, S.G., Pate, R.R., Freedson, P.S., Sallis, J.F., & Taylor, W.C. (2000). Using objective physical activity measures with youth: How many days of monitoring are needed? *Medicine and Science in Sports and Exercise, 32*(2), 426–431.

Williams, D.P., Going, S.B., Lohman, T.G., Harsha, D.W., Webber, L.S., & Bereson, G.S. (1992). Body fatness and the risk of elevated blood pressure, total cholesterol and serum lipoprotein ratios in children and youth. *American Journal of Public Health, 82,* 358–363.

Willms, J., Tremblay, M. & Katzmarzyk, P. (2003). Geographic and demographic variation in the prevalence of overweight Canadian children. *Obesity Research, 11,* 668–673.

 Weblinks

Health Canada: www.healthcanada.ca/paguide

Canada's Physical Activity Guide for Children and Youth is available on this website. Physical activity guides for adults are also available. *Canada's Food Guide to Healthy Eating* is available from this website.

Canadian Cross Country Fitness Challenge: www.c2cfitcanada.com

This online program allows students to track their walking/running/cycling mileage across Canada from St. John's, NL, to Vancouver, BC.

Canadian Cycling Association: www.canadian-cycling.com/cca/home.shtml

Includes *Sprockids,* an introductory cycling program for kids that focuses on riding skills and techniques, safety, fitness, and health.

Canadian Lung Association: www.lung.ca

Website includes teaching resources, student learning activities, and links to provincial lung associations.

Terry Fox National School Run Day: www.terryfoxrun.org

The Terry Fox National School Run Day is held every September as part of the annual Terry Fox Run. Website includes information about Terry Fox and provincial/territorial contacts.

CHAPTER 13

Wellness: Developing a Healthy Lifestyle

Essential Components

I	Organized around content standards
II	Student-centred and developmentally appropriate
III	Physical activity and motor skill development form the core of the program
IV	Teaches management skills and self-discipline
V	**Promotes inclusion of all students**
VI	Focuses on process over product
VII	**Promotes lifetime personal health and wellness**
VIII	Teaches cooperation and responsibility and promotes sensitivity to diversity

Physical Education Standards

1	Students are able to move competently using a variety of fundamental and specialized motor skills.
2	**Students can monitor and maintain a health-enhancing level of physical fitness.**
3	Students are able to apply movement concepts and basic mechanics of skill performance when learning and refining motor skills.
4	**Students comprehend the basic principles of wellness and are able to apply concepts that enable them to make meaningful decisions that positively impact their health and wellness.**
5	**Students participate in a wide variety of physical activities and learn how to maintain a personalized active lifestyle.**
6	Students demonstrate empathy, understanding, and respect for the numerous differences exhibited by people in an activity setting.
7	Students exhibit responsible and self-directed behaviours that lead to positive social interactions in physical activity.

understand their feelings, values, and attitudes. They need to help students learn decision-making strategies, leading toward thoughtful and productive choices. This chapter suggests learning experiences to help youngsters begin to comprehend and synthesize knowledge necessary for wellness.

OVERVIEW

This chapter provides an overview of the concept of human wellness. The first phase of wellness is understanding how the body functions and needs to be maintained for good health. A number of roadblocks to wellness occur on the path to good health, and students need to develop the ability to avoid such deterrents. Effective teachers help students

OUTCOMES

- Describe how wellness instruction can be implemented in physical education.

- Identify various techniques used to help students develop awareness and decision-making skills.

- List teaching behaviours associated with the effective leadership of class discussions.

- Identify various roadblocks to wellness.

- Implement learning experiences related to wellness.

- Define health-related physical fitness and the relationship between total physical fitness and activity.

- Describe the value of proper nutrition.

- Understand the importance of dealing with stress and tension.

If a child were asked what the concept of wellness means, a typical answer might be to "feel good." The term means more, however, than just adequate health. It means attainment of a special type of lifestyle driven by nurturing the body and avoiding substances that are destructive to a healthy body. Wellness education establishes a fundamental basis for effective living. The concept of wellness appears in most provincial and territorial physical education guides as "healthy active living" and receives considerable direct emphasis in the curriculum.

Teaching Wellness in the Physical Education Setting

Nowhere is it assumed that the achievement of wellness is the concern solely of physical education. In some provinces the physical education curriculum and health curriculum are closely linked in the same guide (for example, in Manitoba and Ontario). Other provinces have a variety of separate yet overlapping curriculum documents that address the concept of wellness (for example, British Columbia and Alberta). The reader is encouraged to examine how his or her respective province/territory incorporates the concept of wellness and resulting learning outcomes into the elementary school curriculum.

There are various approaches to teaching wellness in elementary school physical education classes. Physical activity is still the cornerstone of physical education, and it is not recommended that teachers substitute a knowledge-discussion program for activity. On the other hand, a strong case can be made that activity, without a knowledge base of how and why, will be ineffective in the long run.

In general, the approach at the elementary school level is threefold. First, the physical education program imparts *knowledge* that contributes to the concept of wellness. A child needs to understand the human body and how it functions. This involves rudimentary anatomy, simple physiology, and body movement principles. The information must be relevant to situations that students face.

The second part is an *understanding of lifestyles* that contribute to or are destructive of wellness. Wellness is not an entity in itself, but comprises a balance of lifestyle choices. Youngsters need to understand and practise healthy

lifestyles that help them achieve wellness. The final step is to provide opportunity for *applying concepts* through a variety of learning experiences. Knowledge is not enough; knowledge must be used in a context directly related to enhancing wellness. Examples of learning outcomes that appear as part of most provincial and territorial physical education curriculum guides include the following:

- Learning how to measure the heart rate
- Knowing which activities are aerobic and which are anaerobic
- Identifying which muscles are strengthened by different exercises
- Understanding why strength is important in skill performance
- Knowing how to choose a balanced diet
- Understanding how weight is maintained through caloric balance of exercise and eating
- Developing a personalized level of physical fitness

Also see Chapter 11 to review a thematic approach to wellness/healthy active living concepts in physical education.

Instructional Strategies for Teaching Wellness

Physical education plays a large role in enhancing the fitness and skill levels of students so they have a background that allows them to develop an active lifestyle. Another program goal should be to help young people make responsible lifestyle decisions. People are faced with many decisions that positively or negatively impact their level of wellness. The ability to make responsible decisions depends on a wide range of factors: an understanding of one's feelings and clarification of personal values, an ability to cope with stress and personal problems, an ability to make decisions, and an understanding of the impact of various lifestyles on health.

Developing Awareness and Decision-making Skills

The focus of wellness instruction should be to view the student as a total being. Stability is predicated on all parts fitting together in a smooth and consistent fashion. When a problem occurs, the balance of physiology, thinking, and function tends to be disrupted. Individuals then need to use their knowledge, coping ability, and decision-making skills to restore the equilibrium associated with personal stability. Teachers can try to help students understand their feelings, values, and attitudes, and the impact these have on coping and decision making.

Coping Skills

Coping is the ability to deal with problems successfully. Learning to cope with life's problems is dependent on and interrelated with knowledge of self, decision-making skills, and the ability to relate to others. Specific strategies for coping include the following:

1. *Admit that a problem exists and face it.* Coping with a problem is impossible when the problem is not recognized.

2. *Define the problem and decide who owns it.* Individuals must identify what needs to be coped with and decide if the problem is theirs or belongs to others.

3. *List alternative solutions to the problem.* A basic step in decision making, problem solving, and coping is to identify what alternatives are open in a given situation.

4. *Predict consequences for oneself and others.* Once alternatives are identified, an important process is weighing the potential consequences of each, and then ranking them in order of preference.

5. *Identify and consult sources of help.* Consider all possible sources of help available to assist in carrying out alternatives. To do this, students need to have some knowledge of the available resources or know how to find resources.

6. *Experiment with a solution and evaluate the results.* If the decision did not produce satisfactory results, try an alternative. Evaluation of results also allows people to keep track of their abilities and come up with satisfying solutions.

Decision-making Skills

Youngsters are faced with many life situations in which decisions must be made. Decision making is something that everyone does every day. Because it is a common act, it receives little attention until a person is faced with an important decision that has long-term consequences. Although schools attempt to help students learn how to make personally satisfying decisions, a major portion of teacher time is spent supplying information to students. While this teacher function is extremely important, it is only one part of the decision-making process. Ask yourself this question: "If you are going to provide information to others, what do you want them to do with that information?" Opportunities should be provided that help students put the information to use.

Decision making is defined as a process in which a person selects from two or more possible choices. A decision

cannot exist unless more than one course of action is available to consider. Decision making enables the individual to reason through life situations, to solve problems, and, to some extent, to direct behaviour. There are no right answers for the decision made; rather, the success of the decision is based on the student's effective use of a process that results in satisfying consequences. This criterion distinguishes decision making from problem solving. Problem solving usually identifies one best solution for everyone involved. When making decisions, students should consider each of the following steps:

1. *Gather information.* If meaningful choices are to be made, gathering all available information is important. Information should be gathered from as many sources as possible. Students will generally consider information valid if they see that it comes from many different sources and that it allows them to view both sides of an issue.

2. *Consider the available choices.* The next step is to consider all of the available choices. It does not make sense to consider alternatives that, in reality, have no possibility of being selected. Considering the choices is an important step if students are to realize that they have many different possibilities from which to choose and that what they choose will influence the direction of their lives.

3. *Analyze the consequences of choices.* When the various choices are delineated, students must consider the consequences that accompany each choice. If the consequences are ignored, the choice made may be unwise and detrimental to good health. Making wise decisions about wellness demands that students be aware of the consequences. This means understanding why some people choose to smoke or drink, even when they understand the negative consequences. The most important role of the teacher is to help students identify both positive and negative consequences of their choices.

4. *Make a decision and implement it.* When all the information has been gathered, students must make a decision and integrate it into their lifestyles. These decisions are personal to each student.

Leading Discussion Sessions

The success of discussions depends on how effectively the teacher is able to establish and maintain the integrity and structure of the lesson and the students' psychological freedom (see Figure 13.1). Through integrity and structure, all students are dealing with the same issue in a thoughtful and responsible way. Psychological freedom means that individual students participate to the degree they want to, by (a) commenting when they choose to do so or refraining from commenting when they so desire, (b) responding to direct

Figure 13.1

Leading a wellness discussion.

questions or choosing to "pass" for the time being, (c) agreeing or disagreeing with what others in the group have said, or (d) deciding what data they need, if any, and reaching out to ask for those data. This demands certain teacher behaviour to establish a safe and meaningful environment. A brief description of the necessary teaching behaviours follows.

Structuring

The purpose of structuring is to create a climate that is conducive to open communication by all parties. This is accomplished by outlining expectations and role relationships for both teacher and students. Structuring includes any of the following:

1. Establish the lesson climate at the beginning of the lesson by providing an explanation of what the students and teacher will be doing and how they will work together.

2. Maintain the established lesson structure by not allowing students to be pressured to respond and by seeing that no one's ideas are put down.

3. When necessary, add to or modify the lesson structure established at the beginning of the lesson.

For example, this might involve changing to small-group sessions rather than continuing a total-class discussion.

Focus Setting

The purpose of focus setting is to establish an explicit and common topic or issue for discussion. Because this teaching behaviour is used in various circumstances, there are several ways in which it can be formulated:

1. A topic can be presented, usually in the form of a question, to the group for their discussion.

2. Focus setting can be used to restate the original question during the lesson or to shift to a new discussion topic when students indicate they have finished discussing the original question.

3. Focus setting can bring the discussion back to the original topic when a student unknowingly shifts to a new topic.

4. Focus setting can label a discussion question presented by a student as a new topic to allow discussion of that topic in place of a previous one.

Acknowledging

Acknowledging informs a student that the teacher understands what the student has said and that the comments have made a contribution to the discussion. Consider carefully how acknowledging is worded and when it is to be used. To use acknowledging only when the teacher understands and *agrees*, but to do something else when the teacher understands and *disagrees*, is a serious misunderstanding of the purpose and function of this teaching behaviour. Acknowledging is intended to be a nonjudgmental way of saying "I understand."

Teacher Silence

Teacher silence is used to communicate to students through nonverbal means that it is their responsibility to initiate and carry on the discussion. Teacher silence is used only in response to student silence. It protects the students' right and responsibility to make their own decisions about the topic being discussed.

Understanding the Body and How It Functions

The material in this section deals with the knowledge and understanding that elementary school students should develop. The areas presented are rudimentary and illustrate examples of knowledge, concepts, and experiences children must understand to develop a value set that enhances personal wellness. This unit should focus on establishing a foundation for developing proper health attitudes for adolescent and adult life.

Students must understand two major categories of wellness concepts. The first is basic knowledge of how the body functions and how it can be maintained through proper care and activity. The second category centres on roadblocks that stand in the path of wellness. Some of these are stress, physical inactivity, less healthy nutrition, obesity, substance abuse, and personal safety problems. Basic concepts and suggested learning activities are listed for each area.

The Skeletal System

The skeletal system (see Figure 13.2) is the framework of the body and consists of 208 separate bones. The bones act as a system of levers and are linked together by connections (*joints*) that allow movement. The bones are held together at the joints by ligaments and muscles. Ligaments are tough and incapable of stretching. They do not contract the way muscles do and are therefore subject to injury when the bones are moved beyond their natural range.

Joints that are freely movable are called *synovial joints*. Synovial fluid is secreted to lubricate the joint and reduce

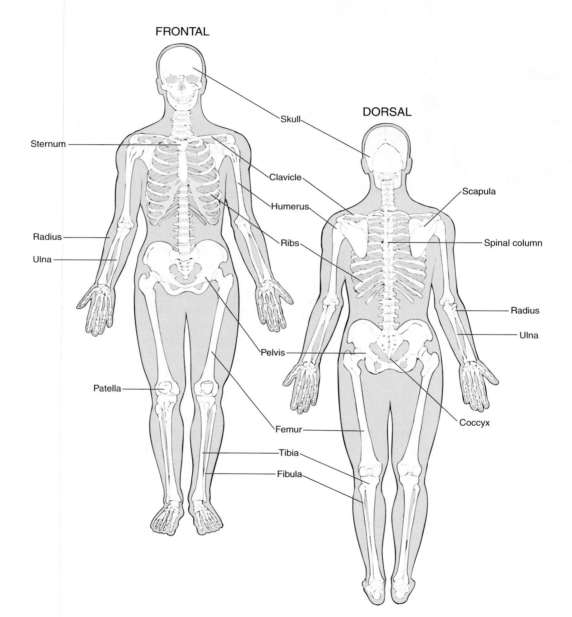

Figure 13.2

Skeletal system.

friction. A thin layer of cartilage also reduces friction at the ends of the bones. A disk, or meniscus, forms a pad between many of the weight-bearing joints for the purpose of absorbing shock. When a cartilage is damaged, joint dysfunction and pain can occur.

Muscular activity increases the weight-bearing stresses on bones. The bones respond to the added stress by increasing in mineral content and density, increasing in diameter, and reorganizing internal elements to cause an increase in bone strength. The bones serve as a mineral reserve for the body and can become deformed as a result of dietary deficiencies.

The bones and joints establish levers, with muscles acting as the force. Three types of levers are identified and classified by the arrangement of the fulcrum, force, and resistance.

The forearm is an example of a first-class lever when it is extended at the elbow joint (fulcrum) by the triceps muscle (see Figure 13.3A). A second-class lever exists where the gastrocnemius raises the weight of the body to the toes (see Figure 13.3B). Examples of third-class lever actions are the movement of the biceps muscle to flex the forearm at the elbow joint (see Figure 13.3C), the sideward movement of the upper arm at the shoulder joint by the deltoid muscle, and the flexion of the lower leg at the knee joint by the hamstring muscles.

Requisite Knowledge

1. The skeletal system consists of 208 bones and determines the external appearance of the body.

2. Joints are places where two or more bones are fastened together to make a movable connection.

3. Bones are held together by ligaments and muscle tissue. The stronger the muscles surrounding the joint, the more resistant the joint is to injury.

4. Good posture results when the bones are in proper alignment. Alignment depends on the muscular system. When antigravity muscles are weak, greater stress is put on the joints, and poor posture results.

5. The bones and joints establish levers with muscles serving as the force.

6. The attachment of the muscle to the bone determines the mechanical advantage that can be gained at the joint. Generally, the farther from the joint the muscle attaches, the greater the force that can be generated.

7. The body has three types of levers. These are classified by the arrangement of the fulcrum, force, and resistance.

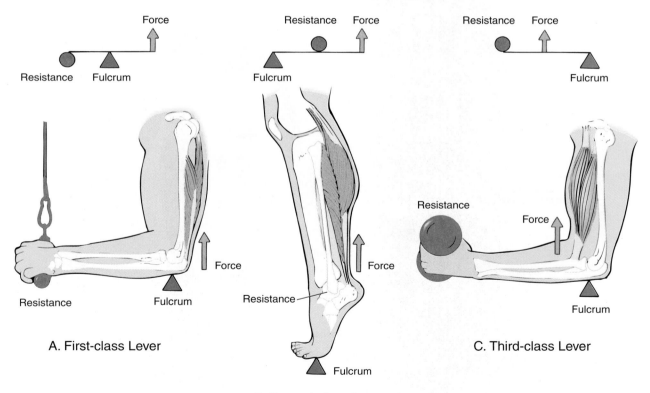

A. First-class Lever

B. Second-class Lever

C. Third-class Lever

Figure 13.3

Types of levers in human joints.

Suggested Learning Experiences

1. Identify and locate major bones significant in body movement. The following are suggested:

   a. head–skull

   b. arm–shoulder girdle–radius, ulna, ribs, humerus, scapula (shoulder blade), clavicle (collarbone)

   c. chest–sternum (breastbone), ribs

   d. back–pelvis–spinal column, pelvis, coccyx

   e. thigh–leg–femur, tibia, fibula, patella (kneecap)

2. Identify the types of movement possible at selected joints. Study the neck, shoulder, elbow, wrist, spinal column, hip, knee, and ankle joints.

3. Catalogue the types of levers found in the body. Illustrate the fulcrum, force, and resistance points.

4. Obtain animal bones from a grocery store and analyze their various components. Cartilage, muscle attachments, ligaments, and bone structure can be studied in this way.

5. Discuss how levers in the body generate force for throwing, striking, and kicking.

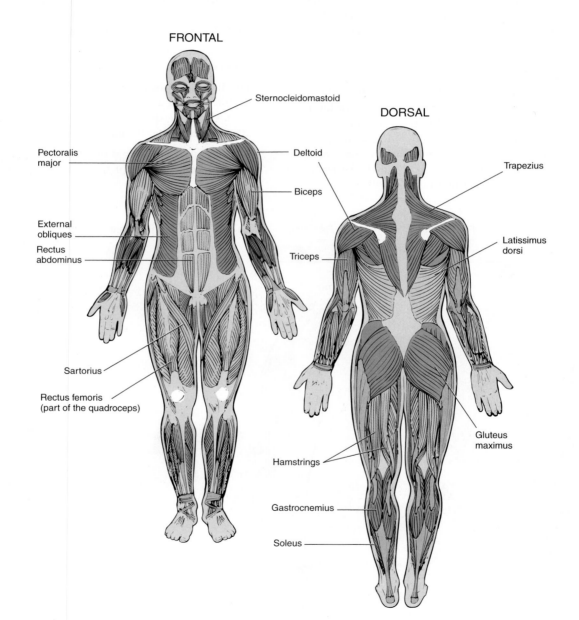

Figure 13.4

Muscular system.

The Muscular System

Muscles (see Figure 13.4) apply force to the bones to create movement. Muscles create movement always through contraction, never by pushing. When one set of muscles contracts, another set that pulls in the opposite direction relaxes. This set is the *antagonistic muscle group.*

People are born with two distinct types of muscle fibre. These are often called slow-twitch and fast-twitch fibres. Slow-twitch fibres respond well to aerobic activities, whereas fast-twitch fibres are suited to anaerobic activities. This is one of the reasons people perform differently in different physical activities. For example, those born with a high percentage of slow-twitch fibres would be suited to distance running but might do poorly in sprint races.

Strength can be increased when muscles are overloaded. Overload occurs when a person does more than a normal amount of work. In young people, strength can be increased without a change in the muscle size. Exercises should overload as many muscle groups as possible to ensure total body development. Strength is an important factor in the development of motor skills. See Chapter 2 for further discussion of muscle development in children.

Flexibility is the range of motion possible at a given joint. Exercises should apply resistance through the full range of motion to maintain flexibility. Extensor and flexor muscle groups are antagonists to each other, and both groups should be exercised equally.

Requisite Knowledge

1. Muscles can pull and shorten (contract); they never push.
2. Flexors cause a decrease in joint angle, and extensors cause an increase. There should be a balance of development between these antagonistic muscle groups.
3. The fixed portion of a muscle (origin) usually has muscle fibres attached directly to the bone or may be attached by a tendon to the bone. The moving portion of the muscle forms a tendon, which attaches to a bone (insertion).
4. Overload with proper progression is necessary for muscle development. Muscles become strong in both boys and girls through exercise. After puberty, boys' muscles will increase in size owing to the male hormone testosterone. Girls' muscles do not show the same degree of increase.
5. Muscles are important for proper posture. Good muscle tone makes good posture comfortable and puts a minimum amount of strain on the joints.
6. Different types of training are necessary for aerobic and anaerobic activity.
7. Muscles are composed of many small fibres. When these fibres contract, they do so according to the all-or-none principle—that is, if they contract, they contract completely. Differences in the contraction strength of a muscle are a function of the percentage of muscle fibres recruited and asked to contract.
8. When muscles are fatigued, the muscle fibres will no longer contract.

Suggested Learning Experiences

1. Identify major muscles or muscle groups and their functions at the joint. Muscle groups suggested for elaboration are the following:
   a. head–neck–sternocleidomastoids
   b. arm–shoulder girdle–biceps, triceps, pectorals, deltoid, latissimus dorsi, trapezius
   c. body–abdominals (rectus abdominis and the obliques)
   d. thigh–leg–gluteus, hamstrings, rectus femoris (the quadriceps), gastrocnemius, soleus, sartorius
2. Learn the significance of the suffix "–ceps" in biceps, triceps, and quadriceps. The suffix refers to the points of origin (heads). The biceps has two points of origin (heads), the triceps has three, and the quadriceps has four.
3. The Achilles and patellar tendons should be identified. How the Achilles tendon got its name makes an interesting story. Achilles' mother dipped the infant Achilles in the River Styx to make him immune from arrows. Unfortunately, she held him by the heel cord, thus preventing that area from coming into contact with the magic water. Achilles was later killed by an arrow that hit his one vulnerable spot, hence the name Achilles tendon.
4. The sartorius muscle is called the tailor's muscle because years ago, tailors sat cross-legged while sewing, thus causing the muscle to shorten. The tailors then had trouble making ordinary leg movements because of the shortened muscle.
5. Know approximately where each muscle originates and how it causes movement at the joint by attaching to a particular bone or bones. Recognize the muscles being developed by various exercises.
6. Study animal muscle under a microscope. Identify various parts of the muscle.
7. Involve students in a project featuring a "Muscle of the Month." The classroom teacher can cooperate by presenting basic facts about the muscle in classroom work. The teacher can post drawings showing the anatomy of the muscle (origin, insertion, and location) (see Figure 13.5) and post these in the gymnasium and classroom.

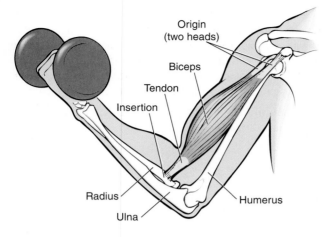

Figure 13.5

Anatomy of a muscle.

8. Discuss how antagonistic muscle groups contract and relax alternately to cause movement. Identify which muscles are relaxed and which are contracting when movement occurs.

The Cardiorespiratory System

The cardiorespiratory system consists of the heart, lungs, arteries, capillaries, and veins. The heart is a muscular organ that pumps blood through the circulatory system—arteries, capillaries, and veins, in that order. The heart has its own blood vessels—the coronary arteries—that nourish it to keep it alive, for the heart draws no nourishment from the blood going through the chambers as it pumps. The blood supply to the heart is critical, and a decreased flow can damage the heart muscle. Decreased flow may result from a build-up of fatty deposits or from a blockage, either of which can be serious enough to be regarded as heart disease.

The heart has two chambers, the right and left ventricles (see Figure 13.6). The left side of the heart pumps blood carrying nutrients and oxygen to the body through the arteries to the capillaries, where the nutrients and oxygen are exchanged for waste products and carbon dioxide. The waste-carrying blood is returned through the veins to the right side of the heart, from which the blood is routed through the lungs to discharge the carbon dioxide and pick up fresh oxygen. This oxygen-renewed blood returns to the left side of the heart to complete the circuit. Other waste products are discharged through the kidneys.

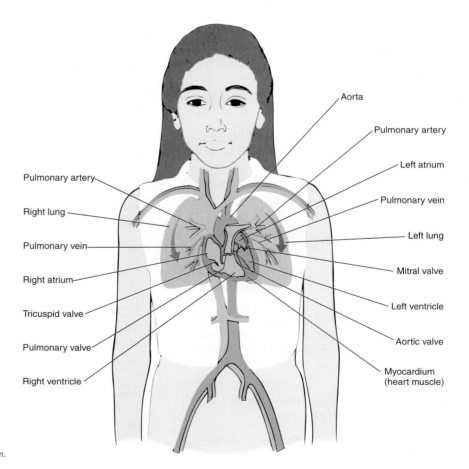

Figure 13.6

Structure of the heart.

Source: The American Heart Association.

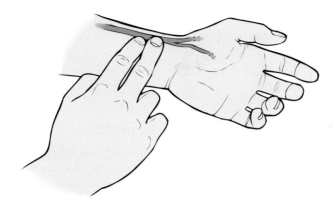

Figure 13.7

Taking the pulse at the wrist.

Each time the heart beats, it pumps both chambers. The beat is called the *pulse,* and its impact travels through the body. The pulse is measured in number of beats per minute called the *heart rate*: a heart rate of 75 means that the heart is beating 75 times each minute. The output of the heart is determined by the pulse rate and by the *stroke volume,* the amount of blood discharged by each beat.

The pulse is measured by placing the two middle fingers of the right hand on the thumb side of the subject's wrist (see Figure 13.7) while the subject is seated. Using the carotid artery (along the neck) is also effective (see Figure 13.9). Heart rate for baseline data should be taken two or three times to make sure that it is accurate. The heart rate is usually taken for 10 seconds and converted to a per-minute rate by using the appropriate multiplier.

The respiratory system includes the entryways (nose and mouth), the trachea (windpipe), the primary bronchi, and the lungs. Figure 13.8 shows components of the system. Breathing consists of inhaling and exhaling air. Air contains 21% oxygen, which is necessary for life. Inspiration is assisted by muscular contraction, and expiration is accomplished by relaxing the muscles. Inspiration occurs when the intercostal muscles and diaphragm contract. This enlarges the chest cavity, and expansion of the lungs causes air to flow in as a result of reduced air pressure. When the muscles are relaxed, the size of the chest cavity is reduced, the pressure on the lungs is increased, and air flows from the lungs. Air also can be expelled forcibly.

The primary function of the lungs is to provide oxygen, carried by the bloodstream, to the cells on demand. The amount of oxygen needed will vary depending on activity level. When an individual exercises strenuously, the

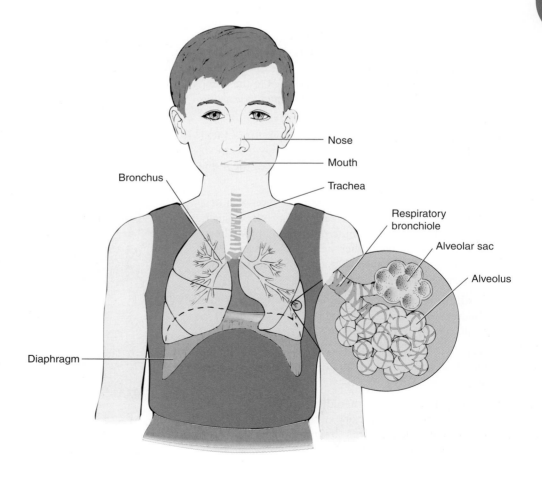

Figure 13.8

Components of the respiratory system.

rate of respiration increases to bring more oxygen to the tissues. If the amount of oxygen carried to the cells is adequate to maintain the level of activity, the activity is termed *aerobic* (endurance) exercise. Examples are walking, jogging, and bicycling for distance. If, because of high-intensity activity such as sprinting or climbing stairs, not enough oxygen can be brought to the cells, the body continues to operate for a short time without oxygen. This results in an oxygen debt, which must be repaid later. In this case, the activity is termed *anaerobic* exercise.

After exercise, the respiratory rate gradually returns to normal. The recovery rate is faster if the oxygen debt built up during exercise was a small one. An individual has recovered from an oxygen debt when blood pressure, heart rate, and respiration rate have returned to pre-exercise levels.

Requisite Knowledge

1. The heart is a muscular organ, and its development and maintenance are a function of the demands placed on it through exercise.

2. The heart beats faster when a person exercises.

3. An important factor in establishing cardiorespiratory conditioning is regular exercise. Regular exercise produces a training effect that results in a decreased resting heart rate and an increased stroke volume (the amount of blood the heart pumps each time it beats) due to hypertrophy of the heart muscle. If the training effect is to occur, the heart rate must be elevated to the training zone for 10 to 20 minutes. (See suggested learning experience number 6, following.)

4. Through exercise and training, the respiratory system is able to move more oxygen into the body because of an increase in the strength and endurance of the respiratory muscles.

5. The heart rate varies depending on the level of fitness and other variables. Heart rate among girls usually averages 10 beats per minute more than among boys. As children grow older, their heart rate decreases. Fear, excitement, or a change in body position also affects the resting heart rate.

6. Cardiorespiratory conditioning is important for children. Many circulatory and respiratory disorders in adults have a childhood origin.

7. Increased levels of cholesterol and other fats in the blood cause build-up of fatty deposits in the coronary arteries.

8. Some factors (such as heredity, sex, race, and age) affect the cardiorespiratory system, but are impossible to control. Risk can be minimized, however, by controlling other factors such as smoking, body weight, diet, blood pressure level, and amount of regular exercise.

9. The immediate effects of exercise are to increase the rate of breathing and the volume of air brought into the lungs.

Suggested Learning Experiences

1. Demonstrate and compare pulse rate in different body positions. Take the baseline heart rate first (two or three times) with the subject in a sitting position. Take the pulse rate with the subject standing and lying down (see Figure 13.9).

2. Using a single subject, show the relationship between exercise and heart action. Take the resting heart rate and record it on the chalkboard. Have the subject run in place for 1 minute. Take the heart rate immediately for 10 seconds and record it. Continue taking the pulse at five 2-minute intervals to demonstrate recovery rate. (The heart rate is approximately doubled after the stipulated exercise.) Discuss why heart rate increases with exercise and how the heart is strengthened through regular exercise.

3. To show how excess weight affects an individual, use two subjects of the same sex who are similar in build. Take the baseline heart rate for each and record it. Give one subject 5 kg in added weight (use two 2.5-kg weights) and have both subjects travel back and forth 10 times across the width of the gym. Immediately take the heart rates and record them. Compare the rates of the two subjects.

4. Compare pulse rate changes after different kinds of exercise—walking, running, rope jumping, and rope climbing. Standardize the exercise time factor at 1 or 2 minutes.

Figure 13.9

Students checking their pulse rate.

5. Calculate the heartbeat range that should be maintained to achieve the training effect and to ensure that the individual is not under- or over-exercising. To do this, first determine the estimated maximum heart rate by taking 220 minus the student's age, and then multiply the difference by 60% and by 80%. An example for a child of age 10 follows:

220 minus 10 = 210

60% of 210 = 126

80% of 210 = 168

The heart rate range for this student to maintain while exercising is 126 to 168. The pulse rate should be checked during exercise to see whether the training effect is occurring. Charts showing exercising heart rate ranges should be placed on bulletin boards in the gymnasium so that students can quickly translate the results.

6. Compare respiration rates before and after exercise.

7. Compare the volume of air moved before and after strenuous activity. Large plastic garbage bags can be used to collect expired air prior to exercise. After 2 minutes of exercise, expired air can be gathered in another bag. Compare the volume of air collected in the two bags.

8. Allow youngsters to listen to their heartbeats with a stethoscope. Have them exercise for a minute or two and listen to their heartbeats again.

Health-related Physical Fitness

Physical fitness is defined as the ability to carry out daily tasks with vigor and alertness, without undue fatigue, and with ample energy to enjoy leisure pursuits and to meet unforeseen emergencies. Physical fitness can best be understood in terms of its components, each of which has a distinctive feature and contributes an essential element to the individual. The most important measurable components of physical fitness are muscular strength and endurance, cardiovascular endurance, flexibility, and body composition. (See Chapter 12 for additional information on health-related physical fitness.)

Strength refers to the ability of a muscle or muscle group to exert force. To develop strength, the child's learning experiences should include a regular program of intense activity involving all large-muscle groups. Strength is necessary in skill performance. *Muscular endurance* is the ability of the muscles to perform a desired activity without excessive fatigue. It is related to strength in that a stronger person is able to keep up muscular effort longer than a weaker person.

Cardiovascular endurance refers to the ability to maintain total body activity for extended periods of time. People with adequate levels of cardiorespiratory fitness can postpone fatigue and can continue performing activities requiring muscular effort. Cardiovascular endurance is based on the movement of oxygen to the muscles at the cellular level so that a constant source of energy is available. Whereas cardiorespiratory endurance is related to general movement (such as walking or running), muscular endurance is related to specific activity (push-ups, throwing, or jumping).

Flexibility is a person's range of movement at the joints. A particularly flexible individual can stretch farther, touch the toes more easily, and bend farther than others. Flexibility allows freedom of movement and the ready adjustment of the body to various movements.

Body composition is the proportion of body fat to lean body mass. Attaining physical fitness is difficult when an individual's body composition contains a high amount of body fat. An understanding of caloric intake and expenditure is important for weight control. It is possible to eat enough to gain weight regardless of the amount of exercise performed.

Requisite Knowledge

1. Physical fitness is acquired only through muscular effort. Activity should be intense, regular, and varied enough to develop all components of physical fitness.

2. The maintenance of physical fitness must be ongoing; gains in fitness levels can be lost in a span of six to eight weeks. Fitness is a lifelong pursuit.

3. Isotonic muscular contractions are the basis of muscular effort, with isometric contractions an important auxiliary.

4. To provide body symmetry, exercises for muscle development should involve similar workloads for extensor and flexor muscle groups. (Flexor muscles decrease the angle of a joint, and extensor muscles cause the return from flexion.)

5. To maintain fitness, a person must have a regular exercise program involving a relatively constant workload. To raise the level of fitness, the workload must be increased progressively.

6. Cardiorespiratory endurance is enhanced by moderate and continued activity, such as jogging, running, or swimming laps, over relatively long periods of time.

7. Exercise, to be beneficial, must be done properly. Certain exercises should be avoided (see Chapter 12).

8. Flexibility activities should feature static stretching. Muscles are stretched slowly and then held in the maximum position for 15 to 30 seconds.

9. Flexibility is specific to a given joint. Students should learn exercises that stretch all joints.

10. Muscles must be strong enough to accomplish tasks and to keep the joints in line for good posture.

Suggested Learning Experiences

1. Acquire a cardboard or wooden box that's about 20 cm high with a flat top. Sit on the floor with legs together and flat on the floor so that the soles are placed against the box side. Begin with arms placed behind the back and palms on the floor to support the body in an erect sitting position. Bring both arms forward slowly and bend the body forward, without bouncing, to touch the toes, the box, or beyond the edge of the box. Measure how many centimetres the student can reach beyond the edge of the box.

2. Discuss what being physically fit means. If a person looks good, is she fit? If a person is active on a regular basis, is he fit? If a person does well on a fitness test, is she fit?

3. Allow students to self-test themselves on a fitness test. Use criterion-referenced health standards and discuss how a minimum level of fitness is related to good health.

4. Have students record their activity levels during a five-day period. Discuss how the volume of activity will enhance or detract from their fitness levels. Compare the amount of activity they participated in to the amount of television they watched.

5. Categorize activities according to their contribution to various components of fitness. Discuss how some activities are excellent for cardiovascular fitness and body composition, some for flexibility, and some for muscular strength and endurance.

6. Discuss the acronym FIT and how it relates to fitness development. Frequency, Intensity, and Time determine fitness workloads. Which of these factors is most important?

Physical fitness concepts and fitness activities are discussed further in Chapter 12.

Understanding Lifestyle Alternatives

The following areas are important for students to understand. Wellness involves knowing which activities to avoid as well as which to do.

The major areas discussed in this section are nutrition and healthy body weight; stress and relaxation; substance abuse; and personal safety. All are areas in which behaviour can be modified to enhance the quality of life. Students' decisions in these areas may affect dramatically how they live and, sometimes, whether they will live.

Nutrition, Physical Activity, and Healthy Body Weight

Proper nutrition is necessary if one is to obtain an optimum level of physical performance from the body. An area of emphasis in the physical education program should be balanced diet and healthy body weight. Students must understand the reasons for maintaining a balanced diet. Students should understand how caloric intake and physical activity work together to establish and maintain a healthy body weight.

Students will become familiar with the elements of a balanced diet. A balanced diet draws from each of the basic food groups. *Eating Well with Canada's Food Guide*, recently updated by Health Canada (2007), shows the four basic food groups and provides recommendations for daily servings from each group. Figure 13.10 displays recommended daily

	Children			Teens		Adults			
	2–3	4–8	9–13	14–18 years		19–50 years		51+ years	
	Girls and Boys			Females	Males	Females	Male	Females	Males
Vegetables & Fruit	4	5	6	7	8	7–8	8–10	7	7
Grain Products	3	4	6	6	7	6–7	8	6	7
Milk & Alternatives	2	2	3–4	3–4	3–4	2	2	3	3
Meat & Alternatives	1	1	1–2	2	3	2	3	2	3
The eating pattern also includes a small amount (30–45ml or about 2 to 3 tablespoons) of unsaturated fat each day.									

Figure 13.10

Recommended Number of Food Guide Servings Per Day.

Source: Health Canada. (2007). *Eating well with Canada's food guide*. Ottawa, ON: Author.

servings for males and females in different age ranges. For additional information included in *Canada's Food Guide* see **www.healthcanada.gc.ca/foodguide**.

Encourage students to moderate their consumption of foods high in cholesterol and fat. Some cholesterol and fat are necessary for proper body function. When too much fat is ingested, however, cholesterol and triglyceride levels in the blood plasma increase. Many studies have shown a relationship between high cholesterol and triglyceride levels and coronary heart disease. (A blood test is needed to determine blood lipid levels.)

Children should be aware of which foods are high in fat and cholesterol. The following are examples of foods high in cholesterol: eggs, cheese, cream, most beef and pork cuts, chocolate milk, shrimp, chocolate candy, cake and cookies, and ice cream.

Approximately 26% of Canadian youngsters are overweight, meaning that their body weight is over the accepted limits for their age, sex, and body build. The majority of cases of obesity occur as a consequence of inactivity or overeating, or both. It is therefore important to learn about the caloric content of foods (as well as their nutritional value) in order to monitor the amount of calories ingested. Learning the amount of calories burned by different physical activities is also important. Students must realize early that when caloric intake exceeds caloric expenditure, fat is stored. Experts agree that obese children do not in general consume more calories than children of normal weight. Rather, they exercise less.

Obesity is a roadblock to wellness. Excessive body fat makes the heart work much harder, and in adulthood increases the chance of high blood pressure and jeopardizes recovery from a heart attack. In youngsters, it has a detrimental effect on self-image, since overweight students find it more difficult than students of normal weight to perform physical tasks.

Requisite Knowledge

1. The diet should be balanced and contain foods from each of the recommended groups. This ensures that the body is receiving essential nutrients.

2. Caloric expenditure (exercise) and intake (eating) must balance if weight is to be maintained. A weight-reduction program should include a reduction in caloric intake and an increase in daily exercise.

3. Activities vary in the energy they require. Consider individual needs when selecting exercise activities.

4. Junk foods add little, if any, nutritional value to the diet and usually are high in calories.

5. Excessive weight makes it difficult to perform physical tasks. This results in less success and in less motivation to be active, thus increasing the tendency toward obesity.

6. Obesity increases the risk of heart disease and related health problems. It is a roadblock to wellness and may decrease the longevity of the individual.

Suggested Learning Experiences

1. Post a list of activities and their energy demands on the bulletin board. Discuss the importance of regular activity.

2. Analyze individual physical activity levels. For one week, record the exercise time and types of activities participated in.

3. Maintain a food diary. Record all the food ingested daily and the amount of calories represented. Compare the amount of calories ingested with the amount of calories expended.

4. On the bulletin board, post a chart that compares the caloric content of junk foods with that of healthier alternatives.

5. Discuss the fat content of various foods. Examine how foods can be modified to reduce the fat content; for example, milk can be reduced to 2%, 1%, and skim. Discuss the benefits of drinking low-fat milk.

6. Discuss the importance of fibre in the diet. Identify foods that are high in fibre content.

7. Identify what happens to people when they diet. Discuss the balance of caloric intake versus caloric expenditure.

Stress and Relaxation

Stress can be defined as a substantial imbalance between environmental demands and the individual's response capability. In situations that induce stress, the failure to meet the environmental demands usually has important consequences. For example, children can feel pressured by their own desires to be accepted by peers, and by their desires to meet teacher and parent expectations. Realistic, challenging, and attainable goals tend to eliminate many frustrating situations that could become stressful. Stress management is learning how to respond to situations that might cause tension. The emphasis in this discussion is on what children should know about stress and what techniques they can adopt to prevent stressful situations.

First, children need to recognize that individuals react differently to stressful situations. Some learn to handle stress productively, so that it actually increases their effectiveness. Some may not sense that a situation is stressful and so may remain calm through a crisis. How an individual perceives a situation usually determines *whether* it is stressful. Teachers can aid youngsters in achieving a productive and healthy outlook on life that will minimize stress.

A second area of concern deals with the effects of stress on the body. Psychologically, stress can take the form of excitement, fear, or anger. Physical changes are also apparent when a person is under stress. The nervous system may respond to the stress through increased heart rate, increased blood pressure, increased respiration rate, increased muscle tension throughout the body, or decreased digestion (often accompanied by queasiness).

Unrelieved stress has detrimental effects on the body. It increases the risk of heart disease and can lead to insomnia and hypertension. Indigestion is common in stressed individuals, as is constipation. Backaches and general body aches often originate from stress.

Studies have shown that moderate physical activity decreases tension. Some experts believe that exercise applies stress to the body in a systematic fashion and thus prepares the body to deal with other stressful situations. One goal of teachers should be to provide students with productive and meaningful ways to relieve tension.

Relaxation is a skill that can be learned. Motor learning promotes patterned movement and inhibits unnecessary muscles from interfering. This results in an ability to relax muscles not specifically required for task performance. Children should learn that relaxation is necessary to achieve top performance in demanding skills, particularly those involving accuracy. A basketball player takes a deep breath, then exhales, to relax before shooting a free throw. Reduction of tension results in conservation of energy and allows the task to be done efficiently and smoothly. Relaxation activities are an important part of a balanced approach to a physical activity program. Taking a few minutes to relax at the end of the lesson can help students return to the classroom in a less stimulated state (see Figure 13.11).

The first step in learning to relax is to recognize stress and tension. At times, children can be given short periods of complete relaxation, generally in a supine position on the floor.

Figure 13.11

Practising relaxation activities.

Requisite Knowledge

1. Stress affects all individuals to some degree. A certain amount of stress is necessary to stimulate performance.

2. The amount of stress that individuals experience depends on how they perceive the situation. Healthy perceptions are needed to cope effectively with stress.

3. When people have difficulty dealing with stress through productive means, they often attempt to relieve it through unhealthy and potentially dangerous means, such as alcohol, tobacco, and drug use, or other inappropriate behaviours.

4. Stress causes changes in body functions. An awareness of these changes is necessary so that students will know when they are under the influence of stress.

5. Stress may increase susceptibility to diseases and can cause psychosomatic illnesses.

6. Exercise is an excellent way to relieve stress and tension.

7. The body works more efficiently if all muscles unrelated to a given task are relaxed.

8. Relaxation is important in skills demanding concentration and accuracy.

9. Deep breathing is a natural relaxant. Teach students to take several deep breaths if they feel tense.

Suggested Learning Experiences

1. Select a particular movement. Identify the muscles necessary for the movement and those that should be relaxed.

2. Hold an isometric contraction at the elbow joint. With the other hand, feel the contraction in the biceps and triceps. Do the same with other joints and muscles.

3. Jacobson popularized the technique of progressive relaxation (Bernstein & Borkovec, 1973). In this technique, a muscle or muscle group is first tensed and then relaxed slowly and smoothly. All the major parts of the body are relaxed as one works down from the head to the toes. An example is: "Frown and squinch up your face, making many wrinkles, and then slowly relax your face and smooth it out." Each time you relax a muscle group, exhale a big breath of air.

4. While standing, slowly take a deep breath and expel the air as completely as possible, while simultaneously dropping the head and collapsing the chest.

5. Try shooting a free throw while holding your breath. Inhale and exhale to relax, and then shoot the free throw. Discuss the difference.

6. Discuss the role of perception in tension-building situations. How does it feel to be scared?

7. Discuss situations in physical education class that build stress: for example, failing in front of others, not being selected for a team, and being laughed at or yelled at for poor performance.

8. Identify physical activities that seem to relieve stress. Discuss the relationship between involvement in activity and the reduction of stress.

9. Identify and discuss unproductive attempts to relieve stress, such as smoking, drinking, and taking drugs.

Substance Abuse

To make wise decisions regarding abused substances, children need to be aware of the impact these substances can have on their lives. The elementary school years are an opportune time to discuss substance abuse, as many youngsters will soon be making decisions related to their use.

Alcohol

Alcohol has both short-term and long-term effects. The short-term effects vary as a result of the depressant effect that alcohol has on the central nervous system. People become relaxed, aggressive, and active in differing degrees. Ultimately, if a great deal of alcohol is ingested, lack of coordination and confusion occur.

Some long-term effects of excessive alcohol consumption may be liver damage, heart disease, and malnutrition. The greatest concern about long-term drinking is the possibility of the person becoming an alcoholic. The disease of alcoholism has the following components: the loss of control of alcohol intake, the presence of functional or structural damage (psychological and physical), and the need to have alcohol to maintain an acceptable level of everyday functioning.

Youngsters may drink for any of several reasons—curiosity, peer pressure, to be like adults and appear more mature, to rebel against the adult world, and because their role models or admired adults drink. Youngsters usually are ambivalent about alcohol: they know its detrimental effects, yet they see many of their friends and role models using it. The problem is difficult, and students need an understanding of what constitutes moderate use.

Tobacco

A long-term tobacco habit significantly increases the possibility of heart attack, stroke, and cancer. Chronic bronchitis and emphysema are diseases prevalent among smokers. Statistics Canada reported that the average age of beginning smokers in Canada is 12 years, while 40% start before they are 14 and 90% before they are 18.

Children need to understand the impact of smoking on a healthy body. Teachers should discuss the reasons that people choose to smoke or not smoke. In the end, however, as with alcohol, youngsters must make a meaningful and personal choice. Youngsters who choose to smoke do so for reasons similar to those related to drinking.

Drug Abuse

The use of marijuana, cocaine, and other drugs should be discussed with students in a nonthreatening setting. Excellent materials are available for teachers to help them give meaningful instruction.

Requisite Knowledge

1. The earlier one begins to smoke, the greater the risk to functional health.

2. Smoking is done for psychological reasons and makes no contribution to physical development.

3. People choose to smoke and drink for reasons of curiosity, status, and peer pressure.

4. Choosing a lifestyle different from the majority of one's friends takes courage.

5. When decisions about substance use are based on a lack of knowledge, they often are poor decisions. Wise and meaningful decisions can be made only after all alternatives and consequences are understood.

6. Substance abuse is often a misguided attempt to cope with problems and stress. Exercise and activity are more productive and healthy ways of coping.

7. The use of alcohol, tobacco, and drugs prevents people from enjoying certain activities.

Suggested Learning Experiences

1. Identify some of the reasons that people choose or choose not to become involved in substance abuse.

2. Discuss the reasons that it is important to be your own person and to make meaningful personal decisions.

3. Develop a bulletin board listing the ways in which the tobacco and alcohol industries attempt to get people to use their products. Reserve a section for advertising that tries to convince people to abstain or to use moderation.

4. Discuss how individuals relieve stress in an attempt to feel good. Discuss productive stress relief activities, such as recreational pursuits, hobbies, and sports.

5. Discuss how peer groups can influence lifestyle choices. Discuss ways to make independent choices without losing friends.

Safety and First Aid

Safety and first aid are often included in the physical education program. Safety is an attitude and involves concern for one's welfare and health. An *accident* is an unplanned event or act that may result in injury or death. Often, accidents occur in situations that could have been prevented. The following are some of the most common causes of accidents: (a) lack of knowledge and understanding of risks; (b) lack of skill and competence to perform tasks safely, such as riding a bike or driving a car; (c) false sense of security, which leads people to think that accidents will happen only to others; (d) fatigue or illness, which affect physical and mental performance; (e) drugs and/or alcohol; and (f) strong emotional states such as anger, fear, or worry, which cause people to do things they might not do otherwise.

Traffic accidents are one area in which many deaths could be prevented. Wearing seat belts could reduce the number of deaths by half. A drinking driver increases the risk of having an accident 20 times over that for a non-drinking driver. Because students are often passengers in automobiles, an awareness of the possibility of serious injury should be a part of the wellness program.

Bicycles are another source of numerous accidents. Car drivers have difficulty seeing bicycles, and the resulting accidents frequently are serious. Students need to learn bicycle safety. Often, the physical education setting is the only place where this is discussed. Instruction in bicycling for safety and fitness is usually well received by elementary school children.

Requisite Knowledge

1. Accidents are unplanned events or acts that may result in injury. Most accidents could be avoided if people were adequately prepared and understood the necessary competencies and risks involved.

2. Wearing seat belts decreases the number of deaths caused by automobile accidents.

3. Bicycles often are not seen by car drivers. Bicycling safety classes can lower the number of bicycle accidents.

Suggested Learning Experiences

1. Discuss the causes of different types of accidents and how many accidents could be avoided.

2. Identify the types of accidents that happen to different age groups and why they happen.

3. Identify the role of alcohol and drugs in the incidence of accidents.

4. Develop a bulletin board that demonstrates how to care for shock victims. Practise carrying out the steps in a mock procedure.

5. Outline the steps to follow in case of a home fire. Discuss how many fires could be prevented.

6. Conduct a bicycle safety fair. Have students design bulletin boards and displays that explain and emphasize bicycle safety.

Active Healthy Schools Initiatives

In addition to direct curricular emphasis, Health Canada's Comprehensive School Health Model (CSH) promotes an integrated framework that combines four main elements of instruction, support services, social support, and a healthy school environment to promote wellness and healthy active living. See Chapter 1 for further information on the Comprehensive School Health Model.

In recent years, the concept of healthy schools has grown exponentially across Canada, with almost every province and/or territory implementing some type of healthy school initiative. In each case the promotion of physical activity plays a predominant role. For example, *Action Schools! BC* is a best-practice model that helps elementary schools promote healthy living, including integrating physical activity throughout the day (see **www.actionschoolsbc.ca**). The catch phrase of this initiative is to provide "*more* opportunities for *more* children to be *more* physically active *more* often (Action Schools! BC, 2005). This model identifies six action zones to help increase physical activity: the school environment; scheduled PE; classroom action; family and community; extra-curricular activities; and school spirit. Other provinces have implemented similar initiatives (e.g., *Everactive Schools*—Alberta; *Healthy Schools in Motion*—Manitoba; *In Motion Elementary Schools*—Saskatchewan; *Wellness-oriented Schools*—Quebec). The concept that is common to all these initiatives is the focus on integrating more physical activity and healthy eating practices throughout the school day. It is also clearly stated that these initiatives are meant to encompass and/or complement the physical education curriculum, not replace it.

Critical Thinking

1. Many provinces and/or individual school boards have implemented healthy food and drink policies in their schools. Discuss the purpose of these policies as they relate to helping students make healthy food choices.

2. Explore how your province or territory offers the health curriculum in the elementary grades. Are health topics integrated with physical education? Are health topics in a stand-alone curriculum guide?

Are health topics integrated across multiple subjects? Discuss the relative merits of each of the preceding alternatives.

References and Suggested Readings

Action Schools! BC. (2005). *Planning guide for schools and teachers—grades 4 to 7*. Vancouver, BC: 2010 Legacies Now.

American Academy of Pediatrics. (2003). Policy Statement: Prevention of pediatric overweight and obesity. *Pediatrics, 112*(2), 424–430.

Bernstein, D.A. & Borkovec, T.D. (1973). *Progressive relaxation training: A manual for the helping professions*. Champaign, IL: Research Press.

British Columbia Legislative Assembly Select Standing Committee on Health. (2006). *A strategy for combating childhood obesity and physical inactivity in British Columbia*. Victoria, BC: Author. Retrieved from www.leg.bc.ca/cmt/38thparl/session-2/health/media/Rel-29Nov2006-Health.htm.

Day, M., Strange, K., Fenton, J., Kopelow, B., Naylor, P.J., McKay, H. (2006). Addressing student obesity using a whole school model—Examples from Action Schools! BC. *PrincipalsOnline, 1*(3), 16–20. Retrieved from www.principalsonline.com.

Corbin, C.B. & Lindsey, R. (2007). *Fitness for life*. (5th ed.). Champaign, IL: Human Kinetics.

Hellsten, L. (2006). Student obesity in Canada. *PrincipalsOnline, 1*(3), 24–28. Retrieved from www.principalsonline.com.

Hayley, D. & Tiggemann, M. (2006). Body image concerns in young girls: The role of peers and media prior to adolescence. *Journal of Youth and Adolescence, 35*(2), 135–145.

Health Canada. (2007a). *Eating well with Canada's food guide*. Ottawa, ON: Author.

Health Canada. (2007b). Eating well with Canada's food guide—a resource for educators and communicators. Ottawa, ON: Author.

Hopper, C., Fisher, B., & Munoz, K. (1997a). *Health-related fitness for grades 1 and 2*. Champaign, IL: Human Kinetics.

Hopper, C., Fisher, B., & Munoz, K. (1997b). *Health-related fitness for grades 3 and 4*. Champaign, IL: Human Kinetics.

Hopper, C., Fisher, B., & Munoz, K. (1997c). *Health-related fitness for grades 5 and 6*. Champaign, IL: Human Kinetics.

Krishnamoorthy, J.S., Hart, C., & Jelalian, E. (2006). The epidemic of childhood obesity: Review of research & implications for public policy. *Social Policy Report, 19*(2), 3–19.

National Association for Sport and Physical Activity. (2005). *Physical best activity guide: Elementary level* (2nd ed.). Champaign, IL: Human Kinetics.

Pate, R., Davis, M., Robinson, T., Stone, E., McKenzie, T., & Young, J. (2006). Promoting physical activity in children and youth—a leadership role for schools. *Scientific Statement from the American Hearth Association, 114*, 1214–1224.

Sallis, J., McKenzie, T., Conway, T., Elder, J., Prochaska, J., Brown, M., Zive, M., Marshall, S., & Alcaraz, J. (2003). Environmental interventions for eating and physical activity—a randomized controlled trial in middle schools. *American Journal of Preventive Medicine, 24*(3), 209–217.

Stewart, S. (2006). The school food & nutrition policy project. *PrincipalsOnline, 1*(3), 29–31. Retrieved from www.principalsonline.com.

Vecchiarelli, S., Prelip, M., Slusser, W., Weightman, H., & Neumann, C. (2005). Using participatory action research to develop a school-based environment intervention to support healthy eating and physical activity. *American Journal of Health Education, 36*(1), 35–42.

 Weblinks

KidsHealth: www.kidshealth.org/kid/index.html

An excellent resource for kid-friendly discussion materials on topics such as dealing with feelings, staying healthy, common injuries, growing up, and child-specific health issues.

Canadian Association for School Health: www.safehealthyschools.org

Active and safe routes to school: www.goforgreen.ca

This program encourages students and parents to walk or cycle to school. Highlights the *Walking School Bus* initiative.

Breakfast for Learning: www.breakfastforlearning.ca

A national, not-for-profit organization that supports child nutrition programs in Canada. Includes a wide range of nutrition resources.

Safe Healthy Schools: www.safehealthyschools.org

A gateway to information on comprehensive schools health (CSH) and health-promoting schools (HPS). Provides wide ranges of educational resources, research reports, and assessment tools.

Provincial and Territorial Non-Mandated School-based Physical Activity and General Healthy Schools Initiatives

British Columbia

Action Schools! BC: www.actionschoolsbc.ca

BC Health-Promoting Schools Framework: www.bced.gov.bc.ca/health/welcome/htm

Alberta

Everactive Schools: www.everactive.org

Schools Come Alive Project: www.schoolscomealive.org

Saskatchewan

Saskatchewan in Motion Children's Strategy: www.saskatchewaninmotion.ca

Saskatchewan in Motion Youth Strategy: www.saskatchewaninmotion.ca

Manitoba

Healthy Schools in Motion: www.gov.mb.ca/ healthyschools

Ontario

Active Schools: www.ophea.net/activeschools.cfm

Living Schools: www.livingschools.ca/Ophea/ LivingSchool.ca/livingschoolinitiative.cfm

ACT NOW ... "the best you can be!": www.actnowprogram.com

Québec

Wellness-oriented School Program: www.mels.gouv.qc.ca/lancement/ecole_forme_sante/ index_en.asp

Kino-Québec: msss.gouv.qc.ca/cn/sujets/santepub/ physical_activity.php

New Brunswick

School Communities in Action: https://www.nbed.nb.ca/action/login.aspx?strLang=E

Nova Scotia

Active Kids, Healthy Kids: www.gov.ns.ca/ohp/ physicalActivity/activeKidsHealthyKids.asp

Prince Edward Island

Active Healthy School Communities Initiative: www.gov.pe.ca/educ/index.php3?number=75664

Newfoundland and Labrador

Living Healthy Schools: www.livinghealthyschools.com

Northwest Territories

Healthy Choices Framework: www.getactivenwt.ca

Yukon

Active Yukon Schools: www.rpay.org

Nunavut

Active Living Strategy: www.gov.nu.ca/cley/english/ activelive.html

SECTION 5

Fundamental Motor Skills

CHAPTER 14

Movement Concepts

Essential Components

I	**Organized around content standards**
II	**Student-centred and developmentally appropriate**
III	Physical activity and motor skill development form the core of the program
IV	Teaches management skills and self-discipline
V	Promotes inclusion of all students
VI	Focuses on process over product
VII	Promotes lifetime personal health and wellness
VIII	Teaches cooperation and responsibility and promotes sensitivity to diversity

Physical Education Standards

1	**Students are able to move competently using a variety of fundamental and specialized motor skills.**
2	Students can monitor and maintain a health-enhancing level of physical fitness.
3	**Students are able to apply movement concepts and basic mechanics of skill performance when learning and refining motor skills.**
4	Students comprehend the basic principles of wellness and are able to apply concepts that enable them to make meaningful decisions that positively impact their health and wellness.
5	**Students participate in a wide variety of physical activities and learn how to maintain a personalized active lifestyle.**
6	Students demonstrate empathy, understanding, and respect for the numerous differences exhibited by people in an activity setting.
7	Students exhibit responsible and self-directed behaviours that lead to positive social interactions in physical activity.

OUTCOMES

- Define how human movement concepts are classified into four major categories.

- Explain the purpose of movement concepts.

- Specify individual activities, partner activities, and group activities to develop movement concepts.

OVERVIEW

This chapter deals with movement concepts—the classification and vocabulary of movement. Students learn the classification of movement concepts, including body awareness, space awareness, qualities of movement, and relationships. Movement concepts form the foundation of all movement experiences.

*I*n the elementary school years, physical education places emphasis on developing skilled movers. It is important to learn fundamental skills in the early years because they are the building blocks for more sophisticated skills. There are two major aspects to becoming a skilled mover: learning the various skills and learning the concepts of movement. It is helpful to treat each area separately for the purpose of explanation. This chapter deals with movement concepts—the classification and vocabulary of movement. Chapter 15 covers motor skills and how to perform the skills correctly. The goals for a performer are to integrate both parts into successful performance. Figure 14.1 shows the components.

Classification of Human Movement Concepts

The movement concept categories of body awareness, space awareness, qualities of movement, and relationships offer structure and direction for planning movement experiences.

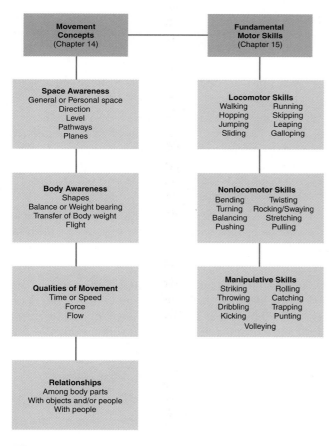

Figure 14.1

The components of movement concepts and fundamental motor skills.

As youngsters experience movement, they also learn the vocabulary of movement in order to increase their understanding of the diversity and openness of movement possibilities. As mentioned in Chapter 1, these concepts are part of a framework designed by Rudolf Laban for analyzing movement. Terminology associated with Laban's framework and movement education provides the basis for many provincial and territorial physical education curriculum guides. For specific examples see Newfoundland & Labrador Department of Education (2004) and Saskatchewan Learning (1999). His conceptual framework has been further developed as a guide for teaching and designing movement experiences for children (often referred to as the *movement education approach*). The teaching methodology features an exploratory and problem-solving approach.

Body Awareness

This category defines *what* the body can perform; the shapes it can make, how it can balance, and how weight is transferred to different body parts. Using these categories to develop challenges can add variety to movement.

1. *Shapes the body makes.* Many shapes can be formed with the body, such as long or short, wide or narrow, straight or twisted, stretched or curled, symmetrical or asymmetrical.

2. *Balance or weight bearing.* Balance demands that different parts of the body support the weight or receive the weight. Different numbers of body parts can be involved in the movements and used as body supports.

3. *Transfer of body weight.* Many skills—such as walking, leaping, and rolling—demand moving the body weight from one body part to another.

4. *Flight.* This category differs from transfer of body weight in that it is explosive movement and involves lifting the body weight from the floor or apparatus for an extended period of time. The amount of time off the floor distinguishes flight from transfer of weight. Examples include running, jumping onto a climbing rope, and hanging.

Space Awareness

Space awareness defines *where* the body can move. The focus is spatial qualities of movement related to moving in different directions and at different levels. The following elements determine how space can be modified and used in movement experiences.

1. *General or personal space.* Personal space is the limited area individual children can use around them, and in most cases is reserved for that individual only. General space is the total space that is used by all youngsters.

2. *Direction.* This refers to the desired route of movement, whether straight, zigzag, circular, curved, forward, backward, sideward, upward, or downward.

3. *Level.* This defines the relationship of the body to the floor or apparatus, whether low, high, or in between.

4. *Pathways.* This trait describes the path a movement takes through space. Examples are squares, diamonds, triangles, circles, and figure eights.

5. *Planes.* Planes are somewhat specific pathways defined as circular, vertical, and horizontal. The application of the concept of planes is usually restricted in elementary school to performing simple activities in a specified plane.

Qualities of Movement

These constructs classify *how* the body moves. The qualities of movement relate closely to mechanical principles used to move efficiently. In addition, they involve the following characteristics:

1. *Time or speed.* This quality deals with the speed and duration of movement. Children learn to move at varying speeds and to control speed throughout a variety of movements. They should learn the relationship between body shape and speed and be able to use body parts to generate speed. Using different speeds—moving to a constant rhythm, accelerating, and decelerating—may vary the time factor.

2. *Force.* Force is the effort or tension generated in movement. Force can be used effectively to aid in executing skills. Learning how to generate, absorb, and direct force is an important outcome. Force qualities may be explored by using words such as *light, heavy, strong, weak, rough,* and *gentle.*

3. *Flow.* This factor establishes how movements are purposefully sequenced to create continuity of movement. Most often this quality is discussed in terms of interrupted (bound) or sustained (free) flow. *Interrupted flow* stops at the end of a movement or part of a movement. *Sustained flow* involves smoothly linking different movements or parts of a movement.

Relationships

This element defines with whom or what the body relates. A *relationship* is defined as the position of the performer to the apparatus or other performers. Examples of relationships are near–far, above–below, over–under, in front–behind, on–off, and together–apart. When done with other people, relationships such as leading–following, mirroring–matching, unison–opposites can be explored.

Additionally, relationships can define the body parts of a single performer, such as arms together–apart or symmetrical–asymmetrical.

Exploring Movement Concepts

Four steps are suggested for designing instructional sequences and implementing movement themes. The instructional process can be keyed by the following directions: "Explore," "Discover and expand," "Analyze and select," and "Repeat and extend."

Step One: Set and Define the Problem

Define a problem for students so they know what to solve. The problem should include the following:

1. *What to do.* An action word directs the activity. Are children to move a certain way, go over and under, explore alternatives, or experiment with some nonlocomotor movement? Direct them to run, jump, or use a fundamental skill.

2. *Where to move.* What space is to be used—personal or general? What directional factors are to be employed—path or level?

3. *How to move.* What are the force factors (light–heavy)? What elements of time are involved (even–uneven, acceleration–deceleration, sudden–sustained)? What are the relationships (over–under–across, in front of–behind)? What body parts are involved for support? For locomotion?

4. *With whom or what to move.* With whom are children to work—by themselves, with a partner, or as a member of a group? Is there a choice involved? With what equipment or on what apparatus are they to perform?

When initiating movement patterns, the challenge can be stated like this: "Let's see you move across the floor, changing direction as you wish, using a quick movement with one foot and a slow movement with the other."

Step Two: Increase the Variety and Depth of Movement

It is effective to use techniques of observation and analysis so you can modify movement patterns when necessary. Encourage youngsters to enhance their movements and variety of responses. Variety can also be achieved by setting limitations and by asking youngsters to solve the problem in a different manner. Present problems in the form of questions or statements that elicit and encourage variety, depth, and extent of movement. Using contrasting terms can be an effective way to increase the depth and variety of movement. A number of examples follow.

Presenting a Problem

1. Show me how a _____ moves. (Show me how an alligator moves.)

2. Have you seen a _____? (Have you seen a kangaroo jump?)

3. What ways can you _____? (What ways can you hop over the jump rope?)

4. How would you _____? How can you _____? (How would you dribble a ball, changing hands frequently?)

5. See how many different ways you can _____. (See how many different ways you can hang from a ladder.)

6. What can you do with a _____? What kinds of things can you _____? (What can you do with a hoop?)

7. Can you portray a _____? (Can you portray an automobile with a flat tire?)

8. Discover different ways you can _____. (Discover different ways you can volley a ball against a wall.)

9. Can you _____? (Can you keep one foot up while you bounce the ball?)

10. Show me different ways to _____. (Show four different ways to move across the floor.)

Securing Variety or Setting Limitations

The following are useful for stimulating movement alternatives or imposing limitations:

1. Try it again another way. Try to _____. (Try to jump higher.)

2. See how far [many times, high, close, low] _____. (See how far you can reach with your arms.)

3. Find a way to _____ or find a new way to _____. (Find a new way to jump over the bench.)

4. Apply _____. (Apply a heavy movement to your run.)

5. How else can you _____? (How else can you roll your hoop?)

6. Make up a sequence _____. (Make up a sequence of previous movements, changing smoothly from one movement to the next.)

7. Now try to combine a _____ with _____. (Now try to combine a locomotor movement with your catching.)

8. Alternate _____ and _____. (Alternate walking and hopping.)

9. Repeat the last movement, but add _____. (Repeat the last movement, but add a body twist as you move.)

10. See if you can _____. (See if you can do the movement with a partner.)

11. Trace [draw] a _____ with _____. (Trace a circle with your hopping partner.)

12. Find another part of the body to _____. Find other ways to _____. (Find another part of the body to take the weight.)

13. Combine the _____ with _____ (Combine the hopping with a body movement.)

14. How do you think the _____ would change if _____? (How do you think the balance exercise we are doing would change if our eyes were closed?)

15. On signal, _____. (On signal, speed up your movements.)

Encouraging Variety Using Contrasting Terms

Another way to increase children's understanding of movement possibilities is to employ terms that stress contrasts. Contrasting terms provide a way to stimulate variety of movement. Instead of challenging children to move quickly, for example, ask the class to contrast a quick movement with a slow movement. The following list includes many common sets of contrasting terms that express relationships between movements.

Above–below, beneath, under

Across–around, under

Around clockwise–around counterclockwise

Before–after

Between–alongside of

Big–little, small

Close–far

Crooked–straight

Curved–flat, straight

Diagonal–straight

Fast–slow

Forward–back, backward

Front–back, behind

Graceful–awkward

Heavy–light

High–low

In–out

In front of–behind, in back of

Inside–outside

Into–out of

Large–small

Near–far

On–off

On top of–under, underneath

Over–under, through

Reach down–reach up

Right–left

Round–straight

Separate–together

Short–long, tall

Sideways–forward, backward

Smooth–rough

Standing upright–inverted

Sudden–sustained

Swift–slow

Tight–loose

Tiny–big, large

Top–bottom

To the right of–to the left of

Up–down

Upper–lower

Upside down–right side up

Upward–downward

Wide–narrow, thin

Zigzag–straight

Some of the terms may be grouped more logically in sets of three contrasts (such as forward–sideways–backward, up–down–in between, or over–under–through). Word meanings also can be emphasized according to rank or degree (as in near–nearer–nearest, or low–lower–lowest).

Step Three: Build Sequences and Combine Movement Patterns

In this step, children combine learned movements into a meaningful sequence. Emphasis is placed on transition (flow) from one movement pattern to another. Challenge youngsters to imagine how they can put movements together. Children can select movements to put in combination or you can specify some limitation on the number of combinations, the types of movements, or the order in

which they are sequenced. Achievement demonstrations stimulate effort because children enjoy showing what they have put together.

Step Four: Incorporate Cooperative Partner and Small-group Activity

Cooperative partner and small-group skills are important educational goals. Make problems realistic and allow opportunity for discussion and decision-making between partners. The following are examples of partner activities that can be developed:

1. One child is an obstacle, and the partner devises ways of going over, under, and around the positions the "obstacle" takes (see Figure 14.2). Additional challenge can involve having one partner hold a piece of equipment such as a wand or hoop to govern movements.

2. One partner supports the weight of the other, either wholly or in part (see Figure 14.3), or the two work together to form different kinds of figures or shapes.

3. One child does a movement, and the other copies or provides a contrasting movement.

4. One child moves, and the other attempts to shadow (do the same movements). Do it slowly with uninterrupted flow predominating.

5. One child moves, and the other provides correction or critique.

6. Partners develop a parallel sequence with both moving together and in the same way.

7. Partners begin 3 to 5 m apart and come together, using the same selected locomotor movement. They reverse direction and part, using another selected locomotor movement.

Figure 14.2

Going under a partner.

Figure 14.3

Supporting a partner's weight.

8. One partner does a movement. The other person repeats the movement and adds another. The first child repeats both movements and adds a third, and so on. Some limit on the number of movements can be set.

9. Children form letters or figures with their bodies on the floor or in erect positions.

For group work in movement activities, groups should be small (three to four children) so that each child makes a significant contribution. The task should be clear so that efforts are directed toward a common goal. Designing, inventing, or modifying a game makes an excellent group problem-solving activity. Here are some examples of movement activities that are feasible for group work:

1. Groups show different ways to support others wholly or in part.

2. Children practise copying activities. One child sets a movement pattern and the rest copy the actions.

3. Groups make a human merry-go-round.

4. Children do parallel movements as a group.

5. Small groups (five is a good number) do over-and-under movements. Each child goes over and under the others in turn.

Body Awareness

BODY SHAPES (FIGURE 14.4)

- "Let's try making shapes and see whether we can name them. Make any shape you wish and hold it. What is the name of your shape, Ali? [Wide.] Try to make

Figure 14.4

Forming different shapes.

different kinds of wide shapes. Show me other shapes you can make. What is the name of your shape, Parker? [Crooked.] Show me different kinds of shapes that are crooked. Make yourself as crooked as possible."

- "Make yourself wide and then narrow. Now tall and then small. How about tall and wide, small and narrow, tall and narrow, and small and wide? Work out other combinations."

- "Select three different kinds of shapes and move smoothly from one to another. This time I will clap my hands as a signal to change to a different shape."

- "Select four different letters of the alphabet. On the floor, make your body shape successively like these letters. Try with numbers. Make up a movement sequence that spells a word of three letters. Show us a problem in addition or subtraction."

- "Use your jump rope and make a shape on the floor. Make a shape with your body alongside the rope."

- "Pretend to be as narrow as an arrow or telephone pole. Pretend to be as wide as a house, store, or hippopotamus."

- "Squeeze into a tiny shape; now grow slowly into the biggest shape you can imagine. Travel to a different spot on the floor, maintaining the big shape. Quickly assume the tiny shape again."

- "Move around the room in groups of three. On signal, form a shape with one standing, one kneeling, and one sitting."

- "Jump upward, making a shape in the air. Land, holding that shape. Begin with a shape, jump upward with a half turn, and land in another shape."

- "What body shapes can you assume standing on one foot?"

- "Show me what body shapes can be made with your stomach in contact with the floor."
- "Look to see where your personal space is in relation to general space. When I say 'Go,' run in general space. On the next signal, return to your space and sit down."

BALANCING: SUPPORTING BODY WEIGHT (FIGURE 14.5)

- "Explore different ways you can balance on different surfaces of your body. Can you balance on three different parts of your body? On two? On one? Put together sequences of three or four balance positions by using different body parts or different numbers of body parts."
- "Can you balance on a flat body surface? What is the smallest part of the body you can balance on? Support the body on two different parts. On three different parts. Support the body on different combinations of body flats and body points."
- "Use two parts of the body far away from each other to balance. Shift smoothly to another two parts."
- "Who can balance on one foot with the arms stretched overhead? Out to the side?"
- "Stand with feet together and eyes closed. Maintain balance while using different arm positions. Balance on one foot for ten counts."
- "From a standing position, raise one leg, straighten the leg in front of you, swing the leg to side and back without losing your balance."
- "Move from a narrow, unstable base to a wide, stable base."
- "Balance on parts of the body forming a tripod." (Explain the term.)

- "In a hands-and-knees position, and later in a crab position, balance on the right arm and right leg, the left arm and left leg, the right arm and left leg, the left arm and right leg."
- "Stand on your toes and balance, using different arm positions."
- "Place a beanbag on the floor. How many different ways can you balance over it? Try with a hoop. How many different ways can you balance inside the hoop?"
- "When I call out a body part or parts, you balance for five seconds on that part or part combination." (Use knees, hands, heels, flats, points, and a variety of combinations.)
- "Keep your feet together and sway in different directions without losing your balance. Can you balance on one foot with your eyes closed? Bend forward while balancing on one foot? Lift both sets of toes from the floor and balance on your heels? Now sit on the floor. Can you lift your feet and balance on your seat without hand support? Can you balance on your tummy without your feet or hands touching the floor?"
- "In a standing position, thrust one leg out sideways and balance on the other foot."
- "Make a sequence by balancing on a narrow surface, change to a wide surface, and back again to a different narrow surface."

BRIDGES (FIGURE 14.6)

- "Show me a bridge made by using your hands and feet. What other kinds of bridges can you make? Can you make a bridge using only three body parts? Only two?"
- "Show me a wide bridge. A narrow one. A short bridge. A long one. How about a high bridge? A low

Figure 14.5

Balancing on different body parts.

Figure 14.6

Making bridges.

one? Can you make a bridge that opens when a boat goes through? Get a partner to be the boat and you are the bridge. If you are the boat, choose three ways of traveling under a bridge."

- "As I touch you, go under a bridge and make another bridge."

- "With a partner, alternate going under a high bridge and going over a low bridge."

- "Can you move one end of the bridge, keeping the other end still?"

- "Make a bridge with one side of the body held upward. Change to the other side."

- "Show me a twisted bridge. A curved bridge."

- "Be an inchworm and start with a long, low bridge. Walk the feet to the hands. Walk the hands forward while the feet are fixed."

- "Make a bridge with three points of contact."

- "Show me a bridge at a high level. At a low level. In between."

- "Work up a sequence of bridge positions, going smoothly from one to the next."

FLIGHT

- "Show me three different ways you can go through space. Try again, using different levels. Lead with different parts of your body."

- "See how high you can go as you move through space. What helps you get height?"

- "Practise various combinations for takeoff and landing. See if you can work out five different possibilities for taking off and landing, using one or both feet." (Possibilities are same to same [hop]; one foot to the opposite [leap]; one-foot takeoff, two-foot landing; two-foot takeoff, two-foot landing [jump]; two-foot takeoff, one-foot landing.)

- "Run and jump or leap through the air with your legs bent. With your legs straight. With one leg bent and the other straight. Try it with your legs spread wide. With your whole body wide. With your whole body long and thin through the air."

- "Project yourself upward beginning with the feet together and landing with the feet apart. Run, take off, and land in a forward stride position. Repeat, landing with the other foot forward."

- "Using your arms to help you, run and project yourself as high as possible. Practise landing with soft knees."

MOVING WITH THE WEIGHT SUPPORTED ON THE HANDS AND FEET (FIGURE 14.7)

- "Pick a spot away from your personal space and travel to and from that spot on your hands and feet. Try moving with your hands close to your feet. Far away from your feet."

- "Move from your personal space for 8 counts. Do a jump turn (180 degrees) and return to your space using a different movement."

- "Lie on your stomach. Move using only your hands."

- "Experiment with different hand–foot positions. Begin with a narrow shape and with hands and feet as close together as possible. Extend your hands from head to toe until they are as far apart as possible. Extend the hands and feet as wide as possible and move. Now try with the hands wide and the feet together. Reverse."

- "Practise travelling so that both hands and feet are off the ground at the same time. Go forward, backward, sideward."

- "With your body straight and supported on the hands and feet [push-up position], turn the body over smoothly and face the ceiling. The body should remain straight throughout. Turn to the right and left. Recover to your original position."

RECEIVING AND TRANSFERRING WEIGHT

- "Support the weight on two different body parts and then transfer the weight smoothly to another pair of parts. Add another pair of unlike parts if you can."

- "Take a deep breath, let the air out, relax, and drop to the floor, transferring the weight from a standing position to a position on the floor. Can you reverse the process?"

Figure 14.7

Taking the weight on hands and feet.

- "Show in walking how the weight transfers from the heel to the ball of the foot with a push-off from the toes. In a standing position, transfer the weight from the toes, to the outside of the foot, to the heel, and back to the toes. Reverse the order."

- "Using three different parts, transfer weight from one to another in a sequence."

- "Travel with a jump or a leap and then lower yourself gently to your back after landing. Repeat, only lower yourself smoothly to your seat."

- "From a standing position, bend forward slowly and transfer the weight partially to both hands. Lift one foot into the air. Return it to the ground gently. Repeat with the other foot. Lift a hand and a foot at the same time and return them smoothly."

- "Lower yourself in a controlled manner to take the weight on your tummy. Can you turn over and take the weight on your seat with your hands and feet touching the floor?"

- "Move from a supine position (on your back) to a standing position without using your arms."

- "Select a shape. See if you can lower yourself to the ground and return to your original position, retaining the shape."

- "Try some jump turns, quarter and half. What is needed to maintain stability as you land?"

- "Project yourself into the air and practise receiving your weight in different ways. Try landing without any noise. What do you have to do? See how high you can jump and still land softly."

- "See how many different ways you can transfer weight smoothly from one part of your body to another. Work up a sequence of three or four movements and go smoothly from one to another, returning to your original position."

STRETCHING AND CURLING

- "In your own space, stretch out and curl. What different ways can you find to do this? Let's go slowly from a stretch to a curl and back to a stretch in a smooth, controlled movement. Curl your upper body and stretch your lower body. Now curl your lower body and stretch your upper body. Work out a smooth sequence between the two combinations."

- "Show different curled and stretched positions on body points and on body flats. Go from a curled position on a flat surface to a stretched position supported on body points. Explore how many different ways you can support your body in a curled position."

- "Stand in your personal space and stretch your arms at different levels. Lift one leg up and stretch it to the front, side, and back. Repeat with the other leg."

- "Stretch with an arm and a leg until it pulls you over."

- "In a sitting position, put your legs out in front. Bend your toes forward as far as possible. Bend them backward so that your heels are ahead of your toes. Turn both toes as far as you can inward. Turn them outward."

- "Lie on the floor on your back. Stretch one leg at a time in different ways in space."

- "Stand. Stretch to reach as far as you can with your hand. Try reaching as far as possible with your toe."

- "Show how you can travel on different body parts, sometimes stretched, sometimes curled."

- "Jump and stretch as high as possible. Now curl and roll on the floor." Repeat several times.

TAKING THE WEIGHT ON THE HANDS (FIGURE 14.8)

Establishing proper hand positioning for taking the weight on the hands (and later for the headstand) is important.

- "Put your hands about shoulder-width apart, with fingers spread and pointed forward. With knees bent, alternate lifting the feet silently into the air, one foot at a time. Pick a point ahead of your hands (60 cm or so), and watch it with your eyes."

- "Place both hands on the floor. Kick up like a mule. Can you kick twice before coming down?"

- "Take the weight on your hands. Make one foot go past the other while in the air."

- "Do as many movements as you can while keeping your hands on the floor."

Figure 14.8

Taking the weight on the hands.

- "See whether you can take the weight on your hands for a brief time. How do you get your body into the air? What is the importance of the centre of gravity? What different movements can you make with your feet while your weight is on your hands? See how long you can keep your feet off the ground. Repeat, trying to get your hips above your hands. Now add a twist at the waist to return your feet to the floor at a different spot."

- "Try again, but shift the weight to one hand and land both feet at a different spot."

- "Begin in a standing position and try to keep your feet over your head for as long as possible. Begin with the arms and hands stretched overhead, and repeat. Kick up one leg and then the other."

Space Awareness Themes (Where the Body Moves)

MOVING IN GENERAL SPACE

Goals in these movement experiences, in addition to developing movement competence, should enhance students' ability to (a) share space with other children, (b) move through space without bumping anyone, and (c) develop consideration for the safety of others.

- "Run lightly in the area, changing direction without bumping or touching anyone until I call 'Stop.' Raise your hand if you were able to do this without bumping into anyone."

- "Let's try running zigzag fashion in the area without touching anyone. This time, when I blow the whistle, change direction abruptly and change the type of movement."

- "Run lightly in general space and pretend you are dodging someone. Can you run toward another runner and change direction to dodge?"

- "Get a beanbag and drop it to mark your personal space. See how lightly, while under control, you can run throughout the area. When the signal is given, run to your spot, pick up your beanbag, put it on your head, and sit down [or some other challenge]. Try this while skipping."

- "What happens when general space is decreased? You had no problem running without touching anyone in the large space. Now let's divide the area in half with cones. Run lightly within this area so as not to touch or bump anyone. Now it's going to get more difficult. I'm going to divide the space in half once more, but first let's try walking in the new area. Now, run lightly." (Decrease the area as feasible.)

- "Get a beanbag and mark your personal space. Run around the beanbag until you hear 'Bang,' and then explode in a straight direction until I call 'Stop.' Return to your personal space."

- "From your beanbag, take five [or more] jumps [hops, skips, gallops, slides] and stop. Turn to face home, and return with the same number of movements. Take the longest steps you can away from home, and then return home with tiny steps."

- "Show me how well you can move with these combinations in general space: run–jump–roll, skip–spin–collapse. Now you devise a series of any three movements and practise them."

- "Today our magic number is five. Can you move in any direction with five repetitions of a movement? Change direction and pick another movement to do five times. Continue."

- "Blow yourself up like a soap bubble. Can you huff and puff? Think of yourself as a big bubble that is floating around. When I touch you, the bubble breaks, and you collapse to the ground. This time, blow up your bubble and float around. When you are ready, say, 'Pop,' so the bubble bursts."

- "I am going to challenge you on right and left movements. Show me how you can change to the correct direction when I say either 'Right' or 'Left.' Now begin running lightly."

- "This time, see whether you can run rapidly toward another child, stop, and bow to each other. Instead of bowing, shake hands, and say, 'How do you do!'"

- "From your personal space, pick a spot on a wall. See whether you can run to the spot, touch it, and return without bumping anyone. This time, it's more difficult. Pick spots on two different walls, touch these in turn, and return."

EXPLORING PERSONAL SPACE

Personal space is space that can be reached from a fixed base. Youngsters can take this personal space with them when they are moving in general space. A graphic way to illustrate personal space is to have youngsters take an individual jump rope and double it. From a kneeling position, they swing it in a full arc along the floor. It should not touch another child or rope.

- "Show us how big your space is. Keeping one foot in place, outline how much space you can occupy. Sit cross-legged and outline your space. Support your weight on different parts of your body and outline your space."

- "Make yourself as wide [narrow, small, large, low, high] as possible. Try these from different positions—kneeling, balancing on the seat, and others. Show us what kinds of body positions you can assume while you stand on one foot. While you lie on your stomach."

- "Stand tall in your space. To the beat of a drum, move in increments to a squat position. Reverse."
- "Move from a lying position to a standing position without using your arms or hands. Return to lying."
- "Can you stay in one place and move your whole self but not your feet? Sway back and forth with your feet together and then with your feet apart. Which is better?"
- "Sitting in your personal space, bend your toes forward; now backward. Bend your feet so that the heels move ahead of your toes."
- "In a supine position (on your back) move your arms and legs from one position slowly and then move them back quickly to where you started. Explore other positions."
- "Keeping one part of your body in place, make as big a circle as you can with the rest of your body."
- "Explore different positions while you keep one leg [foot] higher than the rest of your body. Work out a smooth sequence of three different positions."
- "Pump yourself up like a balloon, getting bigger and bigger. Hold until I say, 'Bang!'"

CIRCLES AND THE BODY (FIGURE 14.9)

- "Can you form full circles with your hands and arms at different joints—wrist, elbow, and shoulder? Now what circle can you make with your legs and feet? Try this lying on your back. Use other body joints to make circles."
- "Travel in general space by skipping [running, hopping, sliding]. Stop on signal and make moving,

Figure 14.9

Forming circles.

horizontal [vertical, inclined] circles with an arm. Repeat, but on signal lie down immediately on your back and make the specified circle with one foot."
- "Show how a swimmer makes circles with the arms when doing the backstroke. Alternate arms and also move them together. Reverse the arm direction to make the crawl stroke. Make vertical circles with one arm and both arms across the body."
- "Keep one foot fixed and make a circle with the other foot by turning completely around."
- "Select a partner. Match the arm circles the partner makes."
- "Can you keep two different circles going at the same time? Make a circle turning one way, and another circle turning the other way. Repeat, using twisting actions of the body parts making the circles."

PLANES OF MOVEMENT

- "Show me a variety of movements in a horizontal plane. In a vertical plane. In a diagonal plane. Put together combinations so that you go in sequence from one type of movement to another."
- "Here is a challenge. Show me a different plane of movement, as I call each one out. Ready?" (Specify the plane of movement.)
- "Using a jump rope doubled in one hand, make circles in the different planes. Try the same with a Hula Hoop."
- "Crouch at a low level, spin upward toward the ceiling, then back to the floor. Spin in the other direction."

LEVELS

- "Choose one way of travelling at a high level and another at a low level. Again, move at a high level and stop at a low level. Move at a low level and stop at a high level. Choose one way of travelling at a medium level and add this somewhere in your sequence— beginning, middle, or end."
- "Select three different kinds of travelling movement with the arms at a high, medium, and low level. Link these movements together in a smooth sequence."
- "Travel around the room raising your arms as high as possible. Travel on your tiptoes. Repeat with your arms as low as possible."
- "Run at different levels. Run as high as you can. Run as low as possible. Run at a medium level."
- "When I clap my hands, change direction and level."
- "Move on all fours with your body at a high level, a medium level, and then as low as possible. Try these movements with your face turned to the ceiling."

- "Use a jump rope or a line or board in the floor as your path to follow. Begin at the far end. Show me a slow, low-level movement down and back. What other ways can you go down and back slowly and at a low level? Change to a fast, high-level movement. On what other levels can you move?"

- "Combine a low, fast movement down with a high, slow movement on the way back. Explore other combinations. Make different movements by leading with different parts of your body."

MOVING IN DIFFERENT WAYS

- "Discover different ways you can make progress along the floor without using your hands and feet. See whether you can walk with your seat. Let your heels help you."

- "What ways can you move sideward or backward? What rolling movements can you make? Look carefully before you move to make sure you have a clear space."

- "Use large movements and travel through general space. Make your body into a straight line and move in straight lines, changing direction abruptly. With your body in a curved shape, move in a curved pathway."

- "Each time you change direction, alternate a straight body and a straight path with a curved body shape and a curved path."

- "Find ways of moving close to the floor with your legs stretched. Now move with your legs bent, keeping at a low level."

- "As you travel forward, move up and down. As you travel backward, sway from side to side."

- "Travel, keeping high in the air. Change direction and travel at a low level. Continue to alternate."

- "Counting the four limbs [two arms, two legs], travel first on all four, then on three, next on an arm and a leg, and then on one leg. Now reverse the order."

- "With your hands fixed on the floor, move your feet in different ways. Cover as much space as possible. With your feet fixed, move your hands around in different ways as far away from the body as you can. Move around general space the way a skater does. Choose other ways."

Qualities of Movement (How the Body Moves)

TIME (SPEED)

Speed involves the pace of action, which can be slow, fast, or any degree in between. Speed involves acceleration and deceleration: that is, the time factor either can be constant or can use acceleration or deceleration. Time also can be even or uneven.

- "With your arms, do a selected movement slowly and then quickly. Move your feet slowly and then as rapidly as you can. Change your support base and repeat."

- "In turn, stretch a part of your body slowly and then return it to place quickly, like a rubber band snapping. Stretch the entire body as wide as possible and snap it back to a narrow shape."

- "Travel through the area without touching anyone. Speed up when there is an open area and slow down when it is crowded."

- "Choose a way of travelling across the floor quickly and then do the same movement slowly. Do a fast movement in one direction and, on signal, change to a slow movement in another direction."

- "Select a magic number between 10 and 20. Do that many slow movements and repeat with fast movements of the same count."

- "Choose a partner. With your partner a little bit away from you, begin moving rapidly toward your partner and decelerate as you draw close. Move away by beginning slowly and accelerate until you return to where you started. Repeat. Select the kinds of movement you wish to use together."

- "Staying in your own personal space, begin with some kind of movement and accelerate until you are moving as fast as you can. Reverse by beginning with a fast movement and then slow down until you are barely moving. Put together a sequence of two movements by beginning with one and accelerating, then changing to another movement and decelerating. Try doing two different body movements at the same time—one that accelerates and one that decelerates."

CONTRASTING MOVEMENTS

Contrasting movements have wide and frequent application in the development of other themes. See page 281 for examples of contrasting words.

- "Show me a fast movement. Now a slow one. Show me a smooth movement. Now a rough, jerky movement."

- "Find three ways to rise from the floor and three ways to sink to the floor. Choose one way to rise and one way to sink. Try to do this three times very smoothly."

- "Make yourself as tall as possible. Now, as short as you can."

- "Move with a small and delicate skip. Change to a large skip."

- "Show me a wide shape. Now, an opposite one. A crooked shape. Now, its opposite. Show me a high-level movement and its contrast. Can you do a balanced movement? What is its opposite?" (Use light–heavy and other contrasts as well.)

- "Pick two contrasting movements. When I clap my hands, do one, and change to the other when I clap again."

FORCE

- "Show me different kinds of sudden movements. Do a sudden movement and repeat it slowly. Put together a series of sudden movements. Put together a series of sustained movements. Mix sudden and sustained movements."

- "Pick a partner and do a quick, strong, movement followed by a quick, light movement."

- "Take five strong, slow jumps, changing your body for each jump."

- "When the drumbeat is loud, walk heavily. When the drumbeat is soft, walk lightly."

- "Reach in different directions with a forceful movement. Crouch down as low as you can and explode upward. Try again, exploding forward. Move as if you were pushing something very heavy. Pretend you are punching a heavy punching bag."

- "What kinds of movements can you do that are light movements? Can you make movements light and sustained? Light and sudden? Heavy and sustained? Heavy and sudden? Which is easier? Why?"

- "Try making thunder [big noise with hands and feet] and then lightning [same movements without any noise], timing each with five slow counts."

TENSION AND RELAXATION

- "Make yourself as tense as possible. Now slowly relax. Take a deep breath and hold it tight. Expel the air and relax."

- "Hug yourself hard! Now, harder. Follow this with the body relaxed. Shake the hands."

- "Reach as high as possible with both hands, relax slowly, and drop to the floor. Tense one part of your body and relax another. Slowly shift the tension to the relaxed part, and vice versa."

- "Run forward, stop suddenly in a tensed position, and then relax. Run in a tensed manner, change direction, and then run in a relaxed manner."

- "Walk forward with tight, jerky movements. Change direction and walk with loose, floppy movements."

Relationship (To Whom and What the Body Relates)

MOVING OVER, UNDER, AROUND, AND THROUGH THINGS

This theme is flexible and can use any available equipment as obstacles to go over, under, around, and through (see Figure 14.10). It can be used effectively in a rotating station system. Equipment can be already arranged, or the children can set it up themselves.

- "Using the equipment, explore different ways you can go over, under, around, or through what you have set up. Lead with different parts of the body."

- "Three of you with jump ropes form a triangle, square, and rectangle, respectively, on the floor. Move in, out, and around the figures."

- "Toss your beanbag in the air. When I call out a body part, sit down quickly, and put the beanbag on that part, or on one of the parts named."

SYMMETRICAL AND ASYMMETRICAL MOVEMENTS

Symmetry increases stability because of the counterbalance effect of the two body halves. Asymmetry, with its weight distributed unequally, leads to quick starts and easier sequential flow due to the unequal weight distribution throughout the body.

- "Show me different kinds of symmetrical movements. Now asymmetrical movements. Put together sequences of symmetrical and asymmetrical movements."

- "Taking the weight on your hands, show symmetrical and asymmetrical movements of your legs."

- "Run and jump high in the air, and place your limbs symmetrically in flight."

Figure 14.10

Moving over and under.

RELATIVE LOCATION OF BODY PARTS

- "We are going to try some special ways of touching. Raise your right hand as high as you can—now down. Raise your left hand as high as you can—now down. Touch your left [or right] shoulder [elbow, knee, hip, ankle] with the right [or left] hand." (Try many combinations.)

- "Now, point to a door [window, ceiling, basket] with an elbow [thumb, toe, knee, nose]. Let's see if you can remember right and left. Point your left [or right] elbow to the window." (Try different combinations.)

- "When I name a body part, let's see if you can make this the highest part of your body without moving from your place."

- "Now, the next task is a little more difficult. Move in a straight line for a short distance and keep the body part named, above all the other body parts. What body parts would be difficult to keep above all the others?" (Possibilities are the eyes, both ears, both hips.)

- "Touch the highest part of your body with your right hand. Touch the lowest part of your body with your left hand."

- "Now move around the room, travelling any way you wish." (The movement can also be limited.) "The signal to stop will be a word describing a body part. Can you stop and immediately put both hands on that part or parts?" (Or, "On 'Stop,' hide the body part.")

LEADING WITH DIFFERENT PARTS OF THE BODY (FIGURE 14.11)

- "As you move between your beanbags [lines, markers], explore ways that different parts of your body can lead

Figure 14.11

Leading with a foot.

movements. Add different means of locomotion. Work at different levels."

- "Have a partner make a bridge and you go under, leading with different parts of the body. Can you find five different ways to go under with different body parts leading? Now try finding five ways to go over or around."

- "What body parts are difficult to lead with?"

Critical Thinking

1. Examine your provincial/territorial elementary physical education curriculum guide. Where and how are the movement concepts mentioned in this chapter incorporated into the document?

2. Movement education has a long history of influence on elementary physical education. Examine the early beginnings of movement education. How has it evolved into present-day physical education?

References and Suggested Readings

Gabbard, C. (2004). *Physical education for children: Building the foundation* (4th ed.). San Francisco, CA: Benjamin Cummings.

Gallahue, D. & Donnelly, F.C. (2003). *Developmental physical education for all children.* (4th ed.). Champaign, IL: Human Kinetics.

Graham, G., Holt/Hale, S.A., & Parker, M. (2007). *Children moving—a reflective approach to teaching physical education* (7th ed.). New York: McGraw-Hill.

Kogan, S. (2004). *Step by step: A complete movement education curriculum* (2nd ed.). Champaign, IL: Human Kinetics.

Kovar, S., Combs, C., Campbell, K, Napper-Owen, G., & Worrell, V. (2007). *Elementary classroom teachers as movement educators* (2nd ed.). Columbus, OH: McGraw Hill.

Laban, R. & Lawrence, F. (1947). *Effort.* London: Union Brothers.

Langton, T.W. (2007). Apply Laban's movement framework in elementary physical education. *Journal of Physical Education, Recreation, & Dance, 78*(1), 17–24, 39, 53.

Logsdon, B.J., Barrett, K.R., Ammons, M., Broer, M.R., Halverson, L.E., McGee, R., & Robertson, M.A. (1984). *Physical education for children: A focus on the teaching process.* Philadelphia: Lea & Febiger.

Newfoundland & Labrador Department of Education. (2004). *Physical education—primary and elementary curriculum guide.* St. John's, NF: Author.

Saskatchewan Learning. (1999). *Physical education 1–5: A curriculum guide for the elementary level.* Regina, SK: Author.

Thompson, M.A. (1993). *Jump for joy! Over 375 creative movement activities for young children.* Englewood Cliffs, NJ: Prentice Hall.

 Weblinks

ACTIV8: www.activ8.org

This is a curriculum-based program to help elementary school children develop their physical skills and fitness. Program includes a variety of warm-ups, cool downs, and physical challenges.

CHAPTER 15

Fundamental Motor Skills

Essential Components

I	Organized around content standards
II	**Student-centred and developmentally appropriate**
III	**Physical activity and motor skill development form the core of the program**
IV	Teaches management skills and self-discipline
V	Promotes inclusion of all students
VI	**Focuses on process over product**
VII	Promotes lifetime personal health and wellness
VIII	Teaches cooperation and responsibility and promotes sensitivity to diversity

Physical Education Standards

1	**Students are able to move competently using a variety of fundamental and specialized motor skills.**
2	Students can monitor and maintain a health-enhancing level of physical fitness.
3	**Students are able to apply movement concepts and basic mechanics of skill performance when learning and refining motor skills.**
4	Students comprehend the basic principles of wellness and are able to apply concepts that enable them to make meaningful decisions that positively impact their health and wellness.
5	**Students participate in a wide variety of physical activities and learn how to maintain a personalized active lifestyle.**
6	Students demonstrate empathy, understanding, and respect for the numerous differences exhibited by people in an activity setting.
7	Students exhibit responsible and self-directed behaviours that lead to positive social interactions in physical activity.

OVERVIEW

Fundamental skills embrace a broad spectrum of skills, from simple to complex. The more precise the motor skill, the more important is the need to establish proper technique. In combination with movement concepts, motor skills form the basis for skilled movement. Fundamental skills are classified into three groups: locomotor, nonlocomotor, and manipulative.

OUTCOMES

■ Understand that teaching fundamental movement is synonymous with providing instruction toward the acquisition of a specific skill.

■ Identify fundamental (basic) and specialized motor skills.

■ Describe the differences between locomotor, nonlocomotor, and manipulative skills.

■ Cite stress points, instructional cues, and suggested movement patterns to enhance the learning of fundamental skills.

■ Demonstrate the various stages of development associated with throwing, catching, kicking, and striking.

■ Identify objects that can be used to help youngsters succeed in manipulative skills.

■ Specify activities designed to develop fundamental and specialized motor skills.

As mentioned in Chapter 14, there are two major aspects to becoming a skilled mover: learning the concepts of movement and learning the various skills. It is helpful to treat each area separately for the purpose of explanation. This chapter deals with motor skills and how to perform the skills correctly. Fundamental skills are skills that form the foundation of human movement, and are usually identified by a single verb, such as walking, batting, bouncing, jumping, or throwing. (Most of the fundamental skills end in the suffix " -ing.")

Fundamental skills embrace a broad spectrum of skills, from simple to complex. Learning fundamental skills implies that proper technique is involved in skill performance. The more precise the skill, the more critical the need to establish proper technique. Teaching correct technique is necessary even when a child is more comfortable with a known departure from accepted form. A child who is right-handed and steps forward with the right foot while throwing should be taught to shift to a left-footed (opposite side) step to be sure the proper pattern is learned.

Learning fundamental skills requires an understanding of correct progressions and consistent practice. Motor skills should be learned under a variety of conditions and practised in as many situations as possible to ensure practice variability. Developing different experiences on which a response foundation is built allows youngsters to respond to the widest possible range of novel situations. Thus, motor learning moves through a complete cycle, from general to specific to general.

Fundamental Skills

Fundamental skills are sometimes labelled *basic* or *functional*. The designation *fundamental skills* is used because the skills are necessary for children to function effectively in the environment. These skills set the foundation for adult activity and form the basis of competent movement. All physical activities use fundamental and specialized skills of one type or another. If children feel incompetent in performing fundamental movement patterns, they may be hesitant to progress to more sophisticated skills. Although the skills are presented here individually, they are performed in a seemingly infinite number of combinations, depending on the sport or activity. Fundamental skills are divided into three categories—locomotor, nonlocomotor, and manipulative.

Locomotor Skills

Locomotor skills are used to move the body from one place to another or to project the body upward. They include walking, running, skipping, galloping, leaping, sliding, jumping, and hopping. They form the foundation of gross motor coordination and involve large muscle movement.

Nonlocomotor Skills

Nonlocomotor skills are performed without appreciable movement from place to place. These skills are not as well-defined as locomotor skills. They include bending and stretching, pushing and pulling, twisting and turning, rocking, swaying, and balancing, among others.

Manipulative Skills

Manipulative skills come into play when children handle an object. Most of these skills involve the hands and feet, but other parts of the body can also be used. The manipulation of objects leads to better hand–eye and foot–eye coordination, which are particularly important for tracking items in space. Manipulative skills form the foundation for many game skills. Propulsion (throwing, batting, kicking) and receipt (catching) of objects are important skills that can be taught by using beanbags and various balls. Rebounding or redirecting an object in flight (such as a volleyball) is another useful manipulative skill. Continuous control of an object, such as a wand or hoop, is also a manipulative activity.

Locomotor Skills

In the descriptions that follow, stress points emphasizing correct technique are listed for each of the locomotor skills. Instructional cues listed are short, concise phrases that remind students how to perform activities correctly. Suggested learning activities fall into two categories. The first, suggested movement patterns, consists of movement-oriented sequences that do not require rhythm. The second category, rhythmic activities, consists of sequences that use rhythmic background. A drum or appropriate recorded music is effective for reinforcing and expanding rhythmic possibilities. These activities focus primarily on developmental level 1.

Walking

When walking, each foot moves alternately, with one foot always in contact with the ground or floor. The stepping foot is placed on the ground before the other foot is lifted. The weight of the body is transferred from the heel to the ball of the foot and then to the toes for push-off. The toes are pointed straight ahead and the arms swing freely from the shoulders in opposition to the feet. The body is erect, with the eyes focused straight ahead and slightly below eye level. The legs swing smoothly from the hips, with knees bent enough to clear the feet from the ground. Marching is a precise type of walk, accompanied by lifted knees and swinging arms.

Stress Points

1. The toes should be pointed reasonably straight ahead.
2. The arm movement should feel natural. The arms should not swing too far.
3. The head should be kept up and the eyes focused ahead.
4. The stride length should not be excessive. Unnecessary up-and-down motion is to be avoided.

Instructional Cues

1. Head up, eyes forward.
2. Point toes straight ahead.
3. Nice, easy, relaxed arm swing.
4. Walk quietly.
5. Hold tummy in, chest up.
6. Push off from the floor with the toes.

Directives for Suggested Movement Patterns

1. Walk in different directions, changing direction on signal.
2. While walking, bring the knees up and slap with the hands on each step.
3. Walk on the heels, toes, and sides of feet.
4. Gradually lower the body while walking (going downstairs) and raise yourself again slowly (going upstairs).
5. Walk with a smooth, gliding step.
6. Walk with a wide base on the tiptoes, rocking from side to side.
7. Clap the hands alternately in front and behind.
8. Walk slowly, and then increase the speed gradually. Reverse the process.
9. Take long strides. Take tiny steps.
10. On signal, change levels.
11. Walk quickly and quietly. Walk heavily and slowly.
12. Walk happily, angrily, sadly. Show other moods.
13. Hold the arms in different positions. Make an arm movement each time you step.

14. Walk in different patterns—circle, square, triangle, figure eight.
15. Walk through heavy mud; on ice; or a slick floor. Walk on a rainy day. Walk in heavy snow.
16. Walk with high knees; stiff knees; one stiff knee.
17. Walk to a spot, turn in place while stepping, and take off in another direction.
18. Walk as if you are on a balance beam. Walk across a tightrope.

Rhythmic Activities

When using recorded music, teach youngsters to hear the phrasing in the selection. Have children walk one way during a phrase and then change to another type of walk during the next phrase. See Chapter 19 for more information on rhythmic activities.

1. Walk forward one phrase (8 counts) and change direction. Continue to change at the end of each phrase.
2. Use high steps during one phrase and low steps during the next.
3. Walk forward for one phrase and sideward during the next. The side step can be a draw step, or it can be of the grapevine type. To do a grapevine step to the left, lead with the left foot, stepping directly to the side. Cross the right foot behind the left, and then in front of the left on the next step with that foot. The pattern is a step left, cross right (behind); step left, cross right (in front), and so on.
4. Find a partner. Face each other and join hands. Pull your partner by walking backward as your partner resists somewhat (8 counts). Reverse roles. Now stand behind your partner and place the palms of your hands on your partner's shoulders. Push your partner by walking forward as your partner resists (8 counts). Reverse roles.
5. Walk slowly, then gradually increase the tempo. Now begin fast and decrease. (Use a drum for this activity.)
6. Walk in various directions while clapping your hands alternately in front and behind. Try clapping the hands under a thigh at each step, or clap the hands above the head in time with the beat.
7. Walk forward four steps, and turn completely around in four steps. Repeat, but turn the other way the next time.
8. While walking, bring the knees up and slap with the hands on each step in time with the beat.
9. On any one phrase, take four fast steps (1 count to each step) and two slow steps (2 counts to each step).
10. Walk on the heels or toes or with a heavy tramp. Change every 4 or 8 beats.

11. Walk with a smooth, gliding step, or walk silently to the beat.

12. Walk to the music, accenting the first beat of each measure.

Running

Running (see Figure 15.1), in contrast to walking, is moving rapidly so that for a brief moment both feet are off the ground. Running varies from trotting (a slow run) to sprinting (a fast run for speed). The heels can take some weight in distance running and jogging. Running should be done with a slight body lean. The knees are flexed and lifted while the arms swing back and forth from the shoulders with a bend at the elbows. Additional pointers for sprinting are found in Chapter 28.

Stress Points

1. The balls of the feet should be used for sprinting.

2. The faster one desires to run, the higher the knees must be lifted. For fast running, the knees also must be bent more.

3. For distance running, less arm swing is used compared with sprinting for speed. Less body lean is used in distance running, with comfort being the key. The weight is absorbed on the heels and transferred to the toes.

Instructional Cues

1. Run on the balls of the feet.

2. Head up, eyes forward.

3. Bend your knees.

4. Relax your upper body.

Figure 15.1

Running.

5. Breathe naturally.

6. Swing the arms forward and backward, not sideways.

Directives for Suggested Movement Patterns

1. Run lightly throughout the area, changing direction as you wish. Avoid bumping anyone. Run zigzag throughout the area.

2. Run and stop on signal. Change direction on signal.

3. Run, turn around with running steps on signal, and continue in a new direction. Alternate turning direction.

4. Pick a spot away from you, run to it, and return without touching or bumping anyone.

5. Run low, gradually increasing the height. Reverse.

6. Run in patterns. Run between and around objects.

7. Run with high knee action. Slap the knees while running.

8. Run with different steps—tiny, long, light, heavy, criss-cross, wide, and others.

9. Run with your arms in different positions—circling, overhead, stiff at your sides.

10. Run free, concentrating on good knee lift.

11. Run with exaggerated arm movements. Run with a high bounce.

12. Run forward 10 steps and backward 5 steps. Repeat in another direction.

13. Run forward, then make a jump turn in the air to face in a new direction.

14. Show how quietly you can run.

15. Run lightly twice around your spot. Then explode (run quickly) to another spot.

Rhythmic Activities

Many of the suggested movements for walking are equally applicable to running patterns. Some additional suggestions for running include the following:

1. Walk during a phrase of music and then run for an equal length of time.

2. Run in different directions, changing direction on the sound of a heavy beat (or on a signal).

3. Lift the knees as high as possible while running, keeping time to the beat.

4. Do European Rhythmic Running (see Chapter 16) to supplement the running patterns described previously.

Hopping

Hopping involves propelling the body up and down on the same foot. The body lean, the other foot, and the arms serve to balance the movement. Hopping can be practised in place or as a locomotor movement.

Stress Points

1. To increase the height of the hop, the arms must be swung rapidly upward.
2. Hopping should be performed on the ball of the foot.
3. Small hops should be used to start, with a gradual increase in height and distance of the hop.

Instructional Cues

1. Hop with good forward motion.
2. Stay on your toes.
3. Use your arms for balance.
4. Reach for the sky when you hop.
5. Land lightly.

Directives for Suggested Movement Patterns

1. Hop on one foot and then on the other, using numbered sequences such as 1–1, 2–2, 3–3, 4–4, 5–5, 2–1, 1–2, 3–2, 2–3, and so on. The first figure of a series indicates the number of hops on the right foot, and the second specifies the number of hops on the left foot. Combinations should be maintained for 10 to 20 seconds.
2. Hop, increasing height. Reverse.
3. See how much space you can cover in two, three, or four hops.
4. Hop on one foot and do a heel-and-toe pattern with the other. Now change to the other foot. See whether a consistent pattern can be set up.
5. Make a hopping sequence by combining hopping in place with hopping ahead.
6. Hop forward, backward, sideward.
7. Hop in different patterns on the floor.
8. Hop with the body in different positions—with a forward lean, a backward lean, a sideward balance.
9. Hop lightly. Heavily. Hop softy so that no one can hear you.
10. Hop back and forth over a line, moving down the line as you hop.

Rhythmic Activities

Combining rhythm with hopping patterns is more difficult than walking, running, or skipping to rhythm because students fatigue rapidly. The suggested patterns combine other locomotor movements with hopping.

1. Walk four steps, hop three times, and rest 1 count.
2. Walk four steps, then hop four times as you turn in place. Repeat in a new direction.
3. Hop eight times on one foot (8 counts) and then eight times on the other.
4. Hop forward and backward over a line to the rhythm, changing feet each phrase (8 counts).
5. Combine skipping, sliding, or galloping with hopping.
6. Practise the step-hop to music. (The child takes a step followed by a hop on the same foot. This is a 2-count movement.)

Jumping

Jumping requires taking off with both feet and landing on both feet (see Figure 15.2). The arms move forward with an upswing, and the movement of the body combined with the force of the feet helps lift the weight. A jumper

Figure 15.2

Jumping.

lands lightly on the balls of the feet with the knees bent. Jumping can be done in place or as a locomotor activity to cover ground.

Stress Points

1. The knees and ankles should be bent before takeoff to achieve more force from muscle extension.

2. The landing should be on the balls of the feet, with the knees bent to absorb the impact.

3. The arms should swing forward and upward at takeoff to add momentum to the jump and to gain distance and height.

4. The legs must be bent after takeoff or the feet will touch the ground prematurely.

Instructional Cues

1. Swing your arms forward as fast as possible.

2. Bend your knees.

3. On your toes.

4. Land lightly with bent knees.

5. Jump up and try to touch the ceiling.

Directives for Suggested Movement Patterns

1. Jump up and down, trying for height. Try small and high jumps. Mix in patterns.

2. Choose a spot on the floor. Jump forward over the spot. Now backward and then sideward.

3. Jump with your body stiff and arms held at your sides.

4. Practise jump turns in place—quarter, half, three-quarter, and full.

5. Increase and decrease your jumping speed. Increase and decrease the height of the jump.

6. Land with the feet apart and then together. Alternate with one foot forward and one backward.

7. Jump and land quietly. How is this done?

8. See how far you can go in two, three, and four consecutive jumps. Run lightly back to place.

9. Pretend that you are a bouncing ball.

10. Jump in various patterns on the floor.

11. Combine a jump for distance with one for height.

12. Jump like a kangaroo. A rabbit. A frog.

13. Combine contrasting jumps: forward and backward. Big and little. Right and left. Light and heavy.

14. Jump and clap hands in front. Behind you. Overhead.

15. Give three preliminary swings of arms and then jump forward.

Rhythmic Activities

Most of the activities suggested for hopping to rhythm are suitable for jumping. Other suggestions follow.

1. Begin jumping slowly to the drumbeat and then accelerate. Begin jumping fast and decelerate to the beat.

2. Toss a ball upward and jump in time to the bounce. (The ball must be a lively one.)

3. Do varieties of the Jumping Jack. First, move your feet without any arm movement. Now add an arm lift to shoulder height, then lift the arm to a full overhead position. Finally, add body turns and different foot patterns.

4. Take a forward stride position. Change the feet back and forth to the rhythm.

Sliding

Sliding is done to the side. It is a 1-count movement, with the leading foot stepping to the side and the other foot following quickly. Since the same foot always leads, practise the movement in both directions. Sliding is done on the balls of the feet with the weight shifted from the leading foot to the trailing foot. Body bounce during the slide should be minimal.

Stress Points

1. Emphasize the sideways movement. Often, students move forward or backward, which is actually galloping.

2. Both directions should be used, so that each leg has a chance to lead as well as to trail.

3. The slide is a smooth, graceful, and controlled movement.

Instructional Cues

1. Move sideways.

2. Do not bounce.

3. Slide your feet.

Directives for Suggested Movement Patterns

1. Lead in one direction with a definite number of slides, do a half-turn in the air, and continue the slide leading with the other leg in the same direction.

2. Begin with short slides and increase length. Reverse.

3. Slide in a figure-eight pattern.

4. Change levels while sliding. Slide so that the hands can touch the floor with each slide.

5. Slide quietly and smoothly.

6. Slide with a partner.

7. Try sliding individually in a circle.

8. Do three slides and a pause. Change the leading foot and repeat.

9. In circle formation, facing in, the whole class does 10 slides one way followed by a pause. Repeat going in the other direction.

Rhythmic Activities

With appropriate music, many of the above movement patterns can be set to rhythm. Use music phrases to signal a change of direction or to insert another challenge.

Galloping

Galloping is similar to sliding, but progress is in a forward direction. One foot leads and the other is brought rapidly forward to it. There is more upward motion of the body than in sliding. A way to teach the gallop is to have children hold hands and slide in a circle, either to verbal cues or to a drumbeat. Gradually ask the class to face the direction the circle is moving. This takes them naturally from a slide into a gallop. Finally, drop hands and permit free movement in general space.

Stress Points

1. The movement should be smooth and graceful.

2. Each foot should have a chance to lead.

Instructional Cues

1. Keep one foot in front of the other.

2. Now lead with the other foot.

3. Make high gallops.

Directives for Suggested Movement Patterns

1. Do a series of eight gallops with the same foot leading, then change to the other foot. Change after four gallops. Change after two gallops.

2. Change the size of the gallops.

3. Gallop in a circle with a small group.

4. Gallop backward.

Rhythmic Activities

Because galloping is essentially a rhythmic movement, many of the patterns described above should be done to rhythm. Use music phrases to signal a change in the lead foot. Check previous sections on locomotor movements for other rhythmic movement suggestions.

Leaping

Leaping is an elongated step designed to cover distance or move over a low obstacle. It is usually combined with running, since a series of leaps is difficult to maintain alone (see Figure 15.3). The suggested movement patterns use combinations of running and leaping.

Stress Points

1. Height and graceful flight are goals to strive for.

2. Landing should be light and relaxed.

Instructional Cues

1. Push off and reach.

2. Up and over, land lightly.

3. Use your arms to help you gain height.

Directives for Suggested Movement Patterns

1. Leap in different directions.

2. See how high you can leap.

3. Leap and land softly.

Figure 15.3

Leaping.

4. Vary your arm position when you leap. Clap your hands as you leap.

5. Leap with the same arm and leg forward. Try the other way.

6. Show a leap in slow motion.

7. Leap and turn backward.

8. Leap over objects or across a specified space.

9. Leap and move into a balanced position.

Rhythmic Activities

Because a leap is essentially an explosive movement through space, it is difficult to apply rhythm to the movement. Children must gather themselves in preparation for the leap, which makes the movement non-rhythmic in nature.

Skipping

Skipping is a series of step-hops done with alternate feet. To teach skipping, first teach youngsters to do a step and small hop on the same foot. A step followed by a hop is then performed on the other foot. Skipping is done on the balls of the feet with the arms swinging to shoulder height in opposition with the feet. Another way to teach skipping is to have youngsters hold a large ball (30 cm or more) in front at waist height. Take a step with one foot followed by raising the other knee to touch the ball. This stimulates the hop. Repeat with the other foot and the opposite knee.

Stress Points

1. Smoothness and rhythm are goals in skipping. Speed and distance are not.

2. The weight must be transferred from one foot to the other on the hop.

3. The arms swing in opposition to the legs.

Instructional Cues

1. Step-hop.

2. Swing your arms.

3. Skip smoothly.

4. On your toes.

Directives for Suggested Movement Patterns

Many of the suggested movement patterns for walking and running can be applied to skipping, particularly those that refer to changing direction, stopping, making floor patterns, and moving at different speeds.

1. Skip with exaggerated arm action and lifted knees.

2. Clap as you skip.

3. Skip twice on one side (double skip).

4. Skip as slowly as possible. Skip as fast as possible.

5. Skip so lightly that your partner cannot hear the movement.

6. Take as few skips as you can to get to a selected spot.

Rhythmic Activities

Almost all the combinations suggested for walking and running are useful for skipping movements, and many combinations of skipping, walking, and running can be devised. The piece "Pop Goes the Weasel" is excellent music for skipping. On the "Pop," some movement challenge can be specified.

Nonlocomotor Skills

Nonlocomotor skills include bending, twisting, turning (in place), moving toward and away from the centre of the body, raising and lowering the parts of the body, and other body movements done in place. Important goals are body control, flexibility, balance, and a variety of movements that lead to effective body management.

Bending

Bending is movement at a joint. Teach how the body bends, why it needs to bend, and how bends are combined in various movements (see Figure 15.4).

Stress Points

1. Bending as far as possible to increase flexibility and range of movement is a key goal.

2. The bending possibilities of many joints should be explored.

3. Time factors can be introduced in slow and rapid bending.

Instructional Cues

1. Bend as far as possible.

2. Bend one part while holding others steady.

Figure 15.4

Bending movements.

Directives for Suggested Movement Patterns

1. Bend your body down and up.
2. Bend forward and backward, left and right, north and south.
3. Bend as many ways as possible.
4. Bend as many body parts as you can below your waist. Above your waist. Bend with your whole body.
5. Sit down and see whether you can bend differently from the ways you bent in a standing position.
6. Lie down and bend six body parts. Can you bend more than six?
7. Try to bend one body part quickly while you bend another part slowly.
8. Make a familiar shape by bending two body parts. Add two more parts.
9. Think of a toy that bends; see whether you can bend in a similar fashion.
10. Find a partner and bend together.

Rocking and Swaying

Rocking occurs when the centre of gravity is fluidly transferred from one body part to another. In rocking, the body is in a rounded position where it touches the floor. The term *swaying* implies a slower movement than rocking and is somewhat more controlled than rocking. The base of support is unchanged in swaying movements.

Stress Points

1. Rocking is done best on a body surface that has been rounded. Arm movements and movements of other body parts can facilitate the rocking motion.
2. Rocking should be done smoothly and in a steady rhythm.
3. Rocking can be started with small movements and increased in extent, or vice versa.
4. Rocking and swaying should be done to the full range of movement.
5. Swaying maintains a stable base.

Instructional Cues

1. Rock smoothly.
2. Rock in different directions. At varying speeds.
3. Rock higher (farther).
4. Sway until you almost lose your balance.

Directives for Suggested Movement Patterns

1. Rock in as many different ways as you can (see Figure 15.5).
2. Show how you can rock slowly; quickly; smoothly.
3. Sit cross-legged with arms outstretched to the sides, palms facing the floor. Rock from side to side until the hands touch the floor.
4. Lie on your back and rock. Now point your arms and legs toward the ceiling as you rock.

Figure 15.5

Rocking variations.

5. Lie on your tummy with arms stretched overhead and rock.

6. Try to rock in a standing position.

7. Rock and twist at the same time.

8. Show two ways to have a partner rock you.

9. From a standing position, sway back and forth. Right and left. Experiment with different foot positions. Sway slowly and rapidly. What effect does rapid swaying have?

10. Repeat swaying movements from a kneeling position.

11. Start with a small rocking motion and make it progressively bigger.

12. Choose three (or more) ways of rocking and see if you can change smoothly from one to the next.

Swinging

Swinging involves the movement of body parts in a motion that resembles a swinging rope or pendulum of a clock. Most swinging movements are confined to the arms and legs.

Stress Points

1. Swinging should be a smooth, rhythmic action.

2. The body parts involved in swinging should be relaxed and loose.

3. The extent of the swing movement should be the same on both sides of the swing.

4. Swinging movements should be as full as possible.

Instructional Cues

1. Loosen up; swing easy.

2. Swing fully; make a full movement.

3. Swing in rhythm.

Directives for Suggested Movement Patterns

1. Explore different ways to swing your arms and legs.

2. Work out swinging patterns with the arms. Combine them with a step pattern, forward and back.

3. Swing the arms back and forth, and go into full circles at times.

4. With a partner, work out different swinging movements (see Figure 15.6). Add circles.

5. Develop swinging patterns and combinations. Form sequences with swinging and full-circle movements.

Figure 15.6

Partner swinging.

Turning

Turning is rotation around the long axis of the body. The terms *turning* and *twisting* are sometimes used interchangeably to designate the movements of body parts. However, turning refers to movements of the body as a whole. Most turns are initiated by a twist. In the movement experiences suggested here, action involves movement of the entire body. Movements of body parts are discussed under "Twisting."

Stress Points

1. Maintaining balance and body control is important.

2. Turning should be tried in both directions, right and left.

3. Turns in standing position can be made by jumping, hopping, or shuffling with the feet.

4. Most turns are made in increments or multiples of quarter-turns. Multiples should be practised.

5. Turns should be practised in body positions other than standing—seated, on the tummy or the back, and so on.

Instructional Cues

1. Keep your balance.

2. In jump turns, land in a relaxed way with the knees relaxed.

3. Be precise in your movement, whether it is a quarter-, half-, or full turn.

Directives for Suggested Movement Patterns

1. In standing position, turn your body to the left and right, clockwise and counterclockwise.

2. Turn to face north, east, south, and west. (Post directions on the wall.)

3. Stand on one foot and turn around slowly. Now turn around quickly. Now turn with a series of small hops. Try to keep good balance.

4. Show how you can cross your legs with a turn and sit down. Can you get up again in one movement?

5. Every time you hear the signal, see whether you can turn around once, moving slowly. Can you turn two, three, or four times slowly on signal?

6. Lie on your tummy on the floor and turn your body slowly in an arc. Turn over so that you are on your back. Turn back to your tummy again.

7. Play Follow the Leader with a partner. You make a turn and your partner follows.

8. Begin with a short run, jump into the air, and turn to land facing in a new direction. Practise both right and left turns.

9. Lying on your back, turn and rest on your side. Return. Repeat on the other side.

10. Walk in general space and turn completely around on signal.

Twisting

Twisting is the rotation of a selected body part around its own long axis (see Figure 15.7). The joints of different body parts can be used for twisting: spine, neck, shoulders, hips, ankles, and wrists. *Twisting* involves movement around the body part itself whereas *turning* focuses on the space in which the entire body turns.

Stress Points

1. Twisting should be extended as far as possible with good control.

Figure 15.7

Twisting movements.

2. The body parts on which the twist is based should be stabilized.

3. A twist in one direction should be countered by a reverse twist.

4. Some joints are better for twisting than others. (Explain why this is so.)

Instructional Cues

1. Twist far (fully).

2. Twist the other way.

3. Hold the supporting parts firm.

Directives for Suggested Movement Patterns

1. Glue your feet to the floor. Can you twist your body to the left and to the right? Can you twist your body slowly? Quickly? Can you bend and twist at the same time? How far can you turn your hands back and forth?

2. Twist two or more parts of your body at the same time.

3. Twist one body part in one direction and another in the opposite direction.

4. Try twisting the lower half of your body without twisting the upper half.

5. See what parts you can twist while sitting on the floor.

6. Try to twist one body part around another part. Is it possible to twist together even more parts?

7. Balance on one foot and twist your body. Can you bend and twist at the same time?

8. Show some different shapes that you can make by twisting your body.

9. Twist like a pretzel; like a licorice stick.

Stretching

Stretching is a movement that moves body parts away from the body centre. Stretching sometimes involves moving a joint through the range of movement. Stretching is necessary for maintaining and increasing flexibility.

Stress Points

1. Stretching should be extended to the full range of movement.

2. Stretching exploration should involve many body parts.

3. Stretching should be done in many positions.

4. Stretching can be combined with opposite movements, such as curling.

5. Stretching is done slowly and smoothly.

6. Hold full stretching position for 10 seconds.

Instructional Cues

1. Stretch as far as possible.

2. Find other ways to stretch the body part [joint].

3. Keep it smooth. Do not jerk.

Directives for Suggested Movement Patterns

1. Stretch as many body parts as you can.

2. Stretch your arms, legs, and feet in as many different directions as possible.

3. Try to stretch a body part quickly. Slowly. Smoothly.

4. Bend a body part and say which muscle or muscles are being stretched.

5. See how many ways you can stretch while sitting on the floor.

6. From a kneeling position, see whether you can stretch to a mark on the floor without losing your balance.

7. Stretch your right arm while you curl your left arm.

8. Try to stretch and become as tall as a giraffe. (Name other animals.)

9. Stretch and make a wide bridge. Find a partner to go under, around, and over your bridge.

10. Bend at the waist and touch your toes with your fingers.

11. Combine stretching with curling. With bending.

12. Make a shape with your body. Now stretch the shape so that it is larger.

13. Find a position in which you can stretch one side of the body.

14. Find a position in which you can stretch both legs far apart in the air. Now make the legs as narrow as possible.

15. Stretch like a rubber band. When I say "Snap!" move the part quickly back to original position.

Pushing

Pushing is a controlled and forceful action performed against an object to move the body away from the object or to move the object in a desired direction (see Figure 15.8).

Stress Points

1. A forward stride position should be used to broaden the base of support.

2. The body's centre of gravity should be lowered.

3. The line of force is directed toward the object.

Figure 15.8

Pushing.

4. The back is kept in reasonable alignment, and the body forces gathered for a forceful push. Do not bend the waist.

5. The push should be controlled and steady.

Instructional Cues

1. Broaden your foot base.

2. Use all your body forces.

3. Push steadily and evenly.

4. Lower yourself for a better push.

Directives for Suggested Movement Patterns

1. Stand near a wall and push it from an erect position, then push with the knees bent and one foot behind the other. In which position can you push with more force?

2. Push an imaginary object that is very light. Now push one that is very heavy.

3. Push an object with your feet without using your arms or hands.

4. Sit down and push a heavy object with your feet. Can you put your back against the object and push it?

5. See how many different ways you can find to push the object.

6. Find a partner and take turns trying to push each other over a line.

7. Lie on the floor and push your body forward, backward, and sideward.

8. Lie on the floor and push yourself with one foot and one arm.

9. Put a beanbag on the floor and push it with your elbow, shoulder, nose, or other body part.

10. Show how you can push a ball to a partner.

Pulling

Pulling is a controlled and forceful action that moves an object closer to the body or the body closer to an object. If the body moves and an object is being pulled, pulling causes the object to follow the body.

Stress Points

1. For forceful pulling, the base of support must be broadened and the body's centre of gravity must be lowered.

2. The vertical axis of the body should provide a line of force away from the object.

3. Pulling should be a controlled movement with a minimum of jerking and tugging.

4. The hand grips must be comfortable if pulling is to be efficient. Gloves or other padding can help.

5. Pulling movements can be isolated in the body, with one part of the body pulling against the other.

Instructional Cues

1. Get your body in line with the pull. Lower yourself.

2. Widen your base of support.

3. Gather your body forces and pull steadily.

Directives for Suggested Movement Patterns

1. Reach for the ceiling and pull an imaginary object toward you quickly. Slowly and smoothly.

2. From a kneeling position, pull an object.

3. Try to pull with your feet while you sit on the floor.

4. Pretend to pull a heavy object while you are lying on the floor.

5. Clasp your hands together and pull as hard as you can.

6. Hold hands with a partner, and pull slowly as hard as you can.

7. Have your partner sit down, and then see how slowly you can pull each other. Take turns.

8. With your partner sitting on the floor, see whether you can pull each other to your feet. Take turns.

9. Reach for the stars with both hands and pull one back to you.

10. Balance on one foot. Try to pull something. What happens?

Pushing and Pulling Combinations

Combinations of pulling and pushing movements should be arranged in sequence. Musical phrases can signal changes from one movement to the other. Balance-beam benches are excellent for practising pulling and pushing techniques. Partner tug-of-war ropes provide effective pulling experiences. Partner resistance exercises are also useful pulling and pushing experiences.

Fleeing, Chasing, and Tagging

Many physical education games involve fleeing, chasing, and tagging. Speed and reaction are essential for dodging by the person being chased and the response of the chaser to the movements of the target child.

Stress Points

1. Run under control.

2. The fleeing child should be in a moderate crouch position with the feet wider than usual. This position enables the student to move laterally in either direction quickly.

3. The fleeing child should become adept at faking, which means making a preliminary movement in one direction before determining the final path to take.

4. All runners should move on the balls of their feet.

5. The chaser should maneuver the fleeing youngster into a confined area to facilitate tagging.

6. Eyes should be focused on the centre of the dodger's body to negate the effectiveness of the fake.

7. The tag should be made between the knees and shoulders in a gentle but firm manner.

Instructional Cues (Chaser)

1. Run under control.

2. Move on the balls of the feet and maintain a slightly crouched position when approaching the dodger.

3. Focus on the waistline of the dodger.

4. Tag gently but firmly.

Directives for Suggested Movement Patterns

1. Run in general space with the stipulation to run toward other classmates and dodge at the last moment. Avoid contact. To vary the activity, change direction on signal.

2. In general space, run and stop on signal.

3. In partners, have one person run and the other shadow (follow closely). The runner should change direction often. Change roles.

4. Move into squads, with the leader 5 m away from and facing the rest of the squad column. All members of the squad take turns running and dodging around a passive captain. Replace the squad captain regularly.

5. Partners mark a small area (3 m by 3 m) with cones. Chase and dodge within this area. Try with two chasers and one dodger.

Manipulative Skills

Manipulative skills are basic to a number of specialized sport skills—catching, throwing, striking, and kicking, among others. These are complex motor patterns, and stages of development have been identified, from initial stages through mature patterns of performance. Most complex skills should be practised at near-normal speed. Whereas locomotor skills can be dramatically slowed down to promote learning, doing so with throwing, striking, or kicking will destroy the rhythm of the skills. Analysis of the following skills is listed by developmental stages rather than age because of the wide maturity differences among children of similar ages. Suggested activity challenges for developing throwing, catching, striking, and kicking skills are found in Chapter 18.

Throwing

In throwing, an object is thrust into space and is accelerated through the movement of the arm and the total coordination of the body. Young children often go through two preliminary tossing stages before entering the stages of throwing. The first toss is a two-handed underhand throw that involves little foot movement. A large ball, such as a beach ball, is best for teaching this type of throw, which begins with the ball held in front of the body at waist level. The toss is completed using only the arms. Youngsters often have difficulty maintaining balance when encouraged to throw the ball any distance. The second preliminary toss is a one-handed underhand throw. In this toss, which resembles pitching a softball, body torque is generated and weight shifted from the rear to the front foot. This toss requires a smaller object such as a beanbag, a fleece ball, or a small sponge ball.

The following skill analysis considers overhand throwing only. Teach proper form before concentrating on distance or accuracy. Velocity, not accuracy, is the primary goal when trying to develop mature patterns characterized by a full range of motion and speed. Throwing for accuracy is practised only after a mature form of the skill is in place.

Stage One

Stage One throwing is generally observed between the ages of 2 and 3 years. This stage is basically restricted to arm movement from the rear toward the front of the body. The feet remain stationary and positioned at shoulder width, with little or no trunk rotation occurring (see Figure 15.9). Most of the movement force originates from flexing the hip, moving the shoulder forward, and extending the elbow.

Figure 15.9

Throwing form, Stage One.

Figure 15.10

Throwing form, Stage Two.

Stage Two

Stage Two throwing develops between the ages of 3 and 5 years. Some rotary motion is developed in an attempt to increase the amount of force. This stage is characterized by a lateral fling of the arm, with rotation occurring in the trunk (see Figure 15.10). Often, children step in the direction of the throw, although many keep their feet stationary. This throwing style sometimes looks like a discus throw rather than a baseball throw.

Stage Three

Typically, Stage Three is found among children ages 5 to 6 years. The starting position is similar to that of stages one and two in that the body is facing the target area, the feet are parallel, and the body is erect. In this stage, however, a step is made toward the target with the foot on the same side of the body as the throwing arm. This allows rotation of the body and shifting of the body weight forward as the step occurs. The arm action is nearer to the overhand style of throwing than is the fling of stage two, and there is an increase in hip flexion. Unfortunately, the throwing pattern of many students never matures beyond this stage.

Stage Four

Stage Four is a mature form of throwing, and more force is applied to the object being accelerated. The thrower uses the rule of opposition in this stage, taking a step in the direction of the throw with the leg opposite the throwing arm. This develops maximum body torque. The target is addressed with the non-throwing side of the body and strides toward the target to shift body weight. Beginning with the weight on the back leg, the movement sequence is as follows: (a) step toward the target, (b) rotate the upper body, and (c) throw with the arm (see Figure 15.11). The

Figure 15.11

Throwing pattern, Stage Four.

cue phrase used is "Step, turn, and throw." The elbow should lead the way in the arm movement, followed by forearm extension, and a final snapping of the wrist. This pattern must be practised many times to develop total body coordination. Through a combination of sound instruction and practice, the majority of youngsters are able to develop a mature pattern of throwing by age 8 or 9 years.

Stress Points

1. Stand with the non-throwing-arm side of the body facing the target. The throwing-arm side of the body should be away from the target.

2. Step toward the target with the foot opposite the throwing arm.

3. Rotate the hips as the throwing arm moves forward.

4. Bend the arm at the elbow. The elbow should lead the forward movement of the arm.

5. Body weight remains on the rear foot (away from the target) during early phases of the throw. Just prior to the forward motion of the arm, the weight is shifted from the rear foot to the forward foot (nearer the target).

TEACHING TIPS

1. Offer a variety of projectiles during throwing practice so that youngsters understand how varying the weight and diameter can affect throwing distance and speed.

2. When youngsters are learning to throw, they should throw for distance and velocity. Throwing for accuracy will discourage the development of a mature throwing form. Youngsters must be encouraged to "throw as hard as possible." Stress distance and velocity before introducing accuracy.

3. It is ineffective to work on throwing and catching at the same time. If learning to throw is the objective, youngsters will throw inaccurately and with velocity. This makes it difficult for a partner to catch the throw. Throwing should be practised against a wall (velocity) or on a large field (distance).

4. Carpet squares or circles drawn on the floor can be used to teach youngsters proper foot movement (stepping forward).

5. Beanbags and yarn balls are excellent for developing throwing velocity since they do not rebound throughout the area.

Catching

Catching uses the hands to stop and control a moving object. Catching is more difficult to learn than throwing, because the object must be tracked and the body moved into the path of the object simultaneously. Another element that makes catching more difficult to master is the child's fear of being hurt by the oncoming object. When teaching the early stages of catching, use objects that cannot hurt the receiver. Balloons, fleece balls, and beach balls move slowly, make tracking easier, and do not hurt if they hit a child in the face.

Stage One

In Stage One of catching, hold the arms in front of the body, with elbows extended and palms up, until the ball makes contact. Then bend the arms at the elbows (see Figure 15.12). The catch is actually more of a trapping

Figure 15.12
Catching form, Stage One.

movement, since the arms press the ball against the chest. Children often turn their heads away or close their eyes because of the fear response. Eliminate the fear of being hurt by a hard object (see Teaching Tips below) and encourage them to watch the object rather than the person throwing the object.

Stage Two

In Stage Two, much of the same behaviour as in stage one is repeated. Rather than waiting for the ball to contact the arms, however, an anticipatory movement is made and the ball is cradled somewhat.

Stage Three

In Stage Three, lifting the arms and bending them slightly prepare for the catch. The chest is used as a back-stop for the ball. During this stage, contact is made with the hands first, and then the object is guided to the chest (see Figure 15.13).

Figure 15.13

Catching form, Stage Three.

Stage Four

The fourth and final stage of catching, which occurs at approximately age 9 years, is characterized by catching with the hands. Encourage catching with the hands by decreasing the size of the ball to be caught. Demonstrate "giving" with the arms (absorbing force) while catching. The legs bend, and the feet move in anticipation of the catch.

Stress Points

1. Maintain visual contact with the projectile.
2. Reach for the projectile and absorb its force by bringing the hands in toward the body. This "giving" makes catching easier by reducing the chance for the object to rebound out of the hands.
3. Place the feet in a stride position rather than a straddle position. A fast-moving object will cause a loss of balance if feet are in the straddle position.
4. Place the body in line with the object rather than reaching to the side of the body to make the catch.

TEACHING TIPS

1. Remove the fear factor by using projectiles that will not hurt the youngster. It is a normal reaction to dodge an object when one feels it could cause harm. The use of foam balls, yarn balls, beach balls, and balloons will facilitate learning to "keep your eye on the ball."
2. The size of the projectile should get smaller as youngsters improve their catching skills. Larger objects move more slowly and are easier to track visually than smaller projectiles.
3. Prepare youngsters for a catch by asking them to focus on the ball while it is in the thrower's hand. Use a verbal cue such as "Look (focus), ready (for the throw), catch (toss the ball)."
4. Balls and background colours should strongly contrast to facilitate visual perception.
5. If the trajectory of the projectile is raised, it will offer the youngster more opportunity for successful tracking. Beach balls will move slowly throughout a high trajectory, giving children time to focus and move into the path of the oncoming object.
6. Bounce objects off the floor so that youngsters learn to judge the rebound angle of a projectile.

Kicking

Kicking is a striking action executed with the feet. There are different types of kicking. Punting (in which the ball is dropped from the hands and kicked before it touches the ground), and placekicking (kicking the ball in a stationary position on the ground) are two. A third type is soccer kicking, which is probably the most difficult of all kicking skills because the ball is moving before the kick is executed.

Stage One

In Stage One, the body is stationary, and the kicking foot is flexed in preparation for the kick. The kicking motion is carried out with a straight leg and with little or no flexing at the knee. There is minimal movement of the arms and trunk, and concentration is on the ball.

Stage Two

In the second stage of kicking, the kicking foot is lifted backward by flexing at the knee. Usually, the child displays opposition of the limbs. When the kicking leg goes forward, the opposite arm moves forward. In Stage Two, the kicking leg moves farther forward in the follow-through motion compared to Stage One.

Stage Three

In Stage Three, movement toward the object to be kicked is added. There is an increase in the distance the leg is moved, coupled with a movement of the upper body to counterbalance the leg movement.

Stage Four

Mature displays of kicking involve a preparatory extension of the hip to increase the range of motion. The child makes a run to the ball and a small leap to get the kicking foot in position. As the kicking foot is carried forward, the trunk leans backward, and a small step forward is made on the support foot to regain balance (see Figure 15.14).

Stress Points

1. Students need to step forward with the non-kicking leg. Stand behind and slightly to the side of the ball. Eyes should be kept on the ball (head down) throughout the kick.
2. Practise kicking with both feet.
3. Use objects that will not hurt children. Foam balls are excellent projectiles that can be used for kicking practice.

Figure 15.14

Kicking a soccer ball, Stage Four.

4. Encourage kickers to move their leg backward in preparation for the kick. Beginners often fail to move the leg backward, making it difficult for them to generate kicking force.
5. Arms should move in opposition to the legs during the kick.
6. After speed and velocity of the kick have been developed, focus on altering the force of the kick. Activities such as soccer demand both soft "touch" kicks and kicks of maximum velocity.

TEACHING TIPS

1. When teaching kicking skills, focus on velocity and distance rather than accuracy. If youngsters are asked to kick accurately, they will poke at the ball rather than develop a full kicking style.
2. Kicking is similar to throwing in that all youngsters should have a ball to kick. Foam balls (for primary grades) are excellent as they do not travel a long distance and the youngster can kick and retrieve the ball quickly.
3. Stationary balls are easier to kick than moving balls. Use this progression when teaching beginners to kick.
4. Teach various types of kicks: the toe kick, instep kick, and the side-of-the-foot kick.

Striking

Striking occurs when an object is hit with an implement. The most common forms of striking are using a bat to hit a softball, using a racket for striking in tennis and racquetball, and using the hand to strike a ball as in volleyball.

Stage One

In this stage, the feet are stationary and the trunk faces the direction of the tossed ball (or ball on a tee). The elbows are fully flexed, and extending the flexed joints in a downward plane generates the force. Little body force is generated because there is no trunk rotation and the motion developed is back to front. The total body does not play a role in generation of forces; rather, its force comes from the arms and wrists.

Stage Two

In Stage Two, the upper body begins to generate force. The trunk is turned to the side in anticipation of the ball. The weight shifts from the rear foot to the forward foot prior to contacting the ball. The trunk and hips are rotated into the ball as the swing takes place. The elbows are less flexed, and extending the flexed joints generates force. Trunk rotation and forward movement are in an oblique plane.

Stage Three

When performing mature striking skills, stand sideways to the path of the oncoming object. Shift the weight to the rear foot and rotate the hips, followed by a shift of weight toward the ball as it approaches the hitter. Striking occurs with the arms extended in a long and horizontal arc. The swing ends with weight on the forward foot. Mature striking is characterized by a swing through the full range of motion and a sequential transfer of weight from the rear to the front plane of the body.

Stress Points

1. Track the ball as soon as possible and keep tracking until it is hit. Even though it is impossible to see the racket hit the ball, this encourages tracking the object as long as possible.

2. Grip the bat with the hands together. If batting right handed, the left hand should be on the bottom (near the small end of the bat).

3. Keep the elbows away from the body. Emphasis should be placed on making a large swing with the elbows extended as the ball is hit.

4. Swing the bat in a horizontal plane. Beginners have a tendency to strike downward in a chopping motion.

TEACHING TIPS

1. Striking should be done with maximum force and bat velocity when the focus of instruction is on developing a mature striking form.

2. Practise hitting stationary objects before progressing to moving objects. Batting tees and balls suspended on a string are useful for beginners.

3. Use slow-moving objects such as balloons and beach balls in the early stages of striking practice. This helps the child track the moving projectile.

4. As skill in striking increases, the size of the projectile and bat (or racket) can be decreased.

5. Ensure that there is contrast between the ball and the background to enhance visual perception.

Critical Thinking

1. Accurate verbal cues are important guides to help students effectively practise fundamental motor skills. Identify three cues for two of the motor skills presented in this chapter. Compare your cues with a partner who choses the same skill.

References and Suggested Readings

Burton, A. & Miller, D. (1998). *Movement skill assessment.* Champaign, IL: Human Kinetics.

Gabbard, C.P. (2004). *Lifelong motor development* (4th ed.). San Francisco, CA: Benjamin Cummings.

Gallahue, D. & Donnelly, F.C. (2003). *Developmental physical education for all children.* (4th ed.). Champaign, IL: Human Kinetics.

Haubenstricker, J.L. & Seefeldt, V.D. (1986). Acquisition of motor skills during childhood. In V.D. Seefeldt (Ed.), *Physical activity and well-being.* Reston, VA: AAHPERD.

Haywood, K. & Getchell, N. (2001). *Life Span Motor Development.* (3rd ed.). Champaign, IL: Human Kinetics.

Magill, R.A. (2004). *Motor learning and control: Concepts and application* (7th ed.). New York: McGraw-Hill.

Malina, R.M., Bouchard, C., & Bar-Or, O. (2004). *Growth, maturation, and physical activity* (2nd ed.). Champaign, IL: Human Kinetics.

Payne, V.G. & Isaacs, L.D. (2005). *Human motor development: A lifespan approach.* (6th ed.). New York, NY: McGraw-Hill.

Wickstrom, R.L. (1983). *Fundamental movement patterns.* Philadelphia: Lea & Febiger.

Weblinks

Healthy Opportunities for preschoolers and primary: www.educ.uvic.ca/faculty/temple/vtstd/ HOP/frameset.htm

This website highlights developmentally appropriate movement activities for daily physical activity. Includes downloadable instructional manual.

Sask Sport: www.sasksport.sk.ca

Highlights the *Children in Sport: A Fundamental Skill Development Program.* This program focuses on building fundamental skills through games and skill progressions.

CHAPTER 16

Introductory Activities: Applying Fundamental Motor Skills

Essential Components

I	Organized around content standards
II	Student-centred and developmentally appropriate
III	**Physical activity and motor skill development form the core of the program**
IV	Teaches management skills and self-discipline
V	**Promotes inclusion of all students**
VI	**Focuses on process over product**
VII	Promotes lifetime personal health and wellness
VIII	Teaches cooperation and responsibility and promotes sensitivity to diversity

Physical Education Standards

1	**Students are able to move competently using a variety of fundamental and specialized motor skills.**
2	Students can monitor and maintain a health-enhancing level of physical fitness.
3	Students are able to apply movement concepts and basic mechanics of skill performance when learning and refining motor skills.
4	Students comprehend the basic principles of wellness and are able to apply concepts that enable them to make meaningful decisions that positively impact their health and wellness.
5	**Students participate in a wide variety of physical activities and learn how to maintain a personalized active lifestyle.**
6	Students demonstrate empathy, understanding, and respect for the numerous differences exhibited by people in an activity setting.
7	Students exhibit responsible and self-directed behaviours that lead to positive social interactions in physical activity.

OVERVIEW

Introductory activities are vigorous, challenging, unstructured movements designed to allow children maximum participation. These activities allow freedom of movement and challenge each child. Introductory activities make up the initial phase of the lesson and are approximately 2 to 3 minutes in duration. They are used to help the children to warm up physiologically and to prepare them for the fitness activity that follows. Introductory activities also allow an opportunity for teachers to practise management skills and focus on the learning outcomes of the lesson.

OUTCOMES

- Describe the rationale for including introductory activities in the lesson plan.

- Characterize various features of the introductory phase of the lesson.

- Develop an introductory activity that meets established criteria for preparing children physiologically and psychologically.

- Describe the type of movements that are used in introductory activities.

*I*ntroductory activities represent the first activity youngsters experience when entering the activity area. Vigorous fundamental locomotor movements that require minimal instruction characterize introductory activities. Introductory activities are used during the first 2 or 3 minutes of the lesson. There are a number of reasons for using introductory activities, including the following:

1. To practise management skills. Introductory activities require little instruction, so use this time to have students practise stopping, listening, and moving on signal.

2. To offer youngsters activity when entering the gym. This satisfies their need to move and gives you an opportunity to establish a positive learning atmosphere for the class.

3. To allow children to warm up physiologically and prepare them for activity to follow.

4. To focus students on the learning outcomes of the lesson.

Introductory activities are active and exciting and help children prepare themselves for the activities that follow. Introductory activities in this chapter are drawn from a variety of sources, including Chapters 12, 14, 15, 17, and 20. Refer to these chapters for additional ideas. In general, the activities should require minimal instruction and review basic skills and concepts.

European Rhythmic Running

Rhythmic Running is used in many European countries to open the daily lesson. The European style is light, rhythmic running to the accompaniment of some type of percussion, usually a drum or tambourine. Skilled runners do not need accompaniment but merely keep time with a leader. Much of the running follows a circular path, but it can be done in scatter formation (see Figure 16.1). To introduce a group of children to Rhythmic Running, have them clap to the beat of the drum. Next, as they clap, have them shuffle their feet in place, omitting the clapping. Finally, the class can run in single-file formation, if desired. The running should be light, bouncy, and rhythmic in time with the beat. When running in single file, youngsters should stay behind the person in front, maintain proper spacing, and lift the knees in a light, prancing step.

A number of movement ideas can be combined with the rhythmic running pattern. Here are some examples:

1. On signal (a whistle or a double beat on the drum), runners freeze in place. They resume running when the regular beat begins again.

2. On signal, runners make a full turn in four running steps, lifting the knees high while turning.

Figure 16.1

European running.

3. Children clap hands every fourth beat as they run. Instead of clapping, runners sound a brisk "Hey!" on the fourth beat, raising one arm with a fist at the same time.

4. Children run in squad formation, following the path set by the squad leader.

5. On signal, children run in general space, exercising care not to bump into each other. They return to a circular running formation on the next signal.

6. Students alternate between running with high knee action and regular running.

7. Runners change to a light, soundless run and back to a heavier run. The tone of the drum can control the quality of the movement.

8. Students use Rhythmic Running while handling a parachute.

9. On the command "Centre," children run four steps toward the centre, turn around (four steps), and run outward for four steps to resume the original circular running pattern.

10. On signal, runners go backward, changing the direction of the circle.

11. Students carry a beanbag or a ball. Every fourth step, they toss the item up and catch it while running.

12. A leader moves the class through various formations. A task that is enjoyable and challenging is crossing lines of children, alternating one child from one line in front of one youngster from another line.

13. The class moves into various shapes on signal. Possible shapes might be a square, rectangle, triangle, or pentagon. The Rhythmic Running must be continued while the youngsters move into position.

14. When a signal is given, each class member changes position with another student and then resumes the activity. An example might be to change position with the student opposite in the circle.

15. Because the movement is rhythmic, students can practise certain skills, such as a full turn. The turn can be done to a four-count rhythm and should be more deliberate than a quick turning movement that lacks definition.

16. When the drum stops, children scatter and run in random fashion. When the beat resumes, they return to circular formation and proper rhythm.

Gross Motor Movements

Most movements of the gross movement type stress locomotor activities, but some include manipulative and nonlocomotor activities. The movements should involve the body as a whole and provide abrupt change from one movement pattern to another. A routine can begin with running and then change to another movement pattern that is either specified by the teacher or determined by the youngsters. Signals for change can be supplied with a voice command, whistle, drumbeat, or handclap. Children enjoy being challenged by having to change with the signal. Continue each part of a routine long enough for good body challenge and involvement.

Running provides much of the basis for gross movement activities, but other activities of a vigorous nature can be used. The suggested activities are classified roughly according to type and whether they are individual-, partner, or group-oriented.

Individual Running and Changing Movements

FREE RUNNING

Students run in any direction, changing direction at will.

RUNNING AND CHANGING DIRECTION

Children run in any direction, changing direction on signal. As a progression, specify the type of angle (right, obtuse, 45-degree, or 180-degree). Alternate right and left turns.

RUNNING AND CHANGING LEVEL

Children run high on their toes and change to a lower level on signal. Require runners to touch the floor sometimes when at the lower level.

RUNNING AND CHANGING THE TYPE OF LOCOMOTION

On signal, runners change from running to free choice or to a specified type of locomotion (such as walking, jumping, hopping, skipping, sliding, or galloping).

RUNNING AND STOPPING

Students run in various directions and, on signal, freeze. Stress stopping techniques and an immobilized position.

RAT RACE RUN

Place four cones in the corners of the gym to create a running track. Students jog/run outside the cones in the same direction while music plays. When the music stops, each student must find a partner (who is ahead of him or her) while continuing to move in a forward direction. When everyone finds a partner, music starts again.

MOVE AND PERFORM ATHLETIC MOVEMENTS

Students move and stop on signal. They then perform an athletic skill move, such as a basketball set shot, lacrosse throw, volleyball pass, or soccer kick. Students should place emphasis on correct form and timing. A variation of the activity is for students to move with a partner and throw a pass on signal or shoot a basket. The partner catches the ball or rebounds the shot.

RUNNING AND ASSUMING A POSE

Pupils run and, on signal, assume a statue pose. Allow choice or specify a limitation.

TORTOISE AND HARE

When the teacher calls out "Tortoise," the children run slowly in general space. On the command "Hare," they change to a rapid, circular run. During the latter, stress good knee lift.

PONIES IN THE STABLE

Each child has a stable—his or her spot or place on the floor. This can be marked with a beanbag or a hoop. On the initial signal, children gallop lightly (like ponies) in general space. The next signal tells them to trot lightly to their stable and to continue trotting lightly in place.

HIGH FIVES

Students move in different directions throughout the areas. On signal, they are challenged to run toward a partner, jump, and give a "high five" (slap hands) while moving. Emphasis should be placed on timing so that the high five is given at the top of the jump. Encourage them to develop combinations of changing the level as well as changing the speed of the movement.

ADDING FITNESS CHALLENGES

Running (or other locomotor movements) can be combined with fitness activities. During the signalled stop, have students perform exercises such as push-ups and curl-ups.

Youngsters move and perform a task on signal. Tasks can be individual or partner activities. Examples are Seat Circles, Balances, Wring the Dishrag, Partner Hopping, Twister, and Back-to-back Get-up (see Chapter 20).

RUN, STOP, AND PIVOT

Students run, stop, and then pivot. This is an excellent activity for game skill development. Youngsters enjoy it especially when they are told to imagine that they are basketball or soccer players.

TRIPLE'S ROUTINE

The triple S's are *speed, style,* and *stop*. Children are in scatter formation throughout the area. On the command "Speed," they run in general space rapidly while avoiding contact with others. On "Style," all run with style (easy, light, loose running) in a large, circular, counterclockwise path. On the command "Stop," all freeze quickly under control. Repeat as necessary.

AGILITY RUN

Pick two lines or markers 3 to 5 m apart. Students run (or use other locomotor movements) back and forth between the lines for a specified time (10, 15, or 20 seconds). Students can add a personal challenge by seeing how many times they can move back and forth within the given time limit.

Other Individual Movement Combinations

UPRIGHT MOVEMENT TO ALL FOURS

Youngsters begin with a movement in upright position and change to one on all fours.

AIRPLANES

Children pretend to be airplanes. When told to take off, they zoom with arms out, swooping, turning, and gliding (see Figure 16.2). When they are commanded to land, they drop to the floor in prone position, simulating a plane at rest. To start their engines and take off, they can perform a series of push-ups and move up and down while simulating engine noise.

COMBINATION MOVEMENT

Directives for combination movement can establish specified movements or allow some choice. The limitation might be to run, skip, and roll, or to jump, twist, and shake.

Figure 16.2

Performing airplanes.

Another approach is to set a number for the sequence and let the children select the activities. Say, "Put three different kinds of movement together in a smooth pattern."

COUNTDOWN

The teacher begins a countdown for blastoff: "Ten, nine, eight, seven, six, five, four, three, two, one—blastoff!" The children are scattered, and each makes an abrupt, jerky movement on each count. On the word *blastoff*, they jump up in the air and run in different directions until the stop signal is given.

MAGIC-NUMBER CHALLENGES

A challenge can be issued like this: "Ten, ten, and ten." Children then put together three movements, doing 10 repetitions of each. Or the teacher could say, "Today we are going to play our version of Twenty-one." Twenty-one becomes the magic number that is to be fulfilled with three movements, each of which is done seven times.

CROSSING THE RIVER

A river can be set up as the space between two parallel lines about 10 m apart, or it can be the crosswise area in a gymnasium. Each time the children cross the river, they use a different type of locomotor movement. Children should be encouraged not to repeat a movement. Play is continuous over a minute or so.

FOUR-CORNERS MOVEMENT

Lay out a square with a cone at each corner. As the student passes each corner, he or she changes to a different locomotor movement with an agility emphasis. Challenge students with some of the following sport agility movements: backward running, leaps, grapevine step, front crossover, back crossover, high knees, and slide steps. Add variation by changing the qualities of movement (for example, soft, heavy, slow, fast). Students can pass to the outside of the area if they are doing a faster movement.

JUMPING AND HOPPING PATTERNS

Each child has a home spot. The teacher provides jumping and hopping sequences to take children away from and back to their spot. The teacher could say, "Move with three jumps, two hops, and a half turn. Return to place the same way." The teacher should have on hand a number of sequences. Action can extend beyond simply jumping and hopping.

MOVE, ROCK, AND ROLL

Each youngster procures an individual mat and places it on the floor. Students are challenged to move around, over, and on the mats. When a signal is given, children move to a mat and try different ways of rocking and rolling. Rocking on different parts of the body can be specified, and different body rolls can be suggested. As another challenge, tell the children to do a rock or a roll or both on a mat, get up and run to another mat, and repeat the sequence.

Individual Rhythmic Movements

As well as the introductory rhythmic activities described below, see Chapter 19 for more ideas.

MUSICAL RELAXATION

Musical relaxation can be conducted with a drum or appropriate recorded music. Children run in time to the rhythm. When the rhythm stops, children recline on their backs, close their eyes, and remain relaxed until the music begins again.

MOVING TO RHYTHM

The possibilities with rhythm are many. Rhythm can guide locomotor movements, with changes in tempo being part of the activity. The intensity of the sound can be translated into light or heavy movements.

MOVING TO MUSIC

Musical pieces can provide a basis for creative movement. Look for two-part musical pieces, so a nonlocomotor movement can be done to the first part and a locomotor movement to the second.

Individual Movements with Manipulation

In addition to the introductory manipulative activities described below, see Chapter 17 for more ideas.

INDIVIDUAL ROPE JUMPING

Each child runs with rope in hand. On the signal to change, the child stops and begins to jump rope.

HOOP ACTIVITIES

Each child runs holding a hoop. When the signal is given to stop, the child either does Hula-Hooping or lays the hoop on the floor and uses it for hopping and jumping patterns.

BALL ACTIVITIES

Youngsters dribble balls (indoors) as in basketball or (outside) as in soccer. When a change is signalled, they stop, balance on one leg, and pass the ball under the other leg, around the back, and overhead, keeping both control and balance. Supply other challenges that involve both movement with the ball and manipulative actions performed in place.

BEANBAG TOUCH AND GO

Beanbags are spread throughout the area. On signal, children move and touch as many different beanbags as possible with their hands. Specify different body parts for children to use for touching. Select different colours of beanbags, and the command might be "Touch as many blue beanbags as possible with your elbow."

Children can also move to and around a beanbag. The type of movement can be varied; for example, they might skip around the yellow beanbag with the left side leading. Change the movement as well as the direction and leading side of the body. Another enjoyable activity for younger students is to trace out a shape (for example, triangle, circle, square) as they move from beanbag to beanbag.

LONG-ROPE ROUTINE

Students begin in a loose column composed of four people holding a long jump rope in their right hands at waist level. Give a series of four commands. On the first signal, youngsters jog lightly in a column. On the second signal, the group shifts the rope overhead from the right side to the left side of the body while jogging. At the third signal, the two inside students release the rope and being jumping as soon as the two students at the end of the rope start turning the rope. On the fourth signal, the turners become jumpers and vice versa. The sequence is repeated a number of times.

DISAPPEARING HOOPS

Each child gets a hoop and places it somewhere on the floor. Offer challenges such as "Move through five blue hoops, jump over four yellow hoops, and skip around six green hoops." On signal, the children move to find a hoop and balance inside it. As youngsters are moving, take away two or three hoops. At the signal, some students will not find a hoop. Those left out then offer the class the next movement challenge. Specify different challenges and stunts inside the hoops.

Partner and Group Activities

MARKING

Each child has a partner who is somewhat equal in ability. Under control, one partner runs, dodges, and tries to lose the other, who must stay within 1 m of the runner. On signal, both stop. Chasers must be able to touch their partners to say that they have marked them. Partners then change roles.

FOLLOWING ACTIVITY

One partner leads and performs various kinds of movements. The other partner must move in the same fashion. This idea can be extended to squad organization.

MEDIC TAG

Three or four students are designated as "taggers." They try to tag other students; when tagged, a student kneels as if injured. Another student (not one of the taggers) can "cure" the injured player with a touch, enabling the student to resume play.

HOSPITAL TAG

Every player is a tagger. Any player who is tagged must cover with one hand the body area that was touched. Students may be tagged twice but must be able to hold both tagged spots and keep moving. A student who is tagged three times must freeze. Restart the game when most of the students have been frozen.

GROUP OVER AND AROUND

Half of the children are scattered. Each is in a curled position, face down. The other children leap or jump over the curled children (see Figure 16.3). On signal, reverse the groups quickly. Instead of being curled, the children form arches or bridges, and the moving children go around these. A further extension is to have the children on the floor alternate between curled and bridge positions. If the moving child goes over the curled position, the floor child changes immediately to a bridge. The moving children react accordingly.

POPCORN

Half the class is scattered throughout the area and assume the push-up position. The other half of the class will move and "pop the popcorn." This is done by moving over and around the students who are in push-up position. When a

Figure 16.3

Group over and around.

student moves around a student, that youngster lowers to the floor. When a student moves over a student lying on the floor, that student raises to the push-up position. Moving students should exchange places with those on the floor after a designated time.

BRIDGES BY THREES

Three children in a group can set up an interesting movement sequence using bridges. Two of the children make bridges, and the third child goes under both bridges and sets up a bridge. Each child in turn goes under the bridges of the other two. Different kinds of bridges can be specified, and the bridges can be arranged so that children change direction. An over-and-under sequence also provides interest.

RUBBER BAND

Students gather around the teacher in the centre of the area. On signal, students move away from the teacher with a designated movement such as a run, hop sideways, skip backward, double-lame dog, or grapevine step. On signal, they sprint back to the central point, jump, and give a shout.

NEW LEADER MOVEMENTS

Squads or small groups run around the area, following a leader. When the change is signalled, the last person goes to the head of the line to lead. Groups of three are ideal for this activity.

BODY PART IDENTIFICATION

Scatter on the floor enough beanbags for the whole class. The children either run between or jump over the beanbags. When a body part is called out, the children place that body part on the nearest beanbag.

LEAPFROG

Two, three, or four children can make up this sequence. The children form a straight or curved column, with all except the last child in line taking the leapfrog position. The last child leaps over the children in turn, and after going over all, assumes the leapfrog position at the head of the column. Lines should be scattered to avoid children running into other jumpers.

Creative and Exploratory Opportunities

Another approach of interest to children is providing creative and exploratory opportunities at the beginning of a lesson. Some examples follow:

- Put out enough equipment of one type (hoops, balls, wands, beanbags) so that all children have a piece of equipment with which to explore. This can be open exploration, or the movement can follow the trend of a prior lesson, thus supplying extension to the progression.

- Have available a range of apparatus, such as climbing ropes, climbing apparatus, mats, boxes, balance beams, balance boards, and similar items. Manipulative items also can be a part of the package. The children choose the area in which they want to participate.

Tambourine-directed Activities

The tambourine can signal changes of movement because it can produce two different kinds of sound: the tinny noise made by vigorous shaking and the percussive sound made by striking the instrument. Signal movement changes by switching from one sound to the other.

SHAKING SOUND

1. Remain in one spot but shake all over. (These should be gross movements).
2. Shake and gradually drop to the floor.
3. Scurry in every direction.
4. Run lightly with tiny steps.

DRUM SOUND

1. Make jerky movements to the percussive beat.
2. Jump in place or through space.
3. Do locomotor movements in keeping with the beat.
4. Responding to three beats, collapse on the first beat, roll on the second, and form a shape on the third.

COMBINATIONS

To form a combination of movements, select one from each category (shaking or percussive). When the teacher makes the shaking sound, children perform that movement. When the teacher changes to the drum sound, the children react accordingly.

References and Suggested Readings

Byl, J. (2004). *101 fun warm-up and cool-down games.* Champaign, IL: Human Kinetics.

Faigenbaum, A. & McFarland, J. (2007). Guidelines for implementing a dynamic warm-up for physical education. *Journal of Physical Education, Recreation and Dance, 78*(3), 25–28.

Landy, J.M. & Landy, M.J. (1992). *Ready-to-use P.E. activities for grades K–2.* West Nyack, NY: Parker Publishing.

Landy, J.M. & Landy, M.J. (1992). *Ready-to-use P.E. activities for grades 3–4.* West Nyack, NY: Parker Publishing.

Landy, J.M. & Landy, M.J. (1992). *Ready-to-use P.E. activities for grades 5–6.* West Nyack, NY: Parker Publishing.

Landy, J.M. & Landy, M.J. (1992). *Ready-to-use P.E. activities for grades 7–9.* West Nyack, NY: Parker Publishing.

 Weblinks

Moving Ahead: http://members.tripod.com/movingahead/index.html

This site is dedicated to teaching children how to perform skilful movements as they learn and develop motor skills.

CHAPTER 17

Manipulative Skills

Essential Components

I	Organized around content standards
II	Student-centred and developmentally appropriate
III	**Physical activity and motor skill development form the core of the program**
IV	Teaches management skills and self-discipline
V	**Promotes inclusion of all students**
VI	**Focuses on process over product**
VII	**Promotes lifetime personal health and wellness**
VIII	Teaches cooperation and responsibility and promotes sensitivity to diversity

Physical Education Standards

1	**Students are able to move competently using a variety of fundamental and specialized motor skills.**
2	Students can monitor and maintain a health-enhancing level of physical fitness.
3	**Students are able to apply movement concepts and basic mechanics of skill performance when learning and refining motor skills.**
4	Students comprehend the basic principles of wellness and are able to apply concepts that enable them to make meaningful decisions that positively impact their health and wellness.
5	**Students participate in a wide variety of physical activities and learn how to maintain a personalized active lifestyle.**
6	Students demonstrate empathy, understanding, and respect for the numerous differences exhibited by people in an activity setting.
7	Students exhibit responsible and self-directed behaviours that lead to positive social interactions in physical activity.

OVERVIEW

Activities in this chapter develop manipulative skills. A manipulative skill is one in which a child handles an object with the hands, feet, or other body parts. Children develop sport skills from practising and learning the advanced activities in this chapter. Jump-rope activities develop specialized motor skills, particularly visual–tactile coordination. Rope-jumping activities in this chapter progress from individual movements using rope patterns, to long-rope jumping with turners, to individual rope-jumping challenges.

OUTCOMES

- Incorporate creative opportunities in teaching manipulative skills.

- Identify instructional procedures related to different types of manipulative skills.

- Outline skill progressions, activities, and instructional hints associated with using balloons, beanbags, balls, paddles, discs, hoops, jump ropes, parachutes, and other objects to teach manipulative skills.

- Identify beginning, intermediate, and advanced rope-jumping skills and routines using individual and long ropes.

- List progressions to use when teaching rope jumping.

Manipulative activities are characterized by the use of some type of implement, usually with the hands but possibly with the feet or other body parts. Manipulative activities develop both hand–eye and foot–eye coordination as well as dexterity. Activities with balloons, hoops, beanbags, balls of various types, discs, and scoops round out a basic program. Activities with jump ropes are important in the program because they offer multiple possibilities: manipulative activity, rhythmic activity, and fundamental movement.

Balloons, beanbags, and sponge balls provide early throwing and catching activities for younger children. A soft object reduces the fear younger children have of being hurt while catching an object. After children master the introductory skills, the teacher can initiate activities with other types of balls and more demanding skills.

The start-and-extend approach is sound for teaching manipulative activities. Start children with a challenge that allows all to achieve success, and then extend the skills and concepts from that base. Concern for progression usually emphasizes that most activities begin with the individual approach and move later to partner activity.

Progression and Movement Concepts

Activities within each unit in this chapter are presented in progression and take the form of movement themes or movement tasks and challenges. Where possible, movement tasks should blend the basic skills in logical progression with movement concepts (see Chapter 14) in order to expand students' movement potential. Creative expression is a valuable outcome of this blend. This gives youngsters a chance to practise their favourite skills, work on learning new skills, or invent different ways of performing. The recommended activities in this chapter help the teacher integrate skills and concepts.

Activities with Balloons and Beach Balls

Balloons provide interesting movement experiences and emphasize hand–eye coordination. Success can be achieved with balloons when students are not ready for faster moving ball skills. Keeping a balloon afloat is within the capability of young children and special education students. Beach balls are larger, move slowly, and are more predictable in movement. Both objects allow youngsters to learn to catch without fear of being hurt by the projectile. Place emphasis on proper footwork. Because these objects move slowly, there is ample time for students to learn proper footwork—preparing for a volley, catching, and striking, for example.

Balloons are inexpensive and readily available. Extras are needed, as there is always breakage. The balloons should be of good quality and spherical in shape. At times, however, oddly shaped balloons can provide a change of pace. Balloons should be inflated only moderately, because high inflation increases the chance of breakage. Beach balls should be inflated with a ball pump. When they are no longer needed for instruction, they can be deflated and stored.

Instructional Procedures

1. Use the following instructional cues when teaching balloon and beach ball skills:

   a. Catch and control with the fingertips.

   b. Keep your eyes on the object.

   c. Move your body into the path of the oncoming object.

   d. Reach, catch, and move the object to the body (giving).

Recommended Activities

1. Begin with free exploration, having children play under control with their balloon (see Figure 17.1). The objective is to have the children gain a sense of the balloon's flight.

2. Introduce specific hand, finger, and arm contacts. Include using alternate hands; contacting at different levels (low, high, in-between); jumping and making high contact; using different hand contacts (palm, back, side, and different fist positions); using different finger combinations (two fingers, index finger, thumb only, others); and using arms, elbows, and shoulders.

3. Expand the activity to use other body parts. Establish contact sequences with three or four body parts. Use various levels and body shapes. Make some visual cards with names of body parts. Students must take their eye off the balloon to see the named body part. This is an excellent challenge to help young children learn to track a moving object.

4. Contact balloon from various body positions—kneeling, sitting, and lying.

5. Use an object to control the balloon (a paddle).

Figure 17.1

Batting balloons from different body positions.

6. Restrict movement. Keep one foot in place. Keep one or both feet within a hoop or on a mat or carpet square.

7. Work with a partner by alternating turns, batting the beach ball back and forth, employing follow-the-leader patterns, and so on.

8. Have four to six children seated on the floor in a small circle. Each circle gets two balloons to be kept in the air. Children's seats are "glued" to the floor. Once a balloon hits the floor, it is out of play. Play for a specified time (30 to 60 seconds). Increase the challenge by using beach balls.

Activities with Beanbags

Activities with beanbags provide valuable learning experiences for elementary school children at all levels. All parts of the body can be brought into play. For tossing and catching, though, the beanbag encourages children to manipulate with their hands. Beanbag activities can be used with older youngsters provided the activities are carefully selected to challenge students. The more challenging partner activities—juggling, different and unique methods of propulsion, and the split-vision drill (Figure 17.2)—are examples of suitable activities.

Instructional Procedures

1. Use the following instructional cues when teaching beanbag activities:

   a. Stress a soft receipt of the beanbag by "giving" with the hands, arms, and legs. "Giving" involves the hands going out toward the incoming beanbag and bringing it in for a soft landing.

   b. Keep your eyes on the beanbag when catching.

   c. When tossing and catching, toss slightly above eye level.

2. Make sure that beanbags are at least 15 cm square. This size balances well and can be controlled on various parts of the body, thus offering greater challenge to intermediate-level children.

3. Throwing and catching skills involve many intricate elements. Emphasize the principles of opposition, eye focus, weight transfer, and follow-through. It is important that children track the object being caught and focus on the target when throwing.

4. Stress laterality and directionality when teaching throwing and catching skills. Children should be taught to throw, catch, and balance beanbags with both the left and right sides of their bodies, and catch and throw at different levels.

5. Throw at chest height to a partner, unless a different type of throw is specified. Practise all types of return: low, medium, high, left, and right.

6. In partner work, keep distances between partners reasonable, especially in introductory phases. Three metres is a reasonable starting distance.

7. In partner work, emphasize skilful and varied throwing, catching, and handling of the beanbag.

Most activities are classified as individual or partner activities. A few activities are for groups of three or more.

Individual Activities

TOSSING TO SELF IN PLACE

1. Toss with both hands, with right hand only, and with left hand only. Catch the same way. Catch with the back of the hands.

2. Toss the beanbag progressively higher, then progressively lower.

3. Hold the beanbag in one hand and make large arm circles (imitating a windmill). Release the bag so that it flies upward, and then catch it.

4. Toss from side to side, right to left (reverse), front to back (reverse), and around various body parts in different combinations.

5. Toss upward and catch with hands behind the back. Toss upward from behind the body and catch in front. Toss upward and catch on the back, on the knees, on the toes, and on other body parts.

6. Hold the bag at arm's length in front of the body, with palms up. Withdraw hands quickly from under the bag, and catch it from on top in a palms-down stroke before it falls to the floor.

7. Toss upward and catch as high as possible; as low as possible. Work out a sequence of high, low, and in between.

8. Toss upward and catch with the body off the floor. Try tossing as well as catching with the body off the ground.

9. Toss in various fashions while seated and while lying.

10. Toss two beanbags upward and catch a bag in each hand.

ADDING STUNTS IN PLACE

1. Toss overhead to the rear, turn around, and catch. Toss, do a full turn, and catch.

2. Toss, clap the hands, and catch. Clap the hands more than once. Clap the hands around different body parts.

3. Toss, touch different body parts with both hands, and catch. Touch two different body parts, calling out the name of the parts. Touch two body parts, clap hands, and catch.

4. Toss, kneel on one knee, and catch. Try this going to a sitting or lying position. Reverse the position order, coming from a lying or sitting position to a standing position to catch.

5. Toss, touch the floor, and catch. Explore with other challenges.

6. Bend forward, reach between the legs, and toss the bag onto the back or shoulders.

7. Reach one hand over the shoulder, drop the beanbag, and catch it with the other hand behind the back. Reverse the hands. Drop the beanbag from one hand behind the back and catch it with the other hand between the legs. Put the beanbag on the head, lean back, and catch it with both hands behind the back. Catch it with one hand.

LOCOMOTOR MOVEMENTS

1. Toss to self, moving to another spot to catch. Toss forward, run, and catch. Move from side to side. Toss overhead to the rear, run back, and catch.

2. Add the various stunts and challenges described previously. Vary with different locomotor movements.

BALANCING THE BEANBAG ON VARIOUS BODY PARTS

1. Balance the beanbag on the head. Move around, keeping the beanbag in place. Sit down, lie down, turn around, and so on.

2. Balance the beanbag on other parts of the body and move around. Balance on top of the instep, between the knees, on the shoulders, on the elbows, under the chin. Use more than one beanbag.

PROPELLING WITH VARIOUS BODY PARTS

1. Toss to self from various parts of the body: the elbow, the instep, the knees, the shoulders, between the feet, between the heels.

2. Sit and toss the bag from the feet to the hands.

OTHER ACTIVITIES

1. From a standing wide-straddle position, place the beanbag on the floor and push it between the legs as far back as possible. Jump in place with a half turn and repeat.

2. Take the same position as above. Push the bag back as far as possible between the legs, bending the knees. Without moving the legs, turn to the right and pick up the bag. Repeat to the left.

3. Stand with feet apart and hold the beanbag with both hands. Reach as high as possible (with both hands), bend backward, and drop the bag. Reach between the legs, and pick up the bag.

4. On all fours, put the bag in the small of the back. Wiggle and force the bag off the back without moving the hands or knees from place.

5. In crab position, place the beanbag on the stomach, and try to shake it off.

6. Push the beanbag across the floor with different body parts, such as the nose, shoulder, or knee.

7. Each student drops a beanbag on the floor. See how many different ways students can move over, around, and between the beanbags. As an example, jump three bags, crab-walk around two others, and cartwheel over one more.

Partner Activities

TOSSING BACK AND FORTH

1. Begin with various kinds of two-handed throws: underhand, overhead, side, and over the shoulder. Change to one-handed tossing and throwing.

2. Throw at different levels, at different targets, right and left.

3. Throw under the leg, around the body.

4. Have partners sit about 3 m apart. Throw and catch in various styles.

5. Use follow activities, in which one partner leads with a throw and the other follows with the same kind of throw.

6. Jump, turn in the air, and pass to partner.

7. Toss to partner from unexpected positions and from around and under different body parts.

8. Stand back-to-back and pass the bag around both partners from hand to hand as quickly as possible.

9. Toss in various directions to make the partner move and catch.

10. Run around the partner in a circle, tossing the bag back and forth.

11. Propel two beanbags back and forth. Each partner has a bag, and the bags go in opposite directions at the same time. Try having one partner toss both bags at once in the same direction, using various types of throws. Try to keep three bags going at once.

PROPELLING BACK AND FORTH WITH DIFFERENT BODY PARTS

1. From a sitting position, toss the bag to a partner with foot or toes, from on top of the feet, and from between the feet, with elbow, shoulder, head, and any other body part.

2. With back to a partner, take a bunny-jump position. With the bag held between the feet, kick the bag back to partner. Try kicking with both feet from a standing position.

3. Partners lie supine on the floor with heads pointing toward each other, about 15 cm apart. One partner has a beanbag between the feet and deposits it in between their heads. The other partner picks up the bag with the feet (reaching over the head) and places it on the floor by the feet after returning to a lying position. With both partners in backward curl position, try to transfer the bag directly from one partner to the other with the feet.

Group Activities and Games

SPLIT-VISION DRILL

A split-vision drill from basketball can be adapted to beanbags. An active player faces two partners about 3 m away. They are standing side by side, a short distance apart. Two beanbags, one in the hands of the active player and the

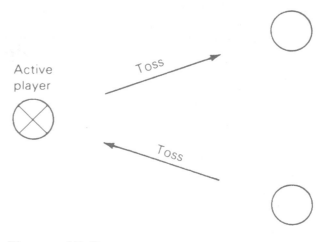

Figure 17.2

Split-vision drill for beanbags.

other with one of the partners, are needed for the drill. The active player tosses to the open partner and at the same time receives the bag from the other partner. The two bags move back and forth between the active player and the other two, alternately (see Figure 17.2). After a period of time, change positions.

TARGET GAMES

Wastebaskets, hoops, circles drawn on the floor, and other objects can be used as targets for beanbag tossing. Target boards with holes cut out are available from commercial sources. Holes can be triangles, circles, squares, and rectangles, thus stressing form concepts.

BEANBAG QUOITS

The game is played in the same way as horseshoes. A court is drawn with two spots on the floor about 5 m apart. Spots can be made with masking tape and should be 2.5 cm (1 inch) in diameter. Each competitor has two bags, a different colour for each player. Tosses are made from behind one spot to the other spot. The object is to get one or both bags closer to the mark than the opponents do. If a bag completely blocks out the spot, as viewed from directly overhead, the player scores 3 points. Otherwise, the bag nearest the spot scores 1 point. Games are played to 11, 15, or 21 points. In each round, the player winning the previous point tosses first.

Activities with Balls

Included in this section are the ball skills in which the child handles balls without the aid of other equipment, such as a bat or paddle. Ball skills are mostly of two types: (a) hand–eye skills, including throwing, catching, bouncing, dribbling (as in basketball), batting (as in volleyball), and rolling (as in bowling); and (b) foot–eye skills, including kicking, trapping, and dribbling (as in soccer).

Types of Balls

For younger children, foam balls and fleece balls are all excellent for introductory throwing and catching, because they help children overcome the fear factor. The 20-cm foam balls generally last longer and have more utility for youngsters. The foam balls are easy to catch and pass, and youngsters will not get hurt if accidentally hit by one. There are many different types of foam used to make these balls and it is important to make sure that the balls are dense and have adequate bounce. An even better (but more expensive) alternative is the "tough-skin" balls—foam balls covered with a tough plastic coating that causes the balls to bounce better and to resist damage. The inflated rubber playground ball (20-cm size) may be used for most ball-bouncing experiences. Inflate balls moderately so that they bounce well, but avoid overinflating, which makes them difficult to catch. The whiffle ball, a hollow plastic ball with holes cut in the surface, is also useful. Scoops provide an extension of whiffle ball activities.

Types of Organization

Begin instruction with younger children with individual work and progress to partner and group activities. After the children have acquired some skill, a lesson can include both individual and partner activities. In propelling the ball back and forth between partners, the children can progress from rolling the ball, to throwing with one bounce, to throwing on the fly. Be sure that a disparity in skill level between partners does not cause a problem for either one.

Distance between partners should be short at first and then lengthened gradually. The concept of targets is introduced by directing the children to throw the ball to specified points. Later, maintain progression by changing from a stationary target to a moving target.

Group work should be confined to small groups (of three to six), so that each child can be active, and should include activities not possible in individual or partner activity.

Instructional Procedures

1. Use the following instructional cues when teaching ball skills:
   a. Keep your eyes on the ball.
   b. Catch and dribble the ball with the pads of the fingers.
   c. Use opposition and weight transfer when passing the ball.

2. In catching, achieve soft receipt of the ball by "giving" with the hands and arms. The hands should reach out somewhat to receive the ball and then cushion the impact by bringing the ball in toward the body in a relaxed way.

3. To catch a throw above the waist, position the hands so that the thumbs are together. To receive a throw below the waist, the little fingers should be kept toward each other and the thumbs kept out.

4. In throwing to a partner, unless otherwise specified, the throw should reach the partner at about chest height. At times, specify different target points—high, low, right, left, at the knee, and so on.

5. Laterality is an important consideration. Give practice in turn to right and left members of the body.

6. Split-vision should be incorporated in bouncing and dribbling. Children should learn to look forward, rather than at the ball, when bouncing and dribbling.

7. Enhance children's tactile senses by having them dribble or bounce the ball with eyes closed.

8. Rhythmic accompaniment, particularly for bouncing and dribbling activities, adds another dimension to ball skills.

Activities with balls are presented with a 20-cm ball in mind. Some modification is needed if the balls used are smaller or are of the type that does not bounce.

Individual Activities

For individual activities, each child has a ball and practises alone. In the first group of individual activities, the child remains in the same spot. Next, the child rebounds the ball against a wall. (The wall should be reasonably free of projections and irregular surfaces so that the ball can return directly to the student.) In the third group of activities, the child performs alone while on the move.

CONTROLLED ROLLING AND HANDLING IN PLACE

1. In a wide-straddle position (other possible positions are seated with legs crossed or outstretched, and push-up position), place the ball on the floor, and roll it with constant finger guidance between and around the legs.

2. Roll the ball in a figure-eight path in and out, around the legs.

3. Reach as far to the left as possible with the ball and roll it in front of you to the other side. Catch it as far to the right of the body as possible.

4. Turn in place and roll the ball around with one hand in a large circle.

5. With the back moderately bent, release the ball behind the head, let it roll down the back, and catch it with both hands.

6. Make different kinds of bridges over the ball while using the ball as partial support for the bridge.

BOUNCING AND CATCHING IN PLACE

1. Beginning with two hands, bounce and catch the ball. Bounce a given number of times. Bounce at different levels. Bounce one-handed in a variety of ways. Bounce under the legs. Close the eyes and bounce and catch.

2. Bounce, perform various stunts (a body turn, or hand clap), and catch.

3. Bounce the ball around, under, and over the body.

4. Practise various kinds of bounces, catching all with the eyes closed.

5. Bounce the ball with various body parts, such as the head, elbow, or knee.

TOSSING AND CATCHING IN PLACE

1. Toss and catch, increasing height gradually. Toss from side to side. Toss underneath the legs, around the body, and from behind. Add challenges while tossing and catching. Clap the hands one or more times, make body turns (quarter, half, or full), touch the floor, click the heels, sit down, lie down, and so on.

2. To enhance body part identification, toss while performing some of the following challenges: touch the back with both hands, touch the back with both hands by reaching over both shoulders, touch both elbows, touch both knees with crossed hands, touch both heels with a heel slap, and touch the toes. Be sure to catch the ball after completing each challenge.

3. Toss upward and catch the descending ball as high as possible; as low as possible. Work out other levels and create combinations. Catch with crossed arms.

4. Practise catching by looking away after the ball is tossed upward. Experiment with different ways of catching with the eyes closed.

BATTING TO SELF IN PLACE

1. Bat the ball as in volleyball by using an open hand, or the side of the hand.

2. Bat and let the ball bounce. Catch in different ways.

3. Rebound the ball upward, using different parts of the body. Let it bounce.

4. Bat and rebound the ball so that it does not touch the ground.

5. Bat the ball, perform a stunt, and bat again.

FOOT SKILLS IN PLACE

1. Put the toes on top of the ball. Roll the ball in different directions, keeping the other foot in place but retaining control.

2. Use a two-foot pickup, front and back. This is done by putting the ball between the feet and hoisting it to the hands.

3. From a seated position with legs extended, toss the ball with the feet to the hands.

4. In a supine position, hold the ball on the floor above the head. Do a curl-up, bring the ball forward, touch the toes with it, and return to supine position.

5. Drop the ball, and immediately trap it against the floor with one foot. Try to bounce it with one foot.

DRIBBLING SKILLS IN PLACE

1. Dribble the ball first with both hands and then with the right and the left. (Emphasize that the dribble is a push with good wrist action). Dribble under the legs in turn and back around the body. Kneel and dribble. Return to standing position. Dribble the ball at different levels and at various tempos.

2. Dribble without looking at the ball. Dribble and change hands without stopping the dribble. Use various number combinations with the right and left hands. Dribble with the eyes closed.

THROWING AGAINST A WALL (CATCHING ON THE FIRST BOUNCE)

1. Throw the ball against the wall, and catch the return after one bounce. Practise various kinds of throws: two-handed, one-handed, overhead, side, baseball, chest pass.

2. Throw at a target mounted on the wall.

THROWING AGAINST A WALL (CATCHINGON THE FLY)

Repeat the throws used in the previous activity, but catch the return on the fly. It may be necessary to move closer and to have the ball contact the wall at a higher point.

HITTING AGAINST A WALL

1. Drop the ball, and contact it with open palm after it bounces. Keep the ball going with multiple hits.

2. Serve the ball against the wall as in volleyball. Experiment with different ways to serve.

KICKING AGAINST A WALL AND TRAPPING (FOOT–EYE SKILLS)

1. Practise different ways to control kicking against the wall and stopping (trapping) the ball on the return. Try using the foot to keep returning the ball against the wall on the bounce.

2. Put some targets on the wall and kick the ball at a target.

ROLLING ON THE MOVE

1. Roll the ball, run alongside it, and guide it with the hands in different directions.

2. Roll the ball forward, then run and catch up with it.

TOSSING AND CATCHING ON THE MOVE

1. Toss the ball upward and forward. Run forward and catch it after one bounce. Toss the ball upward in various directions (forward, sideward, backward), run under it, turn, and catch it on the fly.

2. Add various stunts and challenges, such as touching the floor, clicking the heels, or turning around.

HITTING ON THE MOVE

With first the right and then the left hand, bat the ball upward in different directions, and catch it on the first bounce or on the fly.

PRACTISING FOOT SKILLS ON THE MOVE

Dribble the ball (soccer style) forward and in other directions. Dribble around an imaginary point. Make various patterns while dribbling, such as a circle, square, triangle, or figure eight.

DRIBBLING ON THE MOVE

1. Dribble (basketball style) forward using one hand, and dribble back to place with the other. Change direction on a signal. Dribble in various directions, describing different pathways.

2. Place a hoop on the floor. Dribble inside the hoop until a signal is sounded, then dribble to another hoop and continue the dribble inside that hoop. Avoid dribbling on the hoop itself.

PRACTISING LOCOMOTOR MOVEMENTS WHILE HOLDING THE BALL

1. Hold the ball between the legs and perform various locomotor movements.

2. Try holding the ball in various positions with different body parts.

Partner Activities

ROLLING IN PLACE

Roll the ball back and forth to a partner. Begin with two-handed rolls and proceed to one-handed rolls. When partner rolls the ball, pick it up with the toes and snap it up into the hands.

THROWING AND CATCHING IN PLACE

1. Toss the ball to a partner with one bounce, using various kinds of tosses. Practise various kinds of throws and passes to partner.

2. Throw to specific levels and points: high, low, right, left, at the knee, and so on.

3. Throw and catch over volleyball net.

4. Work in a threesome, with one person holding a hoop between the two partners playing catch. Throw the ball through the hoop held at various levels. Try throwing through a moving hoop.

HITTING IN PLACE (VOLLEYBALL SKILLS)

1. Toss the ball upward to self, contact it two-handed to a partner, who catches and returns it in the same manner. Serve as in volleyball to a partner. The partner makes a return serve. Toss the ball to the partner, who makes a volleyball return. Keep distances short and keep the ball under control. Try to keep the ball going back and forth as in volleyball.

2. Hit the ball back and forth on one bounce. Hit it back and forth over a line, jump rope, or bench.

KICKING IN PLACE

1. Practise different ways of controlled kicking between partners and different ways of stopping the ball (trapping).

2. Practise a controlled punt, preceding the kick with a step on the non-kicking foot. Place the ball between the feet and propel it forward or backward to partner.

3. Practise foot pickups. One partner rolls the ball, and the other hoists it to self with extended toes.

THROWING FROM VARIOUS POSITIONS IN PLACE

Practise different throws from a kneeling, sitting, or lying position.

TWO-BALL ACTIVITIES IN PLACE

Using two balls, pass back and forth, with balls going in opposite directions.

Throw or propel the ball in any manner desired. The partner returns the ball in the same fashion.

THROWING AND CATCHING AGAINST A WALL

Alternate throwing and catching against a wall. Alternate returning the ball after a bounce, as in handball.

THROWING ON THE MOVE

1. One child remains in place and tosses to the other child, who is moving. The moving child can trace different patterns, such as back and forth between two spots. Receiver provides a target with outstretched arms for the tosser. (Tosser's spatial judgment must be adequate to anticipate where the moving child should be to receive the ball.

2. Practise different kinds of throws and passes as both children move in different patterns. (Considerable space is needed for this type of work.) Practise foot skills of dribbling and passing.

3. Carrying a ball, run in different directions while the partner follows. On signal, toss the ball upward so that the child following can catch it. Now change places and repeat the activity.

Juggling

Juggling is a novel task that is exciting to elementary school students. It is challenging and demands practice and repetition.

An excellent medium for teaching beginners is sheer, lightweight scarves that measure 45 to 60 cm square. These move slowly, allowing children to track them visually. Juggling with scarves teaches children correct patterns of object movement; however, it does not transfer easily to juggling with faster-moving objects such as beanbags, tennis balls, and rings. Therefore, two distinct sections for juggling are offered: a section dealing with learning to juggle with scarves and a second discussion explaining juggling with balls. Youngsters who have mastered the scarves can move to balls and other objects.

Juggling lessons should allow opportunity for children to move, at will, between scarves and faster-moving objects. Much practice is necessary to learn to juggle, and there will be a lot of misses during the acquisition of this skill. Because children tire quickly if they are not having success, it may be desirable to introduce juggling skills in small doses throughout a school year.

Juggling with Scarves

Hold scarves by the fingertips near the centre. To throw the scarf, it should be lifted and pulled into the air above eye level. Scarves are caught by clawing, a downward motion of the hand, and grabbing the scarf from above as it is falling. Scarf juggling should teach proper habits (for example, tossing the scarves straight up in line with the body rather than forward or backward). Many teachers remind children to imagine that they are in a phone booth—to emphasize tossing and catching without moving.

CASCADING

Cascading is the easiest pattern for juggling three objects. The following sequence can be used to learn this basic technique.

1. *One scarf.* Hold the scarf in the centre. Quickly move the arm across the chest and toss the scarf with the palm out. Reach out with the other hand and catch the scarf in a straight-down motion (clawing). Toss the scarf with this hand using the motion and claw it with the opposite hand. Continue the tossing and clawing sequence over and over. The scarf should move in a figure-eight pattern as shown in Figure 17.3.

Figure 17.3

Clawing a scarf.

2. *Two scarves—two hands.* Hold a scarf with the fingertips of each hand. Toss the first one across the body as described in step 1. When it reaches its peak, look at it, and toss the second scarf across the body in the opposite direction. The first scarf thrown is caught (clawed) by the hand throwing the second scarf and vice versa (see Figure 17.4). Verbal cues such as "Toss, claw, toss, claw" are helpful.

3. *Two scarves—one hand.* This sequence is a requisite if students are going to juggle three scarves. Start with both scarves in one hand (hold them as described below in three-scarf cascading). The important skill to learn is to toss the first scarf, and then the second scarf, and then catch the first and the second. Verbal cues to use are *toss, toss, catch, catch.* If students cannot toss two scarves before catching one, they will not be able to master juggling with three scarves.

4. *Three-scarf cascading.* A scarf is held in each hand by the fingertips as described in step 2. The third scarf is held with the ring and little fingers against the palm of one hand. The first scarf to be thrown will be from the hand that is holding two scarves. Toss this scarf from the fingertips across the chest as learned earlier. When scarf 1 reaches its peak, scarf 2 from the other hand is thrown across the body. As this hand starts to come down, it catches scarf 1. When scarf 2 reaches its peak, scarf 3 is thrown in the same path as that of scarf 1. To complete the cycle, as the hand comes down from throwing scarf 3, it catches scarf 2. The cycle is started over by

throwing scarf 1 with the opposite hand. Figure 17.5 illustrates the figure-eight motion that is used in cascading. Tosses are always alternated between left and right hands with a smooth, even rhythm.

REVERSE CASCADING

Reverse cascading involves tossing the scarves from waist level to the outside of the body and allowing the scarves to drop down the midline of the body (see Figure 17.6).

1. *One scarf.* Begin by holding the scarf as described previously. Throw away from the midline of the body over the top, releasing the scarf so that it falls down the centre of the body. Catch it with the opposite hand and toss it in similar fashion on the opposite side of the body.

2. *Two scarves.* Begin with a scarf in each hand. Toss the first as described in step 1. When it begins its descent, toss the second scarf. Catch the first scarf, then the second, and repeat the pattern in a toss, toss, catch, catch manner.

3. *Reverse cascading with three scarves.* Think of a large funnel fixed at eye level directly in front of the juggler. The goal is to drop all scarves through this funnel so that they drop straight down the centre of the body. Begin with three scarves as described previously for three-scarf cascading. Toss the first scarf from the hand holding two scarves.

Figure 17.4

Tossing and clawing with two scarves.

Figure 17.5

Three-scarf cascading.

Figure 17.6

Reverse cascading.

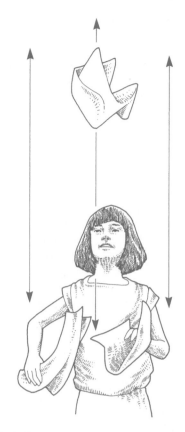

Figure 17.7

Column juggling.

COLUMN JUGGLING

Column juggling is so named because the scarves move straight up and down as though they were inside a large pipe or column and do not cross the body. To perform three-scarf column juggling, begin with two scarves in one hand and one in the other hand. Begin with a scarf from the hand that has two scarves, and toss it straight up the midline of the body and overhead. When this scarf reaches its peak, toss the other two scarves upward along the sides of the body (see Figure 17.7). Catch the first scarf with either hand and toss it upward again. Catch the other two scarves and toss them upward, continuing the pattern.

SHOWERING

Showering is more difficult than cascading because of the rapid movement of the hands. There is less time allowed for catching and tossing. The scarves move in a circle following each other. It should be practised in both directions for maximum challenge.

Start with two scarves in the right hand and one in the left. Begin by throwing the first two scarves from the right hand. Toss the scarves in a large circle away from the mid-line of the body and overhead as high as possible. As soon as the second scarf is released, toss the scarf across from the left hand to the right, and then toss the scarf that's in the

opposite hand and catch the first scarf with the same hand. Finish by tossing the last scarf (see Figure 17.8). All scarves are caught with the left hand and passed to the right hand.

JUGGLING CHALLENGES

TEACHING TIP

1. While cascading, toss a scarf from behind the back.

2. Instead of catching one of the scarves, blow it upward with a strong breath of air.

3. Try juggling three scarves with one hand. Do not worry about establishing a pattern; just catch the lowest scarf each time. Try both regular and reverse cascading as well as column juggling.

4. While doing column juggling, toss up one scarf, hold the other two, and make a full turn. Resume juggling.

5. Juggle three scarves while standing alongside a partner with inside arms around each other.

6. Try juggling more than three scarves (up to six) with a partner.

Figure 17.8

Showering with scarves.

Juggling with Balls

Two balls can be juggled with one hand, and three balls can be juggled with two hands. Juggling can be done in a crisscross fashion, which is called cascading, or it can be done in a circular fashion, called showering. Cascading is considered the easier of the two styles.

Instructional Procedures

1. Juggling requires accurate, consistent tossing, and this should be the first emphasis. The tosses should be thrown to the same height on both sides of the body, about 60 to 70 cm upward and across the body, since the ball is tossed from one hand to the other. Practise tossing the ball parallel to the body; the most common problem in juggling is that the juggler tosses the balls forward and has to move forward to catch them.

2. The fingers, not the palms, should be used in tossing and catching. Stress relaxed wrist action.

3. The student should look upward to watch the balls at the peak of their flight, rather than watching the hands. Focus on where the ball peaks, not on the hands.

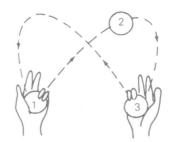

Figure 17.9

Cascading with three balls.

4. The balls should be caught about waist height and released a little above this level.

5. Jugglers must master the art of carrying two balls in the starting hand, and releasing only one.

6. Progression should be working successively with first one ball, then two balls, and finally three balls (see Figure 17.9).

Recommended Progression for Cascading

1. Using one ball and one hand only, toss the ball upward (60 to 70 cm), and catch it with the same hand. Begin with the dominant hand, and later practise with the other. Toss quickly, with wrist action. Then handle the ball alternately with right and left hands, tossing from one hand to the other.

2. Now, with one ball in each hand, alternate tossing a ball upward and catching it in the same hand so that one ball is always in the air. Begin again with a ball in each hand. Toss across the body to the other hand. To keep the balls from colliding, toss under the incoming ball.

3. Hold two balls in the starting hand and one in the other. Toss one of the balls in the starting hand, toss the ball from the other hand, and then toss the third ball.

Recommended Progression for Showering

1. The showering motion is usually counterclockwise. Hold one ball in each hand. Begin by tossing with the right hand on an inward path and then immediately toss the other ball from the left directly across the body to the right hand. Continue this until the action is smooth.

2. Now, hold two balls in the right hand and one in the left. Toss the first ball from the right hand on an inward path and immediately toss the second on the

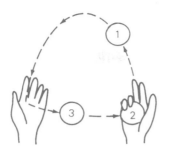

Figure 17.10

Showering with three balls.

same path. At about the same time, toss the ball from the left hand directly across the body to the right hand (see Figure 17.10).

3. A few children may be able to switch from cascading to showering and vice versa. This is a skill of considerable challenge.

Activities with Scoops and Balls

Scoops (see Figure 17.11) are excellent for practising catching and tossing skills using an implement rather than the hands. The following activities are recommended.

Individual Activities

1. Put the ball on the floor and pick it up with the scoop. Toss the ball upward and catch it with the scoop. Throw the ball against a wall and catch it in the scoop. Put the ball in the scoop, throw it in the air, and catch it. Throw the ball against a wall with the scoop and catch it with the scoop.

2. Throw the ball, switch the scoop to the opposite hand, and catch in the scoop. Toss the ball upward from the scoop, perform a body turn, and catch the ball in the scoop.

3. Toss the ball upward and catch it as low as possible. Toss it a little higher each time, and catch it in the scoop. Tell students to toss the ball so that they have to stretch to catch it.

Partner Activities

1. One partner rolls the ball on the floor, and the other catches it in the scoop. Partners throw the ball back and forth and catch it in the scoop. Take a step back

Figure 17.11

Catching a whiffle ball with a scoop.

with each successful catch, a step forward with each missed catch.

2. One partner tosses the ball from the scoop and the other partner catches. Throw the ball from the scoop at different levels and catch it at different levels. Throw and catch from various positions, such as sitting, prone, and kneeling.

Games

Many games can be played using scoops. Modified lacrosse can be played using the scoops and a whiffle ball. Set up a lesson in which children devise games for themselves that use the scoop and a ball.

Bowling Activities

Younger children should practise informal rolling. As they mature, the emphasis should change from informal rolling to bowling skills. Bowling skills begin with a two-handed roll and progress to one-handed rolls, alternating between the right and left hand. They can use various targets, including bowling pins and small cones.

The 20-cm foam or playground ball is excellent for teaching bowling skills. Stress moderate speed in the motion of the ball. The ball should roll off the tips of the fingers with good follow-through action.

The four-step approach is the accepted form for 10-pin bowling, and its basis can be set in class work. The technique, in brief form, for a right-handed bowler follows:

Starting position: Stand with the feet together and the ball held comfortably in both hands in front of the body.

Step One: Step forward with the right foot, pushing the ball forward with both hands and a little to the right.

Step Two: Step with the left foot, allowing the ball to swing down alongside the leg on its way into the backswing.

Step Three: Step with the right foot. The ball reaches the height of the backswing with this step.

Step Four: Step with the left foot and bowl the ball forward.

For instructional cues, the teacher can call out the following sequence for the four steps: "Out," "Down," "Back," and "Roll."

Bowling activities are organized mostly as partner or group work. When using targets, it's desirable to have two children on the target end. One child resets the target, while the other recovers the ball. The following are partner activities unless otherwise noted.

Recommended Activities

1. Use a wide-straddle stance, and begin with two-handed rolls from between the legs.

2. Roll the ball first with the right and then with the left hand. The receiver can use the foot pickup, done by hoisting the ball to the hands with the extended toes.

3. Practise putting different kinds of spin (English) on the ball. (For a right-handed bowler, a curve to the left is called a hook ball, and a curve to the right is a backup ball.)

4. Get into groups of three (see Figure 17.12) and use human straddle targets. The target child stands in a straddle position (60- to 70-cm straddle). Targets must keep their legs straight and motionless during the bowling. Otherwise, they can make or avoid contact with the ball and upset the scoring system. Start from a moderate distance (3 m) at first, and adjust as proficiency increases.

5. Use cones or bowling pins as targets. Begin with one and progress to two or three.

Figure 17.12

Bowling through a human straddle target.

Activities with Paddles and Balls

The current popularity of racquet sports makes it imperative that the schools give attention to racquet skills. For primary-level children, use the plastic or wooden paddle to introduce racquet sports. Much of this early activity is devoted to informal, exploratory play. Different types of objects can be batted: table tennis balls, sponge balls, shuttlecocks, and tennis balls. Use plastic or wooden paddles and appropriate balls to establish a basis for future play in table tennis, badminton, and tennis.

Instructional Procedures for Wooden or Plastic Paddles

1. Use the following instructional cues:

   a. Hold the wrist reasonably stiff.

   b. Use a smooth arm action.

   c. Stroke through the ball and follow through.

   d. Watch the ball strike the paddle.

2. All paddles must have wrist thongs. The hand goes through the loop before grasping the paddle. No play should be permitted without this safety precaution.

3. Emphasize proper grip—seeing that children maintain this is a constant battle. The easiest method to teach the proper grip is to have the student hold the paddle perpendicular to the floor and shake hands with it (see Figure 17.13). Young people tend to revert to the inefficient hammer grip, so named because it is similar to the grip used on a hammer.

4. Accuracy and control should be the primary goals.

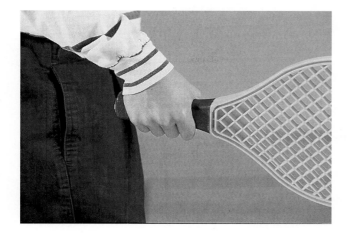

Figure 17.13

Handshake grip.

5. Attempt early activities with both the right and the left hand, but the dominant hand should be developed in major throwing and striking skill progressions.

6. Practice in racquet work should move from individual to partner work as quickly as is feasible, because partner work is basic to racquet sports.

7. For the forehand stroke, the body is turned sideways; for a right-handed player, the left side points in the direction of the hit.

8. For the backhand stroke, the thumb is placed against the handle of the racquet for added support and force, and the body is turned sideways so the shoulder on the side of the racquet hand points in the direction of the stroke.

9. During either type of stroke, a step is made with the foot that is forward with respect to the direction of the stroke.

10. A volley is made with a sort of punch stroke. The hitter faces in the direction of the hit, and pushes the racquet forward rather than stroking. To practise volleys, students need a firm surface from which the ball can rebound.

Individual Activities

1. Place a ball on the paddle and attempt to keep it from falling off. As skill increases, attempt to roll the ball around the edges of the paddle.

2. Using the paddle, rebound the ball upward. Bounce it on the paddle without letting it touch the floor. Increase the height of the bounce.

3. Dribble the ball with the paddle, first while stationary and then while moving. Change the paddle from hand to hand while the ball is bouncing off the floor.

4. Alternate bouncing the ball in the air and on the floor.

5. Bounce the ball off the paddle upward and catch it with the paddle. This requires the child to "give" with the paddle to create a soft home for the ball.

6. Put the ball on the floor and scoop it up with the paddle. Start dribbling the ball without touching it with the hands. Put a reverse spin on the ball and scoop it up into the air.

7. Bounce the ball off the paddle into the air and turn the paddle to the other side as you bounce the ball.

Partner Activities

Beginning partner activity should involve the feed (controlled throw) by one partner and the designated stroke return by the other. In this way, the child can concentrate on the stroke without worrying about the competitive aspects of the activity.

1. Return partner's feed with a forehand stroke. Return backhand. Switch roles.

2. Stroke back and forth with partner, first forehand and then backhand.

3. Play back and forth over a net. The "net" can be a jump rope lying on the floor crosswise to the field of play, or a bench.

4. Volley partner's feed. Volley back and forth with partner. (In the volley, the ball does not touch the floor.)

5. Play doubles. Partners on each side alternate turns returning the ball.

6. Volley using a whiffle ball. (A whiffle ball moves slowly and allows children time to position their feet properly.) Play with a partner. Allow the ball to bounce before returning it. Perform stunts while the ball is in the air.

7. While moving with a partner, keep the ball in the air by alternating bounces.

8. Develop a cooperative partner routine with five individual tasks in sequence.

Activities with Discs

Disc activities are popular with children of all ages, but younger children may need considerable guidance to develop skills. The following are the basic skills that should be taught before a variety of activities are presented.

Throwing the Disc

BACKHAND THROW

The backhand grip (see Figure 17.14) is used most often. The thumb is on top of the disc, the index finger along the rim, and the other fingers underneath. To throw the disc with the right hand, stand in a sideways position with the right foot toward the target. Step toward the target and throw the disc in a sideways motion across the body, snapping the wrist and trying to keep the disc flat on release.

UNDERHAND THROW

The underhand throw uses the same grip as in the backhand throw, but the thrower faces the target and holds the disc at the side of the body. Step forward with the leg opposite the throwing arm while bringing the disc forward. When the throwing arm is out in front of the body, release the disc. The trick to this throw is learning to release the disc so that it is parallel to the ground.

Catching the Disc

THUMB-DOWN CATCH

Use the thumb-down catch when the disc is received at waist level or above. The thumb is pointing toward the ground. The disc should be tracked from the thrower's hand. This clues the catcher about any tilt on the disc that may cause it to curve.

THUMB-UP CATCH

Use the thumb-up catch when the disc is received below waist level. The thumb points up, and the fingers are spread.

SANDWICH CATCH

In preparation for making the catch, one hand is placed around the chin and the other around the stomach. As the disc approaches and the location of the arrival of the disc becomes apparent, the hands move closer to that location. To catch the disc, one hand is one the top and one is on the bottom with the disc in the middle, thus forming a disc sandwich.

Instructional Procedures

1. Use the following instructional cues:

    a. Release the disc parallel to the ground. Tilting it results in a curved throw.

    b. Step toward the target and follow through on release of the disc.

    c. Snap open the wrist and make the disc spin.

2. If space is limited, have all students throw discs in the same direction. Students can line up on either side of the area and throw across to each other.

3. Most activities are best practised by pairs of students using one disc.

4. Children can develop both sides of the body by learning to throw and catch the disc with either hand. The teacher should design the activities so that children get both right-hand and left-hand practice.

5. Because a disc is somewhat different from the other implements that children usually throw, devote some time to teaching form and style in throwing and catching.

Recommended Activities

1. Throw the disc at different levels to a partner.

2. Catch the disc, using various catching styles and hand positions.

3. Throw a curve by tilting the disc. Try curving it to the left, the right, and upward.

4. Throw a bounce pass to partner. Throw a low, fast bounce. Throw a high, slow bounce.

5. Throw the disc with the nondominant hand. Try to throw for accuracy first, and then strive for distance.

Figure 17.14

Gripping the disc for backhand throw.

6. Make the disc respond like a boomerang. Throw into the wind at a steep angle and see whether it comes back to you.

7. Throw the disc into the air, run, and catch it. Try to increase the throwing distance and still make the catch before the disc touches the ground.

8. Have partner hold a hoop as a target. See how many times you can throw the disc through the hoop. Play a game of One Step, in which you move back a step each time you throw the disc through the hoop. When a student misses twice in a row, the partner gets a chance to try.

9. Place a series of hoops on the ground. Different coloured hoops can signify different point values. Have a contest with your partner to see who can earn more points in five throws.

10. Play catch while both partners are moving. Try to throw the disc so that your partner does not have to break stride to catch it.

11. Throw for distance. Try to throw farther than your partner by using a series of four throws.

12. Throw for both distance and accuracy. Using a series of four or more throws, try to reach a goal that is a specified distance away. Many different objects can be used as goals, such as basket standards and fence posts. (This could be the start of playing Disc Golf, which is becoming a popular recreational sport.)

13. Working in groups of three, try to keep the disc away from the person in the middle. The children can establish their own rules as to when someone else must move to the middle.

Disc Games

DISC KEEPAWAY

Playing Area: Designated outdoor activity area, 3 m by 3 m

Players: Groups of four to five students

Supplies: One disc per group

Skills: Throwing and catching

Two players start on defence. The remaining players spread out around the designated area and are the offense. Cones can be used to establish boundaries if necessary. The players on offense attempt to make three consecutive throws. Defensive players attempt to break up the consecutive throws by knocking the disc down or catching it. Once the disc is caught, it cannot be taken away or knocked to the ground. If the disc is caught or knocked from the air to the ground, the person who threw the disc becomes a member of the defence, and the defensive player who knocked the disc down or caught it is on offense. If three consecutive throws are made, two players from offense switch with the defensive players and the game continues.

STEP BACK

Playing Area: Gymnasium or outdoor designated activity area

Players: Partners

Supplies: One disc per set of partners

Skills: Throwing and catching

Partners begin standing 2 to 3 m apart. With each successful catch, one partner steps back. If the disc is dropped, the partners return to the start point and begin again.

DISC BOWLING

Playing Area: Gymnasium or outdoor designated activity area, in 3-by-5-m lanes

Players: Groups of three students

Supplies: Two discs and six to ten bowling pins

Skills: Throwing

Each group is assigned 3-by-5-m lanes with 6 to 10 bowling pins. Two students take on the role of pinsetters and stand beside the pins. The other student is the bowler. The bowler stands 5 m from the pins and has two throws to knock down as many pins as possible. After the first throw the setters remove only the disc. All pins are left as they are. After the second throw, the setters quickly tell the bowler how many pins were knocked down. One setter then collects both discs and reports to the bowling line while the other setter sets the pins up. After the pins are set, the next bowler begins. This process then continues with every student rotating to each role. The setters can also retrieve errant throws when they see they are not going to hit the pins. Allow for adequate buffer zones between lanes.

DISC GOLF

Playing Area: Large outside playing area

Players: Groups of two to four students

Supplies: One disc per child, 8 to 10 hoops, 8 to 10 cones

Skills: Throwing

Disc Golf is played exactly like golf except the disc is thrown rather than a ball hit with a club. Prior to playing, an overview of golf is given. Students are informed that the idea is to get their disc from the cone, which is called the tee, to the hole, or hoop, in the fewest number of steps. To begin, each group is assigned a starting tee. This will minimize waiting after each hole. Each person in the group throws his disc, one at a time. Students then move to their disc for the second throw. The person farthest from the hole goes first. For safety reasons, all members of the group should watch the throw. This process continues until all players have thrown the disc into the hoop. The next tee is located close to the previous hole. Before beginning the hole, students must wait until the group in front of them is finished and has moved on to the next hole.

Activities with Hoops

Hoops provide the potential for a variety of movement experiences. They are often used to expand "creative potential" and play a general purpose in target activities.

Instructional Procedures

1. Hoops can be a creative medium for children. Allow them free time to explore their own ideas.

2. Give the children an adequate amount of space in which to perform, for hoops require much movement.

3. Hoops can serve as a "home" for various activities. For instance, the children might leave their hoops to gallop in all directions and then return quickly to the hoop on command.

4. Hoops are good targets. A hoop can be made to stand by placing an individual mat over its base.

Recommended Activities

HOOPS AS FLOOR TARGETS

Each child has a hoop, which is placed on the floor. A number of movement challenges can give direction to the activity.

1. Show the different patterns you can make by jumping or hopping in and out of the hoop.

2. Do a Bunny Jump and a Frog Jump into the centre and out the other side.

3. Show the ways you can cross from one side of the hoop to the other by taking the weight on your hands inside the hoop.

4. On all fours, show the kinds of movements you can do, with your feet inside the hoop and your hands outside, and then with your hands inside the hoop and your feet outside. Then try with one foot and one hand inside, and one foot and one hand outside.

5. (Set a time limit of 10 to 15 seconds.) See how many times you can jump in and out of your hoop during this time. Now try hopping.

6. Curl your body inside the hoop. Bridge over your hoop. Stretch across your hoop. See how many different ways you can move around the hoop.

7. Get into the hoop by using two different body parts. Move out by using three parts. Vary the number of body parts used.

HOOP HANDLING

1. Spin the hoop like a top. See how long you can make it spin. Spin it again, and see how many times you can run around it before it falls to the floor.

2. Hula-Hoop using various body parts such as the waist, legs, arms, and fingers. While Hula-Hooping on the arms, try to change the hoop from one arm to the other. Lie on the back with one or both legs pointed toward the ceiling and explore different ways the legs can twirl the Hula Hoop. Hula-Hoop with two or more hoops.

3. Jump or hop through a hoop held by a partner. Add further challenge by varying the height and angle of the hoop.

4. Roll the hoop and run alongside it. Change direction when a command is given.

5. Hula-Hoop on one arm. Throw the hoop in the air and catch it on the other arm.

6. Hold the hoop and swing it like a pendulum. Jump and hop in and out of the hoop.

7. Use the hoop like a jump rope.

8. Roll the hoop with a reverse spin to make it return to you. The key to the reverse spin is to pull down (toward the floor) on the hoop as it is released. Roll the hoop with a reverse spin, jump over it, and catch it as it returns. Roll the hoop with a reverse spin, and as it returns, hoist it with the foot and catch it. Roll the hoop with a reverse spin, kick it up with the toe, and go through the hoop. Roll the hoop with a reverse spin, run around it, and catch it. Roll the hoop with a reverse spin, pick it up, and begin hooping on the arm—all in one motion.

9. Play catch with a partner. Try with two or more hoops.

10. Have one partner roll the hoop with a reverse spin and the other attempt to crawl through the hoop.

Games with Hoops

COOPERATIVE MUSICAL HOOPS

Hoops, one per student, are placed on the floor. Players are given a locomotor movement to do. On signal, they cease the movement, find a hoop, and sit cross-legged in the centre of it. Music can be used, with the children moving to the music and seeking a hoop when the music stops. Teachers can remove the hoops, challenging students to share hoops with each other. This can continue until all students are in three or four hoops.

AROUND THE HOOP

The class is divided into groups of three, with children in each group numbered 1, 2, and 3. Each threesome sits back-to-back inside a hoop. Their heels may need to be outside the hoop. The leader calls out a direction (right or left) and names one of the numbers. The child with that number immediately gets up, runs in the stipulated direction around the hoop, then runs back to place and sits down. The winner is the first group sitting in good position after the child returns to place.

HULA HOOP CIRCLE

Four to six children hold hands in a circle, facing in, with a hoop dangling on one pair of joined hands. They move the hoop around the circle and back to the starting point. This requires all bodies to go through the hoop. Children can use their hands to help the hoop move, but cannot release their grips.

HULA HOOP RELAY

Place relay teams of four to six players, each with a hoop, in line or circle formation. The hoop must be held upright with the bottom of the hoop touching the floor. On signal, designated starters drop their hoops and move through the hoops held by squad members. Players repeat the sequence until every player has moved through the hoops.

Activities with Jump Ropes

Rope jumping is an excellent activity for conditioning all parts of the body. It increases coordination, rhythm, and timing, while offering a wide range of challenges. Rope jumping is regarded as an excellent medium for fitness development. It can be designed to suit the activity needs of all individuals regardless of age or condition. Workloads can easily be measured and modified by changing the amount of time jumped or the number of turns. It is a useful activity to teach children, because it offers carry-over value for activity in later life.

Rope jumping has increased in popularity during the past decade, with the Jump Rope for Heart program. This program has spawned school teams, exhibitions, and competitions. Rope-jumping is a creative medium with an incredible number of variations possible. Rope-jumping skills presented in this chapter are those deemed suitable for inclusion in an elementary school physical education program. Not included are highly advanced and complex activities that are often used in more advanced settings. For more information about advanced activities, review the references at the end of the chapter. Rope-jumping activities in this chapter are grouped into three categories: movements guided by rope patterns, long-rope jumping, and individual rope jumping.

Movements Guided by Rope Patterns

Ropes can be placed on the floor in various fashions to serve as stimuli for different locomotor and nonlocomotor movements. The activities should stress creative responses within the limits of the challenge. The concepts of space, time, force, and flow can be interwoven in the activity. The child can move as an individual, with a partner, or as a member of a small group. Generally, ropes are placed in a straight line or in a circle. They can form geometric figures and numbers or letters of the alphabet. The discussions are organized around these patterns.

ROPE FORMING A STRAIGHT LINE

When the rope is placed in a straight line, one approach is for children to begin at one end and to perform activities as they move down the line. Much of the movement can be based on hopping or jumping. The children then return, back up the line, to the starting point. Movement suggestions follow.

1. Hop back and forth across the rope, moving down the line. Return, using the other foot.
2. Jump lightly back and forth down the line. Return.
3. Hop slowly, under control, down the line. Hop rapidly back.
4. Jump so that the rope is between the feet each time, alternately crossing and uncrossing the feet.
5. Do Crouch Jumps back and forth across the rope. Vary with three points and then two points of contact.
6. Jump as high as possible going down the line and as low as possible coming back.
7. Hop down with a narrow shape and back with a different shape.
8. Do a movement with the rhythm slow–slow, fast–fast–fast, going down the line, and repeat coming back.

For the following movements, the child is positioned close to the centre of the line and simply moves back and forth across it without materially changing the relative position.

1. Hop back and forth across the line. Jump back and forth.
2. Go over with a high movement. Come back with a low one.

3. Do a Bunny Jump across and back; a Frog Jump; a Crouch Jump.

4. Take a sprinter's position with the rope between the feet. Alternate the feet back and forth over the rope.

6. Jump back and forth lightly on the tiptoes.

7. Pretend that the rope is a river. Show different kinds of bridges that you can make over the river.

ROPE FORMING A CIRCLE

With the rope in a circle, children can do movements around the outside clockwise and counterclockwise—walking, skipping, hopping, sliding (facing toward and away from the circle), jumping, running, and galloping.

1. Hop in and out of the circle, moving around. Jump.

2. Jump directly in and then across. Jump backward.

3. Jump in, collapse, and jump out, without touching the rope.

4. Begin in the centre of the circle. Jump forward, backward, and sideward, each time returning to the centre.

5. Place the feet in the circle and walk the hands all around the outside of the circle. Place the hands inside and the feet outside. Face the floor, the ceiling, and to the side.

6. Make a bridge over the circle. How many types of bridges can you make?

7. Do a Tightrope Walk clockwise and counterclockwise.

8. Do jump turns inside the circle without touching the rope: quarter turns, half turns, and full turns.

Partner Activity

Partner activity with ropes is excellent. Partners can work with one or two ropes, and can do matching, following, or contrasting movements. Add-on is an interesting game: One partner does an activity and the other adds on an activity to form a sequence. Using the suggested rope forms (multiple ropes) in Figure 17.15, one partner makes a series of movements. The other partner has to try to duplicate the movements.

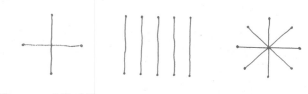

Figure 17.15

Suggested rope forms.

Group Activity

Group activity with jump ropes also has good possibilities. Each child brings a rope to the group. They can arrange patterns with the ropes for hopping, jumping, and other locomotor movements. An achievement demonstration after a period of practice allows each group to show the patterns that they have arranged and the movements that can be done in the patterns.

Long-rope Jumping

Long-rope jumping is an excellent activity for beginning jumpers. Youngsters can concentrate on jumping the rope without learning the skill of turning. Many activities with two or more long ropes add a great deal of variety to long-rope jumping and can make it challenging for the most skilled jumpers. Long jump ropes should be 3 to 5 m in length, with 4 to 5 m the most commonly used. The exact length depends on the age and skill of the children: the longer the rope, the more difficult it is to turn. For primary-grade children, individual jump ropes are shorter and can be used to teach beginning skills because they are easier for young children to turn.

Many of the jumping sequences can use chants. Rope-jumping chants represent a cultural heritage. In many cases, children have their own favourites.

Instructional Procedures

1. Four or five children is an appropriate group size for practising long-rope skills. Two members of the group turn the rope while the others practise jumping. It is important to have a plan for rotating turners, so that all children receive similar amounts of practice jumping.

2. Turning the rope is a difficult skill for young children. It must be practised regularly until children can maintain an even, steady rhythm. Effective turning is one key to successful jumping. If turning is not rhythmic, even skilled jumpers will have problems.

3. When learning to turn the rope, incorporate the following points:

    a. Keep the elbow close to the body and concentrate on turning the rope with the forearm.

    b. Keep the thumb up during the turning motion of the hands. This will emphasize turning with the forearm.

    c. Hold the rope in front of the body at waist level. Keep the body perpendicular to the rope.

4. To practise turning, youngsters are motivated by turning the rope under a lively bouncing ball. Turners stand ready, and a third child tosses a ball upward so

that it will remain in one spot while bouncing. Turners adjust the speed of the turning as the bounces become smaller and more rapid. Children can keep a count of the number of successful turns before the ball ceases bouncing.

5. Children of all ages can perform long-rope jumping. To check the readiness of the children, see if they are capable of jumping in place with both feet leaving the ground simultaneously.

6. Children should understand the terms used to describe entry into the long jump rope. *Front door* means entering from the side where the rope is turning forward and toward the jumper after it reaches its peak. *Back door* means entering from the side where the rope is turning backward and away from the jumper. To enter front door, the jumper follows the rope in and jumps when it completes the turn. To enter back door, the jumper waits until the rope reaches its peak and moves in as the rope moves downward. Learning to enter at an angle is usually easier, but any path that is comfortable is acceptable.

7. Teachers can introduce and teach youngsters long-rope jumping skills using the following steps:

   a. Use a shorter long rope (3 to 5 m). Lay the rope on the floor and have youngsters jump back and forth across the rope. Emphasis should be on small, continuous jumps and learning how to jump back and forth continuously without stopping. Jumps should not be high, just enough to clear the rope.

   b. Turners slowly move the rope back and forth along the floor while the jumper moves over the rope each time it moves near. They slowly increase the speed of the rope moving along the floor. Encourage the jumper to jump up and down with as little forward, backward, or sideways movement as possible.

   c. The jumper stands near the centre of the rope. The turners move the rope in pendulum fashion back and forth while the jumper clears the rope each time it hits the floor.

   d. The jumper starts by facing the centre of the stationary rope. Use three pendulum swings followed by a full turn of the rope rotating from the jumper's back to the front. The jumper continues jumping until a miss occurs. Verbal cueing helps most beginners find success; each time the rope hits the floor, say, "Jump." If youngsters are having difficulty, have them stand behind a turner and jump (without the rope) each time the rope hits the floor.

   e. When jumpers have difficulty with the rhythm, they can practise off to one side without actually jumping over the rope. A drumbeat can reinforce the rhythm with alternating heavy (jump) and light (rebound) beats.

   f. Teach front-door and back-door entry, making sure that the jumper enters at an angle rather than perpendicular to the rope.

INTRODUCTORY SKILLS

Some introductory skills and routines follow:

1. Holders hold the rope in a stationary position 15 cm above the ground. Jumpers jump over, back and forth. Holders raise the rope a little each time, being sure to hold the rope loosely in the hands. This is called Building a House.

2. Ocean Wave is another stationary jumping activity. Turners make waves in the rope by moving the arms up and down. Jumpers try to time it so that they jump over a low part of the wave.

3. Holders stoop down and wiggle the rope back and forth on the floor. Jumpers try to jump over the rope and not touch it as it moves. This activity is called Snake in the Grass.

4. The jumper stands in the centre between the turners, who carefully turn the rope in a complete arc over the jumper's head. As the rope completes the turn, the jumper jumps over it and exits immediately in the direction in which the rope is turned.

5. Children run through the turning rope (front door) without jumping, following the rope through.

6. While the rope is being turned, the jumper runs in (front door), jumps once, and runs out immediately.

7. When children can jump a number of times consecutively, add motivation by using some of the chants that follow.

INTERMEDIATE SKILLS, ROUTINES, AND CHANTS

Intermediate routines require the jumper to be able to go in front door, jump, and exit front door, and to do the same sequence back door. Have students practise enough simple jumping skills and exits that their confidence is fortified; students then can turn to more intricate routines. Entries and exits should be varied in the following routines:

1. Jumpers run in, jump a specified number of times, and exit.

2. Children can add chants that dictate the number of jumps, which are followed by an exit. Here are some examples.

Tick tock, tick tock,
What's the time by the clock?
It's one, two, [up to midnight].

I like coffee, I like tea,

How many people can jump like me?

One, two, three, [up to a certain number].

Hippity-hop to the butcher shop,

How many times before I stop?

One, two, three, [and so on].

Michael, Michael [student's name] at the gate,

Eating cherries from a plate.

How many cherries did he [she] eat?

One, two, three, [and so on].

3. Kangaroo gets its name from the jump required for back-door entry, in which the jumper resembles a kangaroo. The jumper calls out, "Kangaroo!" and takes the entry jump through the back door, then exits. Next time, the same jumper calls out, "Kangaroo one!" and adds a jump. Jumpers call successive jumps until a designated number is reached.

4. An interesting challenge is to turn the rope over a line parallel to it and have the jumper jump back and forth over the line. The jumper can vary foot position: feet together, feet apart, stride forward and back.

5. Jumpers can vary the pattern with turns. Make four quarter turns until facing the original direction. Reverse the direction of the turns.

6. In Hot Pepper, turners turn the rope faster and faster, while the jumper tries to keep up with the increased speed. The following chant is good for Hot Pepper:

Charlie, Charlie [student's name], set the table.

Bring the plates if you are able.

Don't forget the salt and

Red hot pepper!

(On the words "Red hot pepper," the rope is turned as fast as possible until the jumper misses.)

7. In Calling In, the first player enters the rope and calls in a second player by name. Both jump three times holding hands, and then the first runs out. The second player then calls in a third player by name. Both jump three times holding hands, and the second player exits. Players should be in an informal line, since the fun comes from not knowing when one is to enter.

8. Children can enter and exit according to the call in the following chants.

In the shade and under a tree,

I'd like [student's name] to come in with me.

She's [he's] too fast and I'm too slow.

He stays in and I must go.

Calling in and calling out,

I call [student's name] in and I'm getting out.

9. In High Water, turners turn the rope so that it becomes gradually higher and higher off the ground.

At the beach, at the sea,

The waves come almost to the knee.

Higher, higher, [and so forth].

10. In Stopping the Rope, the jumper (a) stops and lets the rope hit the feet, (b) stops the rope by straddling it, (c) stops with the legs crossed and the rope between the feet, or (d) stops the rope by stamping on it.

11. Two, three, or four children can jump at a time. After some skill has been achieved, children in combination can run in, jump a specified number of times, and run out, keeping hands joined all the time.

12. The jumper takes in a ball or other object. He or she bounces the ball while jumping. Alternatively, the jumper can try balancing a beanbag on a body part while jumping.

13. A partner stands ready with a ball and tosses it back and forth to the jumper.

14. For Chase the Rabbit, four or five jumpers are in single file with a leader, the Rabbit, at the head. The Rabbit jumps in any manner he or she may wish, and all of the others must match the movements. Anyone who misses must go to the end of the line. A Rabbit who misses or stops the rope goes to the end of the line, and the next child becomes the new Rabbit. Set a limit on how long a Rabbit can stay at the head of the line.

15. In Setting the Table, a jumper enters and starts jumping. A partner stands ready with at least four beanbags. While the following verse is recited, the partner tosses in the beanbags one at a time, and the jumper catches and places them in a row on the side (with the upward swing of the rope) and then exits.

Debbie, Debbie [student's name], set the table [toss in one bag],

Bring the plates if you are able [toss in another bag],

Don't forget the bread and butter [toss in the other two bags].

16. Children can enter and begin with a hop (one foot), then make a jump (two feet), add a hand touch next (two feet, one hand), and then jump with both hands and feet (two feet, two hands).

17. For jumping with the eyes closed, single or multiple jumpers enter and begin jumping to this chant:

Peanuts, popcorn, soda pop,

How many jumps before you stop?

Close your eyes and you will see

How many jumps that this will be!

The eyes remain closed during the jumping, which continues to a target number or a miss.

Double Dutch (Two-rope) Jumping

Double Dutch rope jumping (see Figure 17.16) is popular on playgrounds and in gymnasiums across the country. This type of jumping requires two rope turners using two long ropes that are turned in opposite directions. It takes practice for children to learn to turn two ropes simultaneously, and teachers must allot time for this. Handling two ropes is tiring, so rotate turners frequently.

Instructional Procedures

1. Arm positions and turning motions are similar to turning a single long rope. In short, keep the upper arm stationary, rotate at the elbow with locked wrist, and keep the thumb up. Avoid crossing the midline of the body, and establish an even cadence. Rotate the hands inward toward the midline of the body (right forearm counterclockwise and left forearm clockwise). Students should concentrate on the sound of the ropes hitting the floor so that they make an even and rhythmic beat.

2. Double Dutch turning takes considerable practice. Take time to teach it as a skill that is necessary for successful jumping experiences.

3. When entering, stand beside a turner and run in to the ropes when the back rope (farther from the jumper) touches the floor. Turners should be taught to say, "Go" each time the back rope touches the floor.

Figure 17.16

Double Dutch rope jumping.

4. Concentrate on jumping in the centre of the ropes facing a turner.

5. Exit the ropes by facing and jumping toward one turner and exiting immediately after jumping. The exit should be made as close to the turner's shoulder as possible.

DOUBLE DUTCH SKILLS

1. *Basic Jump on both feet.* Land on the balls of the feet, keeping ankles and knees together with hands across the stomach.

2. *Turnaround.* Circle left or right using the basic jump. Begin circling slowly at first and then increase speed. To increase the challenge, try the turnaround on one foot.

3. *Straddle Jump.* Jump to the straddle position and return to closed position. Try a *Straddle Cross Jump* by crossing the legs on return to the closed position. Perform the straddle jumps facing away from the turners.

4. *Scissors Jump.* Jump to a stride position with the left foot forward and the right foot back about 20 cm apart. Each jump requires reversing the position of the feet.

5. *Jogging Step.* Run in place with a jogging step. Increase the challenge by circling while jogging.

6. *Hot Peppers.* Use the Jogging Step and gradually increase the speed of the ropes.

7. *Half turn.* Perform a half turn with each jump. Remember to lead the turn with the head and shoulders.

8. *Ball tossing.* Toss and catch a beanbag or playground ball while jumping.

9. *Individual rope jumping.* Enter Double Dutch with an individual rope and jump. Face the turner and decrease the length of the individual jump rope.

10. The following activities are interesting variations for reviving motivation:

    a. *Double Irish.* Turn two ropes in the reverse directions used in Double Dutch. The left hand turns counterclockwise and the right hand clockwise. Jumpers enter when the near rope hits the floor. They should time their entry by following the near rope on its downward swing.

    b. *Egg Beater.* Four turners turn two long ropes at right angles simultaneously (see Figure 17.17). Jumpers enter at the quadrant where both ropes are turning front doors. The number of ropes being turned can be increased to three or four. This activity is easier than jumping Double Dutch since the jumping action is similar to single-rope jumping. It is an excellent activity for helping students build confidence in jumping more than one long rope.

Figure 17.17

Egg Beater.

FORMATION JUMPING

For formation jumping, four to six long ropes with turners can be placed in various patterns, with tasks specified for each rope. Ropes can be turned in the same direction, or the turning directions can be mixed. Several formations are illustrated in Figure 17.18.

Individual Rope Jumping

When teaching individual rope jumping, place emphasis on establishing basic turning skills and letting children create personal routines. Individual rope jumping is particularly valuable as part of the conditioning process for certain sports. It lends itself to prescribed doses based on number of turns, length of participation, speed of the turning rope, and various steps. Because rope jumping is of a rhythmic nature, adding music is a natural progression. Music adds much to the activity and enables the jumper to create and organize routines to be performed to the musical pieces. The most effective approach is probably a combination of experiences with and without music.

There are a number of types of jump ropes on the market, all of which are satisfactory, depending on the likes and dislikes of the instructor. The most popular appear to be the solid plastic speed (often called licorice) ropes and the beaded or segmented ropes. The speed rope is excellent for rapid turning and doing tricks. It does not maintain momentum as well as the segmented ropes. The momentum created with segmented ropes is an important support for beginners.

Instructional Procedures

1. The length of the rope depends on the height of the jumper. It should be long enough so that the ends reach to the underarms (see Figure 17.19) or slightly higher when the child stands on its centre. Preschool children generally use 2-m ropes, and the primary-level group needs mostly 2.5-m ropes, with a few longer lengths.

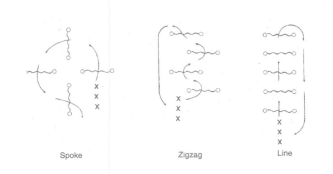

Spoke   Zigzag   Line

Figure 17.18

Formations for jumping rope.

Figure 17.19

Correct jump rope length.

Grades 3 through 6 need a mixture of 2-, 2.5-, and 3-m lengths. A 2- to 3-m rope works well for tall students and most instructors. Ropes or handles can be colour-coded for length.

Two types of ropes are available—the beaded (plastic segment) and the plastic (licorice) rope. For beginning jumpers, the beaded ropes are heavier and seem easier to turn. The drawback to the beaded ropes is that they hurt when they hit another student. Also, if the segments are made round, the rope will roll easily on the floor and cause children to fall when they step on it. The plastic licorice ropes are lighter and give less wind resistance. For experienced jumpers, more speed and control can be gained with this type of rope. An ideal situation would be to have a set of each type.

2. Posture is an important consideration in rope jumping. The body should be in good alignment, with the head up and the eyes looking straight ahead. The jump is made with the body in an erect position. A slight straightening of the knees provides the lift for the jump, which should be of minimal height (about 3 cm). The wrists supply the force to turn the rope, with the elbows kept close to the body and extended at a 90-degree angle. A pumping action and lifting of the arms is unnecessary. Jumpers should land on the balls of the feet, with the knees bent slightly to cushion the shock. They should usually keep the feet, ankles, and legs together, except when a specific step calls for a different position.

3. Students should hold the rope by the index finger and thumb on each side, with the hands making a small circle. They should hold their elbows near their sides to avoid making large arm circles with the rope.

4. Try introducing and teaching youngsters individual rope-jumping skills using the following steps:

   a. Students should first jump without the rope until they learn the correct rhythm and footwork. For slow time, this would be a jump and then a rebound step. Children can pretend that they are turning the rope. Remember that rope jumping involves learning two separate skills: jumping a rope and turning a rope. Some children need to practise the parts separately before putting the skills together.

   b. Turn the rope over the head of the jumper and catch it with the toes.

   c. The jumper holds the rope stationary in front of the body and jumps forward and backward over the rope. To increase the challenge, the jumper swings the rope slightly. He can gradually increase the swing until the rope makes a full turn.

   d. Hold the rope to one side with both hands, swing the rope forward, and jump each time the rope hits the floor. If swinging the rope is a challenge, practise without jumping first.

5. Music can be added when jumpers have learned the first stages of jumping. Music provides a motivation for continued jumping.

6. Children who are struggling with their jumping skills may be helped by the pendulum swing of the long rope, or another student jumping with the child inside an individual rope. Cues such as "Jump" or "Ready, jump" are helpful.

7. Most steps can be done with either slow-time or fast-time rhythm. In slow-time rhythm, the performer jumps over the rope, rebounds, and then executes the second step (or repeats the original step) on the second jump. The rebound is simply a hop in place as the rope passes over the head. Better jumpers bend the knees only slightly, without actually leaving the floor on rebound. The object of the rebound is to carry the rhythm between steps. The rope is rotating slowly, passing under the feet on every other beat; the feet also move slowly, since there is rebound between each jump.

   In fast-time rhythm, the rope rotates in time with the music, one turn per beat (120 to 180 turns per minute, depending on the tune's tempo), and the performer executes a step only when the rope is passing under the feet.

8. Instructional cues to use for improving jumping technique are as follows:

   a. Keep the arms at the side of the body while turning. (Some children lift the arms to shoulder level, trying to move the rope overhead. This makes it impossible for the youngster to jump over the elevated rope.)

   b. Turn the rope by making small circles with the wrists.

   c. Jump on the balls of the feet.

   d. Bend the knees slightly to absorb the force of the jump.

   e. Make a small jump over the rope.

9. To collect ropes at the completion of a rope-jumping activity, have two or three children act as monitors. They put both arms out to the front or to the side at shoulder level. The other children then drape the ropes over their arms (see Figure 17.20). The monitors return the ropes to the correct storage area.

Basic Steps

The basic steps presented here can be done in slow or fast time. After youngsters have mastered the first six steps in slow time, teachers can introduce fast time. The Alternate-foot

Figure 17.20

Collecting the ropes.

Basic Step and Spread Legs Forward and Backward are two steps that work well for introducing fast-time jumping.

SIDE SWING

Swing the rope, held with both hands to one side of the body. Switch and swing the rope on the other side of the body.

DOUBLE SIDE SWING AND JUMP

Swing the rope once on each side of the body. Follow the second swing with a jump over the rope. The sequence should be swing, swing, jump.

TWO-FOOT BASIC STEP

In the Two-foot Basic Step, jump over the rope with feet together as it passes under the feet, then take a preparatory rebound while the rope is over the head.

ALTERNATE-FOOT BASIC STEP

In the Alternate-foot Basic Step, as the rope passes under the feet, the youngster shifts weight alternately from one foot to the other, raising the unweighted foot in a running position.

BIRD JUMPS

Jump with the toes pointed in (pigeon walk) and with the toes pointed out (duck walk). Alternate toes in and toes out.

SWING-STEP FORWARD

The Swing-step Forward is the same as the Alternate-foot Basic Step, except that the free leg swings forward. The youngster keeps the knee loose, and the foot swings naturally.

SWING-STEP SIDEWARD

The Swing-step Sideward is the same as the Swing-step Forward, except that the free leg is swung to the side. The knee should be kept stiff. The sideward swing is about 30 cm.

ROCKER STEP

In executing the Rocker Step, one leg is always forward in a walking-stride position. As the rope passes under the feet, the child shifts weight from the back foot to the forward foot. The rebound is taken on the forward foot while the rope is above the head. On the next turn of the rope, the weight is shifted from the forward foot to the back foot, repeating the rebound on the back foot.

SPREAD LEGS FORWARD AND BACKWARD

For Spread Legs Forward and Backward, start in a stride position (as in the Rocker) with weight equally distributed on both feet. As the rope passes under the feet, jump into the air and reverse the position of the feet.

STRADDLE JUMP

Alternate a regular jump with a straddle jump. The straddle jump is performed with the feet spread to shoulder width.

CROSS LEGS SIDEWARD

In Cross Legs Sideward, as the rope passes under the feet, spread the legs in a straddle position (sideward) to take the rebound. As the rope passes under the feet on the next turn, jump into the air and cross the feet with the right foot forward. Then repeat with the left foot forward and continue this alternation.

TOE-TOUCH FORWARD

To do the Toe-touch Forward, swing the right foot forward as the rope passes under the feet and touch the right toes on the next count. Then alternate, landing on the right foot and touching the left toes forward.

TOE-TOUCH BACKWARD

The Toe-touch Backward is similar to the Swing-step Sideward, except that the toes of the free foot touch to the back at the end of the swing.

SHUFFLE STEP

The Shuffle Step involves pushing off with the right foot and sidestepping to the left as the rope passes under the feet. Land with the weight on the left foot and touch the right toes beside the left heel. Repeat the step in the opposite direction.

SKIER

The Skier is a double-foot jump similar to a technique used by skiers, and requires a chalked or painted line. The jumper stands on both feet to one side of the line. Jumping is done sideways back and forth over the line. Children should try it in a forward and backward direction also.

HEEL–TOE

In the Heel–Toe, as the rope passes under the feet, jump with the weight landing on the right foot while touching the left heel forward. On the next turn of the rope, jump, land on the same foot, and touch the left toes beside the right heel. This pattern is then repeated with the opposite foot bearing the weight.

LEG FLING

On the first jump, bring the right leg up so that it is parallel to the floor, with the knee bent. On the second jump, kick the same leg out and up as high as possible. Try with the other leg.

HEEL CLICK

Do two or three Swing-steps Sideward, in slow time, in preparation for the Heel Click. When the right foot swings sideward, instead of a hop or rebound when the rope is above the head, raise the left foot to click the heel of the right foot. Repeat on the left side.

STEP–TAP

In the Step–Tap, as the rope passes under the feet, push off with the right foot and land on the left. While the rope is turning above the head, brush the sole of the right foot forward and then backward. As the rope passes under the feet for the second turn, push off with the left foot, land on the right, and repeat.

SKIPPING

Do a Step–Hop (skip) over the rope. Start slowly and gradually increase the speed of the rope.

SCHOTTISCHE STEP

The Schottische Step can be done to double-time rhythm, or it can be done with a varied rhythm. The pattern is step, step, step, hop (repeat), followed by four step-hops. In varied rhythm, three quick turns in fast time are made for the first three steps and then double-time rhythm prevails. The step should be practised first in place and then in general space. Schottische music should be introduced along with the steps.

CROSSING ARMS

Once students have mastered the basic steps, crossing the arms while turning the rope provides an interesting variation. Crossing the arms during forward turning is easier than crossing behind the back during backward turning. During crossing, the hands exchange places. This means that for forward crossing, the elbows are close to each other. This is not possible during backward crossing. Students can cross and uncross at predetermined points after a stipulated number of turns. Crossing can be accomplished during any of the routines.

DOUBLE TURNING

The double turn of the rope is also interesting. The jumper does a few basic steps in preparation for the double turn. As the rope approaches the feet, the child gives an extremely hard flip of the rope from the wrists, jumps from 15 to 20 cm in height, and allows the rope to pass under the feet twice before landing. The jumper must bend forward at the waist somewhat, which increases the speed of the turn. A substantial challenge for advanced rope jumpers is to see how many consecutive double-turn jumps they can do.

SHIFTING FROM FORWARD TO BACKWARD JUMPING

To switch from forward to backward jumping without stopping the rope, any of the following techniques can be used.

1. As the rope starts downward in forward jumping, rather than allowing it to pass under the feet, the performer swings both arms to the left (or right) and makes a half turn of the body in that direction (that is, facing the rope). On the next downward swing, the jumper spreads the arms and starts turning in the opposite direction. This method also works for shifting from backward to forward jumping.

2. When the rope is directly above the head, the performer extends both arms, causing the rope to hesitate momentarily, at the same time making a half turn in either direction and continuing to skip with the rope turning in the opposite direction.

3. From a crossed-arm position, as the rope is going above the performer's head, the jumper may uncross the arms and turn simultaneously. This starts the rope turning and the performer jumping in the opposite direction.

SIDEWAYS SKIPPING

In sideways skipping, the child turns the rope laterally with one hand held high and the other extended downward. The rope is swung around the body sideways. To accomplish this, the jumper starts with the right hand held high overhead and the left hand extended down the centre of the body. Then she swings the rope to the left, at the same time raising the left leg sideways. Usually the speed is slow time, with the rebound taken on each leg in turn. Later, better jumpers may progress to fast-time speed. The rope passes under the left leg, and the jumper then is straddling the rope as it moves around her body behind her. The jumper takes the weight on the left foot, raising the right foot sideways. A rebound step on the left as the rope moves to the front brings the jumper back to the original position.

COMBINATION POSSIBILITIES

Numerous combinations of steps and rope tricks are possible in rope jumping. Here are some ideas:

1. Make changes in the speed of the turn—slow time and fast time. Children should be able to shift from one speed to another, particularly when the music changes.

2. Help children develop expertise in various foot patterns and steps. Children should practise changing from one foot pattern to another.

3. Try the crossed-hands position both forward and backward. To add challenge, many of the basic steps can be combined with crossed-hands position.

4. Practise moving from a forward to a backward turn and returning. Perform the turn while doing a number of different basic steps.

5. Attempt double turns combined with basic steps, which are impressive-looking and challenging.

6. Try moving forward, backward, and sideward, employing a variety of the basic steps.

7. Attempt backward jumping, which is exciting as it is a skill quite different from forward jumping. Most basic steps can be done backward or modified for the backward turn.

8. Practise speedy turns (Hot Peppers). Have children see how fast they can turn the rope for 10 or 20 seconds.

INDIVIDUAL ROPE JUMPING WITH PARTNERS

Many interesting combinations are possible when one child turns the individual rope and one or more children jump it. For those routines in which the directions call for a child to run into a jumping pattern, it may be more effective to begin with the child already in position, before proceeding to the run-in stage.

1. The first child turns the rope and the other stands in front, ready to enter.

   a. Run in and face partner, and both jump (see Figure 17.21).

   b. Run in and turn back to partner, and both jump.

   c. Decide which steps are to be done; then run in and match steps.

   d. Repeat with the rope turning backward.

   e. Run in with a ball and bounce it during the jumping.

Figure 17.21

Rope jumping with a partner.

2. Partners stand side by side, clasp inside hands, and turn the rope with outside hands.

   a. Face the same direction and turn the rope.

   b. Face opposite directions, clasp left hands, and turn the rope.

   c. Face opposite directions, clasp right hands, and turn the rope.

   d. Repeat routines with inside knees raised.

   e. Repeat routines with elbows locked. Try other arm positions.

3. The first child turns the rope while the second is to the rear, ready to run in. The second child runs in and grasps the first child's waist or shoulders, and they jump together (engine and caboose).

4. The children stand back to back, holding a single rope in the right hand.

   a. Turn in one direction—forward for one and backward for the other.

   b. Reverse direction.

   c. Change to left hands, and repeat.

5. Three children jump. One turns the rope forward; one runs in, in front; and one runs in behind. All three jump. Try with the rope turning backward.

6. Two jumpers, each with a rope, face each other and turn both ropes together, forward for one and backward for

the other, jumping over both ropes at once. Turn the ropes alternately, jumping each rope in turn.

7. One partner jumps in a usual individual rope pattern. The other is positioned to the side. The turning partner hands over one end of the rope, and the other maintains the turning rhythm and then hands the rope back.

   a. Try from the other side.

   b. Turn the rope backward.

8. Using a single rope held in the right hand, partners face each other and turn the rope in slow time. With the rope overhead, one partner makes a turn to the left (turning in) and jumps inside the rope, exiting by turning either way. See if both can turn inside.

Footbag/Hacky Sack® Activities

A footbag, or Hacky Sack®, is a specific object used for footbag skills and games. The construction varies with the manufacturer, although most footbags are spheres constructed of leather and are stitched internally for durability. Normal size is about 5 cm in diameter. The object of the activities is to keep the bag in the air by means of foot contact.

The kicking motion used for footbag activities is new to most participants because of the lift, which is performed by lifting the foot upward, not away from the body. The lifting motion enables the child to direct the footbag flight upward for controlled consecutive kicks and passes. The ball is soft and flexible, with no bounce. It must be designed specifically as a footbag.

Several points contribute to successful footbag work. The basic athletic stance (ready position) is used with the feet at approximately shoulder width and pointed straight ahead. Knees are bent slightly, with the weight lowered.

There should be equal use of both feet for lifting and kicking. The support (non-kicking) foot is important for maintaining balance and keeping the body in a crouched position. Eye focus on the footbag is essential. Kicking speed should be slow; most beginners tend to kick too quickly. The kicking speed should be about that of the descending footbag. "Slow" and "low" are the key words in kicking.

The arms and upper body are used for balance and control. For the outside and back kicks, an outstretched arm, opposite to the kicking foot and in line with it, aids in maintaining balance. The near arm is carried behind the body so as not to restrict the player's vision. For inside kicks, the arms are relaxed and in balanced position.

To begin, start with a hand toss to self or with a courtesy toss from another player. A restriction is made that touching the footbag with any part of the body above the waist is a foul and interrupts any sequence of kicks. Three basic kicks are recommended.

1. *Inside kick.* This kick is used when the footbag falls low and directly in front of both shoulders. Use the inside of the foot for contact by turning the instep and the ankle upward to create a flat striking surface. Curling the toes under aids in creating a flat striking surface. Contact with the footbag is made at about knee level.

2. *Outside kick.* This kick is used when the footbag falls outside of either shoulder area. The outside of the foot is used by turning the ankle and knee in to create a flat striking surface. With the kicking foot now parallel to the playing surface, use a smooth lifting motion, striking the footbag at approximately knee level. Pointing the toes up aids in creating a flat surface.

3. *Back kick.* This kick is somewhat similar to the outside kick and serves when the footbag goes directly overhead or is approaching the upper body directly. The hips and body must rotate parallel to the flight direction to enable the footbag to pass, while the player maintains constant eye contact. Lean forward in the direction of the footbag's flight and allow it to pass by before executing the kick.

Play can take different forms.

1. *Individual play.* Individuals attempt to see how many consecutive times they can keep the footbag in play. One point is scored for each kick.

2. *Partner play.* Partners alternate kicking the footbag. Score 1 point for each alternate successful kick.

3. *Group play.* A circle of four or five individuals is the basic formation. Rules governing consecutive kicks are (a) all members of the circle must have kicked the footbag for a consecutive run to count, and (b) return kicks are prohibited: that is, kickers may not receive return kicks from the person to whom they kicked the footbag.

Gymnastics Ribbon Movements

Ribbon movements are spectacular and make effective demonstrations. Official ribbon length is around 7 m with the first metre doubled, but for practical purposes shorter lengths are used at the elementary school level.

Ribbons can be made easily in a variety of colours. A rhythmic flow of movement is desired, featuring circular, oval, spiral, and wavelike shapes. A light flowing movement is the goal, with total body involvement. The dowel or wand to which the ribbon is attached should be an extension of the hand and arm. Laterality is also a consideration.

The following are basic ribbon movements:

1. *Swinging movements.* The entire body should coordinate with these large, swinging motions:

   a. Swing the ribbon forward and backward in the sagittal plane.

   b. Swing the ribbon across and in front of the body in the frontal plane.

   c. Swing the ribbon overhead from side to side.

   d. Swing the ribbon upward and catch the end of it.

   e. While holding both ends of the ribbon, swing it upward, around, and over the body.

2. *Circling movements.* Large circles should involve the whole arm; smaller circles involve the wrist. Circles are made in different planes: frontal, sagittal (parallel), and horizontal.

   a. Circle the ribbon at different levels.

   b. Circle the ribbon horizontally, vertically, or diagonally.

   c. Circle the ribbon in front of the body, around the body, and behind the body.

   d. Run while circling the ribbon overhead; leap as the ribbon is circled downward and under the legs.

   e. Add dance steps and turns while circling the ribbon.

3. *Figure-eight movements.* Figure eights are also made in the three planes. The two halves of the figure eight should be the same size and on the same plane level. The figure can be made with long arm movements or with movements of the lower arm or wrist. While performing a figure eight, hop through the loop when the ribbon passes the side of the body.

4. *Zigzag movements.* Zigzag movements can be made in the air or on the floor. These are done with continuous up-and-down hand movements, using primarily wrist action. The following are suggested:

   a. Execute the zigzag in the air in front, around, and behind the body.

   b. Run backward while zigzagging the ribbon in front of the body. Perform at different levels.

   c. Run forward while zigzagging behind the body at different levels.

5. *Spiral movements.* The circles in the spiral can be of the same size or of an increasing or decreasing progression. Spirals can be made from left to right or the reverse.

   a. Execute spirals around, in front of, or beside the body while performing locomotor dance steps.

   b. Execute spirals while performing forward and backward rolls.

6. *Throwing and catching movements.* These skills are usually combined with swinging, circling, or figure-eight movements. The ribbon is tossed with one hand and is caught with the same hand or with the other hand. Throwing and catching is a difficult maneuver.

7. *Exchanges.* During group routines, the ribbon is handed or tossed to a partner.

Critical Thinking

1. The manipulative skills in this chapter have a variety of learning activities for all three developmental levels. For one of the skills mentioned, discuss how you will develop progressive learning activities across several grade levels (e.g., how will you develop juggling skills in grades 1 through 3; 4 through 6).

References and Suggested Readings

Carpenter, J. (2003). *Mix, match, and motivate.* Champaign, IL: Human Kinetics.

Colvin, A.V., Markos, N., & Walker, P. (2000). *Teaching the nuts and bolts of physical education.* Champaign, IL: Human Kinetics.

Finnigan, D. (2002). *Juggling.* Champaign, IL: Human Kinetics.

Hackett, P. & Owen, P. (1997). *The juggling book.* New York: Lyons & Burford.

Kalbfleisch, S. E. (2002). *Jump 2bfit: Rope skipping fitness & activity program.* Ancaster, ON: CETA Publishing.

Loredo, E. (1996). *The jump rope book.* New York: Workman Publishers.

Marrott, B. (1997). *Getting a jump on fitness.* New York: Barricade Books.

Mitchelson, M. (1997). *The most excellent book of how to be a juggler.* Brookfield, CT: Copper Beech Books.

Poppen, J.D. (1989). *Action packet on jumping rope.* Puyallup, WA: Action Productions.

Robertson-Williams, J. (1994). *So, you want to learn how to Double Dutch?* Pittsburgh: Dorrance Publishers.

 Weblinks

Info-Skip Canada: www.jumprope.ca

If your class includes skipping enthusiasts, direct them to this Canadian website devoted to rope skipping, with links to skipping associations across Canada and the world, competitions, techniques, and the history of rope skipping.

teachervision.com: www.teachervision.fen.com/physical-education/lesson-plan/5870.html?detoured=1

This website provides a variety of lesson plans based on Hula Hoop activities.

Heart and Stroke Foundation of Canada: www.heartandstroke.ca

Includes information on two in-school programs (Jump Rope for Heart and Hoops for Heart). Both focus on cardiovascular fitness, while raising funds for the Hearth & Stroke Foundation.

JumpFit: www.jumprope.com

This website highlights jump-rope skills and workout program. Includes basics skills and advance jump rope tricks.

World Footbag Association: http://worldfootbag.com

This website includes information on footbag events, organizations, and teaching resources.

Ultimate Handbook: www.ultimatehandbook.com/uh

This website highlights information on skills and strategies for "ultimate players of all levels." Also includes educational materials for teachers and coaches.

CHAPTER 18

Body Management Skills

Essential Components

I	Organized around content standards
II	**Student-centred and developmentally appropriate**
III	**Physical activity and motor skill development form the core of the program**
IV	Teaches management skills and self-discipline
V	**Promotes inclusion of all students**
VI	**Focuses on process over product**
VII	Promotes lifetime personal health and wellness
VIII	Teaches cooperation and responsibility and promotes sensitivity to diversity

Physical Education Standards

1	**Students are able to move competently using a variety of fundamental and specialized motor skills.**
2	Students can monitor and maintain a health-enhancing level of physical fitness.
3	Students are able to apply movement concepts and basic mechanics of skill performance when learning and refining motor skills.
4	Students comprehend the basic principles of wellness and are able to apply concepts that enable them to make meaningful decisions that positively impact their health and wellness.
5	**Students participate in a wide variety of physical activities and learn how to maintain a personalized active lifestyle.**
6	Students demonstrate empathy, understanding, and respect for the numerous differences exhibited by people in an activity setting.
7	Students exhibit responsible and self-directed behaviours that lead to positive social interactions in physical activity.

OVERVIEW

Body management skills are required for control of the body in a variety of situations. Body management skills require an integration of agility, coordination, balance, and flexibility. Activities in this chapter help students learn to control their bodies using a wide variety of apparatus. This chapter offers organizational hints, instructional strategies, and activities for helping youngsters develop body management skills.

OUTCOMES

- Know how to help students develop body management skills using large and small apparatus.

- Apply proper instructional procedures to a wide variety of apparatus activities.

- Design a safe environment when teaching large apparatus activities.

- Teach a variety of activities on large apparatus, including climbing ropes, benches, balance beams, horizontal ladders, exercise bar, jumping boxes, and parachute.

B*ody management skills are an important component of movement competency. Efficient movement demands integration of a number of physical traits, including agility, balance, flexibility, and coordination. In addition, youngsters must develop an understanding of how to control their bodies while on large apparatus, such as beams, benches, and jumping boxes. A basic understanding of movement concepts and mechanical principles used in skill performance is necessary for quality movement.*

The focus of this chapter is on developing body management skills using large apparatus. Children have an innate desire to run, jump, swing, and climb. This chapter includes activities for climbing ropes, benches, balance beams, horizontal ladders, exercise bars, jumping boxes, and parachutes. Most large apparatus activities offer an opportunity for children to learn body management skills while free of ground support. In addition, this chapter is a strong complement to Chapter 20 (Gymnastics Skills) and provides children with an excellent opportunity to explore and develop movement skills and concepts (see Chapters 14 and 15). In many cases, moving to large apparatus can extend the concepts and skills first explored on the floor.

Return Activities

The use of return activities increases the movement potential of apparatus. Return activity requires children to perform a movement task (jumping, hopping, skipping, and so on) after they have performed on the apparatus. This reduces the time children stand in line waiting for another turn after completion of their task on the apparatus. To increase the amount of time youngsters are actively engaged, increase the distance children have to travel. Return activities demand little supervision. An example of a return activity to use when teaching balance beam activities would be the following: Walk across the beam, do a straddle dismount, and crab-walk to a cone and back to place.

Safe Use of Apparatus

Apparatus often has to be placed in position before a class arrives. Youngsters should understand they are not to use the equipment until the teacher gives approval. Establish procedures for setup, storage, and safe use of apparatus and mats. The following are examples of safety guidelines that can be applied to appropriate situations:

1. Placement of tumbling mats for shock absorption is critical. Tumbling mats should be positioned for safety in dismounting and where falls are possible (e.g., directly under climbing ropes).

2. Demonstrate how to lift and carry the apparatus properly. Practise proper setup and storage of apparatus. For particular pieces that need cooperation among the children, designate the number of children and the means of carrying. Apparatus should be carried, not dragged, across the floor.

3. Activity on apparatus should occur only when supervised by teachers. Children should be instructed to stay away from all apparatus in the area that has been prearranged for later use.

4. Because improper use of apparatus can result in injury, instruction must precede apparatus activity. Place signs reminding students of proper use of apparatus on cones near individual pieces of equipment. Also include regular verbal safety reminders.

Activities with Climbing Ropes

Climbing ropes offer high-level developmental possibilities for the upper trunk and arms as well as training in coordination of different body parts (see Figure 18.1). Adequate grip and arm strength are prerequisites for climbing. Important early goals for children are becoming accustomed to the rope and gaining confidence.

Figure 18.1

Rope climbing on an eight-rope set.

Instructional Procedures

1. Mats should be placed under all ropes.

2. The hand-over-hand method should be used for climbing and the hand-under-hand method for descending.

3. Caution the children not to slide; sliding can cause rope burns on the hands and legs.

4. A climber who becomes tired should stop and rest. Proper rest stops should be taught as part of the climbing procedure.

5. Children also should be taught to leave enough margin for a safe descent.

6. Spotters should be used for activities in which the body is inverted.

7. Rosin in powdered form and magnesium chalk aid in gripping. It is particularly important that they be used when the rope becomes slippery.

8. Marks to limit the climb can be put on the rope with adhesive tape. A height of 2 m above the floor is reasonable.

Preliminary Activities

Progression is important in rope climbing, and the fundamental skill progressions should be followed.

SUPPORTED PULL-UPS

In Supported Pull-up activities, a part of the body remains in contact with the floor. The Pull-up is hand-over-hand and the return is hand-under-hand.

1. Kneel directly under the rope. Pull up to the tiptoes and return to kneeling position.

2. Start in sitting position under the rope. Pull up; legs are supported on the heels. Return to sitting position.

3. Start in a standing position. Grasp the rope, rock back on the heels, and lower the body to the floor. Keep a straight body. Return to standing position.

HANGS

In a Hang, the youngsters pull the body up in one motion and hold it for a length of time (5, 10, or 20 seconds). Progression is important.

1. From a seated position, reach up as high as possible and pull the body—except for the heels—from the floor. Hold.

2. Same as the previous stunt, but pull the body completely free of the floor. Hold.

3. From a standing position, jump up, grasp the rope, and hang. This should be a Bent-arm Hang, with the hands about even with the mouth. Hold.

4. Repeat the previous stunt, but add leg movements—one or both knees up, bicycling movement, Half Lever (one or both legs up, parallel to the floor), Full Lever (feet up to the face).

PULL-UPS

In the Pull-up, the child raises and lowers the body repeatedly. The initial challenge should be to accomplish one Pull-up in the defined position. The number of repetitions should be increased with care. All of the activities described for Hangs are adaptable to Pull-ups. The chin should touch the hands on each Pull-up.

INVERTED HANG

For the Inverted Hang, both hands reach up high. The rope is kept to one side. The performer jumps to a bent-arm position, and at the same time brings the knees up to the nose to invert the body, which is now in a curled position. In a continuation of the motion, the feet are brought up higher than the hands, and the legs are locked around the rope. The body should now be straight and upside down. In the learning phase, teachers should spot.

Climbing the Rope

SCISSORS GRIP

For the Scissors Grip, approach the rope and reach as high as possible, standing with the right leg forward of the left. Raise the back leg, bend at the knee, and place the rope inside the knee and outside the foot. Cross the forward leg over the back leg, and straighten the legs with the toes pointed down (see Figure 18.2). This should give a secure hold. The teacher can check the position.

To climb using the Scissors Grip, raise the knees up close to the chest, the rope sliding between them, while supporting the body with the hand grip. Lock the rope between the legs and climb up, using the hand-over-hand method and stretching as high as the hands can reach. Bring the knees up to the chest and repeat the process until you have climbed halfway. Later, strive for a higher climb.

LEG-AROUND REST

To do the Leg-around Rest (see Figure 18.3), wrap the left leg completely around the rope, keeping the rope between the thighs. The bottom of the rope then crosses over the instep of the left foot from the outside. The right foot stands on the rope as it crosses over the instep, providing

Figure 18.2

Scissors Grip.

Figure 18.3

Leg-around Rest.

pressure to prevent slippage. To provide additional pressure, release the hands and wrap the arms around the rope, leaning away from the rope at the same time.

To climb using the Leg-around Rest, proceed as in climbing with the Scissors Grip, but loosen the grip each time and re-form higher up on the rope.

Descending the Rope

There are four methods to descend the rope. The only differences are in the use of the leg locks, as the hand-under-hand is used for all descents.

SCISSORS GRIP DESCENT

From an extended Scissors Grip position, lock the legs and lower the body with the hands until the knees are against the chest. Hold with the hands, and lower the legs to a new position.

LEG-AROUND REST DESCENT

From the Leg-around Rest position, lower the body until the knees are against the chest. Lift the top foot, and let the feet slide to a lower position (see Figure 18.3). Secure with the top foot and repeat.

INSTEP SQUEEZE DESCENT

Squeeze the rope between the insteps by keeping the heels together. Lower the body while the rope slides against the instep.

STIRRUP DESCENT

Have the rope on the outside of the right foot and carry it over the instep of the left. Pressure from the left foot holds the position. To get into position, let the rope trail along the right leg, reach under, and hook it with the left instep. When the pressure from the left leg is reduced, the rope slides smoothly while the youngster descends with the hands.

Stunts Using Two Ropes

Two ropes hanging close together are needed for the following activities.

STRAIGHT-ARM HANG

To do the Straight-arm Hang, jump up, grasp one rope with each hand, and hang with the arms straight.

BENT-ARM HANG

Perform as for the Straight-arm Hang, but bend the arms at the elbows.

ARM HANGS WITH DIFFERENT LEG POSITIONS

1. Do single- and double-knee lifts.
2. Do a Half Lever. Bring the legs up parallel to the floor and point the toes.
3. Do a Full Lever. Bring the feet up to the face and keep the knees straight.
4. Do a Bicycle. Pedal as on a bicycle.

PULL-UPS

The Pull-up is the same as on a single rope, except that each hand grasps a rope.

INVERTED HANGS

1. Hang with the feet wrapped around the ropes.
2. Hang with the feet against the inside of the ropes.
3. Hang with the toes pointed and the feet not touching the ropes (see Figure 18.4).

Figure 18.4

Spotting an Inverted Hang on two ropes. (Holding the performer's hands ensures confidence and safety.)

SKIN THE CAT

From a bent-arm position, kick the feet overhead and continue the roll until the feet touch the mat. Return to the starting position. A more difficult stunt is to start from a higher position so that the feet do not touch the mat. Reverse to original position.

CLIMBING

1. Climb up one rope, transfer to another, and descend.
2. Climb halfway up one rope, cross over to another rope, and continue to climb to the top.
3. Climb both ropes together without using the legs. This is difficult and requires the climber to slide one hand at a time up the ropes without completely releasing the grip.
4. Climb as on a single rope, with hands on one rope and feet on the other rope.

Activity Sequences

Rope-climbing activities are conducive to forming sequences through which the child can progress. The following sequence represents the kind of progressive challenges that children can meet:

1. Jump and hang (10 seconds).
2. Pull up and hold (10 seconds).
3. Scissors Climb to blue mark (3 m).
4. Scissors Climb to top (4.5 m).
5. Demonstrate Leg-around Rest (3 m).
6. Do an Inverted Hang, with body straight (5 seconds).

Activities on the Balance Beams

Balance-beam activities contribute to control in both static and dynamic balance situations (see Figure 18.5).

The balance-beam side of a balance-beam bench is ideal for such activities. You may wish to have beams and benches of varying widths to provide for a wider range of challenges.

Instructional Procedures

1. Move with controlled, deliberate movements. Speed is not a goal. Advise performers to recover their balance before taking another step or making another movement.

Figure 18.5

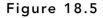

Walking on a balance-beam bench.

2. In keeping with the principle of control, step slowly on the beam, pause momentarily in good balance at the end of the activity, and dismount with a small, controlled jump from the end of the beam when the routine is completed.

3. Mats can be placed at the end of the bench to cushion the dismount and to allow for rolls and stunts after the dismount.

4. Visual fixation is important. Look straight ahead rather than down at the feet. Eye targets can be marked on or attached to walls to assist in visual fixation. This fixation allows balance controls other than vision to function more effectively. From time to time, movements can be done with the eyes closed, entirely eliminating visual control of balance.

5. Children should be told to step off the beam when they lose their balance, rather than teetering and falling off awkwardly. Allow the performer to step back on the beam and to continue the routine.

6. Both laterality and directionality are important. Give right and left feet reasonably equal practice. For example, if a performer does steps leading with the right foot, the next effort should be made leading with the left foot.

7. The child next in line should begin when the performer ahead is about three-quarters of the distance across the beam.

8. A child or the teacher can assist the performer. The assistant holds the hand palm up, ready to assist the performer if and when help is needed.

Activity Sequences

Activities for the balance beam are presented as a progression of movement concepts and skills.

ACTIVITIES ON PARALLEL BEAMS

Activities on two parallel beams are presented first as lead-up practice for the single-beam tasks. The beams should be placed about 25 to 75 cm apart. The parallel-beam activities can be done alone, or with a partner when more security is desired.

1. With a partner, join inside hands and walk forward, backward, and sideward. Walk sideward, using a grapevine step. Hold a beanbag in the free hand.

2. Without a partner, perform various animal walks, such as the Crab Walk, Bear Walk, Measuring Worm, and Elephant Walk.

3. With one foot on each beam, walk forward, backward, and sideward.

4. Progress to the middle of the beam and perform various turns and stunts, such as picking up a beanbag and moving through a hoop.

MOVEMENTS ACROSS THE FULL LENGTH OF A SINGLE BEAM

1. Perform various locomotor tasks, such as walking, follow steps, heel-and-toe steps, side steps, tiptoe steps, the grapevine step (step behind, step across), and so on.

2. Follow different directions—forward, backward, sideward.

3. Use different arm and hand positions—on the hips, on the head, behind the back, out to the sides, pointing to the ceiling, folded across the chest.

4. Move across the beam as you assume different shapes.

5. Balance an object (beanbag) on various body parts—on the head, on the back of the hands, on the shoulders.

6. Explore different mounts and dismounts.

HALF-AND-HALF MOVEMENTS

Half-and-half movements repeat the movements, arm positions, and balancing stunts described previously, except that the performer goes halfway across the beam using a selected movement and then changes to another type of movement on the second half of the beam.

Designing Movement Sequences

For a typical sequence task, the performer mounts the beam, moves halfway across the beam with a selected movement, performs a particular balance, turn, and shape at the centre, finishes the movements on the second half of the beam, and dismounts.

Use the movement concepts discussed in Chapter 14 to guide the design of movement sequences. For example, you may provide a challenge such as "design a sequence that includes a mount, two different ways to travel along a beam, a low turn, and include a shape in your dismount." This will allow students to explore travel, levels, shape, and flight. In general, sequences may be informal or formal—the informal being primarily exploration, and the more formal sequences requiring more practice and refinement, perhaps for a demonstration (for example, "Polish your sequence so you can show it to the class.")

Sequences can also be designed to include a partner. The following are some basic examples.

1. Partners start on opposite ends of the beam and move toward each other with the same kind of movement, do a balance pose together in the centre, and return to their respective ends of the beam.

2. Partners start on opposite ends of the beam and attempt to pass each other without losing their balance and without touching the floor. Find different ways to pass.

Activities on Benches

The balance-beam bench is effective in helping students to develop strength and balance. Bench activities are challenging to children and offer a variety of movement possibilities. Many of the ideas from the preceding beam section can also be used on the wider benches.

Instructional Procedures

1. All activities on the benches should be broken down into three distinct parts: the approach to and mounting of the bench, the actual activity on the bench, and the dismount from the bench.

2. Mats should be placed at the ends of the bench to facilitate the dismount and various rolls and stunts executed after the dismount.

3. Benches can be positioned horizontally or inclined. They can also be combined with other equipment for variation and greater challenge.

4. Three to four children is the maximum number that should be assigned to one bench.

5. Return activities add to the activity potential.

6. Speed is not a goal in bench activities. Movements should be done deliberately and carefully, with attention given to body control and body management.

7. Attention also should be paid to laterality and directionality. For example, if a child hops on the right foot, the next effort should be made on the left foot. In jump turns, both right and left movements should be used.

Perform various locomotor movements along the length of the bench, such as stepping or jumping on and off the side of the bench, hopping on and off the side of the bench, or skipping and galloping on the bench.

Pull the body along the bench, using different combinations of body parts. Use the arms only, the legs only, the right leg and the left arm, or the left leg and the right arm. Pull along the bench, using the following positions:

1. Prone position (head first and feet first) (see Figure 18.6).

2. Supine position (head first and feet first) (see Figure 18.7)

3. Side position (head first and feet first)

Various leg positions (such as legs up in a half-lever position, knees bent, and so on) should be used in performing pulls and pushes. Those body parts not being used to pull can be used to carry a piece of manipulative equipment, such

Figure 18.6

Prone movements, head first.

Figure 18.7

Supine movements, feet first.

Figure 18.8

Crouch jumping.

as a beanbag or ball. Employ different body shapes. Try the Submarine (one foot in the air like a periscope).

MOVEMENTS ALONG THE SIDE OF THE BENCH

Proceed alongside the bench in the following positions with the hands on the bench and the feet on the floor as far from the bench as possible.

1. Prone position
2. Supine position
3. Turn-over (Proceed along the bench, changing from prone to supine position.)

Repeat these positions with the feet on the bench and the hands on the floor as far from the bench as possible.

SCOOTER MOVEMENTS

Sit on the bench and proceed along it without using the hands in the following ways:

1. Do a Scooter. Proceed with the feet leading the body. Try to pull the body along with the feet.
2. Do a Reverse Scooter. Proceed as for the Scooter but with the legs trailing and pushing the body along the bench.
3. Do a Seat Walk. Proceed forward by walking on the buttocks. Use the legs as little as possible.

CROUCH JUMPS

Place both hands on the bench and jump back and forth over it. Progress the length of the bench by moving the hands forward a few inches after each jump.

1. Do a regular Crouch Jump (see Figure 18.8). Use both hands and both feet. Jump as high as possible.
2. Do a Straddle Jump. Straddle the bench with the legs, take the weight on the hands, and jump with the legs as high as possible.
3. Use one hand and two feet. Do a Crouch Jump, but eliminate the use of one hand.
4. Use one hand and one foot. Perform the Crouch Jump, using only one hand and one foot.
5. Stand to one side, facing the bench, with both hands on it. With stiff arms, try to send the seat as high as possible into the air.

BASIC TUMBLING STUNTS

Basic tumbling stunts can be incorporated into bench activities: the Back Roller, Backward Curl, Forward Roll (see Figure 18.9), Backward Roll, and Cartwheel (see Chapter 20).

DISMOUNTS

All bench activities in which the child moves from one end of the bench to the other should end with a dismount.

Many stunts can be used, but the following dismounts are suggested:

1. Single jump (forward or backward) (see Figure 18.10).
2. Jump with turns (half turn, three-quarter turn, or full turn).
3. Jackknife. Jump, kick the legs up, and touch the toes with the fingertips. Keep the feet together.

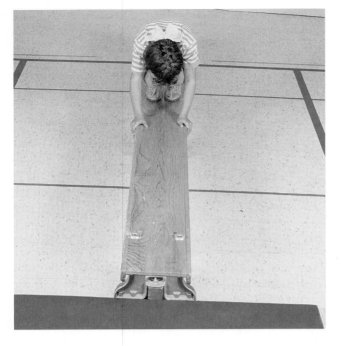

Figure 18.9

Preparing to do a Forward Roll on the bench.

4. Jackknife Split. Same as the Jackknife, but spread the legs as far as possible.
5. Jump to a Forward Roll.
6. Side jump to a Side Roll.
7. Judo Roll.
8. Jump with combinations of the stunts noted in this list.

Figure 18.10

Dismounting from a bench.

Figure 18.11

Challenge course using benches.

Additional Experiences on Benches

1. The range of activities can be extended with the addition of balls, beanbags, and hoops. Hoops can be used as obstacles to go over, under, around, or through. Basic balance and manipulative skills can be incorporated into the activity with balls and beanbags.
2. Two can perform at one time, each child near an opposite end of the bench, doing different balance positions on the bench.
3. Children like to go over and under a row of benches arranged in a kind of obstacle course.
4. Benches can be placed in a square formation, with children moving around the square and doing a different movement on each bench.
5. Benches are appropriate for some partner activities. Partners can start on each end and pass over, under, or around each other, reversing original positions. Wheelbarrow Walks are also suitable.
6. Another enjoyable activity is arranging the benches in a course as illustrated in Figure 18.11. A student is chosen to lead a small group through the challenge course. A different activity must be performed at each bench.

Activities with Jumping Boxes

Jumping boxes provide opportunities for children to jump from a height and propel their bodies through space. Boxes can be of varying heights; 20 cm and 60 cm are suggested.

Instructional Procedures

1. Attention should be given to landing in proper form. Lightness, bent-knee action, balance, and body control should be stressed.

2. Mats should be used to cushion the landing.

3. The exploratory and creative approach is important; there are few standard stunts in jumping box activities.

4. No more than two or three children should be assigned to each series of boxes.

5. Additional challenges can be incorporated using hoops and balls. Extend the movement possibilities with rolling stunts after the dismount.

Activity Sequences

The activities that follow can be augmented easily. Encourage the children to expand the activity.

APPROACHES TO THE BOXES

Performing movements such as these can vary the approach to the boxes:

1. Fundamental locomotor movements: run, gallop, skip, and hop.

2. Animal walks: Bear Walk, Crab Walk, and so on.

3. Moving over and under various obstacles: jumping over a bench, moving through a hoop held upright by a mat, doing a Backward Roll on the mat.

4. Rope jumping to the box: students try to continue jumping while mounting and dismounting the box.

MOUNTING THE BOX

Many different combinations can be used to get onto the box.

1. Practise stepping onto the box (mounting) by taking the full weight on the stepping foot and holding it for a few seconds. This helps the student develop a sense of balance and tends to stabilize the support foot.

2. Mount the box, using locomotor movements such as a step, jump, leap, or hop. Perform various turns—quarter, half, three-quarter, and full—while jumping onto the box.

3. Use a Crouch Jump to get onto the box.

4. Back up to the box and mount it without looking at it.

5. Mount the box while a partner tosses you a beanbag.

Figure 18.12

Jump dismounting.

6. Make various targets on top of the box with a piece of chalk, and try to land on the spot when mounting.

DISMOUNTING THE BOX

The following dismounts can be used to develop body control:

1. Jump off with a quarter turn, half turn, or full turn.

2. Jump off with different body shapes: stretching, curling up in a ball, jackknifing.

3. Jump over a wand or through a hoop.

4. Jump off, and perform a Forward Roll.

5. Change the foregoing dismounts by substituting a hop or a leap for the jump.

6. Increase the height and distance of the dismount.

7. Dismount in various directions, such as forward (see Figure 18.12), backward and sideward.

8. Jump off using a jackknife or wide-straddle dismount.

9. Perform a balance stunt on the box and then dismount.

After the class has learned the basic movements used with jumping boxes, try incorporating continuous squad motion. Choose a student to lead the group through different approaches, mounts, and dismounts. Change the leader each time.

Activities with Horizontal Ladders

Horizontal ladders are manufactured in a variety of models. The most usable ladder is one that can be stored against the wall, out of the way. If the ladder can be inclined, the movement possibilities are extended. Horizontal ladders provide a good lead-up activity for rope climbing, because their rigidity makes them easier to climb. Children can enhance grip strength and increase arm–shoulder girdle development by suspending body weight. This development can help improve students' posture.

Instructional Procedures

1. The opposed-thumb grip, in which the thumb goes around the bar, is important. In most activities, the back of the hands should face the child. (This is the upper grip.) The grip should be varied occasionally, making use of the lower grip (palms toward the face) and the mixed grip (one hand facing one way and one the other).

2. Whenever the child is doing an Inverted Hang, make sure spotters are present.

3. Speed is not a goal of climbing activity. In fact, the longer the child hangs from the ladder, the more beneficial the activity is. There is value in simply hanging.

4. In activities involving movement across the ladder, all children should travel in the same direction.

5. Mats must be placed under the apparatus when it is in use.

6. Children should be instructed in the dismount. They should land in a bent-leg position, on the balls of the feet.

Activity Sequences

HANGS

Hangs should be performed with the opposed-thumb grip and usually with straight arms. Encourage children to hang in a bent-arm position, however, to involve more muscles in the upper arm. The following variations of the hang are suggested:

1. Keep the legs straight and point the toes toward the ground.

2. Lift the knees as high as possible toward the chest.

3. Lift the knees and pedal a bicycle.

4. Bring the legs up parallel to the ground, with the knees straight and the toes pointed.

5. Touch the toes of one or both feet to a rung or to the side of the ladder.

6. Bring the feet up and over one rung and hook the toes under a second rung. Release the hand grip and hang in an inverted position.

7. Stand on a box if necessary to get into position for a Flexed-arm Hang. Hang as long as possible with the chin even with the hands.

8. Swing the body back and forth.

9. Swing back and forth and jump as far as possible. Vary with turns.

10. Hang from the ladder, first with one hand and then with the other.

TRAVELLING ACTIVITIES

Throughout the suggested travelling activities, have the children use different body shapes.

1. Travel the length of the ladder, using the rungs. Start by travelling one rung at a time, and then skip one or more rungs to add challenge.

2. Travel the length of the ladder, using both side rails. Now use one rail only to travel the ladder.

3. Hang with both hands on the side rails. Progress the length of the ladder by jumping both hands forward at once.

4. Hang with both hands on the same rung. Progress by jumping both hands forward simultaneously.

5. Travel underneath the ladder in monkey fashion, with both hands and feet on the rungs. Try with the feet on the side rails.

6. Travel the length of the ladder carrying a beanbag, a ball, or any similar object.

7. Travel the length of the ladder sideways and backward.

8. Travel the length of the ladder, doing a half turn each time a move is made to a new rung.

9. Get a partner. The children start at opposite ends of the ladder, and they pass each other along the way.

Activities on the Exercise Bar (Low Horizontal Bar)

Horizontal bars should be installed on the playground in a series of at least three at different heights. Indoor bars can be freestanding and have adjustable heights. The primary program focuses on hangs, travels, and simple stunts. To perform many of the more complicated stunts on the bar, children need sufficient arm strength to pull the body up and over the bar.

Instructional Procedures

1. Only one child should be on a bar at one time.
2. The bar should not be used when it is wet.
3. The basic grip is the opposed-thumb grip, facing away.

Activity Sequences

HANGS

To hang from the bar, point the feet, one or both knees up, in a Half or Full Lever. Bring the toes up to touch the bar inside the hands. Outside the hands. Use different body shapes.

SWINGS

Swing back and forth, release the grip, and propel the body forward. Land in a standing position.

MOVING ALONG THE BAR

Begin at one side and move hand against hand to the other end of the bar. Move with crossed hands. Travel with different body shapes.

SLOTH TRAVEL

Face the end of the bar, standing underneath. Grasp the bar with both hands and hook the legs over the bar at the knees like a sloth. In this position, move along the bar to the other end. Return by reversing the movement.

ARM AND LEG HANG

Grasp the bar with an upper grip. Bring one of the legs up between the arms and hook the knee over the bar.

DOUBLE-LEG HANG

Perform as in the preceding stunt, but bring both legs between the hands and hook the knees over the bar. Release the hands and hang in the inverted position. If the child's hands touch or are near the ground, she can dismount by releasing the legs and dropping to a crouched position on the ground.

SKIN THE CAT

Bring both knees up between the arms as in the previous stunt, but continue the direction of the knees until the body is turned over backward. Release the grip and drop to the ground.

SKIN THE CAT RETURN

Perform as in the preceding stunt, but don't release the hands. Bring the legs back through the hands to original position.

FRONT SUPPORT

Grasp the bar with an upper grip, and jump to a straight-arm support on the bar. Jump down.

FRONT SUPPORT PUSH-OFF

Mount the bar in the same way as for a Front Support. In returning to the ground, push off straight with the arms and jump as far back as possible.

TUMMY BALANCE

Jump to the bar as in preceding stunt. Position the body so you can balance on the tummy with hands released.

TUMBLE OVER

Jump to a Front-support position. Change the grip to a lower grip. Bend forward and roll over to a standing position under the bar.

SINGLE-KNEE SWING

Using the upper grip, swing one leg forward to hang by the knee. Using the free leg to gain momentum, swing back and forth.

SIDE ARC

Sit on the bar with one leg on each side, both hands gripping the bar in front of the body. Lock the legs and fall sideways. Try to make a complete circle back to position. Good momentum is needed.

SINGLE-LEG RISE

Using the position of the Single-knee Swing, on the backswing and upswing rise to the top of the bar. The down leg must be kept straight. Swing forward (down) first, and on the backswing, push down hard with straight arms. A spotter can assist by pushing down on the straight leg with one hand and lifting on the back with the other.

KNEE CIRCLES

Sit on top of the bar, with one leg over and one under the bar. Lock the feet. With the hands in an upper grip, shift the weight backward so that the body describes a circle under the bar and returns to place. Try this with a forward circle, with hands in a lower grip. Note that children must have considerable initial momentum to complete the circle.

Activities with Parachutes

Parachute play can be enjoyed by children of all ages and can be a useful apparatus to develop a variety of movement skills and concepts. Many movement possibilities, some of which are rhythmic, can be used in parachute play. Locomotor skills can be practised while manipulating the parachute. Rhythmic beats of the tom-tom or appropriate music can guide locomotor movements. Parachute play provides many excellent cooperative group learning experiences. In addition, parachutes provide an interesting means of accomplishing physical fitness goals: a good development of strength, agility, coordination, and endurance. Strength development focuses especially on the arms, hands, and shoulder girdle. At times, however, strength demands are made on the entire body.

Parachutes range in size from about 3 m to 10 m, with the larger size appropriate for a class of 24 to 30 students. Each parachute has an opening near the top to allow trapped air to escape and to keep the parachute shaped properly.

Grips

The grips used in handling the parachute are comparable to those employed in hanging activities on an apparatus. Grips can be with one or two hands, overhand (palms facing away), underhand (palms facing toward), or mixed (one hand underhand and the other overhand).

Instructional Procedures

1. Certain terms peculiar to parachute activity must be explained carefully. Clarify terms such as inflate, deflate, float, dome, and mushroom when they are introduced.

2. For preliminary explanations, stretch the parachute out on the ground in its circular pattern, with the children seated just far enough away so that they cannot touch the parachute during instructions. When the children hold the parachute during later explanations, encourage them to retain their hold lightly, letting the centre of the parachute drop to the ground.

3. The teacher explains the activity, demonstrating as needed. If there are no questions, initiate the activity with a command such as "Ready—begin!"

4. The teacher must watch for fatigue, particularly with younger children.

Activities are presented according to type, and include variations and suggestions for supplementary activities. Unless otherwise specified, activities begin and halt on signal.

Exercise Activities

Exercises should be done vigorously and with enough repetitions to challenge the children. In addition to the exercises presented, others can be adapted to parachute play.

TOE TOUCHER

Sit with feet extended under the parachute and hold the chute taut with a two-hand grip, drawing it up to the chin. Bend forward and touch the grip to the toes. Return parachute to stretched position.

CURL-UP

Extend the body under the parachute in Curl-up position, so that the chute comes up to the chin when held taut. Do Curl-ups, returning each time to the stretched chute position.

DORSAL LIFT

Lie prone, with head toward the parachute and feet pointed back, away from it. Grip the chute and slide toward the feet until there is some tension on it. Raise the chute off the ground with a vigorous lift of the arms, until head and chest rise off the ground. Return.

V-SIT

Lie supine, with head toward the chute. Do V-sits by raising the upper and lower parts of the body simultaneously into a V-shaped position. The knees should be kept straight.

BACKWARD PULL

Face the parachute and pull back, away from its centre. Pulls can be made from a sitting, kneeling, or standing position.

ELEVATOR

Begin with the chute taut and at ground level. On the command "Elevator up," lift the chute overhead while keeping it stretched tight. On the command "Elevator down," lower the chute to starting position. Children can raise and lower quickly, or in increments. Levels can also bring in body part identification, with children holding the chute even with their head, nose, chin, shoulders, chest, waist, thighs, knees, ankles, and toes.

RUNNING IN PLACE

Run in place while holding the chute at different levels.

ISOMETRICS

Hold the chute taut at shoulder level and try to stretch it for 10 seconds. Many other isometric exercises can be performed with the parachute to develop various body parts.

Dome Activities

To make a dome, children begin with the parachute on the floor, holding it with two hands and kneeling on one knee. To trap air under the chute, children stand up quickly, thrusting their arms above the head (see Figure 18.13), and then return to starting position (see Figure 18.14).

Some or all of the children can change to the inside of the chute on the down movement. Domes can also be made while moving in a circle.

STUDENTS UNDER THE CHUTE

Teachers can specify tasks for under the chute, such as taking a certain number of turns with a jump rope, throwing and catching a beanbag, or bouncing a ball a number of times. The needed objects should be under the chute before children make the dome.

Figure 18.13

Making a dome.

Figure 18.14

Holding the air inside a dome.

NUMBER EXCHANGE

Children are numbered from one to four. The teacher calls a number as the dome is made, and those with the number called must change position to be under the dome before the chute comes down. Locomotor movements can be varied.

BLOOMING FLOWER

Children make a dome and kneel with both knees on the edge of the chute. Youngsters hold hands around the chute and lean in and out to represent a flower opening.

LIGHTS OUT

While making a dome, the children take two steps toward the centre and sit inside the chute. They can hold the chute with the hands at the side or by sitting on it.

Mushroom Activities

To form a mushroom, students begin with the chute on the ground, kneeling on one knee and holding with two hands. They stand up quickly, thrusting the arms overhead. Keeping the arms overhead, each walks forward three or four steps toward the centre. They hold their arms overhead until the chute is deflated.

MUSHROOM RELEASE

All children release at the peak of inflation and either run out from under the chute or move to the centre and sit down, with the chute descending on top of them.

MUSHROOM RUN

Children make a mushroom. As soon as they move into the centre, they release holds and run once around the inside of the chute, counterclockwise, back to place.

Parachute Activities with Equipment

BALL CIRCLE

Place a basketball on the raised chute. Make the ball roll around the chute in a large circle, controlling it by raising or lowering the chute. Try the same with two balls.

POPCORN

Place a number of beanbags (from six to ten) on the chute. Shake the chute to make them rise like corn popping (see Figure 18.15).

CIRCULAR DRIBBLE

Each child has a ball suitable for dribbling. The object is to run in circular fashion counterclockwise, holding onto the chute with the left hand and dribbling with the right hand, retaining control of the ball. Switch hands, try the dribbling clockwise. The dribble should be started first, and then, on signal, children start to run. A child who loses a ball must recover it and try to hook on at her original place.

HOLE-IN-ONE

Use four or more plastic whiffle balls of various sizes. The object is to shake the other team's balls into the hole in the centre of the chute. Try to maneuver larger foam balls through the centre of the chute.

Figure 18.15

Popping popcorn.

Other Parachute Activities

MERRY-GO-ROUND MOVEMENTS

Merry-go-round movements, in which children rotate the chute while keeping the centre hole over the same spot, offer many opportunities for locomotor movements, either free or to the beat of a tom-tom. European Rhythmic Running is particularly appropriate. Also appropriate are fundamental movements, such as walking, running, hopping, skipping, galloping, sliding, draw steps, and grapevine steps. The parachute can be held at different levels. Holds can be one- or two-handed.

SHAKING THE RUG AND MAKING WAVES

Shaking the Rug involves rapid movements of the parachute, either light or heavy. Making Waves involves large movements to send billows of cloth up and down. Waves can be small, medium, or high. Different types of waves can be made by having children alternate their up-and-down motions, or by having the class work in small groups around the chute. These small groups take turns showing what they can do. For a more demanding activity, children can perform locomotor movements while they shake the rug.

RUNNING NUMBER GAME

The children around the chute count off by fours; then they run lightly, holding the chute in one hand. The teacher calls out one of the numbers. Children with that number immediately release their grip on the chute and run forward to the next place vacated. They must put on a burst of speed to move ahead.

ROUTINES TO MUSIC

Like other routines, parachute activities can be adapted to music. A sequence should be based on 8 counts, with the routine composed of an appropriate number of sequences.

Critical Thinking

1. For one of the apparatus mentioned, discuss how you will develop progressive learning activities across several grade levels for your gymnastics unit (e.g., how will you develop learning activities that utilize the climbing ropes in grades 1 through 3; 4 through 6).

References and Suggested Readings

Allison, P.C. & Barrett, K.R. (2000). *Constructing children's physical education experiences.* Boston, MA: Allyn & Bacon.

Spalding, A., Kelly, L., Santopietro, J., & Posner-Mayer, J. (1999). *Kids on the ball: Using swiss balls in a complete fitness program.* Champaign, IL: Human Kinetics.

Stiehl, J. & Ramsey, T. (2005). *Climbing wall.* Champaign, IL: Human Kinetics.

Strong, T. & LeFevre, D. (2006). *Parachute games* (2nd ed.). Champaign, IL: Human Kinetics.

Wall, J. & Murray, N. (1994*). Children and movement— physical education in the elementary school* (2nd ed.) Dubuque, IA: WC Brown and Benchmark.

 Weblinks

Moving & Learning: www.movingandlearning.com

This site includes a variety of educational resources for teaching body management skills to children in preschool and primary grades.

CHAPTER 19

Dance and Rhythmic Movement Skills

Essential Components

I	Organized around content standards
II	**Student-centred and developmentally appropriate**
III	**Physical activity and motor skill development form the core of the program**
IV	Teaches management skills and self-discipline
V	Promotes inclusion of all students
VI	**Focuses on process over product**
VII	Promotes lifetime personal health and wellness
VIII	**Teaches cooperation and responsibility and promotes sensitivity to diversity**

Physical Education Standards

1	**Students are able to move competently using a variety of fundamental and specialized motor skills.**
2	Students can monitor and maintain a health-enhancing level of physical fitness.
3	Students are able to apply movement concepts and basic mechanics of skill performance when learning and refining motor skills.
4	Students comprehend the basic principles of wellness and are able to apply concepts that enable them to make meaningful decisions that positively impact their health and wellness.
5	**Students participate in a wide variety of physical activities and learn how to maintain a personalized active lifestyle.**
6	**Students demonstrate empathy, understanding, and respect for the numerous differences exhibited by people in an activity setting.**
7	**Students exhibit responsible and self-directed behaviours that lead to positive social interactions in physical activity.**

OVERVIEW

Activities in this chapter are selected for the purpose of developing rhythmic movement skills. The activities are listed in a progression from easy to more complex, and by developmental level. Dance and rhythmic activities should be scheduled in the same manner as other phases of the year-long physical education program.

OUTCOMES

- Know where to find sources of rhythmic accompaniment.

- Understand the inherent rhythmic nature of all physical activity.

- Outline components of the dance and rhythmic movement program and identify accompanying activities and skill progressions.

- Describe instructional procedures and ideas to facilitate implementation of rhythmic skills into the program.

- Cite creative rhythms, folk dances, and other dance activities that are used as learning experiences in physical education.

- Describe dance progressions for the various levels of development.

Rhythm is the basis of music and dance. Rhythm in dance is simply expressive movement made with or without music. All body movements tend to be rhythmic—the beating of the heart, swinging a tennis racquet, wielding a hammer, throwing a ball. Most movements that take place in physical education class contain elements of rhythm. Movement to rhythm begins early in the child's school career and continues throughout. Since rhythmic activities are particularly appropriate for younger children, a sizable portion of the developmental level I program is devoted to such activities.

Early experiences centre on functional and creative movement forms. Locomotor skills are inherently rhythmic in execution, and the addition of rhythm can enhance development of these skills. An important component of children's dance is fundamental rhythms. Instruction begins with and capitalizes on locomotor skills that children already possess—walking, running, hopping, and jumping. Rhythmic activities provide a vehicle for expressive movement. As children personalize their responses within the framework of the idea, these activities offer opportunity for broad participation and personal satisfaction for all.

Implementing the Rhythmic Movement Program

A major factor in program construction is the progression of basic and specific dance steps. Dances employing the following skills and steps appear in each of the respective developmental level programs.

Skill Progressions

Developmental Level I

In the early primary grades, fundamental locomotor skills are stressed. (Skipping and sliding are taught and practised, but students are not expected to master them.) Combinations of two or more fundamental movements— e.g., the Bleking Step—are presented.

Developmental Level II

At this level, rhythmic activities should include fundamental locomotor skills, more combinations of locomotor skills, the step-hop, and the grand right and left. Marching, basic tinikling steps (Filipino folk dance), and introductory square dancing steps are taught as skill improves.

Developmental Level III

By level III, students are able to master longer and more complex dance steps and sequences, intermediate and advanced tinikling steps, the two-step, and introductory social dance.

Understanding Rhythmic Accompaniment

Music has essential characteristics that children should recognize, understand, and appreciate. These characteristics are also present to varying degrees in other purely percussive accompaniment.

Tempo is the speed of the music. It can be constant or show a gradual increase (acceleration) or decrease (deceleration).

Beat is the underlying pulse of the music. Beat is continuous (though not always heard), and may be strong or weak throughout the music. The beat can be even or uneven. Music with a pronounced beat is easier to follow.

Metre refers to the organization of beats into a regular recurring pattern of measures or bars, commonly in groups of 2, 3, or 4 (indicated by the time signature shown at the beginning of a piece of music: 2/4, 3/4, or 4/4).

Certain notes or beats in a rhythmic pattern receive more force than others, and this defines *accent*. Usually, accent is applied to the first beat of a measure and is generally expressed by a more forceful movement in a sequence of movements.

The *intensity* of music can be loud, soft, light, or heavy. *Mood* is related to intensity but carries the concept deeper into human feelings. Music can reflect many moods— happiness, sadness, gaiety, or fear, for example.

A *phrase* is a natural grouping of measures, coherent segments that make up the melody. Phrases of music are put together into rhythmic *patterns*. Children should learn to recognize when the pattern repeats or changes.

Sources of Rhythmic Accompaniment

Essential to any rhythmic program is accompaniment that encourages desired motor patterns and expressive movement. If children are to move to a rhythm, it must be stimulating, appropriate for the expected responses, and appealing to the learners. Skilful use of a drum or tambourine adds much to rhythmic experiences. A major use of the drumbeat is to guide the movement from one pattern to another by signalling tiny increments of change with light beats that control the flow.

Each school and teacher should build a collection of recorded music. Sets created especially for physical education movement patterns and dance are available from a number of sources. Storage should be arranged so that each recording has its assigned place and is readily available. Keeping extra copies of the more frequently used pieces in reserve is an excellent practice.

Fundamental Rhythms

Fundamental rhythms can be added to the movement activities with which the children are already familiar, such as walking (stepping), running, jumping, and hopping. Fundamental rhythms are emphasized in the primary grades and are extended to the intermediate level on a smaller scale. The general purpose of a fundamental rhythms program is to provide a variety of fundamental movement experiences so the child can learn to move effectively and efficiently, and develop a sense of rhythm. Although the creative aspect of fundamental rhythms is important, even more important is first establishing a vocabulary of movement competencies for each child. The skills in a fundamental rhythm program are important as the background for creative dance and also as the basis for the more precise dance skills of folk, and social dance, which follow later in school programs. Fundamental skills are described, together with teaching hints and stress points, in Chapter 15.

Locomotor Skills

Even rhythm locomotor skills are walking, running, hopping, leaping, jumping, draw steps, and such variations as marching, trotting, stamping, and twirling. Uneven movements are skipping, galloping, and sliding.

Nonlocomotor Skills

Simple nonlocomotor skills are bending, swaying, twisting, swinging, raising, lowering, circling, and rotating various parts of the body. Mimetic movements include striking, lifting, throwing, pushing, pulling, hammering, and other common tasks.

Instructional Procedures

1. Success depends on initiating and guiding simple patterns. Of prime importance is the class atmosphere, which should be one of enjoyment. Furthermore, the accompaniment must be suitable for the movements to be experienced.

2. The element of creativity should not be stifled in a program of fundamental rhythms. The instruction can be directed toward a specific movement (such as walking), and a reasonable range of acceptable

performance, which permits individual creativity, can be established.

3. If you feel awkward or insecure about developing rhythmic programs with a strong creative approach, fundamental rhythms are a good starting point. Combining rhythmic movement with movements students enjoy can be the beginning of a refreshing and stimulating experience for both you and your students.

4. The approach to fundamental rhythms should be a mixture of direct and indirect teaching. Many of the movements do have standard or preferred techniques. For example, there is a correct way to walk. Children should recognize and learn such fundamentals. Within the framework of good technique, however, a variety of movement experiences can be elicited.

Suggestions for Teaching Fundamental Rhythmic Movements

Children enjoy change and the challenge of reacting to change. They can be encouraged to change the movement pattern or some aspect of it (direction, level, body leads, and so on) at the end of a musical phrase. Changes can be signalled by variations in the drumbeat. A heavy, accented beat, for example, can signal a change in direction or type of movement. Stops and starts, changes to different rhythms, and other innovations are within the scope of this process. The intensity of the drumbeat can call for light or heavy movements or for different levels of movement: high, middle, or low. As an example of how to do this, picture a class of children walking heavily in general space to a heavy, even beat. The teacher sounds one extra-heavy beat, whereupon students change direction abruptly, now moving very lightly on the toes to a light, even beat. This sequence finishes with another heavy beat, which signals the children again to change direction and their movement as indicated by the next sequence of beats. The opportunities for movement combinations are many.

The use of different parts of the body, singly and in various combinations, is important in establishing movement variety. Different positions of the arms and legs can vary the ways of moving. Children can perform high on the toes, with toes in or out; on the heels, with stiff knees; kicking high in front or to the rear, with knees brought up high; in a crouch; or any number of different positions. The arms can swing at the sides or be held stiff, be held out in front, or be held overhead. The arms can move in circles or in different patterns. The body can bend forward, backward, or sideward, and it can twist and turn. By combining different arm, leg, and body positions, the children can assume many interesting positions. Changes in body level and patterns of movement for outlining circles, squares, triangles, and other shapes also add interest. Ideas and suggestions for using fundamental skills with rhythm are found in Chapter 15.

Creative and Rhythmic Movement

Creativity should be part of all dance and rhythmic activities, with the scope of the activity determining the degree of freedom. Creativity manifests itself in the opportunity for each child to respond expressively within the scope of the movement idea, which can range from total freedom to stated limits. The child's judgment should be respected, and the teacher should look for original interpretations. Stimulation should be positive in nature, guiding the movement patterns by suggestions, questions, encouragement, and challenges that help children structure their ideas and add variety. Careful guidance is necessary to fan the spark of self-direction, because freedom in itself does not automatically develop creativity.

Instructional Procedures

1. Appropriate music or rhythmic background is important; otherwise, movement can become stilted. An atmosphere of creative freedom must be established. The class should be comfortable and relaxed.

2. When analyzing the setting, ask, What is the basic idea? What expressive movements can be expected? What are the guidelines or boundaries of movement? What space are the children to use?

3. Listening is an important element, because children must understand the mood or sense of the rhythmic background. Some questions that can be posed to children are as follows: "What does the music make us think of?" and "What does the music tell us to do?" If the movement or interpretation is preselected, little time need be wasted in getting under way. Provide enough music that children can grasp the impact. Have them clap the beat if necessary and then move into action.

4. Use action-directing statements such as, "Let's pretend we are . . ."; "Let's try being like . . ."; "Try to feel like a . . ."; and "Make believe you are . . . ."

5. In some lessons, the initial focus may be on the selection of appropriate rhythmic background. In this instance children formulate a creative rhythm of the dramatic type and then seek suitable music for their dance.

6. Give children time to develop and try their ideas. This is an open-ended process that has a variety of solutions. Coaching and guidance are important aspects at this stage. Application of time, space, force, flow, and body factors is essential. Encourage large, free movement of all body parts. Use the entire area and fill in the empty places in general space. Allow time for exploration.

7. Teachers can bring in the idea of metre (2/4, 3/4, 4/4, and 6/8 time) and have children move in time to the metre. Other movements can illustrate even and uneven time, accents, phrasing, and other elements of rhythmic structure.

An example that shows how an idea can be developed for a lesson on creative rhythm is called "The Wind and the Leaves." One or more children are chosen to be the wind, and the remaining children are the leaves. Two kinds of rhythm are needed; a tambourine can be used. The first rhythm should be high, fast, and shrill, indicating the blowing of the wind. The second rhythm should be slow, measured, and light, to represent the leaves fluttering in the still air and finally coming to a rest at various positions on the ground. During the first rhythm, children representing the wind act out a heavy gust. While this is going on, the leaves show what it is like to be blown about. During the second rhythm, the wind is still and the leaves flutter to the ground. Teachers can add other characterizations. For example, street sweepers can come along and sweep up the leaves.

Creative Dance

Basic creative rhythms can be extended toward the broader term of creative dance. The conceptual framework used to describe movement (see Chapter 14) provides an excellent vehicle for designing learning experiences in creative dance. Figure 19.1 shows how the concepts displayed in the framework can be used as an organizer for dance elements. Most importantly, it provides a structure to help movement be developed as a form of artistic expression.

For example, children can express moods and feelings and show reactions to colours and sounds by improvising dances or movements that demonstrate different aspects of force, or gestures that depict different feelings. The teacher should play a piece of music and follow up with a discussion of its qualities and how it makes the children feel. Children may interpret the music differently. Moods can be described as happy, lighthearted, sad, brave, fearful, cheerful, angry, solemn, silly, sleepy, funny, cautious, bold, or nonchalant.

It is important to note that in some cultural and religious communities various dance forms are not considered to be appropriate. In such instances, physical educators

Figure 19.1

Dance elements.

Source: Reprinted with permission of Calgary Board of Education.

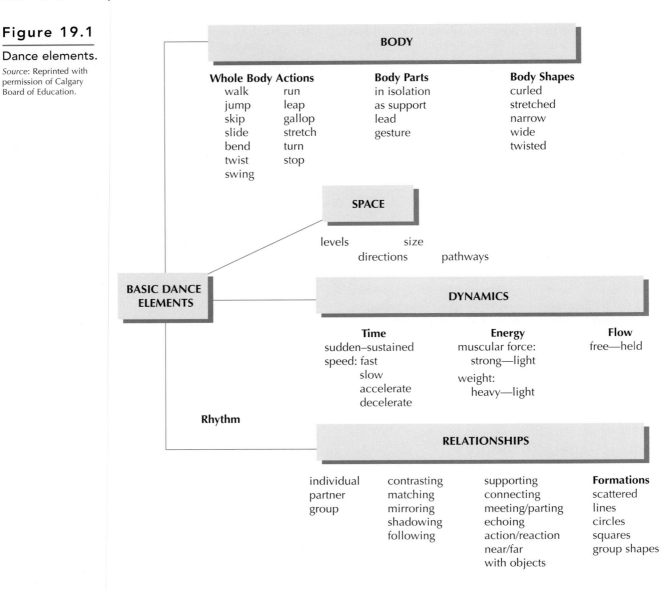

may need to provide alternative movement activities. Gaining an understanding of the cultures that make up a school community is an important step for physical education teachers.

The Creative Process in Dance

The creative process depicted in Figure 19.2 provides teachers with a helpful structure for developing creative dance lessons. The *stimulus* represents the starting point for creative efforts. The stimulus may come from a variety of sources such as poetry, action words, and pictures. An effective stimulus should provide plenty of creative movement potential. Next, encourage students to explore the various movement elements highlighted in the stimulus. Figure 19.3 shows a sample of how to use

the dance elements from the movement framework (see Figure 19.1) to expand possibilities in the exploration phase. *Selecting* and *refining* helps the student to narrow down movement options into a sequence or performance. For example, you may ask students to combine their two favourite leap tasks from the right-hand section of Figure 19.3 (for example, combine a high leap with a partner shadow). The *refining* and *performing* phases provide students with the opportunity to polish movement sequences to a performance level. The performance level may vary from an informal performance for classmates during a class period, to a more formal and refined performance for parents.

The degree to which you move through the phases of the creative process will vary depending on the needs of your students and the learning outcomes you are working toward. A wide range of creative endeavour is possible

Creative Dance offers a unique opportunity to combine cognitive, affective, and motor development. Each creator moves through steps in a creative process, beginning with perceiving a task and ending with a created product.

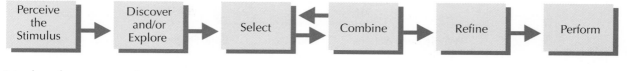

| Perceive the Stimulus | Discover and/or Explore | Select | Combine | Refine | Perform |

Introduce the challenge through observing, brainstorming, perceiving.

Expand "movement vocabulary" through exploring the movement elements to find:
a) many possible solutions;
b) many different kinds of solutions;
c) unique, original solutions;
d) elaborations and extensions of solutions.

Evaluate explored movements and choose those that best solve the problem or create the desired image.

Combine selected movements into sequences or rhythmical patterns. Evaluate, then re-select or re-order as desired.

When the most effective sequence is selected, the student refines and polishes the performance of the work. A performance includes a:
a) beginning;
b) action sequence;
c) conclusion.

(optional)
The dance may be performed for:
a) each other;
b) other classes;
c) parents;
d) the public;
e) teachers.

Figure 19.2

The creative process.

Source: Reprinted with permission of Calgary Board of Education.

through this process. Efforts can vary from informal free exploration in daily lessons to more formal construction of simple routines or sequences, to choreography of a polished dance performance.

Folk Dances

A folk dance is defined as a traditional dance of a particular culture. In this concept, a definite pattern or dance routine is usually specified and followed. Folk dancing is one phase of a child's education that can assist in bringing about international understanding. A country's folk music reflects its way of life. From these dances, children gain an understanding of why people from certain countries act and live as they do, even though modern times may have changed their lifestyle.

Time-period Dances

Each culture also includes dances that may be unique to a particular time and place—e.g., dance crazes and fads. For example, the 1970s in Canada witnessed the disco dance craze; in the 80s western line dance and aerobic dance were popular; and in the 90s the hip-hop dance was developed. Although various dance crazes come and go, in most cases, elements of each craze contribute to the next popular dance form. Examples of these dances have been included at each level.

Teaching New Dances Successfully

Dances in developmental level I consist of simple fundamental locomotor skills, either singly or in combination. Dances such as the two-step, polka, and schottische, with more specialized steps, are found in developmental level II and III. The first consideration when teaching folk dance is to determine whether children know the basic skills required for the dance. If a skill needs to be taught, it can be handled in one of two ways. The first way is to teach the skill separately, before teaching the dance. The second is to teach the dance in its normal sequence, giving specific instruction at the time when the skill appears. The first method is often best, because children can concentrate solely on learning the skill.

The underlying goal of dancing is to learn to move rhythmically. Effective teachers have long recognized the need for progressions in sport activities to ensure that students learn skills correctly and experience success. Progressions in dance and rhythmic activities are also necessary to make dances appealing and easier to learn. To increase the probability of success in dance and rhythmic activities, the following teaching progression is suggested:

1. Listen and move to the music.

   • Include explanation, clap to rhythm, move to tempo and beat.

   • Show dance.

   • Help students distinguish changes in music.

Select a dance element to experiment with...

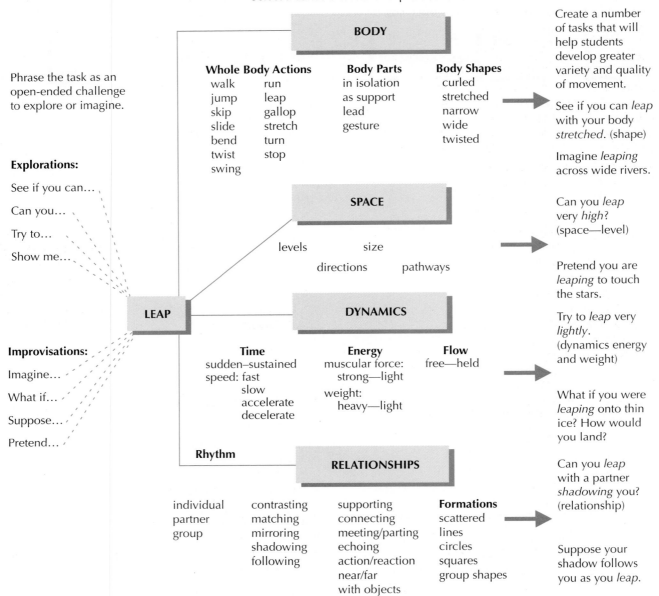

Figure 19.3

Directing students through the exploration process.

Source: Reprinted with permission of Calgary Board of Education.

2. Teach parts of dance without music.
   • Add verbal cues.
3. Teach each part with music.
   • With verbal cues.
4. Put dance together without music.
   • With verbal cues.
5. Put dance together with music.
   • Gradually phase out verbal cues (use only as needed).

Arranging for Partners

An effective method of arranging for partners must avoid the situation in which some children are looked over and overlooked. Some suggestions follow:

1. Dancing boy–girl fashion in the traditional mode is not necessary. When starting a dance program with students who are uncomfortable with each other, allow students to dance with a partner of their choice. If this places boys with boys and girls

with girls, allow that arrangement. Partners can be referred to as number 1 and number 2 or coloured pinnies can be placed on one of the partners. Instead of giving directions for the girl's part, call it out as "The people in red on the outside of the circle do . . ." Be careful not to label one group as playing the role of boys or girls. Change partners frequently; sooner or later the members of both sexes will dance with members of the opposite sex. In this chapter we use the designations "partner A" and "partner B" for the leading and following positions, respectively. Gender references, where they appear, will alternate by example.

2. In a follow-the-leader approach, put on some brisk marching music and begin walking among the students, who are scattered in general space. As you pass students, tap them on the shoulder and ask them to fall in behind you. Subsequent students go to the end of the line when tagged, until all students are chosen. This allows you to arrange students as desired—boy–girl—or just to separate children who do not work well together.

3. Boys join hands in a circle formation, and each girl steps behind a boy. Reverse the procedure, and have girls make the circle, or have half of the class wear red pinnies and form the circle.

4. Boys stand in a circle facing counterclockwise, while girls form a circle around them facing clockwise. Both circles move in the direction in which they are facing and stop on signal. The boy takes the girl nearest him as his partner.

5. For square dances, take the first four couples from any of the previous formations to form a set. Continue until all sets are formed.

Formations for Dances

Figure 19.4 illustrates the formations used with the folk dances that follow in this chapter. Each folk dance description begins with a listing of records, skills, and the formation to be used. If teachers are unsure about how the class should be arranged, they should consult the figure. The formations are grouped into categories of single-circle, double-circle, triple-circle, and others.

Dance Positions

In most dance positions, partner A holds a hand or hands palms up, and partner B joins the grip with a palms-down position. The following dance positions or partner positions are common to many dances.

Partners-facing Position

In partners-facing position, as the name suggests, the partners are facing. Partner A extends hands forward with palms up and elbows slightly bent. Partner B places hands in A's hands.

Side-by-side Position

In side-by-side position (see Figure 19.5), partner A always has partner B to the right. Partner A offers the right hand, held above the waist, palm up. B places the left hand in A's raised hand.

Closed Position

Closed position is the social dance position. Partners stand facing each other, shoulders parallel and toes pointed forward. Partner A holds partner B's right hand in A's left hand out to the side, at about shoulder level, with elbows bent. Partner A places the right hand on B's back, just below the left shoulder blade. B's left arm rests on A's upper arm, and B's left hand is on A's right shoulder.

Open Position

To get to open position from closed position, partner A turns to the left and partner B to the right, with their arms remaining in about the same position. Both face in the same direction and are side by side.

Promenade Position

Promenade position (see Figure 19.6) is the crossed-arm position in which dancers stand side by side, facing the same direction, with the right hand held by partner's right and the left by partner's left.

Varsouvienne Position

Partners stand side by side and face the same direction. Partner B is slightly in front and to the right of Partner A. A holds B's left hand in his left hand in front and at about shoulder height. B brings the right hand directly back over the right shoulder, and A reaches behind B at shoulder height and grasps that hand with his right hand.

Progression of Dances

The dances in this section are listed in progression, beginning with the easiest and progressing to the most difficult dance. Three developmental levels are listed to give you

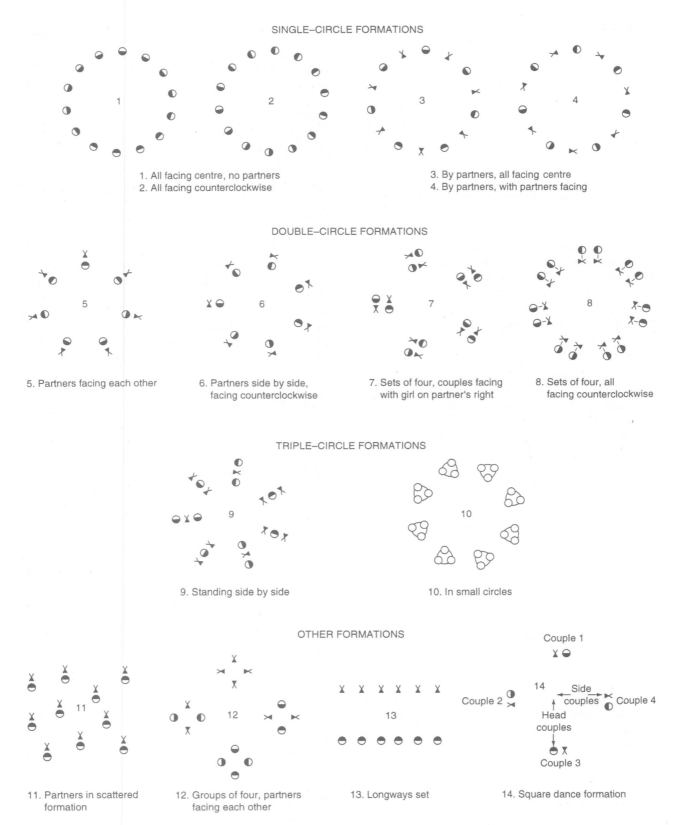

Figure 19.4

Dance formations.

Figure 19.5

Side-by-side position.

Figure 19.6

Promenade position.

the widest possible latitude in selecting dances that fit the maturity and skill of the youngsters. Table 19.1 lists all dances in alphabetical order by developmental level and lists skills required for the dance.

Regarding level of difficulty, teachers must keep in mind that if a group of students is lacking in rhythmic background, the dances in the progression may be too difficult. A grade 6 class, for example, lacking in dance skills, may need to begin with developmental level II dances. On the other hand, avoid boring a class by starting children on material below their maturity level.

Developmental Level I Dances

Dances in this section contain movement songs and folk dances that are introductory in nature and involve simple formations and uncomplicated changes. The movements are primarily basic locomotor skills and hand gestures or clapping sequences. There are dances both with and without partners. As the difficulty of the dances increases, patterns become more definite and more folk dances are included. The movements are still primarily of the simple locomotor type, with additional and varied emphasis on more complicated movement patterns. Basic rhythm or lummi sticks may be introduced at this level.

BLEKING (SWEDISH)

Music Source: Folkcraft, 1188

Skills: Bleking step, step-hop

Formation: Single circle, partners facing, both hands joined. Partners A face counterclockwise and partners B clockwise.

Directions:

Part I—The Bleking Step: Cue by calling, "Slow-slow, fast-fast-fast."

TABLE 19.1

Alphabetical listing of dances by developmental level

DEVELOPMENTAL LEVEL I

Name of Dance	Skills
Bleking	Bleking step, step-hop
Bombay Bounce	Hesitation step, side step
Carousel	Draw step, sliding
Children's Polka	Step-draw
Chimes of Dunkirk	Turning, changing partners
Cowboy Count Down	Counting, heel-tow, sliding
Danish Dance of Greeting	Running or sliding, bowing
Grapevine Line Dance	Grapevine step
How D'Ye Do, My Partner	Bowing, curtseying, skipping
Jingle Bells, Var. 1	Elbow swing, skipping, sliding
Jump	Jumping, walking, arm movements
Jump Jim Jo	Jumping, running, draw step
Larger than Life	Walk, clap, step-close
Mayim, Mayim	Walk, clap, toe point
Rhythm Sticks (Small, Small World)	Rhythmic tapping, stick manipulation
Seven Jumps	Step-hop, balance, control
Shoemaker's Dance	Skipping, heel and toe

DEVELOPMENTAL LEVEL II

Name of Dance	Skills
At the Hop	Step, kick, partner synchronization
Bird Dance (Chicken Dance)	Skip or walk, elbow swing
Cshebogar	Skip, slide, draw step, elbow swing
Cumberland Reel	Walk, star, sashay, grand marche
Gustaf's Skoal	Walking (stately), skip, turn
Jingle Bells, Var. 2	Skip, promenade, slide, elbow swing
La Bastringue	Walk, turn, elbow swing
La Raspa	Bleking step, run, elbow swing
Lummi Sticks	Rhythmic movements
Pata Pata	Toe touches, knee lifts, quarter-turns
Patty Cake (Heel-toe) Polka	Heel-tow, slide, elbow swing
Popcorn	Toe touch, knee lifts, jump
Raise the Roof	Grapevine, bankhead bounce
Ruby Baby	Heel touch, kick, turn, touch
Tinikling	Tinikling steps
Troika	Running steps, turn under
Wild Turkey Mixer	Walking, elbow swing, partner change

(continued)

TABLE 19.1

Alphabetical listing of dances by developmental level (*continued*)

DEVELOPMENTAL LEVEL III

Name of Dance	Skills
Bus Stop	Grapevine, touch, slide, heel splits
Cotton-eyed Joe	Heel-toe, two-step
Electric Slide	Slide, tap, stomp
Hora	Side step, step swing
Korobushka	Schottische step, balance step
Jessie Polka	Step and touch, polka step
Limbo Rock	Touch step, swivel, jump clap step
Lollipop	Grapevine, twist, lindy step
Maple Leaf Stomp	Walk, stamp, slide
Men in Black	Cross-over, walk, neck bob
Miserlou	Grapevine, side step
One, two step	Slide, walk
Space Jam	Grapevine, dribble, bankhead bounce
Teton Mountain Stomp	Walk, banjo position, side care position, two-step

Measures	Action
1	Hop on the left foot and extend the right heel forward with the right leg straight. At the same time, thrust the right hand forward. Hop on the right foot, reversing the arm action and extending the left foot to rest on the heel. (Slow, slow)
2	Repeat the action with three quick changes—left, right, left. (Fast, fast, fast)
3–4	Beginning on the right foot, repeat the movements of measures 1 and 2. (Slow, slow, fast, fast, fast)
5–8	Repeat measures 1–4.

Part II—The Windmills: Partners extend their joined hands sideways at shoulder height.

Measures	Action
9–16	Partners turn in place with a repeated step-hop. At the same time, the arms move up and down like a windmill. The turning is done clockwise, with A starting on the right foot and B on the left. At the completion of the step-hops (16), the partners should be in their original places ready for Part I again. (Step-hop, 2-hop, 3-hop, . . . 16-hop)

TEACHING TIP

Variations:

1. Change from original positions to a double circle, partners facing, A partners with back to the centre. Part I is as described. For Part II, all face counterclockwise, and partners join inside hands. Partners do the basic schottische of "step, step, step, hop" throughout Part II.

2. Another excellent variation is to do the dance with partners scattered in general space. Part I is as described. For Part II, the children leave their partners and step-hop in various directions around the dancing area. When the music is about to change back to Part I, performers find a partner wherever they can, and the dance is repeated.

3. Bleking is excellent music for creative dance, with the stipulation that the children maintain individually the bleking rhythm of "slow-slow, fast-fast-fast" during Part I and do any kind of movement in place that they wish. During Part II, they may do any locomotor or other movement that they choose.

BOMBAY BOUNCE (CONTEMPORARY)

Music Source: Any music with a definite and moderately fast beat (4/4 time)

Skills: Hesitation step, side step

Formation: Scattered, all facing forward

Part I (16 counts): A hesitation step to the left is performed by taking a short step to the left followed by touching the right foot near the left while the weight remains on the left foot. A hesitation step to the right is similar except that it begins with a step to the right. To begin the dance, eight hesitation steps are performed in place with a handclap on each touch. (Left, touch and clap; right, touch and clap.) Repeat 4 times.

Part II (16 counts): Take two side steps to the left, then two to the right. Clap on counts 4 and 8. (Left, close; left, close and clap; right, close; right, close and clap). Repeat the pattern.

Part III (16 counts): Take four side steps left and four side steps right. Clap only on count 8. (Left, close, left, close, left, close, left, close and clap). Repeat to the right.

Part IV (16 counts): Take four steps forward and four steps backward, four steps forward and four steps backward. Clap on counts 4, 8, 12, and 16. (Forward, 2, 3, 4 and clap; backward, 2, 3, 4 and clap; forward, 2, 3, 4 and clap; backward 2, 3, 4 and clap)

TEACHING TIP

Variations are possible (for example, in Part IV, instead of four steps, use three steps and a kick [swing].)

CAROUSEL (SWEDISH)

Music Source: Folkcraft

Skills: Draw step, sliding

Formation: Double circle, facing centre. The inner circle, representing a merry-go-round, joins hands. The outer players, representing the riders, place their hands on the hips of the partner in front.

Directions:

Measures	Verse Action
1–16	Moving to the left, children take 12 slow draw steps and stamp on the last 3 steps. (Step, together, 2, 3, . . . 12, stamp, stamp, stamp, rest)

Measures	Chorus Action
17–24	Moving left, speed up the draw step until it becomes a slide or gallop. Sing the chorus. (Slide, 2, 3, . . . 8)
25–32	Repeat measures 17–24 while moving to the right. (Slide, 2, 3, . . . 8)

During the chorus, the tempo is increased and the movement is changed to a slide. Children should take short, light slides to prevent the circle from moving out of control.

TEACHING TIP

Variation: The dance can also be done with youngsters holding the perimeter of a parachute.

CHILDREN'S POLKA (GERMAN)

Music Source: Folkcraft

Formation: Single circle of couples, partners facing

Skills: Step-draw

Directions:

Measures	Action
1–2	Take two step-draw steps toward the centre of the circle, ending with three steps in place. (Draw, draw, step, 2, 3)
3–4	Take two step-draw steps away from the centre, ending with three steps in place. (Draw, draw, step, 2, 3)
5–8	Repeat the pattern of measures 1 to 4.
9	Slap own knees once with both hands; clap own hands once. (Slap, clap)
10	Clap both hands with partner three times. (Clap, 2, 3)
11–12	Repeat the pattern of measures 9 and 10.
13	Hop, placing one heel forward, and shake the forefinger at partner three times. (Scold, 2, 3)
14	Repeat the "scolding" pattern with the other foot and hand. (Scold, 2, 3)
15–16	Turn once around in place with four running steps and stamp three times in place. (Turn, 2, 3, 4; stamp, 2, 3)

CHIMES OF DUNKIRK (FRENCH-BELGIAN)

Music Source: Folkcraft

Skills: Turning in a small circle with a partner, changing partners

Formation: Double circle, partners facing

Directions:

Measures	Action
1–2	Stamp three times in place, right-left-right. (Stamp, 2, 3)
3–4	Clap hands three times above the head (chimes in the steeple). (Clap, 2, 3)
5–8	Partner A places both hands on partner B's hips; B places both hands on A's shoulders. Taking four steps, they turn around in place. (Turn, 2, 3, 4) On the next four counts,

partner B (on the outside) moves one person to the left with four steps. (Change, 2, 3, 4) Repeat the sequence from the beginning.

TEACHING TIP

An alternative to the turn described is to do an elbow turn by linking right elbows.

COWBOY/COWGIRL COUNTDOWN (CONTEMPORARY)

Music source: Any medium tempo 4/4 western line dance music

Skills: Heel-toes, slide steps

Formation: Lines, facing forward, thumbs in belt

Directions: Designed to help students learn to count to the music

Measures	Action
Part I	Four heel-toes (on right foot); four slide steps to right
	Four heel-toes (on left foot); four slide steps to left
Part II	Three heel-toes (on right foot); three slide steps to right
	Three heel-toes (on left foot); three slide steps to left
Part III	Two heel-toes (on right foot); two slide steps to right
	Two heel-toes (on left foot); two slide steps to left
Part IV	One heel-toe (on right foot); one slide step to right
	One heel-toe (on left foot); one slide step to left
Part V	Eight stomps in place (turning in opposite direction)

DANISH DANCE OF GREETING (DANISH)

Music Source: Folkcraft

Skills: Running or sliding, bowing

Formation: Single circle, all face centre. Partner A stands to the left of partner B

Directions:

Measures	Action
1	All clap twice and bow to partner. (Clap, clap, bow)
2	Repeat but turn back to the partner and bow to the neighbour. (Clap, clap, bow)
3	Stamp right, stamp left. (Stamp, stamp)
4	Turn around in four running steps. (Turn, 2, 3, 4)
5–8	Repeat the action of measures 1–4.
9–12	All join hands and run to the left for four measures. (Run, 2, 3, 4, . . . 16)
13–16	Repeat the action of measures 9–12, taking light running steps in the opposite direction. (Run, 2, 3, 4, . . . 16)

TEACHING TIP

Variation: Instead of a running step, use a light slide.

GRAPEVINE (CONTEMPORARY WESTERN)

Music source: Any medium tempo 4/4 western line dance music

Formation: Introductory line dance, all facing forward

Directions:

Measures	Action
1–4	Grapevine right foot, left, right foot, and touch left foot.
5–8	Grapevine left foot, right, left foot, and touch with right foot.
9–12	Step forward with right foot and bounce two times (on right).
13–16	Step forward with left foot and bounce two times (on left).

On last bounce, make a quarter turn to left. Repeat dance.

HOW D'YE DO, MY PARTNER? (SWEDISH)

Music Source: Folkcraft

Skills: Bowing, curtsying, skipping

Formation: Double circle, partners facing, partner A on inside

Directions:

Measures	Action
1–2	Partners A bow to their partner. (Bow)
3–4	Partners B bow. (Bow)
5–6	A offers the right hand to B, who takes it with the right hand. (Join right hands) Both turn to face counterclockwise. (Face counterclockwise)

7–8	Couples join left hands in promenade position in preparation to skip when the music changes. (Join left hands)
9–16	Partners skip counterclockwise in the circle, slowing down on measure 15. (Skip) On measure 16, Bs stop and As move ahead to secure a new partner. (New partner)

JINGLE BELLS—VARIATION 1 (DUTCH)

Music Source: Any version of "Jingle Bells"

Skills: Elbow swing, skipping, sliding

Formation: Double circle, partners facing, with both hands joined

Directions:

Measures	Action
1–2	Partners take eight slides counterclockwise. (Slide, 2, 3, . . . 8)
3–4	Partners turn so they are standing back to back, and take eight more slides in the line of direction. This move is best made by dropping the front hands and swinging the back hands forward until the dancers are standing back to back. They rejoin the hands that are now in back. Make this move with no loss of rhythm. (Slide, 2, 3, . . . 8)
5–6	Repeat the action of measures 1 and 2. To get back to the face-to-face position, let go of the back hands and swing the front hands backward, allowing the bodies to pivot and face again. (Slide, 2, 3, . . . 8)
7–8	Repeat measures 3 and 4. (Slide, 2, 3, . . . 8)

Chorus Action

1	Clap own hands three times. (Clap own, 2, 3)
2	Clap both hands with partner three times. (Clap both, 2, 3)
3	Clap own hands four times. (Clap own, 2, 3, 4)
4	Clap both hands with partner once. (Clap both)
5–8	Right elbow swing with partner. Partners hook right elbows and swing clockwise with eight skips. (Swing, 2, 3, 4, 5, 6, 7, 8)
9–12	Repeat clapping sequence of measures 1 to 4.

13–16	Left elbow swing with partner for eight skips, finishing in the original starting position, ready to repeat the entire dance with the same partner; or do a left elbow swing with partner for four skips, which is once around, then all children in the inner circle skip forward to the outer dancer ahead and repeat the entire dance from the beginning with a new partner. (Swing, 2, 3, 4, 5, 6, 7, 8)

JUMP (CONTEMPORARY)

Music Source: "Jump for Your Love" (Pointer Sisters)

Skills: Jumping, walking, arm movements

Formation: Lines, facing forward

Directions:

Introduction (20 counts):	Free body shaking (in place)
Part I (16 counts):	Starting with right foot—alternate toe taps forward (R-L x 4); four toe taps to right, four toe taps to left (R-R-R-R, L-L-L-L).
Part II (16 counts):	Starting with right foot—two side kicks to right, two side kicks to left (Repeat sequence); Starting with right foot alternate slalom ski jumps right to left for 8 counts).
Part III (16 counts):	Sit and kick feet in air (8 counts); Stand starting with right hip movement, hips side to side (8 counts).
Chorus (32 counts):	Jump up and down turning in place (8 counts); Jumping Jacks (8 counts); Walk forward four steps punching motions with arms (R-L-R-L); Walk backward four steps punching motions with arms (R-L-R-L); Jump up and down turning in place (8 counts).
	Repeat Parts I and III.
	Repeat Chorus.

JUMP JIM JO (AMERICAN)

Music Source: First Folk Dances, RCA

Skills: Jumping, running, draw step

Formation: Double circle, partners facing, both hands joined

Directions:

Measures	Action
1–2	Do two jumps sideward, progressing counterclockwise, followed by three quick jumps in place. (Slow, slow, fast, fast, fast)
3–4	Release hands and turn once around in place with four jumps (two jumps per measure). Finish facing partner and rejoin hands. (Jump, turn, 3, 4)
5	Take two sliding steps sideward, progressing counterclockwise. (Slide, slide)
6	Partners face counterclockwise with inside hands joined and tap three times with the toe of the outside foot. (Tap, tap, tap)
7–8	Take four running steps forward, then face partner, join both hands, and end with three jumps in place. (Run, 2, 3, 4; jump, 2, 3)

LARGER THAN LIFE (CONTEMPORARY)

Music Source: "Larger Than Life" (Backstreet Boys)

Skills: Walking, clap, turn, side step

Formation: Lines, facing forward

Directions:

Measures	Action
1–8	Starting with feet together. Four steps forward (start on right)—clap on four. Four steps backward—clap on four.
9–16	Step to right, close with left foot (9–10). Step to left, close with right foot (11–12). Repeat for 13–16.
17–24	Turn to left in place (17–20). Turn to right in place (21–24). Repeat dance.

TEACHING TIP

This is a line dance that can easily be adapted to a variety of different tempos. Try to use current music to spark student interest.

MAYIM, MAYIM (ISRAEL)

Music Source: Folkcraft

Skills: Walking steps, clap, toe tap

Formation: Single circle, no partners, join hands

Directions:

Part I

Measures	Action
1–16	Take 16 walking steps to left, then face centre.

Part II

Measures	Action
1–8	Four walking steps to centre (deep knee bend on first step). Four walking steps backward. (Raise hands as you move to centre, lower hands as you move backwards.)
9–16	Repeat 1–8.
17–24	Clap hands four times.

Part III

Measures	Action
1–8	Point left foot forward and tap eight times.
9–16	Point right foot forward and tap eight times. Repeat Parts 1–3.

RHYTHM STICKS—IT'S A SMALL, SMALL WORLD (AMERICAN)

Music Source: Disney Soundtrack

Skills: Rhythmic tapping and manipulation of sticks

Formation: Children sitting cross-legged individually scattered around the area

Rhythm sticks or lummi sticks are 30 to 40 cm in length. Activities may be done individually or in partners. This routine is done individually. The sticks are held in the thumb and the forefinger at about the bottom third of the stick.

Directions:

Measures	Call	Action
1–2	Down, cross, down, cross	Tap ends of both sticks on the floor, and then cross the arms over, tapping the sticks on the floor again.
3–4	Down, cross, down, cross	Repeat
5–6	Down, cross, down, cross	Repeat
7–8	Chorus: It's a small, small world	Lean forward touching head to knees (curl forward).
9–10	Tap, tap, knees, knees	Tap sticks two times in front of the chest, and then lightly tap the knees twice.

11–12	Tap, tap, knees, knees	Repeat
13–14	Tap, tap, knees, knees	Repeat
15–16	Chorus: It's a small, small world	Lean forward touching head to knees (curl forward).

The sequence above repeats a number of times with touches to the toes, shoulders, head, and nose. As a variation, youngsters can face a partner and tap both of their sticks to their partner's sticks.

SEVEN JUMPS (DANISH)

Music Source: Folkcraft

Skills: Step-hop, balance, control

Formation: Single circle, hands joined

Directions: There are seven jumps to the dance. Each jump is preceded by the following action.

Measures	Action
1–8	The circle moves to the right with seven step-hops, one to each measure. On the eighth measure, all jump high in the air and reverse direction. (Step-hop, 2-hop, 3-hop, . . . 7-hop, change direction)
9–16	Circle to the left with seven step-hops. Stop on measure 16 and face the centre. (Step-hop, 2-hop, 3-hop, . . . 7-hop, face centre)
17	All drop hands, place their hands on hips, and lift the right knee upward with the toes pointed downward. (Knee up)
18	All stamp the right foot to the ground on the signal note, then join hands on the next note. (Stamp)
1–18	Repeat measures 1–18, but do not join hands.
19	Lift the left knee, stamp, and join hands.
1–19	Repeat measures 1–19, but do not join hands.
20	Put the right toe backward and kneel on the right knee. Stand and join hands.
1–20	Repeat measures 1–20; do not join hands.
21	Kneel on the left knee. Stand and join hands.
1–21	Repeat measures 1–21; do not join hands.
22	Put the right elbow to the floor with the cheek on the fist. Stand and join hands.

Measures	Action
1–22	Repeat measures 1–22; do not join hands.
23	Put the left elbow to the floor with the cheek on the fist. Stand and join hands.
1–23	Repeat measures 1–23; do not join hands.
24	Put forehead on the floor. Stand, join hands.
1–16	Repeat measures 1–16.

TEACHING TIP

Men performed this dance originally in Denmark as a control-elimination competition. Those who made unnecessary movements or mistakes were eliminated.

Variation: To increase motivation, the dance can be done with a parachute. The dancers hold the parachute taut with one hand during the step-hops. The chute is kept taut with both hands for all jumps except the last, during which the forehead touches the chute on the floor.

SHOEMAKER'S DANCE (DANISH)

Music Source: Folkcraft

Skills: Skipping, heel and toe

Formation: Double circle, partners facing, with partner A's back to the centre of the circle

Directions:

Part I

Measures	Action
1	With arms bent and at shoulder height, and with hands clenched to form fists, circle one fist over the other in front of the chest. (Wind the thread)
2	Reverse the circular motion and wind the thread in the opposite direction. (Reverse direction)
3	Pull the elbows back vigorously twice. (Pull and tighten the thread)
4	Clap own hands three times. (Clap, 2, 3)
5–7	Repeat the pattern of measures 1–3.
8	Tap own fists together three times to drive the nails. (Tap, 2, 3)

Part II

Measures	Action
9–16	Partners face counterclockwise, inside hands joined. Skip counterclockwise, ending with a bow. (Skip, 2, 3, . . . 15, bow)

TEACHING TIP

Variation of Part II Action:

9	Place the heel of the outside foot forward (counts 1 and), and point the toe of the outside foot in back (2 and).
10	Take three running steps forward, starting with the outside foot and pausing on the last count.
11–12	Repeat the pattern of measures 9–10, starting with the inside foot.
13–16	Repeat the pattern of measures 9–12, entire "heel and toe and run, run, run" pattern dance, four times singing Part II verse.

Developmental Level II Dances

Developmental level II dances increase in complexity. Locomotor skills are still the basis of the movement patterns, but in most of the dances, the patterns are more difficult than those in developmental level I. At this level, each dance always has at least two parts and may have three or more. Because the movement patterns are longer, the part–whole teaching method is used more often with this age group. These dances are vigorous and fast moving, which makes them exciting for youngsters to perform.

Tinikling and lummi sticks are continued at this level, which lends challenge and novelty to the progression. Emphasis should be on participation and enjoyment without excessive concern for perfection.

AT THE HOP (NOVELTY)

Music Source: "At the Hop" (A. Singer and D. Madara –Singular Music)

Skills: Walking, kicking, partner cooperation

Formation: Scattered, partners facing holding hands

Directions:

Measures	Actions
1–2	Pulling with hands, move in toward partner—step right foot front, left foot forward together with right. Step right foot front. (2 counts)
3–4	Moving away from partner. Step left foot back, right foot backward together with left. Step left foot back. (2 counts)

	Step back with right foot; step in place with left foot. (2 counts)
7–8	Small kick front with right foot, step back with right foot, step in place with left.

Keep repeating. Add creative arm movements.

THE BIRD DANCE (CHICKEN DANCE)

Music Source: K-Tel Fun Party

Skills: Skipping or walking, elbow swing or star

Formation: Circle or scatter formation, partners facing

Directions:

Part I

Measures	Action
1	Four snaps—thumb and fingers, hands up
2	Four flaps—arms up and down, elbows bent
3	Four wiggles—hips, knees bent low
4	Four claps
5–16	Repeat action of measures 1–4 three times

Part II

Measures	Action
1–8	With a partner, either do a right-hand star with 16 skips or 16 walking steps, or do an elbow swing. (Skip, 2, 3, . . . 15, change hands)
9–16	Repeat with the left hand. On the last four counts of the last swing, everyone changes partners. If dancing in a circle formation, partners B advance forward counterclockwise to the next partner A. If dancing in a scattered formation, everyone scrambles to find a new partner. (Skip, 2, 3, . . . 12, change partners)

TEACHING TIP

Perform the dance individually, with everyone moving to find a new partner on the skipping sequence. The locomotor movements can be varied to include sliding or galloping.

CSHEBOGAR (HUNGARIAN)

Music Source: Folkcraft

Skills: Skipping, sliding, draw step, elbow swing

Formation: Single circle, partners facing centre, hands joined with partners B on the right

Directions:

Part I

Measures	Action
1–4	Take seven slides to the left. (Slide, 2, 3, 4, 5, 6, 7, change)
5–8	Take seven slides to the right. (Back, 2, 3, 4, 5, 6, 7, stop)
9–12	Take three skips to the centre and stamp on the fourth beat. Take three skips backward to place and stamp on the eighth beat. (Forward, 2, 3, stamp; backward, 2, 3, stamp)
13–16	Hook right elbows with partner and turn around twice in place, skipping. (Swing, 2, 3, 4, 5, 6, 7, 8)

Part II Partners face each other in a single circle with hands joined.

Measures	Action
17–20	Holding both of partner's hands, take four draw steps (step, close) toward the centre of the circle. (Step-close, 2-close, 3-close, 4-close)
21–24	Take four draw steps back to place. (Step-close, 2-close, 3-close, 4-close)
25–26	Go toward the centre of the circle with two draw steps. (In-close, 2-close)
27–28	Take two draw steps back to place. (Out-close, 2-close)
29–32	Hook elbows and repeat the elbow swing, finishing with a shout and facing the centre of the circle in the original formation. (Swing, 2, 3, 4, 5, "Cshebogar")

TEACHING TIP

Instead of an elbow swing, partners can use the Hungarian turn. Partners stand side by side, put the right arm around the partner's waist, and lean away from partner. The left arm is held out to the side, with the elbow bent, the hand pointing up, and the palm facing the dancer.

CUMBERLAND REEL (CELTIC)

Music source: Any moderate-tempo reel

Skills: Controlled walking, marching, grand march figures

Formation: Long set formation (four couples facing)

Directions:

Part I

Measures	Action
1–8	Join hands with opposite pair. Circle counterclockwise with walking steps 8 counts (back to starting position).
9–16	Make a right-hand star with opposite couple. Circle clockwise with walking steps 8 counts (back to starting position).

Part II

Measures	Action
1–16	Head couple join hands. Sashay down the set and back.
17–32	Head couple turn to outside and walk down set (others follow). Head couple make arch at opposite end, other couples go under and return to opposite end. There will be a new head couple.

Start again.

TEACHING TIP

The head couples should maintain an even, steady pace and not hurry, or the march becomes a race. When the head couple forms arches for the other sets of couples to tunnel under, the arches should be made with both arms, and the couples should continue marching while they form the arches.

GUSTAF'S SKOAL (SWEDISH)

Music Source: Folkcraft

Skills: Walking (stately), skipping, turning

Formation: The formation is similar to a square dance set of four couples, each facing centre. Partner A is to the left of partner B. Couples join inside hands; the outside hand is on the hip. Two of the couples facing each other are designated the head couples. The other two couples, also facing each other, are the side couples.

Directions: The dance is in two parts. In Part I, the music is slow and stately. The dancers perform with great dignity. The music for Part II is light and represents fun.

Part I

Measures	Action
1–2	The head couples, inside hands joined, walk forward three steps and bow to the opposite couple. (Forward, 2, 3, bow)

3–4	The head couples take three steps backward to place and bow to each other. (The side couples hold their places during this action.) (Back, 2, 3, bow)
5–8	The side couples repeat action of measures 1–4 while the head couples hold their places. (Forward, 2, 3, bow; back, 2, 3, bow)
9–16	The dancers repeat measures 1–8.

Part II

Measures	Action
17–22	The side couples raise joined hands to form an arch. Head couples skip forward four steps, release partners' hands, join inside hands with opposite person, and skip under the nearest arch with new partner. After going under the arch, they drop hands and head back home to their original partner. (Head couples: Skip, 2, 3, 4; under, 2, 3, 4; around, 2, 3, 4)
23–24	All couples join both hands with partners and swing once around with four skipping steps. (Swing, 2, 3, 4)
25–30	Head couples form arches while side couples repeat the action of measures 17–22. (Side couples: Skip, 2, 3, 4; under, 2, 3, 4; around, 2, 3, 4)
31–32	All couples then repeat the movements in measures 23–24. (Swing, 2, 3, 4)

TEACHING TIP

During the first action sequence of Part I (in which the dancers take three steps and bow), a shout of "Skoal" and raising the right fist high above the head as a salute can be substituted for the bow. The word *skoal* is a toast. (Note that the dancers' hands are not joined.)

JINGLE BELLS—VARIATION 2 (DUTCH)

Music Source: Any version of "Jingle Bells"

Skills: Skipping, promenade position, sliding, elbow swing

Formation: Circle of couples facing counterclockwise, partner B on partner A's right. Promenade position, hands crossed in front, right hands joined over left, right foot free.

Directions:

Part I

Measures	Action
1–2	Take four skips forward and four skips backward, starting with the right foot free. (Forward, 2, 3, 4; back, 2, 3, 4)
3–4	Repeat the pattern of measures 1 and 2. (Forward 2, 3, 4; back, 2, 3, 4)
5	Do four slides to the right, away from the centre of the circle. (Out, 2, 3, 4)
6	Now do four slides left, toward the centre. (In, 2, 3, 4)
7–8	Execute eight skips, making one turn counterclockwise, with partner A pivoting backward and partner B moving forward. Finish in a double circle, partners facing, with A's back to the centre. (Skip, 2, 3, 4, 5, 6, 7, 8)

Part II

Measures	Action
1	Clap own hands three times. (Clap, 2, 3)
2	Clap both hands with partner three times. (Both, 2, 3)
3	Clap own hands four times. (Clap, 2, 3, 4)
4	Clap both hands with partner once. (Both)
5–8	Right elbow swing with partner. Partners hook right elbows and swing clockwise for eight skips. (Swing, 2, 3, 4, 5, 6, 7, 8)
9–12	Repeat clapping pattern of measures 1–4.
13–16	Left elbow swing with partner using eight skips and finishing in the original starting position to repeat the entire dance with the same partner; or left elbow swing with partner once around, then all of the children in the inner circle skip forward to the outer dancer ahead and repeat the entire dance with a new partner. (Swing, 2, 3, 4, 5, 6, 7, 8)

LA BASTRINGUE (FRENCH CANADIAN)

Music source: DC 123321 "La Bastringue"

Skills: Walk, elbow swing, promenade

Formation: Single circle, holding hands. Partners stand side by side.

Directions:

Part I

Measures	Action
1–16	All dancers take four walking steps to the centre of the circle. Take four walking steps backward. Repeat. (Forward 2-3-4; back 2-3-4; repeat)
17–32	Drop hands. Girls take four walking steps to the centre of the circle and back with four steps. Boys take four steps to the centre of the circle, turn to face partner and take four steps back to partner. (Girls 2-3-4; back 2-3-4; boys 2-3-4; back 2-3-4).

Part II

Measures	Action
1–8	Swing your partner with right elbows, then with left elbows. (Swing 2-3-4-5-6-7-8)
9–24	Promenade with your partner (holding hands or skater's position) for 15 steps in counterclockwise direction. On the 16th step, turn to face centre of circle and repeat from beginning. (Promenade 2-3-4-5-6-7-8-9 . . . 15, Ready, start)

TEACHING TIP

To make this dance a mixer, boys, after turning while in the centre of the circle, walk to face the next girl to the left of their former partner.

LA RASPA (MEXICAN)

Music Source: Folkcraft

Skills: Bleking step, running, elbow swing

Formation: Partners facing, couples scattered around room

Directions: *La raspa* means "the rasp" or "the file," and the dance movements are supposed to represent a rasp or file in action. Directions are the same for both partners.

Part I: To begin, the partners face each other, partner B with hands at sides and partner A with hands behind the back.

Measures	Action
1–4	Beginning right, take one Bleking step (pages 377, 379). (Slow, slow, fast, fast, fast)
5–8	Turn slightly counterclockwise away from partner (right shoulder to right shoulder) and, beginning with a jump on the left foot, repeat measures 1–4. (Slow, slow, fast, fast, fast)

Measures	Action
9–12	Repeat action of measures 1–4, facing opposite direction (left shoulder to left shoulder). (Slow, slow, fast, fast, fast)
13–16	Repeat action of measures 1–4, facing partner. (Slow, slow, fast, fast, fast)

Part II: Partners hook right elbows; left elbows are bent and left hands are pointed toward the ceiling.

Measures	Action
1–4	Do a right elbow swing, using eight running or skipping steps. Release and clap the hands on count 8. (Swing, 2, 3, 4, 5, 6, 7, clap)
5–8	Do a left elbow swing, using eight running or skipping steps. Release and clap the hands on count 8. (Swing, 2, 3, 4, 5, 6, 7, clap)
9–16	Repeat the actions of measures 1–8.

TEACHING TIP

Variations:

1. Face partner (all should be in a single-circle formation for this version) and do a grand right and left around the circle. Repeat Part I with a new partner.

2. All face centre or face a partner and do the Bleking or raspa step. On each pause, clap own hands twice.

LUMMI STICKS

Music Source: n/a

Skills: Rhythmic tapping, flipping, and catching of sticks

Formation: Couples scattered throughout the area

Lummi sticks are smaller versions of wands; they are 30 to 35 cm long. Their origins remain obscure. Some believe that lummi sticks were a part of the culture of the Lummi Indians in northwest Washington; others give credit to South Pacific cultures.

Most lummi stick activities are done by partners, although some can be done individually. Each child sits cross-legged, facing a partner at a distance of 45 to 50 cm. Children adjust this distance as the activities demand. The sticks are held in the thumb and fingers (not the fist) at about the bottom third of the stick.

Routines are based on sets of six movements; each movement is completed in 1 count. Many different routines are possible. Only the basic ones are presented here. The following 1-count movements are used to make up routines.

Vertical tap: Tap both sticks upright on the floor.

Partner tap: Tap partner's stick (right stick to right stick, or left to left).

End tap: Tilt the sticks forward or sideward and tap the ends on the floor.

Cross-tap: Cross hands and tap the upper ends to the floor.

Side tap: Tap the upper ends to the side.

Flip: Toss the stick in air, giving it a half turn, and catch other end.

Tap together: Hold the sticks parallel and tap them together.

Toss right (or left): Toss the right-hand stick to partner's right hand, at the same time receiving partner's right-hand stick.

Pass: Lay the stick on the floor and pick up partner's stick.

Toss right and left: Toss quickly right to right and left to left, all in the time of one count.

A number of routines, incorporating the movements described, are presented here in sequence of difficulty. Each routine is to be done four times to complete the 24 beats of the chant.

1. Vertical tap, tap together, partner tap right, vertical tap, tap together, partner tap left.

2. Vertical tap, tap together, pass right stick, vertical tap, tap together, pass left stick.

3. Vertical tap, tap together, toss right stick, vertical tap, tap together, toss left stick.

4. Repeat numbers 1, 2, and 3, but substitute an end tap and flip for the vertical tap and tap together. Perform the stated third movement (that is, end tap, flip, partner tap right, end tap, flip, partner tap left).

5. Vertical tap, tap together, toss right and left quickly, end tap, flip, toss right and left quickly.

6. Cross-tap, cross-flip, vertical tap (uncross arms), cross-tap, cross-flip, vertical tap (uncross arms).

7. Right flip side—left flip in front, vertical tap in place, partner tap right. Left flip side—right flip in front, vertical tap in place, partner tap left.

8. End tap in front, flip, vertical tap, tap together, toss right, toss left.

9. Vertical tap, tap together, right stick to partner's left hand, toss own left stick to own right hand. Repeat. This is the circle throw.

10. Same as in number 9, but reverse the circle.

Four children can do the activity with a change in the timing. One set of partners begins at the start, and the other two start on the third beat. All sing together. In this way, the sticks are flying alternately.

Music Source: Folkcraft

Skills: Toe touches, knee lift, quarter turns

Formation: Single lines facing in one direction

Directions:

Measures	Action
1–2	Start with feet together; touch right foot sideward right and return next to left foot. (Right touch, together)
3–4	Same as above with left foot. (Left touch, together)
5	With feet together, move toes out keeping heels on the ground. (Toes out)
6	Turn heels out keeping toes on the ground. (Heels out)
7	Turn heels in keeping toes on the ground. (Heels in)
8	Turn toes in keeping heels on the ground. The feet should now be together. (Toes in)
9–12	Raise right knee diagonally in front of the body and then touch right foot next to left foot. Repeat for counts 11–12. (Lift, touch, lift, touch)
13–16	Kick left foot forward while turning a quarter turn to the right with weight on the right foot. Step backward left, right, left. Feet should be together at the end of count 16. (Kick, left, right, left)

Repeat the dance.

TEACHING TIP

When youngsters learn the footwork, it is enjoyable to add some arm movements to the dance. At count 5, with elbows close to the body, raise hands up and straight out, palms up. Count 6 turn palms down with elbows out. Count 7, turn palms up. Count 8, turn palms down.

Music Source: Folkcraft

Skills: Heel and toe polka step, sliding, elbow swing, skipping

Formation: Double circle, partners facing, A in the inner circle with back to the centre. Both hands are joined with partner. A's left and B's right foot are free.

Directions:

Part I

Measures	Action
1–2	Heel-toe twice with A's left and B's right foot. (Heel, toe, heel, toe)
3–4	Take four slides sideward to A's left, progressing counterclockwise. Do not transfer the weight on the last count. Finish with A's right and B's left foot free. (Slide, 2, 3, 4)
5–8	Repeat the pattern of measures 1–4, starting with A's right and B's left foot, progressing clockwise. Finish with the partners separated and facing. (Heel, toe, heel, toe; slide, 2, 3, 4)

Part II

Measures	Action
9	Clap right hands with partner three times. (Right, 2, 3)
10	Clap left hands with partner three times. (Left, 2, 3)
11	Clap both hands with partner three times. (Both, 2, 3)
12	Slap own knees three times. (Knees, 2, 3)
13–14	Right elbow swing with partner. Partners hook right elbows and swing once around with four walking steps, finishing with A's back to centre. (Swing, 2, 3, 4)
15–16	Progress left to a new partner with four walking steps. (Left, 2, 3, 4)

Repeat the entire dance with the new partner.

POPCORN (AMERICAN)

Music Source: Any medium-tempo 4/4 line dance

Skills: Toe touches, knee lifts, jumps, quarter turns

Formation: Single lines of students; no partners

Directions:

Measures	Action
24	Wait 24 counts; gently bounce up and down by bending the knees during the introduction.

Measures	Action
1–4	Touch right toe in front and return; repeat. (Right, together, right, together)
5–8	Touch left toe in front and return; repeat. (Left, together, left, together)
9–12	Touch right toe in back and return; repeat. (Back, together, back, together)
13–16	Touch left toe in front and return; repeat. (Back, together, back, together)
17–20	Lift right knee up in front of left knee and return; repeat. (Knee up, return, knee up, return)
21–24	Lift left knee up in front of right knee and return; repeat. (Knee up, return, knee up, return)
25–26	Lift right knee up in front of left knee and return. (Knee up, return)
27–28	Lift left knee up in front of right knee and return. (Knee up, return)
29–30	Clap both hands together once. (clap)
31–32	Jump and turn a quarter turn to the right. (Jump and turn)

Repeat entire dance to the end of the music.

RAISE THE ROOF (CONTEMPORARY)

Music source: "Raise the Roof" by Luke

Skills: Grapevine, bankhead bounce

Formation: Line dance, all facing forward

Directions:

Part I

Measures	Action
1–8	In place, make the "raise the roof" motion (both hands pushing above head). (eight counts)
9–16	Bankhead bounce. Both hands in front of face, moving arms from side to side while moving shoulders up and down.

Part II

Measures	Action
1–8	Grapevine to right (four counts—step right, left foot steps behind right, step right, touch left to right). Clap on fourth count. Grapevine to left, clap on fourth.
9–24	Hydrolics. (Bend knees slightly and while moving downward turn right knee inward and upward for eight counts). Repeat with left knee.

Substitute different moves for measures bankhead bounce and hydrolics. Ask students for substitute moves.

RUBY BABY (CONTEMPORARY WESTERN)

Music source: Ruby Baby (Columbia Records)

Skills: Heel touch, grapevine, kick, touch, turn

Formation: Line dance, all facing forward

Directions:

Measures	Action
1–8	Start with feet together. Forward right heel touch, back together, forward left heel touch, back together. Repeat.
9–16	Grapevine—step right, left behind, right, kick left with quarter turn right.
17–20	Back left, back right, back left, back right and touch.

Repeat entire dance.

TINIKLING (PHILIPPINE ISLANDS)

Music Source: n/a

Skills: Tinikling steps

Formation: Sets of fours scattered around the room. Each set has two strikers and two dancers (see Figure 19.7).

Note: The dance represents a rice bird as it steps, with its long legs, from one rice paddy to another. The dance is

Figure 19.7

Tinikling set.

popular in many countries in Southeast Asia, where different versions have arisen.

Directions: Two 2.5-m bamboo poles and two crossbars on which the poles rest are needed for the dance. A striker kneels at each end of the poles; both strikers hold the end of a pole in each hand. The music is in waltz meter, 3/4 time, with an accent on the first beat. The strikers slide and strike the poles together on count 1. On the other two beats of the waltz measure, the poles are opened about 30 to 40 cm apart, lifted 2.5 cm or so, and tapped twice on the crossbars in time to counts 2 and 3. The rhythm "close, tap, tap" is continued throughout the dance, each sequence constituting a measure.

Basically, the dance requires that a step be done outside the poles on the close (count 1) and that two steps be done inside the poles (counts 2 and 3) when the poles are tapped on the crossbars. Many step combinations have been devised.

The basic tinikling step should be practised until it is mastered. The step is done singly, although two dancers are performing. Each dancer takes a position at an opposite end and on the opposite side so that the dancer's right side is to the bamboo poles.

Count 1: Step slightly forward with the left foot.

Count 2: Step with the right foot between the poles.

Count 3: Step with the left foot between the poles.

Count 4: Step with the right outside to dancer's own right.

Count 5: Step with the left between the poles.

Count 6: Step with the right between the poles.

Count 7: Step with the left outside to the original position.

The initial step (count 1) is used only to get the dance under way. The last step (count 7) to original position is actually the beginning of a new series (7, 8, 9–10, 11, 12).

Some tinikling dances and records guide the dancers with a different type of rhythm (tap, tap, close), necessitating adjustment of the steps and patterns in these descriptions.

Tinikling steps also can be adjusted to 4/4 rhythm (close, close, tap, tap), which requires the poles to be closed on two counts and open on the other two. The basic foot pattern is two steps outside the poles and two inside. For the sake of conformity, we present all routines in the original 3/4 time (close, tap, tap). If other rhythms are used, adjust accordingly.

Dancers can go from side to side, or can return to the side from which they entered. The dance can be done singly, with the two dancers moving in opposite directions from side to side, or the dancers can enter from and leave toward the same side. Dancers can do the same step patterns or do different movements. They can dance as partners, moving side by side with inside hands joined, or facing each other with both hands joined.

TEACHING TIP

Steps should be practised first with stationary poles or with lines drawn on the floor. Jump ropes can be used as stationary objects over which to practise. Students handling the poles should concentrate on watching each other rather than the dancer to avoid becoming confused by the dancer's feet.

To gain a sense of the movement pattern for 3/4 time, slap both thighs with the hands on the "close," and clap the hands twice for movements inside the poles. For 4/4 time, slap the right thigh with the right hand, then the left thigh with the left hand, followed by two claps. This routine should be done to music, with the poles closing and opening as indicated. Getting the feel of the rhythm is important.

OTHER TINIKLING STEPS AND ROUTINES

Straddle step: Dancers do a straddle jump outside the poles on count 1 and execute two movements inside the poles on counts 2 and 3. Let the dancers explore the different combinations. Jump turns are possible.

Jump step: Dancers begin the side jump with their side toward the poles. They can execute the jump from either side.

Measure 1:

Count 1: Jump lightly in place.

Counts 2 and 3: Jump twice between the poles.

Measure 2:

Count 1: Jump lightly in place (other side).

Counts 2 and 3: Jump twice between the poles.

The feet should be kept close together to fit between the poles. Dancers can exit to the same side from which they entered, or can alternate sides. Another way to enter and exit is by facing the poles and jumping forward and backward rather than sideward. When jumping sideward, one foot can be kept ahead of the other in a stride position. This position can be reversed on the second jump inside the poles.

Rocker step: For the rocker step, dancers face the poles and begin with either foot. As they step in and out (forward and backward), they make a rocking motion with the body.

Crossover step: The crossover step is similar to the basic tinikling step, except that the dancer begins with the right foot (forward step) and steps inside the poles with the left

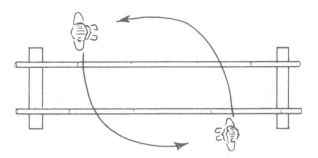

Figure 19.8

Circling poles for Tinikling.

foot, using a cross-foot step. Each time, the dancer must step in or out using a cross-step.

Circling poles: For circling the poles, dancers position themselves as in the basic tinikling step (Figure 19.8) and execute the following movements:

Measure 1:

Count 1: Step slightly forward with the left foot.

Count 2: Step with the right foot between the poles.

Count 3: Step with the left foot between the poles.

Measure 2:

Count 1: Step with the right foot outside the poles to the right.

Counts 2 and 3: With light running steps, make a half circle to a position for the return movement.

Measures 3 and 4: Dancers return to their original position using the same movements as in measures 1 and 2.

Fast tinikling trot: The fast tinikling trot is similar to circling the poles, except that the step goes twice as fast and thus requires only two sets of three counts. Instead of having the side of the body to the poles, as in the basic tinikling step, the dancers face the poles. The following steps are taken:

Measure 1:

Count 1: Shift the weight to the left foot and raise the right foot.

Count 2: Step with the right foot between the poles.

Count 3: Step with the left foot outside the poles and begin turning to the left.

Measure 2:

Count 1: Step with the right foot outside the poles, completing the left turn to face the poles again.

Count 2: Step with the left foot inside the poles.

Count 3: Step outside with the right foot.

The next step is done with the left foot to begin a new cycle. The movement is a light trot with quick turns. Note that the step outside the poles on count 3 in each measure is made with the poles apart.

Cross-step: To do the cross-step, the dancer begins with the basic tinikling position, and uses the following sequence:

Measure 1:

Count 1: Cross-step across both poles with the left foot, hopping on the right side.

Counts 2 and 3: Hop twice on the right foot between the poles.

Measure 2:

Count 1: Hop on the left foot outside the poles to the left.

Counts 2 and 3: Hop twice again on the right foot between the poles.

Line of poles: Three or more sets of poles are about 2 m apart. The object is to dance down the sets, make a circling movement (as in Circling Poles), and return down the line in the opposite direction (see Figure 19.9). The dancer keeps his right side toward the poles throughout.

During measure 1 (three counts), the dancer does a basic tinikling step, finishing on the right side of the first set of poles. During measure 2 (three counts), he uses three light running steps to position himself for the tinikling step at the next set of poles. When he gets to the end, he circles with three steps to get in position for the return journey.

Square Formation: Four sets of poles can be placed in a square formation for an interesting dance sequence (see Figure 19.10). Four dancers are positioned as shown. The movements are as follows: During measure 1, each dancer does a tinikling step, crossing to the outside of the square.

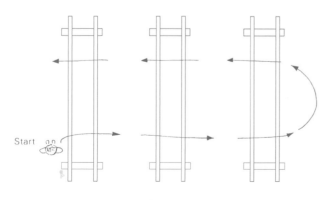

Figure 19.9

Movement through line of poles for tinikling.

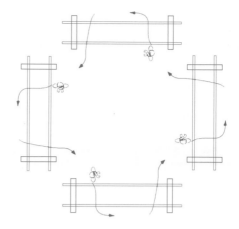

Figure 19.10

Square formation for tinikling.

On measure 2, the dancers circle to position for a return tinikling step. During measure 3, the dancers do a tinikling step, returning to the inside of the square. On measure 4, they rotate counterclockwise to the next set of poles with three running steps.

Children must master the basic tinikling step if they are to enjoy the activity. Tell them to look ahead (not at the poles), so they learn by thinking and doing and not by gauging the pole distances visually.

Four pole set: This arrangement features two longer crossbars, on which two sets of poles rest, leaving a small space between the poles when the sets are open. Four clappers control the poles. Two dancers begin by each straddling a set of poles on opposite ends, so the dancers face each other. Changes in foot pattern should be made every 16 measures, which for most selections is a full pattern of music. The following steps and routines are suggested.

1. Straddle, jump, jump, exiting on measure 16 to the left.

2. Do the basic tinikling step, exiting on the left foot.

3. Do the basic tinikling step, first on one's own set of poles and then on the other set of poles. As the dancer comes out of the first set of poles with the right foot, she makes a half turn to do the tinikling step through the other poles. On the return, she makes another half turn in the middle to face and return to her original position. Repeat the sequence twice.

4. Do the same routine as in number 3, but move diagonally, passing the oncoming dancer with right shoulder to right shoulder, in effect changing places. (Do not use half turns.) Turn around in six steps and return to position. Repeat.

5. Jump to a straddle position with one foot in each of the pole openings. On "close," jump to the space between the sets. On measure 16, the dancer jumps out to the left on both feet.

6. Two-footed step: Jump twice with both feet inside the first set of poles, to the space between, twice inside the second set, and out. Return. Repeat twice.

TROIKA (RUSSIAN)

Music Source: Folkcraft

Skills: Running step, turning under

Formation: Trios face counterclockwise. Start with hands joined in a line of three. The body weight is on the left foot; the right foot is free.

Directions:

Part I

Measures	Action
1	Take four running steps diagonally forward right, starting with the right foot. (Forward, 2, 3, 4)
2	Take four running steps diagonally forward left, starting with the right foot. (Diagonal, 2, 3, 4)
3–4	Take eight running steps in a forward direction, starting with the right foot. (Forward, 2, 3, 4, 5, 6, 7, 8)
5–6	The centre dancer and the left-hand partner raise joined hands to form an arch and run in place. Meanwhile, the right-hand partner moves counterclockwise around the centre dancer with eight running steps, goes under the arch, and back to place. The centre dancer unwinds by turning under the arch. (Under, 2, 3, 4; turn, 2, 3, 4)
7–8	Repeat the pattern of measures 5 and 6, with the left-hand partner running under the arch formed by the centre dancer and the right-hand partner. (Under, 2, 3, 4; turn, 2, 3, circle)

Part II

Measures	Action
9–11	The trio joins hands and circles left with 12 running steps. (Run, 2, 3, 4, 5, 6, 7, 8, 9, 10, 11, 12)
12	Three stamps in place (counts 1–3), pause (count 4). (Stamp, 2, 3, pause)

| 13–15 | The trio circles right with 12 running steps, opening out at the end to re-form in lines of three facing counterclockwise. (Run, 2, 3, 4, 5, 6, 7, 8, open, 10, 11, 12) |
| 16 | The centre dancer releases each partner's hand and runs under the opposite arch of joined hands to advance to a new pair ahead. Right- and left-hand partners run in place while waiting for a new centre dancer to join them in a new trio. (Stamp, 2, line, pause) |

TEACHING TIP

Practise the running steps in groups of three. Then introduce turning under the arch and finish by practising the running circle with accent stamps.

WILD TURKEY MIXER

Music Source: Any piece of music with a moderate 4/4 rhythm is appropriate for this basic mixer

Skills: Walking, elbow swing, partner change

Formation: Trios abreast facing counterclockwise around the circle

Directions:

Measures	Action
1–8	In lines of three, with the right and left person holding the near hand of the centre person, all walk 16 steps forward. (Walk, 2, 3, . . . 16)
9–12	The centre person (Wild Turkey) turns the right-hand person once around with the right elbow. (Turn, 2, 3, 4, 5, 6, 7, 8)
13–16	The Wild Turkey turns the left-hand person with the left elbow, and then moves forward to repeat the dance with the two new people ahead. (Turn, 2, 3, 4; forward, 2, 3, 4)

The same dance can be adapted to other pieces of music. With a faster tempo, the elbow swings are done with a skip instead of a walk.

Developmental Level III Dances

At this level, children should be adept dancers, especially if they have participated in rhythmic activities for several years. If students do not have a well-developed dance background, it is recommended that they first learn dances from developmental levels I and II. Developmental level III dances include dance patterns that must be performed with skill and finesse. At this level, patterns become longer, requiring more concentration and memorization.

BUS STOP (CONTEMPORARY LINE DANCE)

Music source: "Stayin' Alive" (Bee Gees)

Skills: Grapevine, touch, slide step, heel splits

Formation: Line dance, all facing forward

Directions:

Measures	Action
1–4	Start with feet together. Back right, back left, back right, tap left to right.
5–8	Forward left, forward right, forward left, tap right to left.
9–12	Step right, left behind, step right, tap left to right.
13–16	Step left, right behind, step left, tap right to left.
17–20	Step right to right, tap left, step left to left, together left.
21–24	Step right to right, slide together, heel splits, click heels together.
25–28	Tap right forward twice, tap right back twice.
29–32	Tap right forward, tap right back, tap right side, quarter turn left, and stomp right.

Repeat entire dance.

COTTON-EYED JOE (AMERICAN)

Music Source: "Cotton-Eyed Joe" (Rednex)

Skills: Heel-toe, two-step

Formation: Double circle of couples with partner B on the right, holding inside hands and facing counterclockwise. Varsouvienne position can also be used.

Directions:

Measures	Action
1–2	Starting with the left foot, cross the left foot in front of the right foot, kick the left foot forward. (Cross, kick)
3–4	Take one two-step backward. (Left, close, left)
5–6	Cross the right foot in front of the left foot; kick the right foot forward. (Cross, kick)
7–8	Do one two-step backward. (Right, close, right)
9–16	Repeat measures 1–8.
17–32	Perform eight two-steps counterclockwise beginning with the left foot. (Step, close, step; repeat eight times)

TEACHING TIP

During measures 17–32, the last four two-steps may be done in a circle.

ELECTRIC SLIDE (CONTEMPORARY WESTERN)

Music source: "Electric Boogie" (Island Records)

Skills: Slide step, walk, touch step

Formation: Line dance, all facing forward

Directions:

Measures	Action
1–8	Start with feet together. Three slides to right, close with left foot. Three slides to left, close with right foot.
9–16	Walk backward three steps—right, left, right, touch left beside right.
17–20	Step forward with left, touch right beside left. Step backward with right, touch left foot beside right.
21–22	Step forward with left; make a quarter turn to left. Touch right beside left.

Repeat entire dance.

HORA (HAVA NAGILA) (ISRAELI)

Music Source: Folkcraft

Skills: Stepping sideward, step-swing

Formation: Single circle, facing centre, hands joined. The circle can be partial.

The hora is regarded as the national dance of Israel. It is a simple dance that expresses joy. The traditional hora is done in circle formation, with the arms extended sideward and the hands on the neighbours' shoulders. It is easiest to introduce the dance step individually. Once the step is learned, youngsters can join hands and practise the circle formation counterclockwise or clockwise. The clockwise version is presented here.

There are an old and a new hora, as done in Israel. The new hora is more energetic, with the dancers springing high in the air and whirling around with shouts of ecstasy. The hora can be done to many tunes, but the melody of "Hava Nagila" is the favourite.

Directions—Old Hora:

Measures	Action
1–3	Step left on the left foot. Cross the right foot in back of the left, with the weight on the right. Step left on the left foot and hop on it, swinging the right foot forward. Step-hop on the right foot and swing the left foot forward. The same step is repeated over and over. (Side, behind, side, swing; side, swing)

The circle may move to the right also, in which case the same step is used, but the dancers begin with the right foot.

Directions—New Hora:

Measures	Action
1–3	Face left and run two steps. Jump in place. Hop on the left foot, swinging the right foot forward. Take three quick steps in place. Continue in the same manner, moving to the left. (Run, run, jump, hop-swing, step, step, step)

The hora often begins with the dancers swaying in place from left to right as the music builds. Gradually, the dance increases in pace and intensity. Shouts accompany the dance as the participants call to each other across the circle. The words *Hava Nagila* mean, "Come, let us be happy!"

JESSIE POLKA (AMERICAN)

Music Source: Folkcraft

Skills: Step and touch, two-step, or polka step

Formation: Circle, couples facing counterclockwise with inside arms around each other's waist

Directions:

Part I

Measures	Action
1	Beginning left, touch the heel in front, then step left in place. (Left heel, together)
2	Touch the right toe behind. Then touch the right toe in place, or swing it forward, keeping the weight on the left foot. (Right toe, touch)
3	Touch the right heel in front, then step right in place. (Right heel, together)
4	Touch the left heel to the left side, sweep the left foot across in front of the right. Keep the weight on the right. (Left heel, crossover)

Part II

Measures	Action
5–8	Take four two-steps or polka steps forward in the line of direction. (Step, close, step; step, close, step; step, close, step; step, close, step)

TEACHING TIP

The dance may be done as a mixer by having partner B turn out to the right on the last two two-steps and come back to the A behind her. Partners A continue to move forward on the last two two-steps, to make it easier to meet the B coming toward them. Another variation is to perform this activity as a line dance. Youngsters place the hands on the waist or shoulders of the dancer in front of them.

KOROBUSHKA (RUSSIAN)

Music Source: Folkcraft

Skills: Schottische step, balance step, cross-out-together step, walking step

Formation: Double circle, partner A's back to the centre, with partners facing and both hands joined. A's left and B's right foot are free.

Directions:

Part I

Measures	Action
1–2	Take one schottische step away from the centre (partner A moving forward, partner B backward) starting with A's left and B's right foot. (Out, 2, 3, hop)
3–4	Repeat the pattern of measures 1 and 2, reversing direction and footwork. (In, 2, 3, hop)
5–6	Repeat the pattern of measures 1 and 2, ending on the last count with a jump on both feet in place. (Out, 2, 3, jump)
7–8	Hop on the left foot, touching the right toes across in front of the left foot (count 1). Hop on the left foot, touching

the right toes diagonally forward to the right (count 2). Jump on both feet in place, clicking the heels together (count 1), pause, and release the hands (count 2). (Across, apart, together)

Part II

Measures	Action
9–10	Facing partner and beginning with the right foot, take one schottische step right, moving sideways away from partner. (Side, back, side, hop)
11–12	Facing partner and beginning with the left foot, take one schottische step left, returning to partner. (Side, back, side, hop)
13–14	Joining right hands with partner, balance forward and back: Step forward on the right foot (count 1), pause (count 2), rock back on the left foot in place (count 3), pause (count 4). (Forward, hop, back, hop)
15–16	Take four walking steps forward, starting with the right foot, and change places with partner. (Walk, 2, 3, 4)
17–24	Repeat the pattern of measures 9–16, returning to place.

TEACHING TIPS

To use the dance as a mixer, during measures 19 and 20, move left to the person just ahead of your partner and continue with this new partner.

Practise the schottische steps in different directions prior to introducing the dance as a whole.

LIMBO ROCK

Skills: Touch step, swivel step, jump-clap step

Formation: Single circle or scattered

Directions:

Part I

Measures	Action
1–2	Touch left foot in. Touch left foot out. Three steps in place. (In, out, left, right, left)
3–4	Repeat measures 1 and 2 beginning with opposite foot. (In, out, right, left, right)
5–8	Repeat measures 1–4.

Part II

Measures	Action
9–10	Swivel toes right, swivel heels right. Repeat and straighten feet. (Swivel, 2, 3, straighten)
11–12	Repeat beats 1 and 2 beginning with swivel toes left.
13–14	Jump in, clap; jump out, clap. (Jump, clap, jump, clap)
15–16	Repeat measures 13 and 14.

TEACHING TIP

An easier version involves walking eight steps right during measures 9–16.

LOLLIPOP

Music source: "Lollipop" (*Stand By Me* soundtrack)

Skills: Grapevine step, lindy step, slow twist

Formation: Line dance, facing forward

Directions:

Part I

Measures	Action
1–16	Start with feet together. Grapevine to right (step right, left behind, right, touch left beside right). Grapevine to left (step left, right behind left, touch right beside left). Repeat 1–8.
17–28	Twist on toes (heels up) to right (2 counts); twist on toes to left (2 counts). Repeat for total of six twists (12 counts).

Part II

Measures	Action
1–12	Lindy step: Step with right foot to right for two counts—"one step—pause"; step left foot to the left for two counts—"one step—pause." Step right foot back (one count); step left foot back (one count). Repeat.
13–20	Step-clap: Step on right foot (1 count); clap hands (2 count); step on left foot (3 count); clap hands (4 count); step on right (5 count); clap hands (6 count); step on left (7 count); clap hands (8 count).

Repeat the dance.

MAPLE LEAF STOMP (FRENCH CANADIAN)

Music source: "Les Marche des Violins"

Skills: Walk, stomp, slide

Formation: Double circle, with partners facing, hands joined. Inside partner with back to centre of circle.

Directions:

Part I

Measures	Action
1–8	Couples move to centre of circle with three walking steps, stomp foot on fourth step (In-2-3-stomp). Repeat moving away from the centre (Out-2-3-stomp).
9–16	Repeat back into centre (In-2-3-stomp). Partners drop hands, and outside partner turns clockwise in place for four steps (Turn-2-3-4).

Repeat 1–16.

Part II

Measures	Action
1–16	Inside partner stands in place and claps hands. Outside partner takes eight sliding steps clockwise around outside or circle (Slide-2-3-4-5-6-7-8). Then reverse direction for eight sliding steps, passing the original partner, and going to next partner (Reverse-2-3-4-5-6-7-8).
17–32	Join hands in skater's position with new partner and promenade 16 steps (Promenade 2-3-4 . . . 16).

Repeat dance from the beginning.

MEN IN BLACK (CONTEMPORARY)

Music source: "Men in Black" (Will Smith)

Skills: Grapevine, neck bobs, cross-over step

Formation: Lines, same direction

Directions:

Part I

Measures	Action
1–8	Step together to right, repeat (4 counts). Clap on fourth count. Step together to left (4 counts). Clap on fourth count.
9–16	Bounce in place with arms out, feet together (8 counts).

Part II

Measures	Action
1–8	Slide diagonally right together, left together, repeat (8 counts). At same time make fists with hands and pump up and down alternately.
9–16	Step on right foot behind left, left foot crosses over right, step on right. (2 counts = "and, 1, 2")
	Step on left foot behind right, right foot crosses over left, step on left. (2 counts = "and, 1, 2")
	Step on right foot behind left, left foot crosses over right, step on right. (2 counts = "and, 1, 2")
	Step on left foot behind right, right foot crosses over left, step on left turning a quarter turn to the left. (2 counts = "and, 1, 2")

Part III

Measures	Action
1–8	Four neck bobs forward and back, while doing four steps in place, turning back a quarter turn to the right (4 counts) (should be facing "starting wall")
	Freeze for 3 counts, clap 2 times (4 counts)

Repeat from beginning.

MISERLOU (GREEK)

Music source: RCA LPM 1620

Skills: Grapevine, swing step, step pause

Formation: Broken circle with dancers facing forward. No partners. Each dancer may hold end of scarf.

Directions:

Measures	Action
1–4	Facing the centre, all dancers step lightly forward and to the side on their right foot and hold for one count. Then touch the left toe forward in front of the right foot without putting weight on it. Pause again.
5–8	Swing left leg in arc around behind the right foot, and step on left foot in back of right. Step sideward right on right foot, cross and step on left foot in front of right foot. Pivot on ball of left foot to face slightly left, swing right foot in front.

(Cues for 1–8 = Point and point, behind, side, front, turn)

9–16   Take three forward steps clockwise: Step forward with the right, close the left foot to the right, then step on the right again. Hold on fourth count, and lift leg slightly (Walk-2-3-up).

17–20   Take three backward steps counter-clockwise: Step back with the left, close the right foot to the left, and then step back with the left again. Hold on the fourth count, lift the right foot slightly, and turn to face the centre (Back-2-3, Turn).

Repeat from beginning.

1, 2 STEP (HIP HOP)

Music Source: 1, 2 Step (Ciara)

Skills: Step, pivot, slide

Formation: Lines, facing forward

Directions:

Measure	Actions
Intro.	Move in place to music until phrase "the princess is here," then 8 counts to lead in to dance.
1–16	Step right, step together with left, hip sway for 2 counts. Step left, step together with right, hip sway for 2 counts. Step forward with right foot, then left, hop twice while rolling shoulders. Bounce in place, bring hands forward with two fingers (peace sign) on each hand (4 counts).
17–32	Using left foot, pivot to right (2 counts), bounce in place with hands on knees (2 counts). With right foot, pivot to left (2 counts), bounce in place with hands on knees (2 counts). Step right, step together (2 counts), punch left arm out and down (2 counts). Step left, step together (2 counts), punch right arm out and down (2 counts).
33–48	Step with left foot forward & transfer weight to right, transfer back to left (2 counts). Step forward with right, forward with left (2 counts). Right foot forward, heel out, right foot back (2 counts), pull right hand across chest from left to right and down (2 counts).

Forward motion—Slide right (2 counts), slide left (2 counts), right (2 counts), Stop, arms out and head down (2 counts).

Repeat dance from 1.

TEACHING THE POLKA STEP

The polka and the two-step are much alike. They both have a step-close-step pattern. The two-step is simply step-close-step, but the polka is step-close-step-hop. Technically, the polka is usually described as hop-step-close-step (or hop-step-together-step). However, the first description is probably more helpful when working with beginning students.

The polka step can be broken down into four movements: (1) step forward left, (2) close the right foot to the left, bringing the toe up and even with the left instep, (3) step forward left, and (4) hop on the left foot. The series begins with the weight on the right foot.

Several methods can be used to teach the polka:

1. *Step-by-step rhythm approach.* Analyzing the dance slowly, have the class walk through the steps together in even rhythm. The cue is "Step, close, step, hop." Accelerate the tempo to normal polka time and add the music.

2. *Gallop approach.* A method preferred by many elementary instructors is the gallop approach. (Review the previous section on teaching the two-step, which uses the gallop.) The approach is the same, but add the polka hop and speed up the tempo. When moving the right foot forward, a hop must be taken on the left foot. When moving the left foot forward, the hop is on the right foot.

3. *Two-step approach.* Beginning with the left foot, two-step with the music, moving forward in the line of direction in a single circle. Accelerate the tempo gradually to a fast two-step and take smaller steps. Without stopping, change to a polka rhythm by following each two-step with a hop. Use polka music for the two-step, but slow it down considerably to start.

4. *Partner approach.* After the youngsters have learned the polka step individually by one of the three methods, the step can be practised with partners in a double-circle formation, partners A on the inside and all facing counterclockwise, with inside hands joined. Partners A begin with the left foot and partners B with the right.

TEACHING THE TWO-STEP

Children can be taught the forward two-step simply by moving forward on the cue "Step, close, step," starting on the left foot and alternating thereafter. The close-step is made by bringing the toe of the closing foot to a point even with the instep of the other foot. All steps are almost slides, a kind of shuffle step.

The two-step just described is nothing more than a slow gallop, alternating the lead foot. One way to help students learn the step-close-step pattern is to put them in a single circle and have them gallop forward. They should all start on the left foot and move forward eight slow gallops. Stop the class and have them put their right foot forward and repeat the gallops. Continue this pattern, and have the students make the change from galloping with their left foot forward to galloping with their right foot forward without stopping. When they make this transition, they should bring the right foot forward in a walking step—the weight being on the left foot. Reverse the procedure when moving the left foot forward. The movement should be very smooth. When the students master this pattern, repeat the sequence, but do four gallops with each foot forward. After this pattern is mastered, repeat the pattern with two gallops on each foot. When students can do this, they are performing the forward two-step.

Next, arrange the children by couples in a circle formation, partners A on the inside, all facing counterclockwise. Repeat the instruction, with both partners beginning on the left foot. Practise the two-step with a partner, with partner A beginning on the left foot and partner B starting on the right. In the next progression, the children move face to face and back to back.

SPACE JAM (CONTEMPORARY)

Music source: *Space Jam* movie soundtrack

Skills: Grapevine, dribble, bankhead bounce

Formation: Line dance

Directions:

Part I

Measures	Action
1–16	Start with two dribble movements with right foot, 2 counts with left. Continue alternating with 2 counts to each side. On 16th count, jump high and slam dunk.

Part II

Measures	Action
1–16	After slam, grapevine to right (4 counts), left (4 counts), right (4 counts), left (4 counts). Clap on every 4th count.

Part III

Measures	Action
1–16	Raise the roof (hands in the air pushing to roof), pivoting on right foot for 8 counts. Second 8 counts "ad lib" (favourite basketball move to rhythm).

Part IV

Measures	Action
1–8	Bankhead bounce (hands in front of chest, move the arms from side to side while moving shoulders up and down) 4 counts forward, 4 counts back.
9–16	Repeat 1–8.

Repeat from beginning.

TETON MOUNTAIN STOMP (AMERICAN)

Music Source: Folkcraft

Skills: Walking, banjo position, sidecar position, two-step

Formation: Form single circle of partners in closed dance position, partners A facing counterclockwise, partners B facing clockwise.

Directions:

Measures	Action
1–4	Step to the left toward the centre of the circle on the left foot, close right foot to the left, step again to the left on the left foot, stomp right foot beside the left but leave the weight on the left foot. Repeat this action, but start on the right foot and move away from the centre. (Side, close; side, stomp; side, close; side, stomp)
5–8	Step to the left toward the centre on the left foot; stomp the right foot beside the left. Step to the right away from the centre on the right foot, and stomp the left foot beside the right. In "banjo" position (modified closed position with right hips adjacent), partner A takes four walking steps forward while partner B takes four steps backward, starting on the right foot. (Side, stomp, side, stomp; walk, 2, 3, 4)
9–12	Partners change to sidecar position (modified closed position with left hips adjacent) by each making a one half turn to the right in place, A remaining on the inside and B on the outside. A walks backward while B walks four steps forward. Partners change back to banjo position with right hips adjacent by each making a left-face one half turn; then they immediately release from each other. A walks forward four steps to meet the second B approaching, while B walks forward four steps to meet

13–16	the second A approaching. (Change, 2, 3, 4; new partner, 2, 3, 4)
13–16	New partners join inside hands and do four two-steps forward, beginning with A's right foot and B's left. (Step, close, step; repeat four times)

TEACHING TIP

If the dancers are skilful enough, use the following action for measures 13–16: New partners take the closed dance position and do four turning two-steps, starting on A's left (B's right) and make one complete right-face turn while progressing in the line of direction.

Introductory Square Dance

Introductory square dance should be just that—introductory. The emphases should be on enjoyment and learning the basics within the maturity capabilities of elementary school children. This can involve, however, considerable skill and polish. Square dancing is a broad and colourful activity with numerous figures, patterns, and dances. Teach the children to listen to the call and understand what the call means.

Free Formation Approach to Square Dance

Many square dance terms can be taught using a free formation approach. The students are scattered in general space. A piece of country and western music with a strong beat is played. Anytime students hear the call, they perform the same task with the person nearest to them. Note that there are no boy or girl roles. The two-handed swing is to be used instead of the regular buzz-step swing.

Two calls are basic. "Hit the lonesome trail" directs students to promenade individually in general space in diverse directions. This call can be inserted at any time to move the students in new directions. The other basic call is "Stop where you are and keep time to the music." Students stop and beat time to the music with light claps. Other calls can be selected from the following list.

Right (or left) arm round. With a forearm grasp, turn your partner once around and return to place.

Honour your partner, honour your corner. Bow to one person, then bow to another.

Do-si-do your partner, do-si-do your corner. Pass around one person, right shoulder to right shoulder, and back to place. Repeat with another person.

Right- (or left-) hand star. Place indicated hands (palm to palm with fingers pointed upward) about shoulder height with elbow somewhat bent. The next call will indicate how far to turn the star.

Two-hand swing. Partners grasp both hands, lean away from each other, and circle clockwise once around.

Go forward and back. Move forward with three steps and a touch toward another person, who is moving similarly toward you. Move back to place with three steps and a touch.

The next teaching strategy is to divide the class into groups of four. Use a call such as, "Circle up, four hands round." Groups of four circle clockwise. There usually will be extras. If there are three extras, one person can pretend to have a partner. Rotate the extras in and out.

Circle fours until all groups are formed. With the call, "Break and swing," the fours separate into pairs within the foursome. Position the pairs so they face each other. Use the terms "left partner" and "right partner" instead of boy and girl. If convenient, when there are mixed pairs put the girl on the right.

The following figures can be practised in fours:

Circle to the left (or right). Join hands and circle once around as indicated.

Form a right- (or left-) hand star. Hold right hands at about shoulder height and turn clockwise. A left-hand star reverses the direction.

Swing your opposite and swing your partner. Left partners walk toward their right partner opposite and swing. They walk back to their own partner and swing. The call can be reversed.

Birdie in the cage and three hands round. One child (the birdie) goes to the centre, while the other three join hands and circle left once around.

The birdie hops out and the crow hops in. The birdie joins the circle and another child goes in the centre.

Go into the middle and come back out; go into the middle and give a little shout. This is done from a circle-right or circle-left formation. The dancers face centre and come together. Repeat again, but with a light shout.

Round and round in a single file; round and round in frontier style. Circle left (or right), drop hands and move into a single file.

Dive for the oyster—dig for the clam. Usually after circling left once around, one couple goes partially under the raised joined hands of the other couple. The other couple repeats the same maneuver. Stepping should be: In, 2, 3, touch; out, 2, 3, touch.

The caller can use the "Hit the lonesome trail" call at any time to break up the makeup of the fours and then reorganize later with different combinations of students.

Square Dance Formation

Each couple is numbered around the set in a counterclockwise direction. It is important that the couples know their position. The couple with their backs to the music is generally couple 1, or the head couple. The couple to the right of them is number 2, and so on. While the head couple is number 1, the term *head couples* includes both couples 1 and 3; couples 2 and 4 are the *side couples*.

With respect to any one left-hand partner (gent), the following terms are used in traditional calls (adjust references to gender as necessary):

Partner: The other (right-hand) dancer of the couple

Corner or corner lady: The right-hand partner on the left

Right-hand lady: The right-hand partner in the couple to the right

Opposite or opposite lady: The right-hand partner directly across the set

Other terms that are used include these:

Home: The couple's original or starting position

Active or leading couple: The couple leading or visiting the other couples for different figures

Once the square dance formation has been introduced, the figures and pattern calls discussed previously should be practised in the full formation of four couples.

Culminating Events for the Dance Unit

The following are two ideas for events that will finish off the dance unit.

Theme Day After all the grade levels have reached a specified performance level in a dance unit, consider organizing a "theme day" (dances from different decades—1950s, 1960s, 1970s, and so on). The decade theme day may be expanded across subject areas.

Dance Festival When the dance unit is drawing to a close, it is exciting to feature a festival of all the dances learned. To have this activity include everyone, each class or grade level should make a dance presentation.

Critical Thinking

1. Brainstorm ideas for helping students who may be reluctant to feel more comfortable and motivated to participate in dance. What are reasons some students may feel reluctant?

References and Suggested Readings

Boorman, J. (1973). *Creative dance and language experience for children.* Toronto, ON: Longman.

Cone, T. & Cone, S. (2005). *Teaching children dance* (2nd ed.). Champaign, IL: Human Kinetics.

Canadian Association for Health, Physical Education and Dance. (1983). *Folk dance in the elementary school—basic skills series.* Gloucester, ON: Author.

Canadian Association for Health, Physical Education and Dance. (1988). *Creative dance—basic skills series.* Gloucester, ON: Author.

Gilbert, A.G. (1992). *Creative dance for all ages: A conceptual approach.* Reston, VA: AAHPERD.

Joyce, M. (1993). *First steps in teaching creative dance to children* (3rd ed.). Mountain View, CA: Mayfield.

Kassing, G. & Jay, D. (2003). *Dance teaching methods and curriculum design.* Champaign, IL: Human Kinetics.

Kaufmann, K.A. (2006). *Inclusive creative movement and dance.* Champaign, IL: Human Kinetics.

McCutcheon, B. (2006). *Teaching dance as art in education.* Champaign, IL: Human Kinetics.

Overby, L., Post, B., & Newman, D. (2005). *Interdisciplinary learning through dance.* Champaign, IL: Human Kinetics.

Price Bennett, J. & Coughenour Riemer, P. (2006). *Rhythmic activities and dance* (2nd ed.). Champaign, IL: Human Kinetics.

Rose, M. (2000a). *Step lively—dances for schools and families.* Vancouver, BC: Community Dance Project.

Rose, M. (2000b). *Step lively 2—Canadian dance favourites.* Vancouver, BC: Community Dance Project.

Sprague, M., Scheff, H., & McGreevy-Nichols, S. (2006). *Dance about anything.* Champaign, IL: Human Kinetics.

Van Gyn, G.H. & Van Sant, D. (1992). *Can you speak dance?* Victoria, BC: University of Victoria.

Wall, J. & Murray, N. (1994). *Children and movement* (2nd ed.). Dubuque, IA: Brown and Benchmark.

Willis, C. (2004). *Dance education tips from the trenches.* Champaign, IL: Human Kinetics.

 Weblinks

Folk Dance Association: www.folkdancing.org/

The Folk Dance Association's mandate is to help newcomers discover folk, contra, Balkan, English country, international, Israeli, Scottish country, square, swing, and all other types of traditional and ethnic dance. Their website includes the Folk Dance Directory, an online resource of folk dance groups, events, and activities in the U.S. and Canada.

Societé pour la Promotion de la Dance Traditionelle Québecoise: www.spdtq.qc.ca

This society is dedicated to the promotion and preservation of traditional dances of Quebec.

CHAPTER 20

Gymnastics Skills

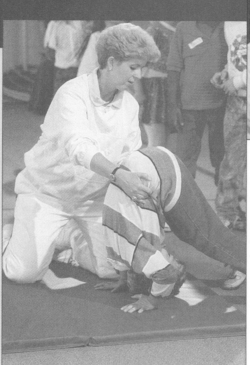

Essential Components

I	Organized around content standards
II	**Student-centred and developmentally appropriate**
III	**Physical activity and motor skill development form the core of the program**
IV	Teaches management skills and self-discipline
V	**Promotes inclusion of all students**
VI	**Focuses on process over product**
VII	Promotes lifetime personal health and wellness
VIII	Teaches cooperation and responsibility and promotes sensitivity to diversity

Physical Education Standards

1	**Students are able to move competently using a variety of fundamental and specialized motor skills.**
2	Students can monitor and maintain a health-enhancing level of physical fitness.
3	**Students are able to apply movement concepts and basic mechanics of skill performance when learning and refining motor skills.**
4	Students comprehend the basic principles of wellness and are able to apply concepts that enable them to make meaningful decisions that positively impact their health and wellness.
5	**Students participate in a wide variety of physical activities and learn how to maintain a personalized active lifestyle.**
6	**Students demonstrate empathy, understanding, and respect for the numerous differences exhibited by people in an activity setting.**
7	Students exhibit responsible and self-directed behaviours that lead to positive social interactions in physical activity.

OVERVIEW

Gymnastics activities make a significant contribution to the overall physical education experience for children in elementary schools by developing body management skills. Participation in gymnastics enhances flexibility, agility, balance, strength, and body control. Students learn specialized motor skills such as body rolling, balance skills, and inverted balances through these activities. Various partner and group activities offer opportunity for social interaction and cooperation. Positive learning experiences in gymnastics activities are dependent on a safe and logical skill progression.

OUTCOMES

- List progressions and developmental level placements for gymnastics activities.

- Organize a comprehensive lesson of gymnastics activities that includes six basic groups: (1) landings, (2) statics, (3) locomotions, (4) swings, (5) rotations, and (6) springs.

- Identify effective management techniques when teaching gymnastics activities.

- Cite safety considerations essential to the gymnastics program.

- Describe gymnastics activities that are appropriate for elementary school children.

Gymnastics activities are an important part of every child's overall experience in physical education, and they can make a significant contribution to the goals of physical education. Because much of the work is individual, children face challenges and have the opportunity to develop resourcefulness, self-confidence, and courage. Through the gymnastics program, such personal characteristics as dedication and perseverance can be furthered, as stunts are seldom mastered quickly. When a challenging stunt is mastered, satisfaction, pride of achievement, and a sense of accomplishment contribute to improved self-esteem. Social interplay is provided through various partner and group stunts requiring cooperative effort. The social attributes of tolerance, helpfulness, courtesy, and appreciation for the ability of others grow out of the lessons.

Important physical values emerge from a gymnastics program. Body management opportunities are presented, and coordination, flexibility, and agility are enhanced. Many activities present the opportunity to practise balance. The demands of holding positions and executing stunts contribute to the development of strength and power in diverse parts of the body. Many stunts require support, wholly or in part, by the arms, thus providing development of the musculature of the arm–shoulder girdle.

Progression and Developmental Level Placement

Progression is important in the gymnastics program. In this book, activities are listed in progression within the three developmental levels. To avoid safety problems, the order of these activities should be reasonably maintained. Adherence to developmental level is secondary to the principle of progression. If children have little or no experience in these activities, start them on activities specified in a lower developmental level.

At the heart of the gymnastics program is the concept of Dominant Movement Patterns (DMP). The DMP approach forms the basis for gymnastics education in Canada (Russell, 1986). The approach is based on the premise that every skill performed in gymnastics belongs to one of the following six patterns of body movement: (1) landings, (2) statics, (3) locomotions, (4) swings, (5) rotations, and (6) springs. This arrangement allows the teacher to pick activities from each movement pattern for a well-balanced lesson and unit. Activities in this chapter are divided into these six basic patterns. Activities in Chapter 18 (Body Management Skills) are also incorporated in this framework.

The following section provides a brief description of each of the six dominant movement patterns:

1. *Landings*—Russell (1986) describes landings as the most important movement pattern because the gymnast has to land from all other DMPs. Therefore it is the most common of the six movement patterns. Four key categories in this DMP include landings on the feet and hands, landings with rotation, and landings flat on the back.

2. *Statics*—This DMP comprises "held" or "still" positions and is further subdivided into supports, hangs, and balances. *Support* activities are those Static Positions that are stable and are done with the shoulders above the apparatus, as opposed to *Hangs*, which are done with the shoulders below the apparatus, and *Balances*, which are unstable (Russell, 1986, p. 60).

3. *Locomotions*—Locomotions are defined as "repetitive displacements of the body" (Russell, 1986, p. 72). In other words, locomotions are movement patterns in which we move distances in space (for example, running, skipping). Three categories of locomotions include on the feet, from support, and from a hang.

4. *Swings*—One of the more advanced DMPs, swing activities are defined as rotation around external axes (on bars and rings, and so on). Swings may be included after establishing a sound grounding in Hangs and Supports (Russell, 1986). Two key swinging skills include (a) swings from hangs, and (b) swings from support.

5. *Rotations*—This DMP deals with rotation around the three primary internal axes (transverse—for example, rolls; longitudinal—for example, pirouettes; and anterior-posterior—for example, cartwheels).

6. *Springs*—Springs include activities that produce rapid displacement of the body in a spring-like movement (for example, leap, vault). Subcategories include springs from two legs, one leg, or two arms (Russell, 1986).

For further information on the Dominant Movement Pattern approach to gymnastics, the reader is directed to Russell (1986) and Russell (1994).

The developmental level I program relies on dominant movement patterns as the framework for organizing skills in the three developmental levels. Skills requiring exceptional body control, critical balancing, or substantial strength should be left for higher levels of development. The developmental level II and III programs are built on activities and progressions developed earlier. Emphasis is placed on learning more standard gymnastics activities. Most skills at developmental level I can be performed with a certain degree of choice, whereas at developmental levels II and III more conformance to correct technique is desirable. In general, the upper developmental level activities place higher demands on strength, control, form, agility, balance, and flexibility.

Most activities at developmental level I can be done—at least in some fashion—by most students; but certain activities at levels II and III may be too challenging for some students. Arrange lessons that include a variety of activities: skills that everyone can do, skills that are moderately challenging, and skills that are more challenging.

Instructional Methodology for Gymnastics

Warm-up and Flexibility Activity

Normal introductory activity and fitness development activity usually supply sufficient warm-up for the gymnastics lesson. Consider the following as a regular sequence for gymnastics warm-up:

1. Aerobic warm-up (e.g., jogging, skipping).
2. General warm-up including dynamic stretching (for example, swinging of legs and arms, followed up by a slower sustained total body stretch from head to toe).
3. Specific stretches that focus on the target skills in the lesson.

Also note that a general warm-down at the end of the lesson is recommended.

Extra flexibility may be required in the wrists, ankles, and neck. The following activities can be used prior to participating in the gymnastics activities.

Wrists

1. Extend one arm forward. With the other hand, push the extended hand down, thus stretching the top of the wrist and forearm muscles. Hold the position for 8 counts. Next, pull the hand backward and hold for 8 counts to stretch the wrist flexor muscles.
2. Clasp the fingers of both hands in front of the chest. Make circles with both hands and stretch the wrists.

Ankles and Quadriceps

1. Kneel and sit on both feet. Smoothly and gently lean backward over the feet, using the arms to support the body.
2. In a sitting position, cross one leg over the other. Use the hands to help rotate each foot through its full range of motion. Reverse legs and repeat.

Neck

1. In a sitting position, slowly sway head from right through centre, to left through centre. Full "neck circles" are not recommended.
2. In the same position, hold the chin against the chest for 8 counts. Repeat with the head looking backward as far as possible. Look to each side and hold for 8 counts.

Lower Back and Shoulders

Begin in a supine position. Place the hands back over the head on the mat so that the fingers point toward the toes. Bridge up by extending the arms and legs. While in the bridge position, slowly rock back and forth.

Effective Class Management

Organization should focus on providing maximum practice opportunity in a safe environment. How children are arranged depends on the activities selected and whether mats are required. The following ideas help establish priorities:

1. Whenever possible, all children should be active and performing. When mats are not required for the activities, there is little problem. Individual mats can be used for many of the simple balances and rolling stunts, particularly at developmental level I. When larger mats are required, consider using small groups. Ideally, each group of three students should have a mat. When teachers use return activities in conjunction with groups as small as three, there is little standing around.
2. When the number of mats is limited, perform across the mats sideways. On a 2-m-long mat, two children can tumble sideways. Three performers can use a 2.5-m-long mat at the same time. With this arrangement, the focus is on single rolls, but an occasional series of rolls lengthwise on the mat is not ruled out.
3. Consider station teaching if equipment is limited. Include a range of skills at each station in order to be inclusive of diverse skill levels. The arrangement might include rolls at the first station, inverted balances at the second, turns and upright balances at the third, and partner stunts at the fourth. Wall charts listing the activities in progression provide excellent guidance.

Formations for Teaching

Following are some effective formations for teaching gymnastics:

Squad formation. Mats are placed in a line, with squads lined up behind the mats. Each child takes a turn and then goes to the end of the squad line, with the others moving up.

Semicircular formation. Students are positioned in a semicircular arrangement. This formation directs attention toward the teacher, who stands in the centre.

U-shaped formation. The mats are placed in the shape of a large U. This formation offers an excellent view for the teacher, and children are able to see what their classmates are doing.

Demonstration mat. One mat is placed in a central position and is used exclusively for demonstrations. Little movement is necessary to see demonstrations.

Description and Demonstration of Gymnastics Activities

To enhance student learning when presenting an activity, the following sequence may be helpful:

1. *Significance of the name.* Most activities have a characteristic name that should be learned.

2. *Description of the activity.* Stunts can be approached in terms of three parts: starting position, execution, and finishing position. Most stunts have a defined starting position that must be performed properly. As a first step, explain the position. Next, present key movements (and cues) for proper execution of the activity. The teacher can clarify such factors as how far to travel, how long to balance, and how many times a movement should be done. In some gymnastics activities, a definite finishing position or action is part of the stunt.

3. *Demonstration of the activity.* Three parts of demonstration are recognized: (a) show the entire skill (whole); (b) follow with a slow, step-by-step demonstration of the entire stunt, identifying three simple cues that help the student perform the skill correctly (part); and (c) execution of the stunt as it is normally done accompanied by the cues (whole). Add further details and refinements as the instruction progresses. Keep in mind that children also need to analyze and solve problems.

Safety Considerations

Safety is a foremost consideration in the gymnastics program. The inherent hazards of an activity and how to avoid them must be included in the instructional procedures.

Spotting

Spotting is a term used to describe external assistance provided to a performer by a third party. When spotting, the goals are to assist the performer and help support the body weight. The Dominant Movement Pattern (DMP) approach to gymnastics (Russell, 1986) emphasizes the development of the physical attributes and motor attributes associated with specific dominant movement pattern as an alternative to spotting. In other words, rather than having a student attempt a skill with a "spot," try introducing more progressions leading to the skill. Inclusion of the Landings DMP provides additional support for reducing performer dependence on spotting to feel safe performing a skill. Where the DMP approach has been embraced, the need for spotting has been deemphasized. For example, in the Saskatchewan Physical Education Safety Guidelines (1998), the following statement appears:

Spotting manual assistance provided to participants while performing skills on the floor or equipment is not appropriate in the elementary gymnastics program. Many gymnastics injuries are the result of attempting skills that students are not ready to perform. If the student needs spotting, this is a good indication that the student lacks the necessary physical or motor skills. Rather than have the student attempt the skills with a "spot," more activities that lead up to the skill can be provided. Not only does this approach prevent the tendency for students to become dependent on a spotter, it reflects that reality that in a larger group setting the teacher cannot spot all the students. (p. 44)

This is not to totally negate the use of physical assistance (spotting) in some instances. The *Ontario Physical Education Safety Guidelines* (1997) offers the following suggestions. It is appropriate to expect students to perform the following spotting duties:

1. Primary students can do non-contact spotting like keeping runways and landing areas clear. (developmental level I and II)

2. Students in intermediate grades can be involved in non-contact spotting as above as well as giving verbal cues and checking placement of mats and stability of equipment. (developmental level III)

3. Students in intermediate grades can also provide contact-spotting roles such as helping peers maintain a static balance and assisting peers with forward rotations (for example, rolls on mats).

Any contact spotting should be limited to minor stability control (for example, stabilizing hips on headstand). Spotting is mentioned in this chapter where it can play this minor stabilizing role. If the performer requires major physical assistance by a spotter, she is not ready to perform the skill and additional progressions are necessary.

Instructional Procedures

1. Although mats are not necessary for some stunts, it is wise to include stunts requiring mats in every lesson.

Children like to perform on mats, and rolling stunts using mats are vital to the gymnastics program.

2. Many partner stunts work well only when partners are about the same size. If the stunt requires partner support, the support child should be strong enough to hold the weight of the other.

3. No two children are alike. Respect individual differences, and allow for different levels of success.

4. Relating new activities to those learned previously is important. An effective approach is to review the lead-up stunt for an activity.

5. When a stunt calls for a position to be held for a number of counts, use a standard counting system (for example, "One thousand one, one thousand two . . ." or "Monkey one, monkey two . . .").

6. When appropriate, have children work in pairs, with one child performing and the second providing support and feedback.

7. Shifting of mats should not be necessary during the course of instruction.

Start-and-Extend Technique

The start-and-extend technique should be applied to stunts when feasible. Consider someone teaching a Heel Click. The teacher begins by saying, "Let's see all of you jump high in the air and click your heels together before you come down." (This is the start.) "Now, this time when you jump into the air, click your heels, and land with your feet apart with a soft bent-knee action to absorb the shock." (This is the extension.) Further extension could be adding a quarter or half turn before landing, clapping the hands overhead while clicking the heels, or clicking the heels twice before landing. In general, the start is made simple, so that all children can experience a measure of success. The instruction then extends to other elements of the stunt, with variations and movement factors added and refined as indicated.

Basic Mechanical Principles

Certain mechanical principles should be established as the foundation of an effective gymnastics program. Instruction is facilitated if children can build on these basic principles:

1. Momentum needs to be developed and applied, particularly for rolls. Tucking, starting from a higher point, and preliminary raising of the arms are examples of ways to increase momentum.

2. The centre of weight must be positioned over the centre of support in balance stunts, particularly in the inverted stands.

3. In certain stunts, such as the headspring, the hips should be projected upward and forward to raise the centre of gravity for better execution.

4. In stunts where the body is wholly or partially supported by the hands, proper positioning of the hands is essential for effective performance. The hands should be approximately shoulder width apart, and the fingers should be spread and pointed forward.

Basic Gymnastics Positions

Students should be able to recognize and demonstrate basic positions that are unique to gymnastics.

Tuck Position

The tuck position is performed with the legs bent and the chin tucked to the chest. Students can be cued to "curl up like a ball." There are three different tuck positions, and students should know all of them: the Sitting Tuck (see Figure 20.1), the Standing Tuck, and the Lying Tuck.

Pike Position

The pike position is performed by bending forward at the hips and keeping the legs straight. The three basic pike positions are the Sitting Pike (see Figure 20.2), the Standing Pike, and the Lying Pike.

Straddle Position

The straddle position is accomplished by bending forward at the hips and spreading the legs apart to the sides as far as

Figure 20.1

Tuck position.

Figure 20.2

Pike position.

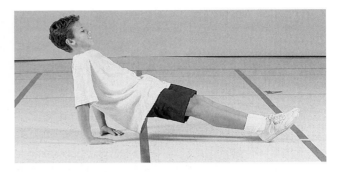

Figure 20.4

Back-support position.

possible. The legs should be kept straight. Variations of the straddle position are the Sitting Piked Straddle (see Figure 20.3), the Standing Piked Straddle, and the Lying Piked Straddle.

Front-support Position

This position is similar to the push-up position. The body is straight with the head up, with fingers flat to the floor.

Back-support Position

The back-support position is an inverted push-up position. The body is kept as straight as possible (see Figure 20.4).

Gymnastics Dance Positions

Attitude

An attitude is a position in which the body weight is supported on one leg while the other leg is lifted and bent

at the knee. The arm on the side of the lifted leg is usually bent over the head, and the other arm is extended at the side (see Figure 20.5).

Lunge Position

In lunge position, the non-supporting rear leg is straight, while the forward, supporting leg is bent at the hip and knee. Most of the weight is placed on the forward leg. The arms are extended, and the head is up with the eyes forward (see Figure 20.6).

Figure 20.5

Attitude.

Figure 20.3

Straddle position.

Figure 20.6

Lunge position.

Figure 20.7

Arabesque.

Plié

A plié is the bending of the knees. Both knees are bent, the arms are extended at right angles to the sides, and the seat is tucked to maintain a flat abdominal wall. The plié teaches children how to absorb the force of the landing. There are different plié positions, but the basic purpose of the plié in gymnastics instruction is to teach landing with grace and control.

Relevé

The relevé is an extension movement from the plié position. The movement goes from the plié (knees bent) position to the extended position. Extension should be complete through all of the joints, stretching upward from the balls of the feet.

Arabesque

In the arabesque position, the weight is supported on one leg while the other leg is extended to the rear. The extended leg is kept straight with the toe pointed, and the chest is kept erect (see Figure 20.7). The Back Extension and the Cartwheel are often brought to completion with an Arabesque.

Jumps

Three jump variations are used commonly in gymnastics dance. They are the Tuck Jump, the Pike Jump, and the Straddle Jump. These jumps are simply a jump with the prescribed position added. The arms are raised in a lifting motion to increase the height of the jump and to enhance balance. The impact of the landing is absorbed at the ankles and knee joints.

Chassé

The Chassé is a slide. This basic locomotor movement involves one leg chasing the other out of position. It is done close to the floor with a light spring in the step.

Table 20.1 shows additional skills from the dominant movement patterns for the apparatus discussed in Chapter 18. These include climbing ropes, balance beams and benches, low horizontal bar, and jumping boxes. These apparatus allow for development of several of the movement patterns, most importantly Swings and Springs, and Hangs within Statics.

TABLE 20.1					
Dominant movement patterns with apparatus (from Chapter 18)					
Landings	**Statics**	**Locomotions**	**Swings**	**Rotations**	**Springs**
Soft Knees on landing (all apparatus)	Climbing Ropes (p. 346)	Climbing Ropes (pp. 346–347)	Climbing Ropes	Climbing Ropes (p. 348)	
Balance Beams (pp. 349–350)	Balance Beams (p. 349)	Balance Beams (pp. 349–350)	Balance Beams	Balance Beams	Balance Beams (pp. 349–350)
Balance Benches (pp. 351–352)	Balance Benches (p. 351)	Balance Benches (pp. 350–352)	Balance Benches	Balance Benches (p. 352)	Balance Benches (pp. 351–352)
Jumping Boxes (p. 353)	Jumping Boxes (p. 351)	Jumping Boxes (pp. 352–353)	Jumping Boxes	Jumping Boxes (p. 353)	Jumping Boxes (p. 353)
	Low Horizontal Bars (p. 355)	Low Horizontal Bars (p. 355)	Low Horizontal Bars (pp. 355–356)	Low Horizontal Bars (pp. 355–356)	

Gymnastics Activities

The gymnastics activities are organized in order of difficulty into three developmental levels. Table 20.2 lists all the activities in each of the levels. A brief discussion of each of the developmental levels follows.

Developmental Level I Activities

Developmental level I consists primarily of imitative walks and movements, plus selected balance skills and rolls. The Forward Roll is practised, but its refinement is left to later levels. The Back Roller is practised as a prelude to the Backward Roll.

Emphasis should be placed on the creative aspects of the activities as well as on performance standards. Children at this level tend to do stunts in different ways because of their different interpretations of what is required. Directional concepts and a basic understanding of common movement terminology should have a prominent place in the instruction. The "why" of an activity should be explained to children.

Animal Movements

ALLIGATOR CRAWL

Lie facedown on the floor with elbows bent. Move along the floor in alligator fashion, keeping the hands close

Figure 20.8

Alligator Crawl.

to the body and the feet pointed out (see Figure 20.8). First, use unilateral movements—that is, right arm and leg moving together—then change to cross-lateral movements.

KANGAROO JUMP

Carry the arms close to the chest with the palms facing forward. Place a beanbag or ball between the knees. Move in different directions by taking small jumps without dropping the object.

BEAR WALK

Bend forward and touch the ground with both hands. Travel forward slowly by moving the hand and foot on the same side together (that is, first the right hand and foot,

TABLE 20.2

Developmental Level Activities Organized by Dominant Movement Patterns

Developmental Level I

Landings	Statics	Swings	Locomotions	Rotations	Springs
Lowering the Boom	Three Point Tip-up		Alligator Walk	Rolling Log	Jump Turns
Soft Knees	Climb-up		Kangaroo Walk	Side Roll	Heel Slaps
Bouncing Ball	Mountain Climber		Bear Walk	Forward Roll	Heel Click
Duck	Switcheroo		Gorilla Walk	Back Roller	Tuck Jump
Jump Turns	One-leg Balance		Rabbit Walk	Forward Straddle Roll	
Tuck Jump	Double Knee Balance		Elephant Walk	Pogo Stick	
Rubber Band	Head Touch		Siamese Twin Walk	Turn Over	
	Head Balance		Lame Dog Walk	Heel Slap & Turn	
	Balance Touch		Crab Walk	Top	
	Kimbo Stand		Directional Walk	Seat Circle	
	Knee-Lift Stand		Line Walking	Wring the Dish Rag	
	Stork Stand		Walking in Place	Roly-Poly	
	Forward Balance		Crazy Walk		
	Backward Balance		Double Top		
	Side Balance				
	Hand & Knee Balance				
	Cross-legged Balance				
	Elevator				
	Fluttering Leaf				
	Rising Sun				
	Thread the Needle				
	Turk Stand				
	Push-up				
	See-saw				
	Partner Toe Toucher				

(continued)

TABLE 20.2

Developmental Level Activities Organized by Dominant Movement Patterns (continued)

Developmental Level II

Landings	Statics	Locomotions	Swings	Rotations	Springs
Knee Drop	Headstand	Cricket Walk		Forward Roll to Walkout	Frog Jump
Forward Drop	Headstand Climb-up	Seal Crawl		Backward Roll	Mule Kick
Dead Body Drop	Headstand Kick-up	Walrus Walk		Backward Roll Incline	Balance Jump
	Frog Handstand (Tip-up)	Double-lame Dog		Backward Shoulder Roll	Heel Stand
	Half–Teeter-Totter	Turtle		Cartwheel	Knee Jump to Stand
	Teeter-Totter	Walrus Slap		Forward Roll (Pike)	Leap Frog
	Handstand	Hip Walk		Forward Roll Combinations	
	One-leg Balance Reverse	Long Bridge		Coffee Grinder	
	Tummy Balance	Scooter		Egg Roll	
	Leg Dip	Toe Tug Walk		Partner Twister	
	Seat Balance	Partner Hopping		Dump the Wheelbarrow	
	Face-to-knee Balance	Wheelbarrow			
	Reach Under				
	Stiff Person Balance				
	Tanglefoot				
	Partner Pull-up				
	Back-to-Back Get-up				
	Row Boat				
	Double Bear				
	Table				
	Hip–Shoulder Stand				

(continued)

Developmental Level Activities Organized by Dominant Movement Patterns (continued)

Developmental Level III

Landings	Statics	Locomotions	Swings	Rotations	Springs
Flip Flop	Headstand Variations	Walk-through		Roll Combinations	Heel Click (side)
	Handstand against the Wall	Double Scooter		Back Extension	Jump Through
	Freestanding Handstand	Tandem Bicycle		Cartwheel	Jackknife
	Straddle Press to Handstand	Injured Person Carry		Round Off	Heel & Toe Spring
	Walking on Hands	Merry-Go-Round		Judo Roll	
	V-up			Walk over	
	Push-up Variations			Single-leg Circle	
	Handstand Stunts			Double Roll	
	Front Seat Support			Triple Roll	
	Wall Walk-up			Quintuple Roll	
	Skier's Sit				
	Dead Person Lift				
	Front Sit				
	Flying Dutchman				
	Knee & Shoulder Balance				
	All-fours Balance				

Figure 20.9

Bear Walk.

then the left hand and foot) (see Figure 20.9). Make deliberate movements.

TEACHING TIP

Variation: Lift the free foot and arm high while the support is on the other side.

GORILLA WALK

Bend the knees and carry the trunk forward. Let the arms hang at the sides. Touch the fingers to the ground while walking.

TEACHING TIP

Variation: Stop and beat on the chest like a gorilla. Bounce up and down on all fours with hands and feet touching the floor simultaneously.

RABBIT JUMP

Crouch with knees apart and hands placed on the floor. Move forward by reaching out with both hands and then bringing both feet up to the hands. The eyes look ahead.

Emphasize that this is a jump rather than a hop because both feet move at once. Note that the jump is a bilateral movement.

TEACHING TIPS

Variations:

1. Try with knees together and arms on the outside. Try alternating with knees together and apart on successive jumps. Go over a low hurdle or through a hoop.
2. Experiment with taking considerable weight on the hands before the feet move forward. To do this, raise the seat higher in the air when the hands move forward.

ELEPHANT WALK

Bend well forward, clasping the hands together to form a trunk. The end of the trunk should swing close to the ground. Walk in a slow, deliberate, dignified manner, keeping the legs straight and swinging the trunk from side to side (see Figure 20.10). Stop and throw water over the

Figure 20.10

Elephant Walk.

back with the trunk. Recite the following verse while walking, and move the trunk appropriately.

The elephant's walk is steady and slow,
His trunk like a pendulum swings to and fro.
But when there are children with peanuts around
He swings it up and he swings it down.

SIAMESE TWIN WALK

Stand back to back with a partner. Lock elbows (see Figure 20.11). Walk forward, backward, and sideward in unison.

TIGHTROPE WALK

Select a line, board, or chalked line on the floor as the high wire. Pretend to be on the high wire and do various tasks with exaggerated loss and control of balance. Add tasks such as jumping rope, juggling balls, and riding a bicycle. Pretend to hold a parasol or a balancing pole while performing.

Children should give good play to the imagination. The teacher can set the stage by discussing what a circus performer on the high wire might do.

LAME DOG WALK

Walk on both hands and one foot. Hold the other foot in the air as if injured. Walk a distance and change feet. The eyes should look forward. Move backward also and in other combinations. Try to move with an injured front leg.

CRAB WALK

Squat down and reach back, putting both hands flat to the floor without sitting down. With head, neck, and body level, walk forward, backward, and sideward.

Figure 20.11

Siamese Twin Walk.

Children have a tendency to lower the hips. The teacher should emphasize that the body is kept in a straight line.

TEACHING TIP

Variations:

1. Move the hand and foot on the same side simultaneously.
2. Try balancing on one leg and the opposite hand for five seconds.

Rolls and Inverted Balances

ROLLING LOG

Lie on the back with arms stretched overhead (see Figure 20.12). Roll sideways the length of the mat. The next time, roll with the hands pointed toward the other side of the mat. To roll in a straight line, keep the feet slightly apart.

TEACHING TIP

Variation: Alternately curl and stretch while rolling.

Figure 20.12

Rolling Log.

SIDE ROLL

Start on the hands and knees, with one side toward the direction of the roll. Drop the shoulder, tuck both the elbow and the knee under, and roll over completely, returning to the hands-and-knees position. Momentum is needed to return to the original position. Practise rolling back and forth from one hand-and-knee position to another.

FORWARD ROLL

Stand facing forward, with the feet apart. Squat and place the hands on the mat, shoulder width apart, with elbows against the insides of the thighs. Tuck the chin to the chest and make a rounded back. A push-off with the hands and feet provides the force for the roll (see Figure 20.13). Carry the weight on the hands, with the elbows bearing the weight of the thighs. If the elbows are kept against the thighs and the weight is assumed there, the force of the roll is transferred easily to the rounded back. Try to roll forward to the feet. Later, try with the knees together and no weight on the elbows.

TEACHING TIP

Consider practising forward rolls on inclined mats. This helps students build momentum and get a good "feel" for the rotational motion required for an effective roll.

Figure 20.13

Forward Roll.

Figure 20.14

Back Roller.

Figure 20.15

Three-point Tip-up.

FORWARD ROLL (STRADDLE POSITION)

Start with the legs spread in the straddle position. Bend forward at the hips, tuck the head, place the hands on the mat, and roll forward. A strong push with the hands at the end of the roll is necessary to return to the standing position.

BACK ROLLER

Begin in a crouched position with knees together and hands resting lightly on the floor. Roll backward, securing momentum by bringing the knees to the chest and clasping them with the arms (see Figure 20.14). Roll back and forth rhythmically. On the backward movement, go well back on the neck and head. Try to roll forward to original position. If you have difficulty rolling back to original position, cross the legs and roll to a crossed-leg standing position. (This stunt is a lead-up to the Backward Roll.)

CLIMB-UP

Begin on a mat in a kneeling position, with hands placed about shoulder width apart and the fingers spread and pointed forward. Place the head forward of the hands, so that the head and hands form a triangle on the mat. Walk the body weight forward so that most of it rests on the hands and head. Climb the knees to the top of the elbows. (This stunt is a lead-up to the Headstand.) A spotter may help stabilize the hips.

TEACHING TIP

Variation: Raise the knees off the elbows.

THREE-POINT TIP-UP

Squat down on the mat, placing the hands flat with fingers pointing forward. The elbows should be inside and pressed against the inner part of the lower thighs. Lean forward, slowly transferring body weight to the bent elbows and hands until the forehead touches the mat (see Figure 20.15). Return to starting position.

The Three-point Tip-up ends in the same general position as the Climb-up, but with the elbows on the inside of the thighs. Some children may have better success by turning the fingers in slightly, thus causing the elbows to point outward more and offering better support at the thigh contact point. This stunt is a lead-up to the Headstand and the Handstand done at later levels.

TEACHING TIP

Variation: Tuck the head and do a Forward Roll as an alternative finishing act.

MOUNTAIN CLIMBER

This activity is similar to the exercise known as the Treadmill. The weight is taken on the hands with one foot forward and one foot extended back, similar to a sprinter's start. When ready, the performer switches foot position, with both feet moving simultaneously. This activity is a lead-up to the Handstand and teaches children to support the body weight briefly with the arms.

SWITCHEROO

This Handstand lead-up activity begins in the front lunge position with the arms overhead. In one continuous movement, bend forward at the hips, place the hands on the mat, and invert the legs over the head. Scissor the legs in the air, and then reverse the position of the feet on the mat. Repeat in a smooth and continuous motion.

Balance Stunts

ONE-LEG BALANCE

Lift one leg from the floor. Later, bring the knee up. The arms should be free at first and then assume specified positions: folded across the chest, on the hips, on the head, or behind the back.

DOUBLE-KNEE BALANCE

Kneel on both knees, with the feet pointed to the rear. Lift the feet from the ground and balance on the knees. Vary the position of the arms. Experiment with different arm positions.

Figure 20.16

Head Touch.

HEAD TOUCH

On a mat, kneel on both knees, with feet pointed backward and arms outstretched backward for balance. Lean forward slowly and touch the forehead to the mat. Recover to position (see Figure 20.16). Vary the arm position.

HEAD BALANCE

Place a beanbag, block, or book on the head (see Figure 20.17). Walk, stoop, turn around, sit down, get up, and so on. Balance the object so that the upper body is in good posture. Keep the hands out to the sides for balance. Later, vary the position of the arms—folded across the chest or placed behind the back or down the sides. Link together a series of movements.

Figure 20.17

Head Balance.

ONE-LEG BALANCE STUNTS

Each of the following stands should be done with different arm positions, starting with the arms out to the sides and then folded across the chest. Have children devise other arm positions.

Each stunt can be held first for three seconds and then for five seconds. Later, the child should close eyes during the count. The child should recover to original position without loss of balance or excessive movement. Stunts should be repeated, using the other leg.

1. *Kimbo Stand.* With the left foot kept flat on the ground, cross the right leg over the left to a position in which the right foot is pointed partially down and the toe is touching the ground.

2. *Knee-lift Stand.* From a standing position, lift one knee up so that the thigh is parallel to the ground and the toe is pointed down. Hold. Return to starting position.

3. *Stork Stand.* From a standing position, shift all of the weight to one foot. Place the other foot so that the sole is against the inside of the knee and thigh of the standing leg (see Figure 20.18). Hold. Recover to standing position.

BALANCE TOUCH

Place an object (fleece ball or beanbag) a metre away from a line. Balancing on the line on one foot, reach out with the other foot, touch the object (no weight should be placed on it) (see Figure 20.19), and recover to the starting position. Reach sideward, backward.

Figure 20.18

Stork Stand.

Figure 20.19

Balance Touch.

TEACHING TIP

Variation: Try placing the object at various distances. On a gymnasium floor, count the number of boards to establish the distance for the touch.

SINGLE-LEG BALANCES

1. *Forward Balance.* Extend one leg backward until it is parallel to the floor. Keeping the eyes forward and the arms out to the sides, bend forward, balancing on the other leg (see Figure 20.20). Hold for five seconds without moving. Reverse legs. (This is also called a Forward Scale.)

Figure 20.20

Forward Balance.

2. *Backward Balance.* With knee straight, extend one leg forward, with toes pointed. Keep the arms out to the sides for balance. Lean back as far as possible. The bend should be far enough back so that the eyes are looking at the ceiling.

3. *Side Balance.* Stand on the left foot with enough side bend to the left so that the right (top) side of the body is parallel to the floor. Put the right arm alongside the head and in line with the rest of the body. Reverse, using the right leg for support. (Support may be needed momentarily to get into position.)

HAND-AND-KNEE BALANCE

Get down on all fours, taking the weight on the hands flat to the floor, knees, and feet, and with toes pointed backward. Lift one hand and the opposite knee. Keep the free foot and hand from touching during the hold. Reverse hand and knee positions.

SINGLE-KNEE BALANCE

Perform the same action as in the previous stunt, but balance on one knee (and leg), with both arms outstretched to the sides (see Figure 20.21). Use the other knee.

Individual Stunts

DIRECTIONAL WALK

For a left movement, begin in standing position. Do all of the following simultaneously: Take a step to the left, raise the left arm and point left, turn the head to the left, and state crisply "Left." Close with the right foot back to standing position. Take several steps left and then reverse.

The Directional Walk is designed to aid in establishing right–left concepts. Ingredients of this stunt are definite and forceful simultaneous movements of the arm, head

Figure 20.21

Single-knee Balance.

(turn), and leg (step) coupled with a crisp enunciation of the direction.

LINE WALKING

Use a line on the floor, a chalked line, or a board. Walk forward and backward on the line as follows. First, take regular steps. Next, try follow steps—the front foot moving forward and the back foot moving up. The same foot always leads. Then do heel-and-toe steps, bringing the back toe up against the front heel on each step. Finally, hop along the line on one foot. Change to the other foot. The eyes focus ahead.

TUCK JUMP

From a stand, jump as high as possible (with vigorous arm swing), grasping the knees in the "tuck" position by pulling knees to chest. Bring knees down quickly to cushion landing.

DUCK

Start in a kneeling position with hands and knees. On the "Duck" signal, stretch out arms and legs to flop to mat. Keep head up and use arms and hands to cushion fall.

FLUTTERING LEAF

Keeping the feet in place and the body relaxed, flutter to the ground slowly, just as a leaf would do in autumn. Swing the arms back and forth loosely to accentuate the fluttering.

ELEVATOR

With the arms out level at the sides, pretend to be an elevator going down. Lower the body a little at a time by bending the knees, but keep the upper body erect and the eyes forward. Return to position. Add a body twist to the downward movement. (Try using a drum.)

CROSS-LEGGED STAND

Sit with the legs crossed and the body bent partially forward. Respond appropriately to these six commands:

"Touch the right foot with the right hand."

"Touch the left foot with the right hand."

"Touch the right foot with the left hand."

"Touch the left foot with the left hand."

"Touch both feet with the hands."

"Touch the feet with crossed hands."

Give the commands in varied sequences. The child must interpret that his right foot is on the left side, and vice versa. If this seems too difficult, have children start with the feet in normal position (uncrossed).

TEACHING TIP

Variation: Have the children do the stunt with a partner, one child giving the commands and the other responding as directed.

WALKING IN PLACE

Pretend to walk vigorously by using the same movements as in walking but without making any progress. This is done by sliding the feet back and forth. Make exaggerated arm movements. (Children can gain or lose a little ground. Two children can walk alongside each other, with first one and then the other going ahead.)

JUMP TURNS

Do jump turns (use quarter turns and half turns) right and left, as directed. The arms should be kept outstretched to the sides. Land lightly without a second movement. Jump turns reinforce directional concepts. Number concepts can also be developed with jump turns. Call out the number as a preparatory command and then say, "Move." Number signals are as follows: "One" for a left quarter-turn, "Two" for a right quarter-turn, "Three" for a left half-turn, and "Four" for a right half-turn. Give children a moment after the number is called and before the "Move" command.

RUBBER BAND

Get down in a squat position with the hands and arms clasped around the knees. On the command "Stretch, stretch, stretch," stretch as tall and as wide as possible. On the command "Snap," snap back to original position.

TEACHING TIP

Variation: Pumping Up the Balloon. One child, the pumper, is in front of the other children, who are the balloons. The pumper pretends to use a bicycle pump to inflate the balloons. The balloons get larger and larger until the pumper shouts "Bang," whereupon the balloons collapse to the floor. The pumper should give a *"shoosh"* sound every time a pumping motion is made.

RISING SUN

Lie on the back. Using the arms for balance only, rise to a standing position.

TEACHING TIP

Variation: Fold the arms over the chest. Experiment with different positions of the feet. The feet can be crossed, spread wide, both to one side, and so on.

Figure 20.22

Heel Click.

HEEL CLICK

Stand with the feet slightly apart, jump up, and click the heels, coming down with the feet apart (see Figure 20.22). Try with a quarter turn right and left.

TEACHING TIPS

Variations:

1. Clap the hands overhead as the heels are clicked.

2. Join hands with one or more children. Count "One, two, THREE," jumping on the third count.

3. Begin with a cross-step to the side, then click the heels. Try both right and left.

4. Try to click the heels twice before landing. Land with the feet apart.

LOWERING THE BOOM

Start in push-up (front-leaning rest) position. Lower the body slowly to the floor. The movement should be controlled so that the body remains rigid.

TEACHING TIPS

Variations:

1. Pause halfway down.

2. Go down in stages, 2 to 3 cm at a time.

3. Go down slowly to the accompaniment of noise simulating air escaping from a punctured tire. Try representing a blowout, initiated by an appropriate noise.

4. Go down in stages by alternating lowering movements of the right and left arms.

5. Vary the stunt with different hand-base positions, such as fingers pointed in, thumbs touching, and others.

TURN-OVER

From a front-leaning rest position, turn over so that the back is to the floor. The body should not touch the floor. Continue the turn until the original position is reassumed. Reverse the direction. Turn back and forth several times. The body should be kept as rigid as possible throughout the turn.

THREAD THE NEEDLE

Touch the fingertips together in front of the body. Step through with one foot at a time while keeping the tips in contact (see Figure 20.23). Step back to the original position. Next, lock the fingers in front of the body, and repeat the stunt. Finally, step through the clasped hands without touching the hands.

HEEL SLAP

From an erect position with hands at the sides, jump upward and slap both heels with the hands (see Figure 20.24).

TEACHING TIP

Variation: Use a one-two-three rhythm with small preliminary jumps on the first and second counts. Make a quarter or half turn in the air. During a jump, slap the heels twice before landing.

Figure 20.23

Thread the Needle.

Figure 20.24

Heel Slap.

POGO STICK

Pretend to be on a pogo stick by keeping a stiff body and jumping on the toes. Hold the hands in front as if grasping the stick (see Figure 20.25). Progress in various directions. (The teacher should stress upward propelling action by the ankles and toes, with the body kept stiff, particularly at the knee joints.)

Figure 20.25

Pogo Stick.

TOP

From a standing position with arms at the sides, try jumping and turning to face the opposite direction, turning three-quarters of the way around, or making a full turn to face the original direction. Land in good balance with hands near the sides. No movement of the feet should occur after landing. Turn both right and left. (Number concepts can be stressed in having children do half turns, three-quarter turns, and full turns.)

TEACHING TIP

Variation: Fold the arms across the chest.

TURK STAND

Stand with feet apart and arms folded in front. Pivot on the balls of both feet, and face the opposite direction. The legs are now crossed. Sit down in this position. Reverse the process. Get up without using the hands for aid, and uncross the legs with a pivot to face in the original direction. Little change should occur in foot position (see Figure 20.26).

PUSH-UP

From a front-leaning rest position, lower the body and push up, back to original position. Be sure that the only movement is in the arms, with the body kept rigid. (Because the Push-up is used in many exercises and testing programs, it is important for children to learn proper execution early.)

TEACHING TIP

Variation: Stop halfway down and halfway up. Go up and down by a few centimetres.

Figure 20.26

Turk Stand.

Figure 20.27

Crazy Walk.

CRAZY WALK

Progress forward in an erect position by bringing one foot behind and around the other to gain a little ground each time (see Figure 20.27).

TEACHING TIP

Variation: Reverse the movements and go backward. This means bringing the foot in front and around to gain distance in back.

SEAT CIRCLE

Sit on the floor, with knees bent and hands braced behind and flat to the floor. Lift the feet off the floor and push with the hands, so that the body spins in a circle with the seat as a pivot. Spin right and left.

TEACHING TIP

Variation: Place a beanbag between the knees or on the toes and spin without dropping it.

Partner and Group Stunts

BOUNCING BALL

Toss a lively utility ball into the air and watch how it bounces lower and lower until it finally comes to rest on the floor. From a bent-knee position with the upper body erect, imitate the ball by beginning with a high bounce and gradually lowering the height of the jump to simulate the ball coming to rest. Children should push off from the floor with the hands to gain additional height and should absorb part of the body weight with their hands as well. Toss a real ball into the air and move with the ball.

TEACHING TIP

Variation: Try this with a partner, one partner serving as the bouncer and the other as the ball (see Figure 20.28). Reverse positions. Try having one partner dribble the ball in various positions.

SEESAW

Face and join hands with a partner. Move the seesaw up and down, one child stooping while the other rises.

WRING THE DISHRAG

Face and join hands with a partner. Raise one pair of arms (right for one and left for the other) and turn under, continuing a full turn until back to original position (see Figure 20.29). Take care not to bump heads. Reverse.

TEACHING TIP

Variation: Try the stunt at a lower level, using a crouched position.

PARTNER TOE TOUCHER

Partners lie on their backs with heads near each other and feet in opposite directions. Join arms with partner using a

Figure 20.28

Bouncing Ball.

Figure 20.29

Wring the Dishrag.

hand–wrist grip, and bring the legs up so that the toes touch partner's toes. Keep high on the shoulders and touch the feet high (see Figure 20.30). Strive to attain the high shoulder position, as this is the point of most difficulty. (Partners should be of about the same height.)

TEACHING TIP

Variation: One child carries a beanbag, a ball, or some other article between the feet, and transfers the object to the partner, who lowers it to the floor.

Figure 20.30

Partner Toe Toucher.

Figure 20.31

Double Top.

DOUBLE TOP

Face partner and join hands. Experiment to see which type of grip works best. With straight arms, lean away from each other and at the same time move the toes close to partner's (see Figure 20.31). Spin around slowly in either direction, taking tiny steps. Increase speed.

ROLY-POLY

Review the Rolling Log. Four or five children lie facedown on the floor, side by side. The last child does a Rolling Log over the others and then takes a place at the end. Continue until all have rolled twice.

Developmental Level II Activities

In developmental level II, more emphasis is placed on form and quality of performance than at the previous level. Stunts such as the Frog Handstand, Mule Kick, Teeter-Totter, and Handstand give children experience in taking the weight totally on the hands. Partner support stunts are introduced. Falls to hands are another addition.

Animal Movements

CRICKET WALK

Squat. Spread the knees. Put the arms between the knees and grasp the outside of the ankles with the hands. Walk forward or backward. Turn around right and left. See what happens when both feet are moved at once!

Figure 20.32

Frog Jump.

Figure 20.33

Seal Crawl.

FROG JUMP

From a squatting position, with hands on the floor slightly in front of the feet, jump forward a short distance, landing on the hands and feet simultaneously (see Figure 20.32). Note the difference between this stunt and the Rabbit Jump. Emphasis eventually should be on both height and distance. The hands and arms absorb part of the landing impact to prevent excessive strain on the knees.

SEAL CRAWL

Start in the front-leaning rest position, the weight supported on straightened arms and toes. Keeping the body straight, walk forward, using the hands for propelling force and dragging the feet (see Figure 20.33). Keep the body straight and the head up.

TEACHING TIPS

Variations:

1. Crawl forward a short distance and then roll over on the back, clapping the hands like a seal.

2. Crawl with the fingers pointed in different directions, out and in.

3. Reverse Seal Crawl. Turn over and attempt the crawl, dragging the heels.

MEASURING WORM

From a front-leaning rest position, keeping the knees stiff, inch the feet up as close as possible to the hands. Regain position by inching forward with the hands. Keep the knees straight, with the necessary bending occurring at the hips (see Figure 20.34).

MULE KICK

Stoop down and place the hands on the floor in front of the feet. The arms are the front legs of the mule. Kick out with the legs while the weight is supported momentarily on the arms (see Figure 20.35). Taking the weight on the hands is important. The stunt can be learned in two stages. First, practise taking the weight momentarily on the hands. Next, add the kick.

TEACHING TIP

Variation: Make two kicks before the feet return to the ground.

WALRUS WALK

Begin in a front-leaning rest position, with fingers pointed outward. Make progress by moving both hands forward at the same time (see Figure 20.36). Try to clap the hands with each step. (Before doing this stunt, review the similar Seal Crawl—see Figure 20.33—and its variations.)

Figure 20.34

Measuring Worm.

Figure 20.35

Mule Kick.

Variation: Move sideways so that the upper part of the body describes an arc while the feet hold position.

DOUBLE-LAME DOG

Support the body on one hand and one leg (see Figure 20.37). Move forward in this position, maintaining balance. The distance should be short (1 to 2 m), as this stunt is strenuous. Different leg–arm combinations should be employed, such as cross-lateral movements (right arm with left leg and left arm with right leg).

TEACHING TIP

Variation: Keep the free arm on the hip.

TURTLE

Hold the body in a wide push-up position with the feet apart and the hands widely spread (see Figure 20.38). From this position, move in various directions, keeping the plane of the body always about the same distance from the floor. Movements of the hands and feet should occur in small increments only.

WALRUS SLAP

From the front-leaning rest position, push the body up in the air quickly by force of the arms, clap the hands together, and recover to position. Before doing this stunt, review the Seal Crawl and the Walrus Walk.

TEACHING TIPS

Variations:

1. Try clapping the hands more than once.

2. Move forward while clapping the hands.

3. Reverse Walrus Slap. Turn over and do a Walrus Walk while facing the ceiling. Clapping the hands is quite difficult in this position and should be attempted only by the more skilled. Work on a mat.

Figure 20.36

Walrus Walk.

Figure 20.37

Double-lame Dog.

Figure 20.38

Turtle.

Rolls and Inverted Balances

FORWARD ROLL TO A WALKOUT

Perform the Forward Roll as described previously, except walk out to a standing position. The key to the Walkout is to develop enough momentum to allow a return to the feet. The leg that first absorbs the weight is bent while the other leg is kept straight.

BACKWARD ROLL (REGULAR)

In the same squat position as for the Forward Roll, but with the back to the direction of the roll, push off quickly with the hands, sit down, and start rolling over onto the back. The knees are brought to the chest, so that the body is tucked and momentum is increased. Quickly bring the hands up over the shoulders, with palms up and fingers pointed backward. Continue rolling backward with knees close to the chest. The hands touch the mat at about the same time as the head. It is necessary at this point to push hard with the hands to release pressure on the neck. Continue to roll over and to push off the mat until the roll is completed (see Figure 20.39). Emphasize proper hand position by telling children to point their thumbs toward their ears and spread their fingers for better push-off control.

BACKWARD SHOULDER ROLL

Start from a squat position. Fall backward onto the hands (hands pointing forward). Next roll onto the back, lifting knees overhead to one side of the head (across one shoulder). Continue rolling over shoulder, ending in a kneeling position.

BACKWARD ROLL (INCLINED)

If possible, the Backward Roll should be practised on an inclined mat. The gentle incline allows the youngster to learn to develop momentum in a nonthreatening manner. An inclined mat can be made by leaving one mat folded and laying a crash pad or another mat over it.

HEADSTAND

Two approaches are suggested for the Headstand. The first is to relate the Headstand to the Climb-up, and the second is to go directly into a Headstand, using a kick-up to achieve the inverted position. With either method, it is essential to maintain the triangle position of the hands and the head.

In the final inverted position, the feet should be together, with legs straight and toes pointed. The weight is evenly distributed among the three points—the two hands and the forward part of the head. The body should be aligned as straight as possible.

The safest way to come down from the inverted position is to return to the mat in the direction that was used in going up. Recovery is helped by bending at both the waist and the knees. The child should be instructed, in the case of overbalancing, to tuck the head under and go into a Forward Roll. Include both methods of recovery from the inverted position in the instructional sequences early in the presentation.

HEADSTAND CLIMB-UP

Take the inverted position of the Climb-up and move the feet slowly upward to the Headstand position (see Figure 20.40). A spotter may steady the hips and upper thighs as needed.

Figure 20.39

Regular Backward Roll.

Figure 20.40

Headstand based on Climb-up.

Keeping the weight on the forward part of the head and maintaining the triangle base, walk the feet forward until the hips are high over the body, somewhat similar to the Climb-up position. Keep one foot on the mat, with the knee of that leg bent, and the other leg extended somewhat backward. Kick the back leg up to the inverted position, following quickly with a push by the other leg, thus bringing the two legs together in the inverted position (see Figure 20.41). The timing is a quick one–two movement.

Emphasize the importance of the triangle formed by the hands and the head and the importance of having the weight centred on the forward part of the head. Most problems that occur during performance of the Headstand come from an incorrect head–hand relationship. The correct positioning has the head placed the length of the performer's forearm from the knees and the hands placed at the knees. A useful technique to aid children in finding the proper triangle is to mark the three spots on the mat with chalk.

It is not desirable to let children stay too long in the inverted position or to hold contests to see who can remain in the Headstand longest. The responsibility for getting into the inverted position should rest with the performer. Spotters may help some by stabilizing hips and upper thighs, but they should avoid wrestling the performer up. The goal of the kick-up method is to establish a pattern that can be used in other inverted stunts.

Squat down on the mat, placing the hands flat, with fingers pointing forward and elbows inside and pressed against the inner part of the knees. Lean forward, using the leverage of the elbows against the knees, and balance on the hands (see Figure 20.42). Hold for five seconds. Return to position. The head does not touch the mat at any time. The hands

Figure 20.42

Frog Handstand.

may be turned in slightly if this makes better contact between the elbows and the insides of the thighs. (This stunt follows from the Three-point Tip-up.)

This comprises continued lead-up activity for the Handstand. Begin in the lunge position and shift the weight to the hands. Kick the legs up in the air to a 135-degree angle, then return to the feet. This activity is similar to the Switcheroo, except that the feet are kicked higher without switching foot position.

Start with the body in an erect position, arms outspread and legs shoulder width apart. Bend the body to the right and place the right hand on the floor. Follow this, in sequence, by the left hand, the left foot, and the right foot (see Figure 20.43). Perform with a steady rhythm. Each body part should touch the floor at evenly spaced intervals. The body should be straight and extended when in the

Figure 20.41

Headstand based on Kick-up.

Figure 20.43

Cartwheel.

inverted position. The entire body must be in the same plane throughout the stunt, and the feet must pass directly over the head.

Children who have difficulty with the Cartwheel should be instructed to concentrate on taking the weight of the body on the hands in succession. They need to get the feel of the weight support and later can concentrate on getting the body into proper position. After the class has had some practice in doing Cartwheels, a running approach with a skip can be added before takeoff.

FORWARD ROLL (PIKE POSITION)

Begin the piked Forward Roll in a standing pike position. Keep the legs straight and bend forward at the hips. Place the hands on the mat, bend the elbows, and lower the head to the mat. Keep the legs straight until nearing the end of the roll. Bend at the knees to facilitate returning to the feet.

FORWARD ROLL COMBINATIONS

Review the Forward Roll, with increased emphasis on proper form. Combinations such as the following can be introduced:

1. Do a Forward Roll preceded by a short run.
2. Do two Forward Rolls in succession.
3. Do a Forward Roll to a vertical jump in the air, and repeat.

BACKWARD ROLL COMBINATIONS

Review the Backward Roll. Continue emphasis on the push-off with the hands. Also teach these combinations:

1. Do a Backward Roll to a standing position. A strong push by the hands is necessary to provide enough momentum to land on the feet.
2. Do two Backward Rolls in succession.
3. Add a jump in the air at the completion of a Backward Roll.

TEETER-TOTTER

The Teeter-Totter is the final lead-up activity for the Handstand. It is performed in a manner similar to the Half Teeter-Totter, except that the feet are held together for a moment in the handstand position before returning to the standing position.

HANDSTAND

Start in the lunge position. Do a Teeter-Totter to the inverted position. The body, which is extended in a line from the shoulders through the feet, should be kept straight with the head down. It is helpful to teach the correct position first in a standing position with the arms overhead and the ears between the arms.

Figure 20.44

Single spotting for handstand, first stage. (The performer's shoulder is against the spotter's leg.)

In single spotting, the spotter takes a stride position, with the forward knee bent somewhat (see Figure 20.44). The performer's weight is transferred over the hands, and the body goes into the Handstand position with a one–two Kick-up. The performer must be able to kick up to vertical under his or her own power. The spotter stabilizes the hips, but does not help pull the performer into a vertical position.

Balance Stunts

ONE-LEG BALANCE REVERSE

Assume a forward balance position. In a quick movement, to give momentum, swing the free leg down and change to the same forward balance position facing in the opposite direction (a 180-degree turn) (see Figure 20.45). No unnecessary movement of the supporting foot should be made after the turn is completed. The swinging foot should not touch the floor.

Figure 20.45

One-leg Balance Reverse.

Figure 20.46

Tummy Balance.

TUMMY BALANCE

Lie prone on the floor with arms outstretched forward or to the sides, with palms down. Raise the arms, head, chest, and legs from the floor and balance on the tummy (see Figure 20.46). The knees should be kept straight.

LEG DIP

Extend both hands and one leg forward, balancing on the other leg. Lower the body to sit on the heel and return without losing the balance or touching the floor with any part of the body. Try with the other foot. (Another child can assist from the back by applying upward pressure to the elbows.)

BALANCE JUMP

With hands and arms out to the sides and body parallel to the ground, extend one leg back and balance the weight on the other leg (see Figure 20.47). Quickly change balance

Figure 20.47

Balance Jump, starting position.

Figure 20.48

Balance Jump.

to the other foot, maintaining the initial position but with the feet exchanged (see Figure 20.48). Keep the body parallel to the ground during the change of legs. Try with arms outstretched forward. Working in pairs might be helpful. One student provides feedback for a partner's performance to make sure that the arms and body are straight and parallel to the floor.

SEAT BALANCE

Sit on the floor, holding the ankles in front, with elbows inside the knees. The feet are flat on the floor, and the knees are bent at approximately a right angle. Raise the legs (toes pointed) so that the knees are straight (see Figure 20.49), and balance on the seat for five seconds.

FACE-TO-KNEE TOUCH

Begin in a standing position with feet together. Placing the hands on the hips, balance on one foot, with the other leg extended backward. Bend the trunk forward and touch the knee of the supporting leg with the forehead (see Figure 20.50). Recover to original position.

Teachers can have children begin by keeping the arms away from the sides for balance and then stipulate the

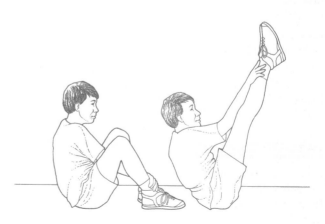

Figure 20.49

Seat Balance.

Figure 20.50

Face-to-Knee Touch.

hands-on-hips position later. In the learning stages, the teacher can assist from behind by supporting the leg extended backward, or the child can place one hand against a wall.

Individual Stunts

REACH-UNDER

Take a position with the feet pointed ahead (spaced about 60 cm apart) and toes against a line or a floor board. Place a beanbag two boards in front of, and midway between, the feet. Without changing the position of the feet, reach one hand behind and between the legs to pick up the beanbag. Now pick it up with the other hand. Repeat, moving the beanbag a board farther away each time.

TEACHING TIP

Variation: Allow the heels to lift off the floor.

STIFF PERSON BEND

Place the feet about shoulder-width apart and pointed forward. Place a beanbag a few centimetres behind the right heel. Grasp the left toes with the left hand, thumb on top. Without bending the knees, reach the right hand outside the right leg and pick up the beanbag without releasing the hold on the left toes. Gradually increase the distance of the reach. Reverse sides (see Figure 20.51).

COFFEE GRINDER

Put one hand on the floor and extend the body to the floor on that side in a side-leaning rest position. Walk around the hand, making a complete circle and keeping the body straight (see Figure 20.52). The stunt should be done slowly, with controlled movements. The body should remain straight throughout the circle movement.

Figure 20.51

Stiff Person Bend.

SCOOTER

Sit on the floor with legs extended, arms folded in front of the chest, and chin held high. To scoot, pull the seat toward the heels, using heel pressure and lifting the seat slightly

Figure 20.52

Coffee Grinder.

Figure 20.53

Scooter.

Figure 20.54

Long Bridge.

(see Figure 20.53). Extend the legs forward again and repeat the process. (This is an excellent activity for abdominal development.)

HIP WALK

Sit in the same position as for the Scooter, but with arms in thrust position and hands making a partial fist. Progress forward by alternate leg–seat movements. The arm–leg coordination is unilateral.

LONG BRIDGE

Begin in a crouched position with hands on the floor and knees between the arms. Push the hands forward a little at a time until an extended push-up position is reached (see Figure 20.54). Return to original position. (The teacher should challenge children to extend as far forward as they can and still retain the support.)

TEACHING TIPS

Variations:

1. Begin with a forward movement, then change to a sideward movement, establishing as wide a spread as possible.

2. Work from a crossed-hands position.

HEELSTAND

Begin in a full-squat position with the arms dangling at the sides. Jump upward to full leg extension with the weight on both heels and fling the arms out diagonally. Hold momentarily, and then return to start position (see Figure 20.55). Several movements can be done rhythmically in succession.

KNEE JUMP TO STANDING

Kneel, with seat touching the heels and toes pointing backward (top of feet against the floor). Jump to a standing position with a vigorous upward swing of the arms (see Figure 20.56).

TEACHING TIP

Variation: Jump to a standing position, doing a quarter turn in the air in one quick motion. Try a half turn.

INDIVIDUAL DROPS OR FALLS

Drops, or falls, can challenge children to achieve good body control. Mats should be used. The hands and arms absorb the

Figure 20.55

Heelstand.

Figure 20.56

Knee Jump to Standing.

impact of a forward fall. During the fall, the body should maintain a straight-line position. Make sure that little change in body angle occurs, particularly at the knees and waist.

KNEE DROP

Kneel on a mat, with the body upright. Raise the feet up off the floor, and fall forward, breaking the fall with the hands and arms (see Figure 20.57).

FORWARD DROP

From a forward balance position on one leg with the other leg extended backward and the arms extended forward and up, lean forward slowly, bringing the arms toward the floor. Continue to drop forward slowly until over-balanced, then let the hands and arms break the fall (see Figure 20.58). The head is up and the extended leg is raised high, with knee joints kept reasonably straight. Repeat, changing position of the legs.

DEAD BODY FALL

Fall forward from an erect position to a down push-up position (see Figure 20.59). A slight bend at the waist is

Figure 20.58

8 Forward Drop.

permissible, but the knees should be kept straight, and there should be no forward movement of the feet.

TANGLEFOOT

Stand with heels together and toes pointed out. Bend the trunk forward and extend both arms down between the knees and around behind the ankles. Bring the hands around the outside of the ankles from behind and touch the fingers to each other (see Figure 20.60). Hold for a five-second count.

EGG ROLL

In a sitting position, assume the same clasped-hands position as for Tanglefoot. Roll sideways over one shoulder, then to the back, then to the other shoulder, and finally back up to the sitting position (see Figure 20.61). The movements are repeated in turn to make a full circle back to place. The secret is a vigorous sideward movement to secure initial momentum. If mats are used, two should be placed side by side to cover the extent of the roll. (Some children can do this stunt more effectively from a crossed-ankle position.)

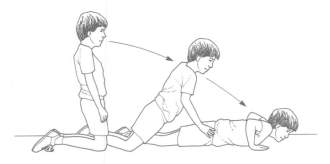

Figure 20.57

Knee Drop.

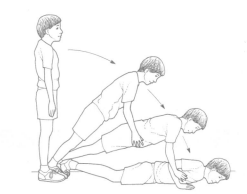

Figure 20.59

Dead Body Fall.

Figure 20.60

Tanglefoot.

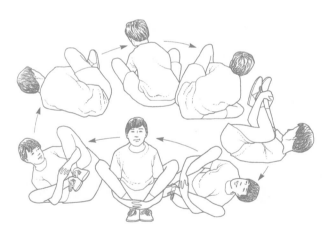

Figure 20.61

Egg Roll.

Figure 20.62

Toe Tug Walk.

Partner and Group Stunts

PARTNER HOPPING

Partners coordinate hopping movements for short distances and in different directions and turns. Three combinations are suggested.

1. Stand facing each other. Extend the right leg forward to be grasped at the ankle by partner's left hand. Hold right hands and hop on the left leg (see Figure 20.63).

2. Stand back to back. Lift the leg backward, bending the knee, and have partner grasp the ankle. Hop as before.

3. Stand side by side with inside arms around each other's waist. Lift the inside foot from the floor and make progress by hopping on the outside foot.

If either partner begins to fall, the other should release the leg immediately. Reverse foot positions.

PARTNER TWISTER

Partners face and grasp right hands as if shaking hands. One partner swings the left leg over the head of the other and turns around, taking a straddle position over partner's arm (see Figure 20.64). The other swings the right leg over the first partner, who has bent over, and the partners are

TOE TUG WALK

Bend over and grasp the toes with thumbs on top (see Figure 20.62). Keep the knees bent slightly and the eyes forward. Walk forward without losing the grip on the toes. Walk backward and sideward to provide more challenge. Walk in various geometric patterns, such as a circle, triangle, or square. (This stunt can be introduced in an easier version by having children grasp the ankles, thumbs on the insides, and perform the desired movements.)

Figure 20.63

Partner Hopping.

now back to back. First partner continues with the right leg and faces in the original direction. Second partner swings the left leg over the partner's back to return to the original face-to-face position. Partners need to duck to avoid being kicked by each other's feet as the legs are swung over.

TEACHING TIP

Variation: The stunt can be introduced by grasping a wand instead of holding hands.

Figure 20.64

Partner Twister.

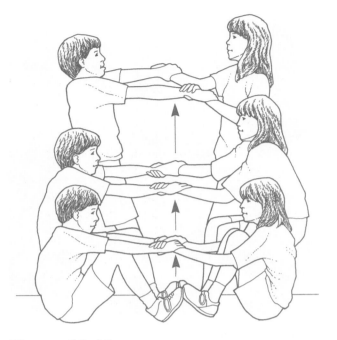

Figure 20.65

Partner Pull-up.

PARTNER PULL-UP

Partners sit facing each other in a bent-knee position, with heels on the floor and toes touching. Pulling cooperatively, they come to a standing position (see Figure 20.65).

TEACHING TIP

Variation: Try with feet flat on the floor.

BACK-TO-BACK GET-UP

Partners sit back to back and lock arms. From this position, they try to stand by pushing against each other's back (see Figure 20.66). Sit down again. If the feet are sliding, do the stunt on a mat.

Figure 20.66

Back-to-Back Get-up.

Variations:

1. Try with three or four children.

2. Try from a halfway-down position, and move like a spider.

ROWBOAT

Partners sit on the floor or on a mat, facing each other with legs apart and feet touching. Both grasp partner's forearms. Pretend to row a boat. Seek a wide range of movement in the forward–backward rowing motion.

LEAPFROG

One student forms a back. A leaper takes a running start, lays hands flat on the back at the shoulders, and vaults over the low student. Backs are formed at various heights (see Figure 20.67). To form a low back, crouch down on the knees, curling into a tight ball with the head tucked well down. To form a medium back, reach down the outside of the legs from a standing position and grasp the ankles. The feet should be reasonably spread and the knees straight. The position must be stable in order to absorb the shock of the leaper. To form a high back, stand stiff-legged, bend over, and brace arms against the knees. The feet should be spread, the head down, and the body braced to absorb the vault.

Leapfrog is a traditional physical education activity, but the movement is actually a jump-and-vault pattern. The takeoff must be made with both feet. At the height of the jump, the chest and head must be held erect to avoid a forward fall. The teacher should emphasize a forceful jump to achieve height, coordinated with light hand pressure to vault over the back. Landing should be done lightly and under good control, with a bent-knee action.

Figure 20.67

High, medium, and low Leapfrog positions.

Variations:

1. Work in pairs. Alternate leaping and forming the back while progressing around the room.

2. Have more than one back for a series of jumps.

3. Using the medium back, vault from the side rather than from the front. The vaulter's legs must be well spread, and the back must keep the head well tucked down.

4. Following the Leapfrog, do a Forward Roll on a mat.

WHEELBARROW

One partner gets down on the hands with feet extended to the rear and legs apart. The other partner (the pusher) grasps partner's legs on upper thighs, just above the knees. The wheelbarrow walks forward on the hands, supported by the pusher. Movements should be under good control.

The pusher must not push too fast. The wheelbarrow should have the head up and look forward. Fingers should be pointed forward and well spread, with the pads of the fingers supporting much of the weight. The pusher should keep the arms extended.

DUMP THE WHEELBARROW

Get into the wheelbarrow position. Walk the wheelbarrow over to a mat. The lower child ducks the head (chin to waist), raises the seat (bending at the waist), and exits from the stunt with a Forward Roll. The pusher gives a little push and a lift of the feet to help supply momentum.

Partner Support Stunts

Several considerations are important in the conducting of partner support stunts at this level. The lower child (the support) should keep the body as level as possible. This means widening the hand base so that the shoulders are more nearly level with the hips. The support performer must be strong enough to handle the support chores. The top child should avoid stepping on the small of the lower child's back. When holding the final pose, the top child should fix the gaze forward and relax as much as possible while maintaining the position.

DOUBLE BEAR

The bottom child gets down on the hands and knees. The top child assumes the same position directly above the support, with hands on the shoulders and knees on the hips of the support (see Figure 20.68). Touch up the final position by holding heads up and backs straight.

TABLE

The bottom performer assumes a crab position. The top performer straddles this base, facing the rear, and positions

Figure 20.68

Double Bear.

the hands on the base's shoulders, fingers pointing toward the ground. The top child then places the feet on top of the base's knees, forming one crab position on top of another (see Figure 20.69). As a final touch, the heads are positioned so that the eyes look up toward the ceiling, and the seats are lifted so that the backs are straight.

HIP–SHOULDER STAND

The support is on the hands and knees, with hands positioned out somewhat so that the back is level. The top child faces to

Figure 20.69

Table.

the side and steps up, first with one foot on support's hips and then with the other on the shoulders (see Figure 20.70).

A spotter should stand on the opposite side and aid in the mounting. The spotter must take care to avoid stepping on the small of the support's back.

Developmental Level III Activities

Children at this level should be skillful in both the Forward and the Backward Roll. Routines involving these rolls can also be expanded. The Judo Roll, Cartwheel with Round-off, and Double Roll continue the mat-type activities. Improvement in the Headstand is expected. Such stunts as the Front Seat Support, Straddle Press to Headstand, and Walk-over provide sufficient breadth for even the most skilled. It is unrealistic to expect all children to accomplish the entire list of stunts at this level.

Particular attention should be paid to the gymnastics-type stunts. Although there is still opportunity at this level for exploration and individual expression, more emphasis is placed on execution and form.

Rolls and Inverted Balances

FORWARD AND BACKWARD ROLL COMBINATIONS

Combinations from developmental level II should be reviewed. The following routines can be added:

Figure 20.70

Hip–Shoulder Stand.

Figure 20.71

Alternating Forward and Backward Rolls.

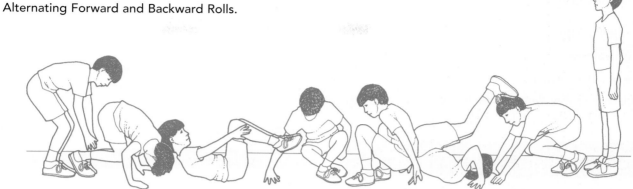

1. Begin with a Forward Roll, coming to a standing position with feet crossed. Pivot the body to uncross the feet. Square shoulders to the line of direction for the Backward Roll (see Figure 20.71).

2. Hold the toes, heels, ankles, or a wand while rolling. Use different arm positions, such as out to the sides or folded across the chest. Use a wide straddle position for both the Forward Roll and the Backward Roll.

BACK EXTENSION

Carry the Backward Roll to the point where the feet are above and over the head. Push off vigorously with the hands, shoot the feet into the air, and land on the feet.

HEADSTAND VARIATIONS

Review the various aspects of the Headstand, using the single-spotter technique as needed. Vary with different leg positions. Add the two-foot recovery. After the stand has been held, recover by bending at the waist and knees, pushing off with the hands, and landing on the feet back in the original position.

HANDSTAND AGAINST A WALL

Using a wall as support, do a Handstand. The arms must be kept straight, with the head between the arms. Some performers like to bend the knees so that the soles of the feet are against the wall.

A critical point in the Handstand against a Wall is to position the hands the correct distance from the wall. It is better to be too close than too far. Being too far can cause the performer to collapse before the feet gain the support of the wall. Use a mat in the preliminary stages.

FREESTANDING HANDSTAND

Perform a Handstand without support. Students must learn to turn the body when a fall is imminent, so that

they land on the feet. Move the hands to help control the balance.

CARTWHEEL AND ROUND-OFF

Practise the Cartwheel, adding a light run with a skip for a takeoff. To change to a Round-off, place the hands somewhat closer together during the early Cartwheel action. Bring the feet together and make a quarter turn to land on both feet, with the body facing the starting point. A Backward Roll can follow the Round-off.

JUDO ROLL

For a left Judo Roll, stand facing the mat with the feet well apart and the left arm extended at shoulder height. Bring the arm down and throw the left shoulder toward the mat in a rolling motion, with the roll made on the shoulder and the upper part of the back (see Figure 20.72). Reverse for a right Judo Roll. Both right and left Judo Rolls should be practised. Later, a short run and a double-foot takeoff should precede the roll. The Judo Roll is a basic safety device to prevent injury from tripping and falling. Rolling and taking the fall lessen the chances of injury. The Judo Roll is essentially a Forward Roll with the head turned to one side. The point of

Figure 20.72

Judo Roll.

impact is the back of one shoulder and the finish is a return to the standing position.

TEACHING TIPS

Variations:

1. Roll to the feet and to a ready position.

2. Place a beanbag about 1 m in front of the toes and go beyond the bag to start the roll.

ADVANCED FORWARD AND BACKWARD ROLL COMBINATIONS

Put together different combinations of Forward Rolls and Backward Rolls. The emphasis should be on choice, exploration, and self-discovery. Variations can involve different approaches, execution acts, and finishes. Try the following variations of the Forward Roll.

1. Roll while holding the toes, heels, or ankles.

2. As above, but cross the hands.

3. Roll with hands on the knees or with a ball between the knees.

4. Roll with arms at the sides, folded across the chest, or on the back of the thighs.

5. Press forward from a front-leaning rest position and go into the roll.

Try the following suggestions with the Backward Roll:

1. Begin with a Stiff-legged Sitdown and go into the roll.

2. Push off into a Back Extension, landing on the feet.

3. Roll to a finish on one foot only.

4. Roll with hands clasped behind the neck.

5. Roll with a ball between the knees.

In addition to these, combine Forward Rolls with Backward Rolls in various ways.

STRADDLE PRESS TO HEADSTAND

Begin by placing the hands and head in the Triangular Headstand position. The feet are in a wide-straddle position and the hips are up. Raise the hips slowly by pressing to a point over the base of support. Slowly raise the legs to a straddle position and finish with the legs brought together in regular Headstand position. All movement is done as a slow, controlled action. (This is a more difficult stunt than the regular Headstand.)

WALKING ON THE HANDS

Walk on the hands in a forward direction, bending the knees slightly, if desired, for balance. (Walking can be done first with a spotter supporting, but this support should be minimal.)

WALK-OVER

Do preliminary movements as if for the Handstand. Let the legs continue beyond the Handstand position and contact the floor with a one–two rhythm. The body must be well arched as the leading foot touches the floor. Push off with the hands and walk out. The spotter gives support under the upper shoulder girdle. Also practise against support such as a stacked mat.

Balance Stunts

V-UP

Lie on the back, with arms overhead and extended. Keeping the knees straight and the feet pointed, bring the legs and the upper body up at the same time to form a V shape. The entire weight is balanced on the seat (see Figure 20.73). Hold the position for five seconds.

This exercise, like the Curl-up, is excellent for development of the abdominal muscles. It is quite similar to the Seat Balance, except for the starting position.

TEACHING TIP

Variation: Place the hands on the floor in back for support. (This makes the stunt easier for those students having trouble.)

PUSH-UP VARIATIONS

Begin the development of Push-up variations by reviewing proper Push-up techniques. The only movement is in the arms. The body should come close to, but not touch, the floor. Explore the following variations.

Monkey Push-up	Point the fingers toward each other. Next, bring the hands close enough for the fingertips to touch.

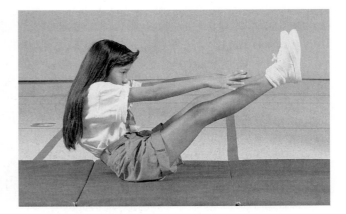

Figure 20.73

V-up.

Circle-O Push-up Combinations	Form a circle with each thumb and forefinger.
Fingertip Push-up	Get up high on the fingertips.
Different Finger	Do a Push-up using the thumb and three or two fingers only.
Extended Push-up	Extend the position of the hands progressively forward or to the sides.
Crossed Push-up	Cross the arms. Cross the legs. Cross both.
One-legged Push-up	Lift one leg from the floor.
One-handed Push-up	Use only one hand, with the other outstretched or on the hip.
Exploratory Approach	See what other types of Push-ups or combinations can be created.

FLIP-FLOP

From a Push-up position, propel the body upward with the hands and feet, doing a Turn-over (see Figure 20.74). Flip back. The stunt should be done on a mat. (Review the Turn-over before having students try this stunt.)

LONG REACH

Place a beanbag about 1 m in front of a line. Keeping the toes behind the line, lean forward on one hand and reach out with the other hand to touch the beanbag (see Figure 20.75). Recover in one clean, quick movement to the original position, lifting the supporting hand off the floor. Increase the distance of the bag from the line.

HANDSTAND STUNTS

Try these challenging activities from the Handstand position against a wall:

1. Turn the body in a complete circle, maintaining foot contact with the wall throughout.

Figure 20.74

Flip-Flop.

Figure 20.75

Long Reach.

2. Shift the support to one hand and hold for a moment.

3. Do an Inverted Push-up, lowering the body by bending the elbows and then returning to Handstand position by straightening the elbows.

FRONT SEAT SUPPORT

Sit on the floor, with the legs together and forward. Place the hands flat on the floor, somewhat between the hips and the knees, with fingers pointed forward. Push down so the hips come off the floor, with the weight supported on the hands and heels. Next, lift the heels and support the entire weight of the body on the hands for three to five seconds. (Someone can help the performer get into position by giving slight support under the heels.)

Individual Stunts

WALL WALK-UP

From a Push-up position with feet against a wall, walk up the wall backward to a Handstand position (see Figure 20.76). Walk down again.

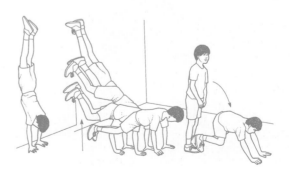

Figure 20.76

Wall Walk-up.

SKIER'S SIT

Assume a sitting position against a wall with the thighs parallel to the floor and the knee joints at right angles. (The position is the same as if sitting in a chair, but, of course, there is no chair.) The hands are placed on the thighs with the feet flat on the floor and the lower legs straight up and down (see Figure 20.77). Try to sit for 30 seconds, 45 seconds, and 1 minute.

The Skier's Sit is an isometric type of activity and is excellent for developing the knee extensor muscles. It is done by skiers to develop the muscles used in skiing.

TEACHING TIP

Variation: Support the body with crossed legs. A more difficult stunt is to support the body on one leg, with the other leg extended forward.

WALK-THROUGH

From a front-leaning rest position, walk the feet through the hands, using tiny steps, until the body is fully extended with the back to the floor (see Figure 20.78). Reverse the body to the original position. The hands stay in contact with the floor throughout.

Figure 20.77

Skier's Sit.

Figure 20.78

Walk-through.

JUMP-THROUGH

Starting in a front-leaning rest position, jump the feet through the arms in one motion. Reverse with another jump and return to original position. The hands must push off sharply from the floor, so the body is high enough off the floor to allow the legs to jump under. (The child may find it easier to swing a little to the side with one leg, going under the lifted hand, as indicated in Figure 20.79).

BOUNCER

Start in a Push-up position. Bounce up and down with the hands and feet leaving the ground at the same time. Try clapping while doing this. Move in various directions. Turn around.

JACKKNIFE

Stand erect with hands out level to the front and a little to the side. Jump up and bring the feet up quickly to touch the hands. Vary by starting with a short run. Be sure the feet come up to the hands, rather than the hands moving down to the feet (see Figure 20.80). Do several Jackknives in succession. The takeoff must be with both feet, and good height must be achieved.

HEEL-AND-TOE SPRING

Place the heels against a line. Jump backward over the line while bent over and grasping the toes. (Lean forward slightly to allow for impetus and then jump backward over the line.) Try jumping forward to original position. To be successful, the child should retain the grasp on the toes.

Figure 20.79

Jump-through.

Figure 20.80

Jackknife.

The teacher can introduce the stunt by first having children grasp their ankles when making the jumps. This is less difficult.

SINGLE-LEG CIRCLE (PINWHEEL)

Assume a squatting position, with both hands on the floor, left knee between the arms and right leg extended to the side. Swing the right leg forward and under the lifted right arm, under the left leg and arm, and back to starting position (see Figure 20.81). Make several circles in succession. Reverse position and try with the left leg.

Figure 20.81

Single-leg Circle (Pinwheel).

Figure 20.82

Double Scooter.

Partner and Group Stunts

DOUBLE SCOOTER

Two children about the same size face each other, sitting on each other's feet (see Figure 20.82). With arms joined, scoot forward or backward with cooperative movements. When one child moves the seat, the other child should help by lifting with the feet. Progress is made by alternately flexing and extending the knees and hips. (Review the Scooter [Figure 20.53] before doing this stunt.)

DOUBLE ROLL

One child lies on a mat with his feet in the direction of the roll. The other takes a position with feet on either side of the first child's head. The first child reaches back and grasps the other's ankles with thumbs on the inside and then raises his own feet, so that the other child can similarly grasp his ankles. The second child propels her hunched body forward, while the first sits up and takes the position originally held by the other (see Figure 20.83). Positions are then reversed and the roll continues.

Be sure that the top child hunches well and ducks the head to cushion the roll on the back of the neck and shoulders. Also, when the top child propels herself forward, bent arms should momentarily take the weight. It is important that the underneath child keeps the knees bent.

Figure 20.83

Double Roll.

TANDEM BICYCLE

One child forms a bicycle position, with back against a wall and knees bent, as if sitting. The feet should be placed under the body. The second child backs up and sits down lightly on the first child's knees. Other children may be added in the same fashion, their hands around the waist of the player immediately in front for support (see Figure 20.84). Moving the feet on the same side together makes forward progress.

CIRCLE HIGH JUMP

Stand in circles of three, each circle having children of somewhat equal height. Join hands. One child tries to jump over the opposite pair of joined hands (see Figure 20.85). To be completely successful, each circle must have each child jump forward in turn over the opposite pair of joined hands. (Jumping backward is not recommended.) To reach good height, an upward lift is necessary. Try two small preliminary jumps before exploding into the jump over the joined hands.

TEACHING TIP

Variation: Precede the jump with a short run by the group. A signal can be sounded so that all know when the jump is to occur during the run.

TRIPLE ROLL

Three children get down on their hands and knees on a mat, with heads all in the same direction to one of the sides. The

Figure 20.85

Circle High Jump.

performers are about 1 m apart. Each is numbered—1, 2, or 3—with the number 1 child in the centre. Number 2 is on the right and number 3 is on the left. Number 1 starts rolling toward and under number 2, who projects upward and over number 1. Number 2 is then in the centre and rolls toward number 3, who projects upward and over number 2. Number 3, in the centre, rolls toward and under number 1, who, after clearing number 3, is back in the centre. Each performer in the centre thus rolls toward and under the outside performer (see Figure 20.86). (Review the Side Roll before doing this stunt.)

Children should be taught that as soon as they roll to the outside, they must get ready to go over the oncoming

Figure 20.84

Tandem Bicycle.

Figure 20.86

Triple Roll.

Figure 20.87

Quintuplet Roll.

child from the centre. There is no time for delay. Very important is the upward projection of the body to allow the rolling child to go under.

QUINTUPLET ROLL

Five children can make up a roll series. They are numbered 1 through 5, as shown in Figure 20.87. Numbers 3 and 5 begin by going over numbers 2 and 4, respectively, who roll under. Number 1 goes over number 3 as soon as possible. Each then continues to go alternately over and under.

DEAD PERSON LIFT

One child lies facing the ceiling, with body stiff and arms at the sides. Two helpers stand, one on each side of the "dead" person, with hands at the back of the neck and fingers touching. Working together, they lift the child, who remains rigid, to a standing position (see Figure 20.88). From this position, the child is released and falls forward in a Dead Body Fall.

INJURED PERSON CARRY

The "injured" child lies on the back. Six children, three on each side, kneel down to do the carry. The lifters work their hands, palms upward, under the person to form a human stretcher, then lift up (see Figure 20.89). (The "injured" child must maintain a stiff position.) They walk a short distance and set the person down carefully.

MERRY-GO-ROUND

From 8 to 12 children are needed. Half of the children form a circle with joined hands, using a wrist grip. The remaining children, the riders, stand within the circle and each one leans back against a pair of joined hands. The riders stretch out their bodies, faces up, toward the centre of the circle, with the weight on the heels. Each rider then connects hands, behind the circle of standing children, with the riders on either side. There are two sets of joined hands—the first circle, or merry-go-round, and the riders (see Figure 20.90). The movement of the Merry-Go-Round is counterclockwise. The circle children, who provide the support, use sidesteps. The riders keep pace, taking small steps with their heels.

Figure 20.88

Dead Person Lift.

Figure 20.89

Injured Person Carry.

Figure 20.90

Merry-Go-Round.

Developing Gymnastics Routines

The teacher can put together in sequence various stunts and other movements. The problems might be structured in the following way:

1. Specify the number and kind of stunts and movements to be done and the sequence to be followed. For example, tell the child to do a balance stunt, a locomotor movement, and a rolling stunt.

2. Arrange the mats in some prescribed order so that they become the key to the movement problems. Two or three might be placed in succession, three or four in a U shape, or four in a hollow-square formation. There should be some space between mats, depending on the conditions stated in the problem. The problem could be presented like this: "On the first mat, do a Forward Roll variation and then a movement to the next mat on all fours. On the second mat, do some kind of balance stunt, and then proceed to the next mat with a jumping or hopping movement. On the third mat, you have a choice of activity." The problem can also be stated in more general terms, and children can do a different stunt or variation on each mat and a different movement between mats.

3. Have partners work out a series of stunts. The paired children should be of equal size and strength so that they can alternate as the support. After children have practised for a period of time, each partnership can demonstrate the routines they have developed.

Partner Support Stunts

The basic instructions for partner support stunts should be reviewed.

FRONT SIT

The support partner lies on the back, with arms outstretched and palms down for support. The top partner straddles the support so that the support and the top partner are looking at each other. The top partner backs up to sit on the support's feet. As the support raises the top partner into a seated position, the top partner extends the legs forward so that the support can reach up and grasp them to stabilize the seated position (see Figure 20.91).

FLYING DUTCHMAN

The support partner lies on the back, with arms outstretched and palms down for support. The top child takes a position facing the support, grasping support's hands and at the same time bending over support's feet. The support then raises the top partner from the floor by extending the knees. The top child arches the back and can then release the grip and put the arms out level to the sides in a flying position (see Figure 20.92). A little experimentation determines the best place for the foot support.

KNEE-AND-SHOULDER BALANCE

The support partner is lying supine, knees well up and feet flat on the floor. Support puts the hands out, ready to brace the shoulders of the top child. The top child takes a

Figure 20.91

Front Sit.

Figure 20.92

Flying Dutchman.

position in front of the support's knees, placing the hands on them. The top performer leans forward so that the shoulders are supported by the hands of the bottom partner, and kicks up (see Figure 20.93). Key points for the top partner are to keep the arms straight and the head up, and to look directly into the support partner's eyes. Spotters may be needed to help stabilize the hips of the top child.

PRESS

The bottom partner lies on the back, with knees bent and feet flat on the floor. The top partner takes a stradle

Figure 20.93

Knee-and-Shoulder Balance.

Figure 20.94

Press.

position over the bottom partner, facing the support's feet. Performers then join hands with each other. The top partner sits on the joined hands, supported by the bottom partner, and rests the legs across the bottom partner's knees (see Figure 20.94). Both performers should keep the elbows quite straight. Hold for a specified time.

ALL-FOURS SUPPORT

The bottom performer lies on the back with legs apart and knees up. The hands are positioned close to the shoulders with palms up. The top performer stands on the partner's palms and leans forward, placing the hands on the support performer's knees. The support raises the top performer by lifting with the arms. The top performer is then in an all-fours position, with feet supported by the bottom performer's extended arms and hands supported by the bottom performer's knees (see Figure 20.95).

Figure 20.95

All-Fours Support.

Critical Thinking

1. Dominant movement pattern approach (DMP) provides a framework for gymnastics education in Canada. Discuss how the dominant movement patterns are related to the movement concepts in Chapter 14.

References and Suggested Readings

Canadian Association for Health, Physical Education, Recreation & Dance. (1979). *Gymnastics—a movement approach.* Gloucester, ON: Author.

Malmberg, H.C. (2003). *KIDnastics— a child-centered approach to teaching gymnastics.* Champaign, IL: Human Kinetics.

Mitchell, D., Davis, B., Lopez, R., & Gunther, S. (2002). *Teaching fundamental gymnastics skills.* Champaign, IL: Human Kinetics.

Ontario Physical and Health Education Association. (1997). *Physical education safety guidelines.* North Yorth, ON: Author.

Palmer, H.C. (2003). *Teaching rhythmic gymnastics.* Champaign, IL: Human Kinetics.

Russell, K. (1986). *Coaching certification manual: Introductory gymnastics* (4th ed.). Vanier City, ON: Canadian Gymnastics Federation.

Russell, K. (1994). *Up, down, all around: Gymnastics lesson plans (Gr. 1–2).* Winnipeg, MB: Ruschkin Publishing.

Russell, K. (1994). *Up, down, all around: Gymnastics lesson plans (Gr. 3–4).* Winnipeg, MB: Ruschkin Publishing.

Russell, K. (1994). *Up, down, all around: Gymnastics lesson plans (Gr. 5–6).* Winnipeg, MB: Ruschkin Publishing.

Saskatchewan Education. (1998). *Saskatchewan physical education: Safety guidelines for policy development.* Regina, SK: Author.

Wall, J. & Murray, N. (1994). *Children and movement* (2nd ed.). Dubuque, IA: WCB Brown and Benchmark.

Wedmann, W., Johnson, N., Kopelow, B., & Fenton, J. (2001). *Gymnastics—Teaching the basics resource manual.* Victoria, BC: BC Ministry of Small Business, Tourism & Culture.

Werner, P.H. (2004). *Teaching children gymnastics: A developmentally appropriate approach* (2nd ed.). Champaign, IL: Human Kinetics Publishers.

 Weblinks

Ayden Elementary School Gymnastics: http://schools.eastnet.ecu.edu/pitt/ayden/PHYSED3.HTM

From a real gymnastics fanatic (and elementary physical education teacher), this site provides dozens of different gymnastics lessons plans, links to gymnastics websites, instructions on how to teach specific skills, and general enthusiasm for the sport.

Kids Can Move School program: www.kidscanmove.com

This website includes a program and resources to help teachers introduce gymnastics to elementary school students.

Canadian Gymnastics Federation: www.gymcan.org

Canadian Gymnastics Federation is the governing body for the sport of gymnastics in Canada, and their website offers information on the national team, on programs and upcoming events, and on news from the gymnastics community.

CHAPTER 21

Alternative Environment Activities

Essential Components

I	Organized around content standards
II	Student-centred and developmentally appropriate
III	**Physical activity and motor skill development form the core of the program**
IV	**Teaches management skills and self-discipline**
V	**Promotes inclusion of all students**
VI	**Focuses on process over product**
VII	Promotes lifetime personal health and wellness
VIII	**Teaches cooperation and responsibility and promotes sensitivity to diversity**

Physical Education Standards

1	**Students are able to move competently using a variety of fundamental and specialized motor skills.**
2	Students can monitor and maintain a health-enhancing level of physical fitness.
3	**Students are able to apply movement concepts and basic mechanics of skill performance when learning and refining motor skills.**
4	Students comprehend the basic principles of wellness and are able to apply concepts that enable them to make meaningful decisions that positively impact their health and wellness.
5	**Students participate in a wide variety of physical activities and learn how to maintain a personalized active lifestyle.**
6	**Students demonstrate empathy, understanding, and respect for the numerous differences exhibited by people in an activity setting.**
7	**Students exhibit responsible and self-directed behaviours that lead to positive social interactions in physical activity.**

OVERVIEW

Canadian climate and terrain provide opportunity for a wide variety of physical activities. Three alternative environment activities—orienteering, cross-country skiing, and curling—are presented in this chapter. Orienteering and cross-country skiing are examples of activities that may be offered in the outdoors during different seasons. Curling is one of the most popular winter recreational activities in many communities across Canada. Suggestions for including these activities in an elementary physical education program are provided. The reader is encouraged to use the alternative environment activities (land-based or water-based) available in their community.

OUTCOMES

- Understand the purpose of including alternative environment physical activities in elementary physical education.

- Describe instructional procedures for orienteering, curling, and cross-country skiing.

- Describe the terminology and rules associated with each of these physical activities.

Orienteering

Orienteering is an outdoor sport that combines jogging and running with navigational skills (use of map and/or compass). Improvement of cardiovascular endurance is an important fitness outcome associated with orienteering. Often the challenge of navigating a particular course takes the focus off the fitness outcome. The skills learned in orienteering can be used for recreation purposes on hikes and various wilderness outings. On a competitive level, an orienteering course consists of a series of designated control points, which competitors try to reach in the shortest amount of time. Orienteering provides excellent opportunity for making curriculum connections with various classroom subjects such as social studies, math, science, and environmental studies.

Basic Terminology

Following are the definitions of some basic orienteering terms.

Bearing: Provides the direction of travel in terms of degrees on a compass.

Cardinal directions: These include North, East, South, West. Inter-cardinal directions include Northeast, Northwest, and Southeast, Southwest (see Figure 21.1).

Contours: Lines on a map that join points of the same elevation. Contour lines that are close together denote a steep slope; widely spaced lines show a more gradual slope.

Control: A red and white nylon cube (20 cm by 20 m) used to mark a particular location on an orienteering course.

Legend: Identifies all features that appear on a map.

Scale: Ratio of distance on the ground to distance on the map.

Symbol: A feature on a map is marked by a unique symbol on the legend. Starting position on an orienteering map is marked with a triangle (Δ), and finishing position with a circle within a circle.

Pacing: A way of measuring distance travelled by counting paces.

Map Skills

Using a Legend on a Map

Using a legend is a key part of effective orienteering. It allows the participant to assess obstacles, terrain, and make decisions about the most efficient and safe route to travel. Many beginning orienteering exercises involve drawing maps of the local area with sample legends. This helps students become familiar with maps and legends. See Figure 21.2 for a sample map and legend.

Orienting the Map

The map should always be oriented to north by matching magnetic north (lines) on the map to the direction of magnetic north on the ground by using the compass (see Figure 21.3).

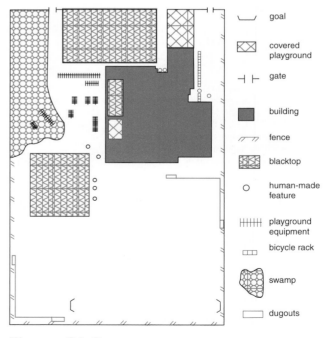

Figure 21.2

Sample map.

Source: Reprinted with permission of Premier's Sports Awards Program. Wedmann, W., Fenton, J., & Kopelow, B. (2001). *Orienteering: Teaching the basics resource manual.* Victoria, BC: British Columbia Ministry of Small Business, Tourism and Culture.

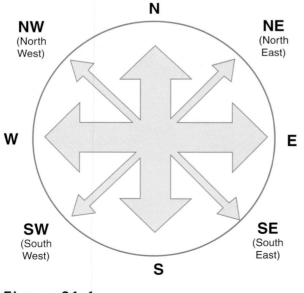

Figure 21.1

Cardinal directions and Inter-cardinal directions.

Compass Skills

Parts of a Compass

Figure 21.4 shows the basic parts of a compass.

A. The base plate is the clear surface that forms the base of the compass.

B. The direction-of-travel arrow is engraved on the base plate.

C. The north sign is on the compass housing.

D. The orienting arrow is engraved on the base plate. The compass is oriented when the red part of the magnetic needle is aligned with the orienting arrow (striped).

E. The red and white magnetic needle. The red end of the needle will always point to magnetic north.

F. The compass housing is the moveable part of the compass and is engraved with 360° marks and cardinal directions.

Handling a Compass

Learning to hold a compass correctly is one of the basic skills. Consider the following points for teaching and practising handling a compass. Figure 21.5 shows the correct technique for holding a compass:

1. Hold the compass between first two fingers and thumb at waist height.

2. Direction-of-travel arrow should point in front.

3. Cord is attached around the wrist.

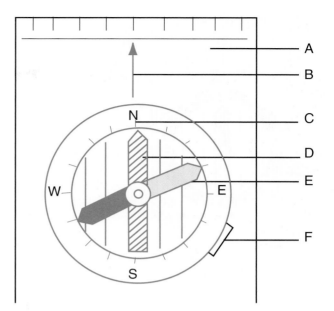

Figure 21.4

Parts of a compass.

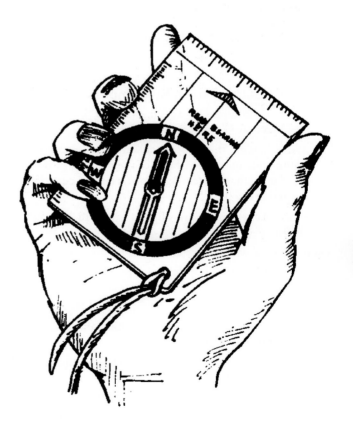

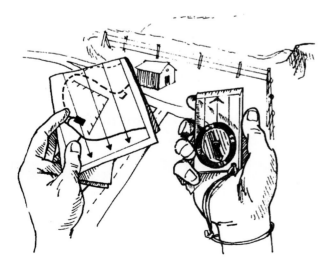

Figure 21.3

Orienting the map.

Source: Reprinted with permission of Premier's Sports Awards Program. Wedmann, W., Fenton, J., & Kopelow, B. (2001). *Orienteering: Teaching the basics resource manual*. Victoria, BC: British Columbia Ministry of Small Business, Tourism and Culture.

Figure 21.5

Holding a compass.

Source: Reprinted with permission of Premier's Sports Awards Program. Wedmann, W., Fenton, J., & Kopelow, B. (2001). *Orienteering: Teaching the basics resource manual*. Victoria, BC: British Columbia Ministry of Small Business, Tourism and Culture.

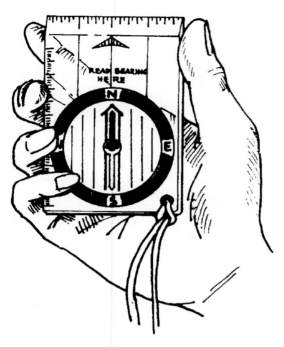

Figure 21.6

Orienting self to north by compass.

Source: Reprinted with permission of Premier's Sports Awards Program. Wedmann, W., Fenton, J., & Kopelow, B. (2001). *Orienteering: Teaching the basics resource manual.* Victoria, BC: British Columbia Ministry of Small Business, Tourism and Culture.

Orienting Self to North by Compass

1. Rotate the compass housing until the "N" lines up with the direction-of-travel arrow.

2. While holding the compass at waist level, rotate your entire body until the red end of the magnetic arrow is lined up with the orienting arrow. A helpful cue is "put the red in the shed."

3. Once these arrows are aligned you will be facing north.

Figure 21.6 shows an example of how the compass should look when oriented to north.

Taking a Bearing

Consider the following points for teaching and practising taking a compass bearing:

1. Hold the compass between first two fingers and thumb at waist height.

2. Point the compass in the intended direction of travel.

3. Rotate the compass housing until the red end of the magnetic needle is directly over the orienting arrow (striped) in the compass housing.

4. Read the bearing off the compass housing at the base of the direction-of-travel arrow.

Activities for Developmental Level I

CHALKBOARD ORIENTEERING

Draw a map of the classroom with symbols marking various features. Include a legend to list these symbols. Place small coloured stickers as controls around the room (each labelled with a number and letter). Circle these markers on the map. The purpose of the game is for students to use the map and symbols to find the controls, record the numbers and letters, and unscramble the letters. Letters can spell simple words and phrases. The activity introduces students to map scale, symbols, legends, controls, and orienting oneself to the map.

MAP DRAWING

Have students draw a simple map of a common area (for example, lunchroom, gymnasium, playground). They must include a system of symbols and a legend. Ask students to mark two or three controls on their map, and see if their partner can follow the map to find the controls. This activity introduces students to map scale, symbols, controls, and legends.

ROUTE ORIENTEERING

Students follow a route marked with flags, with several control markers along the route. When students find a control, they mark the location on their map. At the end, students compare their control locations with the master map. The purpose of route orienteering is to practise translating actual location to map location.

LINE ORIENTEERING

The purpose of line orienteering is to follow a line drawn on the map (see Figure 21.7). If the students follow the line correctly, the controls will be found. Students mark the position of the controls on their map.

Activities for Developmental Level II & III

MAP SYMBOL RELAY

The purpose of this game is to review universal orienteering map symbols. Create a set of matching cards with the symbol on one card and the written description on the other. Each team of four or five students receives the same number of cards (either the symbol or written description). In a relay format, one player from each team chooses a card and runs to the designated area to find the matching card. When the match is found, the runner returns to his team. If the runner returns with an incorrect match, the next runner must take the card back and try again. The relay continues until each team has found all correct matches.

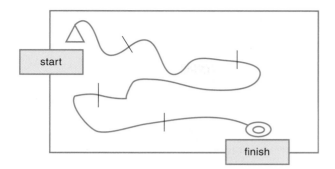

Figure 21.7

Line orienteering.

SARDINES

Use a simple map of a familiar area (for example, school ground, local park). Place 8 to 10 controls at various points around the course. Circle the control locations on the map. Each student (or partner) receives a copy of the map with the controls clearly marked. One student has two to three minutes to hide at one of the controls. On the "go" signal, the other students attempt to find the correct control with their hidden classmate. When a student finds the hiding place, she stays there until all students arrive. Encourage students to disguise their search so as to misguide their classmates!

SCHOOL YARD SCORE ORIENTEERING

Draw a simple map of the school yard including symbols to mark the features (for example, goal posts, bike racks). Place 10 to 15 controls at various points around the school yard. Each control should have a number and code letter. Circle the control locations on the map. Assign a point value to each control (the higher point value for more difficult locations). Each student (or partner) receives a copy of the map with the controls and point values.

On the "go" signal, students try to collect as many points as possible (in any order) in a set time limit. Strategy will involve decisions on collecting controls with different point values (that is, fewer controls with higher point values).

MEMORY ORIENTEERING

This is a challenging partner exercise. Partners view controls marked on a master map of an area (for example, school yard, park) for a designated time period (two minutes). After viewing the map, partners try to find as many controls as possible within the time limit. This is a challenging cooperative activity where partners can develop strategies to work together to find as many controls as possible. Include the rule that partners must arrive back to the command centre together. This can also be used as an exciting team activity (teams of four or five).

POINT-TO-POINT ORIENTEERING

Draw a simple map of a familiar area (for example, school yard, local park). Place 6 to 10 controls at various points around the course. Each control should have a number and code letter. Circle the control locations on the map. Each student (or partners) receives a copy of the map with the controls clearly marked in order.

On the "go" signal, students try to find all the controls in order in the shortest amount of time.

FOLLOW THE LEADER

Divide students into groups of four or five, with one map per group. One student in each group is responsible for leading his group to the first control; other group members follow the exact route taken by the leader. When a group reaches the control, the map is passed to another student in the group, to lead to the next control. Only the student with the map can look at it; others must follow the leader. Each group must find all the controls in order as quickly as possible.

FIND YOUR BEARINGS

All students start at a similar point (for example, large tree). Working in pairs, they map out a series of predesignated directions and distance (for example, 40 paces 40°NE). Students record positions for each bearing on their map. Positions are compared with the master map.

Safety and Etiquette

When participating in an actual orienteering meet or when practising orienteering during a class period, the following safety and etiquette guidelines should be observed:

1. For an official orienteering meet, each participant must carry a whistle. Six long blasts on your whistle signals you are in an emergency situation and require assistance. Three short blasts will be made in reply when someone is searching for you. Carrying a whistle for class orienteering is also advised if students are in unfamiliar areas.

2. Participants should be familiar with emergency procedure (for example, return to prearranged meeting place).

3. Each participant or group should carry a watch to keep track of time limits.

4. Consider having students work in pairs or small groups for both support and safety.

5. Do not enter restricted or out-of-bounds areas, and respect the environment.

6. Do not follow other participants, or remove any controls.

7. All participants must stop to aid an injured participant.

For an excellent resource on teaching orienteering in elementary physical education, consult *Orienteering: Teaching the Basics Resource Manual*, by Wedmann, Fenton, and Kopelow.

Curling

Curling is one of the most popular winter sports in Canada. Many small and remote communities as well as large urban areas in Canada have curling rinks. In terms of popularity, the 2001 Canadian Men's Curling Championships drew more television viewers in Canada than the Stanley Cup! Providing children with the opportunity to develop basic curling skills in elementary school increases the likelihood that they will continue in this sport throughout their lifetime. Many curling clubs welcome school groups, especially since they tend to come to the rink during underused ice times. Clubs will often provide qualified instructors and the necessary equipment, such as sliders and brooms, as well as the rocks and sheets.

Curling provides an excellent opportunity for making curriculum connections with various classroom subjects such as physics and math (for example, Why is it called curling? Why does the rock curl in the opposite direction of the "turn"? What effect does sweeping have on the curl of the rock?)

Some of the basic curling skills (for example, sliding beanbag to target) can be introduced in the gymnasium as early as developmental levels I and II; however, more in-depth focus on curling skills should be introduced later, in level III. For further information on teaching curling in elementary school see the Canadian Coaching Association's (1995) *Getting Started in Curling: Teacher's Resource Guide*.

Basic Rules

A curling team (known as a rink) is made up of four players, each delivering two rocks each end. Rocks are delivered alternately with players from the opposing team. The basic intent of the game is to complete each end with your team's rocks closer to the centre of the house than the opposition.

Only one team can score on any end. A team scores one point for shot rock and one point for each additional rock that is closer to the centre of the house than the closest opposition rock. A rock must be touching the house in order to score. The team that scores delivers the first rock of the next end.

For every shot, the skip will ask a curler to throw an in-turn or an out-turn. This allows a rock to curl behind guards for protection or hit an opponent's rock hidden behind a guard. The force or weight of each throw will depend on whether the skip wants the rock to take out another rock or draw into the house. More force is required for take-out weight.

Basic Terminology

Following are some definitions of common terms used in curling.

Bonspiel: A curling competition.

Curl: Bend in the line of travel as a rock moves down the ice.

Weight: The force imparted on a rock upon release. Draw weight is the force required for the rock to reach the house. Take-out weight refers to the amount of force needed to hit another rock and remove it from the house.

End: A portion of a game that is completed when each team throws eight rocks. A blank end occurs when no points are scored. A standard curling games consists of 10 ends.

Guard: A rock that is placed in a position to protect another.

Hack: Foothold from where the rock is delivered (see Figure 21.8).

House: The four rings at each end of the ice toward which the rocks are thrown. The button is the centre of the house. The tee line passes through the centre of the house at right angles to the centre line (see Figure 21.8).

Hog Line: Line 10 m from the hack at each end. To be in play, a rock must pass completely over the hog line.

In-turn: The rotation imparted on a rock that starts it turning clockwise for a right-hander and counterclockwise for a left-hander.

Lead: Player who throws the first and second rocks each end for her team.

Out-turn: The rotation imparted on a rock that starts it turning counterclockwise for a right-hander and clockwise for a left-hander.

Pebble: A fine spray of water droplets applied to the sheet before each game. Rocks slide along the frozen pebble.

Raise: When one rock bumps another rock.

Roll: Movement of a rock after it strikes another rock.

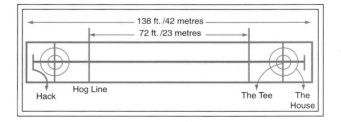

Figure 21.8

Curling sheet.

Second: Player who throws the third and fourth rocks at each end for her team.

Shot Rock: At any time during an end, the rock that is closest to the button.

Skip: Player who throws the seventh and eighth rocks at each end for her team and also directs the tactics and strategy for the team.

Sweeping: To sweep in front of the curling rock with a curling broom. Helps to adjust speed and direction of the rock. Lead and second are responsible for most sweeping duties during a curling game.

Third: Player who throws the fifth and sixth rocks at each end for her team.

Basic Curling Skills

Rock delivery is the fundamental skill in curling. Consider the following points for teaching and practising curling rock delivery:

Stance: Squat down and place gripper foot in the left hack. Gripper foot and sliding foot both point in the direction of the target. Upper body is square to the target, with eyes focused on the line of delivery (see Figure 21.9). Position the rock handle in preparation for either an in-turn or an out-turn.

Start up and step back: Keeping square to the target, lift hips into a semi-crouch. Pull the rock back toward the hack, at the same time move back the sliding foot so it is almost even with the hack foot (see Figure 21.9).

Forward slide and extension: From the start-up position, initiate forward motion with a forward thrust from the hack leg, the sliding foot and throwing arm pointing in the direction of the target (see Figure 21.9). After leaving the hack, the curler's weight should be over the sliding foot. Figure 21.10 shows the distribution of weight in the slide and extension position. The trailing leg extends backward to establish a balanced position. With throwing arm fully extended, release the rock with handle in the 12 o'clock position.

Stance · Start-up · Step back · Forward Slide

Figure 21.9

Curling delivery (right-handed).

Source: Reprinted with permission of Premier's Sports Awards Program. Wedmann, W., Fenton, J., Kopelow, B., & Parsons, A. (1999). *Curling: Teaching the basics resource manual*. Victoria, BC: British Columbia Ministry of Small Business, Tourism and Culture.

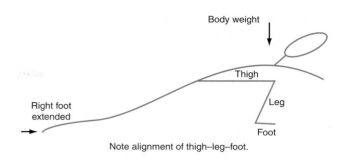

Note alignment of thigh–leg–foot.

Figure 21.10

Weight distribution of release position.

In-turn Delivery

To throw an in-turn, the right-handed curler rotates the handle of the rock in a clockwise direction from the 10 o'clock position, releasing at the 12 o'clock position. A left-handed curler rotates the handle in a counterclockwise direction from 2 o'clock and releasing at 12 o'clock. Initiate the turn during the forward slide portion of your delivery.

Out-turn Delivery

To throw an out-turn, the right-handed curler rotates the handle of the rock in a counterclockwise direction from the 2 o'clock position, releasing at the 12 o'clock position. A left-handed curler rotates the handle in a clockwise direction from 10 o'clock and releasing at 12 o'clock. Initiate the turn during the forward slide portion of your delivery.

Sweeping

Effective sweeping footwork involves a "push and glide" motion. Leading with the sliding foot, the sweeper pushes with the back foot and glides alongside and slightly ahead of the rock. The sweeping motion of the broom is back and forth across the face of the rock. Sweepers are not allowed to contact the rock with the broom or any part of their bodies (for example, the foot).

Equipment

Curling rocks (also called stones) weigh 18 kg, with junior curling rocks half the standard weight (8.5 kg). Each sheet of ice has a set of 16 rocks, 8 for each team. The rocks for each team are identified by the colour of their handles. The rocks should never be lifted off the ice. If a curling rock is dropped from even a short distance, there is significant risk of damage to the rock, the ice, and the curler. Tip the rock up on its side when cleaning the bottom.

For an effective modified curling rock for the gymnasium setting, fill 4-litre plastic milk jugs with about 8–10 cm of sand. These also work on substitute ice surfaces (for example, outdoor ice rinks). Also use bean-bags and modified scooter boards (with added handles) to simulate the delivery action of the rock in the gymnasium setting.

Brooms are used to control the speed and direction of the curling rock. In most cases, curling rinks have curling brooms available for use. When students are practising their delivery technique in the gymnasium, it is helpful to have them hold a floor hockey stick as a substitute for the broom.

Footwear should include a form of sliding material to cover one shoe. Slip-on curling sliders are made to cover shoes. A reasonable substitute for beginners is to put duct tape around the sole of the sliding shoe. For gymnasium practice, put a heavy sock over the shoe of the sliding foot. Most running shoes are appropriate footwear for beginners. However, the shoes must be thoroughly cleaned before going on the ice to avoid leaving debris on the ice surface.

Gymnasium Activities for Curling

Many lead-up activities for curling may be practised in the gymnasium prior to making trips to the curling rink. This will allow the teacher to organize maximum practice opportunity, and ensure students are prepared when they go to the curling rink. The following activities are designed for the gymnasium (using modified equipment to simulate the curling equipment). Also note that many of the on-ice activities listed in the next section can be modified for the gymnasium.

SLIDER AND GRIPPER

Have students establish a slider foot (nondominant) and gripper foot (dominant). In most cases, right-handed participants will use their left leg as a slider and right leg as the gripper (reverse for left-handers). Place a heavy sock over the slider foot to allow this foot to slide on the gym floor. Allow students to experiment with the slider on either foot.

STANCE—START-UP—SLIDE

Have students practise the proper hack position, start-up, and slide. Mark a spot on the floor with tape to simulate the hack position. It is helpful to establish a slow and deliberate cadence for students to practise (for example, Set—Start-up, and Push off or Stance—Hips up—Push forward). During this practice, check for balance and body alignment (see Figures 21.9 and 21.10).

Next, have students hold a floor hockey stick in their non-throwing hand to simulate holding the broom. To simulate a curling rock, beanbags make a good substitute for children. As a next step, consider using 4-litre milk cartons partially filled with sand as modified curling rocks.

STANCE—START UP—SLIDE TO TARGET

Complete the same sequence as above, allowing students to release the "curling rock" toward an established target. Targets may be pylons, bowling pins, or an area marked on the floor (for example, the basketball circle can be the house or curling rings). Allow students to develop "target games" to practise their delivery skills (see Closest to the Button Contest in next section).

LINE OF DELIVERY

Students practise their delivery technique and line of delivery by trying to knock down targets (for example, bowling pins).

DRAW TO THE WALL

Students practise their draw weight by trying to deliver their rock as close to the wall as possible without having it hit the wall. This can be practised in partners, small groups, or one large group. It is fun to develop a Draw to the Wall contest to be held throughout the unit.

DRAW CONTEST

Establish targets at various distances. Students practise adjusting their draw weight to hit the various targets.

On-ice Activities for Curling

In addition to the following, most of the preceding gymnasium activities are used for on-ice practice with curling equipment.

CLOSEST TO THE BUTTON CONTEST

Divide students into groups of eight, four at each end. One at a time, students deliver a proper shot. When the rock stops, the distance to the button is measured. The rock is removed and the next student shoots. At the end of each round, the player closest to the button wins. This is a fun "tournament," with the winners from each group continuing to play off.

HIDING THE ROCK

Place several guards on the ice. Have students practise delivering their rocks behind the guards.

PROBLEM-SOLVING ENDS

Move the rocks into a variety of "final rock" scenarios. Students attempt to deliver what they think is the best shot. It is helpful for students to work in small groups to discuss various options. These scenarios can also be adjusted to practise single shots (for example, double take-out, hiding behind a guard).

PULL AND SLIDE

In pairs, one partner tows another partner (holding the end of the curling broom) who is in the slide release position. This allows the slider to feel the body weight over his sliding foot.

LEARNING TURNS

In pairs, students line up on opposite sides of the width of the rink. In the hack stance, one student adjusts the handle for the in-turn grip and very lightly pushes the rock toward a partner with the proper release. Partner then repeats. Repeat for the out-turn.

MINI GAME

Students are divided into partners and play against another pair, using only half the ice. Two portable hacks are placed in the centre of the sheet so that two separate games can be played on one sheet of ice.

PUSH AND GLIDE

Have student practise the push-and-glide motion down the ice and back. This is effective lead-up practice to the sweeping footwork.

SWEEPING FOOTWORK

Assume the proper stance (see earlier skill section) with the brush on the centre line. While using the push-and-glide method, students move SLOWLY down the ice, staying parallel to the centre line. Repeat each side of the centre line.

SWEEPING A STONE

In pairs, one partner pushes the rock slowly down the ice with her brush while the other partner sweeps. Pusher gradually increases the speed of the rock. Once the rock has travelled the length of the sheet, partners switch roles. The pusher can provide feedback to the sweeper on her sweeping technique. This drill can be repeated with two sweepers.

SWEEPING A DELIVERED ROCK

One student delivers a rock while two other students sweep it down the ice. Begin with a weight that will travel half the distance of the sheet, and gradually increase weight for the full distance of the ice. Switch roles.

TAKE IT OUT

Set up several rocks in the house. Students must attempt to take out the rocks one at a time. Place rocks in various

parts of the house. To increase the challenge, tell the student whether he also must try to "save the shooter" (keep the shooter in the house after it takes out the rock).

Cross-country Skiing

Cross-country skiing (also called Nordic skiing) offers children the opportunity to enjoy the outdoor environment in winter. It is an effective means of keeping active and an excellent opportunity to explore the natural beauty of the environment during the winter months. In some regions of Canada, teachers have developed cross-country ski programs in their schools, complete with equipment and trails on their school grounds. Consider including basic cross-country skiing programs as early as developmental level II. In some regions, skiing may be introduced earlier; however, in most instances, it is difficult for one teacher to provide for the needs of an entire class of younger students without extra adult assistance. In areas where snow may be less frequent, cross-country skiing may be offered as part of a school ski trip to the mountains. Most ski hills include groomed cross-country ski trails in addition to their downhill skiing and snowboarding facilities.

Basic Skills

Diagonal Stride

The diagonal stride is the basic skill used to move across the snow. Starting with a simple walking movement, the child learns to increase speed and efficiency by shifting weight over each ski and kicking back, much like the shift one makes when changing from walking to jogging. Figure 21.11 shows the classic diagonal stride.

Consider the following points for teaching and practising the diagonal stride:

1. Opposing arm and leg move together (swing your arms). *SWING*

2. Transfer your weight from ski to ski as your stride. *PUSH*

3. Forcefully kick down and back on the weighted ski and glide onto opposite ski. *GLIDE*

Diagonal Stride Activities

Practise diagonal stride without poles first, so students can get used to balancing without developing a dependence on their poles.

Hop-hop drill. Hop quickly in place from ski to ski. Use arms and knees to aid in balance. Vary the tempo of the hops.

Shuffle-shuffle drill. Place ski poles in ground about 30–40 m away. Students shuffle across flat terrain, around

Figure 21.11

Diagonal stride.

Figure 21.12

Herringbone pattern.

the poles and return. Increase tempo from walk, to shuffle, to jog. Have students call out cues as they ski to help develop the rhythmic diagonal stride movement.

Holding Hands. Partners must ski on flat terrain while holding hands. If partner falls, the other must help her back up. Focus on developing a rhythmic stride between partners.

Wagon Wheel Tag. Mark out a giant wagon wheel in the snow, 20–30 m in diameter. Identify three to four students as taggers. They must try to tag other students. When a skier is tagged, he also becomes a tagger. All skiers must stay in the wagon wheel paths.

Partner Stride. Stand in a parallel path to a partner. Try to stride ahead with the same tempo and rhythm. Gradually increase speed. Perform the same action with one partner skiing in front of the other in the same path.

Hare and Hounds. Half the class lines up in alternating parallel ski paths (hares). The other half of the class lines up in alternating paths (hounds). On signal, the teacher calls, "Hares go!" When the hares have travelled about 5–10 m, call, "Hounds go!" The hounds now try to catch up and pass as many hares as possible before they reach the finish area (about 40 m away). On return, switch the hounds and hares.

Ski Soccer. Play soccer on skis, using your hands instead of feet to move the ball. Add extra balls to increase movement.

Herringbone

The herringbone is used for climbing hills and slopes when the diagonal stride no longer works efficiently.

Figure 21.12 shows the herringbone pattern. Consider the following points for teaching and practising the herringbone:

1. Facing directly up the slope, place skis in a V position with tails of skis together.

2. Roll knees and ankles inward to push inside edge to the hill.

3. Place your poles outside the V and behind your boots.

4. Stride upward, setting inside edge on each step, using a strong poling action slightly to the rear.

5. Try to maintain the diagonal stride rhythmic movement throughout.

Herringbone Activities

Edging. Practise pushing inside edge to snow on flat terrain and slight slopes before trying on steeper climbing hills. Look for herringbone pattern in snow.

Obstacle course. Design a simple course with varying flat and uphill slopes.

Hare and Hounds on the Hill. Use the same rules mentioned earlier. Hounds try to overtake the hares. If space is limited, send students off in smaller groups.

Snowplow

The snowplow is the basic downhill technique that allows the skier to control her speed on the slope. This is an important skill to increase safety on the trails. Consider the following points for teaching and practising the herringbone:

1. Bend your knees.
2. Push the tails of your skis out (using your heel plates) to form a V in front of you.
3. Roll the ankles and knees inward in order to set the edges. Adjust pressure on edges to control speed.
4. Hands ahead of hips, with poles pointing to the rear.

TEACHING TIP

Variation: For a snowplow turn, stay in the basic snowplow position, turn feet in the desired direction. Use edges to control the turn.

Snowplow Activities

SNOWPLOW SLALOM

Place three or four ski poles along the downhill slope. Skiers must snowplow between the poles.

NO-POLE SNOWPLOW

Practise snowplow technique on varying slopes without using poles.

SNOWPLOW TRAVERSE

Practise the snowplow technique across the slope in a diagonal path. Go diagonally to the right, then to the left.

STOP ON A DIME

Mark a target on the hill. Using their snowplow, skiers must stop as close to the target as possible.

Static Turns

It is helpful for beginning cross-country skiers to know several ways to change direction from a standing position. Consider the following points for teaching and practising the basic turns:

STAR TURN (TAILS)

Start with skis parallel and keep the tails of skis in place. Move to right or left with comfortable steps, making a V shape with each step. Imagine your steps as opening up a fan or displaying a hand of playing cards. This turn can be reversed by keeping the tips in place and making a V by moving the tails of your skis.

KICK TURN

Plant your ski poles behind your skis for support. Swing the first ski 180 degrees round (opposite direction). Follow with the second ski.

Turn Activities

TURN IN PLACE

Perform multiple turns in succession. Alternate direction of turns.

WHICH WAY?

Skiers must turn in the direction of hand signals provided by the teacher. The teacher can include other skills in a "Simon Says" format.

OBSTACLE COURSE

Design an obstacle course that involves a variety of turns.

POLE CHASE

Students ski a designated distance (for example, 30–40 m), turn, and return. Use a different turn each time.

CIRCLE RELAY

Teams of four or five. Each skier must ski to the designated target (ski pole in the snow), turn around the target twice, and then ski back to tag teammate.

TEACHING TIP

Obstacle courses and orienteering challenges of varying levels of difficulty can be designed to allow students to practise all of the above skills.

Safety

1. Be sure students are dressed appropriately for the weather conditions. Layers, hats, and mitts are a must! Have extra hats and mitts available.
2. Teach students to recognize signs and symptoms of both frostbite and hypothermia. Use regular "buddy checks." See Chapter 21 for more information on exercising in cold weather.
3. If you are skiing on trails away from the school, make sure students are aware of rules of the trails including (a) stay with your group; (b) obey the three-blast

emergency signal (go to designated place immediately); (c) stay on the marked trails; and (d) if lost stay put.

4. Remember that beginning skiers move slowly and tire quickly. Plan day trips accordingly.

Critical Thinking

1. Examine the games presented in Chapter 22 and brainstorm ways they can be adapted to help students practise skills in orienteering or curling, or cross-country skiing.

References and Suggested Readings

Anthony, A. (1980). *Orienteering handbook*. Vancouver, BC: Hancock House.

Braggins, A. (1993). *Trail orienteering: An outdoor activity for people with disabilities*. Perthshire, UK: Harveys.

Bunting, C. (2006). *Interdisciplinary teaching through outdoor education*. Champaign, IL: Human Kinetics.

Canadian Association for Health, Physical Education, Recreation and Dance. (2000). *Snow fun—favourite Canadian winter activities*. Ottawa, ON: Author.

Canadian Curling Association. (1995). *Getting started in curling: Teacher's resource guide*. Gloucester, ON: Author.

Cross Country Canada. (1981). *Skill development program*. Ottawa, ON: Author.

Flemmen, A., Grosvold, O. & Brady, M. (1982). *Teaching children to ski*. Champaign, IL: Leisure Press.

Gilbertson, K., Bates, T., McLaughlin, T., & Ewert, A. (2006). *Outdoor education methods and strategies*. Champaign, IL: Human Kinetics.

Gilchrist, J. & Lee, J. (1984). *Orienteering instructor's manual*. Willowdale, ON: Orienteering Ontario.

Hammerman, D., Hammerman, W., & Hammerman, E. (2001). *Teaching in the outdoors* (5th ed.). Danville, IL: Interstate.

Landry, L. (1987). *SchoolSki program manual: Cross-country skiing for schools*. Gloucester, ON: Cross Country Canada.

Logue, V., Logue, F. & Carroll, M. (1996). *Kids outdoors— skills and knowledge for outdoor adventurers*. Camden, ME: Ragged Mountain Press.

Lowry, R. & Sidney, K. (1987). *Orienteering: Training and performance*. Willowdale, ON: Orienteering Ontario.

Loy, J. (2003). *Follow the trail—A young persons guide to the great outdoors*. New York: Henry Holt.

McNeill, C., Cory-Wright, J., & Renfrew, T. (1998). *Teaching orienteering* (2nd ed.) Champaign, IL: Human Kinetics.

Wedmann, W., Fenton, J., & Kopelow, B. (2001). *Orienteering: Teaching the basics resource manual*. Victoria, BC: British Columbia Ministry of Small Business, Tourism and Culture.

Wedmann, W., Fenton, J., Kopelow, B., & Parsons, A. (1999). *Curling: Teaching the basics resource manual*. Victoria, BC: British Columbia Ministry of Small Business, Tourism and Culture.

Wilson, N. (2002). *The SAS handbook of tracking and navigation*. London, UK: Amber Books.

 Weblinks

Canadian Orienteering Federation: www.orienteering.ca

The website of the Canadian Orienteering Federation has information about the history of orienteering in Canada, junior participation, technical articles, standards and rules, upcoming events, and a newsletter.

Canadian Curling Association: www.curling.ca

This site offers links to curling events in Canada and internationally. Explains the *Getting Started in Curling* program, which includes excellent educational resources for teachers and students.

Cross Country Canada: www.cccski.com/main.asp? cmd= doc&ID=565&lan=0

Cross Country Canada presents a great article on "Jackrabbit," Norwegian-Canadian ski legend Herman Smith-Johanssen. This wonderful story will inspire children.

Sportfit: www.sportfitcanada.com

An online resource that helps students explore a variety of winter sports. This resource includes athlete interviews, teacher resources, and mini-lessons.

Canada Winter Games: www.canadagames.ca

This website includes Canada Winter Games Resource Kit with information to organize and promote a school-wide Canada Games Day.

Trans Canada Trail: www.tctrail.ca

This website includes information on the national trail system through every province and territory. Four initiatives are highlighted: Bridges across Canada, Yester years, Our National Roots, and Discovery Program.

Essential Components

I	Organized around content standards
II	Student-centred and developmentally appropriate
III	Physical activity and motor skill development form the core of the program
IV	Teaches management skills and self-discipline
V	Promotes inclusion of all students
VI	Focuses on process over product
VII	Promotes lifetime personal health and wellness
VIII	Teaches cooperation and responsibility and promotes sensitivity to diversity

Physical Education Standards

1	Students are able to move competently using a variety of fundamental and specialized motor skills.
2	Students can monitor and maintain a health-enhancing level of physical fitness.
3	Students are able to apply movement concepts and basic mechanics of skill performance when learning and refining motor skills.
4	Students comprehend the basic principles of wellness and are able to apply concepts that enable them to make meaningful decisions that positively impact their health and wellness.
5	Students participate in a wide variety of physical activities and learn how to maintain a personalized active lifestyle.
6	Students demonstrate empathy, understanding, and respect for the numerous differences exhibited by people in an activity setting.
7	Students exhibit responsible and self-directed behaviours that lead to positive social interactions in physical activity.

OVERVIEW

Developmental games provide the opportunity for children to develop the motor skills and tactical understanding to allow for a smooth transition to a variety of sports. Developmental games have few rules and are easily adaptable, allowing the teacher to change the level of challenge to meet the needs of students. Developmental games also provide the opportunity for learning interactive skills such as leading, following, making decisions, and basic teamwork.

OUTCOMES

- Explain various ways in which games can be created or modified.
- Understand safety precautions associated with the teaching of games.
- Cite various ways to teach games effectively.
- Identify games that provide maximum participation and afford an opportunity for skill development.
- Classify various games according to developmental levels and tactical category.

Developmental games (also known as lead-up games) make a valuable contribution to the growth and development of youngsters. Games are a laboratory where children can apply physical skills in a fun setting. Many games help develop large-muscle groups and enhance the child's ability to run, dodge, start, and stop under control while sharing space with others. By applying tactics in these simple games, children are more prepared for the strategic aspect of the more complex sports. Some social learning outcomes that can be accomplished through games are the development of interpersonal skills, an understanding of rules and limitations, and knowledge of how to behave in a variety of competitive and cooperative situations.

As an important part of the physical education program, developmental games should be scrutinized and evaluated in terms of what they offer children. Offering children the opportunity to create and modify games fosters in them an understanding that game components can be changed to make the play experience beneficial for all.

Evaluating Games

A number of factors have an impact on the worth of developmental games, including the skills required, the number of participants, the complexity of rules, and the amount and type of strategy involved. The number of skills required should be consistent with the developmental level of the child. For example, many games at developmental level I focus on one major motor skill (e.g., running) and several complementary skills (e.g., dodging, stopping). More skills are added and combined as children progress. Development games are created for the express purpose of limiting the number of skills needed for successful participation. Evaluate the number of skills required and build a progression of games that gradually increases the use of skill combinations. In addition to required skills, tactical and strategic understanding also increases with developmental level. Whereas games at level I require minimal tactics for the children to be successful, games at levels II and III require more complex and varied tactics and team play.

The number of rules and the amount of strategy required increase the difficulty of a game. Developmental level I children find it difficult (and uninteresting) to play a game that has many rules. If cognitive strategy is required, requisite physical skills should be learned previously (over-learned) so concentration can be applied to the mental aspect of the game rather than the skill. Complex games require team members to play specific roles, and some of these roles (such as goalkeeper or line positions) may not appeal to students in the primary grades.

Youngsters also have to learn how to cooperate with teammates and compete against peers. The greater the number of teammates and competitors, the more difficult the game becomes. Cooperating with teammates is just as difficult as competing in a meaningful fashion. Moving from partner, to small-group, to team games is a natural progression and a formula for success. A number of games are more effective when played in small groups because the participants handle objects more often and have more chances to be active contributors.

In addition to the above factors, also consider the type and amount of meaningful participation that the game provides. Avoid or adjust games that eliminate children from participation. Many elimination games can be easily adjusted to change "elimination" to a momentary "freeze" position. This allows the student to be back in the game very quickly. Also adjust games that have many children stationary with only a few children actually moving, to allow for more movement for all participants. Finally, reconsider the use of games that involve human targets (for example, dodgeball). Few, if any, sports involve the skill of throwing an object at a person for the sole purpose of hitting them. If you want students to develop their ability to dodge or protect a target (goaltending skills), use a game that allows these skills. For example, having students protect a bowling pin while other students attempt to hit the pin allows the students to throw at a target, and to practise goaltending skills without the use of a human target. Certainly you can make traditional dodgeball less painful by using fleece balls and having "hit below the waist" rules. However, one must still question the validity of using a game that provides minimal developmental direction. Also note the position statement *Appropriate Practices for Elementary School Physical Education* in which the Council on Physical Education for Children (2000) identifies dodgeball as an inappropriate activity for K–12 school physical education programs.

Creating or Modifying Games

Games can be modified and new variations created by you and/or your students. For example, you may observe that a specific game is not meeting the desired learning outcomes and may decide to modify or change the game to facilitate skill development. Stop the class and ask them to think of a way to change the game to meet a particular purpose (for example, change the rules to make scoring more difficult). The teacher can use the alternatives suggested by students to create and implement a new game activity. With developmental level II and III students, you can offer some parameters for developing a game and then allow time for the class to create and implement the activity.

If students and teachers are to make meaningful modifications, they must understand how to analyze a game. The most recognized elements of game structure are desired outcomes, skills, equipment, rules or restrictions, number of players, and scheme of organization. Morris and Stiehl (1999) provide an approach to game analysis that may be helpful to teachers interested in game modification. Students need to learn how and what to modify, and they need to practise the process. Some suggestions to start students thinking include the following:

1. Change the distance to be run by decreasing or increasing it.

2. Change the means of locomotion. Use hopping, walking, skipping, or galloping instead of running.

3. Play the game with one or more partners. The partners can move and act as if they were a single person.

4. Change the method of tagging in simple tag games. Call out "Reverse" to signal that the runner is to become the tagger and vice versa.

5. Make goals or restricted areas larger or smaller. In Over the Wall, the restraining area can be made larger or smaller or its shape can be changed.

6. Vary the boundaries of the game by making them larger or smaller, as dictated by the number of players.

7. Change the formation in which the game is played. For example, Circle Kickball could be played in a square or triangular shape.

8. Change the requirements necessary for scoring. In Hand Hockey, players might be required to make four passes before a shot is taken.

9. Increase the number of players, taggers, or runners. The amount of equipment used can also be increased.

10. Change the rules or penalties of the game. For example, allow players a maximum of three dribbles or to hold the ball for no more than three seconds.

Cooperation and Competition

Without cooperation there would be no game activities. If participants chose not to follow the rules and play with teammates, it would be impossible to structure games. Clearly, games require cooperation before competition can be an outgrowth. *Cooperation* involves two or more children working together to achieve a common goal. *Competition* is characterized by opponents working against each other as each tries to reach a goal or reward. Since cooperation precedes competition, place emphasis on this phase of game activity. Through games, players can develop a spirit of working together, a concern for teammates, and an appreciation for the collective skills of the group.

Achieving a balance between offence and defence helps participants understand that both phases are important. In tag and capture games, offer opportunities for children to remain safe as well as the challenge of being at risk and eluding capture. Evaluate game components continually and modify them in the interest of retaining an enjoyable environment. It is the teacher's responsibility to assure that teams offer youngsters a chance to be successful. Emphasizing cooperation reinforces the need for children to play with all classmates regardless of ability level. Rotate students regularly so they have a chance to play with different classmates.

Classifying Games

Almond (1986) offered a classification system for games based on tactics, goals, and conditions. He identified the following four basic games categories: Invasion (e.g., basketball, soccer, hockey), net/wall (e.g., badminton, squash), striking/field games (e.g., softball, cricket), and target (e.g., bowling, curling, golf). Various classifications, according to Almond, utilize similar ways of solving conceptually similar strategic and tactical problems. For example, all invasion games involve the goal of moving an object through an opponent's territory in an attempt to score, while preventing the opposition from accomplishing the same goal. Given this conceptual similarity, practice activities can be easily adapted across a variety of invasion games. In addition to identifying skills involved in a developmental game, the teacher should also consider the classification. Presenting skills combined with the tactical games classification will allow the teacher to more accurately choose appropriate developmental games for his or her students. For an in-depth view of the tactical games approach see Mitchell, Oslin, & Griffin (2003).

Teaching Tactics and Strategy

All players must acquire a variety of general and specialized physical skills in order to participate effectively in a sport. The use of developmental games helps learners practise these skills in a developmentally appropriate fashion. In addition, effective game players require an understanding of basic tactics and strategy. Hopper and Bell (2000) describe strategic understanding as *knowing ways of playing* (e.g., keeping the rally going in volleyball or badminton), and tactical awareness as *knowing ways of playing to gain advantage over opponents* (e.g., outlet pass in basketball). These authors suggest "too often games teaching has focused on the technical aspects of isolated skills that rarely transfer into actual game play." A "tactical-skill approach" is suggested as an alternative. This is defined as getting students playing the game with the skills they have, and allowing them to focus on basic tactics. Once these basic tactics have been acquired, the student is able to use the more advanced skills. For example, the basic tactical concept of many invasion games is the "give and go" play (passing to a teammate and moving to an open space for a return pass). It is possible to allow students to practise this tactic in many developmental games prior to using it during a basketball or soccer game. Therefore, when a teacher is choosing or designing a developmental game, she should also consider the basic tactical and strategic concepts that are required of the more complex sports, and build the basic concepts into the developmental games.

Safety

Safety is a primary consideration in game situations. Check the play area for dangerous objects and hazards. Plan for buffer zones between parallel areas of play and establish a procedure for retrieving a ball from an adjoining area. Teach children to move in a controlled fashion and to use the entire playing area to avoid collisions. Learning to stop play immediately when a signal is given conditions youngsters to play games with referees, and also assures safety. This is an important prerequisite for later sports experiences.

Teaching Games Effectively

Here are some suggestions for more effectively teaching games to students.

1. *Put students in the formation they are going to use prior to presenting a new game to a class.* If they can sit in game formation, they will have an easier time understanding instructions. Make directions as brief as possible. Get the game under way with minimal instruction and gradually implement more subtle rules. Try the game first before answering any questions students may have. This ensures they have some perception of the game and how it is to proceed; many questions are answered through actually playing the game.

2. *Use a trial period (no scoring) during the first stages of learning a game.* This provides the opportunity for the teacher to clarify rules and avoids the possibility of children being caught off guard because they did not understand the activity.

3. *Avoid using games that isolate one child.* Instead, place two to four children in a situation to share the responsibility. An example of a common game where this happens is Birdie in the Cage. This sport lead-up game traditionally puts one youngster in the centre of the circle to try to intercept or touch passes made by circle players. Placing

several students in the centre makes it a team game and passes the responsibility to all centre players.

4. *Develop a rotation plan that allows all children to play for an equal amount of time.* Avoid a situation where winners stay on the court and losers sit out. Keep in mind that the purpose of games is to keep children involved in physical activity.

5. *Do some careful planning before attempting to teach a new game.* Identify safety hazards, anticipate difficult concepts, and adapt the game to the class and the situation. Make physical preparations prior to teaching. Establish boundaries and have equipment ready for distribution.

6. *When playing developmental and sport lead-up games, try to avoid using the out-of-bounds rule.* Instead, make a rule that whoever gets to the ball first gains possession. This speeds up the pace of the game and offers a strong incentive for quickly getting the ball back into play. If playing a game that uses a goal line or involves the children running to a line, establish a *safety zone.* Instead of using the wall or a line near the wall as the goal, draw safety lines 3 m from the wall to allow for deceleration. Use cones or spots to mark the deceleration zone.

7. *Change the makeup of the teams often and play relatively short games.* Playing games for short periods of time means more games can be played.

8. To identify teams, use pinnies or team belts worn around the waist. To ensure safety, insist pinnies are worn correctly.

9. *Games are an excellent platform for learning social skills.* Encourage children to self-referee where possible. Also, teach children to accept calls made by officials as an integral part of any game situation. Encourage players to learn negotiation skills and to resolve differences among themselves rather than having a teacher decide each issue.

Selection of Games

Games in this chapter were selected because they allow for practise of basic motor skills and strategic concepts, and offer activity for all children. Analyze the skills children must practise before playing. Drills and skill practice become more meaningful when children comprehend that the skill will be used in a game situation. Games have been sorted by difficulty and placed into three developmental levels. Table 22.1 lists each of the games alphabetically by developmental level, as well as the skills required for successful play. Games in developmental level I use basic locomotor skills and offer an environment in which children can practise and participate successfully. These games can be modified easily as required to increase or decrease the challenge.

Specialized sport skills are required in many of the games in developmental levels II and III. Ball-handling

TABLE 22.1
Alphabetical listing of games by developmental level

Developmental Level I Games

Games	Skills	Page
Animal Tag	Imagery, running, dodging	465
Aviator	Running, locomotor movements, stopping	467
Ball Passing	Object handling	467
Bottle Bat Ball	Batting, retrieving balls	467
Bottle Kick Ball	Kicking, trapping	468
Cat and Mice	Running, dodging	468
Change Sides	Body management	468
Charlie Over the Water	Skipping, running, stopping, bowling (rolling)	468
Circle Stoop	Moving to rhythm	469
Circle Straddle Ball	Ball rolling, catching	469
Colours	Colour or other perceptual concepts, running	469
Flowers and Wind	Running	469
Forest Ranger	Running	470
Freeze	Locomotor movements to rhythm	470
Hill Dill	Running, dodging	470
Hot Potatoes	Object handling	471
Frost and Thaw	Running, dodging, holding position	471
Leap the Brook	Leaping, jumping, hopping, turning	471
Marching Ponies	Marching, running	471
May I Chase You?	Running, dodging	471
Midnight Wolf	Running, dodging	472
Mix and Match	Fundamental locomotor movements	472
Musical Ball Pass	Passing and handling	472
One, Two, Buckle My Shoe	Running	472
Popcorn	Curling, stretching, jumping	473
Red Light	Fundamental locomotor movements, stopping	473
Right Angle	Rhythmic movement, body management	474
Roly-Poly	Ball rolling, dodging	474
Sneak Attack	Marching, running	474
Soap Bubbles	Body management	474
Squirrel in the Trees	Fundamental locomotor movements	474
Tag Games (Simple)	Fundamental locomotor movements, dodging	475

Stoop	Back-to-back
Stork	Skunk
Turtle	Locomotor
Mirror	Frozen
Elbow Link	Unfrozen

(continued)

(continued)

TABLE 22.1

Alphabetical listing of games by developmental level (continued)

Developmental Level III Games		
Games	**Skills**	**Page**
Frisbee Golf	Frisbee throwing for accuracy	489
Jump-the-shot Variations	Rope jumping	485
Octopus	Maneuvering, problem solving	485
One-base Tagball	Running, dodging, throwing	485
Over the Wall	Running, dodging	486
Pin Knockout	Rolling, dodging	486
Scooter Kickball	Striking with various body parts	486
Strike the Pins	Throwing	487
Sunday	Running, dodging	487
Tetherball	Batting a ball	489
Touchdown	Running, dodging	488
Two Square	Batting a ball	490
Volley Tennis	Most volleyball skills	490

and movement skills, with emphasis on tactics and strategy, are important for success in many of these games.

Sport Lead-up Games

Games in developmental levels II and III fall into two categories: sport lead-up games and developmental games. This chapter includes developmental games only; however, sport lead-up games can also be integrated into the games program. Sport lead-up games limit the number of skills required for successful participation in order to help children experience success in a sport setting. For example, Five Passes is a game designed to develop passing skills. Children do not have to perform other skills (such as dribbling or shooting) required by the regulation sport to achieve success. Table 22.2 lists all sport-related lead-up games presented in chapters 23 to 29. If you are teaching soccer skills and want to finish the lesson with a lead-up game, consult this chart to find an appropriate activity. Many of the lead-up games are excellent choices for skill development, particularly with developmental level III youngsters.

Developmental Level I

Games in the early part of developmental level I feature individual games and creative play. Little emphasis is placed on team play or on games that have a scoring

system. The games are simple, easily taught, and focus on basic locomotor skills. Dramatic elements are present in many of the games, and others help establish number concepts and symbol recognition. As children mature, they enjoy participation in running, tag, and ball games.

ANIMAL TAG

Supplies: None

Skills: Imagery, running, dodging

Formation:

```
X                    O
X                    O
X                    O
X                    O
X                    O
X                    O
X                    O
X                    O
X                    O
X                    O
X                    O
```

Two parallel lines are drawn about 10 m apart. Children are divided into two groups, each of which takes a position on one of the lines. Children in one group get together with their leader and decide what animal they wish to imitate. Having selected the animal, they move over to within 2 m or so of the other line. There they

TABLE 22.2

Lead-up Games from Sport Chapters 23–29*

(continued)

TABLE 22.2

Lead-up Games from Sport Chapters 23–29* (continued)

* Many of these games are used as culminating activities with sport lesson plans.

imitate the animal, and the other group tries to guess the animal correctly. If the guess is correct, the second group chases the first group back to its line, trying to tag as many as possible. Those caught must go over to the other team. The second group then selects an animal, and the roles are reversed. If the guessing team cannot guess the animal, however, the performing team gets another try. To avoid confusion, children must raise their hands to take turns at naming the animal. Otherwise, many false chases will occur. If children have trouble guessing, the leader of the performing team can give the initial of the animal.

AVIATOR

Supplies: None

Skills: Running, locomotor movements, stopping

Formation:

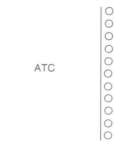

ATC

Players are parked (in push-up position) at one end of the playing area. The air traffic controller (ATC) is in front of the players and calls out, "Aviators, take off!" Players take off and move like airplanes to the opposite side of the area. The first person to move to the other side and land the plane (get into push-up position facing the ATC) is declared the new ATC.

If the ATC yells out some type of stormy weather, all planes must return to the starting line and resume the parked position. Examples of stormy weather commands are *lightning, thunder, hurricane,* and *tornado.* Each ATC is allowed to give only one stormy weather warning.

BALL PASSING

Supplies: Five or six different kinds of balls for each circle

Skill: Object handling

Formation: Circles with 15 or fewer in each circle

The class is divided into two or more circles, with no more than 12 children in any one circle. The teacher starts a ball around the circle; it is passed from player to player in the same direction. The teacher introduces more balls until five or six are moving around the circle at the same time and in the same direction. If a child drops a ball, he must retrieve it and continue. Beanbags can be substituted for balls. On a predetermined signal, players must reverse the passing direction.

BOTTLE BAT BALL

Supplies: A plastic bottle bat, whiffle ball, batting tee home plate, base marker

Skills: Batting, retrieving balls

Formation: Scattered

Each batter hits a fair ball off the batting tee (allowed as many swings as necessary). The batter hits the ball and runs around the base marker and back to home. If the ball is returned to the batter's tee before the batter reaches home, the batter becomes a fielder. If the batter beats the ball back to home plate, she receives another turn at bat (to a maximum of three turns), then trades places with a fielder. The running distance to first base is critical. It can remain fixed or can be made progressively (one step at a time) longer, until it reaches such a point that the fielders are heavily favoured.

TEACHING TIP

Use a plastic bottle bat and whiffle ball. A rotation system should be established when batters switch places with a fielder.

BOTTLE KICK BALL

Supplies: Plastic 4-litre jugs (bleach or milk containers) and 20-cm foam balls

Skills: Kicking, trapping

Formation:

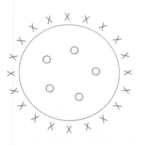

Players form a large circle around 10 to 12 plastic 4-litre jugs (bowling pins) standing in the middle of the circle. Students kick the balls and try to knock over the bottles. Use as many foam balls as necessary to keep all children active. If the group is large, make more than one circle of players.

CATS AND MICE

Supplies: None

Skills: Running, dodging

Formation:

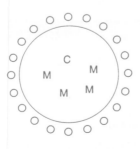

Form a large circle. Two or three children are the cats and four others are the mice. The cats and mice cannot leave the circle. On signal, the cats chase the mice inside the circle. As they are caught, the mice join the circle. The last mouse caught becomes the cat for the next round (and chooses two other cats).

If the cats are having difficulty catching the mice, increase the number of cats and/or decrease the size of the play area.

CHANGE SIDES

Supplies: None

Skill: Body management

Formation:

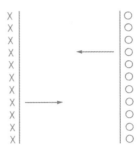

Establish two parallel lines 9 to 10 m apart with half of the class on each line. On signal, all players cross through to the other line, face the centre, and stand at attention. The first group to do all three things correctly wins a point. Children must be cautioned to use care when passing through the opposite group. They should be spaced well along each line; this allows room for them to move through each group. Vary the locomotor movements used by specifying skipping, hopping, long steps, sliding, and so on. The position to be assumed at the finish can also be varied.

CHARLIE OVER THE WATER

Supplies: A volleyball or playground ball

Skills: Skipping, running, stopping, bowling (rolling)

Formation: Scattered

Place the class in circle formation. Two or more children are placed in the centre of the circle, holding a ball. One of the centre players is designated as Charlie (or Sally). The class skips around the circle to the following chant:

Charlie over the water,

Charlie over the sea,

Charlie caught a bluebird,

But can't catch me!

On the word *me,* the centre players toss their balls in the air while the rest of the class runs and scatters throughout the area. When Charlie catches his ball, he shouts, "Stop!" All of the children stop immediately and must stand in a straddle position. All of the centre players attempt to roll their balls through the straddled legs of a classmate. If the roll is successful, that child becomes the new Charlie. If centre players miss, they remain in the centre and the game is repeated. If a centre player misses twice, however, she joins the circle and picks another person as a replacement. Consider using the names of students to replace "Charlie" and "Sally."

CIRCLE STOOP

Supplies: Music or tom-tom

Skills: Moving to rhythm

Formation:

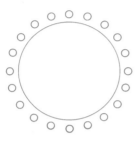

Children are in a single circle, facing counterclockwise. A march or similar music, or a tom-tom beat, can be used to signal movement. The class marches until the music stops, at which point they stoop and touch both hands to the ground without losing balance. The duration of the music should be varied so youngsters don't anticipate the signal.

TEACHING TIPS

Variations:

1. Using suitable music, have children employ different locomotor movements, such as skipping, hopping, or galloping.

2. Vary the stopping position. Instead of stooping, use positions such as the Push-up, Crab, or Lame Dog, balancing on one foot, or touching with one hand and one foot.

CIRCLE STRADDLE BALL

Supplies: Two or more 20-cm foam balls

Skills: Ball rolling, catching

Formation: Circles of 10 to 15 students

Children are in circle formation, facing in. Each player stands in a wide-straddle stance with the side of each foot against the neighbour's foot. Their hands are on the knees. Two or more balls are used. The object of the game is to roll a ball between the legs of another player before that player can get hands down to stop the ball. Keep the circles small so students have more opportunities to handle the ball. Players must catch and roll the ball, rather than bat it.

Children must keep their hands on their knees until a ball is rolled at them. After some practice, the following variation can be played:

TEACHING TIP

Variation: Two or more children are in the centre, each with a ball. The other children are in the same formation as before. The centre players try to roll the ball through the legs of any child, masking intent by using feints and changes of direction. Any child allowing the ball to go through becomes the new centre player.

COLOURS

Supplies: Coloured paper (construction paper) cut in circles, squares, or triangles for markers

Skills: Colour or other perceptual concepts, running

Formation:

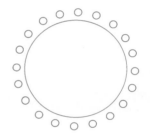

Use five or six differently coloured markers, with a number of children having the same colour. Children are standing or seated in a circle with a marker in front of each. The teacher (or another player) calls out a colour. Everyone having that colour runs counterclockwise around the circle and back to place. The first player seated upright and motionless is declared the winner and calls the next colour. Different kinds of locomotor movement can be specified, such as skipping, galloping, walking, and so on. After a period of play, the children leave the markers on the floor and move one place to the left.

TEACHING TIP

Variation: Shapes (circles, triangles, squares, rectangles, stars, and diamonds) can be used instead of colours, as can numbers or other articles or categories, such as animals, birds, or fish.

FLOWERS AND WIND

Supplies: None

Skill: Running

Formation:

```
X |                    | O
X |                    | O
X |                    | O
X |                    | O
X |                    | O
X |                    | O
X |                    | O
X |                    | O
X |                    | O
X |                    | O
X |                    | O
```

Two parallel lines long enough to accommodate the children are drawn about 8 m apart. Children are divided into two groups: the flowers and the wind. Each team takes a position on one of the lines and faces the other team. The flowers secretly select the name of a common flower. When ready, they walk over to the other line and stand about 1 m away from the wind. The players on the wind team begin to call out flower names—trying to guess the flower chosen. When the flower has been guessed, the flowers run to their goal line, chased by the players of the other team. Any player caught must join the other side. The roles are reversed and the game is repeated. If one side has trouble guessing, a clue can be given as to the colour or size of the flower or the first letter of its name.

FOREST RANGER

Supplies: None

Skill: Running

Formation:

Half of the class forms a circle and faces the centre. These are the trees. The other half of the class stands behind the trees as forest rangers. An extra child, the forest lookout, is in the centre. The forest lookout starts the game by calling, "Fire in the forest. Run, run, run!" Immediately, the forest rangers run around the outside of the circle to the right. After a few moments, the lookout steps in front of one of the trees. This is the signal for each of the rangers to step in front of a tree. One player is left out, who then becomes the new forest lookout. The trees become rangers and the rangers become trees. Each time the game is played, the circle must be moved out somewhat, because the formation narrows when the rangers step in front of the trees.

FREEZE

Supplies: Music or tom-tom

Skills: Locomotor movements to rhythm

Formation: Scattered

Scatter the class throughout the play area. When the music starts, players move throughout the area, guided by the music. They walk, run, jump, or use other locomotor movements, depending on the selected music or beat. When the music is stopped, they freeze and do not move. Any child caught moving after the cessation of the rhythm pays a penalty. A tom-tom is a fine accompaniment for this game, because the rhythmic beat can be varied easily and the rhythm can be stopped at any time.

This game is useful for practising management skills because it reinforces freezing on a stop signal.

TEACHING TIP

Variations:

1. Specify the level at which children must freeze.

2. Have children fall to the ground or balance or go into a different position, such as the Push-up, Crab, Lame Dog, or some other defined position.

HILL DILL

Supplies: None

Skills: Running, dodging

Formation:

```
|                    | X
|                    | X
|                    | X
|                    | X
|                    | X
|        It          | X
|                    | X
|                    | X
|                    | X
|                    | X
|                    | X
```

Two parallel lines are established 10 to 15 m apart. Two or more players are chosen to be taggers and stand in the centre between the lines. The other children stand on one of the parallel lines. One of the centre taggers calls, "Hill Dill! Come over the hill, Or else I'll catch you standing still!"

Children run across the open space to the other line, while the taggers in the centre try to tag them. Anyone caught helps the taggers in the centre. When children cross over to the other line, they must await the next call. Start a new game when a majority of players have been tagged.

HOT POTATOES

Supplies: One to three balls or beanbags for each group

Skill: Object handling

Formation: Circles with 8 to 12 players

Group players in small circles (8 to 12 per circle) so objects can be passed from one to another around the circle. Balls or beanbags or both are passed around the circle. The teacher or a selected student, who is standing with his back to the class, randomly shouts, "Stop!" The point of the game is to avoid being the person who passes the object to the person who caught it when the signal occurs. If this happens, the player(s) who passed the object gets up and moves to the next circle. Begin the game with one object and gradually add objects if the class is capable. Call out, "Reverse" to signal a change in the direction the object is passed.

FROST AND THAW

Supplies: Blue pinnies for Frosts and red ones for Thaws

Skills: Running, dodging, holding position

Formation: Scattered

The class is scattered and moves to avoid being frozen (tagged) by two or three Frosts, who carry a blue pinnie in one hand. Frozen children remain immobile until touched (thawed) by the Thaws, who carry a red pinnie.

LEAP THE BROOK

Supplies: None

Skills: Leaping, jumping, hopping, turning

Formation:

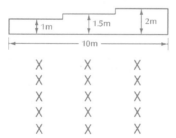

Mark off a brook across the floor. For the first third of the brook, it is about 1 m wide; for the next third, about 1.5 m wide; and for the last third, it is 2.0 m wide. Youngsters line up on one side of the area. On the signal, "Cross the Brook!" players pick a challenge and try to jump across the brook. The wider the brook, the greater the challenge. Use different styles of locomotor movements such as hopping, jumping, and leaping over the brook. The selection of the distances can be changed if they are unsuitable for any particular group of children.

TEACHING TIP

Variation: Use different types of turns—such as right or left; quarter, half, three-quarter, or full—while jumping the brook. Use different body shapes, different arm positions, and so on.

MARCHING PONIES

Supplies: None

Skills: Marching, running

Formation:

Two or three children are ringmasters and crouch in the centre of a circle of ponies formed by the rest of the class. Two goal lines on opposite sides of the circle are established as safe areas. The ponies march around the circle in step, counting as they do so. At a predetermined number (whispered to the ringmasters by the teacher), the ringmasters jump up and attempt to tag the others before they can reach the safety lines. Anyone tagged joins the ringmasters in the centre and helps catch others. Reorganize the game after six to eight children have been caught.

MAY I CHASE YOU?

Supplies: None

Skills: Running, dodging

Formation:

The class stands behind a line long enough to accommodate all. Two or three runners stand about 2 to 3 m in front

of the line. The class asks, "May I chase you?" One of the runners (designated by teacher) replies, "Yes, if you are wearing . . ." and names a colour, an article of clothing, or a combination of the two. All who qualify immediately chase the runners until one is tagged. New runners are chosen and the game is repeated. Encourage players to think of other ways to identify those who run.

MIDNIGHT WOLF

Supplies: None

Skills: Running, dodging

Formation:

A safety line is established about 12 m from a den in which two or three players—the wolves—are standing. The others stand behind the safety line and ask, "What time is it, Midnight Wolf?" One of the wolves is designated to answer in various fashions, such as "one o'clock," "four o'clock," and so on. When the wolf says a certain time, the class walks forward that number of steps. For example, if the wolf says, "six o'clock" the class has to move forward six steps. The wolf continues to draw the players toward him. At some point, the wolf answers the question by saying, "Midnight," and chases the others back to the safety line. Any player who is caught becomes a wolf in the den and helps to catch others.

MIX AND MATCH

Supplies: None

Skills: Fundamental locomotor movements

Formation:

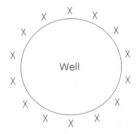

A line is established through the middle of the area. Half of the children are on one side and half are on the other. Two or three extra persons are on one side of the area. The teacher gives a signal for children to move as directed on their side of the line. They can be told to run, hop, skip, or make some other movement. On signal, players run to the dividing line and reach across to join hands with a player on the opposite side. The goal is to find a partner and not be left out. Children may reach over but may not cross the line. The players left out move to the opposite side so that players left out come from alternating sides of the area.

TEACHING TIP

Variation: The game also can be done with music or a drumbeat, with the players rushing to the centre line to find partners when the rhythm stops.

MUSICAL BALL PASS

Supplies: One or two playground balls per group, music

Skills: Passing and handling

Formation:

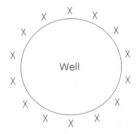

Break the class into a number of small groups (six to seven players) in circle formation facing the centre. One ball is given to a player in each circle and is passed around the circle when the music starts. When the music stops, the player with the ball (or the last player to touch the ball) goes into the "well" in the centre of the circle. The player stays in the centre for one turn. More than one ball may be used.

ONE, TWO, BUCKLE MY SHOE

Supplies: None

Skill: Running

Formation:

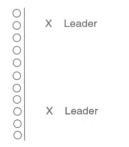

Two parallel lines are drawn on opposite sides of the playing area. Two or three players are selected as leaders and stand in front of the class. The rest of the class is behind one of the lines. The leaders say, "Ready." The following dialogue takes place between the leaders and the children.

Children: One, two.

Leader: Buckle my shoe.

Children: Three, four.

Leader: Close the door.

Children: Five, six.

Leader: Pick up sticks.

Children: Seven, eight.

Leader: Run, or you'll be late!

As children carry on the conversation with the leaders, they toe the line, ready to run. When the leaders say the word *late*, players run to the other line and return. New leaders are chosen after each run. The leaders can give the last response ("Run, or you'll be late!") in any timing desired—pausing or dragging out the words. No player can leave before the word *late* is uttered.

POPCORN

Supplies: None

Skills: Curling, stretching, jumping

Formation:

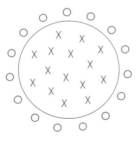

Half of the class is designated as popcorn; they crouch down in the centre of the circle formed by the rest of the class. The circle children, also crouching, represent the heat. One of them is designated the leader, whose actions serve as a guide to the other children. The circle children gradually rise to a standing position, extend their arms overhead, and shake them vigorously to indicate the intensifying heat. In the meantime, the popcorn in the centre starts to pop. This should begin at a slow pace and increase in speed and height as the heat is applied. In the final stages, children are popping up rapidly. After a time, the groups change places and the action is repeated.

RED LIGHT

Supplies: None

Skills: Fundamental locomotor movements, stopping

Formation:

A goal line is established at one end of the area. The object of the game is to move across the area successfully without getting caught. Two or three players are leaders and stand on the goal line. The leaders turn away from the players. One of the leaders claps five times. All leaders turn around on the fifth clap. In the meantime, the players move toward the goal line, timing their movements to end on the fifth clap. If any of the leaders catch any movement by any person, that person is required to return to the starting line and begin anew. After the clapper turns away, she can turn back immediately to catch any movement. Once she begins clapping, however, five claps must be completed before she turns around. The first child to reach the goal line successfully without being caught in an illegal movement is the winner. New leaders are chosen for the next game.

TEACHING TIP

Variations:

1. An excellent variation of the game is to have the leaders face the oncoming players. The designated leader calls out, "Green light" for them to move and "Red light" for them to stop. When the leader calls other colours, the players should not move.

2. Different types of locomotion can be explored. The leader names the type of movement (e.g., hop, crawl, skip) before turning her back to the group.

3. The leader can specify how those caught must go back to place—walk, hop, skip, slide, crawl.

In the original game of Red Light, the leader counts rapidly, "One, two, three, four, five, six, seven, eight, nine, ten—red light," instead of clapping five times. This has proved to be impractical in most gymnasiums, however, because children moving forward cannot hear the counting. Clapping, which provides both a visual and an auditory signal, is preferable.

RIGHT ANGLE

Supplies: Music

Skills: Rhythmic movement, body management

Formation: Scattered

A tom-tom can be used to provide the rhythm for this activity. Children quickly change direction at right angles on each heavy beat or change of music. The object of the game is to make the right-angle change on signal and not to bump into other players.

ROLY-POLY

Supplies: Many 20-cm foam balls

Skills: Ball rolling, aiming at a target

Formation:

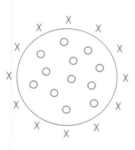

Half of the class forms a circle; the other half is in the centre in straddle position. Balls are given to the circle players. The circle players try to roll the ball through the straddled legs of the centre players. If a circle player makes a successful roll, he switches with the centre player. After a period of time the circle and centre players can all trade places.

SNEAK ATTACK

Supplies: None

Skills: Running

Formation:

Two parallel lines are drawn about 10 to 15 metres apart. The class is divided into two teams. One team takes a position on one of the lines, with their backs to the area. These are the chasers. The other team is on the other line, facing the area. This is the sneak team. The sneak team moves forward on signal, moving toward the chasers. When they get reasonably close, a signal is given, and the sneak team turns and runs back to their line, chased by the other team. Anyone tagged before reaching the line changes to the chase team. The game is then repeated, with the roles exchanged.

SOAP BUBBLES

Supplies: Cones to delineate space, music

Skills: Body management

Formation: Scattered

Four cones are used to delineate the movement area. Each player is a soap bubble floating throughout the area. A locomotor movement is called out, and youngsters perform it, moving within the area designated by the four cones. As the game progresses, the cones are moved toward the centre to decrease the size of the area. The object of the game is not to touch or collide with another bubble. When this occurs, both bubbles burst and sink to the floor, making themselves as small as possible. The space is made smaller until only a few have not been touched. This game teaches the concept of moving in general space without touching.

SQUIRREL IN THE TREES

Supplies: None

Skills: Fundamental locomotor movements

Formation:

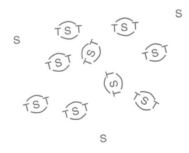

A number of trees are formed by two players facing each other and holding hands or putting hands on each other's shoulders. A squirrel is in the centre of each tree, and one or two extra squirrels are outside. On signal, the trees open up and let the squirrels move around the area. The trees also stay together and move throughout the area. On signal, the trees freeze in place and the squirrels find any available tree. Only one squirrel is allowed in a tree.

Rotation is necessary so all students get to be a squirrel. Once the squirrels are in a tree, ask them to face one of the tree players. The person they are facing becomes their partner for a tree and the other person becomes a new squirrel.

TAG GAMES (SIMPLE)

Supplies: None

Skills: Fundamental locomotor movements, dodging

Formation: Scattered

Tag has many variations. The following are "give up the tag" games because a player is no longer a tagger when she tags another person, who then becomes the new tagger. Children are scattered throughout the area. A number of players are designated as taggers. When a tag is made, that player states, "You're a tagger." The new tagger can chase any player other than the person who tagged him (no tagbacks).

Variations:

1. Touching a specified type of object (such as wood or iron) or line on the floor or an object of a specified colour can make a runner safe.

2. Children can be safe by doing a particular action or by striking a certain pose.

   a. *Stoop Tag.* Players touch both hands to the ground.

   b. *Stork Tag.* Players stand on one foot. (The other cannot touch.)

   c. *Turtle Tag.* Players get on their backs, feet pointed toward the ceiling.

   d. *Mirror Tag.* In order to be freed, a frozen player must mirror the three movements another player performs when standing face-to-face.

   e. *Elbow Link Tag.* Players link elbows with another child.

   f. *Back-to-back Tag.* Players stand back to back with any other child.

   g. *Skunk Tag.* Players reach an arm under one knee and hold the nose.

3. *Locomotor Tag.* The child who is the tagger specifies how the others should move—skipping, hopping, or jumping. The tagger must use the same kind of movement.

4. *Frozen Tag.* Two or more children are taggers. The rest are scattered over the area. When caught, they are "frozen" and must keep both feet in place. Any free player can tag a frozen player and thus release her. The goal of the taggers is to freeze all players.

5. *Unfrozen Tag.* Same rules as Frozen Tag, except that when tagged the frozen player continues to jog in place until freed.

LEADER BALL

Supplies: A volleyball or rubber playground ball

Skills: Throwing, catching

Formation:

One child is the leader and stands about 3 m in front of three other students, who are lined up facing the leader. The object of the game is to move up to the leader's spot by avoiding making poor throws or missing catches. The leader throws to each child in turn, beginning with the child on the left, who must catch and return the ball. Any child making a throwing or catching error goes to the end of the line, on the leader's right. Those in the line move up, filling the vacated space.

A leader who misses a catch or makes a poor throw must go to the end of the line, and the child at the head of the line becomes the new leader.

Variation: The leader can suggest specific methods of throwing and catching, such as, "Catch with the right hand only," or "Catch with one hand and don't let the ball touch your body."

TOE TO TOE

Supplies: None

Skills: Fundamental locomotor movements

Formation: Scattered

Children perform a locomotor movement around the area. On signal, each child must find a partner as quickly as possible and stand toe to toe (one foot only) with that person. Children who can't find a partner within their immediate area must run quickly to the centre of the area (use a marking spot or cone) to find a partner. The goal is to find a nearby partner as quickly as possible and avoid being the last pair formed. Last pair formed calls out the next locomotor skill. If the number of students playing is uneven, the teacher can join in and play.

TWINS (TRIPLETS)

Supplies: None

Skills: Body management, running

Formation: Scattered with partner

Youngsters are scattered throughout the area with a partner (twin). The teacher gives commands such as, "Take three hops and two leaps," or "Walk backward four steps and three skips." When the pairs are separated, the teacher says, "Find your twin!" Players find their twin and stand frozen toe to toe. The goal is to find your twin as quickly as possible and assume the frozen position. Make sure students move away from each other during the movements.

TEACHING TIP

Variation: The game becomes more challenging when played in groups of three (triplets). When using this variation, new partners should be selected each time.

WHERE'S MY PARTNER?

Supplies: None

Skills: Fundamental locomotor movements

Formation:

Children are in a double circle by pairs, with partners facing. When the signal is given, the circles skip (or walk, run, hop, or gallop) to the right. This means that they are skipping in opposite directions. On the command "Halt," the circles face each other to find partners. Partners then perform a challenge (for example, back-to-back stand up). The circles should be reversed after a time.

TEACHING TIP

Variation: The game can also be played with music or a drumbeat. When the music stops, the players seek partners.

Developmental Level II

Compared with the games in developmental level I, the games program undergoes a definite change. Chase and tag games become more complex and demand more maneuvering. Introductory lead-up games with emphasis on strategy and team play make an appearance. The interests of children turn to games that have a sport slant, and kicking, throwing, catching, batting, and other sport skills are beginning to mature.

ADDITION TAG

Supplies: None

Skills: Running, dodging

Formation:

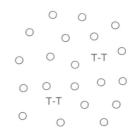

Two or more pairs are taggers, and each stands with inside hands joined. The other children run individually. The pairs move around the area, trying to tag with the free hands. The first person tagged joins the pair, making a trio. The three then chase until they catch a fourth. Once a fourth person is caught, the four divide and form two pairs, adding another set of taggers to the game. This continues until the majority of players are tagged.

TEACHING TIP

Some area restrictions can be established if pairs are having problems catching the runners. The game moves faster if started with more pairs. A tag is legal only when the pair or trio keeps their hands joined.

ALASKA BASEBALL

Supplies: A volleyball or soccer ball

Skills: Kicking, batting, running, ball handling

Formation:

Players are organized in two teams; one is at bat while the other is in the field. A straight line provides the only out-of-bounds line, and the team at bat is behind this

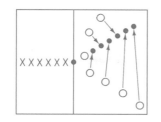

line at about the middle. The other team is scattered around the fair territory.

One player propels the ball, either batting a volleyball or kicking a stationary soccer ball. Teammates are in a close file behind the batter. As soon as the batter sends the ball into the playing area, he starts to run around the line of teammates. Each time the runner passes the head of the file, the team gives a loud count.

There are no outs. The first fielder to get the ball stands still and starts to pass the ball back overhead to the nearest teammate, who moves directly behind to receive it. The remainder of the team in the field must run to the ball and form a file behind it. The ball is passed back overhead, with each player handling the ball. When the last field player in line has a firm grip on it, she shouts, "Stop." At this signal, a count is made of the number of times the batter ran around her team.

Five batters or half of the team should bat; then the teams should change places. This is better than allowing an entire team to bat before changing to the field, because players in the field tire from many consecutive runs.

BAT BALL

Supplies: A 20-cm foam ball

Skills: Batting, running, catching, throwing

Formation:

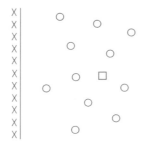

A serving line is drawn across one end of the field, and a 1-by-1-m base is established about 15 m from the serving line. Children are divided into two teams. One team is scattered over the playing area. The other team is behind the serving line, with one player at bat. The batter puts the ball into play by batting it with a hand into the playing area. To be counted as a fair ball, the ball must land in the

playing area or be touched by a member of the fielding team. As soon as the ball is hit, the batter runs to the base and back across the serving line. In the meantime, the fielding team fields the ball and attempts knock a ball off a designated batting tee or cone.

Fielders may not run with the ball. It must be passed from fielder to fielder until thrown at the batting tee.

A run is scored each time the batter hits a fair ball, touches the base, and gets back to the serving line before the ball is knocked off the batting tee. A run is also scored if the fielding team commits a foul. Each player bats once per inning.

BEACH BALL BAT BALL

Supplies: Four to six beach balls or large foam balls

Skills: Batting, tactile handling

Formation:

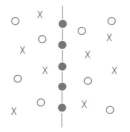

To begin the game, the balls are placed on the centre line dividing the court area. Four to six beach balls are in play at the same time. A score occurs when the beach ball is batted over the end line. Once the ball moves across the end line, it is dead. Players concentrate on the remaining balls in play. If a ball is on the floor, it is picked up and batted into play. At no time may players carry a ball. After all four balls are scored, the game ends. A new game is started after teams switch goals.

BOUNCE BALL

Supplies: Volleyballs or rubber playground balls of about the same size

Skills: Throwing, ball rolling

Formation:

The court is divided into halves. Children form two teams. Each team occupies one half of the court and is given a number of balls. Two players from each team are assigned to retrieve balls behind their own end lines. The object of the game is to bounce or roll the ball over the opponents' end line. A ball thrown across the line on a fly does not count. Two scorers are needed, one at each end line. Players can move wherever they wish in their own area but cannot cross the centreline. After the starting signal, the balls are thrown back and forth at the players' will.

BOX BALL

Supplies: A sturdy box, 60 cm square and about 30 cm deep; four volleyballs (or similar balls)

Skills: Running, ball handling

Formation:

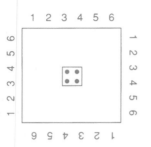

The class is divided into four even teams, with 6 to 10 players per team. Each team occupies one side of a hollow square at an equal distance from the centre. Players face inward and each team numbers off consecutively from right to left.

A box containing four balls is put in the centre. The teacher calls a number, and the player from each team who has that number runs forward to the box, takes a ball, and runs to the head of her line, taking the place of player 1. In the meantime, the players in the line have moved to the left just enough to fill in the space left by the runner. On reaching the head of the line, the runner passes the ball to the next person and so on down the line to the end child. The last child runs forward and returns the ball to the box. The first team to return the ball to the box scores a point.

The runner must not pass the ball down the line until she is in place at the head of the line. The ball must be caught and passed by each child. Failure to conform to these rules results in team disqualification. Runners stay at the head of the line, retaining their original number. The lines are not kept in consecutive number sequence.

BUSY BEE

Supplies: None

Skills: Fundamental locomotor movements

Formation:

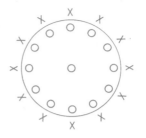

Half of the class forms a large circle, facing in, and is designated the stationary players. The other players seek partners from this group, and stand in front of the stationary players. An extra child in the centre is the busy bee. The bee calls out directions such as "Toe to toe," "Face to face," "Shake hands," "Kneel on one knee [or both]," and "Hop on one foot." The other children follow these directions. The centre child then calls out, "Busy bee." Stationary players stand still, and their partners seek new partners while the centre player also tries to get a partner. The child without a partner becomes the new busy bee.

TEACHING TIP

Teach children a variety of movements they can do if they become the busy bee. When changing partners, children must select a partner other than the stationary player next to them. After a period of time, the active and stationary players are rotated.

CAGEBALL KICK-OVER

Supplies: A cageball, 45-, 60-, or 75-cm size

Skill: Kicking

Formation:

```
O    | X
O    | X
O    | X
O    | X
O    | X
O    | X
O    | X
O    | X
O    | X
O    | X
```

Players are divided into two teams and sit facing each other, with legs outstretched and the soles of their feet about 2 to 3 m apart. While maintaining the sitting position, each player supports his weight on his hands, which are placed slightly to the rear.

The teacher rolls the cageball between the two teams. The object of the game is to kick the ball over the other team, thereby scoring a point. After a point is scored, the teacher rolls the ball into play again. Rotate players by having a player on the left side of the line take a place on the right side after a point is scored, thus moving all the players one position to the left. When the ball is kicked out at either end, no score results, and the ball is put into play again by the teacher.

TEACHING TIP

Children can be allowed to use their hands to stop the ball from going over them.

CLUB GUARD

Supplies: A juggling club or bowling pin and foam rubber ball

Skill: Throwing

Formation:

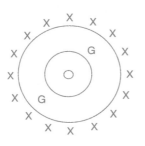

A circle about 4 m in diameter is drawn. Inside the circle at the centre, a 45-cm circle is drawn. The club is put in the centre of the small circle. Two or three youngsters guard the club. The other players stand outside the large circle, which is the restraining line for them.

The circle players throw the ball at the club and try to knock it down. The guards try to block the throws with the legs and body, but must stay out of the small inner circle. The outer circle players pass the ball around rapidly so that one of the players can get an opening to throw as the guards maneuver to protect the club. Rotate in new guards after a short period of time (15 to 20 seconds). The guards are disqualified if they step into the small circle.

TEACHING TIP

Variation: More than one club can be placed in the centre.

COMPETITIVE CIRCLE CONTESTS

Supplies: Volleyballs or 20-cm foam rubber balls, two bowling pins

Skills: Throwing, catching

Formation: Two circles with the same number of students in each

Two teams arranged in independent circles compete against each other. The circles should be of the same diameter; lines can be drawn on the floor to ensure this. The players of each team are numbered consecutively so that each player in one circle corresponds to a player in the other circle. Two numbered players, in sequence, go to the centre of the opponents' circle to compete for their team in either of the following activities:

1. *Circle Club Guard.* The two centre players guard a bowling pin. The circle that knocks down the club first wins a point. The ball should be rolled at the club.

2. *Touch Ball.* The circle players pass the ball from one to another while the two centre players try to touch it. The centre player who touches the ball first wins a point for the respective team. In case neither player is able to touch the ball in a reasonable period of time, the action should be cut off without awarding a point.

After all players have competed, the team with the most points wins. For Circle Club Guard, there must be three passes to different people before the ball can be rolled at the club. It may be necessary to establish circle lines to regulate throwing distance.

COUPLE TAG

Supplies: None

Skills: Running, dodging

Formation:

Two goal lines are established on opposite sides of an area. Players run in pairs, with inside hands joined. All pairs, except two, line up on one of the goal lines. The pairs in the centre are taggers. They call, "Run," and the children, keeping hands joined, run to the other goal line. The pairs in the centre, also retaining joined hands, try to tag any other pair. As soon as a couple is caught, they help the centre couples. The game continues until all are caught.

Variation: Triplet Tag. The game can be played with sets of threes. Tagging is done with any pair of joined hands. If a triplet breaks joined hands, it is considered caught.

CROWS AND CRANES

Supplies: None

Skills: Running, dodging

Formation:

```
X | O
X | O
X | O
X | O
X | O
X | O
X | O
X | O
X | O
X | O
X | O
```

Establish two goal lines on opposite sides of an area. The class is divided into two groups—the crows and the cranes. The groups face each other at the centre of the area, about 2 m apart. The leader calls out either, "Crows," or "Cranes," using a *cr-r-r-r-r* sound at the start of either word to mask the result. If "Crows" is the call, the crows chase the cranes to the goal line. If "Cranes" is the call, then the cranes chase. Any player caught goes over to the other side and becomes a member of that group. The team that has the most players when the game ends is the winner.

Variations:

1. *Toe to Toe.* Instead of facing each other, children stand back to back, about 30 cm apart, in the centre.

2. *Red and Blue.* A piece of cardboard painted red on one side and blue on the other can be thrown into the air between the teams, instead of having someone give calls. If red comes up, the red team chases, and vice versa.

3. *Odd and Even.* Large foam rubber dice can be thrown in the air. If they come up even, the even team chases. If they come up odd, the odd team chases.

4. *Blue, Black, and Baloney.* On the command "Blue," or "Black," the game proceeds as described. On the command "Baloney," no one is to move. The caller should draw out the *bl-l-l-l* sound before ending with one of the three commands.

FOLLOW ME

Supplies: A marker for each child (small cones or beanbags work well)

Skills: All locomotor movements, stopping

Formation:

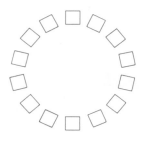

The class is arranged in a rough circle, each youngster standing or sitting with one foot on a marker. Two extra players are guides. They move around the circle, pointing at different players and asking them to follow. Each player chosen falls in behind the guide that pointed at him or her. The guides then take the groups on a tour, and the members of each group perform just as the guide does. The guide may hop, skip, do stunts, or execute other movements, and children following must do likewise. At the signal "Home," all run for places with a marker. Two players will be left without a marker. They can become guides or choose other guides.

FOX HUNT

Supplies: None

Skills: Running, dodging

Formation:

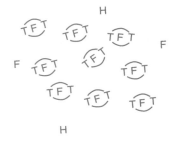

Pairs of players form trees by facing each other and holding hands. A third member of each group is a fox and stands between the hands of the trees. Three players are identified as foxes without trees and three players are designated as hounds. The hounds try to tag foxes that are not in trees. The extra foxes may move to a tree and displace the fox that is standing in the tree. In addition, the foxes in trees may leave the safety of their trees at any time. If the hound tags a fox, their roles are reversed immediately, the fox becoming the hound.

The game should be stopped at regular intervals to allow the players who are trees to change places with the foxes and hounds.

HOME BASE

Supplies: Cones to delineate the area, four pinnies

Skills: Reaction time, locomotor movements, body management

Place a number of marking spots on the floor throughout the area. Divide the class into groups of five or six. Ask each group to quickly line up with one person on a marking spot and the rest of the players behind in single file. The person on the spot is designated as the team captain. A locomotor movement is called and all players do this movement throughout the area. When "Home base" is called, the captains quickly find the closest spot, and their respective team members line up behind them. The first team to return to proper position (standing in a straight line) is declared the winner.

TEACHING TIP

Avoid calling "Home base" until the students are thoroughly mixed. The teacher can specify a number of different formations that students must assume upon return to their home base.

JUMP THE SHOT

Supplies: Five jump-the-shot ropes

Skill: Rope jumping

Formation:

Divide the class into four or five small circles. One player with a long rope stands in the centre. A soft object is tied to the free end of the rope to give it some weight. An old, deflated ball or beanbag makes a good weight (tie the rope to it and use duct tape to keep it from becoming untied). The centre player turns the rope under the feet of the circle players, who must jump over it. A player who touches the rope with the feet must move up to the next group.

TEACHING TIP

Variations:

1. Change the centre player after one or two misses. The centre player should be cautioned to keep the rope along the ground. The rope speed can be varied. Different tasks can be performed, such as hopping, jumping, and turning, or jumping and clapping.

2. Pairs line up in the same formation. They join inside hands and stand side by side when jumping.

LOOSE CABOOSE

Supplies: None

Skills: Running, dodging

Formation:

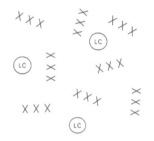

Two or three children are designated as loose cabooses that try to hook onto a train. Trains are formed by three or four children standing in column formation with their hands placed on the shoulders of the child immediately in front. The trains, by twisting and turning, endeavour to keep the caboose from hooking onto the back. Should the caboose manage to hook on, the front child in the train becomes the new caboose. Each train should attempt to keep together. If a train breaks while being chased, the loose caboose becomes the new leader of that train.

NONDA'S CAR LOT

Supplies: None

Skills: Running, dodging

Formation:

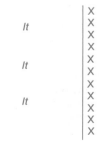

Two or three players are taggers, and stand in the centre of the area between two lines established at opposite ends of the playing area. The class selects four names of cars (e.g., Honda, Corvette, Toyota, Cadillac). Each student then selects or is assigned a name of car.

One of the taggers calls out a car name. All students who selected that name attempt to run to the other line without getting tagged. The tagger calls out the cars until all students have run. When a child (car) gets tagged, he must stand in frozen position at the spot of the tag. He cannot move, but may tag other students who run too near. When the one who is the tagger calls out, "Car lot," all of the cars must go. Change taggers often.

ONE STEP

Supplies: A ball or beanbag for each pair of children

Skills: Throwing, catching

Formation:

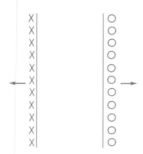

Two children stand facing each other about 1 m apart. One has a ball or a beanbag. The object of the game is to throw or toss the item in the stipulated manner so that the partner can catch it without moving the feet on or from the ground. When the throw is completed successfully, the thrower takes one step backward and waits for the throw from her partner. Children can try to increase their distance to an established line, or the two children who move the greatest distance apart can be declared the winners. When either child misses, moves the feet, or fails to follow directions, the partners move forward and start over. Variables to provide interest and challenge are type of throw, type of catch, and kind of step. Throwing can be underhand, overhand, two-handed, around the back, and so on. Catching can be two-handed, left-handed, right-handed, to the side, and so on.

TEACHING TIP

Variation: *Bowling One Step.* In groups of four to six, each of the players in turn gets a chance to roll the ball at a bowling pin. A minimal distance (2 m) is established. The player takes a step backward each time the pin is knocked down, and keeps

rolling until she misses. The winner is the child who has moved the farthest from the pin.

SQUAD TAG

Supplies: Pinnies or markers for one squad, stopwatch

Skills: Running, dodging

Formation:

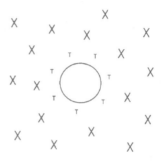

Delineate the running area with cones. An entire squad acts as taggers. The object is to see which squad can tag the remaining class members in the shortest time. The tagging squad should be marked. They stand in a football huddle formation in the centre of the area, with their heads down. The remainder of the class scatters as they wish throughout the area. On signal, the tagging squad scatters and tags the other class members. A class member who is tagged stops in place and remains there. Time is recorded when the last person is tagged. Each squad gets a turn at tagging.

TEACHING TIP

Children should be cautioned to move under control, because there is much chasing and dodging in different directions. Definite boundaries are needed.

STEAL THE TREASURE

Supplies: A bowling pin

Skill: Dodging

Formation:

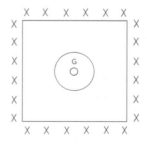

A playing area about 5 m square is outlined, with a small circle in the centre. A bowling pin placed in the small circle (Hula Hoop) is the treasure. Three to four guards are selected to protect the treasure. The guards can move as far from the treasure as they like in order to tag a player. Anyone tagged must remain frozen in place until freed by another player. To successfully steal the treasure, a player must pick it up cleanly without getting tagged. The guards tag them when they come too near. If the treasure is knocked over by a player trying to steal it, that player is frozen in place. There is a delicate balance for the guards between being too far from the treasure and staying too near the treasure and never tagging anyone.

TREES

Supplies: None

Skills: Running, dodging

Formation:

```
X |          It
X |
X |
X |          It
X |
X |
X |          It
X |
X |
X |
```

Two parallel lines are drawn at opposite ends of the playing area. All players, except two or three taggers, are on one side of the area. On the signal "Trees," the players run to the other side of the court. The taggers try to tag as many as possible. Any player tagged becomes a tree, stopping where tagged and keeping both feet in place. Trees cannot move their feet but can tag any runners who come close enough. The taggers continue to chase the players as they cross on signal, until a few are left. New players are selected to be taggers.

WHISTLE MIXER

Supplies: A whistle

Skills: All basic locomotor movements

Formation: Scattered

Children are scattered throughout the area. To begin, they walk or jog around in any direction they wish. The teacher blows a whistle a number of times in succession with short, sharp blasts. Children then form small circles with the number in the circles equal to the number of whistle blasts. If there are four blasts, children form circles of four—no more, no less. The goal is not to be left out and not to be caught in a circle with the incorrect number of

students. After the circles are formed, the teacher calls, "Walk," and the game continues.

TEACHING TIP

Variation: Another version of this game uses a tom-tom. Different beats indicate different locomotor movements—skipping, galloping, slow walking, normal walking, running. The whistle is still used to set the number for each circle.

WOLFE'S BEANBAG EXCHANGE

Supplies: One beanbag per child

Skills: Running, dodging, tossing, catching

Formation: Scattered

Five or six children are identified as taggers. The remaining children start scattered throughout the area, each with a beanbag in hand. The taggers chase the players with beanbags. When a tag is made, the tagged player must freeze, keeping her feet still and beanbag in hand. To unfreeze a player, a non-frozen player can exchange his beanbag for a beanbag held by a frozen player. If two frozen players are within tossing distance, they can thaw each other by exchanging their beanbags through the air using a toss and catch. Both tosses have to be caught or the beanbags must be retrieved and tried again.

TEACHING TIP

Variation: After students have learned the game, tell the taggers that they may interfere with the tossing of beanbags between two frozen players by batting them to the floor. This forces players to try the toss again and to remain frozen until both players make successful catches.

Developmental Level III

Games at this level become more complex and organized. A great deal more cooperation is needed to make the activities enjoyable. In addition, an opportunity exists to use team play tactics. Strategy is important for successful play at this level.

BARKER'S HOOP-LA

Supplies: Hoops, beanbags

Skill: Running

Formation:

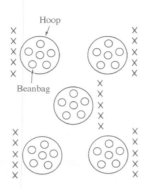

Five hoops are arranged, with one in each corner and the other in the centre of the playing area. Any distance between hoops can be used, but 8 to 10 m is a challenging distance. Five to six beanbags are placed in each hoop. The class is divided into five equal teams, one group near each hoop. This is their home base. The object of the game is to steal beanbags from other hoops and return them to the hoop that is home base for each respective team. The following rules are in effect:

1. A player can take only one beanbag at a time. That player must take the beanbag to the home base before returning for another one.

2. Beanbags cannot be thrown or tossed to the home base, but must be placed on the floor in the hoop before being released.

3. No player can protect the home base or its beanbags with any defensive maneuver.

4. Beanbags may be taken from any hoop.

5. When the stop signal is given, all players must freeze immediately and release any beanbags in their possession. Any follow-through of activities to get a better score is penalized.

The winner is the team with the most beanbags in their home-base hoop.

CAGEBALL TARGET THROW

Supplies: A cageball (60 to 80 cm), 12 to 15 smaller balls of various sizes

Skill: Throwing or rolling

Formation:

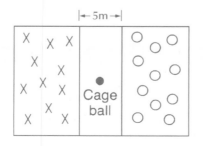

An area about 5 m wide is marked across the centre of the playing area, with a cageball in the centre. The object of the game is to throw the smaller balls against the cageball, thus forcing it across the line in front of the other team. Players may come up to the line to throw, but they may not throw while inside the cageball area. A player may enter the area, however, to recover a ball. No one is to touch the cageball at any time, nor may the cageball be pushed by a ball in the hands of a player. If the cageball seems to roll too easily, deflate it slightly. The throwing balls can be of almost any size—for example, soccer balls, volleyballs, and playground balls.

CHAIN TAG

Supplies: None

Skills: Running, dodging

Formation:

X X X X X X X X X X X

15m

X – X – X

X – X – X

Two parallel lines are established at opposite ends of the playing area. Two groups of three players form a chain with joined hands and occupy the centre. The players with free hands on either end of the chain do the tagging. All other players line up on one of the parallel lines. The players in the centre call, "Come on over," and children cross from one line to the other. The chains try to tag the runners. Anyone caught joins the chain. When the chain grows to six players, it divides into two groups of three players.

TEACHING TIP

Variation: Catch of Fish. The chain catches runners by surrounding them like a fishing net. The runners cannot run under or through the links of the net.

FAST PASS

Supplies: One 20-cm foam rubber ball, pinnies

Skills: Passing, catching, moving to an open area

Formation: Scattered

One team begins with the ball. The object is to complete five consecutive passes without the ball touching the floor. The team without the ball attempts to intercept the ball or recover an incomplete pass. Each time a pass is caught, the team shouts the number of consecutive passes completed. Each time a ball touches the floor or is intercepted, the count starts over.

Players may not contact each other. Emphasis should be placed on spreading out and using the entire court area. If players do not spread out, the area can be broken into quadrants and players restricted to one quadrant.

FLAG CHASE

Supplies: Flags, stopwatch

Skills: Running, dodging

Formation: Scattered

One team wears flags positioned in the back of the belt. The flag team scatters throughout the area. On signal, the chasing team tries to capture as many flags as possible in a designated amount of time. The flags are brought to the teacher or placed in a box. Players cannot use their hands to ward off a chaser. Roles are reversed. The team pulling the most flags is declared the winner.

JUMP-THE-SHOT VARIATIONS

Supplies: A jump-the-shot rope

Skill: Rope jumping

Formation:

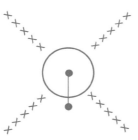

Before the following variations are tried, the jump-the-shot routines and variations listed previously should be reviewed.

1. Two or more squads are in file formation facing the rope turner. Each player runs clockwise (against the turn of the rope), jumping the rope as often as necessary to return to the squad.

2. Each player runs counterclockwise and tries to run around the circle before the rope can catch up with him. If this happens, he must jump to allow the rope to go under him. The best time for a player to start his run is just after the rope has passed.

3. Players can try some of the stunts in which the hands and feet are on the ground, to see whether they can have the rope pass under them. The Rabbit Jump, push-up position, Lame Dog, and others are possibilities.

OCTOPUS

Supplies: None

Skills: Manoeuvring, problem solving

Formation: Groups of six to nine, holding hands, tangled

Octopus is a game that gets its name from the many hands joined together in the activity. Children stand shoulder to shoulder in a tight circle. Everyone thrusts the hands forward and reaches through the group of hands to grasp the hands across the circle. Players must make sure that they do not hold both hands of the same player. Players also may not hold the hand of an adjacent player. The object is to untangle the mess created by the joined hands by going under, over, or through fellow players. No one is permitted to release a handgrip during the unraveling. What is the end result? Perhaps one large circle or two smaller connected circles.

TEACHING TIP

This is a cooperative game that demands teamwork. If, after a period of time, the knotted hands do not seem to unravel, call a halt—and lend a hand. The teacher and group can decide where the difficulty is and allow a change in position of those hands until the knot is dissolved.

ONE-BASE TAGBALL

Supplies: A base (or standard), a volleyball (20-cm foam ball for younger children)

Skills: Running, dodging, throwing

Formation:

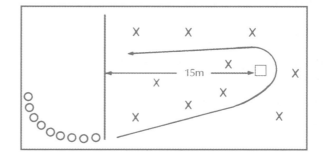

A home line is drawn at one end of the playing space. A base or standard is placed about 12 to 15 m in front of the home line. Two teams are formed. One team is scattered around the fielding area, the boundaries of which are determined by the number of children. The other team is lined up in single file behind the home line.

The object of the game is for the fielding team to tag the runners with the ball (runners must be tagged with the ball rather than have the ball thrown at them). Two runners at a time try to round the base and head back for the home line without being tagged. The game is continuous, meaning that as soon as a running team player is tagged or crosses the home line, another player starts immediately.

The fielding team may run with the ball and pass it from player to player, trying to tag one of the runners. The running team scores a point for each player who runs successfully around the base and back to the home line.

At the start of the game, the running team has two players ready at the right side of the home line. The others on the team are in line, waiting for a turn. The teacher throws the ball anywhere in the field, and the first two runners start toward the base. They must run around the base from the right side. After all the players have run, the teams exchange places. The team scoring the most points wins.

TEACHING TIP

To facilitate tagging a runner, players on the fielding team should make passes to a person close to the runner. They must be alert, because two children at a time are running. The next player on the running team must watch carefully in order to start the instant one of the two preceding runners is back safely behind the line or has been hit.

OVER THE WALL

Supplies: None

Skills: Running, dodging

Formation:

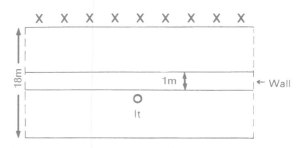

Two parallel goal lines are drawn about 15 to 18 m apart. Two additional parallel lines about 1 m apart are laid out parallel to the goal lines in the middle of the game area. This is the wall. Two or three players are taggers and stand on, or behind, the wall. All the other players are behind one of the goal lines. One of the taggers calls, "Over the wall." All the players must then run across the wall to the other goal line. The taggers try to tag any crossing players. Anyone caught helps catch the others. Players also are considered caught when they step on the wall. They must clear it with a leap or a jump and cannot step on it anywhere, including on the lines. After crossing over to the other side safely, players wait for the next call. The game can be made more difficult by increasing the width of the wall. Taggers can step on or run through the wall at will.

PIN KNOCKOUT

Supplies: Many playground balls, 12 bowling pins

Skills: Rolling, dodging

Formation:

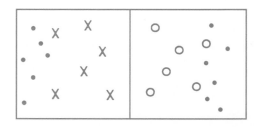

Two teams of equal number play the game. Each team is given many playground balls and six bowling pins. A court 10 by 15 m or larger with a centre line is needed. The size of the court depends on the number of children in the game. The object of the game is to knock down all of the opponents' bowling pins by rolling the balls at their pins. Each team stays in its half of the court.

When a player holds a ball longer than 5 seconds without rolling at the opposing team, play stops, and the ball is given to the opposing team.

The bowling pins are put anywhere in the team's area. Players may guard the pins but must not touch them. When a pin is down, even though a member of the defending team might have knocked it over unintentionally, it is removed immediately from the game. The game is over when all pins on one side have been knocked down.

SCOOTER KICKBALL

Supplies: A cageball, gym scooters for active players

Skill: Striking with various body parts

Formation:

Divide each team into active players (on scooters) and goal defenders. The active players are seated on the scooters, and the goal defenders are seated on the goal line, with feet extended. The object of the game is to kick the cageball over the goal line defended by the opposite team. The players are positioned as shown above.

The game starts with a face-off of two opposing players on scooters at the centre of the court. The face-off is also used after a goal is scored. The active players on scooters propel the ball mainly with their feet. Touching the ball with the hands is a foul and results in a free kick by the opposition at the spot of the foul. A player may also use the head and body to stop and propel the ball.

The players defending the goal are seated on the goal line. They may not use their hands either, but are permitted to use feet, body, and head. (If scoring seems too easy, then the defenders can be allowed to use their hands.) Defenders should be restricted to the seated position at the goal line and are not permitted to enter the field of play to propel or stop the ball.

TEACHING TIP

The number of scooters determines the number of active players. The game works well if half of the players from each team are in the centre on scooters and the other half are goal defenders. After a goal or after a stipulated time period, active players and goal defenders exchange places. Any active player who falls off a scooter should be required to sit again on the scooter before becoming eligible to propel the ball.

TEACHING TIP

Variation: If there are enough scooters for everyone, the game can be played with rules similar to soccer. A more restricted goal (perhaps half of the end line) can be marked with standards. A goalie defends this area. All other players are active and can move to any spot on the floor. The floor space should be large enough to allow some freedom of play.

STRIKE THE PINS

Supplies: 8 to 12 bowling pins per team, 15 to 20 foam rubber balls

Skill: Throwing

Formation:

A line is drawn across the centre of the floor, wall to wall. This divides the floor into two courts, each of which is occupied by one team. Another line is drawn 8 to 10 m

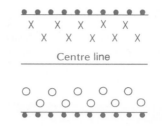

from the centreline in each court. This is the line where each team spaces its bowling pins. Each team has at least five balls. The object of the game is to knock over the other team's pins by rolling the balls. Players roll the balls back and forth, but cannot cross the centre line. Whenever a pin is knocked over by a ball or player (accidentally or not), that pin is removed. The team with the most pins standing at the end of the game is declared the winner. Out-of-bounds balls can be recovered but must be rolled from inside the court.

TEACHING TIP

Variation: Pins can be reset instead of removed. Two scorers, one for each pin line, are needed.

SUNDAY

Supplies: None

Skills: Running, dodging

Formation:

Two parallel lines are drawn at each end of the playing area. Three or more players are taggers and stand in the centre of the area between the two lines. The rest of the class is on one of the two lines. The object is to cross to the other line without being tagged or making a false start.

All line players stand with their front foot on the line. The line players must run across the line immediately when the tagger calls, "Sunday." Anyone who does not run immediately is considered caught. The tagger can call other days of the week to confuse the runners. Runners making false starts join the taggers.

"Making a start" must be defined clearly. To begin, it can be defined as a player moving either foot. Later, when children get better at the game, any forward movement of the body can constitute a start.

TOUCHDOWN

Supplies: A small object (coin, thimble) that can be concealed in the hand

Skills: Running, dodging

Formation:

```
X |                    | O
X |                    | O
X |                    | O
X |                    | O
X |                    | O
X |                    | O
X |                    | O
X |                    | O
X |                    | O
X |                    | O
X |                    | O
```

Two parallel lines are placed at each end of the playing area. Two teams face each other, each standing on one of the parallel lines. One team (offensive) huddles and the members decide which player is to carry an object to the opponents' goal line. The offensive team moves out of the huddle and spreads out along the line. On the signal "Hike," the offensive players move toward the opponents' goal line, each player holding the hands closed as if carrying the object. On the "Charge" signal, the opponents (defence) also run forward and try to tag the players. On being tagged, players must stop immediately and open both hands to show whether or not they have the object. If the player carrying the object reaches the goal line without being tagged, that player calls, "Touchdown," and scores six points. The defensive team now goes on the offence.

Miscellaneous Playground Games

Children enjoy playing the following small group games on the playground during recess and lunch hour.

FOUR SQUARE

(Developmental Levels II and III)

Supplies: 20-cm playground ball or volleyball

Skill: Batting a ball

Court markings:

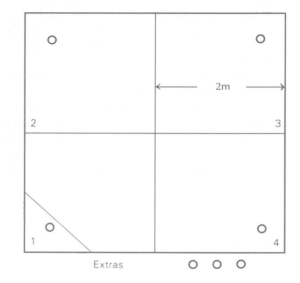

Lines are drawn as shown above. The squares should be numbered 1, 2, 3, and 4. A service line is drawn diagonally across the far corner of square 1. The player in this square always serves, and must stay behind the line when serving.

The ball is served by dropping and serving it underhanded from the bounce. If the serve hits a line, the server is out. The server can hit the ball after it has bounced once in his square. The receiver directs it to any other square with an underhand hit. Play continues until one player fails to return the ball or commits a fault. Any of the following constitutes a fault:

1. Hitting the ball sidearm or overhand.
2. Landing a ball on a line between the squares. (A ball landing on an outer boundary is considered good.)
3. Stepping into another square to play the ball.
4. Catching or carrying a return volley.
5. Allowing the ball to touch any part of the body except the hands.

A player who misses or commits a fault goes to the end of the waiting line, and all players move up. The player at the head of the waiting line moves into square 4.

Variations:

1. A 60-cm circle can be drawn at the centre of the area. Hitting the ball into the circle constitutes a fault.
2. The game can be changed by varying the method of propelling the ball. The server sets the method. The ball can be hit with a partially closed fist, the back of the

hand, or the elbow. The server calls, "Fisties," "Elbows," "Footsies," or "Kneesies" to set the pattern.

3. Chain Spelling. The server names a word, and each player returning the ball must add the next letter in the sequence.

4. Hula hoops can be used so that all students can play at one time.

5. Cooperative scoring can be used with students to see how many consecutive hits they can make without missing.

FRISBEE GOLF

Supplies: One Frisbee per person, hoops for hole markers, cones

Skills: Frisbee throwing for accuracy

Suggested golf course design:

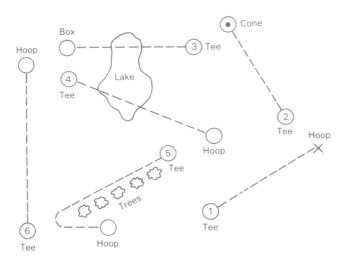

Frisbee Golf, or disc golf, is a favourite game of many students. Boundary cones with numbers can be used for tees, and holes can be boxes, Hula Hoops, trees, tires, garbage cans, or any other available equipment on the school grounds. Draw a course on a map for students and start them at different holes to decrease the time spent waiting to tee off. Regulation golf rules apply. The students can jog between throws for increased activity.

Disc golf is played like regular golf. One stroke is counted for each time the disk is thrown and when a penalty is incurred. The object is to acquire the lowest score. The following rules dictate play:

- *Tee-throws:* Tee-throws must be completed within or behind the designated tee area.

- *Lie:* The lie is the spot on or directly underneath the spot where the previous throw landed.

- *Throwing order:* The player whose disc is the farthest from the hole throws first. The player with the least number of throws on the previous hole tees off first.

- *Fairway throws:* Fairway throws must be made with the foot closest to the hole on the lie. A run-up is allowed.

- *Dog leg:* A dog leg is one or more designated trees or poles in the fairway that must be passed on the outside when approaching the hole. There is a two-stroke penalty for missing a dog leg.

- *Putt throw:* A putt throw is any throw within 3 m of the hole. A player may not move past the point of the lie in making the putt throw. Falling or jumping putts are not allowed.

- *Unplayable lies:* Any disc that comes to rest 2 m or more above the ground is unplayable. The next throw must be played from a new lie directly underneath the unplayable lie (one-stroke penalty).

- *Out-of-bounds:* A throw that lands out-of-bounds must be played from the point where the disc went out (one-stroke penalty).

- *Course courtesy:* Do not throw until the players ahead are out of range.

- *Completion of hole:* A disc that comes to rest in the hole (box or hoop) or strikes the designated hole (tree or pole) constitutes successful completion of that hole.

TETHERBALL

(Developmental Levels II and III)

Supplies: A tetherball assembly (pole, rope, and ball)

Skill: Batting a ball

Court markings:

The first server is picked by lot. One player stands on each side of the pole. The server puts the ball into play by tossing it into the air and hitting in the direction he chooses. The opponent must not strike the ball on the first swing around the pole. On its second swing around the pole, she hits the ball back in the opposite direction. As the ball is hit back and forth, each player tries to hit it so that the rope winds completely around the pole in the direction in which he is hitting the ball. The game is won by the player who succeeds in doing this or whose opponent forfeits the game by committing a foul. A foul is any of the following:

1. Hitting the ball with any part of the body other than the hands or forearms.

2. Catching or holding the ball during play.

3. Touching the pole.

4. Hitting the rope with the forearms or hands.

5. Throwing the ball.

6. Winding the ball around the pole below the 2.5-m (5-foot) mark.

After the opening game, the winner of the preceding game serves. Winning four games wins the set.

TWO SQUARE

(Developmental Levels II and III)

Supplies: A playground ball or volleyball

Skill: Batting a ball

The basic rules and lines are the same as for Four Square, except that only two squares are used. If there are players waiting for a turn, the active player who misses or fouls can be eliminated as in Four Square. The ball must be served from behind the baseline.

VOLLEY TENNIS

Supplies: A volleyball

Skills: Most volleyball skills

Formation: Scattered

The game can be played as a combination of volleyball and tennis. The net is put on the ground, as in tennis, and the ball is put into play with a serve. It may bounce once or can be passed directly to a teammate. The ball must be hit three times before going over the net. Spiking is common because of the low net. A point is scored when the ball cannot be returned over the net to the opposing team.

Critical Thinking

1. Classify the developmental games in this chapter into the four games categories (net/wall, invasion, striking/fielding, target). Discuss how using these categories help students learn games skills along with strategic and tactical concepts.

References and Suggested Readings

Almond, L. (1986). Reflecting on themes: A games classification. In R. Thorpe, D. Bunker, & L. Almond (Eds.). *Rethinking games teaching* (pp. 71–72). Loughborough, England: University of Technology.

Barrett, R. (2005). *Games for the whole child.* Champaign, IL: Human Kinetics.

Byl, J., Baldauf, H., Doyle, P., & Raithby, A. (2007). *Chicken and noodle games—141 fun activities with innovative equipment.* Champaign, IL: Human Kinetics.

Clumpner, R. (2003). *Sport progressions.* Champaign, IL: Human Kinetics.

Council on Physical Education for Children. (2000). *Appropriate practices for elementary physical education: A position statement of the National Association for Sport and Physical Education.* Reston, VA: NASPE/AAHPERD.

DeKoven, B. (2005). *Junkyard sports.* Champaign, IL: Human Kinetics.

Dowson, A. & Morris, K. (2005). *Fun and games—100 sport-related activities for ages 5–16.* Champaign, IL: Human Kinetics.

Griffin, L.L. & Butler, J. (2005). *Teaching games for understanding: Theory, research, and practice.* Champaign, IL: Human Kinetics.

Hanrahan, S.J. & Carlson, T. (2000). *Games skills—A fun approach to learning sport skills.* Champaign, IL: Human Kinetics.

Hopper, T. & Bell, R. (2000). A tactical framework for teaching games: Teaching strategic understanding and tactical awareness. *Physical and Health Education Journal,* 66(4), 14–19.

Hughes, J. D. (2003). *No standing around in my gym.* Champaign, IL: Human Kinetics.

Launder, A. G. (2001). *Play practice—The games approach to teaching and coaching sports.* Champaign, IL: Human Kinetics.

Mandigo, J. & Holt, N. (2000). The inclusion of optimal challenge in teaching games for understanding. *Physical and Health Education Journal,* 66(3), 14–19.

Mitchell, S., Oslin, J., & Griffin, L. (2003). *Sport foundations for elementary physical education: A tactical games approach.* Champaign, IL: Human Kinetics.

Morris, G.S.D. & Stiehl, J. (1999). *Changing kids' games* (2nd ed.). Champaign, IL: Human Kinetics.

 Weblinks

GameCentralStation:
www.gamecentralstation.com

This website acts as a resource for physical educators, recreation specialists, parents, or anyone working with children. The site has hundreds of games for preschool through grade 12. Each game includes instructions, equipment, skills, and related sports activities.

Premier Sport Awards Program: www.psap.jwsporta.ca

A physical education resource program that helps teachers introduce basic sport skills to students. Includes manuals for badminton, basketball, curling, disc sports, field hockey, golf, gymnastics, judo, ice hockey, soccer, orienteering, softball, track & field, and volleyball. Recommended learning resource in BC, MB, AB, SK, NT, NL, and YT.

Playsport: www.playsport.net

Comprehensive database of invasion games, target games, wall/net games.

Provincial Sport Organizations

Alberta Sport, Recreation, Parks & Wildlife Foundation: www.cd.gov.ab.ca/asrpwf

Sport BC: www.sport.bc.ca

Sport Manitoba: www.sportmanitoba.ca

Sport New Brunswick: www.sport.nb.ca

Sport Newfoundland and Labrador: www.sportnl.com

Sport North: www.sportnorth.com

Sport Nova Scotia: www.sportnovascotia.ca

Ontario Sportalliance: www.sportalliance.com

SportPEI: www.sportpei.pe.ca

Sports-Québec: www.sportsquebec.com

Saskatchewan Sports Net: www.sasksport.sk.ca

Sport Yukon: www.sportyukon.com

Sport Skills

CHAPTER 23

Basketball

OVERVIEW

Skills instruction for basketball is introduced primarily during the intermediate grades after students have mastered the basic prerequisite skills. The teaching of rules and tactics for basketball should also be an integral part of the instructional process. Using proper progression is a key to success when teaching fundamental skills and lead-up games associated with basketball. Lead-up games provide an opportunity to emphasize development of selected basketball skills and tactics in a setting that is compatible with the ability of participants.

OUTCOMES

- Structure learning experiences efficiently using appropriate formations, progressions, and teaching techniques.

- Know the basic skills, tactics, and rules of basketball.

- Develop a unit plan and lesson focus for basketball.

- Identify safety precautions associated with playing basketball.

- Describe essential elements for a successful lead-up game.

Basketball is an activity enjoyed by many students. The reinforcement offered when a student makes a basket makes it an attractive game, and this, coupled with the cardiorespiratory benefits, makes basketball a strong contributor to the total curriculum. Basketball instruction in the elementary school focuses on students' developing skills and competence so that they can participate later in life. Place emphasis on lead-up games that allow all students to experience success and enjoyment. Modifying equipment used by elementary school children is important. Smaller balls and lower baskets help develop technically correct patterns, increase the success of the participants, and maintain motivation.

In order to refine their skills, interested students should be given additional opportunities through intramural programs, recreational leagues, or an interschool league.

Instructional Emphasis and Sequence

Table 23.1 shows the sequence of basketball activities divided into two developmental levels. Generally, youngsters are not ready to participate in the activities in this chapter until age 8 or 9.

Developmental Level II

Little emphasis is placed on regulation basketball at this level. Teachers should concentrate on the fundamental skills of passing, catching, shooting, and dribbling. Lead-up games such as Birdies in the Cage, Circle Guard and Pass, and Five Pass–Ten Pass allow participants to learn skills in a setting that offers both enjoyment and success. As children mature at this level, their goal should be to develop a range of skills, including passing, catching, dribbling, and shooting. The layup shot and the one-hand push shot should receive instructional attention. Captain Ball adds elements of simple defence, jump balls, and accurate passing. Choice of lead-up games should also introduce basic tactical concepts (for example, moving into open space to receive a pass).

Developmental Level III

A number of lead-up activities are introduced at this level. Shooting games, such as Twenty-one and Freeze Out, become favourites. Sideline Basketball and Captain Basketball offer meaningful game play. Practice continues on fundamental skills and complementary team play and tactical concepts. Drills and lead-up games increase in complexity and challenge, and teachers present the basic rules for regulation basketball. Introduce basic officiating so youngsters can learn to appreciate the importance and difficulty of refereeing. Allow players to conduct some games through self-officiating.

Basketball Skills

Basketball skills at the elementary level are divided into the following categories: passing, catching, dribbling, shooting, defending, stopping, and pivoting. Teach feinting as part of the passing, dribbling, and offensive maneuvers.

Passing

Certain factors are common to all passes regardless of which pass is used. For firm control, the ball should be handled with the thumb and finger pads, not with the palms of the hands. The passer should step forward in the direction of the receiver. Passes should be made with a quick arm extension and a snap of the wrists, with thumbs and fingers providing momentum. After the pass is released, the palms should be facing the floor. Passers should avoid telegraphing the direction of the pass. They should learn to use peripheral vision and keep their eyes moving from place to place to develop an awareness of their teammates' positions. At the same time, they should anticipate the spot toward which a teammate will be moving to receive the pass.

The following are instructional cues that can be used to help students focus on proper performance of passing:

1. Fingers spread with thumbs behind the ball.
2. Elbows in; extend through the ball.
3. Step forward, extend arms, and rotate hands slightly inward.
4. Throw at chest level to the receiver.
5. For bounce passes, bounce the ball past the halfway point nearer the receiver.

Chest (or Two-hand) Pass

For the chest, or two-hand, pass, one foot is ahead of the other, with the knees flexed slightly. The ball is released at chest level, with the fingers spread on each side of the ball (see Figure 23.1). Pass the ball by extending the arms and snapping the wrists as one foot moves toward the receiver (see Figure 23.2).

Baseball (or One-hand) Pass

For the baseball, or one-hand, pass, the passer imitates the action of a baseball catcher throwing the ball to second base. The body weight shifts from the back to the front foot. Sidearm motion should be avoided, because it puts an improper spin on the ball. Figure 23.3 shows a left-hander throwing the pass.

TABLE 23.1

Suggested basketball program

Developmental Level II	Developmental Level III	Developmental Level II	Developmental Level III
Skills		**Knowledge**	
Passing		*Rules*	
Chest pass	All passes to moving targets	Dribbling	Held ball
One-hand push pass	Two-hand overhead pass	Violations • Traveling • Out-of-bounds • Double dribbling	Personal fouls • Holding • Hacking • Charging • Blocking • Pushing
Bounce pass	Long passes (baseball pass)		
Underhand pass	Three-player weave		
Catching		Scoring	Officiating
Above the waist	While moving	*Offensive Tactics*	
Below the waist		Keeping team possession of ball (on-the-ball and off-the-ball movements)	Keeping team possession of ball while making forward progress (on-the-ball and off-the-ball movements)
Dribbling			
Standing and moving	Figure eight		
Down and back	Pivoting		
Right and left hands	Individual dribbling skills		
Shooting		• pass and move to open space to receive • eluding defender	• give-and-go play • choosing when to dribble, pass, shoot
One-hand set shot	Free-throw shot		
Lay-up, right and left	Jump shot	*Defensive Tactics*	
Defending and stopping		Defending space and player	Defending space, player, and goal
Pivoting	Parallel stop	Clearing the ball	Transition from defence to offense
Feinting	Stride stop		• outlet pass positioning
		Lead-up Games	
		Circle Guard and Pass	Captain Basketball
		Five Passes–Ten Passes	Quadrant Basketball
		Basketball Tag	Sideline Basketball
		Dribblerama	Twenty-one
		Birdies in the Cage	Lane Basketball
		Captain Ball	Freeze out
		Around the Key	Flag Dribble
		Team Five Passes	One-goal Basketball
			Basketball Snatch Ball
			Three-on-three
			Basketrama

Figure 23.1

Ready for a chest pass.

Figure 23.2

Chest pass.

One-hand Push Pass

For a one-hand push pass, the passer holds the ball with both hands but supports the ball more with the left than with the right, which is a little behind the ball. The player pushes the ball forward, with a quick wrist snap by the right hand.

Figure 23.3

Baseball pass.

Bounce Pass

Any of the preceding passes can be adapted to a bounce pass. The object is to get the pass to the receiver on the first bounce, with the ball coming to the receiver's outstretched hands at about waist height. Some experimentation determines the distance. The ball should be bounced a little more than halfway between the two players to make it come efficiently to the receiver.

Underhand Pass

For a two-hand underhand pass, the ball should be held to one side in both hands, with the foot on the opposite side toward the receiver. The ball is "shovelled" toward the receiver and a step is made with the leading foot (see Figure 23.4). The one-hand underhand pass is made like an underhand toss in baseball.

Figure 23.4

Underhand pass.

Figure 23.5

Releasing the two-handed overhead pass.

Two-hand Overhead Pass

The two-hand overhead pass is effective against a shorter opponent. The passer is in a short stride position, with the ball held overhead (see Figure 23.5). The momentum of the pass comes from a forceful wrist and finger snap. The pass should take a slightly downward path.

Catching

Receiving the ball is a most important fundamental skill. Many turnovers involve failure to handle a pass properly. The receiver should move toward the pass with the fingers spread and relaxed, reaching for the ball with elbows bent and wrists relaxed. The hands should give as the ball comes in.

Instructional cues for catching include the following:

1. Move to the ball.
2. Spread the fingers and catch with the fingertips.

3. Reach for the ball.
4. Give with the ball (absorb the force of the ball by reaching and bringing the ball to the chest).

Dribbling

Dribbling is used to advance the ball, break for a basket, or manoeuvre out of a difficult situation. The dribbler's knees and trunk should be slightly flexed (see Figure 23.6), with hands and eyes forward. Peripheral vision is important. The dribbler should look beyond the ball and see it in the lower part of the visual area. The ball is propelled by the fingertips with the hand cupped and relaxed. There is little arm motion. Children should alternate the dribbling hand; practice in changing hands is essential.

Instructional cues for dribbling include the following:

1. Push the ball to the floor. Don't slap it.
2. Push the ball forward when moving.
3. Eyes forward and head up.

Shooting

Shooting is an intricate skill, and students need to develop consistent and proper technique rather than be satisfied when the ball happens to drop into the basket.

1. Good body position is important. Both the toes and the shoulders should face the basket. The weight should be evenly distributed on both feet. In preliminary phases, the student should hold the ball between shoulder and eye level.
2. A comfortable grip is essential—with fingers well spread and the ball resting on the pads of the fingers. One should be able to see daylight between the palm of the hand and the ball. For one-hand shots, the shooting elbow is directly below the ball.

Figure 23.6

Dribbling.

3. As soon as the player decides to shoot, her eye is fixed on the target (the rim or the backboard) for the rest of the shot.

4. As the shot starts, the wrist is cocked.

5. The follow-through imparts a slight backspin to the ball. The child's arms are fully extended, the wrist is completely flexed, and the hand drops down toward the floor. The arc should be 45 degrees or a little higher.

The following instructional cues aid skill development:

1. Use the pads of the fingers. Keep the fingers spread.

2. Keep the shooting elbow near the body.

3. Extend through the ball.

4. Bend the knees and use the legs.

5. Release the ball off the fingertips.

One-hand Set Shot

The one-hand push shot is usually a jump shot at short distances and a set shot at longer distances. The ball is held at shoulder–eye level with both hands; the body is erect, and the knees are flexed slightly in preparation for a jump. For a jump shot, the shooter executes a vertical jump, leaving the floor slightly (see Figure 23.7). (In a set shot, the shooter rises on the toes.) The supporting (non-shooting) hand remains in contact with the ball until the player reaches the top of the jump. The shooting hand then takes over with fingertip control, and the ball rolls off the centre three fingers. The hand and wrist follow through. The child should maintain visual concentration on the target throughout. Emphasize proper technique rather than accuracy.

Lay-up Shot

The lay-up is a short shot taken when going in toward the basket, either after receiving a pass or at the end of a dribble. In a shot from the right side, the takeoff is with the left foot, and vice versa. The ball is carried with both hands early in the shot and then shifted to one hand for the final push. The ball, guided by the fingertips, should be laid against the backboard with a minimum of spin.

Free-throw Shot

Free-throw shooting can be performed successfully with different types of shots. The one-hand foul shot is most popular. The player needs complete concentration, relaxation, and a rhythmic, consistent delivery. Some players find it helpful to bounce the ball several times before shooting. Others like to take a deep breath and exhale completely just before shooting. The mechanics of the shot do not differ materially

Figure 23.7

One-hand Set Shot.

from those of any shot at a comparable distance. Smoothness and consistency are most important.

Jump Shot

The jump shot has the same upper-body mechanics as the one-hand push shot already described. The primary difference is the height of the jump. The jump should be straight up, rather than at a forward or backward angle. The player should release the ball at the height of the jump (see Figure 23.8). Because the legs cannot be used to increase the force applied to the ball, the jump shot is difficult for the majority of elementary school youngsters. It may be best to avoid teaching the shot to youngsters who lack enough strength to shoot the ball correctly and resort to throwing it. If presenting the jump shot, the teacher should ensure that the basket is at the lowest level available and that a junior-size basketball is used so that children develop proper shooting habits.

Another way to practise proper form with the jump shot is to use foam balls. They are light, and children can shoot them easily. Concentrate on proper form rather than on making baskets. Reinforce students who use good technique.

Figure 23.8

One-hand Jump Shot.

Defending

Defending involves a characteristic stance. The defender, with knees bent slightly and feet comfortably spread (see Figure 23.9), faces the opponent at a distance of about 1 m. The weight should be distributed evenly on both feet to allow for movement in any direction. Sideward movement is done with a sliding motion. The defender should wave one hand to distract the opponent and to block passes and shots. A defensive player needs to learn to move quickly and not be caught flatfooted.

Instructional cues for proper defending are as follows:

1. Keep the knees bent.
2. Keep the hands up.
3. Don't cross the feet when moving.

Stopping

To stop quickly, the child drops the weight of his body to lower the centre of gravity and applies the feet as brakes (see Figure 23.10). In the parallel stop, the body turns

Figure 23.9

The defensive position.

sideward and both feet brake simultaneously. The stride stop comes from a forward movement and is done in a one–two count. On the first count, one foot hits the ground with a braking action; the other foot is planted firmly ahead on the second count. The knees are bent, and the centre of gravity is lowered. From a stride stop, the player can move into a pivot by picking up the front foot and carrying it to the rear and, at the same time, fading to the rear.

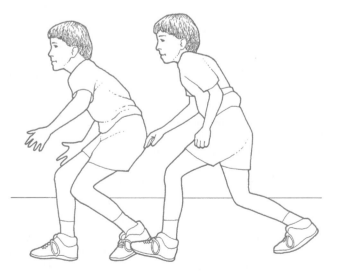

Figure 23.10

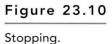

Stopping.

Figure 23.11

Pivoting.

Pivoting

Pivoting is a manoeuvre that protects the ball by keeping the body between the ball and the defensive player. The player holds the ball firmly in both hands, with elbows out to protect it. One foot, the pivot foot, must always be in contact with the floor. Turning on that foot is permitted, but it must not be dragged away from the pivot spot. The lead foot may, however, step in any direction (see Figure 23.11).

If a player has received the ball in a stationary position or during a jump in which both feet hit the ground simultaneously, either foot may become the pivot foot. If a player stops after a dribble on a one–two count, the pivot foot is the foot that made contact on the first count.

Feinting

Feinting (faking) masks the intent of a manoeuvre or pass and is essential to basketball. Feinting is a deceptive motion in one direction when the intent is to move in another direction. The player can achieve this with the eyes, the head, a foot, or the whole body. In passing, feinting means faking a pass in one manner or direction and then passing in another.

Basic Basketball Tactics

The structure and intent of individual skills and team play in basketball (similar to other invasion games) is to move the ball through the opposing team's territory in order to score a basket, while preventing the opposition from achieving the same goal. Within this context, players make tactical decisions either to gain an offensive advantage in order to score, or a defensive advantage in order to prevent

the opposition from scoring. To become an effective invasion game player, it is important to develop both skill and tactical knowledge. Drills and lead-up games in both developmental levels II and III focus on basic offensive and defensive tactics. Table 23.1 lists basic offensive and defensives tactics.

Basic Basketball Rules

The game of basketball played at the elementary school level is similar to the official game played in the secondary schools, but is modified to ensure the opportunity for success and for proper skill development.

Putting the Ball into Play

Each half is started with a jump ball at the centre circle. After each successful basket or free throw, the ball is put into play at the end of the court under the basket by the team against whom the score was made.

Violations

The penalty for a violation is to award the ball to the opponents near the out-of-bounds point. The following are violations:

1. Travelling, that is, taking more than one step with the ball without passing, dribbling, or shooting (sometimes called *walking* or *steps*).

2. Stepping out of bounds with the ball or causing the ball to go out of bounds.

3. Taking more than 10 seconds to cross the centre line from the backcourt to the frontcourt. (Once in the forward court, the ball may not be returned to the backcourt by the team in control.)

4. Double dribbling, which is taking a second series of dribbles without another player's having handled the ball; palming (not clearly batting) the ball; or dribbling the ball with both hands at once.

5. Stepping on or over a restraining line during a jump ball or free throw.

6. Kicking the ball intentionally.

7. Remaining more than three seconds in the area under the offensive basket, which is bounded by the two sides of the free-throw lane, the free-throw line, and the end of the court.

To equalize scoring opportunities, a time limit (30 seconds) may be established during which the offensive team must score or give up the ball.

Fouls

Personal fouls are holding, pushing, hacking (striking), tripping, charging, blocking, and unnecessary roughness. When a foul is called, the person who was fouled receives one free throw. If a child is fouled in the act of shooting and misses the basket, the child receives two shots. If, despite the foul, the basket was made, the score counts and one free throw is awarded. A player who has five personal fouls is out of the game and must go to the sidelines.

Scoring

A basket from the field scores 2 points and a free throw is 1 point. In most cases, the 3-point goal is not a consideration due to the distance of the shot. If desired, teachers could create a 3-point line to simulate the game played by older students.

Instructional Procedures

1. Many basketball skills do not require the use of basketballs. Other balls, such as volleyballs or rubber balls, can be used successfully.

2. Many skills can be practised individually or in pairs with playground balls. This allows all children to develop at their own pace, regardless of skill level. When many balls are used, students have more opportunity to practise dribbling, passing, and catching skills.

3. Baskets should be lowered to 2, 2.5, or 3 m, depending on the size and ability of the children. If the facility is also used for community purposes, adjustable baskets are the key.

4. The program should concentrate on allowing children to practise skills and tactics in drills and modified games. Basketball offers endless possibilities, and using drills and modified games gives variety and breadth to the instructional program.

Basketball Drills

Drills should emulate actual game situations. When using drills, teachers should use the technique suggestions for the skill being practised and apply movement principles. The drills presented here cover both single skills and combinations of skills.

Ball-handling Drills

These drills are practised continuously for about 30 seconds. Players handle the ball with the pads of the fingers. The drills are listed in order of difficulty. These are often appropriate for inclusion during the warm-up phase of a lesson.

AROUND THE BODY DRILLS

1. *Around the waist.* Hold the ball in the right hand, circle it behind the back, and transfer to the left hand. The left hand carries it to the front of the body for a transfer to the right hand. Start with the left hand and move the ball in the opposite direction.

2. *Around the head.* With shoulders back, send the ball around the head in much the same manner described above. Perform in both directions.

3. *Triple play.* Begin by circling around the head; move to waist level and follow by knee-level circles. Move the ball in the opposite direction.

FIGURE EIGHT

1. Begin in a squatting position with the ball in the right hand. Move the ball around the leg to the right and bounce the ball between the legs to the left hand. Circle the ball around the left leg, through the legs to the right hand.

2. Bounce the ball through the legs, front to back, followed by the figure-eight motion.

SPEED DRILL

Feet are placed shoulder-width apart. The ball is held between the legs with one hand in front, and the other behind the back in contact with the ball. In a quick motion, flip the ball slightly upward and reverse the hand positions. Using a quick exchange of the hands, make a series of rapid exchanges. The ball will appear to be suspended between the legs (see Figure 23.12).

DOUBLE CIRCLE DRILL

Beginning with the ball in the right hand, go around both legs, with an assist from the left hand. When the ball

Figure 23.12

Speed drill.

Figure 23.13

Double circle drill.

Figure 23.15

Changing hands control drill.

returns to the right hand, move the left foot away from the right foot. With the ball moving in the same direction, circle the right leg. Move the leg back to the starting position and circle both legs followed by moving the legs apart and circling the left leg (see Figure 23.13). In short, circle both legs, circle the right leg, circle both legs, circle the left leg. Try moving the ball in the opposite direction.

TWO-HAND CONTROL DRILL

Start from a semi-crouched position with the feet shoulder width apart. The ball is held with both hands between the legs in front of the body (see Figure 23.14). Let go of the ball, move the hands behind the body, and catch it before the ball hits the floor. It may be helpful to give the ball a slight upward flip to facilitate the catch. Reverse the action, moving the hands to the front of the body. Perform continuously.

Figure 23.14

Two-hand control drill.

CHANGING HANDS CONTROL DRILL

Begin with the ball in the right hand; move it around the back of the right leg and catch with both hands. The right hand should be in front and the left hand behind. Drop the ball and quickly change the position of the hands on the ball after it has bounced once (see Figure 23.15). Immediately after the catch, bring the ball to the front of

the body with the left hand and switch the ball to the right hand. Repeat continuously. Try moving the ball in the opposite direction.

Individual Dribbling Drills

HOOP DRIBBLING DRILL

Each youngster has a ball and Hula Hoop. Place the hoop on the floor and practise dribbling the ball inside the hoop while walking outside the hoop. Dribble counterclockwise using the left hand and clockwise using the right hand. Repeat with the dribbler inside the hoop and the ball dribbled outside the hoop.

RANDOM DRIBBLING

Each child has a ball. Dribbling is done in place, varied by using left and right hands. Develop a sequence of body positions (standing, kneeling, lying on the side, on two feet and one hand). Encourage players to develop a sequence by dribbling a certain number of times in each selected position. Dribble with each hand.

ONE-HAND CONTROL DRILL

Begin with the right hand holding the ball. Make a half circle around the right leg to the back. Bounce the ball between the legs (back to front), catch it with the right hand, and move it around the body again (see Figure 23.16). After continuing for a short time, switch to the left hand.

FIGURE-EIGHT DRIBBLING DRILL (SPEED)

Start with the right or left hand. Dribble outside the respective leg, between the feet, and continue in front with the opposite hand in figure-eight fashion. Begin slowly and gradually increase the speed of the dribble.

FIGURE-EIGHT DRIBBLING DRILL (ONE BOUNCE)

Assume a semi-crouched position with the feet shoulder-width apart. Start with the ball in the right hand and bounce it from the front of the body between the

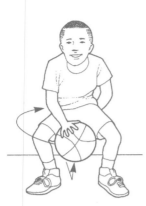

Figure 23.16

One-hand control drill.

Figure 23.17

Figure-eight dribbling drill (one bounce).

legs. Catch it with the left hand behind the legs (see Figure 23.17). Bring the ball to the front of the body with the left hand and start the sequence over with that hand.

FIGURE-EIGHT DRIBBLING DRILL (TWO BOUNCES)

Begin in the same position as described in the preceding drill. Using the right hand, take one dribble outside the right leg (angled toward the back) and a second dribble between the legs to the left hand in front of the body (see Figure 23.18). Repeat, starting with the left hand.

Group Dribbling Drills

Dribbling can be practised as a single skill or in combination with others.

Figure 23.18

Figure-eight dribbling drill (two bounces).

FILE DRIBBLING

In file dribbling, players dribble forward around an obstacle (such as a bowling pin, a cone, or a chair) and back to the line, where the next player repeats (see Figure 23.19). A variation has each player dribbling down with one hand and back with the other.

Figure 23.19

File dribbling.

SHUTTLE DRIBBLING

Shuttle dribbling begins at the head of a file. The head player dribbles across to another file and hands the ball off to the player at the head of the second file. The first player then takes a place at the end of that file (see Figure 23.20). The player receiving the ball dribbles back to the first file. A number of shuttles can be arranged for dribbling crossways over a basketball court.

Figure 23.20

Shuttle dribbling.

OBSTACLE, OR FIGURE-EIGHT, DRIBBLING

For obstacle, or figure-eight, dribbling, three or more obstacles are positioned about 1.5 m apart. The first player at the head of each file dribbles in and around each obstacle, changing hands so that the hand opposite the obstacle is the one always used (see Figure 23.21).

Figure 23.21

Obstacle, or figure-eight, dribbling.

Dribbling and Pivoting Drills

In dribbling and pivoting drills, the emphases are on stopping and pivoting.

FILE DRILL

For the file drill, each player in turn dribbles forward to a designated line, stops, pivots, faces the file, passes back to the next player, and runs to a place at the end of the line (see Figure 23.22). The next player repeats the pattern.

Figure 23.22

File drill.

DRIBBLE-AND-PIVOT DRILL

For the dribble-and-pivot drill, players are scattered by pairs around the floor (see Figure 23.23). One ball is required for each pair. On the first whistle, the front player of the pair dribbles in any direction and fashion on the court. On the second whistle, the player stops and pivots back and forth, and on the third whistle, she dribbles back and passes to the partner, who immediately dribbles forward, repeating the routine.

Figure 23.23

Dribble-and-pivot drill.

Passing Drills

In passing practice, make regular use of the various movement formations (see Chapter 3), including two-line, circle, circle-and-leader, line-and-leader, shuttle turn-back, and regular shuttle formations. Consider a number of other drills.

SLIDE CIRCLE DRILL

In the slide circle drill, a circle of four to six players slides around a person in the centre. The centre person passes to and receives from the sliding players. After the ball has gone around the circle twice, another player takes the centre position.

CIRCLE–STAR DRILL

With only five players, a circle–star drill is particularly effective. Players pass to every other player, and the path of the ball forms a star (see Figure 23.24). The star drill works well as a relay. Any odd number of players will cause the ball to go to all participants, assuring that all receive equal practice.

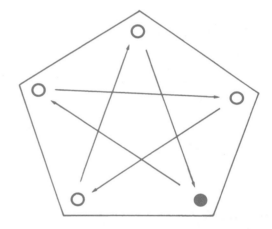

Figure 23.24

Circle–Star formation.

TRIANGLE DRILL

Four to eight players can participate in the triangle drill. The ball begins at the head of a line and is passed forward to a player away from the line. This player then passes to a teammate out at a corner, who then passes back to the head of the line (see Figure 23.25). Each player passes and then

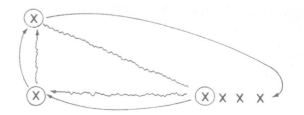

Figure 23.25

Triangle drill formation.

moves to the spot to which he passed the ball, resulting in a continual change of positions.

SQUAD SPLIT-VISION DRILL

This drill requires two basketballs. The centre player holds one ball, while player 1 (see Figure 23.26) has the other. The centre player passes the ball to player 2, while receiving the other ball from player 1. The centre player now passes to player 3 and receives the other ball from player 2, until the balls move completely around the semicircle. To rotate to a new centre player, the centre player becomes player 1 while player 6 (with the ball) moves to the centre spot. All players adjust one space to the right.

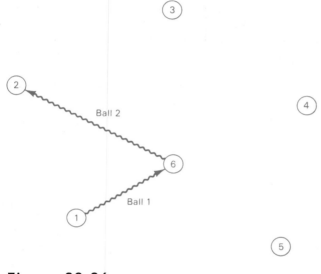

Figure 23.26

Squad split-vision drill.

THREE-LANE RUSH

This is a lead-up to the three-player weave. Youngsters are in three lines across one end of the area. The first three players move parallel down the court while passing the ball back and forth to each other. One player can take a lay-up shot as players near the basket.

THREE-PLAYER WEAVE

This drill requires practice, and children should learn it at slow speed. Walking students through the drill can sometimes help. The player in the centre always starts the drill. She passes to another player coming across in front, and then goes behind that player. Just as soon as she goes behind and around the player, she heads diagonally across the floor until she receives the ball again. The pass from the centre player can start to either side.

Shooting Drills

Shooting drills may involve just shooting or a combination of shooting and other skills.

SIMPLE SHOOTING DRILL

In one simple shooting drill, players form files of no more than four people and take turns shooting a long and then a short shot or some other prescribed series of shots.

FILE-AND-LEADER DRILL

For a file-and-leader drill, the first player in each file has a ball and is the shooter. He passes the ball to the leader, who returns the ball to the spot that the shooter has selected for the shot (see Figure 23.27).

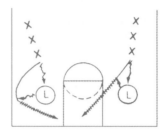

Figure 23.27

File-and-leader drill.

DRIBBLE-AND-SHOOT DRILL

For the dribble-and-shoot drill, two files are established on one end of the floor. One file has a ball. The first player dribbles in and shoots a lay-up. A member of the other file recovers the ball and passes it to the next player (see Figure 23.28). As each person in turn either shoots or retrieves, she goes to the rear of the other file. After children have developed some proficiency in the drill, they can use two balls, allowing for more shooting opportunities.

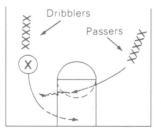

Figure 23.28

Dribble-and-Shoot drill.

SET-SHOT DRILL

In the set-shot drill, players are scattered around a basket in a semicircle, with a leader in charge (see Figure 23.29). Players should be close enough to the basket so that they can shoot accurately. The leader passes to each in turn to take a shot. The leader chases the ball after the shot. A bit of competition can be injected by allowing a successful shooter to take one step back for the next shot, or a player can shoot until he misses.

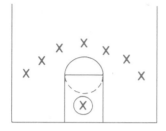

Figure 23.29

Set-shot drill formation.

LAY-UP DRILL

The lay-up drill is a favourite. One line passes to the other line for lay-up shots (see Figure 23.30). Shooters come in from the right side first (this is easier), then from the left, and finally from the centre. Each player goes to the end of the other line.

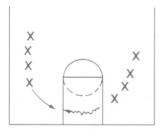

Figure 23.30

Lay-up drill.

JUMP-SHOT DRILL

The jump-shot drill is similar to the lay-up drill, except that the incoming shooter receives the ball, stops, and takes a jump shot. The line of shooters should move back so that there is room for forward movement to the shooting spot. As soon as the passer releases the ball to the shooter, he moves to the end of the shooter's line. The shooter goes to the passer's line after shooting (see Figure 23.31).

Figure 23.31

Jump-shot drill.

One extension of this drill is to allow a second jump shot when the shooter makes the first. In this case, the incoming passer passes to the shooter taking a second shot, as well as to the next shooter. Another extension, which creates a game-like situation, is having both the shooter and the incoming passer follow up the shot when the basket has not been made. As soon as the follow-up shot is made or there are three misses by the followers, the passer passes the ball to the new shooter. Vary the avenues by which the shooters approach, so that children practise shooting from different spots.

Offensive and Defensive Drills

GROUP DEFENSIVE DRILL

For the group defensive drill, the entire class is scattered on a basketball floor, facing one of the sides (see Figure 23.32). The teacher or the student leader stands on the side, near the centre. The drill can be done in a number of ways.

1. The leader points in one direction (forward, backward, or to one side) and gives the command "Move." When the students have moved a short distance, the leader commands, "Stop." Players keep good defensive position throughout.

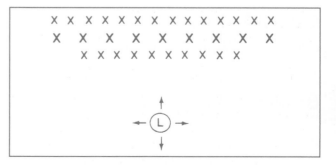

Figure 23.32

Group defensive drill.

2. Commands can be changed so that movement is continuous. Commands are "Right," "Left," "Forward," "Backward," and "Stop." The leader must watch that movement is not so far in any one direction that it causes players to run into obstructions. The leader can give the commands in order, and can point as well.

3. The leader is a dribbler with a ball, who moves forward, backward, or to either side, with the defensive players reacting accordingly.

It is important to stress good defensive position and movement. Movement from side to side should be a slide. Movement forward and backward is a two-step, with one foot always leading.

OFFENSIVE–DEFENSIVE DRILL WITH A POST

The offensive–defensive drill with a post consists of an offensive player, a defensive player, and another player who acts as a passing post. The post player generally remains stationary and receives the ball from and passes to the offensive player. The player on offence tries to maneuver around or past the defensive player to secure a good shot (see Figure 23.33). Plays can be confined to one side of an offensive basket area, thus allowing two drills to go on at the same time on one end of the basketball floor. If there are side baskets, many drills can be operated at the same time. After a player has attempted a basket, rotate players, including any waiting player. The defensive player's job is to cover well enough to prevent shots in front of him. The teacher should match ability; otherwise the drill is nonproductive.

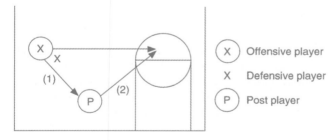

X	Offensive player
X	Defensive player
P	Post player

Figure 23.33

Offensive–defensive drill with post.

Basketball Activities

Developmental Level II

CIRCLE GUARD AND PASS

Playing Area: Any smooth surface with circle markings

Players: 8 to 10 per team

Supplies: A basketball or playground ball

Skills: Passing, catching, guarding

The offensive team is placed in formation around a large (9-m diameter) circle. Two or more offensive players move into the centre. The defensive team is in position around a smaller (6-m) circle inside the larger circle. On signal, the offensive team tries to pass the ball to the centre players. They may pass the ball around the circle to each other before making an attempt to the centre. The defensive team tries to bat the ball away but cannot catch it. After a stipulated time (1 minute), offensive and defensive teams trade positions. If score is kept, 2 points are awarded for each successful pass.

TEACHING TIP

Variation: More than one ball can be used, and different types of passes can be stipulated. The defensive team also can earn points for each time a team member touches the ball.

FIVE PASSES–TEN PASSES

Playing Area: Gymnasium or playground area, 9 by 15 m

Players: 8 to 10 per team

Supplies: A foam-rubber basketball, pinnies

Skills: Catching, passing, dribbling, guarding

Designate three to five players to be taggers and wear a pinnie. The rest of the class passes the ball for five consecutive passes without being intercepted by one of the taggers. The taggers attempt to intercept the ball as the ball is being passed between the other players. If desired, players can use more than one ball. If a tagger intercepts a pass, she can trade places with another player.

DRIBBLERAMA

Playing Area: Any smooth surface with a large circle or square, clearly outlined

Players: Entire class

Supplies: One basketball for each player

Skills: Dribbling and protecting the ball

The playing area is a large circle or square. Dribblerama can be played at two levels of difficulty.

Level 1: All players dribble throughout the area, controlling their ball so that it does not touch another ball. If a touch occurs, both players go outside the area and dribble around the area. Once youngsters have completed dribbling around the area, they re-enter the game.

Level 2: The area is divided in half and all players move to one of the halves. While dribbling and controlling a ball, each player attempts to cause another player to lose control of his ball. When a player loses control, she takes her ball and moves to the opposite half of the area. Play continues against other players who have lost control. When five or six players remain, bring all players back into the game and start over.

BIRDIES IN THE CAGE

Playing Area: Any smooth surface with circle marking

Players: 8 to 15 per team

Supplies: A soccer ball, basketball, or volleyball

Skills: Passing, catching, intercepting

Players are placed in circle formation with two or more children in the centre of the circle. The object of the game is for the centre players to try to touch the ball while circle players are passing it. After a brief time (15 to 20 seconds) choose new players to enter the circle. If scoring is desired, centre players can count the number of touches they made. The ball should move rapidly. Passing to a neighbouring player is not allowed. Teachers can limit play to a specific type of pass (bounce, two-hand, push).

CAPTAIN BALL

Playing Area: Playground or gymnasium area, about 9 by 12 metres

Players: Seven or more on each team

Supplies: A basketball, pinnies, mats or spots

Skills: Passing, catching, guarding

Two games can be played crosswise on a basketball court. A centre line is needed (see Figure 23.34); otherwise, normal boundary lines are used. Carpet squares or marking spots delineate where forwards and the captains must stay. A team is composed of a captain, three or more forwards, and three or more guards. The guards are free to move in their half of the playing area and try to throw the ball to their captain.

The captain and forwards are each assigned to respective spots and must always keep one foot on their assigned carpet square or marking spot. Guarding these four circle players are three guards.

The game is started by a jump at the centreline with two guards from opposing teams. The guards can rove in their half of the court but may not touch the opposing forwards. After a successful basket, an opposing guard immediately puts the ball into play with an inbounds throw. Guards try to throw the ball to their forwards, who maneuver to be open. The forward then tries to throw it to the other forwards or to the captain. Three points are scored when three forwards handle the ball and it is passed to the captain. Two points are scored when the ball is passed to the captain but has not been handled by three forwards.

Stepping over the centre line is a foul. It is also a foul if a guard steps on a forward's spot or mat or makes personal contact with a player on a mat or spot. The penalty for a foul is a free throw. For a free throw, the ball is given to an unguarded forward, who has 5 seconds to get the ball successfully to the guarded captain. If the throw is successful, one point is scored. If it is not successful, the ball is in play. Rotate free-throw shooting among all the forwards.

As in basketball, when the ball goes out of bounds, it is awarded to the team that did not cause it to go out. If a forward or a captain catches a ball without one foot touching their mat or spot, the ball is taken out of bounds by the opposing guard. For violations such as Travelling or kicking the ball, the ball is awarded to an opposing guard out of bounds. No score may be made from a ball that is thrown in directly from out of bounds.

TEACHING TIPS

An effective offensive formation places guards spaced along the centre line (see Figure 23.35—only the offensive team is diagrammed). By passing the ball back and forth among the guards, the forwards have more opportunity to be open, since the passing makes the guards shift position. The guards may dribble, but are restricted to three dribbles for the

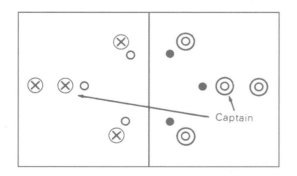

Figure 23.34

Formation for Captain Ball.

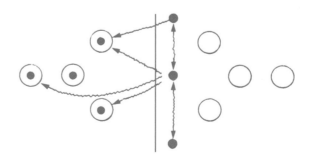

Figure 23.35

An effective offensive formation in Captain Ball.

purpose of advancing the ball. The forwards and captain should shift back and forth to become open for passes. They must keep one foot on the mat or spot. Short and accurate passing uses both chest and bounce passes. Forwards and centres may jump for the ball but must come down with one foot on the mat or spot.

Variations:

1. A five-spot formation like that on a die can be used. Nine players are needed on each team; four forwards, four guards, and one captain. Depending on space and the size of the courts, even more players can be used.

2. Use more than one captain on each side to make scoring easier.

AROUND THE KEY

Playing Area: One end of a basketball floor

Players: Three to eight

Supplies: A basketball

Skills: Shooting

Spots are arranged for shooting as indicated in Figure 23.36. A player begins at the first spot and continues around the key, shooting from each spot. When a miss occurs, the player can stop and wait for the next opportunity and begin from the point at which the miss occurred. The alternative to waiting is to "risk it" and try another shot immediately from the point at which the first try was missed. If the shot is made, the player continues. If the shot is missed, the player must start over from the beginning spot on the next turn. The winner is the player who completes the key first or who makes the most progress.

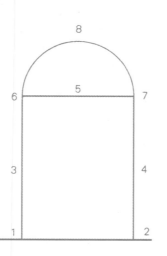

Figure 23.36

Shooting positions for Around the Key.

TEAM FIVE PASSES

Playing Area: Half of a basketball floor

Players: Five or more on each team

Supplies: A basketball, pinnies

Skills: Passing, guarding

Two teams play. Divide the area into smaller areas so many teams can play simultaneously. The object of the game is to complete five consecutive passes, which scores a point. The game is started with a jump ball at the free-throw line.

The teams observe regular basketball rules in ball handling and with regard to travelling and fouling. The team with the ball counts out loud as a pass is completed.

The ball may not be passed back to the person from whom it was received. No dribbling is allowed. If for any reason a player fumbles and recovers, or improperly passes, the ball, start a new count. After a successful score, the scoring team immediately turns the ball over to the other team. A foul draws a free throw, which can score a point. Teams should be well marked to avoid confusion.

Developmental Level III

CAPTAIN BASKETBALL

Playing Area: A basketball court with centre line

Players: Six or more on each team

Supplies: Basketballs, pinnies

Skills: All basketball skills except shooting

A captain's area is laid out by drawing a line (or placing a tumbling mat) between the two foul restraining lines 1.2 m out from the end line. The captain must keep one foot in this area. Captain Basketball is more like regulation basketball than Captain Ball. Captain Ball limits the movements of the forwards. Captain Basketball brings in more natural passing and guarding situations without the movement restrictions on the forwards.

A team typically is composed of three forwards, one captain, and four guards. The captain must keep one foot in the area under the basket. The game is started with a jump ball, after which the players advance the ball as in basketball. No player may cross the centre line, however. The guards must bring the ball up to the centre line and throw it to one of their forwards. The forwards maneuver and attempt to pass successfully to the captain. A throw by one of the forwards to the captain scores 2 points; a free throw scores 1 point.

Fouls are the same as in basketball. In addition, fouls are drawn if a player steps over the centre line or a guard steps into the captain's area. In the case of a foul, the ball is given to a forward at the free-throw line. The player is unguarded and has 5 seconds to pass successfully to the captain, who is guarded by one player. The ball is in play if the free throw is unsuccessful.

TEACHING TIP

Use a folding tumbling mat to designate the captain's area at each end of the court, which discourages intrusion by guards. Even though players are required to remain in their own half of the court, they should be taught to move freely within that area. Stress short, quick passes, because long passes are often ineffective. Captain Basketball offers the chance for practising proper guarding techniques.

QUADRANT BASKETBALL

Playing Area: Basketball court divided into four equal areas

Players: At least eight per team, with a minimum of two placed in each area

Supplies: Basketball, pinnies

Skills: Passing, catching, dribbling, guarding, shooting

Use markers to divide the court by its length and width into four equal areas. Play can be started with a jump ball or by giving the ball to one team. Place two offensive and two defensive players in each quadrant. Players may not leave the quadrant during the course of play. Normal rules of basketball are used, with the exception of limiting the number of dribbles to three. The purpose of this game is to teach youngsters to remain spaced throughout the area. Rotate players to different quadrants so that they have the opportunity to play offence and defence.

TEACHING TIP

Variation: Limit the number of passes that may be made consecutively in one quadrant to encourage passing to other areas. Reduce amount of time a player may hold the ball to five seconds to encourage passing.

SIDELINE BASKETBALL

Playing Area: Basketball court

Players: Entire class

Supplies: A basketball, pinnies

Skills: All basketball skills

Divide the class into two teams, each lined up along one side of the court, facing the other. Three or four active players from each team enter the floor to play regulation basketball. The remainder of the players, who stand on the sideline, can catch and pass the ball to the active players. Sideline players may not shoot, nor may they enter the playing floor. They must keep one foot completely out of bounds at all times.

The active players play regulation basketball, with the additional rule that they must pass and receive the ball three times from sideline players before they can attempt a goal. Sideline players may pass to each other but must pass back to an active player after three sideline passes. The game starts with active players occupying their half of the court. The ball is taken out of bounds under its own basket by the team that was scored on. Play continues until a period of time (one minute) elapses. The active players then go to the end of their line and three new active players come out from the right. All other players move down and adjust to fill the space left by the new players.

No official out-of-bounds on the sides is called. The players on that side of the floor simply recover the ball and, without delay, put it into play with a pass to an active player. Out of bounds on the ends is the same as in regular basketball. If one of the sideline players enters the court and touches the ball, it is a violation, and the ball is awarded out of bounds on the other side to a sideline player of the other team.

TWENTY-ONE

Playing Area: One end of a basketball court

Players: Three to eight in each game

Supplies: A basketball

Skills: Shooting

Players are in file formation by teams. Each player is permitted a long shot (from a specified distance) and a follow-up shot. The long shot, if made, counts 2 points and the short shot counts 1 point. The follow-up shot must be made from the spot where the ball was recovered from the first shot. The normal one–two–step rhythm is permitted on the short shot from the place where the ball was recovered. The winner is the first player scoring a total of 21 points. If on the first shot the player misses the backboard and basket altogether, the second shot must be taken from the corner.

TEACHING TIP

Variations:

1. Start with a simpler game that allows dribbling before the second shot.

2. Allow players to shoot as long as every shot is made. This means that if both the long and the short shot are made, the player goes back to the original position for a third shot. All shots count, and the shooter can continue until a miss.

3. Play with team competition, with each player contributing to the team score.

4. Use various combinations and types of shots.

LANE BASKETBALL

Playing Area: Basketball court divided into six or more lanes

Players: Five per team

Supplies: Basketball, pinnies, cones to mark zones

Skills: All basketball skills

The court is divided into six lanes as shown in Figure 23.37. Players must stay in their lane and cannot cross the midcourt line. Regular basketball rules prevail, with the exception that players cannot dribble more than three times. Play is started with a jump ball. At regular intervals, youngsters rotate to the next lane to ensure they get an opportunity to play both offence and defence.

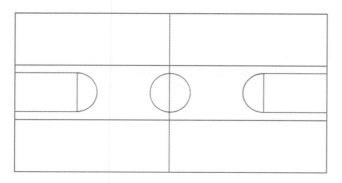

Figure 23.37

Court markings for Lane Basketball.

The teacher can change a number of rules to alter the focus of the game. For example, three passes may be required before shooting may occur. Also, to increase the amount of activity, youngsters can move the entire length of the floor within their lane.

FREEZE OUT

Playing Area: One end of the basketball court

Players: Four to eight

Supplies: A basketball

Skills: Shooting under pressure

There are many types of freeze-out shooting games. This version is an interesting shooting game that culminates quickly and allows players back into the game with minimal wait time. Each player can have three misses before being out. After the first miss, the player gets an *O*; after the second, a *U*; and after the third, a *T*. This spells *OUT* and puts the player out. The winner is the last player remaining.

The first player shoots a basket from any spot desired. If she misses the basket, there is no penalty and the next player shoots. If she makes the basket, the following player must make a basket from the same spot or it is scored as a miss (and a letter). If the player ahead misses, the next player may shoot from any spot without penalty.

FLAG DRIBBLE

Playing Area: One end of a basketball floor or a hard-surfaced area outside with boundaries

Players: 10 to 20

Supplies: A basketball and a flag for each player

Skills: Dribbling

The object is to eliminate other players and avoid being eliminated. Players are eliminated if they lose control of the ball, if their flag is pulled, or if they go out of bounds. Keeping control of the ball by dribbling is interpreted to mean continuous dribbling without missing a bounce. A double dribble (both hands) is regarded as a loss of control.

Start the game with players scattered around the area near the sidelines. Each has a ball, and all have flags tucked in the back of their belts. On signal, all players begin to dribble in the area. While keeping control of the dribble and staying in bounds, they attempt to pull a flag from any other player's back. When players lose control, they move to the perimeter of the area and practise their dribbling skills. As soon as the game is down to a few players, start the game over. Sometimes two players lose control of their basketball at about the same time. In this case, both are eliminated.

Variations:

1. If using flags is impractical, play the game without this feature. The objective then becomes to knock aside or deflect the other basketballs while retaining control of one's own ball.

2. Flag Dribble can be played with teams or squads. In this case, each squad or team is clearly marked.

ONE-GOAL BASKETBALL

Playing Area: An area with one basketball goal

Players: Two to four on each team

Supplies: A basketball, pinnies (optional)

Skills: All basketball skills

This is an excellent class activity if four or more baskets are available. The game is played by two teams according to the rules of basketball but with the following exceptions:

1. When a defensive player recovers the ball, either from the backboard or on an interception, he must take the ball out beyond the foul-line circle before offensive play is started and an attempt at a goal is made.

2. After a basket is made, the ball is taken in the same fashion away from the basket to the centre of the floor, where the other team starts offensive play.

3. Observe regular free-throw shooting after a foul, or use the rule whereby the offended team takes the ball out of bounds.

4. An offensive player who is tied up in a jump ball loses the ball to the other team.

5. Individuals are responsible for calling fouls on themselves.

BASKETBALL SNATCH BALL

Playing Area: Basketball court

Players: 6 to 20 on each team

Supplies: Two basketballs, two hoops

Skills: Passing, dribbling, shooting

Each of two teams occupies one side of a basketball floor. The players on each team are numbered consecutively from the right-hand end of the line. Two balls are placed inside two hoops, one hoop on each side of the centre line. When the teacher calls three or more numbers, players from each team whose numbers were called run to the ball assigned to them. These players pass and dribble to the basket on their right and try to make a basket. Three passes must be made and all players must handle the ball before a basket can be shot. As soon as a basket is made, the players pass and dribble back and place the ball in the hoop. The first team to return the ball after making a basket scores a point for that team. Use a system to keep track of the numbers so that all children have a turn. Numbers are called in any order.

THREE-ON-THREE

Playing Area: Half of a basketball court

Players: Many teams of three players each

Supplies: Basketballs

Skills: All basketball skills

Three teams of three are assigned to a basket. The offensive team stands at the top of the key facing the basket. The defensive team starts at the free throw line. The remaining team waits for their turn beyond the end line. Regular basketball rules are used. The offensive team tries to score. The offensive team plays until they score or the ball is stolen by the defence. In either case, the defensive team moves to the centre of the floor and becomes the offensive unit. The waiting team moves onto the floor and plays defence. The previous offensive team goes to the rear of the line of waiting players. Each of the teams keeps its own score. A class can play many games at the same time depending on the number of available baskets. A team wins when they score 3 points. Rotate winning teams to games at other baskets.

BASKETRAMA

Playing Area: Area around one basket

Players: Usually two

Supplies: A basketball for each player

Skills: Shooting under pressure

On signal, two players, each with a basketball, begin to shoot individually as rapidly as possible, taking any kind of shots they wish, until one scores 10 baskets to become the winner. Each player must handle her own basketball and must not impede or interfere with the other's ball. Naturally, the balls do collide at times, but deliberate interference by knocking the other ball out of the way or kicking it means disqualification.

Mark balls so that there is no argument as to ownership. Try using different types of basketballs or mark with chalk or tape. Each player can count out loud each basket he makes, or another student can keep score for each contestant.

Critical Thinking

1. Using small-sided games (e.g., 2 v 2, 3 v 3) with students at both developmental levels II and III is recommended. Discuss this recommendation as it relates to students learning skills and tactics in a game context.

References and Suggested Readings

American Sport Education Program. (2007). *Coaching youth basketball* (4th ed.). Champaign, IL: Human Kinetics.

B.C. Ministry of Small Business, Tourism and Culture. (2001). *Basketball—teaching the basics resource manual.* Victoria, BC: Author.

Bulger, S., Mohr, D., Rairigh, J., & Townsend, S. (2007). *Sport education seasons.* Champaign, IL: Human Kinetics.

Byl, J. (2006). *Organizing successful tournaments.* Champaign, IL: Human Kinetics.

Fronske, H. (2005). *Teaching cues for sport skills* (3rd ed.). San Francisco: Benjamin Cummings.

Klumpner, R. (2003). *Sport progressions.* Champaign, IL: Human Kinetics.

Launder, A.L. (2001). *Play practice: the games approach to teaching and coaching sports.* Champaign, IL: Human Kinetics.

Nix, C. (2000). *Skills, drills and strategies for basketball.* Scottsdale, AZ: Holcomb Hathaway.

Oliver, J. (2004). *Basketball fundamentals.* Champaign, IL: Human Kinetics.

Prudden, J. (2006). *Coaching girls' basketball successfully.* Champaign, IL: Human Kinetics.

Prusak, K. A. (2005). *Basketball fun & games—50 skill-building activities for children.* Champaign, IL: Human Kinetics.

 Weblinks

Basketball Ontario: www. Basketball.on.ca

This website highlights a game called Basketeers, an intramural style game that uses a modified scoring system and equal playing time for all participants. Focus in on fun and fair play.

Coaching Association of Canada: www.coach.ca

National organization dedicated to improving the effectiveness of coaching across all sports and all levels in Canada.

Basketball Canada: www.basketballcanada.ca

Basketball Canada is the governing body for the sport of basketball in Canada, and their website offers information on the national team, programs and upcoming events, and news and views from the basketball community.

CHAPTER 24

Lacrosse

The skills of lacrosse include catching, throwing, scooping and cradling. This chapter provides an introduction to these basic skills; and describes activities and lead-up games suitable for elementary students at developmental levels II and III.

OUTCOMES

- Identify the instructional cues associated with basic lacrosse skills.
- Develop a unit plan and lesson focus for lacrosse.
- Identify safety precautions associated with teaching lacrosse.
- Describe instructional procedures used for implementing lacrosse activities and lead-up games.

OVERVIEW

Lacrosse is the oldest team sport in North America and its roots can be traced back to Canada's Aboriginal peoples. Lacrosse is classified as an invasion game (like soccer) and the aim is to score points by throwing the ball into the opposition's goal.

Lacrosse is one of the oldest team sports in North America and it is recognized by Parliament as Canada's national summer sport. Lacrosse can trace its roots to Canada's Aboriginal peoples. In 1904, lacrosse was included in the Olympic Games, and the first gold medal won by a Canadian Olympic team was awarded in lacrosse. Lacrosse is a team game that involves passing, catching, running, and scooping the ball off the ground to progress the ball down the field or court. The aim of the game is to score points by shooting the ball into the opposing team's goal. Lacrosse at the elementary level is a lead-up to the four disciplines of lacrosse practised today in Canada: box lacrosse, men's and women's field lacrosse, and the non-contact inter-lacrosse. At the elementary level students should learn the skills, techniques, and strategies of non-contact inter-lacrosse. With plastic sticks and a soft low-bounce ball, lacrosse can be played indoors or out.

Instructional Emphasis and Sequence

Developmental Level I

Developing the fundamental movement skills of throwing and catching will provide a foundation for developing lacrosse skills in the future. See Chapter 15 on fundamental movement skills.

Developmental Level II

Activities are used to develop fundamental skills and basic strategy. Learning to scoop, cradle, catch, and make short passes should receive the majority of attention. Begin by practising the skills in a stationary position, then increase the difficulty by adding movements and supplementary skills. Catching, throwing, and scooping skills can also form part of a unit of instruction on manipulative movement skills (see Chapter 17).

Developmental Level III

At developmental level III, skill development continues, with more emphasis on ball control, passing accuracy, and shooting. Players play lead-up games using skills involved in the game of lacrosse. The rules of lacrosse can be introduced, and students play a non-contact form of the game.

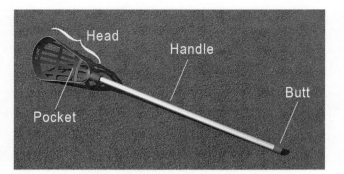

Figure 24.1

Inter-lacrosse stick.

Modified Lacrosse Equipment

At the elementary level, lacrosse is played with a modified stick (inter-lacrosse stick, see Figure 24.1) and soft ball. The sticks are made of a moulded plastic head and a metal handle. The end of the handle is covered with a plastic stopper, and this end of the stick is called the butt. Inter-lacrosse sticks have a built-in or detachable strap across the pocket to assist with catching and to prevent the ball falling out of the stick.

Lacrosse Skills

Ready Position

A stance, which is basic to the performance of the majority of the fundamental skills of lacrosse, is the *ready position* (see Figure 24.2a). The body does not face front-on or side-on, but is halfway between—a *staggered* stance (see Figure 24.2b). This will allow room for the stick to move. Feet are shoulder width apart, knees slightly bent, back straight, and head up. The player carries the stick with both hands. The top hand is placed about two-thirds of the way up the handle, the bottom hand covers the butt of the stick. The palm of the top hand faces away from the body and the palm of the bottom hand faces toward the body. The arm of the top hand is bent at the elbow, and the head of the stick is positioned slightly in front of the shoulder at eye level. The top hand will usually be the player's dominant hand, but lacrosse can also be played ambidextrously.

Instructional cues for the ready position include the following:

1. Staggered stance.
2. Knees slightly bent, back straight, head up.

Figures 24.2a–b

Figure 24.2a

Lacrosse ready position.

Figure 24.2b

Staggered-stance catching.

3. Top hand two-thirds way up the handle, bottom hand cover butt.
4. Head of stick in front of shoulder.

Start in the ready position with the open pocket of the head of the stick facing the passer. The bottom hand points the butt of the stick in the direction of the throw. Keeping the bottom hand fairly still, the thrower extends the upper arm forwards (see Figure 24.3). Watch the ball and move the stick into the path of the ball. When receiving a pass, avoid jabbing or lunging at the approaching ball. Instead, cushion the incoming ball, bringing the stick back to the ready position as the ball enters the stick.

Figure 24.3

Ready to receive a pass.

Instructional cues for catching include the following:

1. Reach forward with the stick head.
2. Watch ball into the stick.
3. Cushion ball.

Passing and Shooting

Start in ready position and move the head of the stick behind the shoulder (see Figure 24.4a). Step forward with the opposite foot to the top hand (left foot for right-handed players) to transfer your weight from the back to the front foot while simultaneously extending the top arm (see Figure 24.4b). The bottom hand starts and stays forward of the body; it does not move very much but stabilizes the bottom of the stick. The top hand should slide down the shaft during the throw. The trajectory of the passes should be fairly flat and the throw should be firm.

Instructional cues for passing and shooting include the following:

1. Ready position with the stick head back.
2. Step with foot opposite top hand.
3. Top arm extends, bottom hand stabilizes the stick.
4. Transfer weight from the back to the front foot.
5. Follow through toward target.

Sco∆oping

When holding the stick with the right hand at the top, position the instep of the right foot beside the ball (left for left-handers). Move the stick across the body and place the back of the stick pocket on the ground slightly outside the line of the body to the left. This action is mainly controlled with the top hand. The grip should not alter through this action. Knees are bent and the body is in a semi-crouched position, keeping the head down and eyes on the ball. Angle of the stick should be approximately 30 degrees. The stick contacts the ground approximately 10 cm before the ball (see Figure 24.5a) and slides under the ball. The stick head should then be brought up toward the chest (Figure 24.5b). Finally, the top hand and arm moves the stick back to the right as a step is taken with the left foot.

Instructional cues for scooping include the following:

1. Right hand at top, right foot beside ball (opposite for left-handed players).
2. Move stick across body.
3. Knees bent, body crouched.
4. Slide stick head under ball and up to chest to "scoop."

Figures 24.4a–b

Lacrosse throwing action.

Figure 24.4a

Figure 24.4b

Figures 24.5a–b

Technique for scooping.

Figure 24.5a

Figure 24.5b

Scooping a Ball Rolling Away from the Player

Use the same action but make sure you catch up to the ball before trying to scoop, then accelerate the stick head faster than the ball is moving.

Cradling

Cradling is a technique used to keep the ball in the pocket of the stick. The stick should be carried in the ready position with the bottom hand loosely holding the butt end of the stick, forming an "O" with the hand. The upper hand should hold the stick firmly above the mid-point of the shaft, approximately one-third of the way down the shaft. A gentle rolling motion of the upper wrist will cause the stick to rotate back and forth, thus "cradling" the ball (see Figures 24.6a–d). Cradling uses centripetal force—the force generated by moving something in a circle—to press the ball into the back of the pocket. Because the moulded plastic inter-lacrosse sticks have a strap (built-in or detachable) across the pocket to help keep the ball from falling out, cradling is not essential when using the modified sticks. However, cradling is an important lacrosse skill, and should be introduced at the elementary level.

Instructional cues for cradling include the following:

1. Bottom hand "O."
2. Rolling motion with upper arm and wrist.

Instructional Procedures

1. For many children, lacrosse is a new experience. Few have played the game, and many may never have seen a game. Showing a short video clip of a lacrosse game as an introduction may be helpful.

2. Lacrosse requires the participants to use a piece of equipment for all aspects of the game. Children catch, pass, shoot, and run while carrying a lacrosse stick. Therefore, it is important to teach children to carry their stick safely in two hands and to use caution when throwing and shooting to ensure no student will be contacted with the follow-through. It is also important to provide students with plenty of opportunities and time to learn to use this new piece of equipment.

3. Lacrosse can be played either indoors or out. A plastic lacrosse ball is a soft, hollow ball, safe for both indoor and outdoor play. Tennis balls or whiffle balls are good substitutes. For indoor play, hockey nets, hoops, or folding mats set on each end make a satisfactory goal. If playing outdoors, hockey nets work best for goals.

4. Lacrosse is an "invasion" game. Like soccer, the purpose of lacrosse is to invade the opponent's space and score a goal by throwing the ball into their net. Modifying game play to promote the use of the skills and use of space concepts will help foster effective team play. Lacrosse is more enjoyable for all when the players pass to open teammates. Discourage excessive control of the ball by one person.

5. The game can be modified by using hoops as nets where no goalie is required. If children are playing the position of goal tender they MUST be fully protected (see Figure 24.7).

Figures 24.6a–d

Technique for cradling the ball.

Figure 24.6a

Figure 24.6b

Figure 24.6c

Figure 24.6d

Figure 24.7

The goal keeper must wear protective equipment.

Suggested Elementary Lacrosse Rules

Lacrosse at the elementary level is a lead-up to the four disciplines of lacrosse practised today in Canada. The safest and most enjoyable game for all participants at the elementary level is a non-contact modified form of inter-lacrosse.

The playing area for lacrosse needs to have easily identifiable boundaries such as a basketball court or a lined soccer field, with a centre line dividing the area in two. A goal of some kind should be placed at either end with a goal crease (area) that only the goalie may go into. To maximize participation, to increase skill development, and to assure the opportunity for success for all participants, it is recommended at the elementary level to keep the playing area smaller by dividing the field in half and having two smaller games going on simultaneously.

The maximum number of players per side should be five: four runners and one goaltender (although not necessary, see point 5 of previous section). Team size can vary depending on the size of the playing area; smaller teams allow more time for individual player–ball control. For the outdoor game, a maximum of 10 players per side is suggested, with 7 per side being encouraged: two attack, two midfielders, two defence, and one goaltender (optional). Players are designated to areas of the field based on their position: attack in the offensive zone,

defence in the defensive zone, while midfielders are permitted to move through both zones. To give everyone a chance at each position, have students switch places after a set time period (attack move to midfield, midfield move to defence, defence move to attack).

The basic suggested rules are as follows:

1. A coin toss to determine possession at the start of the game.

2. A goal scored counts as one point.

3. The first player to cover a loose ball (trapping, see Figure 24.8) using the head of the stick gains possession of the ball. Once the ball is covered, the player then scoops the ball up and all other players must be 1 m away from the player in possession.

4. Any ball out of bounds is the possession of the player who retrieves it. This encourages continuous action.

5. Players must keep both hands on the stick at all times.

6. No body or stick contact is allowed.

7. Except for the goalie (optional), all players must stay out of the goalie's crease (2-m circle around the goal).

8. Continuous play—players must run with the ball, with the exception of stopping to pass, or to shoot.

9. Limit the individual player's time of possession (for example, five seconds).

10. Off-side rule (optional rule for outdoor play)—to avoid crowding and to encourage passing: defence remains behind the centre line (defensive end), offence remains in front of the centre line (offensive end), midfielders are rovers, with access to either zone.

Figure 24.8

Trap the ball for possession in inter-lacrosse.

11. Violation in any of the above rules numbered 5–10 results in a change of possession.

TEACHING TIPS

1. Rules may be adjusted to suit the age and skill of the class.

2. Encourage students to present a target for the passes by moving into free space ahead of the path of the ball.

3. Encourage the skill(s) taught in class to be used during game play by rewarding the students (two points for an assisted goal from a pass caught in the air).

4. Allow play to continue behind the goals if space is available, keeping the game continuous.

5. Emphasize teamwork and skill development by requiring the students to complete certain skills before a goal can be scored (two passes, then shoot for goal).

6. For students using a wheelchair for mobility, cut the length of the shaft to about half its length (depending on the height of the chair and the student's arm length) so that the stick can be manipulated with one hand to the side of the chair.

Lacrosse Activities

Consider the following developmental sequence when choosing activities:

Stationary (Self then Partners) → Movement (S then P) → Multiple skills → Activities

CATCHING AND PASSING ACTIVITIES

1. *Pass Against Wall by Self.* Students stand about 5 m from a wall and toss the ball toward the wall in a pass-type execution. Emphasis should be on proper technique.

2. *Accurate Pass.* Use an inclusive approach (see Chapter 3) and have different target sizes for students to choose to aim at. Targets can be hoops and shapes tied to fences, chalk circles drawn on the wall, or hoops or mats laid flat on the ground (for longer passes).

3. *Toss and Catch.* In a stationary position, toss the ball in the air and attempt to catch the ball with the lacrosse stick. Start with easy tosses, gradually increasing the height of each toss. Increase difficulty by repeating the toss when jogging around the playing area while carrying the stick and cradling the ball.

4. *Partner Catch.* Line up facing a partner 5 m away. One player catches the ball with a stick, while the partner uses her hand to toss the ball in an arc, allowing the receiver to catch with ease.

5. *Wall Catch.* Players line up with a partner about 4 m away from a wall. Each pair will need one ball and one stick. Player A tosses the ball with his hand against the wall so that Player B is able to catch the rebound off the wall with his stick before it hits the ground.

6. *Partner Pass and Catch.* Both students with sticks and a ball line up facing each other about 3 to 5 m away. Partners pass back and forth, while gradually increasing the throwing distance. To increase difficulty, have students pass and catch while jogging around the playing area.

7. *Scoop and Pass Relay.* Players line up in relay fashion 3 to 4 m away from the wall (backs to wall). In front of each team, place a ball and space 3 to 5 pylons, or chairs across the play area 2 to 3 m apart. Players scoop up the ball, weave through the obstacles, and sprint back toward the line. Once the players reach the front obstacle, they must stop and make a pass to the next player in line, before going to the end of the line. To increase difficulty, allow the player to pass while running toward the front of the line and the receiver.

SCOOPING ACTIVITIES

1. *Under the Arch.* In pairs, find a space. One student makes an arch with her body and stick and places the ball under the arch (see Figure 24.9). The other student jogs to scoop up the ball by going under the arch. This encourages students to get down low.

2. *Scooping and Roll.* In their own space students roll their ball a short distance away and jog to scoop up the ball. Repeat.

3. *Continuous Shuttle Pick-up.* Students line up in two lines facing each other, with two or three students per line. One ball is given to each of the three students in one of the lines (ball line). Using their hand, these students will roll the ball toward the opposite line and proceed to run to the end of the opposite line. The first student in the opposite line traps the ball, scoops it up, and cradles on the run to the end of the opposite line.

4. *Roll to Scoop Partner Relay.* Start with the ball placed in front of the first player. First player scoops up the ball and runs around the pylon and back to his partner; then rolls the ball for his partner. The partner then repeats the action. Each player scoops four times.

Figure 24.9a–b

Scoop "Under the arch."

Figures 24.9a

5. *Rats and Rabbits.* In pairs students number themselves 1 or 2. Number 1's become Rats, number 2's become rabbits. Set up as shown in Figure 24.10, each student starts with two hands on his stick. When the teacher calls out, "Rats," the Rats run to scoop up their ball before their Rabbit partner can tag them with his or her hand. Play again, switching up calling out "Rats" and "Rabbits."

CRADLING ACTIVITIES

1. *Cradle Discovery.* Use a convergent discovery approach (see Chapter 3) to introduce the concept of cradling. Ask students to grip their left wrist with their right hand and their right wrist with their left hand. Now ask the students to jog 100 m or so while holding their wrists. When the students have finished their jog ask them how their arms moved and why.

Figure 24.9b

Lead students on a process to discover that their arms rock across their body; and that when they hold and run with a lacrosse stick they will need to engage in a similar rocking action to keep well balanced and to keep the ball in the stick. Then have students practise cradling individually; first at a jog, then running more quickly.

2. *Cradle Pass.* Students can practise in pairs, with partners standing about 5 to 6 m apart. One student cradles the ball while running toward a partner, goes around the partner, and returns to the starting spot. The ball is then passed to the partner, who moves in a similar manner.

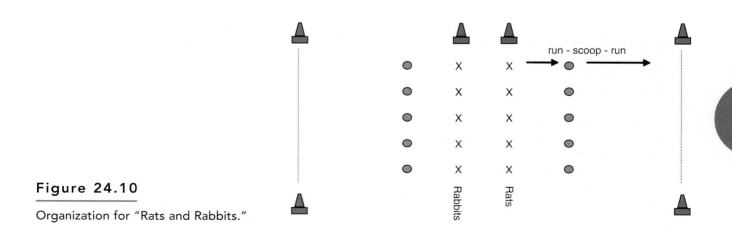

Figure 24.10

Organization for "Rats and Rabbits."

Lacrosse Lead-up Games

Developmental Level II

Most of the games in this section have been adapted from the Canadian Lacrosse Association's (1990) *Inter-lacrosse Instructional Manual*.

HIDEAWAY

Playing Area: Gym or playing field

Players: Entire class divided into four teams

Supplies: One stick per person, as many balls as possible (30+)

Skills: Scooping

Players are divided up into four teams and assigned a corner of the gym for each team's hideaway. Each team receives the same number of balls, which they place in their hideaway. Extra balls may be left in a middle or neutral area. On the signal "go," all players rush out to capture balls from other hideaways. Captured balls are dropped into their new owners' areas. The players then venture out to capture more balls. Players are only allowed to scoop up one ball at a time and no one may touch the balls with their hands or feet. Hideaways may not be guarded. At the end of one minute, stop the game and tally the balls in each hideaway to determine the score for each team.

VOLLEYCROSSE

Playing Area: Gym or playing field

Players: Entire class, two or three students per team

Supplies: One stick per person and one ball per game, volleyball net or pylons (eight per game)

Skills: Catching and throwing

Divide the class up into teams. The aim of the game is to score points by having the ball land in the opposition's court (like volleyball). The ball is thrown over the net and the opposite team tries to catch it. If the ball is caught then this team throws it back over the net. Teams continue to "rally" the ball back and forth until it lands in the court or goes out-of-bounds. If the balls lands in the opposition's court the throwing team scores a point; if the ball lands out of bounds play begins again with no points scored. If you're playing outdoors or don't want to put up nets, create a court with three areas. The middle segment is unoccupied by players. Teams must throw high over the middle section (e.g., higher than the teacher reaching up with her hand) to be a fair throw.

TEACHING TIP

To ensure this game is challenging and there are lots of catching and throwing practise opportunities, team size should be kept to a minimum (two or three students).

AROUND THE CLOCK

Playing Area: Gym or playing field

Players: Entire class; divide class into four teams

Supplies: One ball per team, one stick per person

Skills: Passing and catching

Divide the class into four teams. The objective is to pass the ball between players. Each team forms a large circle with one player in the centre. The player in the centre passes the ball to, and receives it back from, each player in turn around the circle. On completion of the "clock," the team sits down. First team finished gets one point. Change the centre player and repeat. The game ends when each player has had a turn as centre. The team with the most points wins.

Developmental Level III

TARGET BALL

Playing Area: Gym or playing field

Players: Entire class, two teams

Supplies: One stick per player, two balls for every player, cones, utility balls

Skills: Passing and shooting

Place three to four playground balls in the centre of the playing area and sit each ball on a cone. Line up the two teams at opposite ends of the playing area and give each student two balls. The objective of the game is to shoot at the target and knock it off its pedestal (cone). Players cannot retrieve balls from the shooting area until the teacher gives the signal.

KEEP AWAY

Playing Area: Gym or playing field

Players: Entire class, two students per team

Supplies: One stick per player, one lacrosse ball and four pylons per game.

Skills: Passing, catching, moving into free space

Teams of two play against each other. Students select and mark out a playing area with their pylons (about 4 to 5 square metres). The aim of the game is to complete three successive passes to their partner without being intercepted by the opposition. If the ball is intercepted or goes out-of-bounds, possession is turned over to the other team.

Variations: to make this game more difficult the three passes must be caught without the ball bouncing or touching the ground.

END BALL

Playing Area: Gym or playing field

Players: Entire class, no more than four people per team

Supplies: One stick per player, three lacrosse balls

Skills: Passing and catching

Divide the class into two teams, putting one player per team at the end of the playing area. The objective is to pass the ball to your own player at the end. The player at the end may move along the end of the playing area but cannot enter the playing area. The player at the end must catch the pass with her lacrosse stick to score a point. Players move around to get "open," but once they receive a pass, they are no longer allowed to take any steps with the ball. There is no contact and no interference with players attempting to make a pass. One point is scored for getting the ball to the end. When a point is scored possession goes to the opposition. Adding more balls into the field of play can increase difficulty.

LACROSSE SOFTBALL

Playing Area: Gym or playing field

Players: Entire class, two equal teams

Supplies: One stick per player, one ball, bases

Skills: Passing, catching, cradling

For this game, follow basic softball rules with one exception: there is no pitcher. The batter "hits" the ball by throwing it into the field of play. An out may be made if the player catches a pop fly or fields the ball with the stick and throws the runner out.

TEACHING TIP

Variation: Beat the runner. After the batter "hits" the ball, he must try to beat the ball around the bases. The fielding team must try to throw the ball around the bases, 1-2-3-home, before the runner reaches home.

LACROSSE GOLF

Playing Area: Playing field (use lots of space)

Players: Entire class, organized in pairs

Supplies: One stick per player, one ball per pair, targets such as chairs or hoops

Skills: Passing, catching, shooting

The class divides into teams of two and joins with another team of two to play. Each foursome goes to a hole on the course. The objective is to hit the target with as few strokes as possible. Player A "tees off" by passing to B, who is in position toward the target. If the pass is completed, A moves closer to the hole, with B then passing to A. On any incomplete pass (dropped), the ball is returned to the passer for another attempt. Players "leap frog" until one player shoots at the target. Each pass (shot) counts as one stroke. As in golf, teams score eagles, birdies, pars, and bogeys. To increase difficulty, vary length of holes, number of holes, and size of targets. A Par 3 course works well for ease of scoring.

TEACHING TIP

Variation: The first player throws the ball in the direction of the target. The partner makes the next throw from where the ball lands. This activity encourages players to work on throwing skills and accuracy (no catching skills).

Critical Thinking

1. Lacrosse is categorized as an invasion game. Examine the drills and game activities in the invasion games (soccer, basketball, floor hockey) and discuss how to make adjustments so they can be used for lacrosse. For example, how can you adapt the drills and games in other invasion games for use in lacrosse?

References and Suggested Readings

Canadian Lacrosse Association. (1990). *Inter-lacrosse instructional manual—a non-contact skill-oriented activity.* Gloucester, ON: Author.

Canadian Lacrosse Association. (1993). *Women's field lacrosse instructional manual—A non-contact skill-oriented activity.* Gloucester, ON: Author.

Temple, V. A. (2003). Warm-up to Lacrosse. *Strategies, 16,* 31–33.

Temple, V. A. (2002). Lacrosse lead-up games. *Strategies, 16,* 25–28.

 Weblinks

The Canadian Lacrosse Association: www.lacrosse.ca

The Canadian Lacrosse Association's website provides an interesting discussion on why lacrosse is a beneficial sport for children. The different forms of lacrosse (i.e., box, field, inter-lacrosse) are described, and a brief history of the game is provided.

The Canadian Encyclopedia: www.canadianencyclopedia.ca

Provides information about the history and forms of lacrosse, including images from Library and Archives Canada.

CBC Archives: http://archives.cbc.ca

The CBC Archives provides written and visual resources for teachers. Includes an assignment for grade 6 to 8 students that could apply to English, Language Arts, History, Physical Education, and/or Social Studies.

Manitoba Lacrosse Association: www.manitobalacrosse.mb.ca/

This is a great website to view images of a fully equipped box lacrosse player and goalie. The rules of inter-lacrosse can also be downloaded from this website.

Floor Hockey

Essential Components

I	**Organized around content standards**
II	**Student-centred and developmentally appropriate**
III	**Physical activity and motor skill development form the core of the program**
IV	**Teaches management skills and self-discipline**
V	**Promotes inclusion of all students**
VI	**Focuses on process over product**
VII	Promotes lifetime personal health and wellness
VIII	**Teaches cooperation and responsibility and promotes sensitivity to diversity**

Physical Education Standards

1	**Students are able to move competently using a variety of fundamental and specialized motor skills.**
2	Students can monitor and maintain a health-enhancing level of physical fitness.
3	**Students are able to apply movement concepts and basic mechanics of skill performance when learning and refining motor skills.**
4	Students comprehend the basic principles of wellness and are able to apply concepts that enable them to make meaningful decisions that positively impact their health and wellness.
5	**Students participate in a wide variety of physical activities and learn how to maintain a personalized active lifestyle.**
6	**Students demonstrate empathy, understanding, and respect for the numerous differences exhibited by people in an activity setting.**
7	**Students exhibit responsible and self-directed behaviours that lead to positive social interactions in physical activity.**

skills and lead-up games to floor hockey is progression. Lead-up games provide an opportunity for teachers to emphasize development of selected hockey skills and tactics in a setting that is compatible with the abilities of participants.

OVERVIEW

Skills instruction for floor hockey (also called ball hockey and cosom hockey) is introduced during the intermediate grades after children have mastered basic prerequisite skills. Teaching the rules and tactics for hockey is an integral part of the instructional process. The key to success when teaching fundamental

OUTCOMES

- Structure learning experiences efficiently using appropriate formations, progressions, and teaching techniques.

- Know the basic skills, tactics, and rules of floor hockey.

- Develop a unit plan and lesson focus for floor hockey.

- Identify safety precautions associated with teaching floor hockey.

- Describe instructional procedures used for implementing successful practice activities.

Floor hockey is a fast-moving game that can be adapted for use in elementary school. With a plastic puck or soft ball, hockey can be played indoors (see Figure 25.1) and outdoors with a soft ball. Success at floor hockey demands much running and team play. Place emphasis on lead-up games that allow all students to experience success and enjoyment. Teach fundamental skills, tactics, and position play rather than the disorganized "everyone chase the puck" style of floor hockey.

Instructional Emphasis and Sequence

Table 25.1 shows the sequence of floor hockey activities divided into two developmental levels. The actual presentation of activities is dictated by the maturity and past experience of participants.

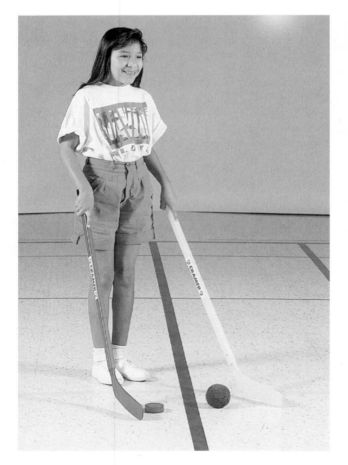

Figure 25.1

Hockey equipment.

Developmental Level II

Drills are used to develop fundamental skills. Emphasize learning to dribble, receiving the puck, and making short passes. Drills and game activities that involve give-and-go plays, and so on, provide the basic tactical focus, and provide the opportunity for all students to practise the skills in a realistic context. Consider using modified games (2 vs. 2, 3 vs. 3, 4 vs. 4) to practise skills and tactics.

Developmental Level III

At developmental level III, skill development continues, with more emphasis on puck control and passing accuracy. Lead-up games use skills involved in regulation hockey. The drills presented are designed to foster team play. Lead-up games are used to help students continue to develop basic offensive and defensive tactics, and field positioning.

TABLE 25.1

Suggested floor hockey program

Developmental Level II	Developmental Level III
Skills	
Gripping and carrying the stick	Controlled stickhandling
Loose stickhandling	Passing to moving target
Passing to stationary and moving target	Wrist shot (refinement)
Wrist shot	Side receiving
Front receiving	Poke check
Face-off	Goal keeping
Stick check	Dodging
Knowledge	
Rules	
Safety and Fair Play	Safety and Fair Play
• no body contact	• no slap shots
• keep stick below waist at all times	• respect for goalie crease
• limit personal infractions (e.g., tripping)	• limit personal infractions

(continued)

TABLE 25.1
Suggested floor hockey program (continued)

Offensive Tactics

Keeping team possession of puck (on-the-puck and off-the-puck movements)	Keeping team possession of puck while making forward progress (on-the-puck and off-the-puck movements)
• pass and move to open space to receive	• give-and-go play
• eluding defender	• choosing when to stickhandle, pass, shoot

Defensive Tactics

Defending space and player	Defending space, player, and goal
Clearing the puck	Transition from defence to offense
	• outlet pass positioning

Game Activities

Stickhandle Competition	Goalkeeper Hockey
Circle Keep-Away	Sideline Hockey
Five Passes	Regulation Elementary Hockey
Lane Hockey	
Pass Hockey	

Hockey Skills

Gripping and Carrying the Stick

The hockey stick should be held with both hands on the stick. The basic grip (for right-handed players) puts the left hand at the top of the stick and the right hand 15 to 30 cm below the left (see Figure 25.2). The player should learn to carry the stick to the right side the body while running, with the blade close to the ground.

Stickhandling

The purpose of stickhandling is to carry and control the puck without looking. Stickhandling is used to advance the puck, break for the goal, or maneuver out of a difficult situation. Instructional cues for stickhandling include the following:

1. Keep the puck under control (within blade length).

2. Move under control and try to "cup" the puck on your stick by pulling it forward and backward.

Figure 25.2

Gripping and carrying.

3. Keep the head up.

4. Keep the elbows away from the body.

Loose Stickhandling

Loose stickhandling is the easiest type of stickhandling. Typically used in open field/court with no defenders around, loose stickhandling involves the player pushing the puck 2 to 3 m ahead and the "chasing" after the puck. Loose stickhandling allows players to move at a faster speed.

Controlled Stickhandling

Controlled stickhandling (Figure 25.3) consists of a series of soft taps in the desired direction of movement (while tapping from side to side of the puck). The puck should be kept far enough away from the feet but less than one stride ahead to allow for control.

Passing

Passing is the basic skill in floor hockey. The quick hit should be taught simultaneously with dribbling skills. Emphasis should be on accuracy. The following instructional cues can be used to help youngsters concentrate on correct technique:

1. Keep the head down and eyes on the puck.

2. Puck starts at heel of blade.

3. Keep stick blade upright and close to puck. Use smooth sweeping motion on contact (minimal back swing).

Figure 25.3

Controlled stickhandling.

4. Roll wrist toward target.

5. Transfer weight from the rear to the front foot.

6. Keep stick below waist level at all times.

Shooting

Wrist Shot

The wrist shot uses the same basic body position as passing. Instructional cues for the wrist shot include the following:

1. There is no backswing on the wrist shot. Start with the blade of the stick cushioning the puck.

2. Keep the puck on the stick as long as possible, and release with a forward "snap" of the wrist. Release the puck from the toe of the blade. Roll wrists over toward target.

3. Transfer weight from back foot to front foot as you carry the puck forward.

Receiving

The term *receiving* refers to stopping the puck and controlling it. Receiving the puck in floor hockey is as important as catching the ball in basketball. As a skill, it requires much practice. Emphasize the following instructional cues:

1. Field with a "soft stick." This means holding the stick with relaxed hands.

Figure 25.4

Receiving a pass from the front.

2. Allow the puck to hit the stick and then "give" to make a soft reception.

3. Keep the hands apart on the stick.

Receiving a Pass from the Front

In order to receive a pass from the front, the player must first move to a point in line with the path of the puck. The flat part of the blade is then extended out toward the puck (see Figure 25.4). The player should receive the puck in front of the body and not permit it to get too close. The faster the puck approaches, the more the player must learn to give with the stick to absorb the momentum of the puck.

Receiving a Pass from the Side

A pass coming from the side is a more difficult skill. In order to field a puck from the side, the player must field the puck on her stick side (see Figure 25.5). Thus, a right-handed player fielding the puck from the left must allow the puck to pass in front of him prior to controlling it with the stick. The player's body and feet should remain facing the direction she wishes to move after controlling the pass.

Individual Defensive Skills

Checking is an individual defensive manoeuvre designed to take the puck away from an opponent.

Figure 25.5

Receiving a pass from the side.

Stick Check

As the offensive player moves with the puck toward the defender, the check is timed so that the blade of the stick is placed against the puck when it is off the opponent's stick (see Figure 25.6), and the checker sweeps the puck away (also called sweep check). After knocking the puck away, the player quickly stickhandles or passes the puck in the desired direction.

Poke Check

The poke check is a one-handed poking motion that attempts to knock the puck away from an opponent. The checker pokes the stick forward to knock the puck away from the opponent's stick.

Dodging

Dodging (also called feinting) is a means of evading a tackler and maintaining control of the puck. The player dribbles the puck directly at the opponent. At the last instant, the puck is pushed to one side of the tackler, depending on the direction the player is planning to dodge. If the puck is pushed to the left, the player should move around the right side of the opponent to regain control of the puck, and vice-versa. Selecting the proper instant to push the puck is the key to successful dodging.

Face-off

The face-off is used at the start of the game, after a goal, or when the puck is stopped from further play by opposing players. Two players take the face-off. Facing opposite sides, players place their sticks on the floor almost touching each other's stick. The right hand can be moved down the stick to facilitate a quick, powerful movement. The referee drops the puck between the player's sticks, and each player attempts to control the puck or to pass it to a teammate.

Goalkeeping

The goalie may kick the puck, stop it with any part of the body, or allow it to rebound off the body or hand. She tries to clear the puck by hitting or kicking it to the side. When a puck is hit toward the goal, the goalie should attempt to move in front of the puck. This allows her body to block the puck should the stick miss it. After the stop, the player passes the puck immediately to a teammate. The goalkeeper is positioned in front of the goal line and moves between the goal posts. Emphasize the following instructional cues:

1. Goalie stands in ready position.

2. Stick is in position in front of body making a triangle with feet and blade flat to the floor.

3. Non-stick hand is open and held out to the side.

Instructional Procedures

1. Ice hockey is a very popular sport in Canada. Students who play ice hockey will have the opportunity to develop more floor hockey skills than other students. The teacher will need to include practice activities for a variety of skill levels and allow ample time for skill development.

2. Floor hockey is an inappropriately rough game if children are allowed to emulate NHL ice hockey (see number 6, guidelines on equipment and special rules).

3. Ample equipment increases individual practice time and facilitates skill development. A stick and a puck for each child are desirable.

Figure 25.6

Stick check.

4. Floor hockey is a team game that is more enjoyable for all when the players pass to open teammates. Discourage excessive control of the puck by one person.

5. Floor hockey is a running game that demands agility and endurance. Frequent rotation and rest periods help prevent fatigue.

6. Provinces have different equipment and safety regulations. The reader is encouraged to consult specific provincial or territorial guidelines. The following points are summarized from the Ontario and Saskatchewan safety guidelines for (a) floor hockey equipment, and (b) special rules:

   (a) Equipment

   - Use only regulation plastic sticks or other approved sticks.
   - Check blades regularly to ensure they are secure.
   - Wearing safety goggles and mouth protection is recommended.
   - Goalies must wear a protective mask (a hockey helmet with cage), chest and leg protection.
   - Use a soft ball or soft rubber puck.

   (b) Special Rules

   - Penalties for infractions strictly enforced.
   - Body contact, stick on body contact, or stick on stick contact are not allowed,
   - Sticks must remain below the waist at all times.
   - Slapshots are not allowed.
   - Implement a crease for protection of goalie (no other players allowed in crease area).

Floor Hockey Drills

STICKHANDLING DRILLS

1. *Phantom Stickhandling.* Successful hockey play demands good footwork and proper stickhandling. To develop these skills, spread players on the field, carrying the stick in proper position, in a group mimetic drill. On command, players move forward, backward, and to either side. Quick reactions and footwork are the focus.

2. *Direction Stickhandling.* Each player with a puck practises dribbling individually. Dribbling should be practised first at controlled speeds and then at faster speeds as skill develops.

3. *Down, Around, and Pass.* Players can practise in pairs, with partners standing about 5 m apart. One player dribbles the puck toward a partner, goes around the partner, and returns to the starting spot (see

Figure 25.7

Down, Around, and Pass drill.

Figure 25.7). The puck is then passed to the partner, who moves in a similar manner. A shuttle type of formation can be used with three players.

4. *Change of Direction Stickhandling.* Players are spread out on the court, each with a puck. On command, they carry the puck left, right, forward, and backward. On the command "Change direction," the players move away from an imaginary checker. Concentrate on puck control and dodging in all directions.

PASSING AND RECEIVING DRILLS

1. *Partner Passing.* In pairs, about 5 m apart, players pass the puck quickly back and forth. Emphasize passing immediately after receiving the puck. The cue phrase might be "Receive and pass."

2. *Pass and Carry.* One player passes the puck to a partner, who receives the puck, carries the puck a few steps to the left or right, and passes back to the other. Passes should be received from various angles and from the right and left sides.

3. Repeat #2, ending with a shot on goal (give-and-go passing).

4. Repeat #3, adding a defender, then two defenders.

5. *Triangle Drill.* Four to eight players can participate in a triangle drill. The puck begins at the head of a line and is passed forward to a player off to one side of the line. This player then passes to a teammate out at a corner, who then passes back to the head of the line. Each player passes and then moves to the spot to where he passed the puck, thus making a continual change of positions.

DODGING AND CHECKING DRILLS

1. *Individual dodging.* Players are spread out on the field, each with a puck. On command, they dribble left, right, forward, and backward. On the command "Dodge," the players dodge an imaginary checker. Players should concentrate on puck control and dodging in all directions.

2. *Cone Dodge.* Three players form the drill configuration as diagrammed in Figure 25.8. Player 1 has the puck in front, approaches the cone (which represents a defensive player), dodges around the cone, and passes to player 2, who repeats the dodging manoeuvre in the opposite direction. Player 2 passes to player 3, and the drill continues in that manner.

Figure 25.8

Cone Dodge drill.

3. *Partner Stick Checks.* Players work in pairs. One partner stickhandles the puck toward the other, who attempts to perform a stick check. Reverse the roles at regular intervals. This drill should be practised at moderate speeds in the early stages of skill development.

4. *Three on Three.* A three-on-three drill affords practice in many skill areas. Three players are on offence and three are on defense. The offence can concentrate on passing, stickhandling, and dodging, while the defense concentrates on checking. A point is given to the offence when they reach the opposite side of the field. Reverse the roles at regular intervals.

SHOOTING DRILLS

1. *Give–and-Go Drill.* Working in partners, Partner 1 starts with the puck and passes to Partner 2. After Partner 1 passes, she moves toward the net in position to take a shot. Partner 2 passes back to Partner 1 who shoots on goal.

2. *Three-Person Rush.* Three files are established at one end of the gym. One line has a puck. One player from each line moves down the gym, passing to the other two players (similar to three-player weave in basketball). As the players near the goal, one of the players takes a shot on goal.

Floor Hockey Game Activities

Developmental Level II

STICKHANDLE COMPETITION

Playing Area: Any clearly defined area

Players: Entire class

Supplies: One stick per person, a puck or ball

Skills: Stickhandling and protecting the puck

The area is divided in half and all players move to one of the halves. While stickhandling and controlling a puck, each player attempts to cause another player to lose control of his puck. When control is lost, that player takes his or her puck and moves to the opposite half of the area. Player continues

against other players who have moved to this area. When five or six players remain, bring all players back into the original area and start over. Reducing the size of the area each time will encourage students to increase the precision of their stickhandling.

CIRCLE KEEP-AWAY

Playing Area: A 6- to 7-m circle

Players: Eight to ten

Supplies: One stick per person, a puck or ball

Skills: Passing, receiving

Players are spaced evenly around the circle, with two or more players in the centre. The object of the game is to keep the players in the centre from touching the puck. The puck is passed back and forth, with emphasis on accurate passing and fielding. Centre players see how many touches they can make during their turn. Allow all youngsters an opportunity to be centre players.

FIVE PASSES

Playing Area: Any defined area

Players: Four to five students per team

Supplies: One stick per person, a puck or ball, pinnies

Skills: Passing, guarding, checking

Two teams play. Divide the area into smaller areas so many teams can play simultaneously. The object of the game is to complete five consecutive passes to score a point. The game is started with a face-off. The teams observe rules prohibiting body or stick contact. The team with the puck counts out loud as a pass is completed. The puck may not be passed back to the person from whom it was received. If the puck is intercepted by the other team or mishandled by the team in possession, the puck is turned over to the other team, who start their five passes. After a successful score, the puck is immediately turned over to the other team.

LANE HOCKEY

Playing Area: Hockey field or gymnasium

Players: Nine per team

Supplies: Hockey stick per player, puck, two goals

Skills: All hockey skills

The field is divided into eight lanes as illustrated in Figure 25.9. Place a defensive and an offensive player in each of the eight lanes. A goalkeeper for each team is also positioned in front of the goal area. Players may not leave their lane during play. Players cannot take a shot on goal until a minimum of two passes has been completed. This rule

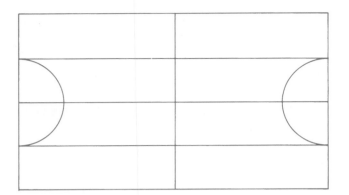

Figure 25.9

Field markings for Lane Hockey.

encourages players to look for teammates and pass to someone in a better position, before taking a shot on goal.

Encourage players to maintain their spacing during play. The purpose of the lanes is to force them to play within a zone rather than rushing to the puck. Rules used for regulation hockey enforce situations not described here. Rotate players at regular intervals.

PASS HOCKEY

Playing Area: Hockey field or gymnasium

Players: Five to six on each team

Supplies: One stick per person, a puck or puck

Skills: Stickhandling, passing, dodging, checking, receiving, face-off

Establish areas at each end of field/court similar to football end zones. No goalies are used. The object of the game is to pass the puck to a teammate in the opponent's end line. A goal is scored when the receiver successfully controls the pass in the end zone. Each goal is worth one point. At the start of the game and after each score, play begins with a face-off.

TEACHING TIP

Consider using the "minimum number of passes before scoring" rule if students are overusing long passes.

Developmental Level III

GOALKEEPER HOCKEY

Playing Area: A square about 10 by 10 m

Players: Two teams of 8–10 players

Supplies: One stick per player, a puck or ball

Skills: Passing, receiving, goalkeeping

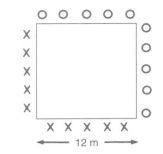

Figure 25.10

Team positions for Goalkeeper Hockey.

Each team occupies two adjacent sides of the square (see Figure 25.10). Team members are numbered consecutively from left to right. The instructor calls two or three numbers. These players enter the playing area and attempt to capture the puck, which is placed in the centre of the square, and to pass it through the opposing team. Teams score a point when the puck goes through the opponent's side. Sideline players are goalies and should concentrate on goalkeeping skills. After a short period of time (1 minute), the active players return to their positions, and new players are called.

TEACHING TIP

Keep track of the numbers called so that all players have an equal opportunity to play. Different combinations can be called.

SIDELINE HOCKEY

Playing Area: Hockey field or gymnasium area

Players: Six to twelve players on each team

Supplies: One hockey stick per player, a puck or ball, two 1-by-2-m folding tumbling mats

Skills: Most hockey skills, except goaltending

Each team is divided into two groups. They are positioned as indicated in Figure 25.11, which shows eight players on each team. Three to six players from each team move onto the court; these are the active players. The others will actively participate on the sidelines. No goalkeeper is used. A face-off at the centre starts the game and puts the puck into play after each score. Each team on the field, aided by the sideline players, attempts to score a goal. The sideline players help keep the puck in bounds and can pass it onto the court to the active players. Sideline players may pass to an active player or to each other.

Any out-of-bounds play on a sideline belongs to the team guarding that sideline and is immediately put into play with a pass. An out-of-bounds shot over the end line that does not score a goal is put into play by the team defending the goal. The group of players on the field changes places

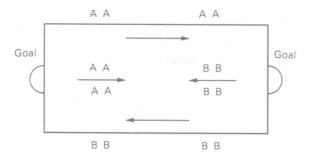

Figure 25.11

Team positions for Sideline Hockey.

with the sideline players on their team as soon as a goal is scored or after a specified time period.

Illegal touching, sideline violations, and other minor fouls result in loss of the puck to the opposition. Roughing fouls and illegal striking should result in banishment to the sideline for the remainder of the competitive period.

TEACHING TIP

Try to encourage team play and passing strategies. An effective rule is to require active players to make three passes to their teammates before taking a shot on goal.

REGULATION ELEMENTARY HOCKEY

Playing Area: Outdoor hockey area or gymnasium area

Players: Six players on court (including goaltender)

Supplies: One stick per player, a puck or ball

Skills: All hockey skills

In a small gymnasium, the walls can serve as the boundaries. In a large gymnasium or on an outdoor court, the playing area should be delineated with traffic cones. The area should be divided in half, with a clearly marked midline. Ensure there is a defined crease area around each goal. Each team has a goalkeeper, who stops shots with her hands, feet, or stick; a centre; two forwards (on either wing); and two defenders.

Play is started with a face-off by the centres at mid-court. If the puck goes out of bounds, it is put back into play by the team that did not hit it last. Whenever the puck passes over the goal line, 1 point is scored. The puck can deflect off a player or equipment to score, but it cannot be kicked into the goal.

The goalkeeper may use his stick and body to clear the puck away from the goal. No other player may enter the crease area.

The following are fouls and are penalized by loss of the puck at the spot of the foul:

1. Illegally touching the puck with the hands.
2. Swinging the stick above waist height (called high-sticking).

3. Player other than the goalie entering the crease area.
4. Holding, stepping on, or lying on the puck.

Personal penalties include any action or rough play that endangers other players. A player committing a penalty must retire to the sidelines for 2 minutes. The following are penalties:

1. Hacking or striking with a stick.
2. Tripping with either the foot or the stick.
3. Pushing, blocking, and dangerous high-sticking.

Critical Thinking

1. Floor hockey and basketball are invasion games. Examine the drills and game activities in both these chapters and discuss how to make adjustments so they can be used for the other sport. For example, how can you adapt the drills and games in basketball for use in floor hockey?

References and Suggested Readings

Chambers, D. (1995). *The incredible hockey drill book.* New York: McGraw-Hill.

Fronske, H. (2005). *Teaching cues for sport skills for secondary school students* (3rd ed.). San Francisco, CA: Benjamin Cummings.

Landy, J.M. & Landy, M.J. (1993a). Floor hockey. In *Ready-to-use PE activities for grades 7–9* (pp. 293–302). West Nyack, NY: Parker Publishing.

Landy, J.M. & Landy, M.J. (1993b). Floor hockey. In *Ready-to-use PE activities for grades 5–6* (pp. 268–277). West Nyack, NY: Parker Publishing.

Mood, D.P., Musker, F.F., & Rink, J.E. (2003). *Sports and recreational activities* (13th ed.). New York: McGraw-Hill.

Nevett, M., Rovengo, I., Babiarz, M. (2001). Fourth grade children's knowledge of cutting, passing and tactics in invasion games after a 12-lesson unit of instruction. *Journal of Teaching in Physical Education, 20,* 389–401.

Trimble, R.M. (1997). *The ultimate hockey drill book.* Indianapolis: Masters Press.

Wilson, G.E. (2002). A framework for teaching tactical game knowledge. *Journal of Physical Education, Recreation and Dance, 73*(1), 20–26 & 56.

 Weblinks

Special Olympics—Floor Hockey: www.specialolympics.org/ Special+Olympics+Public+Website/English/Coach/ Coaching_Guides/Floor+Hockey/default.htm

This Special Olympics' website on floor hockey explains the sport's popularity among disabled athletes.

CHAPTER 26

Soccer

Essential Components

I	Organized around content standards
II	Student-centred and developmentally appropriate
III	Physical activity and motor skill development form the core of the program
IV	Teaches management skills and self-discipline
V	Promotes inclusion of all students
VI	Focuses on process over product
VII	Promotes lifetime personal health and wellness
VIII	Teaches cooperation and responsibility and promotes sensitivity to diversity

Physical Education Standards

1	Students are able to move competently using a variety of fundamental and specialized motor skills.
2	Students can monitor and maintain a health-enhancing level of physical fitness.
3	Students are able to apply movement concepts and basic mechanics of skill performance when learning and refining motor skills.
4	Students comprehend the basic principles of wellness and are able to apply concepts that enable them to make meaningful decisions that positively impact their health and wellness.
5	Students participate in a wide variety of physical activities and learn how to maintain a personalized active lifestyle.
6	Students demonstrate empathy, understanding, and respect for the numerous differences exhibited by people in an activity setting.
7	Students exhibit responsible and self-directed behaviours that lead to positive social interactions in physical activity.

OVERVIEW

Skills instruction for soccer is introduced during the intermediate grades after children have mastered basic prerequisite skills. Teaching the rules and tactics for soccer is an integral part of the instructional process. Using proper progression is a key to success when teaching fundamental skills and lead-up games associated with soccer. Lead-up games provide an opportunity to emphasize development of selected soccer skills and tactics in a setting that is compatible with the abilities of participants.

OUTCOMES

- Structure learning experiences efficiently using appropriate formations, progressions, and teaching techniques.

- Develop a unit plan and lesson focus for soccer.

- Identify safety precautions associated with teaching soccer.

- Describe instructional procedures used for implementing a successful practice activity.

Soccer is a popular sport in Canada for youth, with a tremendous growth rate among girls. Effective soccer stresses position play, in contrast to a group of children chasing the ball. If players are to improve their playing ability, organized practice that emphasizes handling the ball as often as possible is essential. Offer students frequent opportunities on offence to kick, control, dribble, volley, and shoot, and frequent opportunities on defence to mark, guard, tackle, and recover the ball. Success in soccer depends on how well individual skills are coordinated in team play.

Instructional Emphasis and Sequence

Table 26.1 shows the sequence of soccer activities divided into developmental levels. Depending on the amount of experience children have received through community sports programs, the actual sequence may differ in certain areas.

Developmental Level I

Focus on basic sending and receiving skills with younger children. See Chapters 15 and 17 for activities involving kicking a ball.

Developmental Level II

The two basic skills in soccer are (1) controlling or stopping the ball with the foot so that the ball is in a position to be kicked, and (2) passing the ball with the foot to another player or target. Activities at this level should stress games and drills that facilitate practice and use of fundamental skills and basic offensive and defensive tactics. To maximize involvement, make one ball available for every two players.

Developmental Level III

To enhance control of the ball, dribbling skills are introduced and students are taught to control the ball with other parts of the body, such as the thigh and chest. Passing continues to receive major emphasis so that small-side games or mini-soccer, with two to five players per team, can be introduced. The basic goalkeeping skills of catching low and high balls are taught. Further development of basic skills is recommended, along with the introduction of shooting, tackling, heading, jockeying, and the concept of two-touch soccer for more advanced players. Fundamentals of team, positional play, and tactics are taught, along with the rules of the regular game.

TABLE 26.1

Suggested soccer program

Developmental Level II	Developmental Level III
Skills	
Dribbling	Dribbling
Inside-of-the-foot pass	Outside-of-the-foot pass
Long pass	Chest and thigh traps
Foot Trap	Tackling
Passing to goal	Punting
Defensive manoeuvres	Goalkeeping
Throw-ins	Shooting
Jockeying	Heading
Knowledge	
Rules	
Safety and Fair Play	Safety and Fair Play
• slide tackling not recommended	• slide tackling not recommended
• deliberate contact of ball with hands	• offside rule
• personal fouls (e.g., tripping, holding)	• goalkeeper rules
• throw-ins	• penalty kicks
Offensive Tactics	
Keeping team possession of ball (on-the-ball and off-the-ball movements)	Keeping team possession of ball while making forward progress (on-the-ball and off-the-ball movements)
• pass and move to open space to receive	• give-and-go play
• eluding defender	• choosing when to dribble, pass, shoot
Defensive Tactics	
Defending space and player	Defending space, player, and goal
Clearing the ball	Transition from defence to offence
	• outlet pass positioning
Game Activities	
Circle Kickball	Manyball Soccer
Soccer Touch Ball	Addition Soccer
Diagonal Soccer	Over the Top
Dribblerama	Lane Soccer
Bull's-eye	Line Soccer
Pin Kickball	Mini-soccer
Sideline Soccer	Six-spot Keepaway
	Regulation Soccer

Soccer Skills

Offensive skills taught in the elementary grades are passing, kicking, controlling, dribbling, volleying (including heading), and shooting. *Shooting* is defined as taking a shot at the goal with the intent to score. Defensive skills include marking, guarding, jockeying, tackling, and recovering the ball.

Dribbling

Dribbling is moving the ball with a series of taps or pushes to cover ground and still retain control. It allows a player to change direction quickly and to avoid opponents. The best contact point is the inside of the foot, but the outside of the foot will be used at faster running speeds. The ball should be kept close to the player to maintain control. The following instructional cues can be used to emphasize proper form:

1. Keep the head up in order to see the field.
2. Move on the balls of the feet.
3. Contact the ball with the inside, outside, or instep of the foot.
4. Keep the ball near the body so it can be controlled.
5. Dribble the ball with a controlled tap.

Passing

Balance and timing provide the keys to accurate passing. The basic purposes of passing are to advance the ball to a teammate and to shoot on goal. Occasionally, a pass is used to send the ball downfield so that a team has a chance to regroup, with its opponents having an equal chance to recover the ball.

The following are cues to enhance accurate passing:

1. Place the non-kicking foot alongside the ball.
2. Keep the head down and the eyes focused on the ball during contact.
3. Spread the arms for balance.
4. Make contact with the outside or inside of the foot rather than with the toe.
5. Follow through with the kicking leg in the intended direction of the ball.
6. Practise kicking with both the left and right foot.

Inside-of-the-foot Pass Push Pass

The inside-of-the-foot pass is used for accurate passing over distances of up to 10 to 12 m. The non-kicking foot is placed well up, alongside the ball. As the kicking foot is drawn back,

Figure 26.1

An inside-of-the-foot pass.

the toe is turned out. During the kick, the toe remains turned out so that the inside of the foot is perpendicular to the line of flight. The sole is kept parallel to the ground. At contact, the knee of the kicking leg should be well forward, over the ball, and both knees should be slightly bent (see Figure 26.1).

Outside-of-the-foot Pass (Flick Pass)

The non-kicking foot is placed more to the side of the ball than for the inside-of-the-foot kick, and the approach of the kicking leg is from directly behind the ball. The kicking foot is fully extended and contact with the ball is on the outside of the foot between laces and sole-line. Players can use this pass effectively while running, without breaking stride, or for flicking the ball to the side.

Long Pass (Shoelace Kick)

The long pass is the power pass in soccer. It is used for kicking for distance or for power to kick the ball past a goalie. Beginners often use the toes instead of the top of the foot (shoelace) area, which can result in injury or an inaccurate kick. As with all passes, the head is kept down with the eyes focused on the ball. The following cues emphasize correct form:

1. Approach the ball at an angle to the line of flight in a full running stride.
2. The non-kicking foot is placed alongside the ball, with the kicking leg cocked in the backswing. Just before

contact, the ankle of the kicking foot is fixed with the toes pointed down.

3. Contact is made with the top of the foot on the shoelaces.

4. Give the lower leg a good forward snap at the knee.

5. Follow-through in the intended direction of the pass.

To lift the ball, the player makes contact below the midline of the ball, close to the ground, with the body leaning slightly backward. The player places the non-kicking leg to the side and slightly behind the ball so that the kicking foot makes contact just on the start of the upswing of the leg. The lofted pass is made over the heads of opposing players.

Ball Control (Trapping)

Learning to receive a ball and how to place it into the ideal position for making a pass or shot is vital. In fact, one of the best measures of skilled players is how quickly they can bring the ball under control with the feet, legs, or torso. Advanced players are able to achieve this in one smooth movement, with one touch of the ball. The second touch occurs when the pass is made.

For efficient control, a large surface should be presented to the ball. On contact, the surface should be momentarily withdrawn to produce a shock-absorbing action, which decelerates the ball and allows it to drop in an ideal position about a metre in front of the body. The pass or shot can then be made. The following instructional cues will help students develop ball control skills:

1. Move in line with the path of the ball.

2. Reach to meet the ball and give with the contact.

3. Stay on the balls of the feet.

4. Keep the eyes on the ball.

Inside-of-the-foot Trap

This is the most common method of control; it is used when the ball is either rolling along the ground or bouncing up to knee height. The full surface of the foot, from heel to toe, should be presented alongside the ball (see Figure 26.2).

Chest and Thigh Traps

The inside of the thigh and the chest are also used to deflect the ball downward when it is bouncing high. The chest trap requires that the chest be lined up squarely with the direction from which the ball is travelling (see Figure 26.3). On contact, the player draws the chest and waist back, causing a forward body lean. This will

Figure 26.2

Controlling with the inside of the foot.

cause the ball to drop directly to the ground in front of the player. The thigh trap demands that the player turn the body sideways to the flight of the ball. The player contacts the ball with the inside of the thigh. Upon contact with the ball, the thigh is relaxed and drawn backward. This action absorbs the force of the ball and causes it to drop to the ground, ready to be played.

Sole-of-the-foot Trap

This method of control, sometimes called trapping the ball, is used occasionally to stop the ball. With beginners,

Figure 26.3

Chest trap.

it is not as successful a method as the inside-of-the-foot control because the ball can roll easily under the foot. The sole is also used to roll the ball from side to side in dribbling and to adjust for a better passing position.

Heading

Heading is a special kind of volleying in which players change the direction of flight of the ball through contact with the head. Recent research has shown that heading might cause some brain damage. With this in mind, if heading skills are going to be practised, use foam balls in place of soccer balls.

In heading, players use the neck muscles to aid in the blow. The eye must be kept on the ball until the moment of impact. The point of contact is the top of the forehead at the hairline. In preparation for contacting the ball with the head, the player stands in stride position, with knees relaxed and trunk bent backward at the hips. At the moment of contact, the trunk moves forward abruptly, driving the forehead into the ball. Advanced heading is achieved in midair, and is especially useful in beating other players to the ball. Midair heading can be done by a running one-footed takeoff or a standing two-footed jump.

Defensive Manoeuvres

Tackling is a move by a player to take possession of the ball away from an opponent who is dribbling. The most common tackle is the front block, which involves contacting the ball with the inside of the foot just as the opponent touches it. The tackler presents a firm instep to the ball, with weight behind it. The stronger the contact with the ball, the greater the chance of controlling it. Body contact should be avoided, as this may constitute a foul. Other tackles may be made when running alongside the player with the ball.

Limit tackling skills to those that involve the defensive player remaining upright. Methods like the hook slide and split slide are not recommended in elementary school instructional programs.

Jockeying

Knowing when to make a tackle, and when not to, is one of the most difficult skills to learn. A failed tackle may mean that an attacker breaks through with a free shot on goal. Often, defenders should jockey until defensive support arrives. This means backing off while staying close enough to pressure the advancing player. The defender should stay on the toes, watch the ball rather than the opponent's feet, and keep within 1 to 2 m of the ball.

Throw-ins

The throw-in is the only time field players can handle the ball with their hands. The throw-in is guided by rules that must be followed closely or the result is a turnover to the other team. The rules are as follows:

1. Both hands must be on the ball.
2. The ball must be released from over the thrower's head.
3. The thrower must face the field.
4. The thrower may not step onto the field until the throw is released.
5. Both feet must remain in contact with the ground until the ball is released.
6. The thrower cannot play the ball until it has been touched by another player on the field.

The throw-in from out of bounds (see Figure 26.20 on p. 547) may be executed from a standing or running position. Beginning players should learn the throw without a running start. The feet are often placed one behind the other, with the rear toe trailing along the ground. Players should deliver the ball from behind the head, using both arms equally. Release should be from in front of the forehead with arms outstretched. Cues to help students perform correctly are "Drag your back foot" and "Follow through with both hands pointing toward the target."

Shooting

Scoring is the purpose of the game, and students should practise shooting skills both while stationary and while on the run. As with passing, they can use the inside, outside, and top of the foot.

Goalkeeping

Goalkeeping involves stopping shots by catching, stopping, or otherwise deflecting the ball. Goalkeepers should become adept at catching low rolling balls, diving on rolling balls, catching airborne balls at waist level and below (see Figure 26.4), and catching airborne balls at waist height and above.

Youngsters should practise catching low rolling balls in much the same manner as a baseball outfielder does. The goalie gets down on one knee, with her body behind the ball to act as a backstop, and catches the ball with both hands, fingers pointing toward the ground.

If the goalie must dive for the ball, he should throw his body behind it and cradle it with his hands. A goalie should always try to get his body behind the ball.

When catching a ball below the waist, the thumbs should point outward and the arms reach for the ball, with body and arms giving and bringing the ball into the

Figure 26.4

Goalie catching a ball below waist level.

abdomen. For balls above waist level, the thumbs should be turned inward, arms reaching to meet the ball and giving to guide it to the midsection.

Drills for goalies should offer opportunities to catch the different shots described. All students should receive goaltending practice.

Punting

Used by the goalkeeper only, the punt can be stationary or can be done on the run. The player holds the ball in both hands at waist height in front of the body and directly over the kicking leg. For the stationary punt, the kicking foot is forward. A short step is taken with the kicking foot, followed by a full step on the other foot. With the knee bent and the toe extended, the kicking foot swings forward and upward. As the player makes contact with the ball at the instep, he straightens his knee, and derives additional power from the other leg by rising up on the toes or performing a hop (see Figure 26.5).

The goalkeeper who can develop a strong placekick has an advantage. Distance and accuracy are important in setting up the next attack. Over shorter distances, throwing underhand or overhand can be more accurate than kicking. The goalkeeper should use a straight arm for rolling or throwing the ball to players.

Instructional Procedures

1. Controlling the ball and passing predominate in practices. Organize drills and activities to maximize

Figure 26.5

Punt.

the involvement of all children. One ball is needed per two children.

2. Include many combination drills featuring both offence and defence. Drills and lead-up activities can be used to make the skills challenging and appropriate to the developmental level of players.

3. Use small-group games (with two to seven players per team) to ensure maximum activity. Increase the number of team members as skill and tactical understanding improves. Mini-soccer is an excellent game with six or seven players on a side. Two or three games can be played crosswise on a regulation soccer field. The size of the goal should also be scaled down as determined by the needs of the students.

4. Lead-up games are designed to encourage the use of the skills practised in drills. For example, if long passing is the skill of the day, have students play lead-up games requiring long passing.

5. The grid system is useful when organizing drills, activities, and small games. Using cones or chalk, mark a grid system of 9-m squares on the playing field. The number of squares needed depends on the size of the class, but at least one square for every three students is recommended. Possible layouts are shown in Figure 26.6. The squares are used as boundaries for tackling, keeping possession, and passing diagonally or sideways. Drill and game areas can be defined easily, so that a number of small games can be played simultaneously.

6. Use balls that are smaller and lighter than the regulation soccer ball. An effective option for novices is the tough-skin foam-rubber training ball. It withstands heavy usage and does not hurt children on impact. Junior-size soccer balls (No. 4) are also excellent. The key to soccer practice is to have plenty of balls available. Use of a foam ball is recommended for teaching heading skills.

7. Control rough play such as pushing, shoving, kicking, and tripping. Rules need to be strictly enforced.

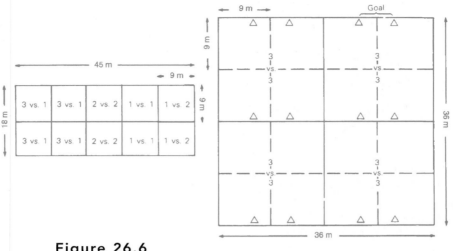

Figure 26.6

Examples of grid layouts and usage.

Soccer Drills

In soccer drills, two approaches are most often used. The first is to practise technique with no action from any defence. The second is the approach, which involves both offensive and defensive players and perhaps a target. In drills using the second approach, the goal is to outmanoeuvre the opponent. Some drills begin with the non-defender approach and then add a defender as warranted.

INDIVIDUAL WORK

Initial dribbling practice is best done individually. Activity can begin by having students dribble in various directions and signalling them to make right and left turns. As a variation, children can react to signals: One whistle means turn left, two means turn right, and three means reverse direction. A number of cones can be scattered around the area. Players then dribble around one cone clockwise and around the next cone counterclockwise.

Have students practise heading skills by tossing a beach ball overhead and heading it. Alternate heading with a short period of dribbling practice. To teach trapping skills, drop a ball and show students how to smother it with a foot. Another drill is to have children toss the ball in the air, let it bounce, and then kick it to themselves with an instep kick. Yet another trick is to toss the ball high and use the instep kick to control the ball.

Rebounding to oneself continuously is an excellent way to learn ball control. (This is sometimes called foot juggling.) Students begin by dropping the ball so that it bounces at waist height, and then practise the following skills:

1. Rebound the ball with alternating feet, letting it bounce between contacts.

2. Play the ball twice with one foot, let it bounce, and then play it twice with the other foot.

3. Toss the ball so it can be handled with the thigh, and then catch. Add successive rebounds with the thigh.

4. Play ball with the foot, thigh, head, thigh, foot, and catch.

The foot pickup is another skill that can be taught in two ways. The first is to have students put the ball between the feet, jump up, and hoist the ball so it can be caught. The second is the toe pickup. Students put the toe on top of the ball and pull the toe back and down so that the ball spins up the instep, and from there hoist it to the hands. Another bit of individual work is toe changing on top of the ball. Students put the ball of the foot on top of the ball. On signal, they change feet.

DRILLS FOR TWO PLAYERS

Many introductory drills can be practised best with a partner. One of the best ways to organize partner drills is to use the grid system mentioned earlier in this chapter. The distance between the grid lines depends on the skills to be practised. Partners position themselves opposite each other so that two lines of players are formed, which gives the teacher a clear view of the class in action (see Figure 26.7). This approach is recommended for introducing all new

Position 2	XXX	XXX	XXX	XXX	
					Teacher
Position 1	XXX	XXX	XXX	XXX	

Figure 26.7

Class organized along grid lines.

skills, such as passing with both sides of the foot, and ball control. Skill combinations can be used, such as throw-ins by one partner and control-and-pass by the other. Within the grids, partners can work on passing, dribbling, keep-away, and one-on-one games.

The following are examples of drills that can be used in partner formation:

1. *Dribbling, marking, and ball recovery.* Pairs are scattered, with one player in each pair having a soccer ball. That player dribbles in various directions, and the second player attempts to stay close to the first (marking). As skill improves, the defensive player attempts to recover the ball from the dribbler. If successful, roles are reversed.

2. *Dribbling.* One player of the pair has a ball and dribbles in various directions. On signal, she passes to her partner, who repeats the dribbling, continuing until another signal is given.

3. *Dribbling, moving, and passing.* Two lines of paired children face each other across a 12- to 18-m distance, as illustrated in the diagram (see Figure 26.8). Each child in one of the lines has a ball and works with a partner directly across from him. A player with a ball from line A moves forward according to the challenges listed below. When he moves near his partner, he passes, and the partner (line B) repeats the same manoeuvre back to line A. Repeating the manoeuvre immediately results in both players returning to their starting place.

   a. Dribble across to partner. Dribble using the outside of either foot.

   b. Gallop across, handling the ball with the front foot only. On return, lead with the other foot.

   c. Skip across, dribbling at the same time.

   d. Slide across, handling the ball with the back foot. On return, lead with the other foot.

   e. Hop across, using the lifted foot to handle the ball. Be sure to change feet halfway across.

   f. Dribble the ball to a point halfway across. Stop the ball with the sole of the foot and leave it there. Continue to the other line. In the meantime, the partner from line B moves forward to dribble the ball back to line A.

   g. Player A dribbles to the centre and passes to player B. Player A now returns to line A. Player B repeats and returns to line B.

4. *Volleying and controlling.* Pairs of players are scattered. One player in each pair has a ball and acts as a feeder, tossing the ball for various receptive skills, including different volleys and control of balls in flight. Controlled tossing is essential to this drill.

DRILLS FOR THREE PLAYERS

With one ball for three players, many of the possibilities suggested for pair practice are still possible. An advantage of drills for three players is that fewer balls are needed.

1. *Passing and controlling.* The trio of players set up a triangle with players about 9 m apart. Students should practise controlled passing and ball control.

2. *Volleying and controlling.* One player acts as a feeder, tossing to the other two players, who practise volleying and controlling receptions.

3. *Dribbling and passing.* A shuttle-type drill can be structured as shown in Figure 26.9. Players keep going back and forth continuously. Player 1 has the ball and dribbles to player 2, who dribbles the ball back to player 3, who in turn dribbles to player 1. Players can dribble the entire distance, or dribble a portion of the distance and then pass the ball to the end player. The teacher can set up obstacles to challenge players to dribble through or around.

4. *Dribbling and stopping the ball.* Three dribblers are in line, each with a ball. The leader moves in various directions, followed by the other two players. On signal, each player controls her ball. The leader circles around to the back ball, and the other two move one ball forward. The dribbling continues for another stop. A third stop puts the players back in their original positions.

5. *Passing.* Players stand in three corners of a 9-m square. After a player passes, he must move to the empty corner of the square, which is sometimes a diagonal movement (see Figure 26.10).

6. *Passing and defence.* One player is the feeder and rolls the ball to either player. As soon as she rolls the ball, she attempts to block or tackle the player receiving

Line A   X X X X X X X X X X X X X X X

                                                12–18 m

Line B   X X X X X X X X X X X X X X X

Figure 26.8

Dribbling, moving, and passing.

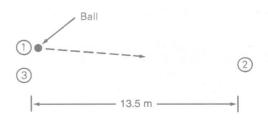
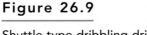

Figure 26.9

Shuttle-type dribbling drill.

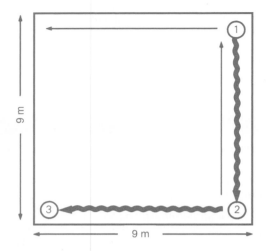

Figure 26.10

Passing drill.

Note: The following symbols are used in soccer game formation diagrams:

×	Defensive player
O	Offensive player
⟶	Player moving without the ball
▬ ▬ ▬ ▶	Player dribbling
∿∿∿▶	Pass, kick, or shot on goal

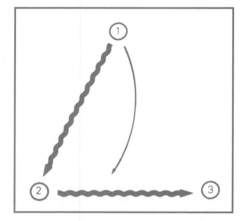

Figure 26.11

Passing and defence drill.

the ball, to prevent a pass to the third player, who, if the pass is completed, attempts to pass back (see Figure 26.11).

DRILLS FOR FOUR OR MORE PLAYERS

Drills for four or more players should be organized so that a rotation gives all players an equal opportunity to practise skills.

1. *Dribbling.* Four players are in line as diagrammed in Figure 26.12. Each player in front has a ball. Both front

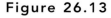

Figure 26.12

Double exchange drill.

players dribble to the centre, where they exchange balls and continue dribbling to the other side. The next players perform similarly. A variation is to have the two players meet at the centre, exchange balls, and dribble back to their starting point. Action should be continuous.

2. *Passing, guarding, and tackling.* Four players occupy the four corners of a square respectively (see Figure 26.13). One player has a ball. Practice begins with one player rolling the ball to the player in the opposite corner, who, in turn, passes to either of the other two players. There should be two attempts each round, so that kicks are possible both ways. The next progression calls for the player who rolled the ball to move forward rapidly to block the pass to either side. Several tries should occur before another player takes over the rolling duties.

3. *Shooting, goalkeeping, and defence.* A shooting drill against defence can be run with four players and a 4- to 5-m goal set off with cones or other markers (see Figure 26.14). One player has the ball. He advances and attempts to manoeuvre around a second player so that he can shoot past the goalkeeper guarding a goal. A fourth player acts as the retriever. Rotate positions.

4. *Dribbling.* Four or five players, each with a ball, form a line. A "coach" stands about 14 m in front of the line. Each player, in turn, dribbles up to the coach,

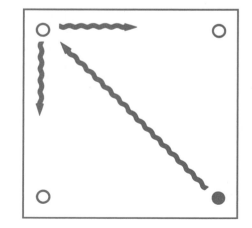

Figure 26.13

Passing, guarding, and tackling drill.

Figure 26.14

Shooting, goalkeeping, and defence.

Figure 26.17

Shooting and goalkeeping.

who indicates with a thumb in which direction the player should dribble past. The coach should give the direction at the last possible moment.

5. *Passing, controlling, and defence.* Four players stand in the four corners of a square, 9 m on a side. Two defensive players are inside the square. The corner players stay in place within the square and attempt to pass the ball among themselves, while the two defenders attempt to recover the ball (see Figure 26.15). After a period of time, another two players take over as defenders.

6. *Shooting.* For two-way goal practice, two to six players are divided, half on each side of the goal. The width of

the goal can vary, depending on the skill of the players. Two types of shooting should be practised: (a) kicking a stationary ball from 9 to 18 m out, and (b) preceding a kick with a dribble. In the second type, a restraining line 12 to 13 m out is needed. This line can be marked by cones, as illustrated (see Figure 26.16). Use at least four balls for this two-way drill. After a period of kicking, the groups should change sides. Ball chasers are the players at the end of each line.

7. *Shooting and goalkeeping.* Scoring can also be practised with a goalkeeper (see Figure 26.17).

Practice should be done with a stationary ball from 12 m out (penalty distance) and with kicks preceded by a dribble. The goalie and the chaser should remain for one complete round and then rotate. Having a second ball to play with saves time because play can continue while the chaser is recovering the previous ball.

8. *Kicking and trapping.* This is an excellent squad drill. Approximately eight players form a circle 14 m in diameter. Two balls are passed back and forth independently. Passes should be kept low, using primarily the side-of-the-foot kick. Also try using three balls.

9. *Passing and shooting.* The drill can be done with four to six players. Two balls are needed. A passer is stationed about 14 m from the goal, and a retriever is behind the goal. The shooters are in line, 18 m from the goal and to the right. The first shooter passes to the passer, and then runs forward. The passer returns the ball to the shooter. The shooter tries to time her run forward so that she successfully shoots

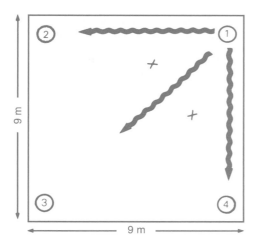

Figure 26.15

Passing, controlling, and defence.

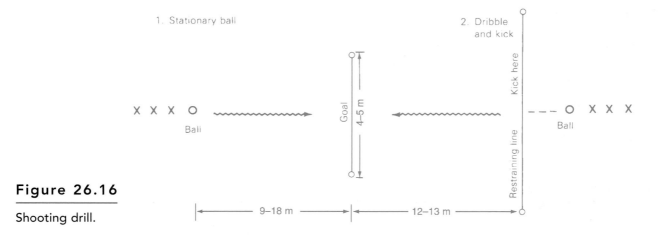

Figure 26.16

Shooting drill.

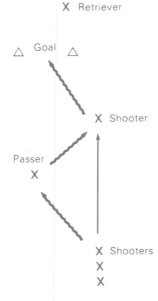

Figure 26.18

routine, passing the ball off to the next player in the line. If the ball goes out of control or is stopped by the defender, it is rolled to the player whose turn is next. Play is continuous, with the defender maintaining his position for several rounds.

Basic Soccer Rules for Lead-up Games

The ball may not be played deliberately with the hands or arms, but disregard incidental or unintentional handling of the ball in the early stages. Eventually, a violation leads to a direct free kick in which the ball is placed on the ground with the opposition a specified distance away (9 m on a full-size field). A goal can be scored directly from this type of kick.

The goalkeeper is allowed to handle the ball within her area by catching, batting, or deflecting with the hands. If the goalie has caught the ball, the opponents may not charge her. While the goalie is holding the ball, official rules limit her to four steps. In elementary school play, the teacher should insist that the goalkeeper gets rid of the ball immediately by throwing or kicking. In some lead-up games, a number of students may have the same ball-handling privileges as the goalie. The rules need to be clear, and ball handling should be done within a specified area.

All serious fouls, such as tripping, kicking a player, holding, or pushing, result in a direct free kick. If a defender commits one of these fouls or a handball in his own penalty area, a penalty kick is awarded. Only the goalkeeper may defend against this kick, which is shot from 11 m out. All other players must be outside the penalty area until the ball is kicked. In lead-up games, consideration should be given to penalty fouls committed in a limited area near the goal by the defensive team. A kick can be awarded to or an automatic goal can be scored by the attacking team.

The ball is out of play and the whistle blown when the ball crosses any of the boundaries, when a goal is scored, or when a foul is called. The team that last touched the ball or caused it to go out of bounds on the side of the field loses possession. The ball is put into play with an overhead throw-in using both hands (see Figure 26.20).

If the attacking team causes the ball to go over the end line, the defending team is awarded a kick from any point chosen near the end line of that half of the field. If the defence last touched the ball going over the end line, then the attacking team is awarded a *corner kick*. The ball is taken to the corner on the side where the ball went over the end line, and the player executes a direct free kick. A goal may be scored from this kick.

The game is normally started by a kickoff with both teams onside. In lead-up games, the teacher can drop the ball for a free ball. In some games, the teacher may find it

the pass through the goal. Both the passer and the retriever should stay in position for several rounds of shooting and then rotate to become shooters. The first pass can be from a stationary ball. Later, however, the kicker can be allowed to dribble forward a short distance before making the first pass. Reverse the field and practise from the left, shooting with the non-dominant leg (see Figure 26.18).

10. *Tackling and ball handling.* A defender is restricted to tackling in the area between two parallel lines, which are 1 m apart. The field is 18 by 36 m (see Figure 26.19). Four to six players can practise this drill. Player 1 advances the ball by dribbling and attempts to manoeuvre past the defender. After he has evaded the defender, he passes to player 2 and takes his place at the other side of the field. Player 2 repeats the

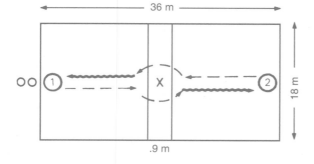

Figure 26.19

Tackling and ball-handling drill.

Figure 26.20

Throwing in, from out of bounds.

advisable simply to award the ball for a free kick in the backcourt to the team not making the score. Lead-up games can continue for a set length of time (by halves) or until a predetermined score is attained.

When the ball is ensnarled among a number of players or when someone has fallen, use a quick whistle. The ball can be put into play by dropping it between players of the opposing teams.

Even though implementation of the offside rule is not crucial in elementary school play, children should understand the rule and the reasons for it. Its purpose is to prevent the "cheap" goal (that is, a player on offence waits near the goal to take a pass behind the defenders and to score easily against the goalkeeper). Although the concept of *offside* involves a number of details, it essentially means that a player on offence who is ahead of the ball must have two defensive players between her and the goal when the ball is kicked forward. One of these players is, of course, the goalie. The offside rule does not apply when the player receives the ball directly from an attempted goal kick, from an opponent, on a throw-in or corner kick, or when the player is in her own half.

Players should not raise their feet high or show the soles or cleats when other players are in the vicinity. This constitutes dangerous play, and an *indirect free kick* is awarded.

Soccer Activities

Developmental Level II

CIRCLE KICKBALL

Playing Area: Playground or gymnasium

Players: 10 to 20

Supplies: Two soccer balls or 20-cm foam rubber balls

Skills: Kicking, controlling

Players are in circle formation. Using the side of the foot, players kick the balls back and forth inside the circle. The object is to kick a ball out of the circle beneath the shoulder level of the circle players. A point is scored against each of the players where a ball leaves the circle between them. If, however, a lost ball is clearly the fault of a single player, then the point is scored against that player only. Any player who kicks a ball higher than the shoulders of the circle players has a point scored against him. Players with the fewest points scored against them win. Players must watch carefully as two balls are in action at one time. A player cannot be penalized if he leaves the circle to recover a ball and the second ball goes through the vacated spot.

SOCCER TOUCH BALL

Playing Area: Playground or gymnasium

Players: 8 to 10

Supplies: Soccer balls or 20-cm foam rubber balls

Skills: Kicking, controlling

Players are spaced around a circle 9 m in diameter with two players in the centre. The object of the game is to keep the players in the centre from touching the ball. The ball is passed back and forth as in soccer. If a centre player touches the ball with a foot, she is awarded a point. Implement a rule that no player may contain or hold the ball longer than 3 seconds, to keep the game moving. Rotate two new players into the centre after 15 to 30 seconds.

DIAGONAL SOCCER

Playing Area: A square about 18 by 18 m

Players: 20 to 30

Supplies: Soccer ball or 20-cm foam rubber ball, pinnies (optional)

Skills: Kicking, passing, dribbling, some controlling, defending, blocking shots

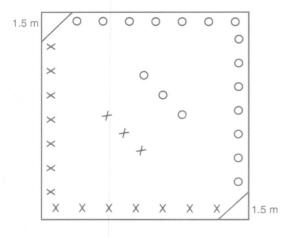

Figure 26.21

Formation for Diagonal Soccer.

Two corners are marked off with cones 1.5 m from the corners on both the sides, outlining triangular dead areas. Each team lines up as illustrated in Figure 26.21 and tries to protect two adjacent sides of the square. To begin competition, three players from each team move into the playing area in their own half of the space. These are the active players who may roam anywhere in the square. The other players act as goalkeepers.

The object of the game is for active players to kick the ball through the opposing team's line (beneath shoulder height) to score. After 30 to 45 seconds, active players rotate to the sidelines and new players take their place. Players on the sidelines may block the ball with their bodies and use their hands. The team against whom the point was scored starts the ball for the next point. Only active players may score. Scoring is much the same as in Circle Kickball, in that a point is awarded for the opponents when any of the following occur:

1. A team allows the ball to go through its line below the shoulders.

2. A team touches the ball illegally.

3. A team kicks the ball over the other team above shoulder height.

DRIBBLERAMA

Playing Area: Playground

Players: 10 to 20

Supplies: Soccer ball or 20-cm foam rubber ball for each player

Skills: Dribbling, protecting the ball

The playing area is a large circle or square, clearly outlined. All players dribble within the area. The game is played on two levels.

Level 1: Each player dribbles throughout the area, controlling the ball so it does not touch another ball. If a touch occurs, both players go outside the area and dribble around the area. Once youngsters have completed dribbling one lap, they may re-enter the game.

Level 2: Two equal playing areas are delineated. All players start in one of the areas. While dribbling and controlling the ball, each player attempts to kick any other ball out of the area. When a ball is kicked out, the player owning that ball takes it to the other area and dribbles. As more players move to the second area, a second game ensues. Players in this area move back to the opposite side. This keeps all players actively involved in the games.

BULL'S-EYE

Playing Area: Playground

Players: 6 to 10

Supplies: Soccer ball or 20-cm foam rubber ball for each player

Skills: Dribbling, protecting the ball

The playing area is a large outlined area—circle, square, or rectangle. One player holds a ball in her hands, which serves as the bull's-eye. The other players dribble within the area. The player with the bull's-eye attempts to throw her ball (basketball set shot) at any other ball. The player whose ball is hit now becomes the new bull's-eye player. The old bull's-eye becomes one of the dribblers. A new bull's-eye cannot hit back immediately at the old bull's-eye. If the group is large, have two bull's-eyes. Do not eliminate players.

PIN KICKBALL

Playing Area: Playground or gymnasium

Players: 7 to 10 on each team

Supplies: 10 or more pins (cones or bowling pins), many soccer or foam rubber balls

Skills: Kicking, controlling

Two teams start about 18 m apart, facing each other. At least 10 pins are placed between the two lines of players. A number of balls are given to each team at the start of the kicking (see Figure 26.22). Players must kick from the line behind which the team is standing. Each pin knocked down scores a point for that team. After all the pins have been knocked down, they are reset, and the game resumes.

TEACHING TIP

This is a flexible game; the number of pins, balls, and players can be varied easily. The teacher can specify the type of kick, or leave it to the player to choose. As accuracy improves, increase the distance between the teams.

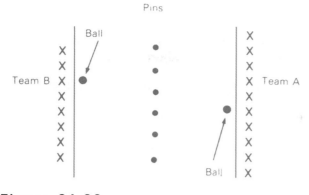

Figure 26.22

Formation for Pin Kickball.

SIDELINE SOCCER

Playing Area: Rectangle about 18 by 30 m

Players: 10 to 12 on each team

Supplies: A soccer or foam rubber ball, four cones, pinnies (optional)

Skills: Most soccer skills, competitive play

Teams line up on the sidelines of the rectangle. Three or four active players from each team are called from the end of the team line (see Figure 26.23). These players remain active until a point is scored; then they rotate to the other end of the line. The object is to kick the ball between cones (goals) that define the scoring area. The active players on each team compete against each other, aided by their teammates on the sidelines.

To start play, the ball can be given to one team or dropped between two opposing players at the centre of the field. To score, the ball must be kicked last by an active player and must go through the goal at or below shoulder height. A goal counts one point. Sideline players can pass to other sideline players or an active teammate, but a sideline kick cannot score a goal.

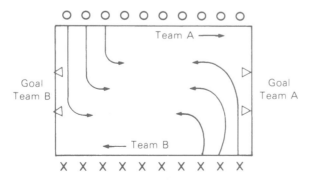

Figure 26.23

Formation for Sideline Soccer.

Regular soccer rules generally prevail, with special attention to the restrictions of no pushing, holding, tripping, or other rough play. Rough play is a foul and causes a point to be awarded to the other team. For an out-of-bounds ball, the team on the side of the field where the ball went out of bounds is awarded a free kick near that spot. No score can result from a free kick. Violation of the no-touch rule also results in a free kick.

TEACHING TIP

Rotate in a new set of players after 30 to 45 seconds. More active players can be added when the class is large. The teacher can mandate a number of passes to sideline players before a shot on goal can be taken. After students acquire some expertise, the cones should be moved in to narrow the goal area. If the ball goes over the end line but not through the goal area, the ball is put into play by a defender with a kick.

Developmental Level III

MANYBALL SOCCER

Playing Area: Soccer field

Players: Entire class

Supplies: Six foam or soccer balls, cones, pinnies

Skills: All soccer skills

Players are divided into two teams and begin in their defensive half of the field. Players are free to roam the entire field with the exception of the goalie boxes, which are delineated with cones. Only the goalie is allowed in the goalie box. Goalies are the only players who can touch the ball with their hands. The goalie tries to keep the balls from going between the cones. The goalie can return the ball to play by punting or throwing. To increase the difficulty of scoring, use more than one goalie.

The object is to kick one of the six balls through the goal. If a ball goes through the goal, the player who scored (not the goalie) retrieves the ball and returns it to the midline for play. All balls are in play simultaneously except when being returned after a goal. Use basic soccer rules to control the game.

ADDITION SOCCER

Playing Area: Playground

Players: 10 to 15

Supplies: One soccer ball per player

Skills: Dribbling, ball control

Five or more players are designated to defend against the other players. The remainder of the players dribble throughout the area, trying to keep the defenders from touching any ball with their feet. When a ball is touched, that player rolls the ball to the side of the playing area and joins hands with the defender to become his partner. They operate as a twosome and must keep hands joined as they try to touch other balls. When another ball is touched, that player takes his ball to the side and joins hands with one of the other defenders. This twosome becomes defenders also, adding their efforts to those of the first twosome. Play continues until all the defenders have touched a ball and have a partner, or for one minute, whichever occurs first. The game then starts over. If, in touching a ball, partners break joined hands, the touch does not count.

OVER THE TOP

Playing Area: Playground

Players: Two teams of five to seven

Supplies: Each player on offence has a ball

Skills: Dribbling, ball control, guarding, tackling

One team is on offence and one on defence, placed according to Figure 26.24. Defensive players stay in their respective areas. On signal, all offensive players dribble through the three areas. A player is eliminated if her ball is recovered by a defensive player or goes out of bounds. The offensive team scores one point for each ball dribbled across the far end line.

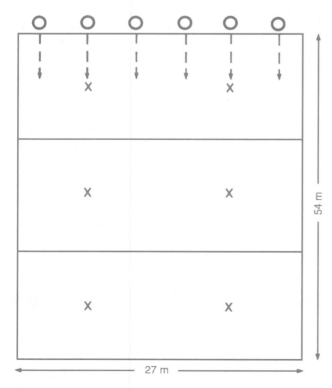

Figure 26.24

Over the Top.

Reverse roles and give the other team a chance to score. Field markings need to be definite to keep the defensive players in their respective zones. A variation is to put neutral zones between the active zones.

LANE SOCCER

Playing Area: Soccer field

Players: Nine per team

Supplies: Soccer or foam rubber balls; pinnies

Skills: All soccer skills

The field is divided into four lanes (eight equal sections) as illustrated in Figure 26.25. A defensive and an offensive player are placed in each of the eight areas. A goalkeeper guards each goal per regulation soccer goals. At least two passes must be made before a shot on goal can be taken. Basic soccer rules guide play. The goalie is the only player who can handle the ball with the hands. A free kick is given to a player who has been fouled by an opponent. Failing to stay within a lane also results in a free kick. Players must be rotated after a goal is scored or a specified amount of time has elapsed. This rotation will enable all students to play four positions: defence, midfield defence, midfield offence, and offence.

TEACHING TIP

The number of lanes can be varied depending on the number of players and the size of the field. Allow players to choose an opponent for their lane. Usually, they will choose an opponent of equal ability.

LINE SOCCER

Playing Area: Soccer field

Players: 8 to 10 players on each team

Supplies: A soccer or foam rubber ball, four cones, pinnies

Skills: Most soccer skills, competitive play

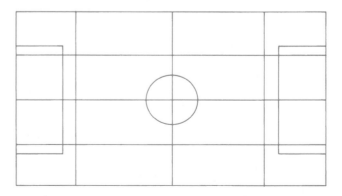

Figure 26.25

Field markings for Lane Soccer.

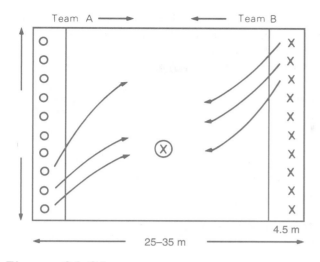

Figure 26.26

Line Soccer.

Two goal lines are drawn 25 to 35 m apart. A restraining line is drawn 4.5 m in front of and parallel to each goal line. Field width can vary from 15 to 25 m. Each team stands on one goal line, which it defends. The referee stands in the centre of the field and holds a ball (see Figure 26.26). At the whistle, three players (more if the teams are large) run from the right side of each line to the centre of the field and become the six active players. The referee drops the ball to the ground, and the players try to kick it through the other team defending the goal line. The players in the field may advance by kicking only.

A score is made when an active player kicks the ball through the opposing team and over the end line (provided that the kick was made from outside the restraining line). Cones should be put on field corners to define the goal line. One point is scored when the ball is kicked over the opponent's goal line below shoulder level. One point is also scored when a personal foul involving pushing, kicking, tripping, and the like is committed.

Line players act as goalies and are permitted to catch the ball. Once caught, however, the ball must be laid down immediately and either rolled or kicked. It cannot be punted or dropkicked.

For illegal touching by the active players, give a direct free kick from a point 11 m in front of the penalized team's goal line. All active players on the defending team must stand to one side until the ball is kicked. Only goalies defend. An out-of-bounds ball is awarded to the opponents of the team last touching it. The regular soccer throw-in from out of bounds should be used. If the ball goes over the shoulders of the defenders at the end line, any end-line player may retrieve the ball and put it into play with a throw or kick.

A time limit of one minute is set for any group of active players. After time is up, play is halted and the players are changed. Use a system of player rotation so all participants get to play.

MINI-SOCCER

Playing Area: Any large area 30 by 45 m, with goals

Players: Seven on each team

Supplies: A soccer ball, pinnies or colours to mark teams, four cones for the corners

Skills: All soccer skills

Each end of the field has a 6-m-wide goal marked by jumping standards. An 11-m semicircle on each end outlines the penalty area. The centre of the semicircle is at the centre of the goal (see Figure 26.27).

The game follows the general rules of soccer, with one goalie for each side. One new feature, the corner kick, is incorporated in this game. This kick is used when the ball, last touched by the defence, goes over the end line but not through the goal. The ball is taken to the nearest corner for a direct free kick, and a goal can be scored from the kick. In a similar situation, if the attacking team last touched the ball, the goalkeeper kick is awarded. The goalie puts the ball down and placekicks it forward.

The players are designated as centre forward, outside right, outside left, right halfback, left halfback, fullback, and goalie. Players should rotate positions. The forwards play in the front half of the field, and the guards in the back half. Neither position, however, is restricted to these areas entirely, and all may cross the centre line without penalty.

A foul by the defence within its penalty area (semicircle) results in a penalty kick, taken from a point 11 m distant, directly in front of the goal. Only the goalie is allowed to defend. The ball is in play, with others waiting outside the penalty area.

TEACHING TIP

Emphasize position play. The lines of three should be encouraged to spread out and stay in their area. The number of players can vary, with some games using as few as three on a side in a more restricted area.

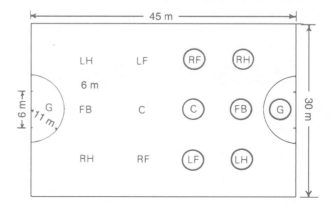

Figure 26.27

Formation for Mini-soccer.

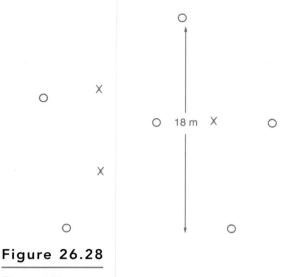

Figure 26.28

Six-spot Keep-away.

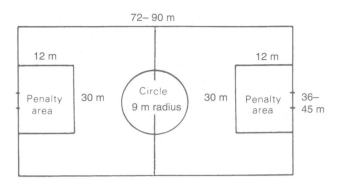

Figure 26.29

Regulation soccer field.

SIX-SPOT KEEP-AWAY

Playing Area: Playground, gymnasium

Players: Two teams, six offensive and three defensive

Supplies: One soccer ball, stopwatch

Skills: Passing, ball control, guarding

There are six offensive and three defensive players in this activity. Five offensive players are arranged in a pentagon formation, with one player in the centre (see Figure 26.28). The pentagon is about 18 m across. Three defenders from the other team enter the pentagon and attempt to interrupt the passing of the offensive team from one to another. A player may not pass the ball back to the person from whom it was received. The game begins with the ball in possession of the centre player.

The object of the game is to make as many good passes as possible against three defenders. After one minute, three offensive players become defensive players and repeat the activity. One more rotation occurs so that all players have been on defence. The threesome scoring the most points is the winner. Offensive players should stay reasonably in position.

REGULATION SOCCER

Playing Area: Soccer field (see Figure 26.29)

Players: 11 on each team

Supplies: A soccer ball, pinnies

Skills: All soccer skills

A team usually consists of three forwards, three midfield players, four backline defenders, and one goalkeeper. More can be placed on a team depending on class size. Forwards are the main line of attack and focus primarily on scoring. Midfield players need good passing and tackling skills as well as a high level of cardiovascular fitness. Defenders work to keep the opponent from scoring. They try to clear the ball away from their own penalty area and avoid dribbling or passing toward their own goal unless it is absolutely safe to do so. Goalkeepers are usually quick and agile and have ball-handling skills.

On the toss of the coin, the winning team gets its choice of kicking off or selecting which goal to defend.

On the kickoff, the ball must travel forward at least about 1 m, and the kicker cannot touch it again until another player has kicked it. The defensive team must be 9 m away from the kicker. After each score, the team not winning the point gets to kick off. Both teams must be onside at the kickoff. The defensive team must stay onside and out of the centre circle until the ball is kicked. Regular soccer rules call for scoring by counting the number of goals made.

When the ball goes out of bounds on the sideline, it is put into play with a throw-in from the spot where it crossed the line. A goal may not be scored, nor may the thrower play the ball a second time until another player has touched it. All opponents are to be 9 m back at the time of the throw.

If the ball is caused to go out of bounds on the end line by the attacking team, a goal kick is awarded. The ball is placed in the goal area and kicked beyond the penalty area by a defending player, who may not touch the ball twice in succession. If a player touches the ball before it goes out of the penalty area, it is not yet in play and should be kicked again.

If the defensive team causes the ball to go out of bounds over the end line, a corner kick is awarded. The ball is placed 1 m from the corner of the field and kicked into the field of play by an attacking player. The 9-m restriction also applies to defensive players.

If the ball is touched by two opponents at the same time and caused to go out of bounds, a drop ball is called. The referee drops the ball between two opposing players, who cannot kick it until it touches the ground. A drop ball also is called when the ball is trapped among downed players.

If a player is closer to the opponent's goal line than to the ball at a time when the ball is played in a forward direction, it is an offside infraction. Exceptions exist, and a player is not offside when he is in his half of the playing field, when two opponents are nearer their goal line than the attacking player at the moment when the ball is played, or when the ball is received directly from a corner kick, a throw-in, or a goal kick.

Penalize personal fouls involving unnecessary roughness. It is forbidden for players to trip, strike, charge, hold, push, or jump an opponent intentionally.

It is a foul for any player, except the goalkeeper, to handle the ball with the hands or arms. The goalkeeper is allowed only four steps and must then get rid of the ball. After the ball has left his possession, the goalkeeper may not pick it up again until another player has touched it. Players are not allowed to screen or obstruct opponents, unless the opponents are in control of the ball.

Penalties are as follows:

1. A direct kick is awarded for all personal fouls and handballs. A goal can be scored from a direct free kick. Examples of infringements are pushing, tripping, kicking a player, and holding.

2. A penalty kick is awarded if a defender in his penalty area commits direct free-kick infringements.

3. An indirect free kick is awarded for offsides, obstruction, dangerous play such as high kicking, a goalkeeper's taking more than four steps or repossessing the ball before another player has touched it, and playing the ball twice after a dead-ball situation. A second player must touch the ball before a goal can be scored. A referee signals if the kick is indirect by pointing one arm upward vertically.

TEACHING TIPS

Players should be encouraged to use the space on the field to the best advantage. When a team is in possession of the ball, players should attempt to find a position where they can pass either behind the player with the ball to give support, or toward the goal to be in a better position to shoot. When a team is forced into defence, the defenders should get goalside of attackers (between the attackers and their own goal) to prevent them from gaining an advantage.

From an early stage, players should be taught to give information to each other during the game, especially when they have possession of the ball.

Valuable help can be given by shouting instructions such as "Player on," "You have time," or "Player behind," and also by a player calling for the ball when she is in position to receive a pass.

Critical Thinking

1. Invasion games utilize similar tactics. Design a practice drill or game that allows students to practise either offensive or defensive tactics and can be easily adapted for use in soccer, basketball, and floor hockey.

References and Suggested Readings

American Sport Education Program. (2006). *Coaching youth soccer* (4th ed.). Champaign, IL: Human Kinetics.

Canadian Soccer Association. (1993). *Getting started in soccer—Helpful hints for first time coaches.* Gloucester, ON: Author.

Garland, J. (2003). *Youth soccer drills* (2nd ed.). Champaign, IL: Human Kinetics.

Luxbacher, J. (2003). *Soccer practice games.* (2nd ed.). Champaign, IL: Human Kinetics.

Luxbacher, J. (1996). *Teaching soccer: Steps to success* (2nd ed.). Champaign, IL: Human Kinetics.

Luxbacher, J. (2005). *Soccer* (3rd ed.). Champaign, IL: Human Kinetics.

National Soccer Coaching Association of America. (2006). *Soccer skills and drills.* Champaign, IL: Human Kinetics.

Turner, A.P., Allison, P.C., Pissanos, B.W. (2001). Constructing a concept of skillfulness in invasion games within a games for understanding context. *European Journal of Physical Education, 6,* 38.54.

Wedmann, W., Kopelow, R., & Fenton, J. (1999). *Soccer—Teaching the basics resource manual.* Victoria, BC: BC Ministry of Small Business, Tourism and Culture.

Wein, H. (2000a). *Developing youth soccer players.* Champaign, IL: Human Kinetics.

Wein, H. (2000b). *105 practical soccer drills.* Orange, CA: Oceanprises.

 Weblinks

Coach's Manual: www.ucs.mun.ca/~dgraham/manual

This website offers just the sort of information a novice to the game of soccer is in need of: rules, the role of referees, necessary skills, and so on. It also offers instructions on how to teach the game to children.

Canadian Soccer Association: www.canadasoccer.com

The Canadian Soccer Association is the governing body for the sport of soccer in Canada, and its website offers information on the national team, on programs and upcoming events, and on news and views from the soccer community.

CHAPTER 27

Softball

Essential Components

I	**Organized around content standards**
II	**Student-centred and developmentally appropriate**
III	**Physical activity and motor skill development form the core of the program**
IV	**Teaches management skills and self-discipline**
V	**Promotes inclusion of all students**
VI	**Focuses on process over product**
VII	Promotes lifetime personal health and wellness
VIII	**Teaches cooperation and responsibility and promotes sensitivity to diversity**

Physical Education Standards

1	**Students are able to move competently using a variety of fundamental and specialized motor skills.**
2	Students can monitor and maintain a health-enhancing level of physical fitness.
3	**Students are able to apply movement concepts and basic mechanics of skill performance when learning and refining motor skills.**
4	Students comprehend the basic principles of wellness and are able to apply concepts that enable them to make meaningful decisions that positively impact their health and wellness.
5	**Students participate in a wide variety of physical activities and learn how to maintain a personalized active lifestyle.**
6	**Students demonstrate empathy, understanding, and respect for the numerous differences exhibited by people in an activity setting.**
7	**Students exhibit responsible and self-directed behaviours that lead to positive social interactions in physical activity.**

OVERVIEW

Skills instruction for softball is introduced during the intermediate grades after children have mastered basic prerequisite skills. Teaching the rules and tactics for softball is an integral part of the instructional process. A key to success is using proper progression when teaching fundamental skills and lead-up games associated with softball. Lead-up games provide an opportunity for teachers to emphasize development of selected softball skills and tactics in a setting that is compatible with the abilities of participants.

OUTCOMES

- Structure learning experiences efficiently using appropriate formations, progressions, and teaching techniques.

- Develop a unit plan and lesson focus for softball.

- Identify safety precautions associated with teaching softball.

- Describe instructional procedures used for implementing successful practice activities.

C*hildren enjoy softball, and a good program should make use of this drive. The emphases in softball should be on skill development and lead-up games. Children have adequate opportunity during recess, at the noon hour, and at other times to play the regulation game.*

Instructional Emphasis and Sequence

Table 27.1 shows the sequence of softball activities divided into two developmental levels. The activities are listed in progression. Children can practise many of the skills of softball but may not be ready to participate in the activities described in this chapter until age 8 or 9.

Developmental Levels I and II

The fundamental skills of batting, throwing, and catching are emphasized at this level. Batting receives attention because softball is little fun unless children can hit. Proper form and technique in all three fundamental skills are parts of the instruction, with teachers paying attention not only to the how but also to the why. Lead-up games provide an introduction to the basic rules and tactics of the game. As children mature, instruction focuses on specific skills for pitching, infield play, base running, and batting.

Developmental Level III

Children at this level develop the background to play the game of regulation softball. Tee Ball provides an opportunity for developing all softball skills except pitching and catching. Home Run and the ever-popular Scrub (Work-up) provide

TABLE 27.1

Suggested softball program

Developmental Level II	Developmental Level III	Developmental Level II	Developmental Level III
Skills		**Pitching**	
Throwing		Simple underhand	Target pitching
Gripping the ball	Throw-in from outfield	Application of pitching rule	Slow pitches
Overhand throw	Sidearm throw		
Underhand toss		**Knowledge**	
Around the bases		*Rules*	
Catching and Fielding		Safety and Fair Play	Safety and Fair Play
Catching thrown balls	Catching flies from fungo bat	• respect for umpire calls	• respect for umpire calls
Catching fly balls	Infield practice	• no sliding permitted	• no sliding permitted
Grounders		Rules of the Game	Rules of the game
Fielding infield grounders		• Strike zone	• Pitching rule
Sure stop for outfield		• Foul and fair ball	• Position and illegal pitches
Batting			
Simple skills	Different positions at plate	• Safe and out	• Infield fly
		• Foul tip	• Keeping score
Tee batting	Bunting	• Bunt rule	• Base running
Fungo hitting		• When batter safe or out	• Situational quiz
Fielding Positions		*Offensive Tactics*	
Infield practice	Backing up other players	Decisions about placement and power of hits	Decisions about placement and power of hits
How to catch	Double play	• to avoid fielders	• situational decisions (e.g., runner on 3rd with one out)
Base Running			
To first base and turn	Fast start off base		
Circling the bases	Tagging up on fly ball	• advance runners	
	Sacrifice		

(continued)

TABLE 27.1			
Suggested softball program (continued)			
Developmental Level II	**Developmental Level III**	**Developmental Level II**	**Developmental Level III**
Decisions by base runners	Decisions by base runners	Decisions about where to throw after ball is fielded (simple)	Decisions about where to throw after ball is fielded (complex)
• stealing	• situational decisions (e.g., one out, runner on 1st, fly ball)	• outfield hit	• situational decisions (e.g., fly ball to right field, one out, runner on 2nd base)
	Defensive Tactics		
Decisions about positioning to field balls (simple)	Decisions about positioning to field balls (complex)	• infield hit	
• adjustments for right hand/left hand batter	• situational decisions (e.g., two out and runner on 3rd base)	*Game Activities*	
• adjustments to monitor base runners		Throw-it-and-run Softball	Five Hundred
		Two-pitch Softball	Batter Ball
		Hit and Run	Home Run
		Kick Softball	Tee Ball
		In a Pickle	Scrub (Work-up)
		Beat Ball	Slow-pitch Softball
			Babe Ruth Ball
			Hurry Baseball (One-pitch)
			Three-team Softball

a variety of experiences, and Batter Ball stresses hitting skills. Batting, throwing, catching, and infield play are practised. Teachers may add new pitching techniques, situation play, and double-play work. Slow-pitch provides lots of action. Babe Ruth Ball emphasizes selective hitting.

Softball Skills

Gripping the Ball

The standard softball grip, difficult for elementary school children, calls for the thumb to be on one side, the index and middle fingers on top, and the other fingers supporting along the other side (see Figure 27.1). Younger children with small hands will find it best to use a full-hand grip, in which the thumb and fingers are spaced rather evenly (see Figure 27.2). Regardless of the grip used, the pads of the fingers should control the ball.

Throwing (Right-handed)

Softball requires accurate throwing. Players must practise proper throwing technique if they are going to be able to perform well in softball. Of all the team sports, softball is probably the most difficult for children because of the fine

motor coordination required. The following instructional cues can be used to help students develop proper throwing technique:

1. Place the throwing-arm side of the body away from the target.

2. Step toward the target with the foot opposite the throwing hand.

Figure 27.1

Gripping the ball: two-finger grip.

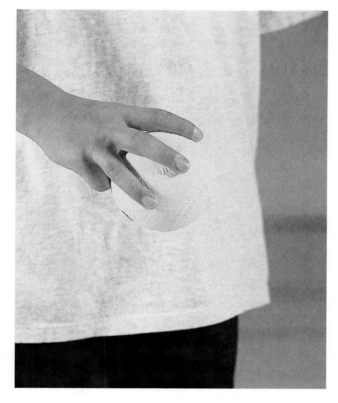

Figure 27.2

Gripping the ball: full grip. The little finger supports on the side.

3. Rotate the hips as the throwing arm moves forward.

4. Bend and raise the arm at the elbow. Lead with the elbow.

5. Shift the weight from the rear foot to the forward foot (nearest the target) prior to the forward motion of the arm.

Overhand Throw

In preparation for throwing, the child secures a firm grip on the ball, raises the throwing arm to shoulder height, and brings the elbow back. For the overhand throw, the hand with the ball is then brought back over the head so that it is well behind the shoulder at about shoulder height. The left side of the body is turned in the direction of the throw, and the left arm is raised in front of the body. The weight is on the back (right) foot, with the left foot advanced and the toe touching the ground. The arm comes forward with the elbow leading, and the ball is thrown with a downward snap of the wrist (see Figure 27.3). The body weight is brought forward into the throw, shifting to the front foot. Follow through so that the palm of the throwing hand faces the ground at completion of the throw. The eyes should be on the

Figure 27.3

Throwing overhand.

target throughout, and the arm should be kept free and loose during the throw.

Sidearm Throw

The sidearm throw is much the same as the overhand throw, except that the entire motion is kept near a horizontal plane. The sidearm throw is used for shorter, quicker throws than the overhand and employs a whip-like action. On a long throw, the sidearm throw curves more than the overhand, because on release it imparts a side-spinning action to the ball. There is generally some body lean toward the side of the throwing arm.

Underhand Throw

For the underhand throw, the throwing hand and arm are brought back, with palm facing forward, in a pendulum swing. The elbow is bent slightly. The weight is mostly on the back foot. The arm comes forward, almost in a bowling motion, and tosses the ball. The weight shifts to the front foot during the toss. The flight of the ball should remain low and arrive at about waist height.

Pitching

Official rules call for the pitcher to have both feet in contact with the pitcher's rubber, but few elementary schools possess a pitching rubber. Instead, the pitcher can stand with both feet about even, facing the batter, and holding the ball momentarily in front with both hands. The pitcher takes one hand from the ball, extends the right arm forward, and brings it back in a pendulum swing, positioning the ball well behind the body. A normal stride taken toward the batter with the left foot begins

Figure 27.4

Pitching.

the throwing sequence for a right-handed pitcher. The pitcher brings the arm forward with an underhanded slingshot motion, and transfers the weight to the leading foot. Only one step is permitted. The follow-through motion is important (see Figure 27.4). Instructional cues for pitching are as follows:

1. Face the plate.
2. Keep your eyes on the target.
3. Swing the pitching arm backward and step forward.
4. Keep the pitching arm extended.

Fielding

Infielders should assume the ready position—a semi-crouch, with legs spread shoulder-width apart, knees bent slightly, and hands on or in front of the knees (see Figure 27.5). As the ball is delivered, the weight shifts to the balls of the feet. The outfielder's position is a slightly more erect semi-crouch. Instructional cues for fielding are the following:

1. Move into line with the path of the ball.
2. Give when catching the ball.
3. Use the glove to absorb the force of the ball.
4. For grounders, keep the head down and watch the ball move into the glove.

Fly Balls

There are two ways to catch a fly ball. For a low ball, the fielder keeps the fingers together and forms a basket with the hands (see Figure 27.6). For a higher ball, the fielder

Figure 27.5

Ready position for infielder.

Figure 27.6

Catching a low fly ball.

Figure 27.7

Catching a high fly ball.

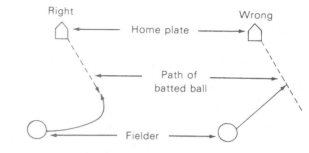

Figure 27.8

Fielding a grounder correctly.

keeps the thumbs together, and catches the ball in front of the chin (see Figure 27.7). The fielder should give with the hands, and take care with a spinning ball to squeeze the hands sufficiently to stop the spinning. The eye is on the ball continually until it hits the glove or hands. The player keeps the knees flexed slightly when receiving, which aids in "giving."

Grounders

To field a grounder, the fielder should move as quickly as possible into the path of the ball (see Figure 27.8) and then move forward and play the ball on a good hop. The eyes must be kept on the ball, following it into the hands or glove. The feet are spread, the seat is kept down, and the hands are carried low and in front (see Figure 27.9). The weight is on the balls of the feet or on the toes, and the knees are bent to lower the body. As the ball is caught, the fielder straightens up, takes a step in the direction of the throw, and makes the throw.

Figure 27.9

Fielding a grounder.

Sure Stop for Outfield Balls

To keep the ball from going through the hands and thus allowing extra bases, the outfielder can use the body as a barrier. The fielder turns half right and lowers one knee to the ground at the point toward which the ball is travelling (see Figure 27.10). The player uses her hands to catch the rolling ball, but if she misses, her body will generally stop the ball.

Figure 27.10

Sure stop.

Figure 27.11

First-base player stretching for a catch.

First-base Positioning

When a ball is hit to the infield, the first-base player moves to the base until the foot is touching it. The player then judges the path of the ball, stepping toward it with one foot and stretching forward. The other foot remains in contact with the base (see Figure 27.11).

Catcher's Position

The catcher assumes a crouched position with the feet about shoulder width apart and the left foot slightly ahead of the right. The catcher should use a glove and wear a mask. A body protector is also recommended. The catcher is positioned beyond the range of the swing of the bat (see Figure 27.12).

Batting (Right-handed)

The batter stands with the left side of the body toward the pitcher. The feet are spread and the weight is on both feet. The body should be facing the plate. The batter holds the bat with the trademark up, and the left hand grasps the bat lower than the right. The bat is held over the right shoulder, pointing both back and up.

Figure 27.12

Catcher's position.

Figure 27.13

Batter's position.

The elbows are away from the body (see Figure 27.13). The swing begins with a hip roll and a short step forward in the direction of the pitcher. The bat is then swung level with the ground at the height of the pitch. The batter keeps eyes on the ball until it is hit. After the hit, there must be good follow-through.

Frequent technique errors include the following: lifting the front foot high off the ground, stepping back with the rear foot, dropping the rear shoulder, chopping down on the ball, golfing, dropping the elbows, or crouching or bending forward. Students should get experience with the choke grip (see Figure 27.14), the long grip (see Figure 27.15), and the middle grip (see Figure 27.16). Beginning batters can start with the choke grip. In any case, the grip should not be too tight. The following are instructional cues for batting:

1. Keep the hands together.
2. Swing the bat horizontally.
3. Swing through the ball.

Figure 27.14

Choke grip.

4. Hold the bat off the shoulder.
5. Watch the ball hit the bat.

Bunting (Right-handed)

To bunt, the batter turns to face the pitcher, the right foot alongside home plate. As the pitcher releases the ball, she runs the upper hand about halfway up the bat. The bunter holds the bat loosely in front of the body and parallel to the ground to meet the ball (see Figure 27.17). The ball can be directed down the first- or third-base line.

The surprise, or drag, bunt is done without squaring around to face the pitcher. The batter holds the bat in a choke grip. When the pitcher lets go of the ball, the batter runs the right hand up the bat and directs the ball down either foul line, keeping it as close as possible to the line in fair territory.

Base Running

A batter who hits the ball should run hard and purposefully toward first base, no matter what kind of hit it is. The runner should run past the bag, tagging it in the process,

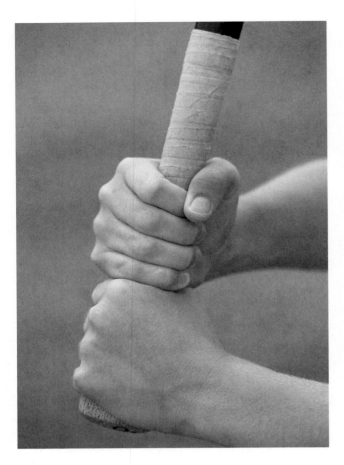

Figure 27.15

Long grip.

Figure 27.16

Middle grip.

and should step on the foul-line side of the base to avoid a collision with the first-base player.

Because a runner on base must hold the base position until the pitcher releases the ball, it is essential to secure a fast start away from the base. With either toe in contact with the base, the runner assumes a body lean, the weight on the ball of the leading foot and the eyes on the pitcher. After the pitch, the runner takes a few steps away from the base in the direction of the next base.

Instructional Procedures

1. Safety is of the utmost importance. The reader is encouraged to consult specific provincial or territorial safety guidelines. The following general precautions should be observed:

   a. There is a danger of the bat being thrown. Members of the batting team must stand well back from the baseline, behind the backstop or fence.

   b. The following are techniques that can teach the batter not to throw the bat:

      - Have the batter touch the bat to the ground before dropping it.
      - Call the batter out if the bat is thrown.
      - Have the batter place the bat in a 1-m circle before running.

   c. Sliding into a base is not permitted.

   d. A catcher must wear a mask and body protector.

   e. Colliding while running for a fly ball can be avoided by teaching players to call for the ball and to stay out of another player's area.

   f. When changing fields at the beginning of an inning, the batting team stays on the first-base side of the infield. The fielding team goes to bat via the third-base side of the infield.

   g. Slo-pitch balls or restricted flight balls should be used. Fleece balls are excellent for introductory fielding skills. Many children fear batted balls, which necessitates using balls that will not hurt them.

2. Batting skills must be stressed. Make sure that students practise the correct stance and proper mechanics of

Figure 27.17

Regular bunt position.

batting. Improved hitting will come with practice. It is helpful to have the batting tee available for all batters.

3. Players should rotate positions often. In physical education classes, everyone, including the pitcher, should rotate to another position at the start of each inning.

4. The distance between the bases greatly affects the game. The distance should be lessened or increased according to the capacities of players.

5. Umpires can be appointed, or the team at bat can umpire. A convenient rule to follow is that the person who made the last out of the previous inning will be the umpire for the next inning. Teach all students how to umpire.

6. Encourage players to recognize and give approval and support to all players. Limit verbal banter to encouraging teammates and complimenting opposing players.

7. Analyze the purpose of lead-up games. Students should practise needed skills before the skills are included in the game.

8. Teach respect for officials and acceptance of the umpire's judgment.

Organizing for Instruction

It is essential that students develop skills in softball and acquire knowledge about the various phases of the game. The amount of field space and the equipment available determine the instructional organization. To cover the various phases of the game, a multiple-activity or station pattern is effective. The following guidelines offer suggestions for instruction:

1. Ensure that children have many opportunities to practise different skills. Even with rotation, there should be as many small groups as possible. For example, throwing and fielding grounders can be practised between two children.

2. Ability differences need to be addressed at times. Since some players have practised more, they often have skill levels higher than those of others in the class.

3. Activities and procedures to be stressed at each station should be carefully planned and communicated to all participants.

4. Complete rotation of stations is not necessary at each class session. During a class session, teams may practise at one station for part of the time and then use the remainder of the time to participate in an appropriate lead-up game.

5. There must be directions listed at each station so students can make the most of the skill development opportunities. Station teaching offers an excellent opportunity for older students to provide assistance. In some school systems, high-school students visit elementary schools on a regular basis for observation and educational experiences.

6. The use of the rotational station system does not rule out activities involving the class as a whole. Mimetic drills (drills without equipment) are valuable for establishing fundamental movement patterns for most skills. Have students practise such techniques as batting, pitching, throwing, and fielding.

7. Move from one station to another in order to provide encouragement, correction, coaching, and motivation for learning.

Basic Softball Rules

The basic rules of the game can be obtained from the following discussion. Consult an official rule guide for an in-depth explanation. Rules may be adjusted as needed to meet the needs of students in your physical education classes.

The official diamond has 18-m baselines and a pitching distance of 14 m. In elementary school it is recommended that youngsters use a diamond with baselines no longer than

13.5 m and a pitching distance of 10.5 m or less. The nine players on a softball team are the catcher, pitcher, first-, second-, and third-base players, shortstop, and left, centre, and right fielders. The right fielder is the outfielder nearest first base.

Batting Order

Players may bat in any order, although having them bat according to their positions in the field is at times convenient in class. Once the batting order has been established, it may not be changed, even if the player changes to another position in the field.

Pitching

The pitcher must face the batter with both feet on the pitching rubber and with the ball held in front with both hands. The pitcher is allowed one step toward the batter and must deliver the ball while taking that step. The ball must be pitched underhanded. The pitcher cannot fake a pitch or make any motion toward the plate without delivering the ball. It is illegal to roll or bounce the ball to the batter. No quick return is allowed before the batter is ready. To be called a *strike,* a pitch must be over the plate and between the knees and shoulders of the batter. A *ball* is a pitch that does not go through this area.

Batting

The bat must be a softball bat. The batter cannot cross to the other side of the plate when the pitcher is ready to pitch. If a player bats out of turn, she is out. A bunt that goes foul on the third strike is an out. A pitched ball that touches or hits the batter entitles the batter to first base, provided she does not strike or bunt at the ball.

Striking Out

A batter is out who misses the ball on the third strike. This is called striking out.

Batter Safe

The batter who reaches first base before the fielding team can field the ball and throw it to first is safe.

Fair Ball

A fair ball is any batted ball that settles on fair territory between home and first base, and home and third base. A ball that rolls over a base or through the field into fair territory is a fair ball. Fly balls (including line drives) that drop into fair territory beyond the infield are fair balls. Foul lines are in fair territory.

Foul Ball

A foul ball is a batted ball that settles outside the foul lines between home and first or between home and third. A fly ball that drops into foul territory beyond the bases is a foul.

Fly Ball

Any fly ball (foul or fair), if caught, is an out. A foul fly, however, must rise over the head of the batter or it is ruled a foul tip. A foul tip caught on the third strike, then, puts the batter out.

Base Running

In base running, no lead-off is permitted. On penalty of being called out, the runner must stay on base until the ball leaves the pitcher's hand. On an overthrow when the ball goes into foul territory and out of play, runners advance one base beyond the base to which they were headed at the time of the overthrow. On an overthrow at second base by the catcher with the ball rolling into centre field, the runners may advance as far as they can. The runner may try to avoid being tagged on a baseline but is limited to a 1-m distance on each side of a direct line from base to base. A runner hit by a batted ball while off the base is out. The batter, however, is entitled to first base. Base runners must touch all bases.

Runners may overrun first base without penalty. On all other bases, the runner must maintain contact with the base or be tagged out. To score, the runner must make contact with home plate.

Scoring

A run is scored when the base runner makes the circuit of the bases (that is, first, second, third, and home) before the batting team has three outs. If the third out is a force-out, no run is scored, even if the runner crossed home plate before the out was actually made.

The situation needing the most clarification occurs when a runner is on base with one out and the batter hits a fly ball that is caught, making the second out. The runner is forced to return to the base previously occupied before the ball reaches that base, or he, too, is out. If he makes the third out as a result of his failure to return to the base in time, no run is scored.

Tactics for Striking/Fielding Games

According to the basic games classification mentioned in Chapter 22, softball is classified as a striking/fielding game (conceptually similar to baseball, cricket, kickball). The intent of basic offensive tactics of these games has the batting team attempting to place its hits in such a way as to reach base and advance runners. Alternatively, the defensive tactics of the fielding team focus on preventing the hitter from reaching base, and limiting progress should he reach base. Choose softball drills and lead-up games that emphasize practice of both skills and tactics.

Softball Drills

Softball drills lend themselves to a station setup. For a regular class of 24 students, four squads with six students each is suggested. Activities at each station can emphasize a single skill or a combination of skills. Situational drills can also be incorporated. Children should realize that constant repetition is necessary to develop, maintain, and sharpen softball skills.

The multitude of softball skills to be practised allows for many different combinations and organizations. The following are examples of combinations and organizations that can be used in station teaching.

BATTING

1. Batting can be organized in many ways. One key to an effective program is to ensure that each child has many opportunities to hit the ball successfully. Sufficient area is needed.

   a. Use a batting tee. For each station, two tees are needed, with a bat and at least two balls for each tee. Three children are assigned to each tee. There should be a batter, a catcher to handle incoming balls, and fielders. Each batter is allowed a certain number of swings before rotating to the field. The catcher becomes the next batter, and a fielder moves up to catcher.

   b. Organize informal hitting practice. A batter, a pitcher, and fielders are needed. Two batting groups should be organized at each station. A catcher is optional.

   c. Practise hitting a foam rubber ball thrown under-handed. The larger ball is easier to hit.

   d. Practise bunting with groups of three: a pitcher, batter, and fielder.

THROWING AND CATCHING

2. Throwing and catching can be practised with the following drills:

   a. Throw back and forth, practising various throws.

   b. Throw ground balls back and forth for fielding practice.

   c. One player acts as a first-base player, throwing grounders to the other infielders and receiving the putout throw.

   d. Throw flies back and forth.

   e. Hit flies, with two or three fielders catching.

   f. Establish four bases and throw from base to base.

PITCHING

3. Proper pitching and catching form should be used for pitching practice:

   a. Pitch to another player over a plate.

   b. Call balls and strikes. One player is the pitcher, the second is the catcher, and the third is the umpire. A fourth player can be a stationary batter to provide a more realistic pitching target.

   c. Pitch toward pitching targets or a similar area outlined on a wall.

4. For infield drills, children are placed in the normal infield positions: behind the plate; at first, second, and third base; and at shortstop. One child acts as the batter and gives directions. The play should begin with practice in throwing around the bases either way. After this, the batter can roll the ball to the different infielders, beginning at third base and continuing in turn around the infield, with each player throwing to first to retire an imaginary runner. Various play situations can be developed. A batter who is skilful enough can hit the ball to infielders instead of rolling it, thus making the drill more realistic. Using a second softball saves time when the ball is thrown or batted past an infielder because players do not have to wait for the ball to be retrieved before proceeding with the next play. After the ball has been thrown to first base, other throws around the infield can take place. The drill can also be done with only a partial infield.

5. Various situations can be arranged for practising base running:

   a. Bunt and run to first. A pitcher, a batter, an infielder, and a first-base player are needed. The pitcher serves the ball up for a bunt, and the batter, after bunting, takes off for first base. A fielding play can be made on the runner.

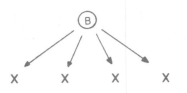

Figure 27.18

Play Pepper.

b. Bunt and run to second base. The batter bunts the ball and runs to first base and then on to second, making a proper turn at first.

6. *Play Pepper* is one of the older skill games in baseball. A line of three or four players is about 8 m in front of and facing a batter. The players toss the ball to the batter, who attempts to hit controlled grounders back to them (see Figure 27.18). The batter stays at bat for a period of time and then rotates to the field.

7. Some of the game-type activities, such as Batter Ball, In a Pickle, Five Hundred, and Scrub, can be scheduled at stations. Stations might be organized as follows (numbers and letters refer to the drills just listed):

Station 1: Batting (see 1a)

Station 2: Throwing, fielding grounders (see 2c)

Station 3: Base running—In a Pickle

Station 4: Bunting and base running (see 5a)

Another example of station arrangement is the following:

Station 1: Batting and fielding—Pepper (see 6)

Station 2: Pitching and umpiring (see 3b)

Station 3: Infield practice (see 4)

Station 4: Batting (see 1b)

Stations might also be arranged as follows:

Station 1: Fly ball hitting, fielding, throwing (see 2e)

Station 2: Bunting and fielding (see 1d)

Station 3: Pitching to targets (see 3c)

Station 4: Batting (see 1a and 1b)

Softball Activities

Developmental Level II

THROW-IT-AND-RUN SOFTBALL

Playing Area: Softball diamond reduced in size

Players: 7 to 11 (usually 9) on each team

Supplies: A slo-pitch or restricted flight softball or similar ball

Skills: Throwing, catching, fielding, base running

Throw-it-and-run Softball is played like regular softball with the following exception. With one team in the field at regular positions, the pitcher throws the ball to the batter, who, instead of batting the ball, catches it and immediately throws it into the field. The ball is then treated as a batted ball, and regular softball rules prevail. No stealing is permitted, however, and runners must hold bases until the batter throws the ball. A foul ball is an out.

TEACHING TIP

Variations: *Beat-ball Throw.* The fielders, instead of playing by regular softball rules, throw the ball directly home to the catcher. The batter, in the meantime, runs around the bases. A point is scored for each base the batter touches before the catcher receives the ball. A ball caught on the fly would mean no score. Similarly, a foul ball would not score points but would count as a turn at bat.

TWO-PITCH SOFTBALL

Playing Area: Softball diamond

Players: 7 to 11 on each team

Supplies: A slo-pitch or restricted flight softball, a bat

Skills: Most softball skills, except regular pitching

Two-pitch Softball is played like regular softball with the following changes:

1. A member of the team at bat pitches. Set up a system of rotation so that every child takes a turn as pitcher.

2. The batter has only two pitches in which to hit the ball, and must hit a fair ball on one of these pitches or is out. The batter can foul the first ball, but if the second is fouled, the batter is out. There is no need to call balls or strikes.

3. The pitcher does not field the ball. A member of the team in the field acts as the fielding pitcher.

4. If the batter hits the ball, regular softball rules are followed. No stealing is permitted, however.

TEACHING TIPS

Since the pitcher is responsible for pitching a ball that can be hit, the pitching distance can be shortened to give the batter ample opportunity to hit the ball. The teacher can act as the pitcher.

Variation: *Three Strikes.* In this game, the batter is allowed three pitches (strikes) to hit the ball. Otherwise, the game proceeds as in Two-pitch Softball.

HIT AND RUN

Playing Area: Softball field or gymnasium

Players: 6 to 15 players on each team

Supplies: A soccer ball or playground ball, home plate, base markers

Skills: Catching, throwing, running

One team is at bat, and the other is scattered in the field. Boundaries must be established, but the area does not have to be shaped like a baseball diamond. The batter stands at home plate with the ball. In front of the batter, 3.5 m away, is a short line over which the ball must be hit to be in play. In the centre of the field, about 12 m away, is the base marker.

The batter bats the ball with the hands or fists so that it crosses the short line and lands inside the area, then attempts to run down the field, around the base marker, and back to home plate before the ball reaches the catcher at home plate (see Figure 27.19). The members of the other team field the ball and throw it to the catcher.

A run is scored each time a batter runs around the marker and back to home plate before the ball is returned to the catcher.

The batter is out in any of the following circumstances:

1. A fly ball is caught.

2. The ball is not hit beyond the short line.

3. The team touches home plate with the ball before the runner returns.

Play the game in innings of three outs each, or make a change of team positions after all members of one team have batted.

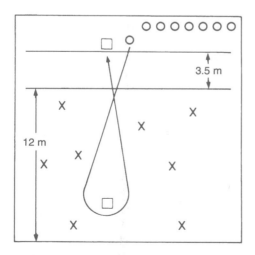

Figure 27.19

Hit and Run.

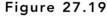

TEACHING TIPS

The distance the batter runs around the base marker may have to be shortened or lengthened, depending on players' abilities.

Variation: Five Passes. The batter is out when a fly ball is caught or when the ball is passed among five different players of the team in the field, with the last pass to a player at home plate beating the runner to the plate. The passes must not touch the ground.

KICK SOFTBALL

Playing Area: Regular softball field with a home base 1 m square

Players: 7 to 11 on each team

Supplies: A soccer ball or another ball to be kicked

Skills: Kicking a rolling ball, throwing, catching, running bases.

The batter stands in the kicking area, a 1-m-square home plate. The batter kicks the ball rolled on the ground by the pitcher. The ball should be rolled at moderate speed. An umpire calls balls and strikes. A strike is a ball that rolls over the square. A ball rolls outside this area. Strikeouts and walks are called the same as in regular softball. Limit the number of foul balls allowed. Otherwise, the game is played like softball.

TEACHING TIP

Variations:

1. The batter kicks a stationary ball. This saves time, as there is no pitching.

2. *Punch Ball.* The batter can hit a volleyball as in a volleyball serve or punch a ball pitched by the pitcher.

IN A PICKLE

Playing Area: Any flat surface with 18 square metres of room

Players: Three or more

Supplies: A slo-pitch or restricted flight softball, two bases 14 to 17 m apart

Skills: Throwing, catching, running down a base runner, tagging

A base runner who gets caught between two bases and is in danger of being run down and tagged is "in a pickle." To begin, both fielders are on bases, one with a ball. The runner is positioned in the base path 3 to 4.5 m away from the fielder with the ball. The two fielders throw the ball back and forth in an attempt to run down and tag the runner between the bases. A runner who escapes and secures a base gets to try again. Otherwise, establish a system of rotation, including any sideline (waiting) players. Do not permit sliding.

BEAT BALL

Playing Area: Softball diamond, bases approximately 9 m apart

Players: Two teams of 5 to 12

Supplies: slo-pitch or restricted flight softball, bat, batting tee (optional)

Skills: All softball skills

One team is at bat, and the other team in the field. The object of the game is for the player to hit the ball and run around the bases before the fielding team can catch the ball, throw it to first base, and then throw it to the catcher at home plate. If the ball beats the hitter home or a fly ball is caught, it is an out. If the hitter beats the ball to home plate, she scores a run. All players on a team bat once before switching positions with the fielding team. The hitter must hit the ball into fair territory before running. Only three pitches are allowed each hitter.

TEACHING TIP

Variations:

1. The hitter has the option of using the batting tee or hitting a pitched ball.

2. The pitcher can be selected from the batting team. This ensures that pitchers will attempt to make pitches that can be hit.

3. Vary the distance so that hitters have a fair opportunity to score. If hitters score too easily, another base can be added.

Developmental Level III

FIVE HUNDRED

Playing Area: Field big enough for fungo hitting

Players: 3 to 12 (or more)

Supplies: A slo-pitch or restricted flight softball, a bat

Skills: Fungo batting, catching flies, fielding grounders

There are many versions of the old game of Five Hundred. A batter stands on one side of the field and bats the ball to a number of fielders, who are scattered. The fielders attempt to become the batter by reaching a score of 500. Fielders earn 200 points for catching a ball on the fly, 100 points for catching a ball on the first bounce, and 50 points for

fielding a grounder cleanly. Whenever the batter changes, all fielders lose their points and must start over.

TEACHING TIP

Variations:

1. The fielder's points must total exactly 500.

2. Points are subtracted from the fielder's score if he mishandles a ball. If he drops a fly ball, for example, he loses 200 points.

BATTER BALL

Playing Area: Softball diamond

Players: 8 to 12 on each team

Supplies: A slo-pitch or restricted flight softball, a bat, a mask

Skills: Slow pitching, hitting, fielding, catching flies

Batter Ball involves batting and fielding, but no base running. It is much like batting practice but adds the element of competition. A line is drawn directly from first to third base. This is the balk line over which a batted ball must travel to be fielded. Another line is drawn from a point on the foul line 1 m behind third base to a point 1.5 m behind second base and in line with home plate. Another line connects this point with a point on the other baseline 1 m behind first base. The shaded area in the diagram is the infield (see Figure 27.20).

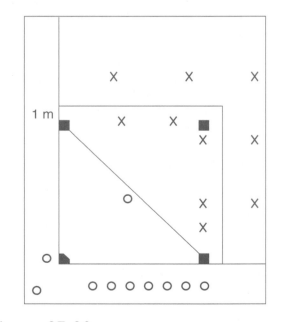

Figure 27.20

Field for Batter Ball.

A member of his own team gives each batter three pitches in order to hit the ball into fair territory across the balk line. The pitcher may stop any ground ball before it crosses the balk line. The batter then gets another turn at bat.

Scoring is as follows:

1. A successful grounder scores one point. A grounder is successful when an infielder fails to handle it cleanly within the infield area. Only one player may field the ball. If the ball is fielded properly, the batter is out.

2. A line drive in the infield area is worth one point if not caught. It can be handled for an out on any bounce. Any line drive caught on the fly is also an out.

3. A fly ball in the infield area scores one point if not caught. For an out, the ball must be caught legally by the first person touching it.

4. A two-bagger scores two points. Any fly ball, line drive or not, that lands fairly in the outfield area without being caught scores two points. If it is caught, the batter is out.

5. A home run scores three points. Any fly ball driven over the head of the farthest outfielder in that area scores a home run.

Three outs can constitute an inning, or all batters can be allowed one turn at bat and then the team changes to the field. A new set of infielders should be in place for each inning. The old set goes to the outfield. Pitchers should be limited to one inning. They also take a turn at bat.

TEACHING TIPS

Many games of this type require special fields, either rectangular or narrowly angled. This game was selected because it uses a regular softball field with the added lines. The lines can be drawn with a stick or can be marked using regular marking methods.

The pitcher has to decide whether to stop the ball. If the ball goes beyond the restraining line, it is in play even if the pitcher touched it.

Variations: Batter Ball can be modified for use as a station in rotational teaching, with the emphasis on individual batting and squad organization. One member of the squad would be at bat and would get a definite number of chances (for example, five) to score. She keeps her own point total. The other squad members occupy the necessary game positions.

HOME RUN

Playing Area: Softball diamond (only first base is used)

Players: 4 to 10

Supplies: A slo-pitch or restricted flight softball, a bat

Skills: Most softball skills, modified base running

The crucial players are a batter, a catcher, a pitcher, and one fielder. Any other players are fielders; some can take positions in the infield. The batter hits a regular pitch and on a fair ball must run to first base and back home before the ball can be returned to the catcher.

The batter is out whenever any of the following occurs:

1. A fly ball (fair or foul) is caught.

2. The batter strikes out.

3. On a fair ball, the ball beats the batter back to home plate.

TEACHING TIPS

To keep skilful players from staying too long at bat, a rule can be made that, after a certain number of home runs, the batter automatically must take a place in the field. Establish a rotation (work-up) system. The batter should go to right field, move to centre, and then go to left field. The rotation continues through third base, shortstop, second base, first base, pitcher, and catcher. The catcher is the next batter. The number of positions depends on the number of players in the game. If there are enough players, an additional batter can be waiting to take a turn.

The game can be played with only three youngsters, eliminating the catcher. With only one fielder, the pitcher covers home plate. The first-base distance should be far enough away to be a challenge but close enough so that a well-hit ball scores a home run. The distance depends on the number playing and the capacities of players.

Variations:

1. This game can be played like softball—allowing the batter to stop at first base if another batter is up.

2. A fly ball caught by a fielder puts that player directly to bat. The batter then takes a place at the end of the rotation, and the other players rotate up to the position of the fielder who caught the ball. The ball belongs to the player in whose territory it falls.

3. *Triangle Ball.* First and third bases are brought in toward each other, thus narrowing the playing field. Second base is not used. The game gets its name from the triangle formed by home plate and the two bases. The batter must circle first and third bases and return home before the ball reaches home plate. This game can also be played with as few as three players, with the pitcher covering home plate.

TEE BALL

Playing Area: Softball field

Players: 7 to 11 on each team

Supplies: A slo-pitch or restricted flight softball, a bat, a batting tee

Skills: Most softball skills (except pitching and stealing bases), hitting a ball from a tee

This game is an excellent variation of softball and is played under softball rules with the following exceptions:

1. Instead of hitting a pitched ball, the batter hits the ball from a tee. The catcher places the ball on the tee. After the batter hits the ball, the play is the same as in regular softball. With no pitching, there is no stealing. A runner stays on the base until the batter hits the ball.

2. A fielder occupies the position normally held by the pitcher. The primary duties of this fielder are to field bunts and groundballs and to back up the infielders on throws.

Teams can play regular innings for three outs or change to the field after each player on the batting team has had a turn at bat.

Figure 27.21

Improvised batting tee.

An improvised batting tee is shown in Figure 27.21. If the tee is not adjustable, three different sizes should be available. The batter should take a position far enough behind the tee so that, in stepping forward to swing, the ball will be slightly in front of the midpoint of the swing.

Tee Ball has many advantages. There are no strikeouts, every child hits the ball, and fielding opportunities abound.

SCRUB (WORK-UP)

Playing Area: Softball field

Players: 7 to 15

Supplies: A slo-pitch or restricted flight softball, a bat

Skills: Most softball skills

The predominant feature of Scrub is the rotation of the players. The game is played with regular softball rules, with individuals more or less playing for themselves. There are at least two batters, generally three. A catcher, pitcher, and first-base player are essential. The remaining players assume the other positions. A batter who is out goes to a position in right field. All other players move up one position, with the catcher becoming the batter. The first-base player becomes the pitcher, the pitcher moves to catcher, and all others move up one place.

If a fly ball is caught, the fielder and batter exchange positions.

SLOW-PITCH SOFTBALL

Playing Area: Softball diamond

Players: 10 on each team

Supplies: A slo-pitch or restricted flight softball, a bat

Skills: Most softball skills

The major difference between regular softball and Slow-pitch Softball is in the pitching, but there are other modifications to the game as well. With slower pitching, there is more hitting and thus more action on the bases and in the field. Outfielders are an important part of the game because many long drives are hit. Rule changes from the game of official softball are as follows:

1. The pitch must be a slow pitch. Any other pitch is illegal and is called a ball. The pitch must be slow, with an arc of 30 cm. It must not rise over 3 m from the ground, however. Its legality depends on the umpire's call.

2. There are 10 players instead of 9. The extra one, called the *roving fielder,* plays in the outfield and handles line drives hit just over the infielders.

3. The batter must take a full swing at the ball and is out if he chops at the ball or bunts.

4. If the batter is hit by a pitched ball, she is not entitled to first base. The pitch is merely called a ball. Otherwise, balls and strikes are called as in softball.

5. The runner must hold base until the pitch has reached or passed home plate. No stealing is permitted.

TEACHING TIP

It may be desirable to shorten the pitching distance somewhat. Much of the success of the game depends on the pitcher's ability to get the ball over the plate.

BABE RUTH BALL

Playing Area: Softball diamond

Players: Five

Supplies: A bat, a slo-pitch or restricted flight softball, four cones or other markers

Skills: Batting, pitching, fielding

Four cones separate the three outfield zones—left, centre, and right field. It is helpful if foul lines have been drawn, but cones can define them (see Figure 27.22). The batter calls the field to which he intends to hit. The pitcher throws controlled pitches so that the batter can hit easily. The batter remains in position as long as he hits to the designated field. Field choices must be rotated. The batter gets only one swing to make a successful hit. He may allow a ball to go by, but if he swings, it counts as a try. There is no base running. Players rotate.

TEACHING TIP

Children play this game informally on sandlots with a variety of rules. Some possibilities to consider are these: What happens when a fly ball is caught? What

limitations should be made on hitting easy grounders? Let the players decide about these points and others not covered by the stated rules.

HURRY BASEBALL (ONE-PITCH SOFTBALL)

Playing Area: Softball diamond

Players: 8 to 12 on each team

Supplies: A slo-pitch or restricted flight softball, a bat

Skills: Slow pitching, most softball skills except stealing bases and bunting

Hurry Baseball demands rapid changes from batting to fielding, and vice versa. The game is like regular softball, with the following exceptions:

1. The pitcher is from the team at bat and must not interfere with, or touch, a batted ball on penalty of the batter's being called out.

2. The team coming to bat does not wait for the fielding team to get set. Because it has its own pitcher, the pitcher gets the ball to the batter just as quickly as the batter can grab a bat and get ready. The fielding team has to hustle to get out to their places.

3. Only one pitch is allowed to a batter. The batter must hit a fair ball or she is out. The pitch is made from about two-thirds of the normal pitching distance.

4. No stealing is permitted.

5. No bunting is permitted.

The batter must take a full swing. Teams in the field learn to put the next hitter as catcher, so that he can bat immediately when the third out is made. Batters must bat in order. Scoring follows regular softball rules.

THREE-TEAM SOFTBALL

Playing Area: Softball diamond

Players: 12 to 15

Supplies: A mask, a slo-pitch or restricted flight softball, bat

Skills: All softball skills

Three-team Softball works well with 12 players, a number considered too few to divide into two effective fielding teams. The players are instead divided into three teams. The rules of softball apply, with the following exceptions:

1. One team is at bat, one team covers the infield (including the catcher), and the third team provides the outfielders and the pitcher.

2. The team at bat must bat in a definite order. This means that because of the small number of batters on each side, instances can occur when the person due to

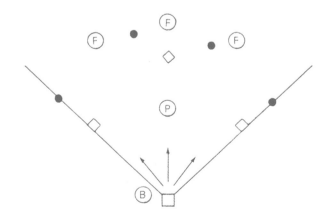

Figure 27.22

Babe Ruth Ball.

bat is on base. To take a turn at bat, the runner must be replaced by a player not on base.

3. After three outs, the teams rotate, with the outfield moving to the infield, the infield taking a turn at bat, and the batters going to the outfield.

4. An inning is over when all three teams have batted.

5. The pitcher should be limited to pitching one inning only. A player may repeat as pitcher only after all members of that team have had a chance to pitch.

Critical Thinking

1. Design a practice activity (drill or lead-up game) for developmental level II that will help students practise fielding skills and basic defensive tactics. Then by making modifications in the same activity increase its complexity and challenge to meet the needs of students at developmental level III.

References and Suggested Readings

American Sport Education Program. (2007). *Coaching youth softball* (4th ed.). Champaign, IL: Human Kinetics.

Garman, J. (2005). *Softball skills and drills* (2nd ed.). Champaign, IL: Human Kinetics.

Joseph, J. (1998). *Defensive softball drills.* Champaign, IL: Human Kinetics.

Noren, R. (2005). *Softball fundamentals.* Champaign, IL: Human Kinetics.

Potter, D.L. (2007). *Softball* (3rd ed.). Champaign, IL: Human Kinetics.

Potter, D.L. & Brockmeyer, G.A. (1999). *Softball: Steps to success* (2nd ed.). Champaign, IL: Human Kinetics.

Softball Canada. (1993). *Getting started in softball—Helpful hints for first-time coaches.* Gloucester, ON: Author.

 **Weblinks**

Softballsearch.com: http://softballsearch.eteamz.com

This site acts as a clearinghouse for softball-related websites, with links to a huge variety of resources: coaching, cheering, drills, leagues, rules, and newsgroups, among others.

Softball Canada: www.softball.ca

Softball Canada is the governing body for the sport of softball in Canada, and its website offers information on the national team, on programs and upcoming events, and on news and views from the softball community.

CHAPTER 28

Track and Field

Essential Components

I	**Organized around content standards**
II	**Student-centred and developmentally appropriate**
III	**Physical activity and motor skill development form the core of the program**
IV	**Teaches management skills and self-discipline**
V	**Promotes inclusion of all students**
VI	**Focuses on process over product**
VII	**Promotes lifetime personal health and wellness**
VIII	**Teaches cooperation and responsibility and promotes sensitivity to diversity**

Physical Education Standards

1	**Students are able to move competently using a variety of fundamental and specialized motor skills.**
2	Students can monitor and maintain a health-enhancing level of physical fitness.
3	**Students are able to apply movement concepts and basic mechanics of skill performance when learning and refining motor skills.**
4	Students comprehend the basic principles of wellness and are able to apply concepts that enable them to make meaningful decisions that positively impact their health and wellness.
5	**Students participate in a wide variety of physical activities and learn how to maintain a personalized active lifestyle.**
6	**Students demonstrate empathy, understanding, and respect for the numerous differences exhibited by people in an activity setting.**
7	**Students exhibit responsible and self-directed behaviours that lead to positive social interactions in physical activity.**

OVERVIEW

Skill instruction for track and field is introduced during the intermediate grades after children have mastered basic prerequisite skills. Teaching the rules and strategies for track and field is an integral part of the instructional process. Using proper progressions is a key to success when teaching fundamental skills and lead-up activities associated with track and field. Lead-up activities provide an opportunity to emphasize the development of selected track and field skills in a setting that is compatible with the abilities of participants.

OUTCOMES

- Structure learning experiences efficiently using appropriate formations, progressions, and teaching techniques.

- Develop a unit plan and lesson focus for track and field.

- Identify rules and safety precautions associated with teaching track and field.

- Describe instructional procedures used for implementing successful lead-up activities and the various track and field events.

- Cite instructional procedures used for analyzing track and field skills.

The elementary program in track and field consists of sprinting (40 to 100 m), middle-distance running, long jump, triple jump, high jump, hurdling, relays, and shot put. The primary emphases are on practice, improvement, and personal accomplishment. Moderate levels of competition are incorporated using a team approach.

Children should experience the differences between walking, jogging, sprinting, striding (for pace), and running. Sprinting techniques are particularly important, with instruction centring on correct form for starting, accelerating, and maintaining speed. Distance running for elementary children focuses on enjoyment, technique, and pacing. Children enjoy jumping and running over obstacles, and this proves to be a great lead-up activity for hurdling. Hurdling may be included in a program using modified equipment. Jumping activities introduce students to a variety of movements that are common among the jumping events. The throwing motion should be introduced to prepare students for participating in the shot put and future throwing events.

Planning and organizing a track and field unit in advance is the key to success for the students. Special considerations about instructional procedures, facilities, equipment, and assessment are important details to include in lesson and unit planning.

Instructional Emphasis and Sequence

Table 28.1 divides track and field activities into two developmental levels. The activities are listed in progression. Because many track and field skills involve locomotor movements, youngsters of all ages can enjoy and participate in these activities.

Developmental Levels I and II

Running and jumping skills are easily mastered by children, so they are introduced in developmental level I. In addition, simple throwing activities are included to prepare students for future throwing events. Early experiences at this level stress running short distances, learning different starting positions, and participating in long jump. Some running for distance is included and relays offer exciting experiences for students to participate in a team activity.

Developmental Level III

More serious efforts to achieve proper form begin at this level. Students may begin to do the following: perform long jump and high jump with modified run-ups; learn the foot sequence for triple jump; learn more advanced throwing

TABLE 28.1 Suggested track and field program	
Developmental Level I & II	Developmental Level III
Track Skills	
40- to 60-m sprints	60- to 400-m sprints
Standing start	Middle distance running (800 to 1500 m)
Crouch start	Long distance (3000 m)
Jogging and cross-country running	Relays
	Hurdling (progressions)
Field Skills	
Jumping activities (progressions)	High jump
Long jump	Triple jump
Throwing activities (progressions)	Shot put
Knowledge	
Safety	Safety
• throw and retrieve procedures	• throw and retrieve procedures
• jumping procedures	• jumping procedures
• care of equipment	• care of equipment

motions; practise proper shot put technique; develop pace in distance running; practise hurdling progressions using modified hurdle heights and distances; and learn passing techniques in the relays.

Track Events

Sprinting

Sprinting is a simple locomotor skill that forms the basic building blocks for a track and field program. The track events that involve sprinting include all distances up to and including 400 m. Effective sprinting (see Figure 28.1) requires quick and powerful actions with sound technical skills.

Here are some important technique points:

- Run tall, slight lean forward at hips.

- Arm swing should be from "chin to hip," elbows bent at 90 degrees.

- Legs and arms drive forward in a straight line.

Figure 28.1

Sprinting technique.

Distance Running

Distance running includes all middle- and long-distance track events, including 800 m, 1,500 m, and 3,000 m. Cross-country races are also considered distance running and cover various distances, depending on the age category. Training for distance running requires good running technique (see Figure 28.2) and cardiovascular fitness. Beginners must start out at shorter distances and gradually build toward long distance running.

Here are some important technique points:

- Heel strikes ground first in most situations (depending on running pace).
- Thigh is not raised as high as in sprinting.
- Arm swing is less vigorous than with sprinting.
- Shoulders are relaxed and posture is straight and erect.

Figure 28.2

Distance running technique.

TEACHING TIP

If students are doing a considerable amount of distance running, appropriate footwear is recommended. A good running shoe with adequate support can help prevent injury. Gradually increase distances, no more than 10% per week.

Sprinting and Distance Running Activities

MARCHING

- Marching is walking with higher knee lift (to waist height).
- Dorsi flex ankle (90 degrees to shin).
- Arms bent at 90-degree angle.
- Push off balls of feet and contact the ground below the hips.
- Body stays tall.

SKIPPING

- Emphasize tall body position.
- Drive knee so that thigh is at waist height.
- Keep arms at 90 degrees; drive opposite arm to knee drive.
- Set up cones or mark lines 30 cm apart and skip from one to the next.
- Speed up skip and then skip into a short run.

CHICKEN WALK SHUTTLE (BOTTOM KICKS)

- Heels come straight to seat.
- At the same time, flap arms like a chicken (to introduce arm action and balance in sprint technique).
- Keep ankle at a 90-degree angle while foot is in the air.
- Keep eyes focused forward at shoulder level.
- Set up relays around a cone (15 to 20 m distance) or in a circuit.
- Chicken-walk short, tall, and backwards.

BEANBAG SHUTTLES OR RELAYS

Set up courses using beanbags and hoops to place them in. Be creative but always give students a focus for each start. For example, in one race you may give them the task of focusing on arm swing. Another race may focus on knee drive or upper-body lean.

TAG ACTIVITIES

Tag activities provide an effective means for children to practise running technique. Be sure, however, to give students a focus. Tag can be a great warm-up activity for a lesson on sprinting, emphasizing looking forward, running tall, and swinging straight, strong arms.

FOLLOW THE LEADER

Students line up in smalls groups of four to six. A designated leader in each group runs in a pattern of her choice, with other students following behind. Change leaders frequently. Each group must keep a pace to allow all members to keep up.

NATURE RUN

- Set up a course approximately 300 to 400 m long in a natural setting. Divide the course alternately into 100-m and 50-m sections, using natural terrain.

- Students walk the 50-m sections and jog the 100-m sections.

- Each student completes the course two to four times.

- With advanced runners, have students sprint the 50-metre sections and jog the 100-m sections. Give ample rest between sets.

RUNNING FOR PACE (ADVANCED)

Children should have some experience in running for moderate distances to acquire an understanding of pace. The running is technique loose and relaxed. Distances up to 1,500 m may be part of the training.

In partners, one student runs, and the other times with a stopwatch. The timer loudly counts the elapsed time second by second, and notes the runner's time as she crosses the finish line. On a track, set a distance, stipulate a target time, and see how close the athlete can come to it.

INTERVAL TRAINING (ADVANCED)

Interval training consists of running at a set speed for a specified distance or time and then walking the same distance or time. As runners become more fit and skilled, the rest or walking time will decrease. Children can run for 100 to 200 m and then walk back to the start, repeating this procedure a number of times. Regardless of the interval time or distance, breathing should return to near normal before the next interval is attempted.

Starting

With all types of starts, it is important to introduce children to the start commands for the different running events. For the sprint events (100 m, 200 m, 400 m) the commands are "on your marks," "set," then the starting gun will sound. To get children used to reacting to a sound rather than saying "go," it can be useful to use noises such as two pieces of wood banged together, a loud clap, or the mimicked sound of a starting gun. Any of the middle-long distance events (800 m or greater) are started with the command "on your mark," then the starting gun.

Starting Techniques

Standing Start

This type of start has a variety of uses in physical education and is generally used in the middle-distance starts and by young athletes as a precursor to using blocks. Figure 28.3 and Figure 28.4, and the following technique points, illustrate and describe the standing start:

Figure 28.3

Standing start—"On your marks."

Figure 28.4

Standing start—"Set."

"On Your Marks"

- Nondominant foot is placed behind starting line. Dominant foot is placed a comfortable stride back (a long stride is not recommended).
- Body position is erect and still.

"Set"

- Bend knees (30 degrees) and at waist so that shoulders are at hip height.
- Opposite arm to front foot is forward, other arm is back. Elbow angle should be at 90 degrees.
- The weight is on the front foot.

"Go" or "Bang"

- Push off back leg and drive opposite arm forward.

Crouch Sprint Start

Once students are familiar with starting technique, they can progress to using the crouched start. Teachers should be aware, however, that some students may not be strong enough for the crouched start to be effective and thus the standing start may be more appropriate.

Figure 28.5

Crouch sprint start—"On your marks."

Foot Placement

- Determine which foot is the most comfortable being forward.
- For the front foot, measure 1 1/2 foot lengths behind the start line.
- For the back foot, measure 1 1/2 foot lengths from the front foot.
- Mark these foot placements with chalk or other marker.

"On Your Marks"

- Student crouches down and places each foot at marks (see Figure 28.5).
- Knee of back leg is down on the ground. Knee of front leg is tucked under chest.
- Hands are placed with fingers behind the line slightly more than shoulder width apart.
- Eyes are looking down at ground, directly below.

"Set"

- Hips are raised up, back knee comes off the ground (see Figure 28.6).
- Front knee angle should be at 90 degrees and the hips should be slightly higher than the shoulders.
- Shoulders should be just ahead of the hands.

Figure 28.6

Crouch sprint start—"Set."

"Go" or "Bang"

- Drive forward (not upward) with back leg and opposite arm.
- Quick, shorter strides with good knee drive.
- Maintain forward body lean and rise gradually rather than standing up suddenly.

Using Blocks

Blocks are not usually used in elementary school track meets. As blocks are expensive for most schools to purchase, students can work in partners to give platforms for a simulated block start. One partner sits on the ground with her back against a wall or some solid structure. She then places her feet at the foot placement markers. The runner uses the partner's feet as "blocks."

Starting Activities

EYES DOWN CONE RUN (USING PROPER COMMANDS)

- Students lie facedown with eyes focused on floor.
- At start signal, students get up and run past the cone (placed 10–15 m away).

- Do not look ahead for the cone, keep eyes focused on the floor.
- Object is to keep eyes low so that the body does not rise too fast at the start.

SPIDER START

- Students start using a spider walk.
- Spider walk from start line to a cone 3–5 m away, then begin to run.
- Student run to a finish line/cone 10 to 15 m away.
- Object is a gradual rise out of the spider position, keeping eyes on ground at the start.

FALLING STARTS

- Students stand with both feet together on the start line.
- Fall forward and whichever foot consistently moves out first will be the back foot for starting.
- Use falling start into a sprint for 10 to 15 m.
- Emphasize eye focus on the ground at first, then to shoulder level afterward.

BLOCK STARTS

- Use the proper commands for all starts.
- Emphasize the following: eye focus, back leg/opposite arm drive, gradual rise, quick steps.

Hurdling

For safety, children should use hurdles that are designed to tip over easily when struck. Scissor hurdles are one of the safest types of hurdles and adjust to low heights for young athletes. Although manufactured hurdles are easier to work with, schools can make their own hurdles from a variety of materials, including sticks placed on top of cones.

For beginners, it is important to learn how to run (not jump) over the hurdles and establish a steady rhythm. Encourage students to run over the hurdles with a tall upper body and to keep their eyes forward (that is, not look down at the hurdle).

Teaching Hurdle Technique

1. Low-Obstacle Running
   - Place five cones, sticks, or other low obstacles approximately 2–3 m apart.
   - Technique points: tall upper body, eyes forward, run, don't jump.

2. Steady Rhythm Running
   * Set up several lines of obstacles with each line having different spacing between obstacles (for example, Line 1: 2 m, Line 2: 2.5 m, Line 3: 3 m, Line 4: 3.5 m, and so on).
   * Emphasize a steady and consistent rhythm between the cones.
   * Students are working toward having three steps between obstacles.

3. Low-Hurdle Running
   * Repeat activities A and B using low hurdles or sticks over cones (but do not exceed knee height).
   * Make sure there are several lines with different spacing between hurdles so that students can choose which one is best for them (see Figure 28.7).
   * Emphasize steady, fast rhythm (running not jumping).

4. Introduction to Hurdling Technique
   * Introduce terms: (i) lead leg—first leg to go over hurdle; (ii) trail leg—the leg that comes through last.
   * Have students practise going over hurdles using both left and right as lead legs.
   * Students will be able to determine which leg feels more comfortable and will now begin to practise with a partner using a consistent lead leg.
   * Using the same lead leg for each hurdle, students should attempt to establish a steady rhythm between hurdles.

5. Advanced Hurdling Technique
   * Take off 20 to 40 cm in front of hurdle.
   * Lead leg is extended straight up and over hurdle (toes up).
   * Opposite arm reaches forward with lead leg.
   * Upper body leans forward over lead leg.
   * Bend trail leg and lift the knee high and to the side.

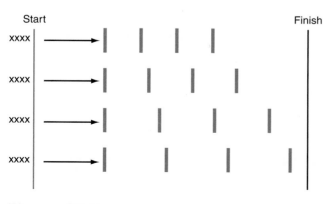

Figure 28.7

Teaching progression for Hurdle Running.

* Pull trail leg heel to seat, keep foot flexed.
* Snap lead leg down to ground.
* Pull trail leg forward, parallel, and then drive forward with it as the first step to the next hurdle.
* Maintain a forward position with hips and shoulder square to the hurdle.
* Use same lead leg for each hurdle, sprinting three strides between hurdles.

Hurdling Activities

LOW-OBSTACLE COURSE

Use cones, benches, hoops, low vaulting boxes, mats, rolled-up mats, sticks, and other equipment to set up obstacle courses. The object is to reinforce running tall and establishing hurdle rhythm.

* Do a walk-through first, and then increase speed gradually as students learn the course.
* Make sure to leave enough room between students when they are on the course.

LEAD LEG DRILLS (ADVANCED)

Set up four hurdles approximately 1 m apart. Hurdle height will depend on the skill level and age of students.

* Students walk beside the row of hurdles, bringing lead leg up in a straight line, not out to side.
* Lead leg immediately "snaps" down in a pawing motion at the ground.
* Intent is to get the lead leg back to the ground as quickly as possible.

TRAIL LEG DRILLS (ADVANCED)

Set up four hurdles approximately 1 m apart. Hurdle height will depend on the skill level and age of students.

* Students walk or march beside the row of hurdles, bringing trail leg laterally over hurdle.
* Lead leg must step at least even with the hurdle, but preferably slightly in front.

Relays

Sprint Relays (4 x 100-m): Non-visual Pass

Short distance relays use a non-visual pass and alternate exchanges where the first and third runners receive, carry, and pass the baton with their right hands and the second and fourth runners use their left hands. Although there are several methods of baton passing, including the downsweep pass and the upsweep pass, the recommended method of passing is called the push pass (also known as the Canadian National Team pass).

The passer carries the baton in a vertical position and pushes it into the open hand of the receiver by simply extending the arm forward. The receiver must give the passer a good target by putting her arm straight back at shoulder level and pointing the thumb down.

General Technique

First and Third Runners

- Passer runs on inside of lane and carries baton in right hand.
- Receiver waits on outside of lane and looks over left shoulder.
- Receiver begins to run when the passer hits the checkmark (see below for determining checkmarks).
- Passer yells a code word ("hand," "hi," or student choice) when he is close enough to pass.
- Receiver keeps looking forward and swings left hand back to shoulder level, ready to receive the baton.
- Passer pushes baton into hand of receiver who has thumb pointing down.
- Receiver grasps the top third of the baton and runs along the outside of the lane.

Second and Fourth Runners   All technique points are the same as for the first and third runners *except:*

- Passer runs on the outside of the lane.
- Passer carries baton in left hand.
- Receiver waits on inside of lane and looks over right shoulder.

Checkmarks and Exchange Zones

Checkmarks in relay races are used to signal the receiver to start running. Because the short distance relays use a non-visual pass, this checkmark is important. The receiver watches the passer until he hits the checkmark, then the receiver starts to run. This helps reduce the likelihood of the two runners colliding, ensures the pass is made within the exchange zone, and keeps the momentum of the baton constant.

To establish the checkmark, practise with the two runners at each exchange area (see Figure 28.8). The baton must be passed within the exchange zone; therefore, students should be encouraged to make the pass early in the zone to avoid running out of space. The receiver should

Figure 28.8

Relay exchange zone.

stand within the 10-m acceleration zone (the exact placement will be determined with practice). Place a checkmark (use a piece of tape or chalk) within the lane 5 to 10 m back from the receiver's position.

To practise the exchange, have the passer run approximately 40 m in her lane toward the receiver. When the passer hits the checkmark, the receiver begins to sprint (remind the receiver to run hard to avoid colliding and to attempt to match the speed of the passer when the exchange is made). Then, to complete the exchange, follow the instructions for baton passing. Adjustments to the checkmark often must be made to ensure the baton is passed within the exchange zone. For example:

- *Runners collide.* Checkmark needs to be moved back OR receiver needs to start running sooner (for example, receiver did not start running as soon as passer hit checkmark).
- *Passer fails to catch up to receiver.* Checkmark distance needs to be moved closer OR receiver starts running too fast and needs to run slower (to match speed of passer).

TEACHING TIP

It is important to emphasize to students that both the passer and receiver have different but equally important responsibilities. It is the receiver's responsibility to make sure she forms a proper, stable target. It is the passer's responsibility to place the baton into the receiver's hand. This gives the students something to focus on, rather than the relay race itself.

Non-visual Exchange Activities

STATIC BATON PASSING

Receiver stands arm's length in front of passer. The partners practise the timing of saying the code word, the receiver swinging hand back, and the passer pushing the baton into the student's hand.

WALKING AND JOGGING BATON PASSING

The passer and receiver practise baton passing while walking. Receiver must make sure his hand provides a steady target. Passer must focus on pushing the baton into the receiver's hand on first attempt. Increase the speed to a jogging pace.

Passer starts at least 20 m back and runs toward receiver. When passer reaches checkmark, receiver begins to run. The baton is passed to the receiver, who then runs 20 m (marked by a cone).

Distance Relays (4 x 200-m, 4 x 400-m): Visual Pass

This pass is the safest type of exchange and is used in longer distance relays. It allows the receiver to watch the passer and the passer's level of fatigue, so that the exchange can be made smoothly. The following technique points describe the visual pass:

- Receiver faces inside of track while holding left hand out to receive baton.
- Fingers are extended, thumb pointed up.
- Receiver begins to run when passer is 3 to 5 m away, and accelerates to match the speed of passer.
- Passer is carrying baton vertical with the right hand and reaches toward receiver.
- Receiver grasps the baton and immediately shifts it from the left to the right hand.

Visual Pass Activities

Practise the visual pass at different paces (for example, walking, jogging, fast running). Partner drills and other relay games are useful activities in developing this pass.

General Relay Activities

CIRCULAR RELAYS

Circular relays make use of the regular circular track. On a 200-m track, relays can be organized in a number of ways, depending on how many runners are spaced for one lap. Four runners can do a lap, each running one quarter of the way; two can do a lap, each running half the distance; or each runner can complete a whole lap. In these races, each member of the relay team runs the same distance. Relays can also be organized so that members run different distances.

SHUTTLE RELAYS

Because children are running toward each other, one great difficulty in running shuttle relays is control of the exchange. In the excitement, the next runner may leave too early, and the tag or exchange is then made ahead of the restraining line. Mark restraining line with a bright coloured cone to reduce early exchanges.

Field Events

Jumping

The basic technique points for the jumping events are similar; therefore, any of the introductory jumping activities and lead-up activities can be used to develop jumping skills. Hopping relays, leap frog, skipping rope games, tag games, one- and two-foot hops, and jumping circuits are great lead-up activities that will introduce students to the jumping motion. All jumping activities involve arm swing, active takeoffs, landing, and dynamic movements, and mini-games that use these skills will help students prepare their muscles and bodies for the jumping events.

Horizontal Jumps

The horizontal jumps include the long jump and triple jump. As the long jump is not as technical, it should be introduced first and used as a progression to teach the triple jump. While the technique points for the two events are different, the general rules and safety considerations are the same.

General Rules

1. Takeoff foot must be completely on/behind board. (That is, if any part of the foot is over the board, the jump is not measured. It is a fault.)
2. Jump is measured from where the performer hits the sand. If the performer falls back or walks backward through the pit, that is where it is measured.

TEACHING TIP

1. Sandpits should be dug up and softened so that sand is loose and free from dangerous objects such as sticks, glass, or animal droppings.
2. Takeoff boards should be level with the run-up surface.
3. For beginners, using a takeoff area instead of a board can increase the level of success (see Figure 28.9).
4. Supervise pits and ensure all rakes or shovels are well clear of the pit area, placed sharp side down.

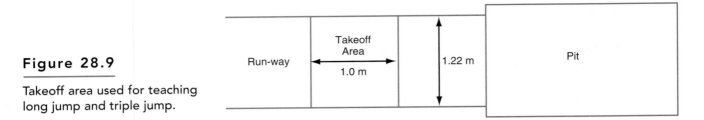

Figure 28.9

Takeoff area used for teaching long jump and triple jump.

Long Jump Technique

The Approach

- Recommended approach distance is 10 to 15 m.
- Accelerate toward the board so that jumper is at maximum speed at the board (if the jumper is slowing down before the board, her run-up is likely too long).
- Last four strides should be quick, with the last stride being short and powerful.

The Jump

- Plant takeoff foot (fully extended) on board.
- Drive free knee up to 90 degrees and opposite arm up.
- Keep eyes and head forward.
- Pull legs up and extend out (in front of hips) parallel to pit.

The Landing

- When feet reach pit, bring arms back behind hips.
- Land on both feet softly with bent knees.
- Continue forward motion through pit and leave pit in a forward direction.

Long Jump Activities

STANDING LONG JUMP

Can be done on mats, grass, or into a sandpit.

- Keep knees flexed and arms back.
- Drive arms up and knees up and out.
- Land softly with bent knees, and sweep arms back to maintain forward momentum.

TAKEOFF ACTIVITIES

1. Start with a one-step approach:
   - Focus on strong and quick knee–arm drive.
   - Keep upper body tall and eyes looking forward.
   - Get as much height in the air as possible.

2. Three- to five-step approach focusing on knee–arm drive.

3. Three- to five-step approach with a flag or ball overhead. Students try to hit the flag or ball with their head.

4. Three- to five-step approach with a stick placed on cones 1 m past the takeoff board. Students jump over the stick and land in the pit.

JUMP AND FLIGHT ACTIVITIES

1. Use cones or rope to land over. Gradually increase the distance from the takeoff board to the cone or rope.

2. *Jump the River.* Put two ropes on ground about 1 m apart at one end and 2 m at the other end. Using a short run up to the river, each student takes off on one foot from one side and lands on the opposite shore on two feet. With each successful crossing, students move to a wider part of the river.

LANDING ACTIVITIES

Use one-step takeoff drills with different targets for landing. Use rope, cones, flags, or chalk on the ground to provide targets for landing and maintaining forward momentum. For safety, ensure students always land with bent knees.

1. *Jump the Shot.* Put students in small groups of four to five. Using a long rope (with bean bag tied to the end for weight), one student spins it in a circle. Other students jump the rope as it comes to them. Students take turns spinning the rope.

Triple Jump

Since this is a very technical event and requires a considerable amount of strength, it is recommended primarily for older children. Although many school districts in Canada do not offer triple jumps at elementary school track meets, it is an event that is popular among young athletes.

To be successful, students need to spend considerable time learning the proper sequence of foot placement, and how to actively hop and develop an effective "hop, bound, jump" rhythm.

In most cases, a student will use for takeoff the opposite foot to that which she uses in long jump. For example, if a student uses the left foot for the long jump takeoff, she will generally use the right foot for the triple jump takeoff.

To begin, teach the technique to students by walking through the activities. For the purposes of explanation, the following is based on a right-foot takeoff.

Triple Jump Technique (Right-foot Takeoff)

The Approach A maximum 10 m is recommended. Controlled acceleration. Speed is not important at this stage and can often cause young jumpers to confuse their footing.

"Hop" Flat-footed takeoff with the right leg. Drive forward and coordinate arms with legs. Land actively on right foot.

"Bound" Strongly swing a bent left leg forward. Swing opposite arm (right) forward. Bound forward. Land actively on the left foot.

"Jump" Drive right knee up and forward. Bring both feet together. Arms are forward and up. Extend legs parallel to pit, keep feet up.

Landing Bring arms back behind hips when feet reach the pit. Land on both feet softly with bent knees. Continue forward motion through pit. Leave pit in a forward direction.

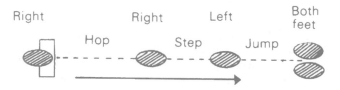

Figure 28.10

Triple Jump foot sequence.

TEACHING TIP

Establish the proper foot sequence first (see Figure 28.10). Then try to emphasize good rhythm and equal phases. The ideal technique is to have consistent rhythm and equal distance for each phase (hop, bound, jump).

Triple Jump Activities

1. *Hopping and bounding activities.* Create games and circuits using single leg hops and bounding for distance. Chalk-marked circles and cones can be used. Set up these activities with students hopping or bounding beside the cones or into the marked circles. The next progression is to hop or bound over low obstacles.

2. To teach proper foot sequence, use cones or chalk circles labelled with the appropriate right or left feet. Set up several lines with hoops at different distances. Children may practise on grass first, and then move to the side of sandpit to add the landing (see Figure 28.11).

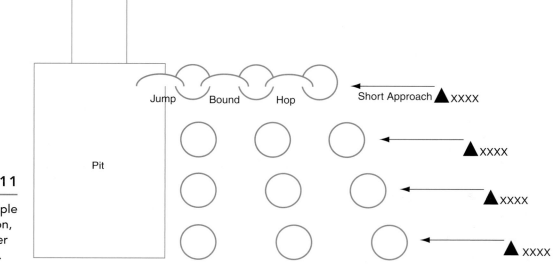

Figure 28.11

Whole-class triple jump instruction, teaching proper foot sequence.

When practising on grass, have students use small movements so that when landing on the jump they do not jar their legs or back. Also, use a soft surface to practise the triple jump sequence and do not repeat more than three times per week in order to prevent injury.

High Jump

High jump is one of the most popular events among elementary school students. Students always enjoy jumping onto the high jump mats and challenging themselves to new heights. However, if students are not instructed and supervised correctly, poor technique and horseplay can quickly lead to injury. Fortunately, if the teaching progressions for high jump are introduced, students can safely practise and experience success.

To minimize safety risks, teachers should consider the following:

1. Follow the progressions to teach proper technique.

2. Limit the approach speed and distance. Students *do not* need to sprint toward the bar.

3. Use a bungee bar or flexible elastic rope as a crossbar. Do not use a regular crossbar with beginners.

4. Ensure the landing surface (high jump mats) is well maintained and will absorb the force of the landing.

5. Figure 28.12 displays the recommended approach and landing area setup to prevent landing injuries.

Teaching Progressions

To introduce the high jump, begin away from the mats. The key to success and safety in this event is teaching proper approach and takeoff. Students must learn a controlled approach so that they do not gain too much momentum on their run-up, which can often cause them to travel over the landing area.

1. Away from the high jump mats, have students choose which leg is most comfortable for takeoff. (For the purposes of this section, the takeoff leg will be the left.)

2. Introduce the knee-drive action. Students stand on the sideline. Right foot on the line. Step forward with left and swing right knee up. Do this activity slowly at first and gradually increase the speed and intensity of the knee drive. Students should then start to get some "air time." Technique points: quick and strong knee drive; back straight, takeoff leg straight (the knee drive lifts the student into the air).

3. Add another step to the above activity. Now students will start with their left foot on the line and take two steps. Instruct students as follows: "Left foot on the line; right–left and up." The same technique points apply.

4. Add one more step to the above activity. Students will start with their right foot on the line and take three steps. This time it will be similar to the first progression. Instruct students as follows: "Right foot on the line; left–right–left and up." At this point, students will start to gain some forward momentum. Therefore, once students have learned the sequence, encourage them to try to take off and land in the same position.

5. Now take the three-step approach to the mats. One at a time, students will practise their three-step approach, but this time landing with their feet on the mat. Do not have the bar set up yet. You will know where to start the students by the approach distance they developed in step 4. Usually, it is approximately 2 to 3 m from the mats, depending on the age and height of the student.

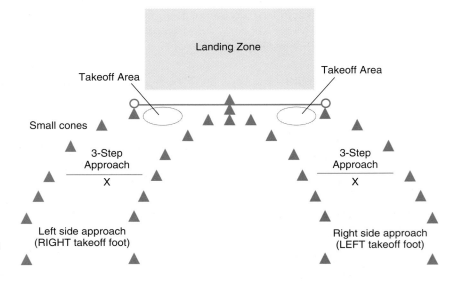

Figure 28.12

High jump approach and landing area setup.

6. Set up the bungee bar or rope just slightly above the height of the mats. Keep assisting students with the technique they've been practising. It is helpful to call out their steps while they approach. Students are still landing on their feet at this point. Add one technique point: Takeoff foot should point toward the back corner of the mat (diagonally).

7. With the bungee bar still low, students will maintain the same technique, except that they now will land on their seat on the mat. Instructors will notice that some students will have done this on their own, as it is a natural progression.

8. Practise the above technique while gradually raising the bungee bar. At this point, students are still using a three-step approach. Once students are comfortable with the technique, increase the approach to five steps. Technique points: last three steps are quick and short; tall at takeoff; knee drives straight up (knee to chest).

After learning the above progressions, students have the basics to eventually perform the flop technique. Many students will not have the skills or will not be old enough to move on, but these students will be able to use the technique they have already learned to experience some level of success. Students who are ready to move on will work toward executing the flop technique. The following technique points describe the flop technique.

High Jump Technique (Flop Technique)

The Approach

- Controlled speed toward the bar. Excessive speed is not necessary and can be dangerous.
- Shape of the approach is an "inverted-J" (see Figure 28.13).
- A five-to-seven-step approach is recommended (maximum eight steps). More than eight steps encourages students to run too fast and thus take their landing too far back into the landing area.
- Lean into curve and away from bar.

Takeoff

- Last step is quick and short.
- Stay tall (avoid leaning forward into bar).
- Take off one arm's-length away from standard and on outside foot.
- Point takeoff foot diagonally to back corner of the mat.
- Keep takeoff leg straight and strong.
- Drive inside knee up and swing both arms up.
- Eyes look "down" the bar.

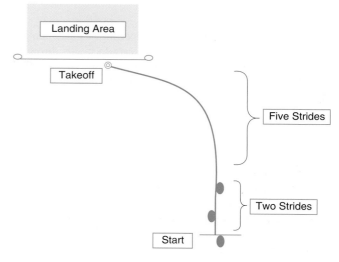

Figure 28.13

Shape of High Jump approach.

Flight

- At the top of knee drive, push inside knee down and lift hips up.
- Tuck feet underneath.

Landing

- Extend legs, then bring chin to chest.
- Land on back and avoid heels landing above the head.

Basic High Jump Rules

1. One-footed takeoff only.
2. Three attempts are allowed to clear each height.
3. The athlete who clears the highest bar wins the competition. In the event of a tie, the jumper with the fewest misses at earlier heights is declared the winner.
4. As an official, ensure that standards are set up so that the platforms that hold the bar are facing inward toward each other.

TEACHING TIP

1. Do not stack mats for the landing area.
2. Check that the landing area is large enough and that the mats are the appropriate thickness of foam (consult district and provincial/territorial safety regulations).
3. Use a bungee bar or other stretchy material (e.g., surgical tubing, elastic).
4. Check that approach area is level, clean, and not slippery.
5. Only one jumper on mats at one time.

Throwing

Shot put is the only throwing event permitted in elementary school; however, it is possible to introduce the throwing motion that is common for all throwing events. The common elements for all throwing events include the following:

1. Preparation—feet shoulder width apart, toes pointed in direction of throw, chin up and hips forward, knees bent.

2. Momentum building—movement from a low to high position, rotation or speed on approach run.

3. Delivery or release—sequence of body parts moving forward is from lower body to upper body (for example, the hips come through before the shoulder or arm).

4. Recovery—throwing arm follows through.

General Throwing Activities

SEATED PASS RELAY

Teams of six with each group member sitting on the floor in a circle, facing out. Pass a utility ball around the circle using two hands. Emphasize sitting up straight and turning the torso to pass the ball. Switch directions or add more balls to modify the activity.

TEAM BEAN BAG TOSS

Teams of six stand behind a start line. On signal, the first team member throws the beanbag as far as possible. Entire team runs to bean bag, with next team member tossing the beanbag from the landing spot of the first toss. Teams run in order from the team with the shortest toss first (so other teams are not in the field of throw). Continue toss from the new landing position, until all team members have made a toss. Team with the greatest cumulative distance wins.

BEANBAG THROW

Using overhead-throwing technique, students can throw beanbags into a hoop. Modify this activity by using a bucket, using both the left and right hands, and varying the distance or style of throw.

HOOP TOSS

Place a target in the middle of the gym floor (e.g., a chair, a large cone). Organize the class into teams of three or four, giving each student a hoop. Students take turns throwing the hoops toward the target (discus style) using the basic stance for throwing preparation. Have them try using both left and right hands. Emphasize dropping the same-side foot back as the throwing hand and releasing the hoop at no more than a 45-degree angle. Also, try to get students thinking about using their hips to rotate the hoop back and forward, instead of swinging the arm.

Shot Put Technique

1. Shot is held on the balls of the fingers and tucked up under chin and below the ear (clean palm, dirty fingers and chin).

2. Knees bent, forward leg is bent slightly. Completely extend forward leg and bend back leg to 90 degrees.

3. Keep throwing elbow up.

4. Drive up with back leg, and as body comes forward use the "blocking" step (hips come through first).

5. Drive to a tall position, releasing the shot put at approximately 45-degree angle. Keep chin up on release.

6. Do not break the wrist.

Shot Put Activities

BACKWARDS THROW

From behind a bench or small obstacle, throw a utility ball using two hands, and attempt to hit the mat. Place the mat approximately 3 to 5 m from the bench. Thrower stands facing the opposite direction of mat. This activity helps the child focus on the body movement used in shot putting. Technique points include knees slightly bent; back and arms straight; throw beginning at hips and using stomach (sideways rotational motion); and head up. Vary the distances and throwing style, or add a net between the bench and the mat to introduce throwing trajectory.

TWO-HANDED THROW

Students work in pairs to practise throwing a utility ball from between their legs. Emphasize bent knees, straight arms and back. Using forward and back hip movement, bring ball back then forward, release, and follow through. Begin introducing throwing trajectory and encourage a 45-degree angle of release. You can modify this activity by adding a target, throwing for distance, and decreasing the size of the ball.

Basic Shot Put Rules

1. Enter and exit from the back of the throwing circle.

2. Feet must remain behind the front of the circle at all times during and after throwing.

3. The shot put must land within boundary lines.

4. The measurement is taken from the front of the circle to where the shot put first hits the ground.

TEACHING TIP

1. To organize a group of students for shot put instruction, use a straight line (see Figure 28.14).

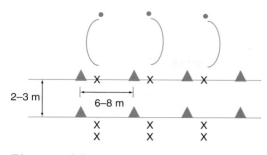

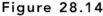

Figure 28.14

Class organization for Shot Put.

2. Establish a command sequence so that students do not retrieve shot puts before they hear the signal from the instructor (e.g., "Throw" or "Retrieve").

3. Students not throwing should remain 3 to 4 m behind throwers.

Organizing for Instruction

A track and field program takes considerable preparation before the classes begin. Consider the following points when planning for instruction:

1. The goal of the program should be to encourage students to participate and to progress at their own pace. Individual goals may be set where students work toward their "personal best." Group activities with a scoring system can be effective motivational elements.

2. When a track is not available, one may be laid out on grass fields with marking lime or paint. Most fields will accommodate a 200-m track and this is adequate for instructional purposes. For the measurements and layout for a 200-m track, see Figure 28.15.

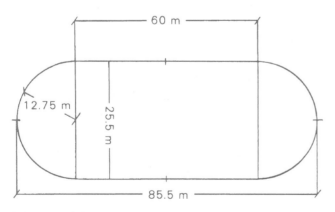

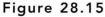

Figure 28.15

200-m track.

3. A hurdling area can be outlined in an appropriate location on the field or track. Use lining paint or marking lime to mark the hurdle positions. It is helpful to measure out the hurdle distances for varying levels of student ability.

4. Check high jump mats every year to ensure that they have not deteriorated and that landing areas provide a safe, cushioned landing surface.

5. It is helpful for instructional purposes to have separate pits for long jump and triple jump. These pits should be spaced well apart to minimize interference.

Instructional Procedures

1. Begin track and field units with sprinting and relays. Encourage a team approach and incorporate relay-type games to build the program. The following outlines lesson progressions for a track and field unit:

Lesson 1:	Sprinting and relay games
Lesson 2	Distance Running Form and Long Jump
Lesson 3:	Running Starts and Triple Jump
Lesson 4:	Baton Passing
Lesson 5:	Hurdles
Lesson 6:	High Jump
Lesson 7:	Shot Put
Lesson 8:	Relays, Jumps Review, and Practice
Lesson 9:	Practice Day
Lesson 10:	Mini-meet

2. Begin the unit with whole-class instruction until enough activities have been introduced to set up stations. Multiple activities maximize students' on-task behaviour. Stations can be selected from the skill areas that have been introduced on previous days. Sample stations include the following: (i) starting and sprinting, (ii) baton passing, (iii) long jump event and/or long jump activities, (iv) triple jump event and/or triple jump activities, (v) high jump, (vi) hurdles, (vii) shot put, (viii) nature run.

3. When working with stations, the instructor should be in a position to see all events. Establish a safety signal (three blasts of the whistle); when students hear the signal, they must immediately stop what they are doing.

4. Provide written directions at each station stating what is to be accomplished and incentives for completing the activity correctly. In addition, be sure to give enough time for students to practise and complete the stated activity.

5. Assessment and evaluation procedures should be based on individual improvement and on the student's executing technique points successfully.

6. Always plan lessons with appropriate warm-up and cool-down. Warm-up activity should include jogging as well as stretching.

Mini-meets

Track and field mini-meets can range in organization from competition within a single classroom to competition among selected classes, to an all-school challenge. In these informal meets, it is recommended that children participate in a run, a jump, and a throw. If time or supervision is not available, students can be limited to their choice of one track and one field event. A team approach using a point system encourages participation and allows all students to experience success, even if they have not done well individually. Schedule the relay races as the last event.

Organizing a Track and Field Meet

The primary goal of an elementary school track and field meet is to encourage maximum participation and present opportunities for students to experience success. Determining individual winners and meet champions should be lower in priority.

While track and field competitions can focus on individual efforts, it is recommended that team scoring be used to encourage participation. When team competition is incorporated, both individual winners and team winners are recognized. Points scored by individual winners are assigned to respective teams and tallied at the end of the meet for a team total. For larger meets, the scoring system most commonly used is a 10-point system:

First place	10 points
Second place	8 points
Third place	6 points
Fourth place	5 points
Fifth place	4 points
Sixth place	3 points
Seventh place	2 points
Eighth place	1 point

For smaller meets, a five-point system for first, second, and third places is scored on a five-, three-, and one-point basis, respectively. Relay races, because of multiple participation, should count double in the point scoring.

Generally, award ribbons to the top finishers in each event. For more formal track meets, have ribbons printed with the name of the meet, date, and designated place. Most often, ribbons are awarded for first, second, and third place. Some larger meets have ribbons for first through eighth place. Distributing the ribbons to the individual competitors can be an onerous task that is easily overlooked. Ensure you have a table designated solely for giving out ribbons, and enough volunteers to distribute the ribbons throughout the meet.

The order of events is dependent upon the size and type of the competition, the facilities available, and the number of officials and volunteers. Usually hurdles are the first event of the day and relays are the last. Other considerations that may be important are the following: scheduling long distance events early in the morning during cooler hours; spacing running events so that there is ample rest for athletes who may be running two different running events; and scheduling the jumping events at different times.

Organizing a track and field meet is not an easy task and requires many volunteers and trained helpers. The following is a list of key officials and their responsibilities:

Meet Director: Overall supervisor and contact person for the meet.

Clerk of the Course: Organizes participants into heats by division based on schedule of events. Directs athletes to appropriate lanes. Works with announcer to call athletes for their events. Explains the starter's commands to athletes.

Announcer: Works with the clerk of the course and the meet director to keep meet on schedule. Announces the next events to be marshalled and where athletes should report. If possible, broadcasts races and results to the audience.

Starter: Starts all races on the track with the appropriate commands. Watches for runners being pushed or tripped, and for false starts. Recalls them by a second starting blast or with a whistle.

Timers: The head timer assigns each timer to a lane or position (sprint races). The head timer signals the start line when all timers have their watches reset and are ready. Timers watch the starter's gun and start their watches when they first see the smoke of the gun. Watches are stopped when the runner's torso (any part between the shoulders and the hip) reaches the finish line. Timers report times to the head timer, who then records the times in the appropriate space on the race sheet.

Place Judges: Decide the order in which the athletes cross the finish line. It is recorded by lane (first—lane 4, second—lane 6, third—lane 5). The head place judge meets with the head timer to match the times to the places. Competitors who have the same time recorded finish according to the place judge's decision.

Messengers (Runners): Runners should be located at the start line and finish line. The start line runner takes the

Figure 28.16

Funnelling runners at the finish line.

event sheet from the clerk of the course to the finish line. The finish line runner takes the final results sheet from the finish line to the results area to be processed and posted. Figure 28.16 shows a system for funnelling runners at the end of a race.

Field Judges and Officials

- Each field event should have enough officials and helpers to keep the event running smoothly.

- For throwing events, make sure there are officials to spot the landing of the implement, measure, and record. Helpers can retrieve implements, carry the measuring tape, and organize athletes.

- With long and triple jump, officials will be needed for measuring and recording. Helpers can rake, and call athletes to the runway.

- High jump officials are responsible for measuring the bar at its lowest point, watching the bar to see if the jump is successful, and recording successes or failures on the record sheet. Helpers replace the bar when it has been knocked off the standards.

- All field officials are responsible for knowing the rules for their specific event.

- The head field judge oversees all field events, verifies record-breaking distances and heights, resolves disputes, and clarifies rules.

Critical Thinking

Track and field events focus on fundamental motor skills including running, jumping, and throwing. Review earlier chapters and identify a range of games and other activities that can be used to help students practise track and field events.

References and Suggested Readings

Alberta Learning. (2001). *Run, jump, throw and away we go! Kindergarten to grade 12 teacher resource*. Edmonton, AB: Author.

Athletics Canada. (1995). *Run, jump, throw instructor's manual*. Ottawa, ON: Author.

Carr, G.A. (1999). *Fundamentals of track and field* (2nd ed.). Champaign, IL: Leisure Press.

Greene, L. (2005). *Training for young distance runners*. Champaign, IL: Human Kinetics.

Guthrie, M. (2003). *Coaching track & field successfully*. Champaign, IL: Human Kinetics.

National Association for Sport and Physical Education. (1994). *Track and field resource materials for upper elementary and middle school students*. Reston, VA: Author.

Schmottlach, N., & McManama, J. (2002). *The physical education handbook* (10th ed.). San Francisco: Benjamin Cummings.

Silvester, J. (2003). *Complete book of throws*. Champaign, IL: Human Kinetics.

Wedmann, W., Fenton, J., Kopelow, B., Viviani, C., & Parsons, A. (2000). *Track & field: Teaching the basics resource manual*. Victoria, BC: Ministry of Small Business, Tourism and Culture.

 Weblinks

KidsRunning.com: www.kidsrunning.com/krresources.html

A great resource on children and running, this website has information on training programs for children, nutrition, competing, games to play, stories, and event listings. The site is geared to both children and to adults looking for information on kids' running.

Athletics Canada: www.athleticscanada.com

The website for Athletics Canada will help you identify the top Canadian athletes in the different disciplines of track and field and learn about their achievements at home and on the international arena.

Athletics Alberta: www. athleticsalberta.com

Includes information on developmental resources focused on the fundamentals of track and field to support teachers and coaches.

Volleyball

Essential Components

I	**Organized around content standards**
II	**Student-centred and developmentally appropriate**
III	**Physical activity and motor skill development form the core of the program**
IV	**Teaches management skills and self-discipline**
V	**Promotes inclusion of all students**
VI	**Focuses on process over product**
VII	Promotes lifetime personal health and wellness
VIII	**Teaches cooperation and responsibility and promotes sensitivity to diversity**

Physical Education Standards

1	**Students are able to move competently using a variety of fundamental and specialized motor skills.**
2	Students can monitor and maintain a health-enhancing level of physical fitness.
3	**Students are able to apply movement concepts and basic mechanics of skill performance when learning and refining motor skills.**
4	Students comprehend the basic principles of wellness and are able to apply concepts that enable them to make meaningful decisions that positively impact their health and wellness.
5	**Students participate in a wide variety of physical activities and learn how to maintain a personalized active lifestyle.**
6	**Students demonstrate empathy, understanding, and respect for the numerous differences exhibited by people in an activity setting.**
7	**Students exhibit responsible and self-directed behaviours that lead to positive social interactions in physical activity.**

SUMMARY

Skills instruction for volleyball is introduced during the intermediate grades after children have mastered basic prerequisite skills. Teaching the rules and tactics for volleyball is an integral part of the instructional process. Using proper progression is a key to success when teaching fundamental skills and lead-up games associated with volleyball. Lead-up games provide an opportunity to emphasize development of selected volleyball skills and tactics in a setting that is compatible with the abilities of participants.

OUTCOMES

- Structure learning experiences efficiently using appropriate formations, progressions, and teaching techniques.

- Develop a unit plan and lesson focus for volleyball.

- Identify safety precautions associated with teaching volleyball.

- Describe instructional procedures used for implementing a successful practice activity.

To play volleyball successfully at the elementary level, students need to learn basic skills properly. This requires sufficient practice in serving and passing skills and the development of hand–eye and body coordination for effective ball control. Attention to proper technique is essential. Informal practice begins with activities that mimic volleyball skills—passing, serving, and rebounding of all types. Blocking is an important skill that youngsters can perform if they anticipate correctly. Spiking progressions may be introduced depending on the abilities and experience of your students.

Instructional Emphasis and Sequence

Developmental Level I

In the primary grades, children can practise ball-handling activities related to volleyball skills. Rebounding and controlling balloons are excellent related experiences, particularly for younger children (see Chapters 15 and 17). These preliminary experiences in visual tracking are advantageous for volleyball skills learned in the upper grades.

Table 29.1 shows a sequence of volleyball activities divided into two developmental levels. In most cases, youngsters are not ready to participate in the activities in this chapter until age 8 or 9.

Developmental Level II

Experiences at this level are based on the use of the beach ball or volleyball trainer. A beach ball is larger and more easily handled than a volleyball and allows children a level of success not possible with a smaller and heavier ball. A volleyball trainer is a light version of a volleyball. Players can practise simple returns and underhand serves with beach balls and trainers. Drills and lead-up games too can be played with a beach ball or volleyball trainer ball. Consider using modified games, 2 vs. 2, 3 vs. 3, and 4 vs. 4, on small courts with modified nets.

Developmental Level III

Shift to volleyball trainer balls when the maturity of the youngsters dictates. Foam rubber and training volleyballs (20 cm) are excellent substitutes for volleyballs (see Figure 29.1). They do not hurt youngsters, and they move slowly and afford an opportunity for successful play. Students should exhibit basic technique in handling high and low passes. Instruction focuses on the underhand serve and the overhand and forearm passes. Teachers can

TABLE 29.1

Suggested volleyball program

Developmental Level II	Developmental Level III
Skills	
Underhand serve	Overhead pass
Simple returns	Forearm pass
	Setup*
	Spike*
	Blocking*
Knowledge	
Rules	
Simple rules (service, number of hits)	Basic game rules (ball handling, scoring, net play)
Rotation	
Offensive Tactics	
Identifying open spaces on court	Identifying open spaces on court
• positioning in court	• basic adjustments in positioning and shot selection
• basic shot placement	• offensive adjustment in response to changes in defensive tactics*
Defensive Tactics	
Defending space	Defending space
• base positioning	• team positioning to cover court
	• backing up teammate
	• shifting to adjust to offensive plays*
Game Activities	
Beach Ball Volleyball	Pass and Dig
Informal Volleyball	Mini-volleyball
Shower Service Ball	Rotation Mini-volleyball
	Regulation Volleyball
	Three-and-over Volleyball
	Rotation Volleyball
	Four-square Volleyball

*Introduce as student ability and experience permits

Figure 29.1

Various balls used in Volleyball.

introduce spiking, blocking, and overhand serve as required. Continue with basic strategy as part of the instructional approach in modified games (2 vs. 2, 3 vs. 3, 4 vs. 4).

Volleyball Skills

Underhand Serve

The serve is used to start play. For elementary school children, the underhand serve is easiest. The overhand serve may be introduced as a challenge and extension if students appear ready.

These directions are for a right-handed serve. The player stands facing the net with the left foot slightly forward and the weight on the right (rear) foot. The ball is held in the left hand with the left arm across and a little in front of the body. The ball is lined up with a straightforward swing of the right hand. The left-hand fingers are spread, and the ball rests on the pads of these fingers. On the serving motion, the server steps forward with the left foot, transferring the weight to the front foot and at the same time bringing the right arm back in a preparatory motion. The right hand now swings forward and contacts the ball just below centre. The ball can be hit with the heel of the hand (hand may be open or in a fist). An effective follow-through with the arm ensures a smooth serve (see Figure 29.2).

The following instructional cues focus on correct performance of the underhand serve:

1. Use opposition. Place the foot opposite the serving hand forward.

Figure 29.2

Underhand serve.

2. Transfer the weight to the forward foot.
3. Keep the eyes on the ball.
4. Follow through in the direction of the serve; don't punch at the ball.

Overhand Serve

Present the overhand serve as an option for students who have mastered the underhand serve. For the right-handed serve, the server stands with the left foot in front and the left side of the body turned somewhat toward the net. The weight is on both feet. The server must master two difficult skills: how to toss the ball and how to contact the ball. The ball is held in the left hand directly in front of the face. The ball must be tossed straight up and should come down in front of the right shoulder. As the ball is tossed, the weight shifts to the back foot. The height of the toss is a matter of choice, but from 1 to 1.5 m is suggested. As the ball drops, the striking arm comes forward, contacting the ball about 30 cm above the shoulder. The server shifts weight to the forward foot, which can take a short step forward, making contact with the open palm.

Overhead Pass

To execute an overhead pass, the player moves underneath the ball and controls it with the fingertips. Feet should be in an easy, comfortable position, with knees bent. The player cups her fingers so that the thumbs and forefingers form a triangle and the other fingers are spread (cupping the ball). The hands are held forehead high, with elbows out and level with the floor. The player, when in receiving position, looks ready to look upward through cupped hands (see Figure 29.3).

The player contacts the ball above eye level and propels it with the force of spread fingers. At the moment of

Figure 29.3

Overhead pass ready position.

contact on the pads of the fingers, the legs are straightened and the hands and arms follow through. If the ball is a pass to a teammate, it should be high enough to allow for control. If the pass is a return to the other side, it can be projected forward with more force.

Using trainer volleyballs will allow youngsters time to move into the path of the volleyball instead of reaching for the ball. Instructional cues for passing include the following:

1. Move into the path of the ball and face the target; don't reach for it.

2. Bend the knees prior to making contact.

3. Contact the ball above the forehead with the pads of the fingers (cupping the ball).

4. Extend the knees upon contact with the ball.

5. Follow through in direction of target after contacting the ball.

Forearm Pass (Underhand Pass)

The forearm pass is the most used skill in elementary school volleyball. Similar to the overhead pass, the player moves into the path of the ball to face the target. Instructional cues for forearm passing include the following (see Figure 29.4a and b):

1. The trunk leans forward and the back is straight, with a 90-degree angle between the thighs and the back.

2. The legs are bent, and the body is in a partially crouched position, with the feet shoulder-width apart.

3. The player clasps the hands together so that the forearms are parallel. The thumbs and wrists are kept parallel and together, with the fingers of one hand clasped within the other.

4. The forearms present an even platform and the elbow joints are locked. The ball is played on the forearms, at hip level. Avoid swinging the arms when contact is made.

5. Extend the knees upon contact with the ball.

Figures 29.4a–b

Ready position for forearm (underhand) pass.

Figure 29.4a

Figure 29.4b

Advanced Volleyball Skills

The spike and block are difficult skills for the majority of youngsters to master. Volleyball lead-up games do not require the use of these skills. Consider introducing these skills on an "as needed" basis.

Spike

The spike is an effective play in volleyball, and when properly done is extremely difficult to return. Its success depends a great deal on the ability of a teammate to set up properly. Consider the following instructional cues for the spike:

1. Approach angled to the net (about the 3-m line).
2. Simultaneous upward leg thrust and arm action at takeoff (step-together-up).
3. Elbow of hitting arm is up and back (elbow by ear).
4. Ball contact is high and in front of the head.
5. Whip action with wrist on follow-through.

Blocking

Blocking involves one or more members of the defensive (receiving) team forming a screen of arms and hands near the net to block a spike. Emphasize individual blocking at the elementary level. To block a ball, a player jumps high with arms outstretched overhead, palms facing the net, and fingers spread. The jump must be timed with that of the spiker, and the blocker must avoid touching the net. The ball is not struck but rather rebounds from the blocker's stiffened hands and arms.

Instructional Procedures

1. Most volleyball-type games begin with a serve, so it becomes critical that students master this skill. Include modifications to increase youngsters' potential for success (for example, closer service line, multiple attempts).

2. To save time, instruct players to roll the ball back to the server. Other players should let the ball roll to its destination without interception.

3. Effective instruction is possible only when children can rebound the balls from the hands and arms without pain. Beach balls are excellent for beginning players. Foam balls and volleyball trainers are the logical next choice. A 20-cm foam rubber training ball has much the same feel as a volleyball but does not cause pain. The foam balls should be used early in skill practice. A new ball, the volleyball trainer, most closely resembles a volleyball but is larger in diameter and lighter in weight. By using either ball, children avoid developing a fear of the fast-moving object.

4. The predominant instructional pattern should be individual or partner work. For individual work, each child needs a ball.

5. Emphasize the forearm pass as the basic reception skill.

6. Rotation should be introduced early and used in lead-up games. Two rotation plans are illustrated in Figure 29.5.

Organizing for Instruction

Practice sessions can be categorized as individual play, partner work, or group work. Teachers can preface these tasks with "Can you . . ." or "Let's see if you can . . ." Students should learn early on the skill of tossing to oneself to initiate a practice routine.

Individual Play

1. For wall rebounding, the player stands 2 m away from a wall. She throws the ball against the wall and passes it

Two lines

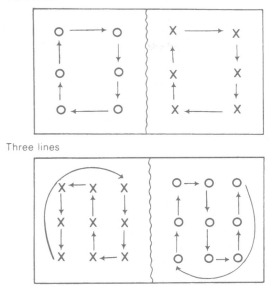

Three lines

Figure 29.5

Rotation plans.

to the wall. Then she catches the ball and begins again. Allow two passes against the wall before the student catches. A further extension is for the child to pass the ball against the wall as many times as possible, using correct technique.

2. From a spot 2 m from the wall, the player throws the ball against the wall and alternates an overhead pass with a forearm pass. Then he catches the ball.

3. In another wall-rebounding exercise, the player throws the ball to one side (right or left) and then moves to the side to pass the ball to the wall. She then catches the rebound.

4. The player passes the ball directly overhead and catches it. She should try making two passes before catching the ball. Later, the player alternates an overhead pass with a forearm pass and catches the ball. A further extension of the drill is to keep the ball going five or six times with one kind of pass or with alternate passes.

5. The player passes the ball 3 m high and 3 m forward, moves rapidly under the ball, and catches it. Later, he should make additional passes without the catch.

6. The player passes the ball 4 m overhead, makes a full turn, and passes the ball again. Vary with other stunts such as touching the floor, making a half turn, clapping the hands at two different spots, and others. Allow the student choice in selecting the stunt.

7. The player stands with one foot in a hoop. She passes the ball overhead and attempts to continue passing while keeping that foot in the hoop. Encourage the student to try with both feet in the hoop.

Partner Work (Passing)

1. Players are about 3 m apart. Player A tosses the ball (controlled toss) to player B, who passes the ball back to A, who catches the ball. Continue for several exchanges and then change throwers. Another option is for player B to make a pass straight overhead, catch the ball, and then toss to player A. A second variation is to have one player toss the ball slightly to the side. Player B then makes a pass to player A. Player A can make the toss in such a fashion that player B must use a forearm return.

2. Two players are about 4 m apart. Player A passes to herself first and then makes a second pass to player B, who catches the ball and repeats. Player B can follow this with a return.

3. Players A and B try to keep the ball in the air continuously.

4. Players are about 4 m apart. Player A remains stationary and passes in such a fashion that player B must move from side to side. An option is to have player B move forward and backward.

5. Players are about 3 m apart. Both have hoops and attempt to keep one foot in the hoop while passing. Try keeping both feet in the hoop.

6. Two players pass back and forth, making contact with the ball while off the ground.

7. Players are about 4 m apart. Player B is seated. Player A attempts to pass to player B. A second method is for both players to stand. Player A passes to player B and then sits down quickly. Player B attempts to pass the ball back to player A, who catches it in the seated position.

8. Player A passes to player B and does a complete turnaround. Player B passes back to player A and also does a full turn. Other stunts can be used.

9. Partners stand on opposite sides of a volleyball net. The object is to keep the ball in the air. The drill can be done by as many as six players.

10. If the net is stretched properly, students can practise recovery. One player throws the ball against the net, and the active player recovers with a forearm pass.

Partner Work (Serving and Passing)

1. Partners are about 6 m apart. Partner A serves to partner B, who catches the ball and returns the serve to partner A.

2. Partner A serves to partner B, who makes a pass back to partner A. They then switch so that partner B serves.

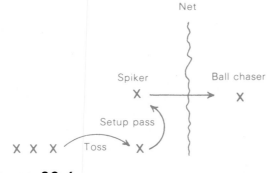

Figure 29.6

Setup and spiking drill.

3. *Service One-step.* Partners begin about 3 m apart. Partner A serves to partner B, who returns the serve with partner A catching. If there is no error and if neither receiver moved the feet to catch, both players take one step back. Players repeat this process each time the receivers commit no error or foot movement. If an error occurs or if appreciable foot movement is evident, the players revert to the original distance of 3 m and start over.

Group Work

1. A leader stands in front of not more than four other players, who are arranged in a semicircle. The leader tosses to each player in sequence around the circle, and they return the ball. After a round or two, another player comes forward to replace the leader.

2. For blocking, six players are positioned alongside the net, each with a ball. The players take turns on the other side of the net, practising blocking skills. Each spiker tosses the ball to herself for spiking. A defensive player moves along the line to block consecutively.

3. Students can practise setup and spiking according to the drill shown in Figure 29.6. A back player tosses the ball to the setup player, who passes the ball properly for a spike. Either the entire group, or just the spikers, can rotate.

4. Two groups of children stand on opposite sides of a net. Eight to ten balls must be available to make this a worthwhile experience. Players serve from behind the end line and recover balls coming from the other team. The action should be informal and continuous.

Tactics for Net/Wall Games

According to the basic games classification mentioned in Chapter 22, volleyball is classified as a net/wall game (conceptually similar to tennis, badminton, table tennis).

The basic offensive tactics of these games emphasize hitting the ball into the opponent's court space with the necessary accuracy and power so the ball cannot be returned. Alternatively, the defensive tactics of the receiving team focus on returning the ball before it lands in their court. Both defensive and offensive tactics involve both on-the-ball and off-the-ball decisions. See Table 29.1 for basic tactical concepts for developmental level II and developmental level III. Choose volleyball drills and lead-up games that emphasize practise of skills as well as applicable tactics.

Basic Volleyball Rules

Officially, six players make up a team, but any number from six to nine make a suitable team in the elementary school program. To begin, the winner of the coin toss can choose to serve or to select a court. The opposing team takes the option that the winner of the toss did not select. At the completion of a game, teams change courts, and the losing side serves.

To be in the proper position to serve, a player must have both feet behind the end line and must not step on the end line during the serve. The server covers the right back position. The server retains the serve, scoring consecutive points, until that side loses a point and is put out. Rally scoring (either team can score a point on serve) has recently been introduced. Members of each team take turns serving, the sequence being determined by the plan of rotation.

Official rules allow the server only one serve to get the ball completely over the net and into the opponent's court. The lines bounding the court are considered to be in bounds: that is, balls landing on the lines are counted as good. Any ball that touches or is touched by a player is considered to be in bounds, even if the player who touched the ball was clearly outside the boundaries at the time. The ball must be returned over the net by the third contact, which means that the team has a maximum of three hits to make a good return.

The following major violations cause the loss of the point or serve:

1. Touching the net during play.

2. Not clearly passing the ball—sometimes called palming or carrying the ball.

3. Reaching over the net during play.

4. Stepping over the centre line. (Contact with the line is not a violation.)

A ball going into the net may be recovered and played, provided that no player touches the net. The first team to reach a score of 15 points wins the game if the team is at least 2 points ahead. Games to 25 points have been recently introduced (when change was made to rally scoring). If not, play continues until one team secures a 2-point lead. Only players in the front line may spike at the net. No player may volley the ball twice in succession.

Volleyball Activities

Developmental Level II

BEACH BALL VOLLEYBALL

Playing Area: Volleyball court

Players: Six to nine on each team

Supplies: A beach ball 30 to 40 cm in diameter

Skills: Most passing skills, modified serving

The players of each team are in two lines on their respective sides of the net. The player behind the back line does serving, as in regulation volleyball. The distance is shortened, however, because serving a beach ball successfully from the normal volleyball serving distance is difficult. The player serves from the normal playing position on the court in the right back position. Scoring is as in regulation volleyball. Play continues until the ball touches the floor.

A team loses a point to the other team when it fails to return the ball over the net by the third volley or when it returns the ball over the net but the ball hits the floor out of bounds without being touched by the opposing team. The server continues serving as long as her team scores. Rotation is as in regulation volleyball.

TEACHING TIPS

The server must be positioned as close to the net as possible while still remaining in the right back position on the court. Successful serving is an important component of an enjoyable game.

Variations:

1. In a simplified version of Beach Ball Volleyball, one player in the front line puts the ball into play, throwing the ball into the air and then passing it over the net. Play continues until the ball touches the floor, but the ball may be volleyed any number of times before crossing the net. When either team has scored 5 points, the front and back lines of the respective teams change. When the score reaches 10 for the leading team, the lines change back. Game is 15.

2. Any player in the back line may catch the ball as it comes initially from the opposing team and may immediately make a little toss and pass the ball to a teammate. The player who catches the ball and bats it cannot send it across the net before a teammate has touched it.

INFORMAL VOLLEYBALL

Playing Area: Volleyball court, 1.8 m net

Players: Six to eight on a team

Supplies: A trainer volleyball

Skills: Passing

This game is similar to regulation volleyball, but there is no serving. Each play begins with a student on one side tossing to herself and passing the ball high over the net. Points are scored for every play, as there is no "side out." As soon as a point is scored, the nearest player takes the ball and immediately puts it into play. Otherwise, basic volleyball rules govern the game. Rotation occurs as soon as a team has scored five points, with the front and back lines changing place. Action is fast, and the game moves rapidly, as every play scores a point for one team or the other.

SHOWER SERVICE BALL

Playing Area: Volleyball court

Players: 6 to 12 on each team

Supplies: Four to six trainer volleyballs

Skills: Serving, catching

A line parallel to the net is drawn through the middle of each court to define the serving area. Players are scattered in no particular formation (see Figure 29.7). The game involves the skills of serving and catching. To start the game, two or three volleyballs are given to each team and are handled by players in the serving area.

Balls may be served at any time and in any order by a server, who must be in the back half of the court. Any ball

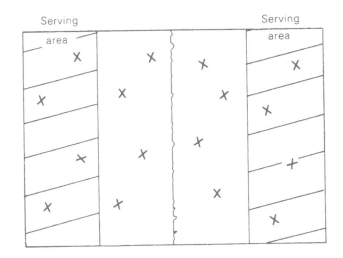

Figure 29.7

Formation for Shower Service Ball.

served across the net is to be caught by any player near the ball. The person catching or retrieving a ball moves quickly to the serving area and serves. A point is scored for a team whenever a served ball hits the floor in the other court or is dropped by a receiver. Two scorers are needed, one for each side.

TEACHING TIP

As children improve, all serves should be made from behind the baseline.

Developmental Level III

PASS AND DIG

Playing Area: Playground or gymnasium

Players: Five to eight on each team

Supplies: A trainer volleyball for each team

Skills: Overhand, forearm, and dig passes

Each team forms a small circle of not more than eight players. The object of the game is to see which team can make the greater number of passes in a specified time or which team can keep the ball in the air for the greater number of consecutive passes without error.

On the signal "Go," the game is started with a volley by one of the players. The following rules are in force:

1. Balls are passed back and forth with no specific order of turns, except that the ball cannot be returned to the player from whom it came.

2. A player may not pass a ball twice in succession.

3. Any ball touching the ground does not count and ends the count.

TEACHING TIP

Players should be responsible for calling illegal returns on themselves and thus interrupting the consecutive pass count. Groups should count the passes out loud, so that their progress is known.

MINI-VOLLEYBALL

Playing Area: Gymnasium or badminton court

Players: Three on each team

Supplies: A volleyball or trainer volleyball

Skills: Most volleyball skills

Mini-volleyball is a modified activity designed to offer opportunities for successful volleyball experiences for beginners. The playing area is 4.5 m wide and 12 m long. The spiking line is 3 m from the centre line. Many gymnasiums are marked for badminton courts that are 6 by 13.4 m with a spiking line 2 m from the centre. This is an acceptable substitute court.

The modified rules used in Mini-volleyball are as follows:

1. A team consists of three players. Two substitutions may be made per game.

2. Players are positioned for the serve so that there are two front-line players and one back-line player. After the ball is served, the back-line player may not spike the ball from the attack area or hit the ball into the attack area unless the ball is below the height of the net.

3. The height of the net is 1.8 m.

4. Players rotate positions when they receive the ball for serving. The right front-line player becomes the back-line player, and the left front-line player becomes the right front-line player.

5. A team wins a game when it scores 15 points and has a 2-point advantage over the opponent. A team wins the match when it wins two out of three games.

The back-line player cannot spike and thus serves a useful function by allowing the front players to receive the serves while moving to the net to set up for the spikers.

TEACHING TIP

This game can be modified to suit the needs of participants. Sponge training balls work well in the learning stages of Mini-volleyball.

ROTATION MINI-VOLLEYBALL

Playing Area: Basketball or volleyball court

Players: Three on each team

Supplies: A volleyball or trainer volleyball

Skills: All volleyball skills

Three games, involving 18 active players, can be played at the same time, crosswise on a regular basketball court. The remaining children, organized in teams of three, wait on the sideline with teams designated in a particular order. Whenever a team is guilty of a "side out," it vacates its place on the floor and the next team in line moves in. Each team keeps its own running score. If, during a single "side in," 10 points are scored against a team, that team vacates its place. Teams in this arrangement move from one court to another and play different opponents. The one or two extra players left over from team selection by threes can be substitutes and should be rotated into play on a regular basis.

REGULATION VOLLEYBALL

Playing Area: Volleyball court

Players: Six on each team

Supplies: A volleyball or trainer volleyball

Skills: All volleyball skills

Regulation volleyball should be played with one possible rule change: In early experiences, it is suggested that the server be allowed a second chance when failing to get the first attempt over the net and into play. Some teachers like to shorten the serving distance during the introductory phases of the game. It is important for the serving to be done well enough to keep the game moving.

A referee should supervise the game. There are generally two calls:

1. *"Side out."* The serving team fails to serve the ball successfully to the other court, fails to make a good return of a volley, or violates a rule.

2. *"Point."* The receiving team fails to make a legal return or is guilty of a rule violation.

TEACHING TIP

Emphasize team play. Backcourt players should be encouraged to pass to frontcourt players rather than merely batting the ball back and forth across the net.

Variation: The receiver in the backcourt is allowed to catch the serve, toss it, and propel it to a teammate. The catch should be limited to the serve, and the pass must go to a teammate, not over the net.

THREE-AND-OVER VOLLEYBALL

Playing Area: Volleyball court

Players: Six on each team

Supplies: A volleyball or trainer volleyball

Skills: All volleyball skills

The game Three-and-Over emphasizes the basic offensive strategy of volleyball. The game follows regular volleyball rules with the exception that the ball must be played three times before going over the net. The team loses the serve or the point if the ball is not played three times.

ROTATION VOLLEYBALL

Playing Area: Volleyball court

Players: Variable

Supplies: A volleyball or trainer volleyball

Skills: All volleyball skills

If four teams are playing in two contests at the same time, a system of rotation can be set up during any one-class period. Divide the available class time roughly into three parts, less the time allotted for logistics. Each team plays the other three teams on a timed basis. At the end of a predetermined time period, whichever team is ahead wins the game. A team may win, lose, or tie during any time period, with the score determined at the end of the respective time period. The best win–loss record wins the overall contest.

FOUR-SQUARE VOLLEYBALL

Playing Area: Volleyball court

Players: Two to four on each team

Supplies: A volleyball or trainer volleyball

Skills: All volleyball skills

Place a second net at right angles to the first net, dividing the playing area into four equal courts. The courts are numbered as in Figure 29.8. There are four teams playing, and an extra team can be waiting to rotate to court number 4. The object of the game is to force one of the teams to commit an error. Whenever a team makes an error, it moves down to court 4 or off the courts if a team is waiting. A team errs by not returning the ball to another court within the prescribed three volleys or by causing the ball to go out of bounds.

The ball is always put in play with a serve by a player from team 1, the serve being made from any point behind the end line of that team. Players must rotate for each serve. The serve is made into court 3 or 4. Play proceeds as in regular volleyball, but the ball may be volleyed into any of the other three courts. No score is kept. The object of the game is for team 1 to retain its position.

TEACHING TIP

The game seems to work best with five or more teams. With four teams, the team occupying court 4 is not penalized for an error, because it is already in the lowest position.

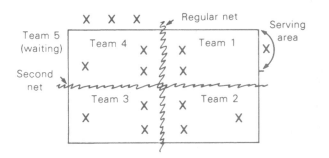

Figure 29.8

Four-square Volleyball courts.

Critical Thinking

1. Design a practice activity (drill or lead-up game) for developmental level II that will help students practise reception skills and basic offensive tactics. Then by making modifications in the same activity, increase its complexity and challenge to meet the needs of students at developmental level III.

References and Suggested Readings

American Sport Education Program. (2003). *Coaching youth volleyball*. Champaign, IL: Human Kinetics.

American Volleyball Coaches Association. (2006). *Volleyball skills and drills*. Champaign, IL: Human Kinetics.

Dearing, J. (2003). *Volleyball fundamentals*. Champaign, IL: Human Kinetics.

Fronske, H. (2005). *Teaching cues for sport skills* (3rd ed.). San Francisco: Benjamin Cummings.

Kus, S. (2004). *Coaching volleyball successfully*. Champaign, IL: Human Kinetics.

Miller, B. (2005). *The volleyball handbook*. Champaign, IL: Human Kinetics.

Mitchell, S., & Oslin, J. (1999). An investigation of tactical understanding in net games. *European Journal of Physical Education, 4,* 162–172.

Viera, B.L. & Ferguson, B.J. (1996). *Teaching volleyball: Steps to success* (2nd ed.). Champaign, IL: Human Kinetics.

Wedmann, W., Fenton, J., & Kopelow, B. (2001). *Volleyball—Teaching the basics resource manual*. Victoria, BC: British Columbia Ministry of Small Business, Tourism and Culture.

 Weblinks

About Volleyball: http://volleyball.about.com

This site is directed at volleyball enthusiasts of all levels, with information ranging from stats for top players and teams, to a variety of drills for beginner players.

Volleyball Canada: www.volleyball.ca

Volleyball Canada is the governing body for the sport of volleyball in Canada, and its website offers information on the national team, on programs and upcoming events, and on news and views from the volleyball community.

GENERAL INDEX

ACTIVITY INDEX

Exercises

Games

Introductory Activities

Jumping Activities

Rhythmic Activities

Sports-Related Lead-Up Games

Basketball

Cross-Country Skiing

Curling

Floor Hockey

Lacrosse

Orienteering

PHOTO CREDITS

Section 1: Bob Daemmrich/The Image Works
Chapter 1: Will Hart
Chapter 2: Bob Daemmrich/The Image Works

Section 2: VCG/FPG International
Chapter 3: Elizabeth Crews
Chapter 4: Bob Daemmrich/The Image Works
Chapter 5: Bob Daemmrich/The Image Works
Chapter 6: Will Faller
Chapter 7: Bob Daemmrich/The Image Works

Section 3: Bob Daemmrich/The Image Works
Chapter 8: Bob Daemmrich/The Image Works
Chapter 9: Bob Daemmrich/The Image Works
Chapter 10: Syracuse Newspapers/Dick Blume/The Image Works
Chapter 11: Bob Daemmrich/The Image Works

Section 4: Ron Chapple/FPG International
Chapter 12: Michael Newman/PhotoEdit
Chapter 13: Stone/Mary Kate Denny

Section 5: Bob Daemmrich/The Image Works
Chapter 14: Bob Daemmrich/The Image Works; Wendy Moran
Chapter 15: Bob Daemmrich/Stock, Boston; Wendy Moran
Chapter 16: Bob Daemmrich/The Image Works
Chapter 17: Elizabeth Crews

Section 6: Bob Daemmrich/Stock, Boston
Chapter 18: Bob Daemmrich/The Image Works
Chapter 19: Bob Daemmrich/The Image Works
Chapter 20: Bob Daemmrich/The Image Works
Chapter 21: Bob Daemmrich/Stock, Boston; Corbis/Magma Photos
Chapter 22: Bob Daemmrich/Stock, Boston

Section 7: Bob Daemmrich/Stock, Boston
Chapter 23: Jeff Kaufman/FPG International
Chapter 26: Nancy Richmond/The Image Works
Chapter 27: David Young-Wolff/PhotoEdit
Chapter 28: Bob Daemmrich/The Image Works; Sandra L. Gibbons
Chapter 29: Stone/Peter Cade